DAVID SYME

DAVID SYME

Man of The Age

ELIZABETH MORRISON

© Copyright 2014

All rights reserved. Apart from any uses permitted by Australia's Copyright Act 1968, no part of this book may be reproduced by any process without prior written permission from the copyright owners. Inquiries should be directed to the publisher.

Monash University Publishing
Building 4, Monash University
Clayton, Victoria 3800, Australia
www.publishing.monash.edu

Published in association with the
State Library of Victoria
328 Swanston Street
Melbourne, Victoria 3000, Australia
slv.vic.gov.au

http://www.publishing.monash.edu/books/ds-9781922235350.html

Design: Les Thomas

Cover images:
> David Syme in later life (courtesy of Dr Veronica Cordon)
>
> Elizabeth Street, Melbourne, in 1863 (Pictures Collection, State Library of Victoria, IAN24/12/63/9)
>
> Masthead of the *Age*, 17 October 1854 (Newspaper Collection, State Library of Victoria).
>
> Author photo courtesy of Sarah Cannon.

National Library of Australia Cataloguing-in-Publication entry:

Author:	Morrison, Elizabeth, 1936-, author.
Title:	David Syme : man of the Age / Elizabeth Morrison.
ISBN:	9781922235350 (paperback)
Series:	Biography.
Notes:	Includes index.
Subjects:	Syme, David, 1827-1908; Journalists--Australia--Biography; Journalism--Australia--History; Australia--History--19th century.
Dewey Number:	070.92

Printed in Singapore by Markono Print Media Pte Ltd.

The great man of the age is the one who can put into words the will of his age, tell his age what its will is, and accomplish it.

    Georg Wilhelm Friedrich Hegel, *The Philosophy of Right*, 1821

Made weak by time and fate, but strong in will
To strive, to seek, to find, and not to yield.

    Alfred, Lord Tennyson, 'Ulysses', 1833

And more, much more than this, I did it my way.

    Paul Anka, 'My Way', first recorded by Frank Sinatra, 1968

CONTENTS

List of illustrations ix
List of abbreviations xi
Preface and acknowledgments. xiii

PART I: PRELUDE

1. The legacy of David Syme 3
2. David and his brothers: formative years. 12
3. David and Ebenezer: first years in Victoria. 25
4. Joining Ebenezer at the *Age* 41

PART II: SUPPORTING A SISTER-IN-LAW

5. 'I felt it to be my duty'
   (March 1860 to March 1866) 53
6. 'Beginning to make progress'
   (April 1866 to December 1870). 79
7. 'Business is good but money scarce'
   (January 1871 to May 1876) 99
8. 'The *Age* has just scored a tremendous Victory'
   (June 1876 to March 1878) 130

PART III: NEGOTIATING WITH A NEPHEW

9. 'I am the man who has made the firm a success'
   (April 1878 to July 1883) 153
10. '<u>Expedition</u> is everything in newspaper work'
    (August 1883 to December 1887) 184

11. 'Everything going on well'
    (1888)...217

12. 'Neither pleasure nor profit in continuing our partnership'
    (January 1889 to March 1891)........................237

PART IV: A FREE HAND

13. 'I am not prepared to make any compromise whatever'
    (April 1891 to July 1896)............................273

14. 'I am sending forth on their travels my two youngest sons'
    (August 1896 to December 1901)......................309

15. 'I will see the thing through'
    (January 1902 to February 1908).....................349

16. Afterwords..386

    Appendix A: Newspapers and periodicals published by the
    Age business under David Syme 405

    Appendix B: David Syme's personal publications..........407

    Sources 409

    Index 423

LIST OF ILLUSTRATIONS

Figure 1.1.   Media House, corner of Collins and Spencer Streets, Melbourne 6

Figure 3.1.   Ebenezer Syme 29

Figure 5.1.   David Syme, circa 1861 53

Figure 5.2.   Elizabeth Street, Melbourne, in 1863 55

Figure 5.3.   Jane Syme (later Hope, Palk, Galgey), circa 1856 57

Figure 5.4.   Masthead of the *Age*, 3 June 1861 60

Figure 5.5.   Masthead of the *Weekly Age*, 31 January 1862 60

Figure 5.6.   Masthead of the *Leader*, 4 January 1862. 60

Figure 5.7.   Masthead, illustrated, of the *Farmers' Journal and Gardeners' Chronicle*, 11 January 1862 64

Figure 5.8.   Masthead of the *Australian News for Home Readers*, 21 April 1862 67

Figure 5.9.   George Syme, brother of David 75

Figure 6.1.   Under the Verandah of the Hall of Commerce, Collins Street West, 1868 86

Figure 6.2.   Masthead of the *Illustrated Australian News for Home Readers*, 27 July 1867 87

Figure 7.1.   Victory rotary printing machines, introduced to Australia by Syme in 1872 101

Figure 7.2.   David Syme and his staff, January 1873 117

Figure 9.1.   The *Age* office, Collins Street, 1879 155

Figure 9.2.   Blythswood, home of David Syme and family from 1882 178

Figure 10.1. The *Age* 'Back Building', 1886 186

Figure 10.2. Attack on the *Age* New Guinea expeditioners, as depicted by one of its members, 1884 205

Figure 11.1.	*Age* newsprint display at Melbourne Centennial International Exhibition, 1888	219
Figure 12.1.	Joseph Syme	258
Figure 14.1.	Annabella Syme	310
Figure 14.2.	The *Age* office, Collins Street, 1899	325
Figure 15.1.	David Syme in later life	350
Figure 15.2.	Geoffrey Syme, 1908	354
Figure 15.3.	Cover of *Every Saturday*, 12 October 1907	356
Figure 15.4.	Melbourne Mansions, Collins Street, 1950s	374
Figure 16.1.	Syme tomb in Boroondara Cemetery	393
Figure 16.2.	David Syme depicted for readers of the *Lone Hand*, June 1907	404

LIST OF ABBREVIATIONS

Note: Abbreviations have been devised for some Syme-related manuscript material held in the Australian Manuscripts Collection of the State Library of Victoria and cited frequently in footnotes:

SFP   Syme Family Papers (MS 9751)

LB1–LB6   The six letterbooks of David Syme, which form part of the Syme Family Papers, MS 9751 (Boxes 1181/1–3 and 1182/1–3), are cited simply as:

    LB1   4 October 1871–25 March 1876 (Box 1181/1)
    LB2   24 April 1876–15 October 1886 (Box 1181/2)
    LB3   15 October 1886–21 November 1892 (Box 1181/3)
    LB4   11 November 1886–11 January 1893 (Box 1182/1)
    LB5   18 September 1890–2 October 1905 (Box 1182/2)
    LB6   4 October 1905–30 September 1907 (Box 1182/3)

Wages Book   Staff Wages Book 1886–1937.
This ledger is filed with Syme, David. Obituaries; Wages Book 1886–1937; Caxton Commemoration Fund (MS 10602)

Members of the Syme family frequently cited in footnotes are given as:

    AS   Annabella Syme (wife of David)
    DS   David Syme
    GS   Geoffrey Syme (son of David)
    Jane   Jane Syme, later Hope, Palk, Galgey (sister-in-law of David)
    JCS   Joseph Cowen Syme (nephew of David)

Other abbreviations:

    MLA   Member of the Legislative Assembly

    MLC   Member of the Legislative Council

    VPD   Victoria. Parliamentary Debates

    VPP   Victoria. Parliamentary Papers

PREFACE AND ACKNOWLEDGMENTS

This biography of Scottish-born David Syme (1827–1908), who was associated with the Melbourne daily *Age* from mid-1856 and responsible for policy and production from March 1860 until his death, necessarily covers much of the same ground as two previous *David Syme* studies – Ambrose Pratt's of 1908 and C.E. Sayers' of 1965. I acknowledge their prior contributions, from which I have both drawn and turned away. The primary focus of those books is their subject's involvement in politics. My *David Syme* focuses primarily on his management of a newspaper business, to help understand how he made the *Age* into a long-running, mass-circulating media outlet. Moreover, it takes into account Syme's many interrelated interests, aims and achievements in the context of his time and place – the 19th and early 20th century in Victoria.

In the search for sources I am indebted to several descendants of David Syme: to his great-grandson Ranald Macdonald, former managing director of David Syme and Co., for inspiration; to Syme's granddaughter Dr Veronica Condon, for access to her collection of documents, correspondence, memorabilia in addition to her own writings, both unpublished and on her website (www.sirgeoffreysyme.com.au), and for provision of several photographs to include in this book; to his great-granddaughter Judith Adams for access to family letters; to his great-grandson Michael Dennis and wife Hélène for generously sharing family lore. Friendly interest shown by great-granddaughter Jennifer Smyth and by Judith Clemons, who married into the Syme clan, is also much appreciated. Marten Syme, descendant of David's brother George, has been most generous, making available his transcripts of the George Syme papers that his family deposited in the State Library of Victoria, sharing his research into the extended Syme family and providing photos for publication. Pru Williams, descendant of Ebenezer, has sent me from England the results of her extensive genealogical and historical research into the life of not only Ebenezer but also, and revealingly, that of his widow Jane. Without assistance from these family members my Syme story would be thin indeed.

Staff at the *Age* library have been interested and helpful. Thanks to John Langdon and Maria Paget, and especially to Michelle Stillman for invaluable information about archival and pictorial material. Thanks also to Gay Alcorn and Kate Cole-Adams for facilitating the publication of an 'Insight' article in the *Age* on the centenary of Syme's death (2008) and to Miranda Ramsay for one in *Age Extra* on the 150th anniversary of his assuming control (2010).

For more than three decades the State Library of Victoria has enabled my research into the history of Victoria's newspaper press and for this my gratitude is immeasurable. Embarking on a David Syme project, in 2007 I was given permission and assistance to digitise copies of some 1370 letters by Syme, preserved in six office letterbooks; thus I could have at hand in Canberra, where I live, the key source for the biography. For this I wish to record my profound gratitude to then State Librarian Anne-Marie Schwirtlich, and to Sandra Burt, Shane Carmody, Kevin Molloy and Peter McGrath. I acknowledge also the courteous help always given by staff when I have needed to consult the Syme Family Papers and other relevant sources.

Other institutions and their staff I wish to thank are the National Library of Australia, the State Library of New South Wales, the State Library of South Australia, the State Library of Tasmania, the Royal Geographical Society of South Australia, Monash University Library Rare Books, Melbourne University Archives, Monash University Archives, the Museum of Victoria, the Victorian Spiritualists Union, and the Gisborne and Mt Macedon Historical Society.

I owe thanks to the following for giving me relevant information and comment on a great range of Syme-related matters: Alison Adams, Ron Armstrong, Chris Bantick, Jenna Reed Burns, Graeme Davison, Paul de Serville, Colin Duncan, Al Gabay, John Hirst, Damien John Hynes, Stuart Mackenzie, Sybil Nolan, Jean Prest, Peter Putnis, Den Robin, James Rundle and Barbara Strange. If I have inadvertently left anyone out, I apologise.

For reading the manuscript I am indebted to Michael Cannon for clarifying aspects of printing technology. Taking the manuscript through to publication, it has been a pleasure to work with Nathan Hollier, Sarah Cannon and Kathryn Hatch of Monash University Publishing and with Margot Jones at the State Library of Victoria.

Finally, I am grateful to friends and family who, through their expressed interest, helped keep my own enthusiasm alive while I tried to track and unearth long-buried and elusive information. In particular to Mimi Colligan, who understands how to undertake 19th-century quests, and to John Mulvaney for listening attentively to my musings, reading my drafts, and producing pertinent contextual material from his extensive library.

PART I

PRELUDE

Chapter 1

THE LEGACY OF DAVID SYME

A legend in his lifetime, David Syme is still regarded as 'the most influential journalist in Victorian history' (Baker 2012, 17). Legends persist through the telling and retelling, and this affirmation in December 2012 by Mark Baker, President of the Melbourne Press Club, serves to remind and reinforce a reputation that might otherwise fade with time. Published in the Melbourne daily *Age* of 8 December and on the Press Club website and relayed to other papers and websites and YouTube, the statement was made at Syme's induction two days earlier into Victoria's newly created Media Hall of Fame (Melbourne Press Club 2012). Syme was one of 20 eminences of the press, ranging from John Pascoe Fawkner, founder of the *Melbourne Advertiser* in 1838, to Second World War correspondents Alan Moorehead and Chester Wilmot, all honoured at a dinner held by the Press Club on 6 December for their 'significant contribution to the craft of journalism' and for enhancing the 'history of the news media'.

Journalism is here used in the wide sense of not only writing for media outlets, but also editing and having responsibility for content, policy and production. Rarely did Syme actually write for the *Age*. Ranald Macdonald, a great-grandson of Syme and managing director of David Syme and Co. Ltd from 1964 to 1983, spoke to the award, saying that Syme's contribution was to build 'a thriving business based on upholding the values of good and fearless journalism', thus developing the *Age* 'into one of the truly great international journals' (Macdonald 2012, 4).

Historical reminders are timely, when the world of print newspapers is breaking up under the impact of digital technology and the associated development of social media (O'Donnell, McKnight and Este 2012; Jericho 2012; Buchanan 2013). With the seeming inexorable trend of readers away from paper and the traditional 'rivers of gold' advertising flowing to online outlets, the established business model no longer holds. While the public appetite for news is undiminished, it is being demanded and supplied in a drastically different timescale than hitherto. The 24-hour news cycle entails problems of synchronised release and maintenance of consistency across multimedia outlets ('platforms'). These factors are transforming the modus operandi of reporters, leader writers and subeditors. In an era of flux, these journalists are inevitably challenged to identify and maintain standards, values and ethics. If the 20th-century style newsroom is now superseded, what of the structure and functioning of David Syme's outfit in the century before last? While his newsroom may now be almost unrecognisable, yet the legacy remains of a great metropolitan daily with a tradition of investigative journalism and breadth of coverage unparalleled in Australia.

If the legend of Syme has shrunk today to the notion of his long and significant association with the *Age*, much more was once known about the man of many parts, and kept in memory until the 1960s, when people who had known him, even as children, were still alive. Once a household word, his name is now less used, although the annual David Syme Research Prize is still being awarded and the David Syme Charitable Trust still distributes funds to a range of causes. Moreover, a portrait of Syme was displayed in the 'For Auld Lang Syne: Images of Scottish Australia' exhibition at the Art Gallery of Ballarat in mid-2014. But the David Syme Business School, established at the Caulfield Institute of Technology in 1978, which in 1990 became the David Syme Faculty of Business at Monash University, turned into the unadorned Faculty of Business and Economics in 1993, and the David Syme Foundation, an educational services consultancy set up in the late 20th century by aficionado Don Veitch, is no longer in existence.

Few today know that Syme's newspaper management extended beyond running the *Age* from 1860 to 1908. Under his control was a newspaper and printing business from which were issued, at various periods, a number of other papers. Older newspaper readers may remember the weekly *Leader*, published from 1856 to 1957, which came to be directed at a rural readership, as is the *Weekly Times*, still in publication. Researchers and writers dealing with 19th-century Australia will be familiar with the monthly *Illustrated Australian News*, an invaluable source of pictorial material that ceased in 1896. But who remembers the three other weeklies and the annual in the Syme stable (listed in Appendix A) or the countless pamphlets reprinted from articles in series in the *Age* and the *Leader*? In their day all significant and influential, and identified with David Syme and Co., these print materials are filed away in State Library storage, largely forgotten. The tiniest fraction of them has been digitised.

Likewise, it is not generally known today that Syme was an author of some standing. In their time his published writings attracted generally favourable

CHAPTER 1

reviews and serious, informed comment. That the man, whose ideas shaped the policies of his paper through his supervision of their editorial articulation, was an intellectual seeker after truths is evident in his four erudite essays in learned journals and four monographs on weighty subjects (listed in Appendix B). While they have been out of print for over a century, and are out of sight in libraries, it is testimony to their value that historian John La Nauze discussed them in the 'David Syme' chapter of his 1949 *Political Economy in Australia* and that in recent years they have been discussed by Stuart Macintyre and other historians of economic theory and political philosophy (Macintyre 1991, 92–97; King 2007, 276–278; Melleuish 2009).

Gone without trace are two splendid buildings that Syme had constructed and which graced Melbourne's most famous street until the mid-20th century, when they were demolished to make way for 'progress'. One was the premises of David Syme & Co. at 233 Collins Street, designed by leading architect Joseph Reed and occupied from 1879. In 1898, at Syme's direction and under the guidance of another prominent architect, Robert Hyndman, the building was doubled in size and remodelled, preserving the classic character and adding greatly to the handsome appearance of the fashionable promenade and thoroughfare until unappealing glass-and-concrete modernising was effected in stages from 1951 to 1961. Soon found inadequate, in 1968 this building was abandoned for squat utilitarian premises at the other end of the city. However, in 2009 Fairfax Media, owner of the *Age* from 1983, moved the newspaper enterprise to imposing, purpose-built glass-and-steel seven-storey premises on the south-west corner of the Spencer and Collins intersection at the perimeter of the new, affluent Docklands area. This is Media House (fig. 1.1), proclaimed 'the 21st century home for Fairfax Media's state-of-the-art multimedia operation' ('Media House' 2010, 1). Suggesting the newspaper's masthead, THE AGE is blazoned in giant capitals across the glass front of the building; above it is the newspaper's lion-and-unicorn British royal coat of arms. On the topmost wall is another large screen displaying the current time, the temperature and items of news from the *Age* online at www.theage.com.au, signalling that the future of newspapers is now.

Syme's other significant contribution in the heart of the city was Melbourne Mansions, to the east at 91–101 Collins Street. A project of his final years, Syme engaged the architectural firm Inskip and Butler to design the six-storey building housing professional suites on the lower floors and residential apartments above. Tenanted from 1905, it was a sought-after address and elegant landmark in the streetscape until sold to raise capital for David Syme & Co. in 1958 and demolished soon after.

Figure 1.1. Media House, corner of Collins and Spencer Streets, Melbourne. (Photographed by the author in June 2011)

Syme's extensive real estate holdings in Melbourne and throughout Victoria have long since passed into other hands, with residences pulled down, gardens dug up and land sub-divided and developed. Of the properties to which he was most attached, Blythswood, the family home on 14 acres running down to the Yarra River in Kew, is now marked by the street Blythswood Court. There is no trace of Seaforth, the holiday house in bayside Mordialloc, now a suburb; nor is there of Rosenheim, until 1884 his Mount Macedon country retreat, where he created a botanical showpiece garden. His Yarra Valley farm, Killara, is now a winery. And there were many more land-holdings, urban and rural, at various times bought, made available to offspring, leased, sold.

CHAPTER 1

Of the architectural creations, only Syme's tomb in the Boroondara Cemetery, Kew, remains intact, a memorial to his aspirations, spiritual and material. Architecture had significance as well as function for him, witnessed in this astonishingly grand mausoleum, provided for in his will and built under the supervision of architect Walter Butler. Striking in its simple lines and intriguing decorations, it is modelled on a very beautiful ancient Egyptian temple.

Bringing Syme back to life, as it were, it is not difficult to visualise his physical appearance, at least as an adult. Photographs taken from time to time from his 20s to late 70s are reproduced in biographies by Ambrose Pratt (1908) and C.E. Sayers (1965), while some published memoirs of journalists who knew and worked for him contain evocative descriptions. Thus we know that he would stand out in a crowd. He was over six feet tall, and lean – 'as lank and long as Abraham Lincoln', wrote journalist Randolph Bedford (1976, 250) – and slightly stooped; his dark hair, which later was grey then white and receding, was slightly wavy; his beard and moustache were neat and well-trimmed (Cockerill 1943, 57; Robinson 1967, 22). Habitually his gaze was direct and, although his mouth was set almost grimly, his eyes could sometimes bespeak a hidden gentleness. A view of the behaviour and personality displayed to his literary and editorial staff in his mature years is provided in the publications of several of the clever and creative men who served time on the *Age* and recorded the not inconsiderable impact of their then late-middle-aged employer. A man of 'magnificent strength', 'iron will' (Grover 1993, 76), he could at worst be cranky and obsessive; at best, behind a formidable mask, be generous and kind (Hoare 1927, 152–157; McKay 1961, 9–10; Waters 1951, 20).

Telling the story of Syme's life requires careful and detailed examination of the disparate material traces and documentary archives to understand how these various pieces of evidence may be pieced together and form a meaningful mosaic. Writing that life requires also a rationale and focus – a point of view.

Most studies published to date, long or short, are expositions of his legendary influence on politics – chiefly Victorian colonial then State, and briefly Australian Federal. They rest on two premises. One is the simplistic equation of Syme and the *Age*, so that 'Syme stated…' means 'the *Age* stated…', and vice versa. The other asserts that the Syme–*Age* entity exercised enormous political power in Victoria during the second half of the 19th century. An early expression of this approach is to be found in the celebratory and widely read *Victoria and Its Metropolis* published in Melbourne's boom year, 1888:

> Between 1860 and 1880 the *Age* was practically the mover in all the democratic agitations which made the political history of the period. Orators and intriguers rounded up their flocks in Parliament; crowds of the free and independent voters took their way at successive elections to give their voice at the polling booths; but the voice was really the voice of David Syme, who, from behind the scenes, stirred up a people that was all unconscious of the secret power that moved it (Sutherland 1888, v.1, 494–495).

Some years later Prime Minister Alfred Deakin, in his introduction to Pratt's biography, referred to the Syme–*Age* congruence, asserting that 'For many years past, so far as the public knew, Mr. Syme was *The Age* and *The Age* was Mr. Syme' (Pratt 1908, v–vi). This was echoed by Pratt himself: 'As a historic Australian figure, Syme...cannot be separated from *The Age*...His identification with *The Age* was complete – absolute, indeed' (xxvi).

Commissioned by Syme in 1907, Pratt's biography is based substantially on reminiscences then written and dictated by his employer. It is organised around and gives primacy to what Syme stated to be his and the *Age*'s key policy campaigns for legislative action: to open up land for settlers; to impose tariffs for the protection of emerging primary and potential secondary industries; to reform the constitution so as to lessen the power of the squatter-dominated Legislative Council; and, later, to reduce government spending ('extravagance'). Published in September 1908 seven months after Syme's death, it has served to mark his place in political history. This was unequivocally endorsed by historian Keith Hancock in his 1930 *Australia*, where Syme is 'the editor-proprietor of a great newspaper, the most dour and formidable of radical chieftains, the maker and unmaker of governments' (Hancock 1930, 224). Sayers' biography, published in 1965, follows Pratt's organisational structure. Stuart Macintyre's study of Syme in his book on three colonial Victorian liberals, deals critically with the same political issues (Macintyre 1991, 66–114). All these studies are essentially political biographies, contributing to political history.

But Syme was not only a political animal. That there are alternative approaches was hinted at by historian John La Nauze in 1949, suggesting it 'may be suspected that Syme did not always create waves, but sometimes rode on their crests' and favouring not only a critical study of his part in the politics of his day (such as later provided by Macintyre and to a lesser extent by Sayers) but also a study of his journalism (La Nauze 1949, 99–100). In his 1963 history of its goldrush years Geoffrey Serle (1977, 381)

CHAPTER 1

accords Syme a major place in the history of Victoria; in his 1971 volume about the boom-time 1880s he devotes several pages to a wide-ranging, succinctly worded description and assessment of him as a many-sided man of the press (Serle 1971, 26–30). Ranald Macdonald went further in his Daniel Mannix Memorial Lecture delivered in September 1981 on behalf of students at Newman College, University of Melbourne, and published as a pamphlet the following year (Macdonald 1982). Sketching Syme's life, he focused on his role and activities in the world of newspapers, as he did in December 2012, speaking to Syme's induction into the Media Hall of Fame. This line was also taken by journalist Ben Hills (2010, 73–80) when writing about Syme in his 2010 biography of the legendary 20th-century *Age* editor, Graham Perkin. Long overdue now is a full-length biography of David Syme, to expand these vignettes of a many-sided man of a bygone age.

A story that focuses on what was a central driving force and vocation for most of the subject's adult life – management of a newspaper business – has to not only encompass longitudinally the trajectory from his birth in Scotland in 1827 to his death in Melbourne in 1908 but also take into account laterally the other dimensions that go to make up the person and bear on this central preoccupation. This means, of course, not ignoring or separating out the private from the public persona. It means seeing Syme as a family man, not to say patriarch, and making the best use of the relatively few records available. It also means recognising that his newspaper business was very much a family concern, involving, at various periods of his life, his two brothers, a brother-in-law, a sister-in-law, nephews and three of his five sons.

Syme's living legacy of course is the extensive set of descendants, branching out from six of the seven surviving children. There were 28 grandchildren descended from David and his wife Annabella (M. Syme 2013, 238–244). They in turn produced scores of great-grandchildren; now the great-great grandchildren are appearing. Many of these descendants have been and are eminent in public and intellectual life. Several helped carry on David Syme & Co until the later 20th century, including a grandson, a granddaughter two grandsons-in-law, a great-grandson and a great grandson-in-law. All belonging to the extensive David Syme family tree appear to be aware and proud of their familial heritage, with a good number in contact with each other, celebrating anniversaries and sharing family memories and lore.

But the family is not all. Syme's public life was multidimensional, and the several facets were interrelated. Syme the man of action who ran a newspaper business (and, some claimed, the colony itself) had other capitalistic–entrepreneurial strings to his bow, which may be summarised as agribusiness, property development, and share trading. Thanks to all of these, the man who came to Victoria in 1852 with little in his pocket, had at his death 56 years later an estate worth almost £980,000 – which would make him a multimillionaire in today's Australian dollars.

Having an integrated approach to telling a story of David Syme, the newspaper manager, requires recognising that his scope for action was moderated, if not absolutely determined, by the terms, constraints and powers of his proprietorship – that is, by actual and perceived legal and family obligations. Accordingly, following a section on his preparatory, formative years, three sections of this book represent successive phases of Syme's ownership: the 50-50 partnership with his sister-in-law Jane for 18 years; the 75–25 partnership with his nephew Joseph for 13 years; his sole proprietorship for the final 17.

Giving a sense of the business as an ongoing concern means recognising the people associated with it – who they were, what they did, their relationships with their employer. Pratt's book names only a handful. While we may glean more names, with dates and remuneration, from those wages books that still exist, it is Syme's directives to staff and contributors, preserved in his in letterbooks, that yield insights into his management style

A newspaper business is and always has been part of a press network in which relations with other such businesses may be collaborative or competitive, depending on circumstances and relative status. Syme worked hard to maintain and negotiate such relationships – whether competing, usually with the Melbourne daily *Argus*, or cooperating, typically with the proprietors of liberal–reformist metropolitan papers in other colonies, in particular the Adelaide *Advertiser*. This vital context for the Syme story may be reconstructed in step-by-step detail through the correspondence of the principals. In this respect, the letters preserved that David Syme and the *Advertiser*'s John Langdon Bonython wrote to each other are valuable both for content and for the contrast displayed between their personal styles.

Maintaining a profitable business, Syme more than kept up with the times, investigating and applying the opportunities offered by innovative technology. In this for many years he was an Australian frontrunner. He applied the latest advances in printing technology to achieve mass production and, thus, mass circulation, managing to far outstrip that of the established and conservative *Argus*. By 1881 the *Age* was claimed to have the largest circulation of any daily in the British Empire outside London. At first in competition with the *Argus* proprietors, later in cooperation, Syme applied

CHAPTER 1

transformative advances in communications to overcome the tyranny of distance and, at the same time, radically change the journalistic content and style as well as the timeliness of its impact. Together with other newspaper proprietors and managers, he ensured that the Australian press system was a contributing part of the fast-developing imperial and global network.

Those who come to this book for more insights into the political history of Victoria and Australia may be disappointed. *David Syme: Man of the Age* is the story of the man behind the legend that grew up about him. Placing Syme and his *Age* business firmly in the world of newspaper publishing in what was arguably its heyday, before the advent of radio, television and the internet, the book is written from the perspective of the subject and his surroundings. So doing, it is hoped that, looking back from today, the reader may gain an understanding not only of the paper's famous proprietor but also of how some of the foundations were laid for a flourishing Australian metropolitan daily press. Necessarily it is a white, British and masculinist story, with Indigenous people barely mentioned, and women mostly peripherally – a world now vastly transformed.

The *Age* has endured, as Syme's chief legacy to the public of Victoria and indeed Australia. Of the nation's surviving metropolitan dailies, it is one of the longest in continuous publication without change of title or frequency of issue since its first appearance on Tuesday 17 October 1854, during the tumultuous period of Victoria's early existence. First associated with the newspaper in 1856, Scotsman David Syme took over the running of it and two associated weeklies in March 1860 and remained in charge until his death in February 1908. Under his management, the *Age* weathered adversity in the 1860s and early 1870s and surged to a triumphal dominance in the 1880s that lasted throughout his lifetime and provided momentum for its survival into the 21st century.

Chapter 2

DAVID AND HIS BROTHERS

Formative Years

During the long period of David Syme's association with the *Age* business, a variety of family circumstances, relationships and obligations influenced the conduct and trajectory of his professional as well as his personal life. It was never a one-man band. There were parents, siblings, spouse, offspring, in-laws, nephews and nieces. Nor was David's early life simply solitary and cramped by an intimidating father, as portrayed in his memoirs and in biographies drawing thereon.[1] David was the youngest in a large family, and the influence of his older brothers seems to have been equally if not more formative. It is noticeable and curious that the substantial assistance given to him by certain people at crucial stages in his life – family and associates – is not mentioned in his memoirs.

David Sime, as the name on his birth certificate is spelled, was born on 2 October 1827 and baptised nine days later, at North Berwick, Scotland, a small coastal town on the southern side of the Firth of Forth, some 40 kilometres from Edinburgh.[2] Now an esteemed seaside resort and golfing centre, and in 2006 winner of an award for the cleanest, most sustainable and most beautiful community, it was then, and before the coming of the railway in 1849, stagnant if not in decline, with no manufacturing or trade to speak of ('North Berwick' 2009). David was the youngest of seven children born to George Alexander Sime and his wife Jean (Jane, in some records). While

---

[1] David Syme notebooks (hereafter DS notebooks), in the possession of Dr Veronica Condon. Unless otherwise indicated, information and quotations in this chapter are taken from her photocopies of these notebooks, described by her at www.sirgeoffreysyme.com.au, where she points out that much of the material is reproduced, sometimes with changes, in Pratt's *David Syme* (1908).

[2] Extract from Register of Births and Baptisms, in Syme Family Papers. MS 9751, Australian Manuscripts Collection, State Library of Victoria (hereafter SFP), Box 1193/3(a)[i].

CHAPTER 2

their surname is spelled as Sime in the parish baptism registers, the offspring in adulthood spelled it Syme, and that will be used here henceforth.[3] David's ancestors were, he believed, 'undistinguished'.

The seven children were born between 1815 and 1827, roughly two years apart. Margaret was the eldest. A son Adam, born in 1817, and a daughter Elizabeth Jane, in 1823, both died in infancy. The brothers, James (1819), George Alexander (1821) and Ebenezer (1825) were, respectively, eight, six and two years older than he.[4] In contrast to his long litany of complaints about a strict and aloof father, David has nothing adverse to say about his mother, and perhaps we may assume that she nurtured the children well. In any case, that her offspring took care of her after the death of George senior may indicate reciprocal fondness as well as a sense of duty.

David described his father as of 'sterling, if stern integrity, & manly character' and commented that it was hard to account for his harsh attitude to his children, recalling that, although he was 'naturally of a kind disposition' and a 'devoted husband', he held the children at arms-length with 'never a kind word or an approving smile' and there was no time for play or sports and no holidays. His sense of humour was 'grim'. As will become apparent, David in adulthood and as a parent evinced these same traits, negative and positive. His recollections, however, tell only part of the story of his formative years. Composed when very ill and near the end of his long life, and after having established a large family of his own and made a quite different life in Australia, they should not be understood as telling the whole truth.

George senior was a man of his place and time. Let us leave David recollecting in Melbourne in 1907, and go back to his father in Scotland of the 1820s and 1830s. With a classical university education, he had been trained as a minister in the Established Church of Scotland and would have been imbued with the strict Calvinist belief that the chief end of man was to know and do the will of God, the corollary to which was a strenuous morality. Along with the doctrine of salvation of the elect formulated by the Swiss John Calvin and brought into Scotland by John Knox in the 16th century, and forming the backbone of Scottish theological orthodoxy, was what is now seen as the 'dark repressive force' of Scottish Calvinism,

---

[3] The first use I have found is in a reference dated 18 November 1843 for David's brother George, in George Syme, Letters to the Reverend George Alexander Syme, MS 4576/7–9, State Library of Victoria.

[4] Old Parish Registers of Births & Baptisms, www.scotlandspeople.gov.uk, accessed 1 December 2009. In most later published sources, Ebenezer's birth year is erroneously given as 1826, and Margaret's said to be unknown.

characterised by harsh discipline, killjoy attitudes and suppression of the arts (Macleod 2001).

George senior may, by temperament and upbringing, have been an extreme exponent, but he was no unquestioning, narrow conformist. Trained for the ministry, he was never ordained and, rather than preaching the gospel and for whatever reason, became a parish schoolmaster, first in Montrose, later in North Berwick. This relatively lowly position was perhaps frustrating for a man of considerable learning who, apparently, did not relate easily to other people, especially to children. Quarrelling unpleasantly with the local minister of the Kirk (Established Church) and consequently dismissed from the position of clerk of the session, for 14 years he doggedly pursued litigation until restitution was obtained, showing a persistence that would be a determining trait of David in his adult working life. David saw him controlling the lives of his children, yet the father apparently did not prevent the son from putting in an appearance at the town's Meeting House Sunday School of the Secession Church (it had broken off from the Established Church of Scotland in 1833). Perhaps, in view of his long-running quarrel with his own church, the father encouraged his son to try that of the opposition. In any case, David disliked the experience and attended only once.

The family lived frugally, which helped their father, whose stipend was modest, to send his three older sons to university. James studied medicine at Glasgow; intended for the ministry, George obtained an MA at the University of Aberdeen then embarked on theological studies at St Andrews University, where Ebenezer was doing likewise. Clearly, George senior was concerned for their education and intellectual development, albeit along lines of his choosing. There was at least one occasion, however, when he engaged them in a discussion on a more or less equal footing, purporting to seek their opinion on whether he should switch from his entrenched Conservative support and vote for the Whig candidate in what must have been the 1841 general election.

The two oldest boys were at home from college for the summer vacation. Their father explained that not voting Tory might, in a Whig-leaning electorate, be better for their interests; the sons, whether intimidated or pragmatic, nevertheless recommended Tory support. In recounting this episode, David does not enlarge on his father's behaviour. Did George senior want to foster his sons' political thinking, or was he genuinely seeking guidance in a situation of multifarious religious and political allegiances (Donaldson 1990, 129; Hutchison 1986)? In any case, George did maintain

CHAPTER 2

his allegiance, and the local Tory candidate was returned by a majority of *one*. This did not please the Whig voters of his electorate and brought opprobrium on the family for a time, for there was then no secrecy about the ballot. Whatever young David observed and understood of the political discussion among the males of the family, and whether or not he contributed to it, his strong memory of the occasion bespeaks a nascent political awareness. And he was interested enough to note and remember that the turning point of the election was the question of free trade and protection, an issue that would later be central to his newspaper policies.

David remembered being very lonely at home after his brothers had all gone away to study, Ebenezer in 1841 the last to leave. With other boys of his age (14) gone to sea he too wanted to be a sailor. One can imagine him viewing the traffic of ships in and out of the harbour of North Berwick, and perhaps watching from the shore as vessels sailed away out of the Firth of Forth into the German Ocean (now the North Sea) and dreaming of his own liberation. His parents predictably rejecting the notion, he thought of running away but refrained for his mother's sake, thinking of the grief it would cause her. In secret, however, he taught himself navigation and began to smoke – a practice that would became a habit and may have contributed to the illness that ended his life.

In 1843, in David's 16th year, there were two radical changes on the Scottish ecclesiastical scene that had ramifications for him and his brothers. These were part of a growing tide of opposition to traditional Scottish Calvinism and the Established Presbyterian Church. One was the founding in Kilmarnock on 16 May 1843 of the Evangelical Union. It was set up by Scottish theologian James Morison (1816–1893), as a grouping for Secessionist and Congregationalist churches and embraced a more universalist view of salvation than was allowed in traditional Scottish theology (Escott 1960, 126–134). Two years later this new organisation would be profoundly important for the Syme brothers.

The other, the so-called 'Disruption', began two days later, on 18 May, with a massive walk-out of ministers from the General Assembly of the Church of Scotland in Edinburgh and the consequent secession of about one third of parish ministers and their congregations. The breakaway Free Church of Scotland was formed, comprising initially some 700 congregations (McCaffrey 1998, 37–38). North Berwick, along with innumerable other towns, acquired an additional church, the Free Kirk, and minister. This man made a very unfavourable impression on young David who, with or without his father's sanction, attended at least some of his services and recalled them as dreary in the extreme – a reaction that characterises all his recorded accounts of religious observance in his youth. While we do not know George senior's views of the happenings, there is on record a hint of accompanying disruption at home when George junior, while studying, decided to join the new Free Church. In a character reference written in 1848, he was said to have shown 'great integrity of principle when placed in painful domestic circumstances'.[5]

During David's adolescent years, when his brothers were away at university and he was lonely – his memoirs do not mention his sister Margaret, then in her late 20s, who had left home in 1839 to be a governess (M. Syme 2013, 7) – he studied unremittingly and, in his own words, gained a 'sound' English education and a 'fair knowledge' of Latin. But apparently there was no discussion of or provision for his future when he was of the age and more that his brothers had been sent to university. The most likely explanation of this uncharacteristic neglect of his youngest son's educational welfare is his father's increasing ill health in the years and months before his death on 28 January 1845 aged 56 (Sayers 1965, 6). Thereupon, Mrs Syme and 17-year-old David moved to the town of Bathgate, some 40 miles away, where his brother James had a medical practice.

Inland on the Edinburgh–Glasgow road, Bathgate was then, like North Berwick, a small community, but had some industry in the environs – the Glenmaris Distillery that had opened in 1800 and numerous mines for the extraction of coal, limestone and ironstone – and would grow after the opening in 1849 of the railway from Edinburgh and the establishment of the Bathgate Chemical Works in 1852 ('Bathgate' 2009). The town would have a population of almost 5000 in 1861. In 1845, it was a crossroads for George, Ebenezer and David, brought together there in a way that set each of them on a course that would take them by stages away from the troubled religious preoccupations of Scotland towards new, secular lives in Australia.

While David's ideas about his future were unclear and plans non-existent, both older brothers had undertaken substantial university and theological study and were on course for careers in the church. George, who from 1843 and while still studying, had been preaching in the Free Church at Lockerbie and elsewhere, was dogged by ill health that interfered with pastoral work and studies. Ebenezer, in the final stages of study at St Andrews University, in October 1844 had seen that it was 'high time to be up and doing', and

---

[5]   T. Duncan to G. Syme, 11 November 1848, George Syme Letters.

CHAPTER 2

considered his 'great work on earth is to labour to bring souls to X [Christ]'.[6] He had soon embarked on itinerant preaching at private meetings and in 'meeting houses', apparently also in the Free Church, and was contemplating a course of theological study at Edinburgh University.

All three were in Bathgate with James early in 1845, following the death of their father. At this time, they resolved to enrol for classes in a theological academy run in Kilmarnock by James Morison, the Evangelical Union founder. For some time, both George and Ebenezer had had misgivings about their theological studies and had come to question the doctrines and dogmas not only of the Established Church but also, in George's case, of the Free Church. Ebenezer recorded in his diary on 26 May 1845, after he had begun study at Edinburgh but obviously did not find it right for him, that he was 'Heaving a sigh over the past', felt the 'importance and necessity of a thorough training for a few years' and saw 'no other open door but the Academy, at Kilmarnock'. He also recorded that 'Since I was at Bathgate my brother's sentiments seem to have undergone a similar change'.[7] The brother is most likely George (rather than David) whose papers yield the fact that he had been in Bathgate with James since September 1844 and was still there in February 1845.[8]

Meanwhile, David, also staying with his older brother James at Bathgate, had been having long talks about matters of sin and salvation. These, he recalled, caused his own religious views to change, and he arrived at a position that seemed 'both scientific and scriptural'. His memoirs refer to accepting an invitation to classes at Kilmarnock for two years study of theology and exegetics beginning in August 1845 but, surprisingly, make no mention of his brothers' similar intentions. The evidence suggests, however, that there was at least a great deal of discussion and consultation, if not collective decision-making, and that the older brothers set an example and provided David with a program, at least in the short term.

Very likely the brothers heard of the Evangelical Union classes run by James Morison through meeting his father, Robert, who lived in Bathgate and shared his son's religious beliefs. Over the next few years, Robert would take a kindly, quasi-paternal interest in the welfare of George, Ebenezer and

---

[6] Diary entry, October 1844, Ebenezer Syme Papers, MS Box 132, Australian Manuscripts Collection, State Library of Victoria.
[7] Diary entry, 26 May 1845, Ebenezer Syme Papers.
[8] R. Johnston to G. Syme, 13 September 1844, 19 February 1845, George Syme Letters.

David. (Their older brother James drops out of the picture, dying in the late 1840s from typhus, contracted from a patient.)⁹

James Morison is seen today as a key person in the 'humanising of Scottish theology in the mid-nineteenth century' with a 'supreme place' in the movement away from Calvinism to 'Universal Atonement theology' (Escott 1960, 107, 116). With the support of the inaugural conference of the Evangelical Union, Morison set up his academy in Kilmarnock, holding classes in the church classroom for the training of ministers. Classes included Hebrew, Old Testament Greek and the scientific exegesis of the New Testament, Systematic Theology and practical sermon-work. Morison was the principal teacher, providing his services gratis. Classes were held in August and September each year, the full course running for five years. Teaching began for the first session in 1843; in 1845, 31 students were enrolled, including the three Syme brothers. The time at Kilmarnock marks the brothers' move still further away from Scottish Calvinism, with George and Ebenezer both leaving the Free Church. Those two attended the academy for one session only, then moved by stages to settle into pastoral appointments and family life.

Ebenezer's diary entry of 4 November 1845 reads: 'During the months of August & September I was at Kilmarnock enjoying the instructions of Mr Morison – will owe much to him throughout eternity…Brothers George & David were there also – the time was a precious one.' Cryptically, the following words are: 'might have been more so.' Does this mean he would have liked longer, or that there was dissension, or something else? In any case, after this session, Ebenezer returned to Bathgate. Whether from a sense of vocation or financial necessity, he thought that he needed to preach rather than study, but saw then that he could not profess Baptist views and neither was an Evangelical Union position possible.

In September 1845 Ebenezer decided to travel to Liverpool and learn Chinese, having been encouraged at Kilmarnock to become a missionary in China. On hearing that the Chinese teacher had left, he went to Liverpool anyway, and preached there and, subsequently, in and around Manchester, where he made friends with and stayed at the house of William Holland, a radical nonconformist (Sayers 1965, 263).¹⁰ At this time he decided definitely to be an independent street preacher, and embarked on travels

---

9   D. Rogers to C. Sayers, 19 May 1964, SFP Box 1196/1(a).
10   Diary entries, November 1845 (recalling events of previous months), Ebenezer Syme Papers.

CHAPTER 2

around Scotland and northern England. This migratory life worried Robert Morison who, in a letter to George in May 1847, advocated a 'permanent station' and regular habits, observing: 'Bustle and tactics will never succeed long. I earnestly wish that Ebenezer would calmly act upon these principles more fully as much as you and David, otherwise he will find out at the last that he has miscalculated his position'.[11]

On 21 April 1848, at the young age of 22, Ebenezer married Jane Hilton Rowan, aged 20, in the Cathedral Parish Church, Manchester, with friend William Holland a witness.[12] By then he was, as shown on the marriage certificate, a Baptist Minister in Glasgow; this notwithstanding an earlier critical stance vis-à-vis the Baptist Church. On 29 November the same year he officiated at the marriage in Glasgow of his sister Margaret to John Gourlay, warehouseman, who will be heard of again, in Melbourne.[13] The following year Ebenezer and Jane had their first child, a son whom they named William Holland, and in 1850 a second, George Alexander, after his paternal grandfather and uncle. Now a family man, Ebenezer finally obtained a fixed appointment, installed on 16 May 1850 as Missionary of the North of England Unitarian Church Association in the Unitarian Chapel, Sunderland, in Durham.[14] Possibly Jane was adding to the family income, for the 1851 Census gives her occupation as milliner and dressmaker.[15]

George, meanwhile, was suffering health problems, as he would for the rest of his life, these mentioned countless times by his correspondents; his great-grandson Marten Syme (2013, 28, 29) has written of his 'debilitating affliction' and 'chronic illness'. In 1846 he was travelling on the Continent, one reason being therapeutic, to take a water cure at Vincent Priessnitz's famous spa in Gräfenberg, Austria (now part of Jesenik in the Czech Republic) ('Vincenz Priessnitz' 2013). Issued in Edinburgh, his passport was for travel to Hamburg, Berlin, Dresden 'and other places' and the legible endorsements thereon indeed show that between March and October he was in Hamburg, Berlin and also Gräfenberg.[16] A note in the passport tells us that the then 25 year-old was a 'Gentleman' (significantly, not a clergyman),

---

[11] R. Morison to G. Syme, 5 May 1847, George Syme Letters.
[12] Family History Report, Ebenezer Syme and Jane Hilton Rowan, dated 23 October 2009, supplied by Pru Williams.
[13] Banns and Marriages 1538–1854, www.scotlandspeople.gov.uk, accessed 1 December 2009.
[14] Installation address, Ebenezer Syme Papers.
[15] Family History Report.
[16] Passport, dated 6 November 1845, in George Syme Letters.

with a fair complexion, grey eyes, brown hair and an oval face. At five feet and nine inches he was considerably shorter than David in adulthood.

Returning to Britain, he was appointed City Missionary in Manchester, and then Railway Missionary in and around Warwick and elsewhere. In the same letter of May 1847 where he expressed concern about Ebenezer, Robert Morison proffered the advice that George, obviously still beset by serious and chronic health problems, should have a 'dogged determination to occupy a permanent position', seeing that no man could expect to be honoured and useful without one. And indeed George did find a position. Moving to Nottingham in late 1848, he was an assistant preacher for a time, then obtained a permanent appointment, at a new Baptist chapel (Wylie 1853, 129). In September 1850 he married Susannah (Susan) Goodier in Chorlton, south of Manchester.[17]

For David, living in Kilmarnock was to experience a much larger place than North Berwick or Bathgate. A substantial, attractive town in a mining, manufacturing, agricultural and commercial district, it had a railway and was home to a weekly newspaper, the Conservative-leaning weekly *Kilmarnock Journal*, established in 1834 (Mitchell 1851). There for two sessions at the academy, David was impressed with the religious views of James Morison, whom he found to be 'an eminent preacher' and 'a man of considerable erudition'. His fellow students he recalled as 'bright and earnest young men', and noted that he met several of them later in Australia, where none of them were preaching. For two years, and it is not known where, or with what financial support, he applied himself between sessions to theological and linguistic studies. He became proficient in Hebrew, and began to learn Arabic, aspiring to become an oriental linguist. But this was a side issue. Driving himself to study, overworked, he reached a point of nervous exhaustion and, most likely, deep depression, seeing himself with no particular linguistic ability and losing heart for biblical studies.

His memoirs record a breakdown in health that obliged him to give up the studies. The time had not been wasted, however, for he had developed scholarly habits and an interest in and quite deep if eclectic knowledge of the pre-Christian world that would surface decades later, a testimony to which is the temple that is his final resting place in the Boroondara Cemetery.

It is not clear exactly when the collapse occurred, but it seems that the trouble was looming and the signs evident to others early in 1847. His brother George was concerned; as was Robert Morison, mentor to all three

---

[17] Marriage record, freebmd.rootsweb.com, accessed 3 December 2009.

CHAPTER 2

brothers. In May he recommended to George that David should be got into active and, desirably, remunerative employment, perhaps as a missionary to the railway workers with George and, if called upon he would 'give a sincere recommendation' to a Mr William Brock.[18] An undated letter from Brock to George shows that this was not successful: 'I regret the failure of my efforts to find any situation…for your brother. The demand…seems very far to exceed the supply'.[19]

David's memoirs continue vague about his movements and source of support in 1847 and 1848. Giving up his theological studies, he was advised, he does not say by whom, to travel to Germany for a water cure. Very likely the advice came from George, who would also been able to recommend specific places, people and activities. David would have left for the Continent some time in 1848. His account is frustratingly brief, particularly considering that he was there in or just following the 'Year of Revolutions' and surely must have heard and talked about the national movements in Germany and elsewhere (Stearns 1974).

En route to the Gräfenberg spa, he stopped in Berlin for several weeks with students he had known in Scotland (at Kilmarnock?). He was at Gräfenberg for three months, then went to Vienna, and from there to Heidelberg for some six months. He wrote of attending classes at the University of Heidelberg for the 1849 session, and that he took more interest in the teachings of the philosopher Wilhelm Friedrich Hegel than in theology. The University website notes that in the nineteenth century the institution was 'widely celebrated for its…liberality and commitment to democratic ideals and its openness to new ideas' and that 'this combination attracted a large number of foreign students' ('History of Heidelberg University' 2013). As the University has no record of Syme's enrolment, it is possible that he attended as a 'guest', with the special permission of the professors concerned.[20]

There is an alternative possibility: Don Veitch (2001, 69–71) has made a case for David's attendance at public lectures of the philosopher Ludwig Andreas Feuerbach, given from December 1848 to March 1849 in the Heidelberg City Hall. Feuerbach had in the 1820s abandoned theological studies to study philosophy under Hegel in Berlin and natural science at Erlangen, and had moved to espouse the view that religion is a projection

---

[18] R. Morison to G. Syme, 5 May 1847, George Syme Letters.
[19] W. Brock to G. Syme, undated, George Syme Letters.
[20] Email to the author from Dr Werner Moritz, Director of Archives, Heidelberg University, 16 April 2009.

of the human mind. After Hegel's death in 1831 he had been a leading member of the radical young Hegelians. Now a hero to young students, he had been invited by them to give public lectures on the essence and role of religion.

This must have been heady stuff for young David. Liberated from the strictures and convolutions of Scottish theological doctrines and dissensions, he would have been able to apply his training in scholarly habits and his native powers of observation and analysis and launch himself on the course of independent thinking that would characterise his intellectual endeavour for the rest of his life. After a year's absence he returned to Scotland, speaking some German he said, acquainted with some philosophical thought and with his health restored. More than that, his travels and study had oriented him to matters secular and given him grounding in political philosophy and economy on which he would draw and build in the years ahead.

David was the first of the three brothers to turn away from a career in the church. After his return from the Continent he had no settled ideas about a future. He applied for many jobs (of what kind we do not know), finally obtaining a position as reader on a Glasgow newspaper. This essential job of checking proofs for compositorial accuracy, what today is termed proofreader, was low in the newspaper office hierarchy. Which newspaper employed him, and exactly when, we do not know. It would probably have been around 1850, when the city's population was approaching 350,000 and growing (Mitchell 1851). Scotland's principal port, the city was a centre for trade in cotton and the manufacture of iron 'on a vast scale'. Culturally, it possessed an 'ancient' university, celebrated schools, literary and scientific institutions and public charities. In fact, the Glasgow experience may well have provided the young man with a template of progress and development that would, in years to come, guide his visions for the growth of Melbourne.

Most important for David, however, there were 14 newspapers in publication: eight weeklies, one issued three times a week, three issued twice, and two recently established dailies. Something foreign to the press of today, all claimed a political and/or religious allegiance. Both of the new dailies – the Glasgow *Daily Mail*, established in 1848, and the Glasgow *North British Mail*, published from 1847 – professed to be 'Liberal' (rather than 'Conservative'). Whichever employed David (it seems impossible to know), he must have become acquainted with the rich newspaper culture of this metropolis – something for future reference, which he would not have gained in his earlier places of residence.

CHAPTER 2

Considering his years of serious study, both imposed and self-driven, it is not surprising that David found the work 'easy' and he believed he was 'giving satisfaction', although the manager did hint that he 'need not be so severe on the leading articles', which suggests that he was going beyond the requirements of his position. This fledgling career in newspaper work ended when David came to consider career advancement on the paper as not very promising compared with the prospects on the Californian goldfields. Reading the letters about the goldrushes sent by the special correspondent of the New York *Tribune* (and presumably published in the paper for which he worked), he decided to try his luck in the New World. ('Here, I said to myself, is a country where there is room & opportunity'.) Albeit relatively brief, his stint on a Glasgow newspaper would have given him some idea of the structure and functioning of this kind of business.

Sailing from London in 1851, David reached San Francisco, arriving at a city severely damaged by the great fire of June that year. Ebenezer's diary entry for 2 August refers to a dream that their brother James had drowned at sea, which he interpreted as referring to David, for, as he wrote, James had been dead for several years, while David had gone to California.[21] Whether this phenomenon occurred while David was on the high seas or after his safe arrival, the five-month voyage had been eventful and dangerous, with the ship battling a severe storm while rounding Cape Horn. David remembered that it was like 'sailing over a series of snow-covered mountain ranges'.

Leaving San Francisco, David embarked on prospecting at a succession of sites around California, finding this physically hard and the books on geology and gold mining he had brought with him of little help. Gradually, after several months of misadventure and perseverance, he was able to settle down to steady work. He liked the country and the climate, but did not take to the people he met in mining camps, finding the average American 'ill-informed' and lamenting the lack of literature, even a newspaper, on the goldfields. (Newspapers there were, notably San Francisco's daily *Alta California*, but apparently he did not come across them.)

David decided to make for goldfields new, on 1 July 1852 setting sail for Melbourne, Australia, on the *Europe*. He had money enough to travel as a cabin passenger, not in steerage.[22] The vessel was very old and unseaworthy and captained by a rogue. With insufficient food and unscheduled, unpleasant stops in Samoa, the New Hebrides and other Pacific Islands, the voyage was

---

21 Diary entry, 2 August 1851, Ebenezer Syme Papers.
22 'Shipping', *Maitland Mercury*, 25 September 1852, p. 2.

distasteful to say the least, and when the ship eventually arrived in Sydney on 21 September, David chose to disembark and four days later took the regular intercolonial steamer service to Melbourne. Voyaging on the *Waratah*, and again with the funds to travel as a cabin passenger, he left Sydney for the city where, several years later, he would settle to his life's work.

During his several months in California David Syme had learned the hard way that the secret of success in some occupations was not through scholarly methods but through hard, practical experience, with a degree of open-minded trial and error. Moreover, he learned to rough it with a range of men, supporting himself by his own labour – experience he would use on the goldfields of Victoria and take with him to apply to the practical, technical and managerial sides of the work he would later be responsible for.

David was the first of the Syme siblings to make Australia home. His brother Ebenezer would make the journey the following year; in 1857 his sister Margaret and husband John Gourlay and the widowed mother Jean Syme would arrive; and in 1863 his brother George. The migration of Syme siblings – the three Scottish dissenters who were becoming singular secularists turning to journalism and their down-to-earth, reliable brother-in-law – would be very important for the *Age* newspaper business during its foundation years, and thereafter.

Chapter 3

DAVID AND EBENEZER

First Years in Victoria

David

David Syme disembarked in Melbourne on 29 September 1852, and the following day set out on foot for the goldfields of central Victoria.[1] His brother Ebenezer, who arrived with his wife and family some nine months later, chose not to join the general exodus from the capital of the young colony but fell on his feet in Melbourne newspaper circles. Within two years he gravitated to the nascent daily *Age,* and 18 months later became its owner. How his younger brother David later came to be associated with this newspaper enterprise will be seen in following chapters.

David recalled being one of the great throng of immigrants to Victoria in 1852 after the news of the gold discoveries of 1851 reached Europe and America.[2] He wrote of 1000 arriving each week; in fact there were even more, for historical statistics show 69,181 persons migrating to Victoria in 1852, swelling the population to almost 168,321 by the end of December – a population growth rate for the colony in that year of almost 73 per cent, never since equalled (ABS 1986, 4). Hobson's Bay teemed with ships arriving in numbers each day, while in the streets and lodging houses of Melbourne there were hordes of men, mostly single, taking their bearings before leaving the metropolis. In fact, the city held only about one-quarter of Victoria's population; the greater part of the other three-quarters was on the goldfields.

---

[1] 'Shipping', *Melbourne Morning Herald*, 30 September 1852. The David Syme, miner, whom the Public Record Office Victoria's shipping records show as having arrived on the *El Dorado* from Liverpool in November is a different person, perhaps the David Syme, 1830–1900, who later joined the *Age* business as a compositor and was there until two months before his death in 1900.

[2] As in the previous chapter, unreferenced material derives from DS notebooks.

For the next four years David was one of these men, prospecting for gold as he had done in California. He set off from Melbourne with scant delay. With little money, he said, he spent five shillings to stay in a hotel overnight, and the next day, with a man met there, began the walk to the Mount Alexander diggings (now Castlemaine) 119 kilometres to the northwest. This would have taken several days; in 1854 it took 25-year-old Danish Claus Gronn four, although he had expected to make the journey in two and a half (Gronn 1981, 62).

During his first day out David was threatened by a character aiming a weapon at short range – the first of numerous unpleasant experiences as a prospector in Victoria. His memoirs, virtually the only source for this period, tell stories of adventures and excitement, of good luck followed by bad, and vice versa. While he took in his stride the turns of fortune, including being cheated and robbed, such experiences left him with a lasting distrust: 'The lesson to me was never to be cock sure of anything', he reflected.

At the Mount Alexander diggings, and in spite of huge rushes and finds since late 1851, David found slim pickings and moved on to the Bendigo fields. These were little better, added to which, his 'friend' made off with David's share of the gold. Learning that Beechworth was the 'centre of attention', he travelled the not inconsiderable distance of more than 320 kilometres (on foot?), armed against bushrangers (he had learned to shoot in California, he wrote). Although it was the site of a big rush in the summer of 1852/53, he found the ground 'worked out' and stayed only a couple of weeks. In Beechworth he teamed up with Jesse Tymons (later spelled Timmins), an American whom he had met on the voyage from California. The two travelled back to the central goldfields district and 'did very well' at Daylesford. They should have stayed longer, but could not resist the attractions of Ballarat, then, as David remembered, 'in the zenith of its glory'. There the pair took up two claims and, demonstrating a considerable degree of enterprise and actual or anticipated funds, employed four men to dig shafts. They were taking risks, for one shaft struck water and was flooded and, after four months' work draining it, no gold was found.

David's sources of information about promising gold-bearing areas probably came by word of mouth rather than from published sources for, although Melbourne and Geelong newspapers were available on the goldfields in the early 1850s, the goldfields press did not become established until well into 1855. Castlemaine's short-lived *Castlemaine Yarner and Digger's Gazette* came out in December 1853, as did the *Bendigo Advertiser* (the first goldfields newspaper to endure), in each case after David had left

CHAPTER 3

the district. It was the same with Beechworth's *Ovens and Murray Advertiser*, which began publication in January 1855. His memoirs refer often to making the acquaintance of fellow gold-seekers, and one may infer that he was sociably open to gleaning useful information in conversation.

After the Ballarat debacle, David had a short spell in Melbourne, 'uncertain what to do next'. This was probably in mid- to late 1854, and one assumes that he would have reunited (and stayed?) with Ebenezer, although he does not say so. But characteristically undeterred (and had he done some research in Melbourne?) and with his erstwhile partner Tymons, he took out a large claim on a quartz reef at Mount Egerton (then spelled Edgerton) east of Ballarat. It was a quiet and out-of-the-way place, he recalled, although the *Age* of 4 September 1855 talked it up, noting there were many steam machines in operation and diggers wanting shares. David and Jesse ordered large crushing machinery, which never arrived (a lesson to be remembered in the trials later over obtaining printing machinery). Six men were brought from Melbourne to work the claim, pegged at the end of 1854. After some six months, with gold-bearing quartz piling up for all to see, their claim was, by stages, encroached on. David, evincing persistence like his father's, sought redress. While the Warden at Ballarat gave some support, subsequently the magistrate at Egerton gave an unfavourable ruling. Ebenezer then wrote at length to the Colonial Secretary in October 1855 and voiced the matter through the columns of the *Age*, leading to a rambling 'Opinion of Law Officers' (Attorney-General William Stawell and Solicitor-General Robert Molesworth) dated December.[3] This failed to address the rights of the issue, instead concluding that the magistrate and assessors 'formed a competent tribunal' (that is, their decision was not to be challenged). This had not been communicated to David when he protested to the Colonial Secretary on 24 January 1856: 'we are left entirely without redress, and are now altogether at the mercy of the jumpers, who have gone one step further and *possessed themselves of the remaining portion of our claim*'. A reply dated 29 January communicating the adverse opinion was then sent to him – the sorry end of a matter propelled by some impetuous lack of caution on the part of David and his partner and bungling and bias from the authorities. Commenting in February on the '*denouement*' of the case, the *Argus* deemed the claim jumping 'an outrage upon law and order [which] seems to have been sanctioned by the Government'.[4]

---

[3] 'Quartz Claim of Messrs Syme and Co.', *Victorian Parliamentary Papers* (hereafter VPP), Legislative Council, 1855–56, no. C 26. The document includes correspondence from the Syme brothers to the authorities.

[4] 'Domestic Intelligence', *Argus*, 27 February 1856, p. 6, col. 1.

The partners sold up and went their separate ways, Tymons to mine in the Omeo district. Although he did not completely lose touch with his American partner, David's career as a miner was over. Making a living in the rough and tumble of mining communities, he had learned, however, to be independent and enterprising. Observing and adapting to conditions and opportunities for individuals, he acquired a sense of what governments might do through legislative measures. At the time of the Eureka uprising he would probably have been in Melbourne or Mount Egerton. By word of mouth and the newspapers, including the *Ballarat Times*, published from March 1854, he would have known about the miners' grievances. To these he was sympathetic, but took no part in the agitation. Law-abiding, he had mining licences for himself and employees. He had also gained valuable business experience in cooperating with a partner, engaging workers, ordering equipment – skills that could well be applied elsewhere.

Ebenezer

Meanwhile in England, at the other end of the earth, Ebenezer (fig.3.1) had given up his religious vocation for a secular occupation. He left the pulpit in 1851, having been a Unitarian minister in Sunderland for less than 18 months. While his decision to leave may have been brewing for a long time, the move was sudden. His diary entry for 4 April 1851 includes a fundamental question about the essential divinity or humanity of Jesus, while that of 8 May records that he was determined at last to engage in business, in a situation having nothing to do with 'speculative opinion' and where success is not dependent on it.[5]

By then, Ebenezer had responded to an advertisement by the London bookseller John Chapman for an assistant. After meeting the applicant, whom he described as 'tall, striking and powerful', Chapman decided to engage him as 'manager' (Haight 1969, 165). Ebenezer moved himself and family to London and began work at the bookshop in early July. While his first task was to re-arrange the window display, his literary and journalistic talents soon came to the fore (Elder n.d.).[6] Shortly after, Chapman took over the *Westminster Review*, a periodical of high standing of which it has been written: 'the history of the *Westminster* is the history of illustrious men and women of the nineteenth century' (Wallins 1983, 429). Chapman published

---

[5] Diary entries, 4 April, 8 May 1851, Ebenezer Syme Papers, MS Box 132, Australian Manuscripts Collection, State Library of Victoria.

[6] Diary entry, 22 July 1851, Ebenezer Syme Papers.

CHAPTER 3

Figure 3.1. Ebenezer Syme. (*Courtesy of Fairfax Media*)

this learned quarterly until 1859, owned it until 1887, and edited it until 1894. Marian Evans, a budding novelist who would become known as George Eliot, was assistant editor from September 1851 to January 1854. Ebenezer became her assistant, working diligently in spite of health problems.[7] He contributed numerous reviews and articles to the *Westminster*. On the whole these were valued, although Evans sometimes had reservations about his style (Eliot 1954, v. 1, 354). He edited and mainly wrote 'The Contemporary Literature of England', a series of articles published in it from April 1852 to April 1853.

---

[7] Chapman's diary entry, 24 September 1851, in Haight (1969, 214).

Through Chapman, Ebenezer met a range of liberal and radical thinkers and writers, possibly including the American Horace Greeley, founder of the New York *Tribune*, who was boarding with Chapman at the time and whom David would years later seek to contact (Haight 1969, 164, 195). He strengthened his friendship with the radical author, publisher and bookseller George Jacob Holyoake, whom he had met in 1850, and whose brother Henry he would come to know in Melbourne (Elder n.d., 5–6). In 1850, Holyoake had helped found a weekly, the radical *Leader*, which may have been a model for the *Melbourne Leader*, published from January 1856 at the *Age* office.

Ebenezer was leading a full life outside his paid employment. Advertisements in the London *Leader* show that in 1852 he was giving lectures in the evenings on subjects ranging from 'Jesus, the Galilean Reformer' to 'Mahomet' to 'Is there a Life after Death', indicating how far he had come from narrow evangelism and towards comparative and secular thinking. In January and February 1853 he moderated a debate between Holyoake and one Reverend Brewer Grant on the question: 'What Advantages would accrue to Mankind in general and to the working classes in particular by the removal of Christianity and the substitution of Secularism in its place?' held in the Royal Institution and drawn out over six weekly sessions. The published text of the debate sold 45,000 copies over the next nine months (Elder n.d., 6).

In March Ebenezer left Chapman's employment, preparatory to migrating with his family to Melbourne. Perhaps this was prompted by his poor health; perhaps a recommendation from David on the goldfields of Victoria was a factor. Ebenezer, however, had been hearing and reading about the Australian colonies. Chapman had lived for a time in South Australia in its early years; Marian Evans was encouraging her widowed sister to emigrate (Elder n.d., 6–7); and Ebenezer would have been familiar with books about Australia regularly reviewed in the *Westminster*. Three were reviewed in the January 1853 issue: *Memoirs of Mrs. Caroline Chisholm*; *Australia As It Is* by F. Lancelott; and Samuel Sidney's *The Three Colonies of Australia*. Leaving London, Ebenezer, Jane and their three sons (a third, Joseph Cowen, named after a supporter of Chartism and revolutionary movements in Europe, had arrived in 1852) travelled to Scotland (to see and farewell friends and relatives?) and in April 1853 left Glasgow on the *Abdalla* for Melbourne, arriving in July.[8]

---

[8] Unassisted Inward Passenger Lists to Victoria 1852–1923, Public Record Office Victoria.

CHAPTER 3

Presumably the brothers' reunion was facilitated by advertisements that each placed in the *Argus* (on 27 July, 'Ebenezer Syme wishes to find his brother David Syme…'; on 29 July and following days, 'Ebenezer Syme will find a letter for him…'). Ebenezer's papers in the State Library of Victoria include a manuscript document entitled 'First Impressions', similar to but more expansive than those in David's memoirs.[9] The newcomer saw 'wave after wave of stalwart men in the variegated and picturesque costume of the gold-digger…form in groups at the corners of the principal streets…where they discuss the probabilities of the last new rush'. This essay must have been written some years later, however, with some literary licence referring anachronistically to the men falling 'easy victim to the news-boys as they ply their daily avocation with desperate energy hinting at wonderful disclosures in the columns of the Hage and Hargus'. Of these two Melbourne dailies, while the *Argus* began publication in 1846, the *Age* did not appear until October 1854, some 15 months after Ebenezer's arrival.

Ebenezer later wrote in the *Age* that 'Three years ago…[he had] landed as an "adventurer" on these shores', in the hope of finding what he could not find without difficulty in England – 'a home for his family, and a sphere of action for his own energies', and noted that since his arrival he had 'labored quietly in his vocation as a journalist'.[10] 'Quiet' is not an adjective that fits with Ebenezer or his writing. It is true that he readily found work as a journalist, although we cannot be sure we know all the newspapers he wrote for, or when, before joining the *Age* in early 1855. John Pascoe Fawkner in January 1838 gave Melbourne its first newspaper, the *Melbourne Advertiser*. Thereafter, new papers were constantly being launched, usually with high hopes but insufficient capital to cover establishment costs, let alone enough advertisers and subscribers to produce even minimal profits for their proprietors. Only the fittest that survived are generally known about today. At the time, however, the newspaper publishing scene of Melbourne, always in flux, was prolific and competitive, and starting to become so in country Victoria also. A colonial press was evolving and, with it, an esprit de corps amongst the newspaper men (Morrison 2005, Chapter 3).

We do not know whether Ebenezer ever contributed to the daily *Melbourne Morning Herald*, the twice-weekly *Banner*, the weekly *Reformer* or the weekly *Express*, all being published in mid-1853. We do know that he joined the daily *Argus*, and came to write also for the weekly *Diggers Advocate*, begun

---

9   'Melbourne: First Impressions', Ebenezer Syme Papers.
10 'To Our Readers', *Age*, 7 June 1856, p. 2.

on 3 November 1853 by miners' leader George Edward Thomson (E. Syme 1977; Darragh 1997, 91 [31.01]). The first extant copy, 10 November, shows a professional-looking four-page newspaper priced at sixpence and carrying, besides many advertisements and notices, news items from the diggings at Bendigo, Forest Creek and Ballarat. It would appear that Ebenezer became a contributor through its editor Henry Holyoake, brother of George in London. This issue advertises in a Missing Friends column: 'If this should meet the eye of the Rev Ebenezer Syme from London, Mr. H. Holyoake would be glad to hear from him. Direct to the Central Office of this paper at Bendigo or the Diggers Advocate Box Post Office Melbourne.'

In December, the paper was sold to miner George Black, who had been a Methodist lay preacher in Nottingham (did he know George Syme?) and an itinerant Chartist lecturer before his migration to Victoria (Crail 2010). Retitled the *Gold Diggers Advocate and Commercial Advertiser* and expanded to eight pages, for several months it bore the old masthead illustration. Holyoake continued as editor and Ebenezer as a contributor (having joined the staff of the *Argus* by this time). The paper on 15 July sported a new engraved masthead illustration: a shield bearing mining motifs above the motto 'Advance Australia' and the exhortation: 'Labour Founds Empires; Knowledge and Virtue Excel and Perpetuate Them'. This issue and subsequent ones take forceful editorial positions about the state and future of Victoria, strongly opposing the government's position vis-à-vis the miners. The last issue extant, which may be the last published, is that of 16 September 1854, when troubles on the Ballarat goldfields were mounting, in the lead up to the Eureka rebellion.

The *Age*

The *Age* was being planned at this very time. Three Melbourne newspapers ceased shortly before it began: the *Gold Diggers Advocate*, the *Express* (last extant issue 2 September) and the *Banner* (last extant issue 22 September). Priced at sixpence a copy, their circulations must have been adversely affected when the daily *Argus* cut its price to threepence some months earlier. (The *Argus* raised the price again to sixpence on 14 September, presumably after the damage was done.)

A look at some of the personnel illustrates the interconnectedness of the community of pressmen, and of their papers, and points to the sharing of scarce printing equipment: the conditions in which the *Age* made its appearance. The proprietor of the *Banner*, Hugh McColl, had been for a

CHAPTER 3

short time responsible for printing both it and the *Gold Diggers Advocate*. In February 1854, the latter was being printed at the *Melbourne Morning Herald* office by Frederick Sinnett, then editor of the *Herald* and also joint proprietor of the new *Mount Alexander Mail* at Castlemaine on the central Victorian goldfields.

In June 1854 Henry Cooke, merchant, together with journalists Jabez Ham and Thomas Lockyer Bright, bought the *Express* (Darragh 1997, 89 [27.09–10]). Henry's brother Francis, also a merchant, provided one of the two sureties required by law. In August the Cooke brothers were planning to bring out a daily, the *Age*, perhaps also intending to stop the *Express*. On 8 September a prospectus for it was issued.[11] The *Age* premises would be those of the *Express*, at 21 Elizabeth Street. The demise of the three weeklies meant access to a ready work force (the newly unemployed compositors, printers, reporters, etc.) and printing equipment, and a potential readership amongst the subscribers to and purchasers of the defunct publications.

With roles reversed, the up and running *Age* would be registered in the name of Francis Cooke and Co, with Henry this time underwriting it (Darragh 1997, 92 [37.01]). Thomas Bright, who had edited the *Express* since mid-1853, was to carry a large share of the editorial responsibilities (Darragh 1997, 89 [27.07]; Pratt 1908, 46, 48). It seems that the proprietors (plural, assuming that both Francis and Henry were involved) intended the new paper to have a distinctive if undenominational religious character. The prospectus declared that the *Age* would be an unaligned force for moderation and, while 'unsectarian', would stand for making 'the power of the press subservient to the diffusion of a pure and Christian morality'. This is not how we think of the 19th-century *Age*. We see it and its rival *Argus* as diametrically opposed, the latter diehard conservative, the former by contrast determinedly radical. This was not the case in 1854, however, when the idealistically reformist Ebenezer Syme was writing for the *Argus* – a paper, then under Edward Wilson's direction and described as pursuing a 'wild Democratic course' (Bonwick 1890, 69). It was dissatisfaction with this course and the desire in 'certain religious circles' for a 'more Christian and moderate journal' that was seen as the reason for the establishment of the *Age*.

The 'religious circles' are, however, hard to pin down. In August Bright visited a number of people to discuss support for and prospects of the new paper being considered. The only one he named, in a public statement some months later, is the Bishop of Melbourne – presumably the Anglican,

---

11   Reproduced in the *Age*, 17 October 1854, p. 1, col. 6.

Charles Perry – who had on 17 August supplied a statement of unqualified support: 'It would afford me great gratification if a daily newspaper could be established upon Christian and in the true sense of the word, catholic principles… I therefore very heartily wish success to this undertaking.'[12]

The issue of morality and religion as a guiding principle for a newspaper had been aired in the short-lived *Reformer*, owned by Thomas McCombie, journalist, businessman and later politician. Formerly, while he was editor and part-proprietor of the *Port Phillip Gazette* from 1844 to 1851, he had printed and published a succession of religious periodicals from the *Gazette* office. The subject would soon be swept away, however, in the dramatic unfolding of political events in late 1854 and early 1855 that had a galvanising effect on the press of Melbourne.

As had been foreshadowed in its prospectus, the *Age* appeared on Tuesday 17 October, also the day of the opening of the 1854 Melbourne Exhibition. An eight-page, six-column broadsheet, it was priced at sixpence per copy. Over the words COLONY OF VICTORIA, the masthead carries an engraved royal lion-and-unicorn '*Honi soit qui mal y pense*' and '*Dieu et Mon Droit*' British royal coat of arms, modified to include two sheep in a pastoral setting – but not a hint of mines and diggers. The format and layout are standard for the time: the first three pages contain advertising and notices including government advertisements, a staple revenue source. Pages 4 to 5 include shipping information, commercial columns, the editorial and sub-leaders, followed by the program of the Exhibition and sundry other local reports. 'Religious Statistics' occupy two and a half columns on page 6, followed by advertisements that continue to page 8, at the bottom of which is the imprint required by law: 'Printed and published by Francis Cooke (for the proprietors Francis Cooke & Co.,) at the *Age* Newspaper and general Printing Office, 21 Elizabeth Street, South, Melbourne, in the Colony of Victoria.'

By prior arrangement this first issue was printed in the Exhibition premises, the Crystal Palace in William Street, later the site of the Royal Mint building. A large poster was also printed, recommending the paper to potential readers and advertisers and advising that subscribers for the first quarter would receive a splendid illustrated supplement, intended as a specimen of colonial art.[13] The poster also informed that a 'unique Copy

---

[12] Perry's statement was reproduced in Thomas Bright's, 'The *Age* and the Bishop of Melbourne', *Age*, 15 January 1855, p. 4.

[13] Facsimile copy of poster, in possession of Mimi Colligan.

CHAPTER 3

will be executed in Gold, on White Satin, for Exhibition in Melbourne, and transmission to The Great Paris Exhibition' (the Paris Exposition Universelle of May to November 1855). Notwithstanding this international reach, the list of agents named in this issue was restricted to parts of Melbourne – Collingwood, Richmond including Prahran, St Kilda and Windsor, Emerald Hill (South Melbourne) and Sandridge (Port Melbourne), North Melbourne and Williamstown, and the growing port town of Geelong some 97 kilometres to the west, on Port Phillip Bay. The editorial page carries an apology for 'imperfections' and omissions, due to printing problems. Although the printing quality is uneven, the newspaper has a thoroughly professional layout. That 33 of its 48 columns carry advertisements bespeaks an inheritance from its predecessor, the *Express*, and expectations of reliable revenue, whatever the initial circulation, which is not known.

The *Argus* acknowledged the new daily in a patronising sub-leader two days later. Entitled 'Puritans of the Press', it purported to be charitable about the 'infant...brought into the world'. Noting that it 'hoists the *religious flag*', it refuted any implication that the *Argus* was irreligious. The *Melbourne Morning Herald* did not mention the new competitor.

The appearance of the *Age* coincided with the disturbances on the Ballarat goldfields, but these, while brewing in the months previous, do not seem to have been determining factors in the newspaper's creation. Unlike the other Melbourne dailies and the daily *Geelong Advertiser* (dating from 1840, it was the colony's oldest country paper), the *Age* had at first no agents or correspondents on the goldfields. The day of first publication and opening of the Exhibition, 17 October, was also the day of a mass protest meeting of miners in Ballarat that turned provocative and violent, with the Eureka Hotel burned down. During the next six weeks, when the Ballarat Reform League was formed, bigger mass meetings were held and mining licences ostentatiously burned. Opposition to the Governor and authorities culminated in the deadly confrontation of the so-called Eureka Stockade – miners and their supporters against government troops, at which 30 of the former were killed, attacked by stealth early on Sunday 3 December.[14]

Until this time, editorials in the *Age* make scant comment on the goldfields unrest, with most devoted to municipal and local matters. Not until Tuesday 5 December was there a coming to grips with what was happening and the causes behind it. 'The Hour of Trial' leader, while acknowledging some 'misconduct' of the Government, calls on the diggers

---

14   For an account of the Eureka uprising, see Serle (1977, Chapter 6).

to stop their 'career of revolt'. For the rest of the month, the several editorials recounting and commenting on the aftermath, including the arrest of the perceived ringleaders for high treason and the editor of the *Ballarat Times*, Henry Seekamp, for sedition (for inflammatory editorials in his paper that were almost certainly not written by him), are generally on the side of law and order and the authorities. At best they are even-handed. Under Francis Cooke and Co. the *Age* did not engage with the literally burning issue of the day.

But this regime was not to last. The editors and staff were diverging from the law and order stance of the proprietors. Moreover, the newspaper business was under-financed. The *Age* of 26 December announced that publication would have to be discontinued. On 4 December Francis Cooke & Co had appealed for a loan to John Fawkner, Melbourne's first newspaper proprietor and now a man of property. The firm had obtained £500 from him, at 10 per cent interest payable when profits would allow, but this amount was far less than the losses the Cookes had sustained.[15] However, on 30 December, the day the *Age* might have to cease, it was instead registered, as required by law, with Francis Cooke as proprietor and publisher and sureties provided by Henry Cooke and the editor Thomas Bright (Darragh 1997, 92 [37.01]).

The *Age* continued to appear, but not with the Cooke brothers as owners. A cooperative of 26 *Age* employees, mostly 'printers' (that is, compositors) pooled their resources to take over and run the business. On 6 January 1855 the *Age* was registered in their names (Darragh 1997, 93 [37.02]). Sureties were provided by Henry Elder (a jeweller) and William Casey, both of Melbourne. An announcement in the *Age* of 10 January dated the changeover from the 1st of the month, and stated that the paper would 'henceforth be conducted with increased energy and ability'.

In January, public support for the 13 Eureka 'rebels' and the editor of the *Ballarat Times* was swelling. Editorials in the *Age* forcefully reflect this. By contrast, the *Argus* swung around to a position of support for the authorities. On the staff of the *Argus*, Ebenezer was caught in the switch. The *Age* of 15 January 1855 reported that the 'temporary' editor of the *Argus*, Frederick Sinnett had been replaced by Mr Syme, opining the *Argus* to be the 'avowed organ of Government'.[16] The *Age* of the next day, 16 January, however, published a disavowal: 'Mr Syme, long known as one of the best and most

---

[15] Receipt for loan from J.P. Fawkner, SFP Box 1193/7(b); Sayers (1965, 27–29).

[16] Employing Sinnett, editor and proprietor of the *Melbourne Morning Herald*, was perhaps a desperate measure.

CHAPTER 3

accomplished journalists in Melbourne, is not necessarily identified with the sentiments of the *Argus*'. Then or soon after – we do not know the exact day – Ebenezer went over to the *Age*.

When on 5 February Henry Seekamp of the *Ballarat Times* was brought for sentencing after having on 25 January been found guilty of sedition, Ebenezer, together with Ballarat newspaperman Andrew Semple, stood bail. This is but one example of Ebenezer's idealistic impetuousness, for he was in no way financially secure. An action surely not to be condoned by his *Argus* employer, it would have triggered his shift, if this had not taken place before. In any case, a reference in the *Age* of 26 February and running until 3 March to 'an accession of strength to our editorial staff' probably refers to Ebenezer. The hearing was postponed until after the State Trials, at which all the accused were acquitted. On 25 March Seekamp, who fortunately for Ebenezer did not abscond, was sentenced to six months' imprisonment, an example to the local press of the boundaries of free speech (Morrison 2005, 94–96).

In addition to bringing out the daily, the cooperative was planning to publish a weekly paper. A notice in issues of the *Age* from 15 January foreshadows a 'Journal of Politics, Literature, and Popular Progress, containing in addition to a great variety of original matter, extracts from the English papers &c.' Primarily for the country districts, it would contain a 'Complete Summary of the Foreign, Colonial and Domestic News of the Week', and cost one shilling. There were precedents for the 'companion' weekly: James Harrison of the *Geelong Advertiser* had been publishing a *News of the Week* since 1852 and the *Melbourne Morning Herald* proprietors started the *Weekly Herald* in 1854. The *Melbourne Weekly Age*, essentially a digest of six daily issues, made its first appearance on Saturday 3 February 1855.[17] A *Weekly Argus* appeared soon after, on 16 March, the first of several instances where the *Age* led and the *Argus* followed.

On Saturday 24 March 1855 the cooperative management moved their newspaper business out of the former *Express* premises to 67 Elizabeth Street. Perceiving brighter prospects, the *Age* leader on 26 March describes the new accommodation as 'splendid'. In 1908, Mitchell Armstrong (1908b), who had been on the staff in the early years, less enthusiastically recalled 'somewhat squat two-storied premises'.

There were considerable difficulties for the group to overcome, with 'untried machinery and a hastily organised staff'.[18] Early in 1855 an

---

[17] Unfortunately, extant copies date only from 21 March 1856.
[18] Editorial and notice above, *Age*, 26 March 1855, p. 5.

advertisement for steam engines (printing machines) was running in the *Age*. In March, during the State Trials, when the demand for copies was too great to meet (4000 were being printed daily, it was claimed – sales double that of the *Herald* and more than half of the *Argus*), 'large and powerful machines were being constructed'.[19] In May, the new equipment was up and running, and the cast-off engine, boiler and fittings were being advertised for sale.

The *Age* policies were being enunciated by three journalists: Thomas Bright, who stayed on after the Cooke departure; Ebenezer Syme; and Irish former clergyman David Blair, who had left the *Argus* in January 1855, probably before Ebenezer, and who had earlier worked in Sydney on Henry Parkes's *Empire* (Roe 1969). It is not clear which of the three wrote any particular leader. With the restoration of relative calm after the Eureka State Trials in early 1855, the newspaper's policies were to do with the future of the young colony, the needs of miners and settlers, and the importance of agricultural resources. The editorial on 9 April, 'The Causes of Colonial Depression', advocates a five-point set of remedies: introduction of responsible government and taxation by representation; throwing open the lands; giving up government immigration; doing away with centralised government; encouraging colonists to produce their own food. Interspersed with the leaders about happenings local and distant (the latter when ships arrived with news from 'Home') were editorials hammering and reinforcing such themes as depressed conditions, too many imports and the need for laws to make land accessible. Later in 1855 many leaders are concerned with Legislative Council elections, and in 1856 with the advent of responsible government and the anticipation of elections for the new bicameral legislature. Scanning the leaders of 1855 and early 1856, it is abundantly clear that foundations for the policies of the *Age* under David Syme 's management were laid well before his appearance on the scene.

The *Age* of 9 July 1855 reported a meeting of the cooperative to celebrate its first six months.[20] It was held at the Criterion Hotel at 40 Collins Street West, with Blair in the chair and Ebenezer Syme designated vice-chair. In responding to the toast to the Press, Ebenezer stated that the 'two great rulers in the political world' are 'the Press and the Stump' (hustings). As will be seen, the new men in Victoria had a certain enthusiastic naivety about the respective roles of and working relations between the press and

---

[19] Notice above editorial, *Age*, 24 March 1855, p. 5.
[20] 'Festive Meeting of the *Age* Proprietors', *Age*, 9 July 1855, p. 5.

CHAPTER 3

the legislature, between newspapermen and politicians – roles yet to evolve and clarify. An *Age* editorial of 7 August 1855, entitled 'Journalism and Legislation', reveals this, refuting a claim by Edward Wilson of the *Argus* that it was 'inexpedient for conductors of public journals to interfere personally in politics'. The editorial asserted instead that journalists have to study the theory of politics, watch the progress of contemporary events, expose wrong and inculcate right, and the best training for this is in a legislative chamber. Was Ebenezer already thinking about going into politics?

The New Year brought a number of obvious changes in the *Age* business. In the first place, from 1 January 1856 the price per copy of the *Age* was reduced from sixpence to threepence and, to offset this, the size from eight to four pages, a regrettable but needed economy. Secondly, at this time, and possibly instigated by Ebenezer, the lion and unicorn royal coat of arms disappears from the masthead: an assertion of republicanism?

Thirdly, there was a significant innovation for the press and people of the city: a new weekly, the *Melbourne Leader*, which began appearing on 4 January 1856, edited by experienced journalist James Smith, who had arrived in Melbourne from England in 1854 (Stuart 1989, 28). A prospectus had been issued in December 1855, and the weekly was registered that month in advance of publication (Darragh 1997, 98 [53.01]). The subtitle, *A Weekly Journal of News, Politics, Literature*, indicates its wide-ranging content. Unlike the *Melbourne Weekly Age*, directed at country readers, the *Melbourne Leader* was intended as an instructive and entertaining family magazine for the young metropolis (rather than the rural paper that it later became). It may well have been the brainchild of Ebenezer, inspired by the radical London weekly *Leader*, co-founded in 1850 by his friend George Holyoake. A clue to this is the description in Mitchell's UK press directory of the London *Leader* as a 'first-class family weekly paper', the exact words used to describe the Melbourne counterpart.[21] How it would in practice be differentiated from the *Melbourne Weekly Age* (which had been advertised as a 'Journal of Politics, Literature, and Popular Progress') was not at all clear then or for many years. Apparent, however, was another lead over the *Argus*, which would not have a second weekly until 18 months later, when the *Examiner* began on 4 July 1857 (the title echoing that of the English literary weekly founded by leading journalist Leigh Hunt in 1808 and in publication until 1881).

---

[21] Advertisement, *Age*, 30 Oct 1856, p. 8.

The *Age* cooperative held for almost 18 months. It had been re-registered on 24 December 1855, the entry indicating the new premises and some changes in the list of proprietors; there were 24 instead of 26, and Ebenezer Syme was one of them (Darragh 1997, 93 [37.03]). But in the early months of 1856, with financial mismanagement and alleged larceny, the cooperative was falling apart. Insolvency threatening, the business, comprising the three newspapers, the plant and the equipment, went to auction on 6 June 1856. Ebenezer purchased it for £2000, having earlier canvassed and secured the support of several Melbourne merchants and professionals to advance funds and provide guarantees. That they did is testimony to confidence in his aims and the viability of the enterprise for, with no capital behind him, he was an unlikely buyer. The business was mortgaged to two of the guarantors, the ironmonger James McEwan and the merchant Thomas Rae.[22]

The *Age* leader on the day of the auction commended the cooperative enterprise:

> One of the most interesting experiments in the way of co-operative enterprise that has ever been tried in Australia. A body of working men undertook the herculean task of establishing a daily journal, solely by means of their combined labour.

Signed 'D.B.', obviously it was written by Blair. The failure he attributed not to an inadequate readership but to a couple of 'plotters' among the partners. This may be so, but the fact was that, with the excitement of Eureka receding, the readership of the *Age* had reduced and the circulation at this time was only about one-sixth that of the *Argus*, which is recorded at 7800 in the city and 4300 in the country in 1856.[23] In no way was the future of the *Age* assured.

---

[22] Ebenezer Syme and the Age business 1856–1862, SFP Box 1185/1.
[23] 'Circulation', Historical Records of "The Argus" and "The Australasian", 1846–1923, compiled by C.P. Smith [1924], MS 10727, Australian Manuscripts Collection, State Library of Victoria.

Chapter 4

JOINING EBENEZER AT THE *AGE*

The *Age* of Thursday 12 June 1856 bore the imprint: 'Printed and Published by Ebenezer Syme, the Sole Proprietor, at the Age Newspaper and General Printing Office, 67 Elizabeth Street, Melbourne, in the Colony of Victoria', as did the next issues of the *Melbourne Weekly Age* and the *Melbourne Leader*. But the new owner failed to register the change of proprietorship. Either he was unaware of the legal requirement, or careless. Foolhardy, impetuous, with no business sense, Ebenezer might have saved his family if not himself or the *Age* by quietly pursuing salaried journalism, instead of venturing almost simultaneously into newspaper ownership and politics. Not long after Ebenezer bought the financially shaky business, David came to have a stake in and help keep it afloat, but he was much less involved until his brother's untimely death, which irrevocably altered the course of his own life.

At a loose end and ready for an occupation other than prospecting, David in mid-1856 was doing some work for the *Age*. Perhaps he was first sent to report on conditions in the mining areas, for financial records show that he was paid £40 for 'Expences to Diggings' in June and July.[1] From August to December, he was on the payroll, at a salary of £5 per week. There is no record of his duties, but Mitchell Armstrong, a compositor at the *Age* and later a newspaper proprietor at the town of Kyneton, 84 kilometres north-west of Melbourne, wrote years after that David was in charge of the mining news of the *Weekly Age*, 'applied himself to many of the details of the business of the paper', and demonstrated a 'talent for economical detail and management' (Armstrong 1908b).

Under Ebenezer's ownership, on 3 July 1856 the cover price of the *Age* was increased to fourpence, and to sixpence in October. During July a feature headed 'News of the Day' was introduced by stages. Placed after the leader and sub-leader/s, it comprised a series of paragraphs providing encapsulations of up-to-date news of happenings in Melbourne and beyond. The *Age* of 1

---

1   Financial statement, D. Syme, SFP Box 1191/1(a)[iii].

DAVID SYME

August announced: 'The "News of the Day" is a new feature in Melbourne journalism, and will maintain the character it has already acquired after only a week's experiment.' Similarly, 'News of the Week' was introduced to the *Melbourne Weekly Age*. In December a set of instructions for intending correspondents (replies to whom appeared in the 'To Correspondents' feature preceding the leader) began to appear and continued to March. Very detailed and prescriptive, this appears a naive and pedantic approach, hardly likely to appeal to the public, and may be the work of an inexperienced enthusiast (David?).

After David had been on the *Age* payroll for some three months, Ebenezer took him into partnership. We do not know when this might have been first discussed, nor what pressure Ebenezer might have exerted; nor do we know whether David had to be persuaded or leapt into the venture. As recorded on a scrap of paper, the co-proprietorship took effect on 26 September 1856:

> Memorandum of partnership between Ebenezer Syme & David Syme as proprietors & publishers of the Age, Weekly Age, & Leader Newspapers, 26 September 1856. The partnership is to date from the present time, but the share of profit to be allowed to David Syme and the way in which it is to be calculated will be settled when Ebenezer Syme returns to town.[2]

The signature of each partner follows the text, which is in Ebenezer's hand. Whatever was subsequently settled, there is no extant documentary record. Given Ebenezer's laxity about legal procedures this need not surprise. As will be seen later, David would always maintain that he and Ebenezer had agreed to hold equal shares, though over subsequent years some of Ebenezer's descendants would dispute this.

A statement announcing the new partnership appeared in the *Age* of Saturday 27 September 1856, preceding the editorial:

> I have this day admitted my brother, David Syme, into partnership with me as proprietor of the *Age*, *Weekly Age* and *Leader* newspapers; and this business will henceforth be carried on under the firm of "E. and D. Syme." Ebenezer Syme. Melbourne, September 26, 1856.

Accordingly, the imprint of the same issue reads: 'Printed and Published by E. and D. Syme, proprietors, at the Age Newspaper and General Printing

---

[2] Memorandum of partnership, SFP Box 1185/1(a)[iii].

CHAPTER 4

Office, Elizabeth Street, Melbourne, in the Colony of Victoria.' But the partnership was not registered in Ebenezer's lifetime.

Ebenezer was to need both financial and practical assistance, for he had put himself forward as a candidate for the new Legislative Assembly and had to take to the 'stump' as well as wield the pen, as did a surprising number of new immigrants to Melbourne who were connected with newspapers. The *Age* of 25 August 1856 supported such involvement, noting 'strong misgivings in the minds of certain "well-meaning" but feeble-hearted journalists of the old fogy class, as to the capability of candidates of their own calibre to breast and brave its force'. Three days later the *Age* editorial, 'Journalism and Politics', named several Melbourne candidates 'connected with the Fourth Estate': Butler Cole Aspinall, David Blair, John Henry Brooke, George S. Evans, Thomas McCombie, Charles Pridham and, last but not least, Ebenezer Syme, standing for the north-central mining district seat of Loddon, who most likely wrote the leader. Although for most of the men, the association was in the past. Blair and McCombie were currently journalists, the latter being editor of the *Melbourne Morning Herald*, but Ebenezer was a proprietor and publisher as well.

In September, as the memorandum of agreement conveys, Ebenezer was out of town, possibly sounding out election prospects. The *Age* of 4 October, late in the campaign process, announced his candidature for the seat of Loddon. On 12 November the paper reported that he, co-editor Blair and no fewer than five *Age* contributors had been elected.[3] On 21 November, parliamentary sessions began, and Ebenezer had to juggle his responsibilities. David did not stay long to help hold the fort, explaining in his memoirs that 'After a few months trial we found that the income was not sufficient to provide a decent income for both'. Remaining a partner, he took up other employment, profits from it to be pooled. Inferentially, he left in the first half of 1857, for an item in the 'Notice to correspondents' column of the *Age* of 2 June 1857 is addressed to him – Mr D. Syme–you will find a letter for you this morning (Tuesday) either at the Agent's, or by coach'; as is an item on 1 July – '"D.S."–We have not overlooked the matter. It shall be attended to in time.' (Was the matter to do with formalising the agreement, one wonders. Or with payment for services?) He must have done work for the newspaper business from time to time, for financial records, which are difficult to interpret, do show that, as well as the payments in

---

[3] 'For English Readers', *Age*, 12 November 1856, p. 5 (immediately preceding the editorial).

DAVID SYME

1856 mentioned earlier, he was paid £5 for expenses in March 1857, £5 wages for a week in March 1858 and £21 for three weeks (at £7 per week) in March 1859.[4] But this was supplementary income, for he had embarked on a successful career as a public works contractor.

Vital infrastructure for the exponentially growing immigrant population spreading over the colony, the need for roads and bridges to be constructed and repaired was highlighted in the report of a public meeting, 'The Roads of the Colony', chaired by Melbourne's mayor and aimed at promoting 'prompt construction' of main roads throughout the colony. Reported in the *Age* of 12 September 1856, it probably came to David's attention. Finding work as an assistant to a road-building contractor, he soon moved to tendering on his own account.[5] Central Roads Board records show that between 2 June 1857 and 15 January 1860 David Syme submitted 36 tenders.[6] They also record that nine of these tenders were accepted, their dates of submission ranging from 25 August 1857 to 27 December 1859. While not obvious if or when David wrote for the *Age*, the thought arises that he may have had a hand in producing the leader on Road Engineering that appeared in *Age* of 11 August 1857, two weeks before submission of the first tender to be accepted.

The first two tenders were for building a log bridge at Lancefield on the Kilmore to Kyneton Road and one at Woodend, both locations less than 80 kilometres from Melbourne, to the north-west. In each case Syme's were the lowest tenders. (He recalled becoming experienced in the 'art of tendering'.) Liking the work and finding it profitable, he gradually acquired knowledge of road-making and bridge-building. There were drawbacks, however: the interval between contracts and having to keep his workmen, overseers and horses together and find regular work for them. He could have received at least £4000 for tenders carried out over some 28 months. Even though he would have had to pay for men and materials, it was clearly more remunerative than being employed in the *Age* office at a rate of £260 per annum (£5 per week), or even £364 (£7 per week).

The work required him to come to grips with technical engineering matters, to hire, supervise and fire, and to keep his books, giving him practical and financial experience. And it took him around areas of Victoria being opened up, providing opportunities to observe the conditions and needs of

---

[4] Financial statement, D. Syme, SFP Box 1191/1(a)[iii].
[5] DS notebooks (as in the previous chapter, unreferenced material derives from Syme's memoirs in DS notebooks).
[6] Central Roads Board, Register of Tenders 1853–1860, VPRS 1145, Public Record Office Victoria.

CHAPTER 4

settlers. All this was valuable preparation for managing and building up the *Age* newspaper business.

Healthy outdoor work, it was also usefully remunerative for one who was to marry and begin a family. We do not know how or when he met young Annabella Johnson, the daughter of John William Johnson, who was on the way to becoming, through investments and land speculation, a man of modest property, and thus a potential source of security for his new son-in-law. The marriage certificate shows bride and groom each then resident in North Melbourne, proximity that may have led to their making acquaintance, although the contracting business would have taken David out of town a great deal.[7] According to Armstrong (1908a), David lived for seven months at Alexander's Temperance Hotel in Kyneton while bridge-building in the district. Annabella was living with her parents, with whom she had come to Victoria from Yorkshire, England, in 1853. On 17 August 1858, 30-year-old David and 20-year-old Annabella were married in St James Church of England, Collins Street West, Melbourne. It would be a fruitful and, to all appearances, happy alliance. There are no accounts or photos of the event, but one year later a letter to 'My dear Belle – my beloved child' from her mother, accompanying an anniversary present, suggests parental satisfaction at the match: she writes of 'your dear Partner whose esteem and love we hope to gain as our acquaintance, or rather intercourse increases'.[8] She also mentions that her daughter was 'about to become a mother'. Some three weeks later, on 5 September 1859, John Herbert (to be known always as Herbert) arrived, the firstborn to Annabella and David.[9]

At this time the *Age* business was carrying on regular publication of the three newspapers, albeit on a shaky financial footing, with credit tight. A letter of 1 February 1858 from David Blair to James McEwan advised that it was difficult to meet his account, having 'forborne to press Mr Syme, knowing his difficulties'.[10] The few and messy financial statements in existence show, for the week ending 17 October 1856, a credit balance of £40.17.11, and for the week ending 12 December 1856, a frighteningly small £14.18.0.[11] There are no extant profit figures for 1857 to 1859. As for paying off the purchase loans, several repayments, to McEwan and others, are recorded

---

[7] Certificate of marriage, SFP Box 1193/3(a)[ii].
[8] S. Johnson to Annabella Syme (hereafter AS), [August 1859], SFP Box 1180/5(a).
[9] Syme Family Date books, SFP Box 1193/6.
[10] D. Blair to J. McEwan, SFP Box 1185/1(a)[iv].
[11] E. & D. Syme miscellaneous financial papers, SFP Box 1191/1(a)[i]–[iii].

in 1856 and 1857; there are none for 1858, but from January 1859 there are regular quarterly payments of £217.1.10 until September 1862, when the loans were discharged.[12] Conjecturally David, whose name had been added to the mortgage document on 17 January 1857, may have set this in motion when he was on the *Age* office payroll for a few weeks in early 1859.[13]

Additional funds would have been needed in 1858 for a program of rebuilding. Although with more space than the original premises at 21 Elizabeth Street down near Flinders Street, those at 67 Elizabeth Street were proving inadequate. For several months after Ebenezer bought the business in June 1856, he had advertised in the *Age* for large premises 'in a central part of Melbourne', the rent not to exceed £400 per annum. Obviously these were not forthcoming for renovations took place instead, between June and August 1858. During this time the business operated from the adjacent building at 65 Elizabeth Street. The *Age* promised that 'With premises more adequate to the growth of the establishment, we shall be enabled in future to secure better organization, and a still higher degree of efficiency in every department.'[14] To further ensure this, as announced in the *Age* of 22 September, a new steam printing machine was ordered from England.

The *Age* cover price continued at sixpence. There is no record of its circulation in the late 1850s, but, had it been rising, one expects this would have been mentioned in the newspaper. Seeking to widen the readership, on 30 April 1857 the paper announced its aim to be within the reach of every man in the colony and to have a 'labor-column' for the working classes as well as a commercial one for the business ones.[15] The *Melbourne Leader* seemed actually to be doing better. The *Age* of 9 January 1857 claimed that it had no equal, with the 'most able writers of the colony contributing and having an editor of 'brilliancy of wit'.[16] As editor James Smith moved to the *Argus* staff during 1856, this may have been Moses Wilson Gray, who had joined the *Age* staff as law reporter in 1855.[17] On 30 April 1857 the *Age* stated that both the *Melbourne Leader* and the *Melbourne Weekly Age* had circulations over 5000 (that is, in each case considerably more than the

---

[12] Cash credit bonds and bank drafts, SFP Box 1185/1 (c).
[13] Mortgage, Ebenezer Syme to James McEwan and Thomas Rae, SFP Box 1185/1(b)[i]
[14] 'Notice', *Age*, 30 August 1858, p. 5.
[15] 'Important Announcements', *Age*, 30 April 1857, p. 4.
[16] Advertisement, *Age*, 9 January 1857, p. 8.
[17] 'Death of Mr. Wilson Gray', *Age*, 17 April 1875, p. 5.

CHAPTER 4

daily).[18] In July 1858 the *Melbourne Leader* was enlarged from 16 to 20 pages and described in the *Age*, as an 'extensive family paper' and the 'favorite' one with the 'working classes'.[19]

Syme family involvement in the *Age* business was strengthened when John Gourlay, brother-in-law of Ebenezer and David, migrated to Melbourne in 1857 and joined the staff. He, with his wife Margaret, their two children and the Syme siblings' widowed mother Jean, arrived on the *Donald McKay*, which docked on 30 September.[20] Whether Ebenezer, or David, or both, played a part in the decision of all three to emigrate, and whether a job at the *Age* was promised in advance is speculation. Gourlay worked in the Counting House (finance section) of the business until his death in 1894, always a valuable stalwart.

In 1859 George, brother to Ebenezer, David and Margaret, also came to Melbourne, on 14 March arriving unaccompanied on the *Mindoro* after a lengthy three and a half months voyage from Liverpool, delayed at Lisbon for repairs.[21] We may only guess at the reason for this visit. Did he have an idea of emigrating and, if so, was he going to inspect the place where his brothers and brother-in-law were making a new life? Was he driven to this by ill-health or a growing untenability of his clerical position (of which more in the following chapter)? David's and Ebenezer's papers yield no clue, let alone any note of this brief stay, though the entry for George's son in *The Cyclopedia of Victoria* (1903–1905, v. 1, 449) mentions visits to the goldfields. He was back in England on 23 October, there to remain for three and a half years, before returning with wife and son to settle permanently in Australia.[22]

Milestones in the history of the *Age* in these early years coincide with momentous happenings in Victoria. The first months of the newspaper's existence saw also the Eureka uprising. The first months of Ebenezer's ownership saw the introduction of self-government for the colony, nomination of candidates and electioneering, the actual elections and, finally, on 21 November the opening of the first Parliament, which would

---

18　'Information for Advertisers', *Age*, 30 April 1857, p. 4.
19　'The Melbourne Leader', *Age*, 19 July 1858, p. 1.
20　Unassisted Inward Passenger Lists to Victoria 1852–1923, Public Record Office Victoria; 'Shipping Intelligence', *Argus*, 1 October 1857, p. 4.
21　'Casualties at Sea', *Sydney Morning Herald*, 12 February 1859, p. 4; 'Shipping', *Age*, 15 March 1859, p. 4.
22　George Syme, Letters to the Reverend George Alexander Syme, MS4576/7–9, Australian Manuscripts Collection, State Library of Victoria.

run until 9 August 1859. First as a candidate, then Member of the Legislative Assembly, Ebenezer was heavily involved in all these processes. Moreover, as *Age* editor and with responsibility for journalistic content, he was involved in the reporting and editorialising upon political happenings. Former co-editor, Thomas Bright had gone, teaming up with William Shaw and Jeremiah Harnett, trouble-makers from the failed cooperative, to produce *My Note Book*, a weekly newsletter of political comment (Stuart 1979, 272). Co-editor Blair, also a Member of the Legislative Assembly (MLA) and even more politically involved, would distance himself from the running of the paper, while remaining for a time on the payroll. Ebenezer bore the editorial responsibility alone. From the time that parliamentary sittings began, and no doubt reflecting the demands of his double life, the general quality of editorials deteriorated. Frequently the leader consisted of jottings about the current parliamentary proceedings. The parliamentary happenings were also repeated in summary form in 'News of the Day' and reported in full in other columns. Many of the leaders were sarcastic and aggressive, and devoid of solid fact or reasoned argument. There were relentlessly fierce, often vicious, attacks on Irish Catholic John O'Shanassy, when Premier briefly in March and April 1857 and again from March 1858 to October 1859. And there were frequent broadsides at the rival *Argus* (sometimes designated 'Professor Gunny Bags').

Later in 1857, however, the quality began to improve, the leaders becoming less scrappy and more focused. The majority deal with Victoria's legislative program – many of these with electoral reform, many others with the perennial question of making land available. Periodically there were editorials that dealt with items in the British and European news, gleaned from overseas newspapers reaching Melbourne by ship. Occasionally there were topics on significant issues not of immediate political import. One that came up late in 1858, and leading up to the Burke and Wills expedition of 1860–61, was the need for exploration of the interior, to find direct routes to the north coast and undiscovered fertile lands.[23]

The pros and cons of free trade and protection were considered in the *Age* of 14 March 1859, and thereafter many leaders take up the topic, tending increasingly to favour and advocate the latter. David Syme has often been credited with having formulated the doctrine that the *Age* promoted under his management ('The Father of Protection in Australia' is the subtitle of Ambrose Pratt's biography), but the topic was being aired regularly in the

---

[23] Editorials, *Age*, 23 August, p. 5, 1 October 1858, p. 4.

CHAPTER 4

Age before he took control of it. And, as will be seen, some years earlier the cause had been taken up by another newspaper.

Ebenezer did not stand again for parliament after the first term ended in August 1859. He was ill and, whether he then knew it or not, was dying from tuberculosis. During the final decline, David returned to the *Age* office, probably in late January 1860, after he had submitted his last tender (15 January). He may have instigated the reduction in the price of the *Age* to threepence on 17 February, and may have written the editorial of 23 February that asks 'why not give protection a go?'

Ebenezer died on 13 March 1860 at his St Kilda home, 'after a lingering illness' the death notice stated.[24] He may have continued writing for the *Age* until near the end for the black-bordered editorial (in fact an obituary) in the *Age* of 15 March, observed that 'his spirit was still a power' on his deathbed.[25] Tributes were published in the rival dailies, praising his journalism (though the *Argus* hinted at personal 'faults') and in many country papers. In retrospect, an eerie coincidence, the *Age* of 24 February reported the death from tuberculosis of 30-year-old Edward Whitty of Boroondara (a Melbourne district). Whitty had been an editor of the London *Leader*, the publication that may have given Ebenezer the idea for the *Melbourne Leader* (Brake 2008).

Ebenezer was buried in the Melbourne General Cemetery on Thursday 15 March, with a graveside service conducted by the Presbyterian Minister to South Melbourne, Hugh Darling.[26] The funeral procession had nothing like the grandeur of his brother David's 48 years later, but for the time, and for a young man who had been in the colony only a few years and was associated with what was then a small newspaper concern, it was fairly remarkable. The cortège, of a size to be noticed, travelled from St Kilda to the Cemetery via Princes Bridge and Swanston Street, the city's major south–north thoroughfare. There were at least several mourning and private carriages. Chief mourners in the first were David, brother-in-law John Gourlay, and the older three of Ebenezer's four sons; there followed medical and editorial staff, MLAs, other newspaper colleagues, and numerous friends.

For five years, from 1855 to 1859, Ebenezer provided journalistic flair that secured a regular readership and a core of advertisers. In this respect, the continuance of the *Age* in these foundation years is due to him. The 15 March

---

24   Death notice in *Age*, 14 March 1860.
25   Editorial, *Age*, 15 March 1860, p. 4.
26   'Funeral of Ebenezer Syme', *Age*, 16 March 1860, p. 5.

Age obituary terms him 'a stern and potent striver in the noble and arduous task of building up a nationhood for this young country', stating that he had introduced a superior style of writing into colonial journalism, wanting to make the *Age* 'a congenial centre of attraction for journalists of intellectual power and progressive tendencies'. But the statement in the *Geelong Advertiser* of that date – 'For several months he was perfectly aware of the probability of an earthly close to his earthly career, and made all necessary dispositions of his affairs with philosophical deliberation' – does not accord with his failure to leave a will, register his newspapers or clarify the basis of and formally document the partnership with his brother.

David was faced with a decision – continue the business, or try to sell it. The latter was probably not attractive, for with a circulation of no more than 2000 copies daily, the *Age* was by no means securely established ('Great Australasian Dailies' 1892, 98). Either way, there was the question of support for two families: the established one comprising Ebenezer's widow and her five children aged 11 down to three years; the one in the making consisting of David, his wife, six months-old son and an unborn child probably just conceived. His decision to continue was announced 10 days after Ebenezer's death.

PART II

SUPPORTING A SISTER-IN-LAW

Chapter 5

'I FELT IT TO BE MY DUTY'

(March 1860 to March 1866)

Figure 5.1. David Syme, circa 1861.
(Ambrose Pratt, *David Syme*, 1908, facing p. 118)

Let us picture David in March 1860, now in the seat of command at the *Age* office. He is 32. A photo (fig. 5.1) taken the following year shows him boyish yet serious, with a steady gaze. He does not yet look strained or exhausted. His dark, wavy hair is slightly unruly, his beard and moustache not quite as neat and trimmed as later they would be. His apparel suggests urbanity with a touch of raffishness, befitting a member of the Grub Street profession. He had only to open his mouth to betray his Scottish origins (Bedford 1976, 266).

It suited David, he recalled, that he could look down from his first floor office and see in advance people coming to visit him.[1] Not that he spent time there in contemplation: rather, he threw himself into unstinting effort. He remembered working for 15 hours a day, unremittingly. If so he could barely do more than go home to sleep – a 10- to 15-minute walk to his residence at 186 Flinders Lane East (*Sands, Kenny* 1860).

An illustration (fig. 5.2) in the *Australian News for Home Readers* (of which, more later) gives some idea of the appearance of the *Age* building at 67 Elizabeth Street. The accompanying text, 'View in Elizabeth Street', talks up the thoroughfare:

> one of the principal cross business arteries, and indeed a main line of communication from the harbor and the…railway, to the northern interior of the country; for, conducting the traveller by a long pathway of street almost up to the University, it places him on the direct road to Sydney on the one hand, and to the gold country around Mount Alexander, and the Murray country beyond, on the other. Elizabeth street, without any stretch of fancy, may fairly be called the Fleet street of Melbourne…[2]

Wishful thinking, for the other newspaper offices were elsewhere. The *Argus* was in Collins Street (it would be almost two decades before the *Age*, too, would be located in this sought-after precinct); the *Herald* was in a laneway off Bourke Street East. The article continues: 'though there is a considerable admixture of the wholesale with retail business.' Just so. The London Tavern was adjacent to the south (and for a time a boot maker, not shown) and a warehouse of wallpaper importer William Dean immediately to the north at 67a. There were some elements of a bookish location, however: next door but one, at 69, was the warehouse of George Robertson, Importer of Books and Stationery, supplier to the *Age* of British magazines for review and to be a useful contact and publisher in the future.[3] And opposite, at 64 Elizabeth Street, was the Glasgow Book Warehouse. Notwithstanding these proclaimed advantages of the location, David would later remember these rented *Age* premises as small and very inconvenient.

---

[1] DS notebooks (as earlier, David Syme's recollections referred to in this chapter are from this source).

[2] 'View in Elizabeth Street', *Australian News for Home Readers*, 24 December 1863, p. 10.

[3] 'The Magazines for March', *Age*, 13 June 1856, p. 2.

CHAPTER 5

Figure 5.2. Elizabeth Street, Melbourne, in 1863. The *Age* office is the two-storey building between the London Tavern and William Dean, Importer. The numbering on the engraving is misleading: the *Age* building was number 67, Dean's, 67a. (Pictures Collection, State Library of Victoria, IAN24/12/63/9)

Why did Syme, as we shall now usually call him, take on the running of the *Age* business? He addressed this question in the memoirs composed some 47 years later, providing a measured and rational retrospective analysis. He wrote that opting for management of the newspaper business had not been to his liking, upsetting all his plans. He had made the decision, primarily, because he saw that it would have been impossible to sell the newspaper business and he had 'sunk a good deal of money' in it and, secondly, because the sole income for Ebenezer and his family had been from it. Thirdly, he declared: 'my political views were very decided. I believed I knew what the country required & I felt it to be my duty to put my views before the public.' These views as he recorded them in 1907, were the urgent need for land settlement to arrest the exodus of an army of ex-miners from the colony, the necessity for protective tariffs to encourage industry and provide employment, strong support for free compulsory and secular education, strong opposition to mining on private property, and 'many other subjects' besides.

Looking back on nearly 50 years of landmark legislation that his *Age* had advocated, Syme may have attributed more developed views to himself than he had at the time. One wonders whether, in March 1860, the youngish neophyte newspaper proprietor saw himself with such a major part to play in the future and progress of Victoria. While this is unanswerable, one may take another approach and try to imagine his situation then. He had, as he saw it, a duty to support Ebenezer's family as well as his own. The newspaper business was a going concern, with an established readership – and with debts to discharge. The line of least resistance was to keep the show on the road. Moreover, and given what we can glean of his personality and experiences, he welcomed and dealt with occupational challenges.

Syme resolved to continue the business in partnership with his sister-in-law Jane (fig. 5.3), the *Age* of 23 March announcing his decision: 'I beg respectfully to intimate that the business of the Firm of E. & D. SYME will in future be conducted by me, on behalf of myself and the widow and family of my late brother.'[4] Accordingly, the E. & D. Syme imprint continued in the three newspapers. Ebenezer, with characteristic improvidence, having died intestate, the Supreme Court granted Jane her late husband's share of the business, after which articles of co-partnership were drawn up. Dated 28 November 1860, and signed by the parties, the agreement states that Jane and Syme were to be 'equal co-partners', making it the first documentary record of the share held by each.[5] Syme was to have 'the management and control of the said business and of all matters connected with the Editorship and Publication' and Jane was 'in no way to interfere with the management control or direction' so long as these were not 'manifestly injurious to the welfare' of the business. Thus, while Syme was taking on a heavy burden of providing for two families, at least he would have a free hand.

On 10 April 1862 Jane left on the *Suffolk* for England with her five children.[6] Through her attorney in Melbourne, William Poole, the partnership agreement was renewed in January 1863 until the end of that year, and again in February 1864, to continue until 31 December 1867.[7] Syme did the work; Jane received her share of the profits and regular reports on the business. Why she left Melbourne, where she had lived for nearly seven years and had friends and family, is a 'truth-is-stranger-than-fiction' story.

Jane wrote to Syme regularly for the monthly mailboat ('My dear David'), and occasionally also to his wife Annabella.[8] Her letters reveal that she was replying to regular ones that had kept her up-to-date with changes and

---

[4] 'Notice', *Age*, 23 March 1860, p. 4.
[5] Articles of co-partnership, SFP Box 1185/2(a)[i].
[6] 'Shipping Intelligence', *Argus*, 11 April 1862, p. 4.
[7] Articles of co-partnership, SFP Box 1185/2(a)[i].
[8] DS inward correspondence, SFP Box 1180/1; AS inward correspondence, SFP Box 1180/5(b).

CHAPTER 5

Figure 5.3. Jane Syme (later Hope, Palk, Galgey), circa 1856. (Courtesy of Hugh Seppelt)

developments in the business and with which were enclosed the remittances to which the partnership agreement entitled her. (Syme's letters for the 1860s are not preserved). Her comments on the newspaper business testify to an intelligent interest in it. They are mostly negative in tone, however, expressing fear of losses rather than commending gains and encouraging plans. Usually, they are accompanied by lamentations about her loss of Ebenezer, the children's fatherless state, and her dire poverty.

That is part of Jane's story. The full one, a pathetic saga of a woman caught in a parlous situation, trying to care for all her children and maintain her dignity, was unknown to Syme at this time. It was omitted by and perhaps not known to biographers Pratt and Sayers, and is only touched on by Macintyre (1991). It involved deception of Syme, which eventually he discovered and which had a profound, lasting and emotionally crippling effect on him. But, given the mores of the time, and the trap into which she had let herself fall, her hiding of the truth of her situation is understandable.

Jane and her children arrived in London on 28 June 1862, met by her father and sisters. In a letter to Syme 12 days later, she said she was staying with her father and looking for lodgings and a school for her boys, and had written to his brother George, still in England, asking for advice about this.[9] Finally, she expressed the hope that Syme would 'keep his promises' for the sake of 'your <u>brother's</u> children'. What she did not mention was that she was then seven months pregnant, which was surely the reason for her departure from Melbourne, to avoid disgrace for herself, her children and, by association, her brother-in-law.

On 8 September she gave birth to a daughter, Alice Maude.[10] The baby's father was 49-year-old Robert Palk, alias Hope. After emigrating from England to Melbourne in 1852, Palk had practised in Melbourne as an apparently unqualified medical practitioner before setting up as a homoeopathist, possibly unregistered. 'Dr Palk' lived in and was a councillor for the local government of Emerald Hill, a suburb contiguous with St Kilda where Ebenezer and Jane had resided. Leaving a wife and three adult daughters in Melbourne, he travelled on the same ship with Jane.[11] Writing to Annabella about the unpleasant voyage, she mentioned the 'kindness of Dr Palk, getting the ships doctor to order me gruel every night, which was clandestinely given to the children'.[12] She did not allude to the clandestine relationship, however, nor to the progeny of it. Never a very happy one, and to turn dreadfully sour, the liaison would nevertheless last some 14 years and produce five children.

Unbeknownst to her brother-in-law, Jane in England lived as Mrs Hope, the name under which the birth of her daughter Alice was registered. Her letters indicate a succession of residences in places far apart. Her father and sisters drop out of the picture; perhaps they knew of her circumstances, were ashamed or disapproving, and ceased contact. Palk may have remained with her, but it is possible that he went back to Melbourne for a time, for shipping records list a Robert Hope sailing on 8 January 1864 for London on the

---

[9] Jane Syme (hereafter Jane) to DS, 9 July 1862, SFP Box 1180/1(a).
[10] Information in email from Pru Williams, 13 November 2008.
[11] 'Shipping Intelligence', *Argus*, 11 April 1862, p. 4.
[12] Jane to AS, 18 November 1862, SFP Box 1180/5(b).

CHAPTER 5

Mediator from Melbourne.[13] On 21 October 1864 Jane gave birth to another child, Robert Carew Hope.[14] If Palk had reunited with Jane in late February or early March 1864 after leaving Melbourne in January, the birth was four to six weeks premature.

All this time, Jane kept in the dark not only David and Annabella, who saw a widowed sister-in-law struggling, with their indispensable assistance, to provide for her and Ebenezer's five children. She also gave no clue to Syme's agent James McEwan in London or to her brother-in-law George and his wife Susan, with whom she corresponded.[15]

During the next six years, Syme discharged the duty of publishing the three newspapers and foregrounding the policies they had been expressing. So doing, he paid off creditors and made enough profit to provide the two livings. What funds he might have brought into the business, and whether he received any assistance from relatives or friends, is not apparent from the few extant financial records for this period. At all events, this was a remarkable achievement. Furthermore, he experimented with additional publications, one in time to prove an outstanding success. All this was done at a cost to his health, as will be seen.

The daily *Age* continued at eight pages and priced at threepence. From 3 June 1861 the British coat of arms, abandoned in 1856 under the rule of the radical collective, was again printed on the masthead (fig. 5.4). While featuring the royal lion-and-unicorn and thus symbolising the newspaper being part of the machinery of state, it lacked the sheep and local touches of the earlier version. Notices in the paper from time to time list a wide and expanding array of agents – suburban, country and intercolonial. Dating from the New Zealand goldrushes of 1861 there were several in that colony. Farther afield, F. Algar was the agent in London. Syme worried about competition, especially from the daily *Herald*, which on 28 March 1863 reduced its price from threepence to a penny, announcing that it was starting its 'new career with eight thousand subscribers' and that it was likely to be the 'leading journal in Victoria'. He must have written of his concern to Jane, who on 23 September replied somewhat unhelpfully: 'You seem to let the Herald bother you. I would just let it go to the dogs…as long as you are able to get along'.[16] It was a niggling worry that would have to be addressed, but not for some years.

---

[13] 'Shipping Intelligence' *Argus*, 9 January 1864, p. 4.
[14] Birth certificate, Robert Carew Hope, SFP Box 1193/4(c)[ii].
[15] Miscellaneous correspondence, Jane Hilton Syme, SFP Box 1180/7(a).
[16] Jane to DS, 23 September 1863, SFP Box 1180/1(a).

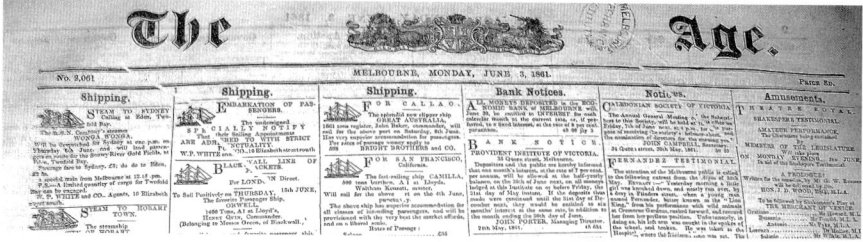

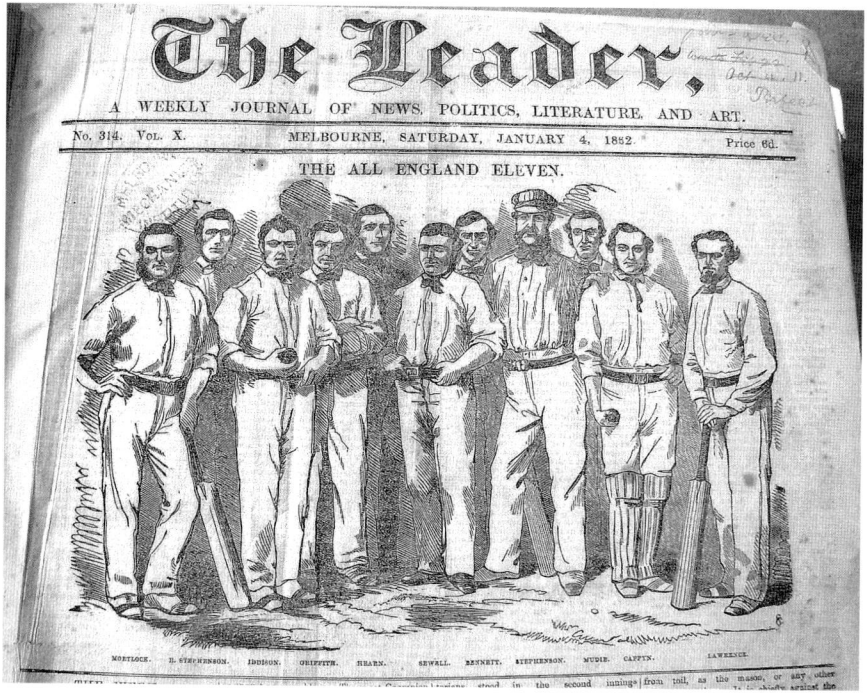

From top to bottom:

Figure 5.4. Masthead of the *Age*, 3 June 1861, featuring the reinstated British coat of arms. (Newspaper Collection, State Library of Victoria)

Figure 5.5. Masthead of the *Weekly Age*, 31 January 1862. '*Melbourne*' has been dropped from title. (Newspaper Collection, State Library of Victoria)

Figure 5.6. Masthead of the *Leader*, 4 January 1862. '*Melbourne*' has been dropped from title. Illustrations begin. (Newspaper Collection, State Library of Victoria)

CHAPTER 5

Syme's two weeklies were heavily promoted in the parent daily *Age*. In January 1862 their titles were modified slightly, the word 'Melbourne' being dropped to make them the *Weekly Age* (fig. 5.5) and the *Leader* (fig. 5.6), in each case perhaps signifying a reach beyond the metropolis. The *Weekly Age* had a wide country circulation and, after the Otago goldrush, an agent as distant as Dunedin, New Zealand.

Also in January 1862, the subtitle of the *Leader* was extended, becoming *A Weekly Journal of News, Politics, Literature, and Art*. With the addition of 'art', there were more illustrations. The 4 January 1862 issue has an engraving of the All England XI cricket team and promises a picture of the Melbourne Cricket Ground in the next. While this did not eventuate, a series of portraits of Victorian politicians began in February. In 1863, there was evidently some problem. Jane wrote on 24 October: 'certainly you are the best judge about the Leader but being a weekly family paper I think it is a pity to withdraw the engraving.'[17] With a good circulation (said in July 1862 to be 10,000), the *Leader* was now reaching out beyond the metropolis to the whole colony.[18] On 18 July 1863 it was enlarged to 24 pages.

As in the past, new printing machinery was purchased from local suppliers when needed, and machines and type no longer wanted were advertised for sale through the *Age*. In 1860 a faster four-feeder Napier Gripper producing 1200 sheets per hour was obtained. In 1862 another steam machine capable of printing 6000 sheets an hour was acquired.[19] Presumably, in each case the need arose primarily because an additional newspaper was being launched.

New publishing ventures

Syme was swift to start two more newspapers, both aiming to extend circulation beyond existing readerships: in 1860 the *Victorian Farmers' Journal and Gardeners' Chronicle*; in 1861, the *Australian News for Home Readers*. While each enriched the print culture of Melbourne, the former had a relatively short life, while the latter, with modifications and improvements and eventually a new title, lasted many years, outliving all similar and rival publications.

On 7 June 1860, barely three months after Syme assumed control, a prospectus for the *Victorian Farmers' Journal and Gardeners' Chronicle* was

---

[17] Jane to DS, 24 October 1863, SFP Box 1180/1(a).
[18] *Age*, 1 July 1862, p. 1, col. 5.
[19] 'Second-Hand Type', *Age*, 15 January 1861, p. 8; 'Wanted, a Four-Feeder', *Age*, 21 January 1862, p. 4; 'Printing Machines for Sale', *Age*, 10 November 1866, p. 7.

published in the *Age*. One month later the first number appeared. This weekly was directed at the growing army of ex-miners and other new settlers seeking a livelihood from the land in Victoria. While the need for unlocking the lands had been a major policy of the *Age* since its beginnings, the new publication was catering for the complementary need for information. Although later claimed to be 'probably the earliest distinctly agricultural paper in Victoria', it was not the first attempt to provide agricultural information through the periodical and newspaper press.[20]

The subject was featured in existing general newspapers, including the *Age* itself. For example, an article, 'The Australian Gardener' in the *Age* of 1 March 1855 dealt systematically with when and how to sow vegetable crops. Moreover, in 1855 there had been a short-lived monthly, the *Rural Magazine*, published in Melbourne and devoted to The Farm, The Garden, Rural & Botanical Features of the Month, Horticultural Notices, etc. It was produced by W.S. Chauncey (author, as 'Rusticus', of *How to Settle in Victoria*), who would become Superintendent of Roads and Bridges. (Possibly, through roads contracting, David knew the man and his several publications.) Still coming out was the monthly *Victorian Agricultural & Horticultural Gazette*, published by the Melbourne printers Heath & Cordell under the auspices of (though not subsidised by) the Governor and of the Agricultural and Horticultural Societies of Geelong and Melbourne. Issued from 21 March 1857, it ceased in December 1861 because, it was stated, of overdue subscriptions; but the underlying cause may have been the advent of Syme's *Victorian Farmers' Journal*. The *Victorian Agricultural & Horticultural Gazette* claimed, possibly rightly, to have been the first journal of its class in the Australian colonies. In South Australia the monthly *Farm and Garden*, edited by Edward William Andrews, part owner of the *South Australian Register*, appeared from July 1858, ceasing in June 1863. Periodical publishing was at best a risky venture in colonial Australia. It remained to be seen if the *Victorian Farmers' Journal* would fare better than these others.

The first number of the *Victorian Farmers' Journal*, 7 July 1860, consists of 32 three-column tabloid size pages. It contains a wide range of agricultural and horticultural features, from advice and instruction and calendars to news about agricultural societies, shows, prizes, ploughing matches, and the like. These were features of the *Victorian Agricultural & Horticultural Gazette* also. The difference is that Syme's was a weekly newspaper, not a monthly magazine. The opening editorial asserts an 'aim to establish a paper

---

[20] 'Death of Mr. Syme', *Age*, 15 February 1908, p. 13.

CHAPTER 5

that will ever be designed to further the best material interests of Victoria', 'to advise, to encourage, and to stimulate the rising agricultural interest of this colony to new exertions'. The contents of the first issue are rich and varied, including an article, 'Farming in Victoria', addressing the difficulties confronting persons commencing farming (the goldfields having drained the country of agricultural labourers), and the first of many more features on irrigation, 'perhaps the most important subject that can engage the study of the Australian farmer' and looking presciently to 'any future time in the history of the colony a general system of irrigation should be carried out'.

During the next year and a half, news features were introduced, including 'General News' (reporting, for example, on the Burke and Wills expedition in the issue of 2 November 1861), and the number of agents increased dramatically to 72, widely spread through Victoria, including Gippsland. The issue for 28 December 1861 foreshadows improvements to come in the New Year: an increase in size, particularly to include 'an epitome of general news to make it in every respect a farmer's newspaper'; and an index.

The first issue for 1862, on 4 January, was a broadsheet with half the number of pages (that is, accommodating the same amount of material as before) and a cover price of sixpence. The following issue apologises that the intended engraved banner was not ready; it appears on the next, however, depicting agricultural produce, livestock and machinery. The word 'Victorian' was removed from the title (fig 5.7), just as the word 'Melbourne' was dropped from the other two weeklies at this time, similarly indicating a wider reach. Regularly advertised in Syme's other papers, the *Age* of 21 April 1862 advises that the *Farmers' Journal* would now be including general news 'on the plan of English agricultural journals'. The monthly *Australian News for Home Readers* (discussed below) of 25 November 1863 states that the *Farmers' Journal* was 'open to the discussion of all subjects affecting the well-being of the agriculturist, the grazier, the settler, the gardener, the vine-grower. The latest and most ample information respecting new crops, plants, new modes of culture, and new or improved machinery, will be constantly supplied'. It refers to adopting the plan of English agricultural papers – that is, providing general news of the week in addition to the usual agricultural intelligence – and notes the journal's 'well-known extensive circulation'.

The rival *Argus* favourably reviewed the new publication, noting that it 'steps in to supply a want which will be more and more felt as the lands of the colony pass into the hands of bonâ fide cultivators'.[21] It was a want that 15

---

[21] *Argus*, 10 July 1860, p. 4, col. 5.

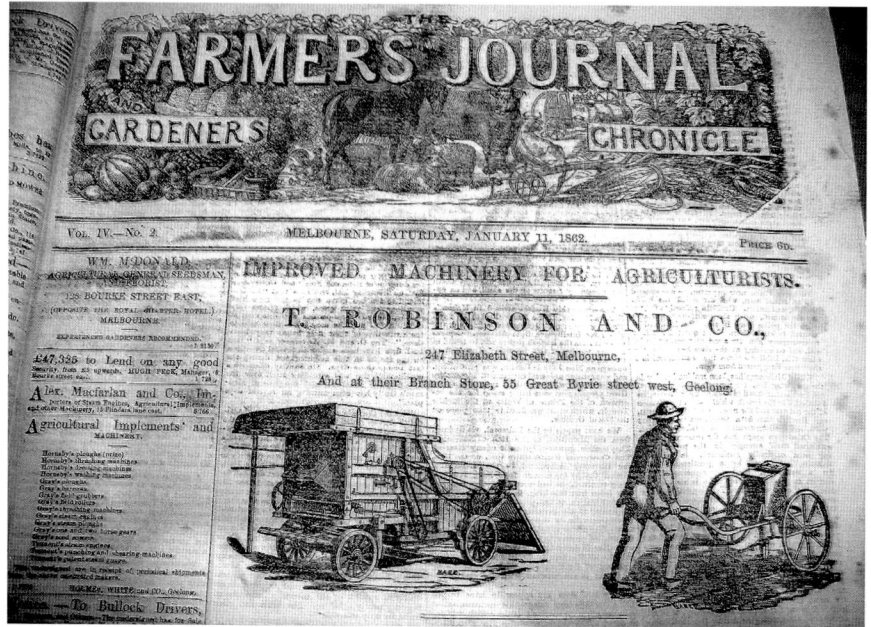

Figure 5.7. Masthead, illustrated, of the *Farmers' Journal and Gardeners' Chronicle*, 11 January 1862. '*Victorian*' has been dropped from title. (Newspaper Collection, State Library of Victoria)

months later the *Argus* proprietors (Edward Wilson, Lauchlan Mackinnon and Allan Spowers) moved also to satisfy. On 5 October 1861 their *Yeoman and Australian Acclimatiser* appeared, priced at 20 shillings per annum (thus undercutting the *Farmers' Journal*, which had a quarterly subscription equal to 30 shillings a year). While no circulation figures are to be found for the *Farmers' Journal*, the appearance of a competing agricultural weekly would suggest a receptive market. In its time the *Farmers' Journal* was known as far away as Scotland, an advertisement in Syme's *Australian News for Home Readers* of 25 June 1862 quoting a tribute from the Edinburgh *North British Agriculturist* – 'best agricultural newspaper in the Australian colonies'.

Increasingly, the *Farmers' Journal* was becoming a regular rather than specialist newspaper. It is hard to distinguish between the clientele for it, the *Weekly Age* and, to a lesser extent, the *Leader*. From today's perspective, it seems hardly rational, if not quite mad, to be publishing three weeklies containing much identical material for greatly overlapping if not near-identical readerships. As companions to the *Age*, there were the *Weekly Age*, the *Leader* and the *Farmers' Journal*. Companions to the *Argus* were the *Weekly Argus*, the *Examiner* and the *Yeoman*. One has to ask, was there

CHAPTER 5

really scope for all these? In particular, was there, with the speedier daily distribution being made possible through the expanding rail network and the comprehensive coach services connecting with it, need for a daily to have a weekly edition as well? There are no records of these issues being aired, but actions speak for themselves.

Moves started in May 1864 with the *Weekly Herald* ceasing publication. The *Argus* proprietors were next to act, on 8 September publishing a prospectus for the *Australasian*: 'a New Weekly newspaper…an Australian paper for all Australians', to be 'liberal, independent, and decided…within the bounds of moderation'. The three existing weekly companions to the *Argus* were to be incorporated in the *Australasian*, its first issue to appear on 1 October 1864. Proprietor Lauchlan MacKinnon later wrote that for years the firm had been losing more than £2000 a year on the *Yeoman* and the *Examiner*.[22]

Apparently taking Syme by surprise, this plan galvanised him to action, though not as drastic. In the last week of September an announcement in his four papers read that 'after a long and prosperous career as an independent paper', the *Farmers' Journal* would be incorporated in the *Weekly Age*. Enlarged from 12 to 16 pages, it would be the largest paper in the Australian colonies, for the same price providing more general news, which farmers wanted. (In fact, the *Weekly Age* was already 16 pages.) The intention was to produce a paper 'superior to anything yet issued for the Victorian press… alike the organ of the farmer, the miner, the man of business, and the general public'. The implementation took place on 30 September, one day before the appearance of the *Australasian*. That the imminent appearance of the *Australasian* drove Syme to this hasty amalgamation is clear from Jane's response of 24 November 1864 to the news of it: 'I was sorry to hear that the Farmers Journal had to be given up but I do not see that anything else could be done after the steps the "Argus" had taken'.

It was a needed and overdue move. The *Weekly Age* of 14 October, under the heading 'The Press and the Weekly Age' carries accolades in the form of extracts from several country papers. The *Daylesford Express* opines that 'the *Age* (presumably meaning the daily and the weekly) has fought its way…to the front rank of Australian journalism'. But clearly, the *Argus* proprietors had stolen the march towards rationalisation; for Syme there was the unresolved matter of the respective roles and readerships of the *Weekly Age* and the *Leader*. This would not be addressed for several more years.

---

22 L. Mackinnon to J. Johnston, 25 February 1869, James Stewart Johnston Correspondence 1836–1911, University of Melbourne Archives.

Syme's other publishing venture, the monthly *Australian News for Home Readers,* which would become the long-running and highly successful *Illustrated Australian News,* began in 1861. The precise date has to be conjectural, for there are no surviving issues until 21 April 1862, and of this there are only the first two pages of, presumably, 16, as in successive ones. These extant issues show that it was then directed primarily, but certainly not exclusively, at readers in the British Isles, in text and pictures laying out aspects of colonial life – the splendid to the curious, the natural to the man-made.

Unillustrated summaries of news for 'home' had been provided by daily newspapers of Melbourne (and other colonial capitals) for many years. The *Age* had been doing this almost since it began: the issue for 24 November 1854 includes a summary published specifically to catch the monthly mailboat, stating this was being done 'in accordance with the established custom of the colonial press'. In late 1856 Francis Robinson and Andrew Semple began an independent publication, the *Australasian News for Home.* It was seen by the December issue of the *News Letter of Australasia,* produced by George Slater and W.H. Williams and printed at the *Herald* Office to be an 'offshoot of the *Age*', but there is no evidence that it was associated; nor is there any indication that it was illustrated (no copies survive and it appears not to have lasted long).[23]

As for illustrations in newspapers, in the 1860s there were artists and engravers in Melbourne seeking livelihoods, and engraved illustrations were making their way into existing weekly papers, including, as mentioned earlier, the *Leader* and, as its fancy masthead, the *Farmers' Journal.* But a host of generic 'illustrated newspapers' had been appearing since the 1850s, for varying, mostly short, periods. Often, the same publishers were involved.[24] Some were specifically for the 'home' (British) market. The second number of the short-lived weekly *Melbourne Illustrated News* (5 November 1853), for instance, reminded readers that it would be 'a means of communicating to their friends at home a more perfect picture in detail of the country they have adopted than any description in words could furnish'. The *News Letter of Australasia* was still in publication when the *Australian News for Home Readers* began.

The earliest advertisements found for Syme's *Australian News for Home Readers* are in the *Argus* for 22, 23 and 25 March 1861; the next found is in the *Age* on 2 October 1861, where Ballarat agent William Young advertises

---

[23] 'News for Home', *Age,* 2 October 1856, p. 7, refers to its prospectus being in circulation.
[24] For examples and discussion, see Dowling, Peter, 'Chronicles of Progress: the Illustrated Newspapers of Colonial Australia, 1853–1896', PhD, Monash University, 1997.

CHAPTER 5

Figure 5.8. Masthead of the *Australian News for Home Readers*, 21 April 1862. First extant issue (fragment only). (Newspaper Collection, State Library of Victoria)

it and the other four Syme papers. Because there are no extant copies before April 1862, we cannot be sure that the earlier issues were illustrated. That the 21 April issue, featuring an engraving from Nicholas Chevalier's depiction of Cape Schanck on page 1 (fig. 5.8), is described in the *Age* of 21 April as 'splendidly illustrated' and that advertisements for the *Illustrated Australian News* in later years give its beginnings as 1862 may well mean that there were no illustrations before April 1862 and explain in part why the earlier issues have not been preserved. The numbering is a curiosity, to be examined. The 21 April 1862 issue is numbered 27, which, at fortnightly issue, would put it roughly near the time of the March 1861 notices in the *Argus*. The issues on file from 21 April 1862 are monthly, however, and explicitly for the monthly mailboat – yet they are numbered as if fortnightly (and there is no sign whatsoever of there having been issues in between). I suggest that from the start of publication there was an intention to make the paper *appear* to be eligible for the penny postage for newspapers. A clue to this is the statement 'Published in accordance with ACT 17 Vic, no. 30', printed on the cover of each issue. This 'skipping' would continue until new postal legislation explicitly included monthly publications in the definition of newspaper.

It is possible that the *Australian News* might have been enhanced from April 1862 onwards to compete with the illustrated monthly begun by the *Herald* proprietors in January 1862. Their *Illustrated Melbourne Post* was to be published several days before the departure of the mailboat each month and may have been inspired by and benefited from the *News Letter of Australasia* being printed at its plant (and may have been the cause of the demise of the *News Letter* in October 1862). The attractive engraved masthead of the *Post* depicts a maritime scene, sea and boats. 'To Our Readers' announces that it will 'exhibit Victoria as she is…a little of everything connected with the colony and its progress'. Priced at sixpence, the eight-page issue includes illustrations of explorers Burke and Wills, Leichhardt, King and Becker, of sports and recreation in Australia, and of the Exhibition building.

Basically the *Illustrated Melbourne Post* was a monthly, although in the early years there were some weekly issues as well. From 1865 it had an Adelaide edition also, something that Syme's monthly would later have. Clearly, for the quality and range of topics illustrated and written about, it was a very serious competitor for the *Australian News for Home Readers*, which, moreover, had neither 'illustrated' in its title nor an illustrated masthead, though both would be provided in due course. The claim made in the December 1863 issue of the *Australian News for Home Readers* that it was 'the oldest monthly Australian Illustrated Paper prepared expressly for transmission to Europe' is questionable. Ultimately, a mystery remains about the beginnings of Syme's *Australian News for Home Readers*.

The 25 June 1862 issue of the *Australian News for Home Readers* is the first complete one extant. Its 16 pages feature a handful of illustrations; subsequent numbers have more. Jane, who would have received issues to September, appears to have been impressed, but apprehensive, writing in November: 'The Australian News is looking very well – you have quite a show of engravings in it but I fear it will swallow a large amount of profit… however I suppose nothing venture nothing win.'[25]

The number of illustrations increases in 1863. The 24 January issue has Cooper's Creek (where Burke and Wills perished) engraved from a sketch by Alfred Howitt; that issued 25 May 1863 has a four-page supplement (text only) and, for the first time, an illustrated masthead. Modified from an illustration in the body of the March issue, it is a view of Melbourne city

---

[25] Jane to DS, 21 November 1862, SFP Box 1180/1(a).

CHAPTER 5

seen from the Botanical Gardens to the south, across the Yarra River, and has Mount Macedon in the background. The December 1863 issue includes the streetscape with the *Age* building, mentioned earlier. The 24 February 1864 issue has a new masthead illustration: ships in Hobson's Bay flanked by a mining scene on one side and wool bales on the other. The front page of the 24 September 1864 issue features lost children being found in the bush by Aboriginal trackers – an engraving by Frederick Grosse of a drawing by Nicholas Chevalier (whose studio was in Elizabeth Street not far from the *Age* office). Jane approved, writing to Syme on Christmas Day: 'I like the appearance of the Australian News very much this month. I think the Engravings are very much improved and altogether the paper looks very well. You would be pleased to hear that one of the London Illustrated papers, a penny one, has taken notice of the Australian News two weeks following and had engravings of the lost children.'[26]

The *Australian News for Home Readers* and the *Illustrated Melbourne Post* survived when other illustrated newspapers did not. This may be due in part to their monthly publication, with deadlines easier for engravers to meet than for weeklies (although *Melbourne Punch* managed). Equally or perhaps more important for viability, each was an offshoot of a daily newspaper, the income from which was the mainstay of the business. The *Argus* proprietors, however, did not produce an illustrated newspaper until launching the *Australasian Sketcher* in 1873.

The policies enunciated by Ebenezer and adopted by David entailed the enactment of legislation, and to this cause the young newspaper proprietor turned his attention. Throughout the 1860s, unlocking the lands, a major policy of the *Age* from the start, would continue to be argued editorially, synchronously with the presentation and passage of successive Land Acts, while on the matter of legislating for tariffs on imports ('protection'), the newspaper moved from a slight tendency in favour to strong advocacy. As described in his memoirs, Syme was in charge of the editorial department, arranging the subject with the leader writer each afternoon and approving, altering or rewriting after it was submitted late at night. *Age* office records are few for the 1860s and thus it is difficult to ascertain precisely who were his leader writers and reporters. According to his memoirs, at first there was one contributor for the 'leading columns' (meaning one leader writer?), one subeditor, three reporters for local news and one for the law courts. One of the reporters usually did musical and dramatic criticism as well. This seems

---

[26] Jane to DS, 25 December 1864, SFP Box 1180/1(a).

a simplification, for there is scattered evidence that, from Ebenezer's regime if not earlier, there were a number of men writing leaders for the *Age*, some regular staff, others contributors, paid by volume.

The *Age* leader writers

Syme wrote that his first leader writer was William Joseph O'Hea, who was fluent and nimble, but had a repertoire limited to the land and the fiscal questions, on each of which he 'never went wrong'. O'Hea, who had been at the *Age* since 1856, assisted in founding the Land League, and was elected an MLA in 1859, had been on the editorial staff of the *Illustrated London News* and had written for the London *Times* (*Men of the Time* 1882, 151–152). According to Syme, he was replaced by Gerald Supple, another Irishman who had been in Melbourne from 1857 and had been recommended to Ebenezer by his friend George Holyoake. Supple was 'difficult', with a 'poetic temperament', Syme stated, and left after a disagreement with another writer, Scottish George Paton Smith, about the latter's treatment of Irish matters. Supple was in fact mentally unstable, in 1870 shooting and wounding Smith and killing a bystander; subsequently convicted, on the grounds of insanity his death sentence was commuted to a prison sentence (Finlay 1976).

George Paton Smith, who came from the same part of the world as Syme (Berwick-on-Tweed, south of North Berwick) and was about his age (two years older), had arrived in Melbourne in 1855 and worked as a draper in Sandhurst until 1857 (Thomson and Serle 1972, 193). From 1859 he was at the *Age* and *Leader*, and studied for the bar, to which he was admitted in 1861. Syme regarded him as a 'well read, best all round contributor' and the first he could trust to carry out policy so that he (Syme) could go home at night and leave the office in his charge. Syme does not call him the *Age* 'editor', but Thomas Cope did, in addressing a public meeting of the Australasian Reform League in June 1864, where he conveyed that Smith was editor from 1861.[27] Smith himself stated in Criminal Sessions of the Supreme Court in October 1865 that he had been editor until January, understanding, though not positive, that Syme and Henry J. Smith were now joint editors.[28] Henry Smith would next move to the *Argus*, becoming chief of staff there in 1867.[29] In 1866 George Paton Smith entered politics as MLA for South Bourke.

---

[27] 'Australasian Reform League', *Leader*, 11 June 1864, p. 6.
[28] 'Criminal Sessions', *Leader*, 29 October 1865, p. 11, col. 2.
[29] 'Chiefs of Staff', Historical Records of "The Argus" and "The Australasian", compiled by C.P. Smith [1924], MS 10727, Australian Manuscripts Collection, State Library of Victoria.

CHAPTER 5

From the historian's perspective, and notwithstanding Syme's praise of Paton Smith's abilities and the trust he placed in him, it seems that the newspaper proprietor was very badly served by this journalist. Vicious personal attacks in editorials written during his 'editorship' and probably or certainly written by him occasioned a series of litigious and other disturbances. A leader in the *Age* in February 1864 calling MLA and *Herald* journalist George Collins Levey a 'Parliamentary flunkey' become 'roguish journalist' led to a physical fight outside the *Age* office – Levey with a horsewhip striking Smith, who retaliated with fisticuffs before rescued by 'his friends' and taken in to the safety of the office.[30] Ironically, Levey would later and for many years be one of Syme's most trusted and reliable contributors and a confidant, while Paton Smith became an implacable enemy.

Under attack

Age attacks on MLA Charles Gavan Duffy and the land legislation then under consideration, for which he was responsible, caused the government of John O'Shanassy to cease placing government advertisements in the *Age* in late April 1862. (Although criticised for the loopholes that allowed for exploitation, the Land Bill passed into law on 18 June 1862.) The reason given in a government circular of 28 April for the withdrawal of advertisements was that the *Age* had a smaller circulation than its contemporaries – true in the case of the *Argus* (with almost 15,000)[31] but not, the *Age* editorial of 30 April claimed, in the case of the *Herald*. This severely affected the *Age* business revenue for a time, but in October government advertisements were back in the paper. By March next year there was no shortage of advertisements of any kind, the *Age* of 31 March apologising that the pressure of advertisements had meant that several letters already in type had been 'crowded out'. The Heathcote *McIvor Times* of 10 July 1863 observed that attempts to stop the *Age* had only increased its circulation.

Jane, writing to Syme in October, expressed the hope that 'by regaining the Government advts you find the paper more prosperous and…feel more independent of the success or otherwise of the Herald' (obviously a continuing worry for Syme).[32] In her letter a year later she was 'glad' that

---

[30] *Argus*, 24 February 1864, p. 4, col. 6.
[31] 'Circulation', Historical Records of "The Argus" and "The Australasian".
[32] Jane to DS, 24 October 1863, SFP Box 1180/1(a).

things were looking good on paper.³³ In fact, through all the trials and strains, Syme kept the business solvent, with a profit of £1063 in 1860, £2352 in 1861 and £982 in 1862; while a mere £266 in 1863, it rose to £3016 in 1864 and £2696 in 1865.³⁴ Moreover, he completed repayment of the purchase loan by September 1862.³⁵ But it was still not in the same league as the *Argus* business, which showed annual profits ranging from £10,321 for 1860 to £19,641 for 1865.³⁶

The strains, however, were manifold. Attorney-General Richard Ireland, prompted by O'Shanassy, introduced a Bill for the registration of newspapers that increased the obligations on its producers. It required editors as well as publishers to make affidavits, and sureties of £1500 (under the existing pre-Separation New South Wales legislation, £300 was required). Ireland claimed that the existing law was becoming a dead letter, with many papers not observing it, citing the *Age*, the *Argus* and the *Herald*, as well as a host of country papers. The parliamentary debate was acrimonious and divisive (Morrison 2005, 154–157). Ebenezer had not registered his three newspapers after he bought the *Age* business. And nor had David, after Ebenezer's death. Whether or not he was aware of this omission, he was now swift to remedy it, and would observe the law punctiliously thereafter. At the end of April and in early May 1864 all five Syme newspapers were registered (Darragh 1997, 93 [37.06], 100 [62.01], 117 [173.01, 174.01, 175.01]). Proprietors were given as David Syme and Jane Hilton Syme, and David Syme also as printer and publisher. In each case, the sureties (still £300) were supplied by brother-in-law John Gourlay and medical practitioner Dr John Downes Ovens, MLA, a former contributor to the *Age*.

There was huge opposition to Ireland's Bill, press solidarity coming to the fore, with the *Age* and *Argus* both against it.³⁷ It was dropped in August 1863. New legislation came into force in June 1864 as part of a general consolidation of the laws. The *Printers and Newspapers Registration Statute*, like the New South Wales Act, had more flexible penalties (for failure to register not less than £25 and not more than £100) and the definition of 'newspaper' was more restricted, excluding monthlies. (Added incentive for the *Australian News* to skip numbers and thus resemble a fortnightly.)

---

33 Jane to DS, 25 October 1864, SFP Box 1180/1(a).
34 E. & D. Syme miscellaneous financial papers, SFP Box 1191/1(a)[iii]–[v].
35 Bank drafts, 15 May 1859–13 September 1862, SFP Box 1185/1(c)[iii].
36 'Profits', Historical Records of "The Argus" and "The Australasian".
37 Editorial, *Age*, 21 April 1863.

CHAPTER 5

Of a spate of actions against Syme as publisher for allegedly libellous statements in editorials, some were successful, some not, but all added to his workload, worry and expenses. Libel actions were a fact of his life as a newspaper publisher, the corollary of his newspaper's campaigns for enlightened lawmaking and against waste and corruption. But this was a particularly bad period, a stressful induction into the newspaper business and a foretaste of the terrible strains to be endured nearly 30 years later, with the Speight case of the early 1890s. An exacerbating factor, at least until he left the employ of the *Age* (although he may well have continued as a writer of occasional leaders) was surely George Paton Smith, with his poison pen.

Some of the cases were relatively trivial and over quickly. One such was *Moorehead v. Syme* in 1863, with a verdict for the plaintiff and Syme to pay £348 damages for libel injuriously affecting a man of business.[38] But actions brought by Henry Brooke, MLA for West Geelong and onetime reporter for the *Herald*, dragged on for months, from June 1864 until finally settled in March 1865, when imputations against the plaintiff (Brooke) were withdrawn, and an apology made and costs paid in full by the defendant (Syme).[39] That the latter was worried is reflected in Jane's letters: in December 1864 anxious to hear how he was getting on with Brooke; in May 1865 relieved the Brooke affair was settled.[40]

An action that threatened to destroy the *Age* and its proprietor was brought following a deadlock in 1865 between the Legislative Assembly and the Council. This 'constitutional crisis' followed attempts of the government of James McCulloch to pass a tariff measure by tacking it to an Appropriation Bill.[41] Politically conservative John Dennistoun Wood, a barrister who had been an MLA until defeated in the 1864 elections, brought a libel action against David Syme, alleging the *Age* had accused him of plotting to overthrow the government' (Eastwood 1976). Syme was committed for trial on 20 September 1865, while the *Age* editorial the following day commented in an outspoken and seemingly fearless manner. Syme's 'The Ethics of the Press' in *Melbourne Punch* took up criticisms made by Attorney-General George Higinbotham in parliament ('a portion of the press – was a disgrace'), proclaiming it 'the duty of journalists to

---

[38] 'Telegraphic News', *South Australian Register*, 4 June 1863, p. 2.
[39] 'Law Report', *Argus*, 10 June 1864, p. 7, 8 March 1865, p. 5, col. 2.
[40] Jane to DS, 24 December 1864, SFP Box 1180/1(a), 19 May 1865, SFP Box 1180/1(b).
[41] For more on this 'constitutional crisis' and the *Age*, see Sayers (1965, 70–72).

uphold constitutional authority by supporting the government of the day' and attacking a 'venal press' and 'hireling editors'.[42] In October and November the jury, twice, failed to reach a verdict. An election looming, the *Age* campaigned against Wood, who was not elected and, finally, the case was dropped.[43] Syme must have told Jane something of this, for in her December 1865 letter she was sorry to hear about the Wood libel case and wanted to be sent newspapers, saying that it almost seemed they were being deliberately kept from her.[44]

An associated civil action, *Tanner v. Syme*, was brought in November 1865, with a verdict for the plaintiff on three of four counts.[45] This, at last, was the end of this protracted and potentially damaging litigation. On 27 January 1866 the *Age* reported on the subscription to a fund to defray the expenses of the trials; members of the public had subscribed £331.3.6 towards the total expenses of £540.15.2.

Family life

There were domestic pressures too. While in good faith Syme continued to support his late brother's dependants in England, he was providing for his own growing family. John Herbert (always known as Herbert), who was six months old at the time of Ebenezer's death, was joined by a brother, George Francis Ebenezer (always known as Francis, perhaps because David already had both brother and nephew named George) on 14 December 1860.[46] A daughter, Caroline Alice, was born on 3 December 1862 but died at 16 months, on 17 April 1864. Another son, Arthur Edward, arrived on 16 October 1864. The family lived in a succession of rented houses, moving from Flinders Lane in the city to Emerald Hill and from there in 1864 to the Saltwater (now Maribyrnong) River bridge area, Essendon (*Sands & McDougall's* 1863–1866). Moving with young children cannot have been easy and it would be many years before the family would settle into their own home.

---

[42] David Syme, 'The Ethics of the Press', *Melbourne Punch*, 28 September 1865, p. 108; 'Parliament', *Argus*, 20 September 1865, p. 7.
[43] 'Police. City Court', *Argus*, 21 September 1865, p. 7, and traceable through *Argus* court reports thereafter, for example in issues for 17, 28, 30 October, 17, 30 November, 1 December 1865.
[44] Jane to DS, 24 December 1865, SFP Box 1180/1(b).
[45] 'Law Report', *Argus*, 14 November 1865, p. 6.
[46] Syme Family Date books, SFP Box 1193/6.

CHAPTER 5

Figure 5.9. George Syme, brother of David. (Courtesy of Marten Syme)

Writing to Annabella in August 1864, Jane expressed her sympathy for Caroline's death and her satisfaction that David was benefiting from the homeopathic treatment that she had recommended (doubtless influenced by her de facto husband's occupation) and said that she was missing Ebenezer very much.[47] (Jane's letters often refer to David's being unwell, and suggest he try and continue with homeopathy!) The same day she wrote to David about 'money misunderstandings' and worries about her sons' futures.[48] She was then seven months pregnant with her first Palk son. And four days after giving birth to Robert, she wrote a pleasantly toned letter to Syme, mentioning that she had sent a box of presents for 'Annie's boys'.[49]

George (fig 5.9), the last of the Syme brothers to emigrate, arrived in Melbourne on 25 September 1863 on the *Champion of the Seas* with his wife Susan and young son George Adlington (to be known to David Syme and

---

[47] Jane to AS, 18 August 1864, SFP Box 1180/5(b).
[48] Jane to DS, 18 August 1864, SFP Box 1180/1(a).
[49] Jane to DS, 25 October 1864, SFP Box 1180/1(a).

family as Addie).⁵⁰ His road to the secular life had been longer than his brothers'. Amongst all his clergy employers, from Free Church to Evangelical to Baptist, he was always respected for his piety, diligence and moral rectitude, although he was regarded as only a mediocre preacher, who could at times labour 'Morisonianism'.⁵¹ But frequently there were expressions of serious concern from clergy and parishioners about his dissenting views on doctrinal matters. No lone dissenter, however, he seems to have been part of a network of like-minded ministers, preaching in their churches and inviting them to do so in his.

For there was another dimension to George's life. He had been in communication with leaders of the 1848 uprisings, who continued to promote national movements in Italy Hungary, Poland and other European countries from bases in England – Giuseppe Mazzini, Lajos Kossuth, Stanislaus Worcell, and others. He and Ebenezer's London friend George Holyoake helped these political refugees in England to find employment and form organisations to further their causes. Travel to Italy by George in 1856 seems to have been part of serving the cause of freedom there.

In spite of intermittent illness, he was able to retain his position at the Baptist church in Nottingham until 1860, when he tendered his resignation. He received glowing testimonials and funds from a subscription acknowledging his 11 years of service. It is not clear how he earned a living for the next couple of years in England. Correspondence to him suggests that he may have been involved in periodical publishing ventures and was trying to recruit journalists for the *Age* business in Melbourne.

In 1862 he and Susan were making preparations to emigrate. This we may trace through several of sister-in-law Jane's letters. In September (16 days after secretly giving birth to Alice, her first child with Robert Palk) she wrote to Susan advising her what to take to Australia.⁵² In November she wrote to David that George had sold his furniture, adding that she was thinking of going to see him about Ebenezer's papers.⁵³ In July 1863, when George and family were already on the high seas, she said in a letter to David that George was going out in the hope of helping him.⁵⁴ Through George, she sent David newspapers from Manchester, where she was then

---

50   'Shipping Intelligence', *Argus*, 26 September 1863, p. 4.
51   The story of these years in England is put together from character references and letters in George Syme Letters.
52   Jane to S. Syme, 24 September 1862, SFP Box 1180/7(a).
53   Jane to DS, 21 November 1862, SFP Box 1180/1(a).
54   Jane to DS, 19 July 1863, SFP Box 1180/1(a).

CHAPTER 5

living, and in subsequent letters sought acknowledgment of their receipt and his views of them. Newspapers of a significantly large provincial city, they may well have been of interest and use then. Certainly in the 1870s Syme looked to English provincial models.

George soon joined the firm. The exact date is not known, nor what his duties were at first – later, he would edit the *Leader*. For the duration of his association with the *Age* business he would be an inconspicuous but invaluable source of intellectual support for his brother.

David Syme, the man who had felt it his duty to carry on the *Age* business, did so in the first six years at great cost to his health. He later recalled this tough time: 'To manage, finance & conduct a daily newspaper is no light matter at any time, but to do so without ample means, without a competent business or literary staff' (which, presumably he could not afford), with a small circulation, two established rivals, 'seemed almost foolhardy'. It was 'killing work', which began to tell. The decision was made to travel abroad and have a long break from newspaper work. We do not know, but may wonder, if Annabella's father contributed to, or even paid entirely for, the cost of this long vacation.

Syme and his wife were to sail on Wednesday 7 March 1866. The departing proprietor gave a farewell dinner at Scott's Hotel for his staff on the preceding Saturday. Henry Smith, on behalf of the guests, presented David with an elegant silver inkstand and everyone expressed wishes that he would return 'in possession of renewed health and vigor'.[55] On Tuesday, the eve of the departure, there was another dinner, this time at Menzies Hotel; it was reported as a 'numerous gathering, including members of the Cabinet and of both branches of the Legislature', and included George Paton Smith, George Syme and Henry Smith.[56] Once again a silver testimonial was presented, a 'massive tea and coffee service valued at 100 guineas'. It was said to be a 'token of admiration' for 'efforts to promote the liberal cause' and stated that the firm could 'ill afford to spare' him. Syme responded that he knew he had made enemies but had not known that he had so many friends; that he had had difficulties with rivals (meaning the *Argus* and perhaps the *Herald*) with connections and capital; that, however, the *Age* was now a commercial success and he had full confidence in the staff during his absence. There were toasts all round.

---

[55] 'The News of the Day', *Age*, 5 March 1866, p. 4.
[56] 'News of the Day', *Age*, 7 March 1866, p. 4.

The following day David and Annabella sailed on the *Sussex* for England via Cape Horn.[57] We do not know if their three small sons went too. Syme's memoirs do not say, nor are they mentioned in official or newspaper shipping lists. Might they have been left in the care of one of their grandmothers? The memoirs do record that George Syme took his brother's place in the *Age* office for the nine months' absence.

---

[57] Outward Passengers to Interstate, UK, NZ and Foreign Ports, 1852–1923, Public Record Office Victoria; 'Shipping', *Age*, 8 March 1866, p. 4.

Chapter 6

'BEGINNING TO MAKE PROGRESS'

(April 1866 to December 1870)

Syme's return to Britain after an absence of 15 years was restorative, he recalled.[1] Beyond the shipping manifests and notices and allusions in later business letters, there is little record of his activities during the nine months from March to December 1866, however, and the biographer has to resort largely to informed speculation. Presumably the long voyage to London was relaxing and the time in England, during the warmest months, June to September, was likewise conducive to his recovery. He and Annabella may have visited her relatives in Yorkshire, as we know happened on later trips. With more time to read and reflect, especially on board ship, this must have been an opportune period for him to begin the gathering of material and developing of ideas to be transformed into the several scholarly articles and books he would write and have published, in parallel with and related to running the newspaper business. Business matters were not overlooked. He appears to have investigated developments in printing machinery and newspaper production, acquiring information and impressions that helped shape the management of his business for the next five years. And we know from Jane's later letters that there was a meeting between the two, possibly in September.

Apparently Syme promised Jane, in person, that he would give 14-year-old nephew Joseph a job at the *Age*, for some 12 months later she sent a reminder: 'you know David you told me you could give him one in his presence'.[2] The two proprietors must also have discussed the partnership agreement, which was to expire at the end of 1867, for its terms were varied by an endorsement dated 25 September 1866, and signed by Jane. The sum

---

[1] DS notebooks (as in previous chapters, unreferenced material derives from DS notebooks).
[2] Jane to DS, 19 August 1867, SFP Box 1180/1(b).

to be paid to each partner per week was £12 (it had been £10) and Syme was to receive an extra £9 for his services.[3]

By this time Jane was married to Robert Palk, whose wife of many years, also named Jane, had died from typhoid fever in Melbourne on 13 September 1865.[4] Legitimising their union on 16 April 1866 in St Peter's Church, Hackney, were they impelled by the knowledge of Syme's impending visit and the risk of his finding out about their relationship (which did not in the event occur)?[5] By the time of the meeting or meetings, Jane was pregnant with a third Palk child, Reginald, who would be born on 17 January 1867.[6] Apparently neither Syme nor Annabella had any inkling that she was married and with child.

With George Syme in charge of the business during his brother's absence, the newspapers continued to be published on schedule, and to propound the same editorial policies, seen particularly in the support of a Tariff Bill introduced in January 1866, and which led to another deadlock between the two houses. It was finally passed in April but the Governor Sir Charles Darling was recalled for becoming embroiled in the politicking (Sayers 1965, 79–82). The thoughtful and informed leaders, urging conferences and compromises, supporting Darling and distinguishing between loyalty to the Crown and submission to the dictates of Downing Street, were probably written by George. He was educated, literate, informed, and without the late Ebenezer's wild streak or George Paton Smith's invective. In his memoirs David does not credit George with able deputising, however, saying only that on his return there was a lot to make up, and that finances were not good because there had been another advertising boycott in his absence.

Under George's management there were modest changes to three newspapers, some foreshadowing bigger ones to come. An announcement in the *Age* of 27 July 1866 informed that the *Leader* would be published on 29 July, for the English Mail, thus extending its targeted readership and complementing (not replacing) the *Australian News for Home Readers* as a source of colonial information, opinion and inspiration for readers at 'home'. The monthly was advertised in the *Age* of 17 May 1866 as the *Illustrated Australian News for Home Readers*, foreshadowing a change of title that

---

[3] Articles of co-partnership, addendum, SFP Box 1185/2(a)[i].
[4] Jane Palk death, Register of Deaths in the Colony of Victoria, 1865, no. 6541.
[5] Marriage certificate details, Family History Report, Ebenezer Syme and Jane Hilton Rowan, dated 23 October 2009, supplied by Pru Williams, descendant.
[6] Birth certificate, Reginald Hope, SFP Box 1193/4(c)[iii].

CHAPTER 6

would appear on the masthead a year later. Its numbering was permanently regularised from 27 July, following the passing of a new Post Office Statute in June, under which a newspaper was defined as 'published at intervals not exceeding one month', and the 'Published in accordance with…' statement on the front page was relegated to the imprint on the back.

Syme and his wife travelled back to Melbourne on the *Lincolnshire* via the Cape of Good Hope, arriving on 20 December 1866.[7] Although still troubled by a cough, Syme considered that his health was greatly improved. In spite or because of some inconclusive medical consultations, he went back to work and got better, he said. Within days of his return many changes were announced in the *Age*. These appear to be first steps in an already thought-out campaign for the supremacy of the *Age* and its companion newspapers.

The program of changes aimed at elevating the *Age* from an also-ran position to the forefront of the Melbourne press field. Achievement of the first steps was assisted by a transformation in the support staff. Two newspaper men, who would be associated with Syme and his papers until the early 1890s, came on the scene – the polymath James Harrison in 1867 and the talented and lively George Levey in 1869. Syme does not mention either in his memoirs, but there is ample evidence in his letters over the years of his respect for and reliance on them. While their valued contributions would continue into the 1890s, their assistance was especially important in the period before Charles Pearson, Arthur Windsor and Alfred Deakin made their appearance, in the 1870s, on the *Age* journalistic stage. Both Harrison and Levey were, at various times, on the staff in Melbourne and contributors based in London.

James Harrison to the rescue

Harrison was a steadying influence for Syme. With a wealth of experience in journalism and newspaper production, he was doubtless the single most valuable member of staff in the 1860s and the mainstay of the *Age* business from 1867 to early 1873. This is not to overlook the significant journalistic support from Syme's talented brother, but to recognise that George was reclusive, dogged by delicate health and did not have the same managerial capabilities.

Harrison came from Geelong to Melbourne to be a juror for the Intercolonial Exhibition of Australasia, October 1866 to February 1867, and joined Syme's staff thereafter. Exactly when has not been established, but

---

[7] 'Shipping', *Age*, 21 December 1866, p. 4.

he was firmly ensconced when Syme was called to the Bar of the House (the Legislative Assembly) on 17 July to answer a charge of Breach of Privilege. This was occasioned by the leader in the *Age* of 12 July, which alleged that some members of the Legislative Assembly had offered Edmund Hargraves their support in his claim for the balance of a reward due for discovering gold, in return for a percentage of the sum claimed. The editorial linked such corrupt practices to the regrettable lack of payment for members of parliament, which left them open to temptation. All Syme would volunteer to the Assembly was that Harrison was the editor of the paper, producing a statutory declaration to that effect, and stating that he, Syme, would not name his informants ('It is not usual for journalists to disclose the sources of information').[8] The subsequent finding by a Parliamentary Select Committee headed by Edward Langton that the allegations in the editorial were unproven was hotly disputed, however, in a *Leader* article that concludes: 'the public will remain convinced that corruption does exist'.[9]

Harrison had experience in printing (his first trade was as a compositor), and in newspaper editing, publishing and proprietorship (Morrison 1997). Scottish-born in 1816, he had worked successively in Glasgow, London, Sydney, Melbourne and, from 1840 to 1865, in Geelong, where for many years he produced the first and most influential country newspaper for Victoria, the *Geelong Advertiser*. His paper was the first to advocate protective tariffs. Politically aware, Harrison was elected a member of the Geelong Town Council in 1850 and, representing Geelong, Member of the Legislative Council (MLC) 1854–56, where he was an early advocate of unlocking the land.[10] A forthright journalist, in 1854 he ran foul of the law for attacking in print the undeniable drunkenness of a Crown Prosecutor during a trial, had conducted his own defence, and been convicted. The fine imposed, an unconscionable £800 plus costs, was offset in part by a public subscription fund, but the whole experience was disheartening, and for a time he left the newspaper world and devoted himself to scientific pursuits that had previously been carried out part-time – ice-making and other inventions. Elected MLA for Geelong in 1859, mounting debts forced him to resign his seat.

Like Syme, he was an emigrant of relatively humble origins from the Scottish Lowlands and significantly self-educated. Like Syme, he was a hard-working man of integrity. Some 11 years older, he was an unacknowledged

---

[8] 'Legislative Assembly, Wednesday 17th July', *Age*, 18 July 1867, p. 6.
[9] 'Legislative Assembly, Wednesday 31st July', *Age*, 1 August 1867, p. 6; 'The Langton Report', *Leader*, 3 August 1867, pp. 17–18.
[10] 'The Land Question' [editorial] *Age*, 4 December 1854, p. 4.

CHAPTER 6

mentor to him. He was responsible for writing leaders and parliamentary reports for the *Age* and science contributions for the *Leader*. It is very likely that he also played a large part in organising the reporting staff and office procedures, as indicated by Syme's acute dismay when he left in 1873. There is a hint of some frustration at being a hack behind-the-scenes journalist, and his relations with Syme were not always smooth – but his scientific pursuits were his priority, and the newspaper work basically an income source.

Syme in England had looked into new printing machinery. He contacted the London agent of American inventor and manufacturer Richard Hoe about a machine to print both *Age* and *Leader*. Probably a rotary press, he considered it, at £2250, too expensive.[11] Hoe had invented and was commercially manufacturing the rotary press, the first model appearing in 1847 ('Richard March Hoe' 2013). Syme would take up the matter of rotary presses again, on a trip to Britain in 1871. On 10 November 1866, while he was still away, the *Age* had begun advertising two machines no longer needed, presumably those used to print the *Age* and *Leader* (four-feeder 6000 sheets per hour and two-feeder 36-inch x 50-inch sheets, 3000 per hour) and on 27 December, coinciding with his return, the paper informed that a 'new and more powerful' machine was being installed, not a rotary press and most likely procured in Melbourne.

Age circulation on the rise

The moves towards ascendancy began only seven days after Syme's return. On 27 December the *Age* announced that its price would be reduced from threepence to twopence from 1 January 1867 and the 'Ourselves' leader of 29 December asserted that the *Age* was entering a new era, with more news and a broader range of topics. On 2 February, five weeks after the reduction, the *Age* claimed its circulation to have nearly doubled, while on 5 May was said to be larger than that of any other metropolitan journal (meaning the *Argus*, which then had a daily average circulation of 8935, and the *Herald*).[12]

A year and a half after the first reduction there was another, the *Age* becoming a penny paper from 1 June 1868, and the number of pages reduced from eight to four. The *Age* of 18 May 1868 announced the looming reductions,

---

[11] DS to Cowan & Co., Edinburgh, 18 June 1872, LB1, pp. 58–61. (Six of David Syme's letterbooks, covering the years 1871–1907, referred to hereafter as LB1–LB6, are among the Syme Family Papers (SFP) in Boxes 1181/1–3 & 1182/1–3.)

[12] 'Circulation', Historical Records of "The Argus" and "The Australasian", 1846–1923, compiled by C.P. Smith, [1924], MS 10727, Australian Manuscripts Collection, State Library of Victoria.

citing as successful precedents the *Manchester Guardian* and the *Manchester Examiner and Times* (perhaps it was copies of these newspapers sent by Jane to Syme in 1863 that first drew his attention; but in any case, he would have had the opportunity to look at practices firsthand in 1866). On 1 June the paper carried a sub-leader tracing the development of the cheap English press. In 1860 dailies had been highly priced, with small circulations; now high-circulating penny dailies were common. For instance, in Newcastle (England) a paper with a high price and circulation of 3000 was now down to a penny, with a circulation of 30,000. The cheapening could be seen to have actually elevated the state of the press for, with the 'dissemination of knowledge among the masses', it had become a strong political force, with people becoming more moderate and tractable and extreme radicalism a thing of the past. This sub-leader conveys that Syme was keenly following the course of press developments.

In July 1868 actual circulation figures begin to appear in the *Age*. On 13 July it announced that circulation had risen from 13,000 to 14,500 in six weeks. But the accompanying reduction to four pages was unfortunate. Although offset by a larger eight-column sheet, the type was smaller, giving a cramped and less visually pleasing appearance. There was little room for more than advertisements and notices (pages 1 and 4); for 'Shipping', 'To Correspondents', editorial and sub-leaders, 'News of the Day' (page 2); and for telegrams, political, Court and City Council reports, and letters to the editor (page 3). Jane wrote in September that she would like to have seen the *Age* in its new form.[13] For some years, this would be the format, until the means of mass production could be acquired for the stated aim of including more news and topics to be implemented.

In parallel with changes to the *Age* there were improvements to the *Leader*, aimed at making it a credible rival to the *Australasian*. On 28 December 1866 a notice in the *Age* informed that from 5 January 1867 the weekly was to be enlarged by eight pages (to 32) and would give 'greater prominence to agriculture, horticulture, sporting, theatrical, literary reviews, social progress here and abroad'. The 'Ourselves' editorial the next day repeated this, adding that the circulation of the *Leader* had doubled again and again and that, while it politically instructed the working class, it should be more than a political organ and a record of 'accidents and offences'. About to enter new era, it would be larger, with more news, sport and theatre, and a broader range of topics, especially relating to agriculture, for 'In this

---

[13] Jane to DS, 12 September 1868, SFP Box 1180/1(b).

CHAPTER 6

country every one should know something of the cultivation and products of the soil…"Earth hunger" is universal'. Syme, through his newspapers and writings, and also through his own ventures, would express and demonstrate a life-long preoccupation with agriculture, and the *Leader* would become a newspaper distinctly for a rural constituency. In 1869 Lauchlan Mackinnon of the *Argus* privately considered the Farmers' section of the *Leader* superior to the Yeoman feature in the *Australasian*.[14]

The *Age* of 12 June 1867 notified a further enlargement of the *Leader*, with a bigger page to give five columns instead of four, and stated that the aim of making it 'the organ of advanced liberalism in the Australian colonies' had succeeded beyond 'the most sanguine expectations'. On 6 July the subtitle became *A Weekly Journal of News, Politics, Literature, Agriculture, Sporting and Science*, replacing '*News, Politics, Literature and Art*', for the *Leader* was expanding its coverage. A new feature, 'Phases of Melbourne Life: Under the Verandah' began in that issue. Dealing with financial and political happenings of the week, its writer was sharebroker Robert Wallen, who explained in the first of what would be nine numbered contributions, that the 'Verandah' was that of the Hall of Commerce at 48 Collins Street West, meeting place for the Stock Exchange and housing stockbrokers and telegraph agencies (fig. 6.1). On 21 September the item, which would be a regular and valued feature of the *Leader* for decades, became simply 'Under the Verandah', unnumbered (Elliott 1958, 216; Adamson 1984, 8–9). Thanks to Harrison, 'Science' began in earnest, an existing 'Scientific' column becoming more substantial and including a 'Patents' sub-section. On 8 August 1868 the first of his Scientific Gossip columns, signed Oedipus, began.

In February 1868 the *Leader* began advertising for a 'really good Tale of Australian Life', and on 1 August the 'Tales & Sketches' feature started. This issue marks the end of the *Weekly Age*, its last number having appeared on 24 July. Its incorporation into the *Leader* was long overdue, the *Weekly Argus* and *Weekly Herald* having ceased in 1864. By 1868 the *Weekly Age* contained little material that was not in the *Leader* and it is hardly surprising that in the issue of 25 July the amalgamation of the two was announced. A circulation of 8000 being claimed for the *Weekly Age* and 13,000 for the *Leader*, it was expected that post-amalgamation the latter would be 21,000 (there is no evidence that it was). Three editions would be published weekly, on Thursday, Friday and Saturday.

---

[14] L. Mackinnon to J. Johnston, 28 January 1869, James Stewart Johnston Correspondence, University of Melbourne Archives.

Figure 6.1. Under the Verandah of the Hall of Commerce, Collins Street West, 1868. (Pictures Collection, State Library of Victoria, IAN05/09/68/9)

Syme made changes also to the *Australian News for Home Readers*, permanently prefixing *Illustrated* to the title with the issue for 27 July 1867 (fig. 6.2). This change was not out of the blue; as seen in the last chapter, the monthly had been referred to by that title in 1866, while the Christmas Supplement to the 27 December issue bears the title 'Supplement to the *Illustrated Australian News*'. On this 27 July issue, the title words *for Home Readers* are in very plain inconspicuous type (perhaps a deliberate step towards their being discarded altogether, suggesting increased catering for the local market). There is a new masthead illustration, presenting Melbourne as a metropolis of some grandeur. A new view shows the Gellibrand lighthouse at the entrance to Hobson's Bay, bordered by garlands and two imposing new buildings: on one side, Parliament House, on the other the General Post Office, which had opened on 1 July. In both cases, the buildings are depicted as they were planned to be when completed, not as they then were!

Takeover of the *Herald*

In spite of these successes, Syme was smitten with fear of the *Age*'s annihilation. In this case the perceived enemy was not its ideological

CHAPTER 6

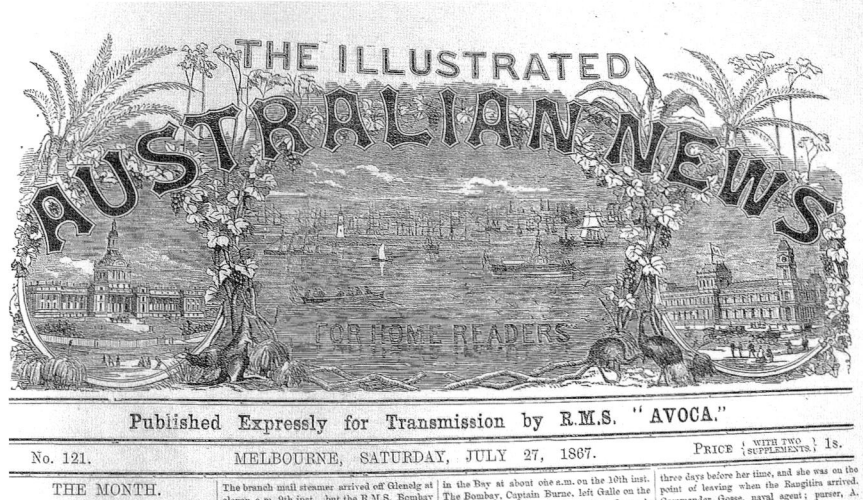

Figure 6.2. Masthead of the *Illustrated Australian News for Home Readers*, 27 July 1867, the first issue with title beginning '*Illustrated*'. (Newspaper Collection, State Library of Victoria)

opponent, the *Argus*; it was the *Herald*, which had been making inroads as a paper for the people ever since its price was reduced to a penny in 1863. And there was the associated competition for the *Illustrated Australian News for Home Readers* from the excellently produced *Illustrated Melbourne Post*, being published by the *Herald* proprietors. A stroke of extraordinary good fortune, the opportunity to purchase the rival business presented in November 1868 when, through a series of financial reverses, the proprietors were forced to sell. George Collins Levey, his brothers Oliver and William, and their father (also George), were involved. In May 1863 the paper was registered in the names of George Levey senior and Francis Franklyn, both resident in England, with sureties provided by Levey sons, George and William, both in Melbourne (Darragh 1997, 87 [23.10–11]). In December 1863 their printer's broker brother Oliver was the new registered owner. By the time of the sale in 1868, George junior was also a vendor. None could afford to carry on the *Herald*.

Syme was swift to act. For £2000 he bought the business (including the two newspapers, printing-presses, plant and stock-in-trade), although attempting to conceal the fact. On the face of it, the purchaser was Jane's attorney William Poole. In the document of assignment dated 28 November, David Syme's name has been crossed out throughout and Poole's substituted, but it is Syme who is shown as accepting the drawing of two bills of exchange for final payment.[15] The vendors are shown as mortgagees Thomas Spalding and John Hodge, wholesale stationers, Drury-Lane, London, and Oliver Levey and George Collins Levey. If Syme wanted to keep his purchase a secret, it was soon out in the *Argus*, which reported all the details of the transaction.[16]

The *Herald* was registered under Poole's name on 2 December 1868, with sureties provided by the general manager of the *Age* business John Macdonald (given as McDonald), and John Gourlay (Darragh 1997, 87 [23.13–14]). The same day the imprint of the *Herald* reflects a change of ownership: 'Printed and published by Richard Brotchie [an *Age* employee] at the Herald Office, Bourke-street, Melbourne, for the Proprietor'. The newspaper continued to be produced at its Bourke Street premises, but for evening, not morning, publication. Implemented on 4 January 1869 with scant notice, a prospectus for the new paper was printed in the *Age* of 31 December. It stated that the evening newspaper would be politically liberal but politics would not occupy too large a place. To be issued at 3 pm, it would be particularly suited to businessmen for the early (that is, updated) news and to working men who only have the chance to read in the evenings. The prospectus also pointed out that Sydney and Adelaide each had an evening paper, as did the provincial towns of Ballarat, Sandhurst and Castlemaine, but Melbourne, 'the most populous, the most bustling (commercially and politically) city of this southern continent' did not. This was not accurate; Melbourne already had the *Evening Star*, which had started on 14 October 1867. It ceased in early 1869 (the last locatable issue is 5 March), presumably knocked out by the new *Herald*.

David must have reported the acquisition promptly to Jane, for in February 1869 she wrote to him, wondering how the speculation would turn out, and whether increased circulation would cover the costs of another manager's salary, extra hands, etc.[17] In the event, the Syme connection lasted less than two years. On 20 September 1870 William Forsyth was registered as the new proprietor of the *Herald*, with Richard Brotchie continuing as printer and publisher (Darragh 1997, 87 [23.15–16]). Disposal must have been contemplated some months before, as Jane wrote to David on 30 August 1870 that she was glad he was willing to

---

[15] Bill of sale, Assignment, SFP Box 1185/5[i]–[ii].
[16] *Argus*, 9 December 1868, p. 5, col. 3.
[17] Jane to DS, 23 February 1869, SFP Box 1180/1(c).

CHAPTER 6

dispose of the *Herald* to advantage and in November that she was 'not sorry to hear that the Herald is sold as it must give you less care and worry'.[18]

Getting rid of the third morning daily did not eliminate competition, however. Just over a month after the evening *Herald* began, a new morning daily started. The *Daily Telegraph* was first issued on 8 February 1869, priced at one penny. Claiming 'purely Liberal principles', its editor was Howard Willoughby, who would join the *Argus* some years later; its manager was Frederick Somerton, who had worked for the *Herald* some years earlier and had been engaged by Syme following his purchase but who resigned soon after.[19] In September 1869 Somerton, who was by then sole proprietor, started the *Weekly Times*. So, Melbourne had three morning dailies with their companion weeklies: the conservative *Argus* and companion *Australasian*; the liberal–reformist *Age* and *Leader*; and the middle-of-the-road-perhaps-conservative-leaning *Daily Telegraph* and *Weekly Times*. It was an era of robust journalism. For the *Age* business, a daily, a weekly and a monthly constituted the stable, which would consolidate and expand over the next quarter-century. The *Age* in particular, already a vehicle for a political program and ideas, would come to cover a much wider range of topics.

Along with Syme's purchase of the *Herald* came the *Illustrated Melbourne Post* – as noted earlier, a serious competitor for the *Illustrated Australian News for Home Readers*. Doubtless in preparation before the sale on 28 November, the issue for 7 December 1868 was the last. To the title of the 140th number of the *Illustrated Australian News for Home Readers*, dated 1 January 1869, was added: 'with which is Amalgamated the *Illustrated Melbourne Post*.' Thus, was that competitor despatched. An Adelaide edition, begun in 1865, renamed the *Illustrated Adelaide Post* in March 1867, and a Tasmanian edition that started in 1867 were part of the package sold to Poole (for Syme). Production and distribution of Tasmanian and Adelaide editions of the *Illustrated Australian News* started in January 1869, with the takeover of the *Illustrated Melbourne Post*. In each case there was much identical content (sometimes re-arranged) and some local features.

Along with the *Herald*, came George Collins Levey. It appears that he had bought into the business only in late 1868, when in Melbourne and writing for the newspaper. There are no staff records to show when he began as member of the *Age* staff, or perhaps as a contributor. From Syme's

---

[18] Jane to DS, 30 August, 29 November 1870, SFP Box 1180/1(c).
[19] 'The "Daily Telegraph": Birth and Death of a Newspaper', *Table Talk*, 6 May 1892, p. 6.

letters to Levey in 1873, in London, one may infer that he was a valued asset, and missed ('I wish you had been here to assist me') [20]. In any case, his engagement could not have been for long at this stage because Levey was appointed secretary to the commissioners for the Sydney Intercolonial Exhibition, held from 30 August to 30 September 1870. This was the first of what would be a succession of positions with exhibitions until 1900 – in Australian cities, London, Vienna, Philadelphia, Paris and Amsterdam (Mellor 1974).

Eight years younger than Syme, English-born Levey had prospered on the goldfields before turning to journalism. After travelling in Europe from 1858 to 1860, he joined the *Herald* as subeditor and rose to editorial responsibilities; partly concurrently he had been an MLA from 1861 to 1867. University educated, flexible, adaptable and lively, he seemed always on the move. He probably spent more time in London than in Melbourne during the quarter of a century he wrote for the *Age* and carried out sundry errands there for Syme. He was the nearest to being treated by Syme as an equal, at least, in correspondence, where he usually seems a confidant with whom Syme felt comfortable. Lauchlan Mackinnon of the *Argus*, by contrast, considered him an 'unprincipled character', not suited to be a contributor.[21]

London connections were coming to the fore in the late 1860s. 'News by the Mail' had long been a regular monthly feature in the *Age*, headlined prominently on page 2 or 3. In 1870 an additional article was introduced: 'The Victorian in London'. Unsigned, as was the practice then, the writer was English-born journalist and playwright William Akhurst, who had been in Melbourne from 1850, had worked for the *Argus* and the *Herald*, and was remembered years later as a 'big, jolly man' (Work 1898). With wife and two children, he sailed for England on the *Kent* in February 1870, sent off with a benefit concert at the Theatre Royal on Thursday 27 January; there was a varied popular program and general jollity (Gibbney and Smith 1987, v.1, 8).[22] Syme may have made arrangements with Akhurst before he sailed, the first contribution appearing in the *Age* of 18 June. In length a little over one column, it discusses the behaviour and treatment of Australian colonials in London, the state of theatricals there ('stale'), and the possible supply of preserved meat to the Austrian cavalry.

---

20   For example, DS to G. Levey, 17 June 1873, LB1, p. 180.
21   L. Mackinnon to J. Johnston, 22 April 1870, Johnston Correspondence.
22   'Mr. Akhurst's Farewell', *Age*, 28 January 1870, p. 3.

CHAPTER 6

The *Age* business profits for the years 1866 to 1870 were smaller than for the first half of the 1860s, where the lowest had been £266 (1863) and the highest £2696 (1865). For the year of Syme's absence, 1866, they were £1078.[23] In 1867 they were an alarming £53 (due to outlay on machinery and a delayed effect of reduced advertising revenue?). Thereafter, they were £572 in 1868, £1428 in 1869 and £1458 in 1870; small beer compared with those for the *Argus* – £18,369 in 1866, £14,968 in 1867 (figures for later years have not been located).[24] But much had been achieved in these years: consolidation of the newspaper 'stable', establishment of the basic requirement for mass circulation (a penny paper) and elimination of the *Herald* competition. Moreover, Syme's policies were taking popular hold, and being reflected in legislation, especially for land selection and tariff protection. In retrospect, Syme saw his protection views 'beginning to make progress'. Overlooking the earlier advocacy of protection by Harrison and his *Geelong Advertiser*, he said that, against strong opposition, he then stood alone as a protectionist in Australia, so far as he knew. Beginning to make progress could well be said of his whole enterprise.

In the late 1860s the press of Victoria was starting to play an *accepted* role in the political system and public life, and exhibiting solidarity. A growing public climate of support for newspapers and against the corruption that was rife in parliamentary circles is seen in the outcomes of libel actions against newspaper publishers during this period. It is also reflected in the fact that probing criticism and exposures tended now not to lead to such actions (Morrison 2005, 162–169; Sayers 1965, 75–133, *passim*). Historian of Victoria Don Garden (1984, 157) refers to the period after the passing of the Grant Land Act in 1865 as marking 'a low point in Victoria's history… [bringing] about a period of parliamentary corruption which is apparently without equal'. The major scandal known as the Quieting of Titles case, which involved trade in certificates of title implicating parliamentarians and a property speculator, and which was uncovered and hammered in the *Age*, but without ensuing litigation, is the prime example (Sayers 1965, 93–99, *passim*).

Jane was critical of David's libel cases, in a September 1867 letter to Syme drawing a comparison with Ebenezer: '"dear Eby" used to be careful about

---

23   Financial statement, SFP Box 1191/1(a)[v].
24   'Profits', Historical Records of "The Argus" and "The Australasian", compiled by C.P. Smith, [1924], MS 10727, Australian Manuscripts Collection, State Library of Victoria.

excising offensive remarks' and advised more watchful supervision.[25] But in contrast to the earlier 1860s, verdicts for defendants (newspaper publishers) in libel cases were becoming more common. In September 1869 a criminal action in the City Police Court against Syme as publisher concerned articles in the *Age* and *Leader* that were critical of anatomical exhibits in Dr Robert Jordan's 'Anthropological Museum' for pandering to 'filthy pruriency'. The case was dismissed by the magistrate, who saw that the writer was only doing his duty to the public. The verdict, endorsed by the *Argus* of 15 September, led to closure of the exhibition and investigation by the Medical Society of Victoria.[26] In 1870 the case of *Wilson v. Syme* in the Supreme Court concerning allegations in the *Age* of improper land dealings was dismissed at the preliminary hearing, the judge considering that the words were not libellous.[27]

Family and partnership complications

In January 1868 the partnership with Jane was renewed for another three years, to the end of 1871. Dated 20 January 1868, this time the document was signed by William Poole in Melbourne, on Jane's behalf.[28] Perhaps an indication of disagreements to come, Jane was increasingly complaining and demanding. From May and for the next two years, in successive letters she requested balance sheets (which presumably Syme sent).[29] In February 1869 she expressed unease about amendments to the deed of partnership that made all overdrawn moneys into debts, which she saw as one-sided.[30] As do many of her letters, it refers to the advances she was requesting and getting. Syme and his wife remained unaware of her marital and family circumstances. On 19 April 1867 she wrote to Annabella that this was the 19th anniversary of her marriage to Ebenezer (but not that three days earlier it was the first anniversary of hers to Palk), while her letter of the same date to Syme raised the matter of 15-year-old son Josephs's employment in the *Age* business: 'Joe is anxiously waiting to hear from you what appointment

---

25 Jane to DS, 25 September 1867, SFP Box 1180/1(b).
26 'Criminal Prosecution for Libel, Jordan v. Syme', *Argus*, 10 September 1869, p. 7, and reported in subsequent issues of the *Argus*, e.g. 14, 15 16, 17, 18 and 24 September 1869.
27 *Argus*, 11 July 1870, p. 5, col. 1.
28 Articles of co-partnership, addendum, SFP Box 1185/2(a)[i].
29 Jane to DS, 21 May 1868, SFP Box 1180/1(b), 17 June 1869, 18 May 1870, SFP Box 1180/1(c).
30 Jane to DS, 23 February 1869, SFP Box 1180/1(c)

CHAPTER 6

you can give him in the office, and upon what terms, he would like to be in the accountants office'.[31] One month later she reminded Syme of his 'promise' made in 1866, adding that she felt 'rather humiliated to ask it as a favour for one of your brother's children'.[32] In monthly letters thereafter, to May 1868, she reiterated her request and also asked for help for 17-year-old son George. Her eldest son, William, had already left home to study medicine in Dublin.

Syme was as good as his word, making arrangements to receive George and Joseph. They left from Gravesend in May 1868 on the *Yorkshire*, arriving in August.[33] Syme's home life for about a year included an extended family. David and Annabella were generous and caring to their nephews, who boarded with them at their house in Cotham Road, Kew, to which they had moved from Essendon (*Sands & McDougall's* 1868). Jane wrote to Annabella thanking her for her kindness to the boys, who stayed with their uncle's family until late 1869, when David and family moved to Alma Road, St Kilda.[34] In January 1870 she repeated her thanks but expressed surprise at the sale of the house and the boys having to leave.[35] A factor in the move may have been Annabella's pregnancy, for a daughter, Lucie, was born in December 1869.[36] Annabella may have had miscarriages during the five and a half years since the birth of Arthur, for Jane wrote in February 1870 that she was sorry about Annie's trouble with confinements and hoped the little girl would 'prosper'.[37] Jane herself had had another successful pregnancy, on 10 April 1869 giving birth to a fourth Palk child, Margaret Hilton Emma.[38] Again masking the true situation, she wrote to David 12 days later that she was not well and confined to her bedroom![39] A family loss was the death on New Year's Day 1870, at the Gourlay residence, of Jean Syme, aged 84, mother of David, George and Margaret.[40]

---

[31] Jane to AS, 19 April 1867, SFP Box 1180/5(b); Jane to DS, 19 April 1867, SFP Box 1180/1(b).
[32] Jane to DS, 19 April 1867, SFP Box 1180/1(b).
[33] Unassisted Inward Passenger Lists to Victoria 1852–1923, Public Record Office Victoria.
[34] Jane to AS, 13 August 1868, SFP Box 1180/5(b).
[35] Jane to DS, 7 January 1870, SFP Box 1180/1(c)
[36] Syme Family Date books, SFP Box 1193/6.
[37] Jane to DS, 14 February 1870, SFP Box 1180/1(c).
[38] Birth certificate, SFP Box 1193/4(c)[ii].
[39] Jane to DS, 22 April 1870, SFP Box 1180/1(c)
[40] 'Deaths', *Argus*, 3 January 1870, p. 4.

In 1869, while living in St Kilda, Syme applied to lease land outside Melbourne. An undated letter to Annabella written at the National Hotel, Gisborne, 'Sunday afternoon' may be related to this. Affectionate, as are all other surviving letters to her, it begins 'Dearest wife' and ends 'My love to yourself and the children'.[41] He was spending the weekend and the Monday following in the Gisborne–Mount Macedon–Woodend area some 60 or so kilometres north-west of Melbourne, parts of which he would have known well from his roads contracting in the 1850s. He tells Annabella about Mount Macedon (the '"Mount" as they call it') – that it is 1500 feet above sea level, with a bracing climate, and that 'English fruit trees,…which wont do well about Melbourne here flourish luxuriantly as at home'. (This last may be hearsay from locals for he also refers to being engaged in 'awful chill work', which suggests winter, when such trees would be bare.)

The 'work' may have been the scouring of the district for suitable land to purchase. Syme would later say that the stockbroker Jonathan Were had suggested he apply for an allotment at Mount Macedon, Were and associates having done so on 3 May 1869.[42] Subsequently, he said, he went with Were to inspect (was this when he wrote the undated letter to his wife?), and on 5 July 1869, applied for 20 acres at Mount Macedon. On 28 July, he applied for two adjoining allotments. Annabella's brother Francis Johnson had made an application then withdrawn it; physician and property investor Dr Godfrey Howitt had done likewise. Granting of the three licences to Syme was finally approved in April 1870, the recommendation to do so being endorsed by Archibald Michie, who had just been appointed Attorney-General in the McCulloch Government (and who had himself applied for a Mount Macedon allotment in 1869). Syme thus obtained some 57 acres on leasehold, and proceeded with clearing the land, fencing and tree planting in compliance with the conditions of the lease under the Land Act.

The legality of these transactions would be challenged almost 30 years later, with claims that Syme acted corruptly in acquiring the extra allotments. As will be seen in Chapter 14, he would be exonerated, but his actions revealed as sharp practice. Exhibiting the same kind of shrewdness as with the *Herald* takeover in December 1868, he was acting within the law, but

---

[41] DS to AS, 'Sunday afternoon', SFP Box 1180/5(c).
[42] Royal Commission into Certain Allegations against the Lands Department 1899, *Land Selection at Mount Macedon: Commission, Report and Evidence*, VPP 1899–1900, no. 33; Sayers 1965, 246–249.

CHAPTER 6

at its boundaries. Clearly he – like a host of men (politicians, civil servants, lawyers, journalists, merchants, etc.) – was seizing the opportunities that the successive Land Acts of the 1860s offered for him to become a man of property and mark in the young colony of Victoria.

From the time of his arrival in Melbourne, nephew Joseph (commonly referred to as Joe) worked in the *Age* Counting House, where his uncle John Gourlay was employed. His first duties were to assist the business manager John Macdonald with the account books.[43] Writing in December 1868, Jane was pleased to learn that her son was 'giving satisfaction'; in October 1869 and again in January 1870 she thanked David for the salary rise and the opportunities being provided for Joseph.[44] In September she wrote suggesting Syme make use of him as an assistant.[45] With what surely amounts to nagging, she seems to have been unduly concerned that Joe would get a rough deal.

Joseph's brother George was the real worry. In March 1868, before the boys left England, Jane wrote David that she was arranging for a letter of introduction for George and asked him if he could find this nephew a position.[46] By December, she was responding to adverse reports, writing that she hoped George would avoid the 'temptations of Melbourne'.[47] From laments in letters over the next few years it appears he did not resist, took to drink, ran up debts, and had no job. One cannot but wonder about the effect that their home circumstances and their mother's relationship with Palk might have had on Ebenezer's children, particularly on George and Joseph, who also had the burden of keeping their mother's secrets from their aunt and uncle, as it appears they did for several years.

William, the eldest son, seems to have assumed a head of the household role, becoming, as a medical practitioner, a qualified member of a respected profession and, later, conducting sensible and on the whole amicable dealings with David on behalf of his mother and siblings; after he reached the adult age of 21 it would be with him that David would deal, rather than Jane. Young Joe conscientiously followed the path laid out for him; only later would destructive bitterness surface. George was the casualty. David for years was finding jobs and funds for his nephew. In her letters

---

[43] Jane to DS, 6 September [inferentially1870], SFP Box 1180/1(e).
[44] Jane to DS, 2 December 1868, SFP Box 1180/1(b), 7 October 1869, 7 January 1870, SFP Box 1180/1(c).
[45] Jane to DS, 6 September [inferentially1870], SFP Box 1180/1(e).
[46] Jane to DS, 26 March 1868, SFP Box 1180/1(b).
[47] Jane to DS, 29 December 1868, SFP Box 1180/1(b).

Jane alternately apologised for his behaviour and upbraided her in-laws for not being sufficiently understanding. In December 1870, for instance, she wrote accusing Annabella of forgetting herself as a mother in complaining of George, for it might be 'her turn' one day.[48] To David she was more restrained, writing on 29 December that she hadn't heard from George that month and hoped he would find employment.[49] It seems that David and Annabella, in the course of their committed and many-sided lives dutifully and stoically expended much time and effort, not to mention expense, in attending to the welfare of George and Joe.

Authorship

Apart from day-to-day newspaper management and laying the foundations for transforming the *Age* into one of the leading dailies in the British Empire, and in addition to taking on responsibilities for his extended as well as his close family, David Syme broke into print in England, albeit at first anonymously and, when his authorship became known, began to establish a position for himself as a serious thinker and writer on a vital issue of the day. In 1870 his 'The Land Question in England' was published in the liberal quarterly journal of ideas, the *Westminster Review*.[50] He had first submitted it unsuccessfully to John Morley of the *Fortnightly Review*.[51] Speculatively, during the recuperative 1866 trip he may have gathered material and formulated ideas, and made the acquaintance of the *Westminster*'s editor, John Chapman. (He would refer to him in 1872 as 'my friend Dr Chapman'.[52]) That Ebenezer worked for Chapman in the early 1850s could have facilitated his brother's *entrée*. The periodical had a high reputation; an editorial in the *Argus* of 9 March 1868 on the English press said that the *Westminster* 'has always been esteemed as one of the ablest and most influential organs of philosophical radicalism in the mother country' and was a 'courageous champion and defender of ultra liberal opinions'.

The 30-page scholarly 'Land Question' article is carefully referenced to a wide range of sources: works on history, agriculture, politics, economics in many countries (England, Ireland, Mexico, Peru, India and others, including the Australian colonies); census data; a letter to the *Times*. All

---

[48] Jane to AS, 1 December 1870, SFP Box 1180/5(b).
[49] Jane to DS, 29 December 1870, SFP Box 1180/1(c).
[50] See Appendix B for details and publishing history of Syme's works.
[51] DS to J. Morley, 28 March 1872, LB1, p. 32.
[52] DS to G. Street, 28 March 1872, LB1, p. 30.

CHAPTER 6

sources that it would have been more convenient to consult and think about away from the day-to-day business and journalistic pressures. The author does not refer to any radical socialist or communist works of the time, although his theories have some affinity with them. The article puts into an international and comparative context, however, matters related to the regulation and reform of land settlement that had been an essential part of the policies of his newspapers during the late 1850s and for most of the 1860s, and demonstrates the clarity and breadth of thinking of which Syme was capable.

The article is the leading one in the October issue. Its author is against large land-holders, whether these be landed families in England or squatters in Australia. He sees this 'system' as producing classes of stupid agricultural labourers and paupers. He puts forward an idiosyncratic version of socialism. A variant of the case for the yeoman farmer, he opposes the alienation of public territory to individual proprietors as a 'modern innovation', unknown to three-fourths of the human race, from the 'American Indian [to the]… aborigines of Africa and Australia'. He advocates farms being of moderate extent and cultivators having security of tenure and, to achieve this, that the Crown resume possession of all agricultural and unreclaimed land, compensate owners, and lease blocks for 30 years, subject to renewal. He admits his proposals are revolutionary, saying that a 'revolution is but another name for a thorough reform, and a thorough reform of our [that is, the English] land system is urgently required'. While the whole concept is idealistic and utopian, the article demonstrates Syme's abilities not only as a thinker but also as a writer, a metier that he would pursue in parallel with his newspaper business, and which would help him to sustain a vision, the big picture. Ironically, in applying just one year earlier to lease 20 acres at Mount Macedon, Syme had, whether intentionally or otherwise, taken the first steps towards what would be huge dealings in rural real estate over the years ahead.

Although the article is unsigned, its authorship was revealed to the reading public two weeks later, in the *Athenaeum* of 15 October and commented upon in another English scholarly periodical. Historian Frederic Seebohm, an authority on the origins of English communal farming, evaluated it in the *Fortnightly Review* of January 1871. Carefully if sceptically examining Syme's argument, he concluded: 'Is it in the interests of the working classes of England that the air should be filled with wild schemes such as this?' In similar vein, the article by agricultural and land writer Chandos Wren Hoskyns, 'The Present State of the Land Question', in the April issue stresses the need for removing obstructions to the acquisition and transfer of land, at 'a time when every privilege is scrutinized and the wildest land theories find support', thus alluding to Syme's proposals. Albeit from the margins, Syme in 1870 was joining a contemporary English debate. It remained to be seen whether he could maintain this position from his newspaper press base in colonial Melbourne.

Chapter 7

'BUSINESS IS GOOD BUT MONEY SCARCE'

(January 1871 to May 1876)

An inauspicious start to the year, on Sunday 8 January 1871 a fire in the upper storey of the *Age* premises destroyed part of the subeditor and reporters' room and back files of newspapers therein. Syme reported this to Jane, who responded from England in March enquiring about the damage.[1] The *Argus* on the day after the fire sympathetically called the loss of the papers 'an injury the extent of which cannot be assessed in money'. The *Age* and *Leader* began advertising for complete files not only of the stable of five Syme newspapers, but also of the daily *Argus* and *Herald*, the weekly *Australasian* and *Bell's Life in Victoria* (which had ceased in 1868), and of the official *Government Gazette*. Notwithstanding these losses and sundry other sources of stress, the years from 1871 to 1876 would see considerable achievements for Syme.

Following the lowering of the price of the *Age* to one penny in 1868, Syme in the early 1870s was deeply and intensely involved in taking the next steps to build the newspaper into a mass-circulating daily and make his other two papers into publications of outstanding quality. He was doing this at a time when the expanding press community was expressing pride in its newspapers, while politicians and the general public were coming to accept them as part of political life and a source of edification and entertainment (Morrison 2005, 186–188). This was a corollary of increasing education and literacy, a more settled middle class with leisure to read, and a growing awareness of the role that newspapers were playing in the operating of representative democratic government.

---

[1] Jane to DS, 23 March 1871, SFP Box 1180/1(c).

DAVID SYME

New printing technology

The *Age* proprietor was responsible for the introduction of revolutionary new printing technology into the Australasian colonies. In 1872 a rotary press was installed in the *Age* office – a machine that printed continuously from reels of paper and folded the finished newspapers. This meant faster production and, thus, the potential for increased circulation. It also required a trip to Britain in 1871, to see the new machines in operation and place an order for one.

In 1868 the London *Times* had produced the Walter rotary press, capable of delivering 12,000 copies per hour, and the firm of Richard Hoe in the United States was working on similar machines ('Tradition Established' 1939, 276, 390). The small Liverpool firm of Duncan and Wilson produced their first Victory machine in 1870, for the Glasgow *Star*. It was capable of printing and folding 10,000 copies per hour, and it was on this that Syme set his sights. A printing textbook of 1888 describes its advent as effecting a 'comparative revolution'; and even without its innovative folding capacity it was 'fully capable of holding its own' against the Hoe and Walter already in use (Wilson and Grey 1888, 208).

Seen off by 'a large number of friends', Syme left Melbourne on 28 March 1871, sailing on the *Geelong*.[2] Prior to his departure he was farewelled at a lunch held at the Criterion Hotel and attended by some 50 persons, including many employees and several politicians.[3] Significantly, editor James Harrison was chair of the proceedings. Travelling alone this time, Syme was away just over five months. In Britain, he spent several weeks investigating the Victory in operation and visiting the makers in Liverpool.[4] In Glasgow he would have been able to see the machines at the *Star* and the *Daily Mail*. At the latter office he made contact with Dr Cameron, proprietor, and F. Dietrichsen, manager.[5] In Edinburgh he discussed technical matters with William McCulloch, machinist of the *Daily Review*.[6] Seemingly satisfied by his inspection, in Liverpool he would have discussed terms of purchase and arrangements for installation. He also saw manufacturers and suppliers of the web (reel) paper he would need for a rotary machine.[7] In due course

---

[2] *Argus*, 29 March 1871, p. 5, col. 1.
[3] 'The News of the Day', *Age*, 29 March 1871, p. 2.
[4] DS to W. Clarson, 12 August 1873, LB1, pp 187–190.
[5] DS to F. Dietrichsen, 25 April 1872, LB1, p. 38; DS to Dr Cameron, 15 June 1874, LB1, pp. 214–215.
[6] DS to W. Clarson, 10 September 1872, LB1, pp. 83–84.
[7] DS to W. Watson, 29 February 1872, LB1, pp. 27–28.

CHAPTER 7

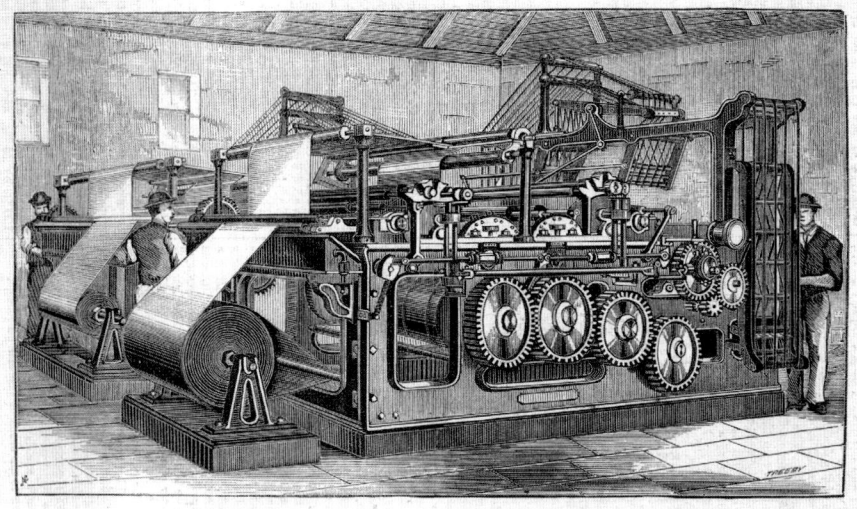

Figure 7.1. Victory rotary printing machines, introduced to Australia by Syme in 1872. (Pictures Collection, State Library of Victoria, IAN10/06/78/104)

he ordered a Victory and web paper for it through the Edinburgh firm of Cowan & Co.[8]

But procurement of new machinery was not the only purpose of his trip. As dealt with later in this chapter, he visited Reuters to discuss a cable news service, and he met sister-in-law and business partner Jane and began to learn the truth of her circumstances. He also gave some time to the writing (on shipboard) and publication of more scholarly articles. On 4 September he arrived back in Melbourne on the *Gothenburg*, via the United States and New Zealand, having accomplished his primary mission.[9]

The Victory machine (fig, 7.1) arrived in Melbourne in January 1872, the fifth to be made and sold by Duncan and Wilson. The office Machinery Register shows the total paid as £1792.6.7.[10] James Duncan, son of the firm's George Duncan, came out to help install it.[11] He would later do likewise at the Sydney *Evening News* and *Australian Town and Country Journal* and the

---

[8] Listed in the Edinburgh *Directory for the Year 1871–2* as 'papermakers, stationers, and envelope manufacturers'.
[9] 'Shipping Intelligence', *Argus*, 5 September 1871, p. 4.
[10] Machinery Register, 1871–1888, SFP Box 1186/1.
[11] DS to J. Cowan, 22 May 1872, LB1, pp. 43–47; information from descendant, Colin Duncan.

Auckland Star in New Zealand when these newspaper businesses followed the lead set by Syme and bought the Victory.

On 2 February 1872 Syme wrote to Jane that the machine was up but not yet running, as there were alterations to be made. Optimistically, he expected it to be operational in a month.[12] Some 10 weeks later, on 13 April 1872, the *Age* announced the use of the new technology and, from 20 April, a corresponding doubling of the Saturday paper to eight pages:

> The proprietors are enabled to make the proposed change from their having imported the newest machinery for printing from the web, without which it would have been nearly impossible to have kept pace with the increasing demand for THE AGE.

So doing, as with the price lowering to one penny in 1868, the *Age* claimed to be following the example of leading provincial papers in Britain, citing the *Manchester Guardian*, the *Manchester Examiner and Times*, the *Leeds Mercury* and the *Scotsman*. (An eight-page paper was no innovation for Melbourne, however: although the *Herald* and *Daily Telegraph* were still only four pages, the *Argus* was eight, as the *Age* had been before its price reduction in 1868.)

But behind the scenes Syme was grappling with technical problems. The Victory was much slower than promised, the folding mechanism would not work and the paper (newsprint) was quite unsuitable, with many copies often damaged. Between April 1872 and June 1874 he wrote at least 50 letters seeking help, some running to several closely written pages.[13] Most are signed David Syme; some, more formally, 'E & D Syme', with disingenuous textual reference to 'our Mr Syme'. He asked Dietrichsen at the Glasgow *Daily Mail* and Major Laurence Knox, publisher of the *Irish News* in Dublin, for details of their experience with the Victory. Time and again he wrote to the supplier James Cowan of Cowan & Co. about his problems and, not all on file, but to be inferred, to the manufacturers Duncan and Wilson. Seeking information about a suitable second machine and appropriate, affordable paper he wrote to London agent George Street and to Scottish A.J. Malcolm, a partner in and later chairman of the London firm of the ironmonger James McEwan, whom he would frequently consult and confide in over the years, until Malcolm's death in 1905.[14]

---

[12] DS to Jane, 22 February 1872, LB1, p. 23.
[13] The first to J. Cowan on 24 April 1872 (LB1, p. 37), the last to Dr Cameron on 15 June 1874 (LB1, pp. 214–215).
[14] 'Personal', *Argus*, 9 March 1905, p. 5.

CHAPTER 7

In September 1872 he commissioned William Clarson of the publishing firm Clarson, Massina & Company, who was travelling to England, to investigate and possibly procure another printing machine and suitable paper, and gave him eight letters of introduction.[15] He asked him to look at the latest machines, including the Walter on display at the Exhibition Building in London, and to see about the availability of second-hand Hoes through the *Printers Register*. Clarson, whom Syme described, in a letter to Jane of 10 September 1872, as 'a friend of mine', was a journalist, publisher and horticulturist.[16] Earlier in the year E. & D. Syme had taken part in a cooperative venture, the *Leader* of 24 February containing an advertisement for a combination subscription to the *Leader* or *Australasian* or *Weekly Times* with the monthly *Australian Journal*, published by Clarson's firm.

In England Clarson was quick to act; too quick for Syme. On 15 December he used the new and expensive cable connection to wire that he had ordered 15 tons of paper and a new Victory machine. Syme had great reservations, and on 18 December cabled to terminate the paper contract 'by mutual consent'. Over the year he and his employees experimented to find the most suitable paper, finding some consignments underweight and poorer quality than promised; and they learned by trial and error how it needed to be dampened before printing. In the process, Syme was casting wide to find the best supplier at the best price, in so doing giving detailed, complicated instructions in letters not only to Clarson but to sundry agents and suppliers. In consequence, there were duplicate orders, cancellations, misunderstandings, ill feeling and threats of litigation. In the course of his delegated investigations and arrangements, he both incurred claims from and made claims against paper suppliers and manufacturers for breach of contract; even at the start of 1876 there were two ongoing serious disputes concerning paper orders.

In spite of grumbling over its operation, Syme reported to Jane in October 1873 that the new machine was 'working well, turning out copies almost at the rate of 10,000 an hour', adding that he expected the second one to be shipped by the next mail.[17] It arrived in November, the 14th to be made by Duncan and Wilson. Obtained this time through McEwan, the cost to

---

[15] DS to W. Clarson, 10 September 1872, LB1, pp. 82–84; letters of introduction, LB1, pp. 85–90; on file are copies of a further 10 letters to Clarson, dates ranging from 10 October 1872 (LB1, pp. 93–95) to 18 May 1874 (LB1, pp. 207–208).

[16] DS to Jane, 10 September 1872, LB1, p. 81.

[17] DS to Jane, 9 October 1873, LB1, pp. 195–196.

Syme, including shipping, was £1682.14.7.[18] He was unhappy about the delay in delivery, having complained to Clarson on 21 May and 12 August 1873 (he feared that the one being made for him was to be on display at the Vienna Exhibition). He had further trouble getting this second one to work properly, however, and took issue with the firm, claiming compensation. On 15 June 1874 he wrote to Dr Cameron at the Glasgow *Daily Mail* that he had experienced nothing but trouble and expense 'It is but too well known in every newspaper office in these colonies that our machines have been a failure' and he wanted Cameron, as a partner in the Victory Machine Company, to see that he (Syme) received justice.[19] In dispute with the makers, Syme was casting his experience in the worst possible light, for these two machines, after the teething troubles were overcome, proved to be anything but failures, and a third Victory would be bought in 1877 (Duncan and Wilson's 53rd). All three were in working order in the 1880s, when Syme upgraded to new Hoes – the first Victory offered for sale in 1889 for £650, the second sold to a New Zealand firm for a hefty £1174.5.6 and the third still in use at the end of 1888, valued at £835.11.5.[20]

The whole episode displays, on the one hand, Syme's initiative and persistence through to eventual success. It shows, on the other, that he expected too much of people, and could be controlling and churlish. Initially courteous, his letters to Clarson eventually became carping, critical, and alienating. Typically, he drove a hard bargain. But it was more of a problem that, apart from young James Duncan, he had no one at hand with any relevant technical experience, and had to wait weeks and months (the new overseas telegraph being too costly except for an emergency) for two-way communication with experts who could only proffer advice without seeing the problems. Moreover, in his anxiety and haste to reach a solution, he pursued several avenues of information and supply virtually simultaneously, without proper individual follow-up, resulting in misunderstandings, duplications of orders and untenable cancellations. It was a pattern to be repeated throughout his life.

Cable connection to London

Another technological development to be embraced by Australian newspapers was the cable connection to London. Introduced to the Australian colonies from the early 1850s, the telegraph had been used by the press for

---

[18] Machinery Register.
[19] DS to Dr Cameron, 15 June 1874, LB1, pp. 214–215.
[20] Machinery Register.

CHAPTER 7

communicating within and between colonies, and had been followed by the emergence of telegraph news agencies to collect and disseminate packages of news to complement individual use. By 1870 all colonies except Western Australia (which became connected in 1877) were linked. A link to Britain and the rest of the world had been contemplated from 1856, and from 1870 its completion was being envisaged and planned for. The last links were completed and, after some false starts, the line was in working order in October 1872. In November, celebration banquets were held in Adelaide, Sydney and London on 15 November (Morrison 2005, 86, 204; Livingston 1996, 83). Now overseas news could be received by cable in hours or less, instead of three to four weeks, and 'telegraph offices replaced the waterfront as the receiving centre for world news' (Blainey 1983, 222). (Previously, news had been sent by cable to ports en route and picked up by ships for carriage to Australia.)

Under the heading 'News from Europe By Submarine Telegraph', the *Age* of 23 October 1872 published some 38 news items, as closely-set paragraphs in no meaningful order, similar to the format of 'News of the Day'. Sourced from Reuters to the newly-formed Australian Press Association (discussed below), the first of the cables had been despatched in London at 4.25 pm on 21 October, were received in the *Age* office, via Adelaide, at 11 pm on 22 October, and were published at 5 am the next day. Allowing for the 10-hour time difference, some 20½ hours had elapsed between despatch in London and receipt at the *Age* office. Better organisation would eventually reduce this. Supposedly selected with a view to Australian needs, the initial news was unremarkable, to say the least, the package of 23 October beginning with a Church Congress at Leeds. Neither the *Argus* nor the *Age* managers were satisfied and, although there was contemporary excitement about the new communications tool, it would be months before actual benefits were experienced and years before the cable facility would be properly utilised by the press. Also extremely expensive to begin with – at 10s.8d per word – its usefulness at the start was limited to the wealthy.

In spite of making early moves, Syme failed to be the frontrunner with this innovation in telecommunications, as he was with advances in printing technology. An alliance of the older conservative papers, the *Sydney Morning Herald* and the *Argus*, moved sooner and more decisively (Putnis 2004). The rival *Argus* was better placed than the *Age*, with a London office from 1869 and its three proprietors living in England. During 1870 the *Argus* and *Sydney Morning Herald* managers in Australia were corresponding about cooperation; in England the *Argus* proprietors were talking of a press association that would be inclusive (encompassing the *Age*) and independent of Reuters. When in November 1870 Syme applied to participate as a full member of the so-styled Australian Press Association, the *Argus* Council of Management in Melbourne turned him down. In June 1871, during his English stay, he visited the Reuters cable news agency, to come to some separate arrangement, only to discover that *Argus* proprietor Edward Wilson had already clinched a deal for obtaining cable news on behalf of the Australian press in April, when he (Syme) was on the high seas. Hugh George of the *Argus*, who had travelled to England on the same ship as Syme, further discussed this deal with Reuters some days after Syme's visit. The upshot was that Syme, through Hugh George, found that he had no option but to subscribe to the Press Association service. The *Argus* proprietors were later to regret having excluded him from its management, finding that, without a united Australian press front (which came more than two decades later), it was not possible to displace the Reuters monopoly.

After his return to Melbourne in September 1871, Syme moved unsuccessfully to establish his own service. On 22 November he wrote to Samuel Bennett in Sydney, publisher of two dailies, the *Empire* and the *Evening News*, and the weekly *Town and Country Journal*, noting that action would be needed to procure English telegrams once the cable was in operation.[21] Saying that his arrangements were in a very chaotic state, he was, however, considering a press association separate from the *Argus*. On 4 December he wrote to Street in London, prematurely and with wishful thinking saying that he was connected with an association of papers locally.[22] He asked Street to find out the best terms for transmission and to arrange for the present correspondent John Plummer to obtain cable news amounting to an average of 40 words daily. He would telegraph Street immediately the line was opened. Whilst the Australian Press Association was professionally organised to obtain Reuters news and sell it on to any Australian newspaper able and willing to pay, Syme was behaving like a rank amateur. His proposals came to naught, at this stage. It became clear, however, that he and the *Age* were not to be totally dependent on the Press Association.

At the same time, he made separate arrangements with a new venture, the Anglo-Australian Telegraph Agency in Melbourne, to obtain six London telegrams per week at a charge of £450 per annum.[23] It was run by Reuben

---

[21] DS to S. Bennett, 22 November 1871, LB1, pp. 10–12.
[22] DS to G. Street, 4 December 1871, LB1, pp. 20–21.
[23] DS to R. Quarrill, 12 December 1872, LB1, p.109.

CHAPTER 7

Quarrill (very likely the Quarrill employed on the *Age* staff in 1875[24]). Study of the cable news in the *Age* fails to reveal use of this service; and Syme found the arrangement unsatisfactory, in May 1873 doubtful that it would continue. It is not clear how long it did, but possibly into early 1875 at the latest.[25] Continuing with the Press Association service, Syme was not happy. He complained that, compared with other papers, he was overcharged – the Sydney *Evening News* paying £300 per annum and getting cables sooner, the *Age* having to pay £500.[26] With complaints flowing both ways between Hugh George and Syme, it was an unsatisfactory situation that would continue until 1877.[27] Moreover, both the *Argus* and the *Age* wished to break the Reuters domination.

When the Saturday *Age* doubled in size from 20 April 1872, Syme had been planning for more advertisements and new and attractive reading matter to fill the additional four pages. Fortuitously or perhaps with intent, the *Age* of 13 April, which announced the Saturday enlargement, was included with the sample issues of newspapers and periodicals published in Victoria on or about 15 April 1872, collected by the Trustees of the Public Library for display at the London Exhibition (Morrison 2005, 187–188). Further publicity in Britain was set in train when on 22 April Syme sent London agent Street a notice of the enlargement to be placed in the *Daily News*, the *Times*, the *Economist*, the *Leeds Mercury*, the *Birmingham Telegraph*, the *Manchester Examiner & Times*, the *Scotsman* and the Glasgow *Mail*.[28] With Street given as advertising agent for the *Age*, clearly the intention of the notice was not simply to trumpet the status of the *Age*, but to present it as a very suitable advertising medium for English commercial interests.

Serial fiction for the *Age*

That the *Age* was to become more than a vehicle of political news and views is strikingly evident in the issue for 20 April, which features the first instalment of bestselling novelist Mary Braddon's *To the Bitter End*, shortly to be published in England as a book. While the *Leader* and the *Australasian* and their weekly counterparts in other colonies had begun the serialising of fiction in the 1860s, the *Age* was the first Australian daily to do so. The

---

[24] Staff Wages Register, 1874–1876, entry for 20 February 1875, SFP Box 1186/2.
[25] DS to G. Levey, 20 May 1873, LB1, p. 173.
[26] DS to H. George, 21 September 1875, LB1, p. 232.
[27] DS to H. George, 14 November 1873, LB1, pp. 199–202.
[28] DS to G. Street, 22 April 1872, LB1, pp.35–36.

Melbourne *Daily Telegraph* was quick to emulate, beginning on 13 December with James Payn's, *At Her Mercy*, but it would be many years before the *Argus* would follow suit, although in October 1872 its three expatriate proprietors were talking about a Saturday supplement for the *Argus*, to compete with the *Age*.[29].

This development was firmly in Syme's hands, working at first through Street's London agency and moving to involve George Levey, then in London, seeing him as more knowledgeable about literature.[30] *To the Bitter End* was surely a popular choice although Syme begrudged spending £129 on rights when he obtained Edmund Yates's *Castaway* for £50 in 1871, for the *Leader*. Braddon's novel ran until mid-January 1873, after which there was a break until mid-November, when Anthony Trollope's Christmas novella *Harry Heathcote of Gangoil* began, much to Syme's pleasure. Appearing in the *Age* concurrently with serialisation in the London *Graphic*, it was published as a book in 1874. In the interval Syme, although expressing dislike of Trollope (the person or his books?) and rejecting his *Phineas Redux*, would have serialised his *The Eustace Diamonds* and also wanted George Eliot's *Middlemarch*, but in each case the weekly *Australasian* had got in first. Following *Harry Heathcote* there was almost unbroken serialisation of new novels by stock bestselling novelists – such as Edmund Yates, Ann Thackeray (Lady Ritchie), James Payn, Wilkie Collins. To augment the income from their books, such authors frequently sold serial rights to newspapers in the UK and beyond, often through Tillotsons Fiction Bureau in Bolton, Lancashire (Morrison 1995). It would appear that after the initial flurry in trying to get fiction copy, someone on the *Age* made arrangements for procurement through Tillotsons, selecting from their circularised list, and Syme pulled back from total hands-on involvement.

Besides the new serial fiction, Syme paid serious attention to improving the regular overseas correspondence. He decided to dispense with two existing correspondents, William Akhurst and his 'The Victorian in London', and London journalist John Plummer, who had founded and edited *London Figaro*, been a correspondent for the *Sydney Morning Herald* and was contributing 'Social and Industrial Topics' to the *Age*. In a letter of 17 June 1873 Syme gave Levey the job of confirming to them

---

[29] L. Mackinnon to J. Johnston, 3 October 1872, James Stewart Johnston Correspondence, University of Melbourne Archives.

[30] DS to G. Street, 22 April 1872, LB1, pp.35–36, and 13 August 1872, LB1, p. 78; DS to G. Levey, 15 July 1873, LB1, pp.181–182, and 12 August 1873, LB1, pp. 185–186.

that they were not wanted.[31] He had in March pressed him to take over the London correspondence, promising a free hand, provided the material was interesting and from an Australian point of view.[32] Levey accordingly accepted. His 'London Notes' began appearing in May, and Syme expressed appreciation in several subsequent letters. In October 1873 he wanted Levey to do something about Paris correspondence while on the Continent, noting that the *Daily Telegraph* had a correspondent there and 'The Victorian in London' had included news from the French metropolis.[33] He pointed out on 12 August that Levey would have to find a successor (and not Akhurst) if he returned to Melbourne to work for Syme (which he did in 1874), but it is not clear that Levey did look for one.[34]

James Harrison, as explained below, was living in London from late 1873 and became a sort of successor to Levey, sending leaders and a correspondence column for the *Age* as well as scientific material for the *Leader*. There is no documentation to show precisely when this began. In August 1875 Syme accepted his offer to review new books and also asked if he ever thought of coming back, assuring him that he would be fully employed if he did.[35] In September Syme wanted a new approach, asking Harrison for three letters: one on English and Continental politics; one on literature and literary gossip; and one on scientific or social matters.[36] Finding this not satisfactory after all, in January 1876 he requested a return to the former arrangement of one monthly letter on politics and home and foreign events generally and five or six leading articles.[37]

Apart from the decisive serial fiction innovation, Syme was clearly feeling his way with literature and the arts for the *Age*. In September 1873 he wrote to Levey that a Miss Zimmern had, through Dr Richard Garnett at the British Museum, offered to 'do the literary & artistic business' – this may have been either the prolific journalist Helen Zimmern or her lesser-known sister Alice (Brake and Demoor 2009, 699).[38] Thinking that a 'really good, clever, gossiping sort of letter on all sorts of things interesting to ladies wd be of more value than one exclusively literary', Syme asked Levey to interview

---

[31] DS to G. Levey, 17 June 1873, LB1, p.180.
[32] DS to G. Levey, 27 March 1873, LB1, pp.153–154.
[33] DS to G. Levey, 10 October 1873, LB1, p.197.
[34] DS to G. Levey, 12 August 1873, LB1, pp.185–186.
[35] DS to J. Harrison, 9 August 1875, LB1, p. 229.
[36] DS to J. Harrison, 6 September 1875, LB1, pp. 230–231.
[37] DS to J. Harrison, 27 January 1876, LB1, p. 241.
[38] DS to G. Levey, 9 September 1873, LB1, pp. 191–192.

her. She did send several contributions, but Syme found them out of date. Paying her £3 for two (30 shillings each) he asked her to discontinue.[39]

In similar manner, in March 1876 Syme responded to a George Oxenpoint who, on the recommendation of Plummer, had sent several contributions on drama and theatre. Telling him that 'there are not a sufficiently large class of readers in the colony who take an interest in dramatic matters to make it worth while to have a special correspondence on the subject', he said he would pay two guineas each for them, but asked that no more be sent.[40] He replied also to Plummer that he thought the Oxenpoint's first letter 'very good indeed' – also saying that he had his (Plummer's) name on a list of possible future correspondents, but nothing seems to have come of this.[41]

There was great acceptance of the new enlarged Saturday issue of the *Age*. Syme wrote to Street on 22 April 1872 that its circulation was 20,000, 'equal to the combined circulation of the Argus, Telegraph & Evening Herald, with a few thousand to spare' and on 13 August that it had risen to 24,000.[42] The average daily circulation of all issues, not just the enlarged Saturday one, rose steadily thereafter, Syme telling an Edinburgh agent in May that the *Age* was 'never in a better position…both as regards circulation & advertising.'[43] For the week ending 6 July 1872 the average daily circulation (actually, accountant-certified number of copies printed) was 17,112.[44] For the last six weeks of 1873 it was 20,027, 'a circulation unprecedented in the Australian colonies', it was claimed.[45]

In 1874 some economies were effected, the Saturday *Age* of 10 January having a smaller page, of seven columns instead of eight, and justifying this as due to the high price of paper. (The *Daily Telegraph* and *Herald* both had seven columns.) The reduction did not arrest the increase in circulation, which, as announced in the *Age*, was over 23,000 at the end of 1874 and 24,000 in August 1875.[46]

Syme made improvements to the *Leader* also. Although his brother George was the editor, David made some key decisions. In late 1873 Scottish-born John Lamont Dow, who had come to Victoria in 1848 at the age of 11 and who

---

[39] DS to Miss Zimmern, 18 May 1874, LB1, p. 211.
[40] DS to G.S. Oxenpoint, 22 March 1876, LB1, p. 245.
[41] DS to J. Plummer, 22 March 1876, LB1, p. 246.
[42] DS to G. Street, 22 April 1872, LB1 pp. 35–6, and 13 August 1872, LB1, p. 78.
[43] DS to J. Cowan, 22 May 1872, LB1, pp. 43–47.
[44] *Age*, 12 July 1872, p. 4, col. 2.
[45] 'Circulation of the Age', *Age*, 1 January 1874, p. 2 .
[46] 'To Advertisers', *Age*, 26 December 1874, p. 4; *Age*, 14 August 1875, p. 4, col. 4.

CHAPTER 7

had extensive farming, exploring (of the Gulf of Carpentaria) and mining experience, began his long and productive association with the *Leader* (Dow 1972). An undated memorandum in David's hand commissions him to tour the Wimmera District of Western Victoria and report weekly, primarily on agricultural matters but also on mining and '<u>anything</u> that you consider of interest to our readers'.[47] His name first appearing on the payroll in March 1874, as reporter, that year his 'Travelling Reporter' articles were published from time to time, in the 'Farm' section of the weekly.[48] Later in 1874 he toured South Australia, with his articles appearing from 3 October until 12 February 1875, reprinted as a book, and at least one as a separate pamphlet. By September 1876 his salary was £6 per week; it is likely that he was then agricultural editor for the paper.[49]

With a heavy emphasis on agriculture, the *Leader* was strengthening its leading position as a rural newspaper, while continuing the topical Melbourne 'Under the Verandah', which Syme described as 'of a light, gossipy nature' and 'eminently readable'.[50] The feature was now written by staff journalist Alfred Telo, a gifted and artistically sensitive writer, who was plagued by epilepsy, Syme writing sympathetically to George Levey in September 1873 that 'Poor Telo' was 'laid up' after several fits.[51] From 1 July 1873, due to a reduction in postage for newspapers, the weekly was post free, costing six shillings and sixpence a quarter, not seven shillings and sixpence, which made it more affordable for country people.

For several months Clarson sent horticultural contributions for the *Leader* from England, besides looking into printing machines and paper on Syme's behalf. It was David, not George, who responded. Pleased with them, he asked the writer not to send any to the *Australasian*.[52] In January 1876 David turned his attention to reorganising the Sporting correspondence. He terminated the appointment of J. Sampson and, through James McCulloch (the businessman, not the politician, then in London), engaged W.S. Martin of the *Bell's Life in London, and Sporting Chronicle* office as 'Ashdown' for three guineas per monthly letter, advising him that the 'Turf' (horseracing) was of most interest, and that comment rather than narrative was required,

---

[47] DS to J. Dow, undated, LB1, p. 203.
[48] Staff Wages Register, entry for 14 March 1874.
[49] Staff Wages Register, entry for 23 September 1876.
[50] DS to G. Levey, 27 March 1873, LB1, pp. 153–154.
[51] DS to G. Levey, 9 September 1873, LB1, pp. 191–192; M.C. [i.e. Marcus Clarke], 'Alfred Telo – A Reminiscence', *Leader*, 11 October 1879, p. 17.
[52] DS to W. Clarson, 30 January 1873, LB1, pp. 131–134.

the latter being available in sporting journals 'out here'.⁵³ McCulloch also negotiated with William Farquharson Lamonby, who was writing for the English *Field* as Skiddaw and for the *Australasian* on coursing (hunting), about coming out to be sporting editor of the *Leader* but Lamonby's reply by sea mail was apparently received too late for the coursing season and Syme did not take him on then.⁵⁴

The *Illustrated Australian News*, for which Telo was also writing, continued to lead the field, and not only in Victoria.⁵⁵ Issued in several intercolonial editions, it is the one example of Syme's 'empire' building. The Tasmanian edition continued until March 1873 if not later; the *Illustrated Adelaide Post* was a virtual Adelaide edition of the *News* until December 1874, and entries in a Staff Register provide evidence of Sydney and New Zealand editions in 1874.⁵⁶ Notwithstanding the acknowledged success of the *Illustrated Australian News*, the *Argus* proprietor Lauchlan Mackinnon in England was very opposed to starting a rival illustrated paper. When the *Australasian Sketcher* was, nevertheless, launched he thought the first number looked inferior to 'Syme's paper', and three months later believed the venture was a 'fatal blunder' – since the *Argus* had been kept in the 'front rank' (was this false complacency?), it was not necessary to have 'grudged the poor wretch Syme his crust'.⁵⁷

Several of Syme's letters of the early 1870s reveal the importance he placed on obtaining illustrations and the degree to which he was personally involved. One of 10 October 1871 to Street in London, asks him to get purchasers for the *Illustrated Australian News* hand-engraved wood blocks.⁵⁸ In 1873, when Syme was very conscious of competition with the new *Australasian Sketcher*, seven of his letters to Levey raise matters of illustrations.⁵⁹ They concern both selling *Illustrated Australian News* blocks in England and buying ones with interesting European subjects – such as the famous meeting of Africa explorer David Livingstone and Henry Stanley on 27 October 1871, the death of Napoleon (surely Napoleon III, whose death was depicted in the *Illustrated London News* shortly after its

---

53 DS to W. Martin, 26 January 1876, LB1, pp. 238–239.
54 DS to W. Lamonby, 26 January 1876, LB1, p. 240.
55 DS to G. Levey, 15 July 1873, LB1, pp. 181–182.
56 Staff Wages Register, for example entries for 21 February, 14 March 1874.
57 L. Mackinnon to J. Johnston, 13 June, 30 September 1873, Johnston Correspondence.
58 DS to G. Street, 10 October 1871, LB1, p. 2.
59 DS to G. Levey, seven letters, 27 March 1873 (LB1, pp. 153–154) to 10 October 1873 (LB1, p. 197).

CHAPTER 7

occurrence in January) and John Rogers Herbert's 'Moses', a replica of which the artist was producing for the National Art Gallery of Victoria. Satisfactory exchange arrangements were frequently made with the London weekly *Graphic*. In September 1873 Syme seemed to be delegating some of the work to business manager John Macdonald, but in October was still involved, suggesting to Levey that suitable illustrations might be obtained cheaply from Continental papers.

A new publication from the *Age* business appeared in February 1875, the *Age Annual* for 1874. It was, as described in the *Age* of 6 February, 'compiled with the object of furnishing the political statistics of Victoria in a compact form, and thus supplying an acknowledged want…of considerable value, not only for commercial purposes, but as a political record or history of the work of our Legislature during the year'. Octavo size, in embossed blue cloth covers (suggestive of the official 'blue books'), this issue comprises 76 pages and includes a calendar of events for 1875, lists and abstracts of Acts of Parliament passed in 1874, and a great deal of directory-type information relating to government, tariffs, railway and steamer timetables, telegraph rates, etc. It must have found appreciative buyers, for a second edition was advertised in March, and in June the *Age* featured 'Opinions of the Press', an entire column of laudatory extracts from 22 newspapers including leading Victorian provincial papers of opposed political persuasion and, intercolonially, the *Sydney Morning Herald* and the *South Australian Register*. An addition to the publications stable, the annual appeared again early in 1876, a larger 88 pages. The *Age* of 12 January 1876 promoted it: 'Advertisers will find this an excellent medium for keeping their announcements before the public as the Annual circulates over all parts of the colony, and is kept for purposes of reference throughout the year.'

Deeply involved in the detail of technical innovation, Syme also had a growing business to manage. As he explained in a letter to his nephew William in May 1872, in connection with partnership negotiations (dealt with below), he saw himself as in control of the whole enterprise, with the editor subservient to him:

> I think your ideas regarding the relative positions of Editor & Manager somewhat peculiar. You think the Editor entitled to a higher salary because he governs the policy of the paper. But have you asked yourself who governs the policy of the Editor? You do not imagine, surely, that he can do as he likes. If you do, all I can say is that you are mistaken. But in using such arguments I can scarcely believe you seriously believe

in them yourself. Besides if the Editor of a paper has a more responsible position than the manager I act in the double capacity.⁶⁰

While he did have a remarkable capacity for attending to different, difficult and continuing matters as well as bringing out the three newspapers, in the early 1870s Syme needed to give huge amounts of attention to the installation of printing machinery and the expansion of content in the *Age*. James Harrison, as editor and a sort of deputy manager, made this possible. One assumes that Harrison, with the support of Syme's family members, held the fort for the five months of his absence in 1871 and continued to shoulder some of the responsibility and workload for the regular production of the daily, the weekly and the monthly published by the *Age* business.

As *Age* editor, Harrison was responsible for the production of editorials, whether written by him or by one of the posse of leader writers who would be paid for their work. As seen above, Syme dictated policy, no deviation from which would be countenanced. Generally, the arrangement worked well, but in late 1872 there was a disagreement between Harrison and Syme about editorial treatment of the proposed education legislation.⁶¹ It was quickly quelled, however, as Harrison, well aware of Syme's autocratic rule, chose to fall into line. In any case, while the *Age* office work provided Harrison with a steady income, his real interests were elsewhere. In addition to his newspaper work, he had been experimenting with the means of transporting frozen meat to England and had exhibited at Victoria's International Exhibition of 1872–3 (Morrison 1997). By March 1873 he was planning to demonstrate feasibility by taking a shipment to England in July.

Syme was well aware of this, and apprehensive, when he wrote to Levey in March: 'Mr Harrison leaves here at the end of June to take a cargo of iced meat home, so I will miss you more than ever', and again in 17 June: 'Mr Harrison has left the Age on my hands before the time arranged upon & I am head over ears in work.'⁶² Before he sailed on 23 July, on the *Norfolk*, Harrison was given a grand farewell luncheon by David and George Syme, attended by some 50 of his press colleagues.⁶³ With an almost overwhelming increase in his workload, Syme wrote to Jane on 9 October: 'You will think me very remiss in not writing you oftener than I have done recently, but

---

60 DS to W. Syme, 25 May 1872, LB1, p. 50.
61 DS to J. Harrison, 26 October 1872, LB1, pp. 96–97, and 6 November 1872, LB1, p. 98.
62 DS to G. Levey, 27 March 1873, LB1, pp. 153–154, and 17 June 1873, LB1, p. 180.
63 'News of the Day', *Age*, 21 July 1873, p. 2.

CHAPTER 7

the fact is my time is so fully occupied since Mr Harrison left'.[64] When his frozen meat export trial turned out a total failure, Harrison made his home in London and, as noted above, returned to journalism, as a regular and prolific correspondent for the *Age* and *Leader*.

Syme's journalists

After Harrison's departure, Syme had to take charge of the editorial work and the day-to-day running of the business. His leader writers were, as named in a letter to Levey: 'Windsor, O'Hea, Bright & G.P.S.'[65] All were contributors, that is, not on the regular staff. As we have seen, George Paton Smith had been on the staff as editor in the early 1860s and William O'Hea had been writing for the *Age* from the mid-1850s. Bright is probably not the T.L Bright of the early months of the *Age*, but Charles Bright, an experienced journalist who had written for the *Argus*, was a strong protectionist, and interested in spiritualism (F.B. Smith 1969). Arthur Lloyd Windsor, who would later join the fulltime staff and be appointed editor, had been contributing for, probably, some months. When Syme wrote in his memoirs that he had to do the editorial work after George Paton Smith left in 1865 and until Windsor took over he failed to give Harrison his due, and record for posterity his editorial work.

He also omitted to acknowledge Levey in that capacity. He worked for Syme as a journalist after he came back from the 1872 London Exhibition and until he left Melbourne in early 1873 for the Vienna Exhibition.[66] In August, September and October 1873, after Harrison's departure, Syme wrote to Levey, who was then in London, almost desperate to get him back.[67] He succeeded, and Levey was on the *Age* payroll as editor from 14 May 1874 to 31 July 1875, at first paid £10, in June 1874 raised to the astonishingly high sum of £12 per week.[68] George Syme, editor of the *Leader*, was receiving £5.

After Levey left in 1875, Windsor was the chief leader writer. Syme was happy with the arrangement so long as Windsor 'keeps his health', he wrote to Harrison on 9 August.[69] Windsor was then still a contributor, not

---

64 DS to Jane, 9 October 1873, LB1, pp. 195–196.
65 DS to G. Levey, 15 July 1873, LB1, pp. 181–182.
66 Evident from DS to G. Levey, 27 March 1873, LB1, pp. 153–154.
67 DS to G. Levey, 12 August 1873, LB1, pp. 185–186, 9 September 1873, LB1, pp. 191–192, and 10 October 1873, LB1, p. 197.
68 Staff Wages Register, for example, entries for 20 and 24 June 1874.
69 DS to J. Harrison, 9 August 1875, LB1, p. 229.

a member of the *Age* staff. His considerable intellectual capacity is evident in his earlier contributions to the English *Quarterly Review* and in his book *Ethica: or, Characteristics of Men, Manners, and Books*, published in 1860. The essays therein testify to his wide and deep learning. Even more important for editorial work, his book exemplifies fine writing: a lively approach, with short, pithy sentences; and arguments presented in a clear, balanced and logical way. Recruited in England, Windsor had come to Melbourne in 1863 to be editor of the *Argus*, but left after two years to edit the *Mount Alexander Mail* at Castlemaine (Sayers 1976). Returning to Melbourne, he was sometime editor of the short-lived weekly *Town and Country Journal* (it started October 1872, ceased late 1875) and contributor to the *Age*. Whether he slowly came to be considered editor of the *Age*, or one day was so appointed by Syme, is not known.[70] Mention in a letter of 30 April 1878 to Levey implies that Windsor was then firmly established in the position.[71] Six years younger than Syme, he was not only very intelligent and highly educated, but he was tractable. With a retiring personality, it suited him to have Syme dictate; yet he was ready enough to improvise when Syme did not give the orders. Only impaired by Windsor's intermittent ill health, the combination was a most workable one until his retirement in 1900.

A bevy of correspondents from suburbs and towns of Victoria contributed local reports regularly or occasionally. Arranging for these was an ongoing task, one in which Syme often played a part. Space precludes identifying all. For instance, on 9 February 1871 Syme wrote to New South Wales politician Henry Parkes at a time when Parkes badly needed money and was working as a journalist, offering him Sydney correspondence, which was accepted.[72] Of particular importance to Syme were reports from the mining centres of Ballarat and Sandhurst (Bendigo). In July 1872 he engaged Robert MacKay, then employed on the *Bendigo Advertiser* produced by his father Angus Mackay, setting out instructions for the supply of daily reports of the mining market (work that Syme himself was familiar with from having done it for the *Age* in 1856) and general local news.[73]

Threatening to outgrow the Elizabeth Street premises, the staff at the *Age* office was many times larger than when Syme took over in 1860. A composite photograph, 'The Employes [sic] of the Age', presented to Syme

---

[70] Sayers (1965, 148 and 1976) errs in dating his editorship from 1872.

[71] DS to G. Levey, 30 April 1878, LB2, pp. 142–143.

[72] DS to H. Parkes, 9 February 1871, Henry Parkes Correspondence, Vol. 37, pp. 154–155, A907, Mitchell Library, State Library of New South Wales.

[73] DS to R. Mackay, 22 July 1872, LB1, p. 73.

CHAPTER 7

Figure 7.2. David Syme and his staff, January 1873. (Courtesy of Fairfax Media)

in January 1873 (fig. 7.2), comprises 115 images of employees, plus Syme looming large in the centre. Prominently near the top of the picture is James Harrison, the image size surely signifying second-in-command status in the establishment. Fourteen images larger than the mass of 100 small ones include George Levey (to the upper left of Harrison) and nephew Joseph (to the right of Syme). Brother George cannot be identified with certainty – there are several possible likenesses amongst the medium-size photos. Possibly the total number of employees was greater than 115, counting the casual unnamed 'boys', compositors, 'flyers', 'feeders', etc. noted in a staff wages register of the time. In addition, there was a host of non-staff contributors, who were paid by line or column.

Making himself ill with overwork when trying to get the Victory operating properly, Syme wished he had stayed longer in Britain to become familiar with the machine. On 22 May 1872, in his regular monthly letter to Jane, he wrote that he'd been very busy of late 'with the new machine, the ministerial crisis of Sunday, other matters too many to mention. For a week at a stretch I never was in bed or undressed'.[74] And in his letter of 12 October 1872 he says he is 'wretchedly out of sorts', as he was seven years ago when ordered home, and that the worry of the office is getting too much for him.[75] Yet he would continue with his multiple and intense involvements for another three and a half years before a third trip to Britain.

He had become part of various professional and special interest networks. Often portrayed as a loner, not a joiner, in fact he was an active member of some Melbourne press and professional groups. He does not appear to have taken an active part in the Victorian Press Association, formed in September 1872, chiefly to lobby the government for reduction in newspaper postage and cable message charges.[76] But he was on the general committee of the Caxton festival to commemorate in 1871 the 400th anniversary of the introduction of printing in England, although absent overseas for most of the planning time (Morrison 2005, 186–187), and he was, with *Argus* editor Frederick Haddon and politician and onetime journalist George Higinbotham, a trustee of the Caxton Fund for the assistance of indigent journalists.[77] Moreover, although he did not join the somewhat bohemian Yorick Club for journalists formed in 1868 (Carrington 1911) – he became a member years later when it was reputable – he had signed up with the Athenaeum Club when it was founded in July of the same year, played a prominent part in opening celebrations (de Serville 2013, x, 34), and gave the club publicity through the *Age*.[78] As discussed below, in the 1870s he along with other leading men of the press became involved with the Victorian Association of Progressive Spiritualists.

From the start of his management of the *Age*, Syme had ensured editorial enunciation of his political policies, and maintained oversight and control of *Age* editorials as the newspaper continued to report and comment on Victorian politics. Between 1870 and 1875 there were seven changes of Premier, with most of the terms short, some stopgap, and little continuity of policy (Waugh 2006). The only sizeable term, that of James Francis from June 1872 to July 1874 (when illness forced his resignation), saw the only major legislation, the *Education Act*, passed in September 1872, providing

---

[74] DS to Jane, 22 May 1872, LB1, p. 49.
[75] DS to Jane, 12 October 1872, LB1, pp. 91–92.
[76] News items in *Argus*, 10, 11 September, 17 October 1872, 4, 5 March, 14, 16, 17 May 1873, 12 February 1874.
[77] Caxton Fund records, 1871–1912, MS 6272, Australian Manuscripts Collection, State Library of Victoria.
[78] 'The News of the Day', *Age*, 1 May, p. 4, 22 July 1868, p. 3.

CHAPTER 7

for education to be compulsory, free and secular. But outside the parliament, in the metropolis and in country towns, moves were afoot from 1875 to change the character of colonial government. While there were as yet no organised political parties, and governments were formed by shifting factional alliances amongst members of parliament, there was in Victoria a polarising movement gaining momentum: a division of the body politic into constitutionalists on the one hand and liberal reformists, on the other. The latter advocated constitutional reform – in particular, reform of the Upper House (the Legislative Council) – and import tariffs that would serve to protect and encourage agriculture and manufacturing in Victoria. In diametric opposition to the *Argus*, the *Age* supported if not led the reformists.

From August 1875 radical–reformist politician Graham Berry was in the ascendancy, forming his first government in August 1875. This would last only two and a half months, being replaced by the rule of James McCulloch. This short Berry premiership saw the formation of the first of two organisations to support and advance his position and policies – the Victorian Protection League, which quickly had branches throughout Melbourne and spread to country areas. The second, the National Reform League, which began in Ballarat in November, spread to country towns and to Melbourne where, on 25 February 1876, David Syme was elected its President, by default.[79] His name having gone forward as one of several Vice-Presidents, he was elected to the headship when the nominee, George Higinbotham, withdrew. His tenure would be cut short three months later, however, and there is no evidence of his playing an active role in the organising of and speaking at the spate of public meetings held in the name of the League. But there is no doubt that, through the *Age* in late 1875 and early 1876, he was pursuing his and the Berry faction's reform agenda. It has been said that he assisted or even dictated the make-up of Berry's first Cabinet, the *Age* providing (or leaking) the names the day before the formal announcement.[80]

In print again

The man of action, David Syme, was also driven by a deep desire to engage with and express ideas. Following his *Westminster Review* article in 1870, another appeared in the same journal in July 1871, the month that Syme

---

[79] Reports in *Argus*, 1, 26 February 1876; James Rundle, Political and Social Tensions in Victoria, 1875–1880, Melbourne, 2010, unpublished manuscript, p. 23, Australian Manuscripts Collection, State Library of Victoria.

[80] Rundle, p. 2.

arrived in England. Whether despatched before his departure or completed during the voyage and submitted on arrival is not known. Apparently John Morley, editor of the *Fortnightly Review*, had rejected it, as he had Syme's 'The Land Question in England'.[81] Possibly the Ebenezer connection was a factor in editor Chapman's acceptance. This time carrying Syme's name, the article, 'On the Method of Political Economy', was published in the Independent Section, an indication that its approach was considered unorthodox.[82] A preliminary note to the Section explains that a 'limited portion of the *Westminster Review* is occasionally set apart for…able articles…containing opinions at variance with the particular ideas or measures it may advocate. The object…is to facilitate the expression of opinion by men of high mental power and culture'.

In this short (12-page) piece, Syme argues succinctly for using inductive rather than deductive approaches to political economy, that is, to what is now more generally termed economics. He wants the study of the operation of production, selling and consumption in relation to human behaviour, law and government to be more empirical and comparative, and to take into account virtuous motives as well as the principle of self-interest. Drawing on and challenging standard authorities (Adam Smith, George Malthus, Thomas Buckle and John Stuart Mill), it reads today somewhat as a clever undergraduate essay, whose author is perhaps not sufficiently aware of changes occurring in the discipline that he analyses. At the same time, written by one who is normally a man of action but who can occasionally shut off from quotidian pressures, it demonstrates a bridging of the world of ideas and practical realities. It found an encouraging response in the United States (mentioned below) and five years later would be expanded as his first book, *Outlines of an Industrial Science*, discussed in the next chapter.

Being in England afforded Syme the opportunity to arrange for the publisher Trübner to reissue 'The Land Question in England'. Newly titled *Landlordism: in its Moral, Social, and Economic Relations*, in 1871 it appeared in pamphlet form, and was one of five works on land tenure, including one by J.S. Mill, discussed in the October issue of the *Edinburgh Review*. While not dismissing Syme's views, the writer suggests they are simplistic, and doubts if Mill would endorse them ('Systems of Land Tenure' 1871). Having arranged for the pamphlets to be despatched in August 1871 to

---

[81] DS to J. Morley, 28 March 1872, LB1, p. 32.
[82] See Appendix B.

CHAPTER 7

Australia, Syme still awaited their arrival in early 1872 and wanted agent Street to circulate surplus copies in England.[83] By this time, the article had been published in Melbourne, with some changes, as Tract no. 2 of William Gresham's Land Reform League (seven Tracts appeared between 1868 and 1873). Whether or not Syme was consulted about this publication, which probably took place in his absence, subsequently he made three small donations to the League, amounting to £5.[84]

A third article, 'Restrictions on Trade. From a Colonial Point of View', was published in the *Fortnightly Review* of April 1873.[85] Written by 28 March 1872 (perhaps on the ship coming home in 1871), Syme sent it to the *Fortnightly* (actually a monthly), whose editor Morley 'believed deeply in progress, science, and rational thought' and whose journal 'looked favorably on new writing' (Spurgeon 1984, 132). Syme promoted his article to Morley, on the grounds that he had 'no recollection of ever having seen the question of tariffs discussed in any English journal from a colonial point of view before' and explained that the 'views set forth are not of the orthodox stamp certainly, but that, I imagine, will not form a formidable objection.'[86] From a colonial standpoint, it explains to the English why tariffs are necessary in colonial communities, outlining their manifold advantages over free trading. It is a serious argument for protective tariffs in newly settled regions, showing a wide and deep knowledge and understanding of interacting social, economic and political factors in Victoria and other newly colonised and developing states.

Very well received in the United States, it was reprinted in Boston and widely circulated; a copy is held in the Library of Congress and two in the National Library of Canada. It is quoted from at length by protectionist R.E. Thompson in his *Political Economy* of 1882 (La Nauze 1949, 124). Syme had already attempted to be part of an American discourse, after William Darrah ('Pig Iron') Kelley, a United States congressman representing the iron and steel districts of Pennsylvania and a self-educated fierce protectionist, had written commending Syme's 'Political Economy' article, and sent a copy of his speeches and letters. In response, Syme had on 28 March 1872 written to thank Kelley and sent him a copy of the *Landlordism* pamphlet and said he would forward a copy of his latest

---

[83] DS to G. Street, 22 April 1872, LB1, pp. 35–36.
[84] Acknowledged in Tracts 5, 6 and 7.
[85] See Appendix B.
[86] DS to J. Morley, 28 March 1873, LB1, p. 32.

should it appear in the *Fortnightly Review*.[87] The same day he wrote to Street asking that, if the article did appear, to send one copy to Kelley and one also to Horace Greeley of the New York *Tribune*.[88] Greeley had supported causes similar to Syme's, but by the time the article appeared in April 1873 he was six months dead.

Syme and the Spiritualists

Outwardly, Syme lived a secular life, having moved away long since from all forms of Scottish Protestantism. But as a man of ideas he was constantly seeking eternal truths. In the 1870s he sought yet another path to enlightenment, becoming associated with the Victorian Association of Progressive Spiritualists (VAPS), a body of freethinkers eschewing formal religion, founded in October 1870. Men of education and attainment were joining. His leader writer Charles Bright, active in the Society, may have aroused Syme's interest. (Gabay 2001, 78). His first recorded attendance at a VAPS meeting is 20 November 1872, when he was elected to its committee for 1873. At the annual meeting in January 1874 he was re-elected. In March, along with Bright, Hugh George of the *Argus*, Henry Gullett of the *Australasian* and several other newspapermen, he attended a session arranged for visiting American medium Charles Forster to display his powers. Reportedly, Forster conveyed meaningful messages to some present, including one from Syme's father George.[89] Whatever the group made of this and other marvels, Syme resigned from the VAPS committee in early 1875. Noting his resignation, the annual report for 1874 describes him as 'always a quiet but earnest worker among us'.[90] He must have been there to observe, not to make waves. Recollecting, weeks before his death more than 30 years later he wrote: 'I have never met anything distinctly proving beyond a shadow of a doubt that there was any connection between the spirit world and the present.'[91] Whether he continued to be a member and attend meetings until his departure for overseas in 1876 is not now knowable, the relevant VAPS records having been lost. As seen in Chapter 9, he was actively involved in the later 1870s.

---

[87] DS to W. Kelley, 28 March 1872, LB1, p. 31.
[88] DS to G. Street, 28 March 1873, LB1, p. 30.
[89] *Observer* editorial, *Advertiser and Observer* (Collingwood and Carlton), 26 March 1874, p. 2.
[90] *Harbinger of Light*, December 1872, February 1874, February 1875, p. 768.
[91] DS notebooks, entry dated 19 January 1908..

CHAPTER 7

Partnership problems

Whether and how to renew his business partnership with Jane, due to expire on 31 December 1871, occupied much of Syme's mind and time in the early 1870s. A complicating factor was that her adult children might claim a financial interest in their late father's enterprise. William, then 23, was a medical practitioner in country Victoria; the black sheep George was about to be 21; Joseph in the office would attain his majority in 1873. The youngest two were still with their mother: Jane Mary (Minnie) would be 21 in 1875 and James (Jimmie) in 1878. On 13 June 1871 David was to meet Jane in London to discuss this.[92]

A few weeks earlier Syme had received a bombshell from her. In a letter dated 12 May, sent to his London address, beginning 'My dear David' and ending 'Yours affectionately, Jane Hope', she explains that she has remarried, to a homeopath from Melbourne, Robert Palk who 'for family considerations that he could better explain' has assumed the name Hope. She assures him that it is out of no disrespect that she has withheld the information, but from a failure of 'moral courage' and her desire to avoid pecuniary suffering for her children.[93] She does not tell him the date of the marriage, nor that she has had four children with Palk, two of these out of wedlock, nor that she is pregnant with a fifth. She invites him to stay at their residence, but in the event she went to London to see him.

Had Syme accepted her invitation, he would probably have been confronted with her Palk/Hope children; but apparently he did not learn of their existence for some years, though he may have become aware of her latest pregnancy when he met her. (A daughter, Lilian, would be born later that year and die in 1874.[94]) In a postscript she advises that Mr Malcolm, Syme's contact at the London office of McEwan & Co., who has dealt with her regular payments from the *Age* business, knows nothing of this information. Whatever the shock to him, Syme's response must have been gentle, for Jane, writing on 2 June, thanks him for his 'kind letter', says she is humbled and alludes to her husband's maltreatment of her and her Syme children.[95]

At their meeting in June Jane proposed the partnership be renewed for 10 years, as she had in her letter of 26 January that year, but there was no

---

[92] Jane to AS, 12 June 1871, SFP Box 1180/5(b).
[93] Jane to DS, 12 May 1871, SFP Box 1180/1(c).
[94] Family History Report, Ebenezer Syme and Jane Hilton Rowan, dated 23 October 2009, supplied by Pru Williams, descendant.
[95] Jane to DS, 2 June 1871, SFP Box 1180/1(c).

written agreement. David had earlier proposed seven.⁹⁶ It is likely that, as well as the renewal, the matter of her large overdraft and the question of the legal entitlements of her five Syme offspring was brought up.

The 44-year-old father of four arrived back in Melbourne on 4 September 1871 to more immediate family concerns. Three days later a daughter, Gabrielle, was born at the family's St Kilda residence. Sadly, this baby died on 24 September 'after a day's illness', Syme wrote to Jane in a letter of 6 November.⁹⁷ He also told her that there was an additional source of grief for him and Annabella when they discovered that Jane had sent written instructions that the family burial plot, in which were Ebenezer's remains and those of Gabrielle's sister Caroline, was not to be disturbed. He had, consequently, to postpone the funeral and obtain 'another piece of ground'.

Syme was prompt in attending to the partnership renewal matter, however, and the complication of nephews William and George being 'of age'. On 4 October 1871 he wrote to William in relation to the partnership being renegotiated, asking for the date of Jane's second marriage and to see his power of attorney for his mother.⁹⁸ William, who wanted the marriage kept a secret, was mistaken about the marriage date, which Syme must have understood from him to be 1868 (not 1866).⁹⁹ Syme also sought legal advice about the status of the partnership in view of Jane's secret marriage and undesirable husband ('not being a proper person to have as a partner'). He was advised that there were no grounds not to renew, but that it was necessary to get the consent of the adult children, and that the husband had to be a party. From that date until mid-June 1872 there were countless complicated letters and discussions between Syme and William on behalf of his siblings and between Syme and Jane. On 6 May 1872 William wrote to David that his position was not enviable, having to mediate between him on the one hand and his brothers Joe and George on the other.¹⁰⁰ Both he and David were patient, courteous and reasonable – explaining and compromising in a very difficult situation. Jane, passive, simply wanted regular remittances, and the payment of school fees for James, which, numerous letters attest, Syme attended to meticulously.¹⁰¹

---

96 Jane to DS, 26 January 1871, SFP Box 1180/1(c).
97 DS to Jane, 6 November 1871, LB1, pp. 8–10.
98 DS to W. Syme, 4 October 1871, LB1, p. 1.
99 W. Syme to DS, 3 October 1871, SFP Box 1180/2(a); Case for the opinion of counsel, SFP Box 1185/2(b)[i] (gives Jane's marriage erroneously as 1868).
100 W. Syme to DS, 6 May 1872, SFP Box 1180/2(a).
101 For example, DS to Jane, 29[?] December 1871, LB1, p. 22.

CHAPTER 7

At first William and George were agreeable about renewing the partnership but, after seeing the draft document, doubted their mother's reliability and wanted her share transferred to them. Also at issue was the duration of a renewal. Jane wanted 10 years, Syme now two, but eventually they settled for four, from 31 December 1871, agreeing at last to renew two years thereafter until James turned 21 in 1878.[102] Weekly drawings were next at issue. At the end of 1870, Syme's capital in the business was £4434, Jane's less than half at £1899. Accordingly, Syme would receive £12 per week but Jane only £6, the other £6 to pay off her overdraft and increase her capital. After much negotiation, William and George finally ratified the agreement on 17 June 1872. Their younger brothers Joseph and James were each to sign when they came of age. The agreement document was sent to Jane on 18 June 1872 for her and Robert Palk, who both duly signed and returned it.

On 25 November 1872 William wrote to Syme that he or Joe would take over the sending of drafts to Jane and paying James's school fees.[103] On 4 January 1873 Syme wrote to Jane, wishing her and the children compliments of the season and saying that he approved of her leaving Palk, which she should have done sooner, but advises her not to come to Melbourne, for she would be in disgrace (though he would be happy to see her).[104] Jane at that stage had not left her husband, but relations between them were abysmal. In his 22 April 1873 letter Syme asked her why did she *have* to marry Palk? ('What had you done that you need be afraid of?')[105] He did not seem to know about the illegitimate children and perhaps was under the impression that Palk deceived Jane into a bigamous marriage.

Syme had introduced a new matter in a letter of 27 March 1873.[106] He referred to money troubles resulting from big investments in equipment, etc. and raised the possibility of taking in a partner. He had discussed these matters with Joe, he said, and asked her to have confidence in both of them. On 20 May, again in relation to having a partner, he suggested giving Joe 'the required authority to be used if necessary'.[107] On 9 October 1873 he reported that things were looking up in the business and noted that Joe was keeping her posted – apparently indicating that he need no longer write

---

[102] Articles of co-partnership, SFP Box 1185/2(b)[ii].
[103] W. Syme to DS, 25 November 1872, SFP Box 1180/2(a).
[104] DS to Jane, 4 January 1873, LB1, pp. 119–120.
[105] DS to Jane, 22 April 1873, LB1, p. 168.
[106] DS to Jane, 27 March 1873, LB1, pp. 163–165.
[107] DS to Jane, 20 May 1873, LB1, p. 174.

regularly.[108] Whether or not he meant by this that Joe should perhaps be taken into partnership (his words do not settle this), he did sow a seed for Jane to cultivate later.

Jane and her children arrived at their own agreement, with a Declaration of Trust dated 30 December 1873 giving her Syme offspring shares in her asset. Syme found it satisfactory.[109] George junior, running up huge debts and unable to keep jobs, assigned his share to William, and on 22 February 1875 Minnie assigned the power to deal with hers.

In May 1872 Syme moved his family from St Kilda to Gisborne Street, East Melbourne, where they lived for the next three years (*Sands & McDougall's* 1873–1875).[110] Belonging to the Unitarian Church, the house was found to be in disrepair and badly drained, with water in the cellar. Syme wrote letters of complaint but there is no sign that these were acted on.[111] Comments in letters from Jane indicate that Annabella had bouts of ill health, possibly associated with her next pregnancy and not helped by the living conditions. However, Syme had a house, Rosenheim, built on his leased land at Mount Macedon, ready for occupancy in February 1872 if not earlier and Annabella stayed there from time to time. Happily, on 3 March 1873 she produced a healthy son, Geoffrey, in Melbourne, and a few weeks later was back at 'the Mount' until about the end of April, Syme informed Jane.[112] During 1874 David had alterations and extensions to Rosenheim.[113] On 8 March 1875 Annabella gave birth to another daughter, Olive.[114] And after expiry of the Gisborne Street lease in May 1875, Rosenheim became the family's principal residence, with Syme staying in Melbourne during the week, possibly at the Athenaeum Club in Collins Street (*Sands & McDougall's* 1876).

The Syme's home life was complicated in May 1874 by the arrival in Melbourne of Jane's youngest two Syme offspring, 19-year-old Minnie and 17-year-old Jimmie. William, taking responsibility for his younger siblings, had travelled to England and brought them back with him on the

---

[108] DS to Jane, 9 October 1873, LB1, pp. 195–196.
[109] Case for the opinion of counsel, additional note re Declaration of Trust, SFP Box 1185/3(a)[i]; Agreement and assignment, SFP Box 1185/3(b)[ii].
[110] DS to J. Duerdin, 27 May 1872, LB1, pp. 51, 52, and 19 July 1873, LB1, pp. 184–185.
[111] DS to W. Allenan, [?] June 1872, LB1, p. 64; DS to Mr Kelton, 24 January 1874, LB1, p. 204.
[112] Syme Family Date Books, SFP Box 1193/6(d); DS to Jane, 22 April 1874, LB1, p. 168.
[113] DS to Secretary, Mutual Insurance Company, 22 February 1874, LB1, p. 206.
[114] Syme Family Date Books.

CHAPTER 7

Cambridgeshire.[115] Writing to Annabella in September, Jane thanked her for kindness to the children, saying there was little to live for 'now that all my dear children are away' (where were her Palk offspring, aged 12, 10, 7 and 5?).[116] Once again Syme and Annabella took in the children of Ebenezer and Jane. It is not known how long they stayed with their aunt and uncle, and whether they moved to Macedon when the family left Gisborne Street. Minnie settled in to the Syme–Johnson fold quite firmly, marrying Annabella's younger brother Francis (also known as Frank) in March 1875 and thus becoming a sister-in-law as well as niece. Syme attended to the welfare and occupation of Jimmie (James), an unsettled lad, although without the severe problems of his elder brother George.[117] In May Jane wrote to thank Annabella for her care of Minnie, noting that she knew Minnie had told her about Lilian's death in 1874.[118] It is not known whether she and Syme were then aware there were four surviving Palk children.

Syme must have suspected or found out some of Jane's secrets when in 1876 he sought legal advice about his right to wind up the partnership, stating that he had 'no difficulty' in carrying it on until November 1875 (what happened then?).[119] The advice, in legalese, is almost impenetrable; in general, renewal of the partnership is supported. Dated 24 May 1876, the document records Syme's stated intention to go to England by the outgoing Californian mail steamer to get Mrs Palk's consent and, with a sum of money if necessary, Mr Palk's. Syme was sick at heart with the whole business, and even unhappy with nephew William, refusing to deal with him until he signed the latest balance sheet (which is not now on file).

Finances

Syme wrote to Jane on 22 April 1873, when in the throes of his Victory problems, 'Business is good but money scarce', and noted that he would have to raise funds somehow.[120] It is not possible to amplify this because there are no financial statements to be found for the years 1871 to 1875. Possibly Syme destroyed them. Certain documents are mentioned: he wrote in January 1873 to Jane that the 1872 balance would show a poor result, and

---

[115] Unassisted Inward Passenger Lists to Victoria 1852–1923, Public Record Office Victoria.
[116] Jane to AS, 2 September 1874, SFP Box 1180/5(b).
[117] DS to W. Syme, 26 July 1875, LB1, pp. 226–227.
[118] Jane to AS, 13 May 1875, SFP Box 1180/5(b).
[119] Case for the opinion of counsel, SFP Box 1185/3(a)[i].
[120] DS to Jane, 22 April 1873, LB1, p. 168.

to William in July 1875 that he was very disappointed for 1874 but reluctant to let information out of the office, for the copying would be a big job![121] There was quite heavy expenditure on the new machines and more expensive paper, but also evidence that he was becoming an investor, dealing in shares in 1872 and 1873.[122] A sign of speculative proclivities, he became a Trustee of the Premier Building Society.[123] Moreover, there was the cost of building and subsequently extending Rosenheim on his Mount Macedon land.

Organising his finances, on 19 October 1871 Syme opened an account for the *Age* business at the Bank of New South Wales (where he already had a private one) and obtained an overdraft. When this bank refused his application of 26 March 1873 to increase it to £4000, he opened an account at the Colonial Bank and got the desired advance.[124] Further funds came his way when in August 1874 he sold Rosenheim to his father-in-law and leased it back.[125] In 1875 William lent him £300, all he could manage, as he was paying off his mother's overdraft![126]

As seen above, in May 1876 Syme had arranged another visit to England. He had this in mind when he wrote to London correspondent Plummer on 22 March: 'It is just possible I may manage to make a run home myself in a short time'.[127] Stating that he was going overseas, on 26 May Syme resigned from the position of President of the National Reform League and the following day from that of Trustee of the Premier Building Society.[128] On 29 May, the day before his departure, he wrote to Jane that he had to attend to business matters (machines and paper), wanted to see her 'on matters of mutual interest', and that he looked forward to the voyage, which would be good for his health, being worn out from the heavy work undertaken since Harrison left.[129] The same day, in a note to nephew William, he testily, and somewhat disingenuously, reiterated that his purpose was solely to 'settle certain outstanding claims we have against certain firms there which we

---

[121] DS to Jane, 31 January 1873, LB1, p. 136; DS to W. Syme, 26 July 1875, LB1, pp. 226–227.

[122] Letters concerning investments, 1872–73: LB1, pp. 26, 69, 105, 147, 170.

[123] DS to Secretary, Premier Building Society, 27 May 1876, LB2, p. 10.

[124] DS to H. Stiles, 9 May 1873, LB1, p. 169; DS to Jane, 20 May 1875, LB1, p. 174.

[125] Lease, John W Johnson to AS, SFP Box 1188/1(a)[ii]; DS to Manager, Imperial Insurance Company, 2 September 1874, LB1, p. 216.

[126] W. Syme to DS, 1 August 1875, SFP Box 1180/2(b).

[127] DS to J. Plummer, 22 March 1876, LB1, p. 246.

[128] DS to Secretary, National Reform League, 26 May, and Secretary, Premier Building Society, 27 May, LB2, p. 10.

[129] DS to Jane, 29 May 1876, LB2, pp. 11–12.

CHAPTER 7

have hitherto failed to get settled by correspondence' and to purchase another machine for the *Age* and one for the *Illustrated Australian News*.[130] Macintyre (1991, 81–82) asserts that Syme lied about the purpose of trip, implying it was solely to confront Jane about the partnership. But, as will be seen in the next chapter, the story is more complex and the imperatives to travel went beyond partnership matters, pressing though these were.

---

[130] DS to W. Syme, 29 May 1876, LB2. p. 13.

Chapter 8

'THE *AGE* HAS JUST SCORED A TREMENDOUS VICTORY'

(June 1876 to March 1878)

The endgame for the Jane and David association was played out with bitterness for some 20 months, beginning with the partners' next meeting in Britain. This period also saw Syme preparing for a new partnership that would take the *Age* into the big league of British newspapers. He turned his mind to management matters. He explored possibilities for new premises. In rivalry with the *Argus* he laid the foundation for a competing cable message service. Most important, in the climate of political and accompanying press polarisation, Graham Berry's liberal–reformist faction came into government, strongly supported by the *Age*, thus strengthening its place as Melbourne's leading daily paper.

In 1876 Syme travelled overseas for the third time since taking control of the newspaper business. Leaving his brother George in charge and doubling his modest weekly salary to £10, he was away for just over seven months.[1] When on 29 May he sailed on the *City of Adelaide* for Sydney to take the California mailboat, Annabella came down from 'the Mount' to farewell him.[2] Four surviving letters that he wrote to her during his absence (there were apparently more) are affectionate and suggest that the two were very close, while frequent references to the children indicate that his family was very much on his mind.[3] They are long letters, allowing a reconstruction of his movements and activities during some four months in Britain.

---

[1] Staff Wages Register, entry for 3 June 1876, SFP Box 1186/2.
[2] DS to Jane, 29 May 1876, LB2, pp.11–12; 'Shipping Intelligence', *Argus*, 30 May 1876, p. 4.
[3] Unless otherwise noted, details of Syme's time in Britain have been taken from his letters to AS, 8? June, 1, 29 September, 26 October 1876, SFP Box 1180/5c.

CHAPTER 8

Writing to Annabella several days later from Fiji, he expected the voyage to take 80 days, thus getting him to London in August. Crossing North America, he 'looked in on' the Philadelphia Exhibition, one of the 'very few Australians' reported to have done so.[4] As in the past, the long sea voyages would have enabled him to relax and recover depleted energies. But no sloth, his chief occupation was rewriting the manuscript of what would be his first published book, *Outlines of an Industrial Science*, produced, he stated in its Preface, 'in hours snatched from a laborious profession, often at wide intervals apart, and generally after an exhausting day's work'. For he had found time to write the first of what would be four published books. Possibly this was during 1874 and 1875, when the initial problems with new printing technology had been overcome, there were no major changes of format or content to his newspapers, and the partnership question was yet to be addressed.

In London Syme left his revised manuscript with the publisher Macmillan & Co and in mid-August travelled to meet Jane and discuss the partnership. Separated from Robert Palk, she was then living at Rothesay, on the Isle of Bute off Scotland's west coast. Arriving by boat, he was met by her on the pier, accompanied by her seven year-old daughter, Margaret, whom he liked ('a nice child she is by the way', he would tell Annabella). Staying in a Rothesay hotel for three nights, he had several fraught and inconclusive meetings with his sister-in-law. Presumably concerned for her and her children's financial welfare, she was agitated and afraid, now that Syme knew more of her life with Palk. He, while bitter about her deception and suspicious about its full extent, primarily wanted to wind up the partnership on a fair, mutually agreeable basis.

During several meetings Jane pressed for her son Joseph to have a financial stake in the newspaper business. Besides working in the Counting House, apparently with aptitude and interest, he had taken up further studies. Having passed the Matriculation examination in 1872, he enrolled in classes (presumably evening ones) in the Law Faculty at the University of Melbourne in 1875, obtaining passes in two out of four subjects in October and in the other two when repeating at supplementary examinations in February 1876, thus passing First year of the Bachelor of Law (LL.B) degree.[5] He did not pursue his studies, however, presumably because of increased involvement

---

4   'Philadelphia Exhibition', *Argus*, 21 September 1876, p. 7.
5   University of Melbourne Student record for Joseph Cowen Syme, University of Melbourne Archives.

in the business. Syme was willing to consider a one-fifth share, but Jane refused to sign an agreement to this effect. According to Syme's account to Annabella, Jane was wildly irrational and emotional, precluding a sensible discussion. Syme's 'last shot', a threat to auction the *Age* and start a new paper, shocked her into an uneasy verbal agreement. She consented to the cabling of her son William in Victoria: 'Mother earnestly desires settlement arbitration, December, Joseph one-fifth interest'. William cabled back agreeing to a settlement but demanding one-fourth share for Joseph. And thus the matter would rest until Syme's return to Melbourne.

Syme broke his journey back to London in Glasgow for some unspecified business (perhaps to do with the Victory machine at the *Star*) and in and around Leeds to visit elderly relations of Annabella. Awaiting him on return to London were birth certificates of Jane's Palk children that he had sought: for Robert born in 1864, Reginald in 1867 and Margaret in 1869, but not for the first, Alice, born in 1862. Syme believed he had proof that the two boys were illegitimate, for he understood, wrongly, that Jane had married Palk in 1868. As Jane married him in 1866, it was actually Alice and Robert who were born out of wedlock. But he seems then not to have known (did he later?) of the existence of Alice, conceived in Melbourne less than two years after Ebenezer's death, something that would surely have shocked him even more, and presumably was the cause of Jane's leaving Australia. He was also concerned about the 'poison' working in his nephews, who had been brought up in ignorance and were now becoming aware of the 'true state of affairs'. An added pressure on Ebenezer's young sons would have been the requested or self-imposed secrecy about the existence of a stepfather and half-siblings, when they came to live in Victoria and were in contact with Syme and his family, although in time these facts got out.

Outlines of an Industrial Science to be published

Negotiating publication of his book turned out far more satisfactorily than attempting to resolve the partnership matters, even though Macmillan was not interested. As Syme reported to Annabella: '[Alexander] Macmillan was abroad & his son [George] who had it in London, for a week didn't seem to like it'. Syme then successfully approached the publishers Henry S. King & Co., noted for their 'International Series of Scientific Works' initiated in 1871, and about to establish the periodical *Nineteenth Century* (Anderson and Rose 1991, 238–244). A memorandum of agreement dated 26 August shows that 750 copies would be printed, Syme to pay £37.10.0 towards costs,

CHAPTER 8

and profits to be shared equally.[6] At the same time Syme's agent, fellow journalist and friend George Levey, was arranging for publication of an American edition.

During September and October Syme spent considerable time checking and correcting the proofs of his book, with help and advice from the political economist Professor Thomas Edward Cliffe Leslie, who is thanked as a 'friend' in the Preface, dated 1 November, for reading over the proofs and making suggestions. *Outlines of an Industrial Science* was published in December, when Syme was on the high seas returning to Melbourne.[7] Another 500 copies (a 'Second Edition') were printed on 29 March 1877. Months later Syme learned of this and that H.S. King had been absorbed into the new firm of Kegan Paul.[8] Steady for the first year, sales would drop off to an annual few, with Syme receiving small remunerations from time to time from Kegan Paul. Copies were sold in Melbourne through George Robertson. Syme may have presented Thomas King of the *South Australian Advertiser* with a copy, for the postscript of a letter to King of 21 May asks if he has read his 'outlines' yet.[9] In 1883, 47 copies were lost in a fire in publishers' warehouses in Paternoster Square that destroyed Kegan Paul's 'whole stock of printed books', but not unbound printed sheets, stored elsewhere (Howsam 1998, 85–86). At 30 June 1894, the last account books entry, there were 30 bound copies of *Outlines* in stock with Kegan Paul in London.

A succinct, concise monograph, *Outlines of an Industrial Science* uses the term 'industrial science' in place of 'political economy' and expands the ideas in Syme's 1871 *Westminster Review* article, 'On the Method of Political Economy'. The book argues for the use of the inductive method to arrive at truths, questions the universality of the self-interest motive, explores the effects of unbridled competition and considers the benefits of regulatory tariffs. It examines what are termed 'egoistic' and 'allostic' (that is, selfless) industrial forces and the concepts of value and price. Finally, with the ground and contours laid out, this 'science' is then compared to the cognate discipline of sociology or social science and distinguished from 'art', which is defined as the industrial legislation that applies the findings of

---

[6] Contracts, *Archives of Kegan Paul, Trench, Trübner and Henry S. King, 1853–1912*, 1974, Bishop's Stortford: Chadwyck-Healey, microfilm, held in Monash University Library.
[7] 'H.S. King Publication Books', *Archives of Kegan Paul*.
[8] DS to A. Malcolm, 27 December 1877, LB2, p. 129.
[9] DS to T. King, 21 May 1877, LB2, pp. 50–51.

industrial science (an odd usage). Based on Syme's wide and careful reading, the book draws on and departs from the theories of John Stuart Mill, Adam Smith and other English economists, presenting a logical exposition of the principles underlying Syme's own economic policies. If the views are somewhat idiosyncratic, the logic is unassailable and the prose spare and clear.

The reception of Syme's book has been examined in depth by historian J.A. La Nauze (1949, 98–135), in his essay on Syme's contribution to economic thought. He notes that, although favourably reviewed by the *Westminster Review*, the *British Quarterly Review* and various English newspapers, the book did not bring fame for its author in Britain.[10] Writing to A.J. Malcolm at McEwans in April 1877, Syme commented that the English press were treating it in a very 'gingerly' manner, as if not sure 'where it would lead them to'.[11] Copies are still held in the British Library, and the libraries of Oxford University and the University of Edinburgh.

The American edition, published by H.C. Baird of Philadelphia in 1877, apparently received more acclaim. It became a textbook in elementary political economy in colleges and schools and was praised by Henry Carey, whose *Principles of Social Science* (1858) Syme is said, by La Nauze (1949, 121 n.63), to have owned and annotated. The Library of Congress holds a copy of *Outlines*, as does the National Library of Canada. The book was praised in the German *Allgemeine Zeitung*, which hoped there would be a translation into German. According to La Nauze (1949, 112), this did in fact take place and, along with Syme's 'On the Method of Political Economy' article, attracted a great deal of attention in print from writers on economic theory then and for some decades thereafter.[12].

While based in London, Syme stayed for a time at the Salisbury Hotel in Fleet Street, going regularly to McEwans in Lombard Street to attend to business correspondence. He found time to do some sightseeing (Kew, Hampton Court, Battersea Park) and occasionally met up with other Australians. In September he received invitations from the Goodiers (relatives of brother George's wife Susan) to visit for a few days and from a Melbourne

---

[10] Extracts from six favourable reviews are, nevertheless, featured in a 'By the Same Author' notice facing the title page of Syme's *Representative Government in England*, 1881.

[11] DS to A. Malcolm, 16 April 1877, LB2, p. 34.

[12] I have not been able to locate a German translation; copies of the book in English are still held in the Thuringer Universitats- und Landes library at Jena and in the Deutsche Zentralbibliothek at Koel.

CHAPTER 8

friend, possibly businessman and pastoralist William McCulloch, to go shooting in Scotland, but does not seem to have acted on them. In October he took Annabella's aunt for a week to Brighton, for her entertainment and for his own health, which was not good – he was suffering badly from insomnia, he told his wife. He enjoyed Brighton, and would have liked to stay longer, albeit going into London every second day!

Syme was not in England on vacation, however, but with three separate objects: publication of his book; dissolution of the partnership with Jane; and solution of technical and associated litigious matters arising from his experimental introduction of new printing technology in 1872. To these last he gave what time he could from the start; later, with his book in press and the partnership negotiations in abeyance, he devoted full attention. He settled his claim on the Victory Company, being paid £100 and the cost of repairs, and he ordered another Victory printing press, which he arranged to be inspected and passed by the machinist, William McCulloch, of the Edinburgh *Daily Review*.[13] He saw a Mr Parsons of Parsons and Davies about two-feeder 'Graphic' machines (developed for use by the London *Graphic*) and 'got a full account'.[14] He made further investigations into the most suitable paper and suppliers thereof, not happy with Spicer Brothers' product. Assembling a list of other possible makers, he turned to the Star Mill Co.

A major lawsuit, which Syme does not specify but could have been an action against the newsprint suppliers Cowan & Company of Edinburgh, proved most demanding and worrying. He wrote to Annabella on 29 September: 'I am in London still. I am every day occupied with the law suit, seeing actuaries & lawyers & trying to master the case. It will be a most expensive case too…all my other work is in arrears.' A month later, writing from Edinburgh on 26 October, he reported having had at least 30 people to visit in all parts of the country and that he had not yet obtained adequate assistance in London. The situation was being exacerbated by errors and omissions by staff at the *Age* office, then beyond his control, and he reached a point of despair over the 'wretched business…I feel as much out of sorts as any man in this wretched country cd well do'.

Syme's letters to Annabella convey that he missed her and their children intensely, and welcomed correspondence and photos from them. All the children are mentioned at one time or another. He is very pleased to hear

---

[13] DS to W. McCulloch, 24 January 1877, LB2, p. 19.
[14] DS to A. Malcolm, 12 May 1877, LB2, p. 40.

from Herbert and Francis, quoting back some of their remarks; he wonders why 'Arty' (Arthur) has not written ('is he lazy?'). He is sad to hear of poor Olive's troubles (mildly intellectually disabled, possibly epileptic, she was to have special needs throughout her life). He finds a photo of Lucie very good. He asks after young Geoffrey. He worries about the health of Annie, his 'Very Dear Wife' and 'My Dearest Wife'. The letter from London dated 1 September ends with several lines of very loving words: 'I think dearest I have no more to say. I often think of you, & what a blank life would be without you', conveying that she was indeed a deeply appreciated source of love and support. This was much needed at this time, with the running sore of the partnership, and the bitterness about Jane's betrayal of trust.

Syme's misery was deepened by the news from Annabella, received in late October, that his brother George, never robust, was unwell. On receiving it he cabled 'Relieve George immediately. Return January' and wrote to Annabella on 26 October that this must happen 'no matter what cost to the paper', seeing that it would be 'absolute murder for him [George] to go on & the paper must just take its chance – he is to look on & only guide its general policy'. For the next three months, responsibilities were taken over, presumably, by editor Arthur Windsor and business manager John Macdonald. This letter has an uncharacteristically deeply despairing tone – and its writer must have moved to a quick settlement of his big lawsuit or have cut his losses and abandoned the oppressing case so he could return home sooner than planned, as there is no further mention of it in his correspondence, although there would be multiple smaller claims.

Syme left England in late November, around the time that Jane also sailed. She had written him that she wanted to travel to Melbourne in order, with her sons, to negotiate settlement of the partnership, and requested him to book her a passage. He complied, ensuring that they were not on the same ship.

Partnership with Jane dissolved

Syme arrived in Melbourne on 7 January on the *Bangalore* and was reunited with Annabella and family now living in Melbourne.[15] On 25 January having 'hardly had time to get properly into harness', he said, he was writing to Malcolm at McEwans in London about paper and machine orders and

---

15   'Shipping Intelligence', *Argus*, 8 January 1877, p. 4.

CHAPTER 8

claims.[16] Soon after, he was giving priority to settling the partnership matter, Jane having arrived on 8 January (listed as Mrs Jane H. Hope) on the suitably named *Nemesis*.[17] He wrote to her on 8 February (this time not 'My dear Jane' but 'Dear Mrs Hope') that his negotiations with her sons had been unsuccessful, asking her to suggest the next step, and adding that he would be available for an interview.[18] After her reply of 10 February that she did not want one, Syme wrote on 13 February setting out his terms – he was willing to concede one quarter share for Joseph in place of one-fifth, to let him have a certain amount of control, and to extend the period from five to seven years.[19] He regrets that she does not want to see him and denies that he had shown her any discourtesy or, what was surely a telling blow, 'done anything but what I thought would suit with your circumstances'. Her terse reply of 17 February (from Swinton, Studley Park, the residence of her daughter Minnie and husband Frank, Annabella's brother) takes issue with his mode of addressing her and keeping her 'in the dark', and requests that in future proposals be put through 'Joe or Willie'.[20]

The next move on record is Syme's offer through his solicitors, dated 27 April and open for seven days, to purchase Jane's share of the business for £8000.[21] This appears to have prompted a series of accusations from Joseph amounting to Syme's failure to treat Jane fairly both as Ebenezer's widow and his uncle's business partner, which Syme, in a letter of 9 May to Joe, wants proven or withdrawn while Jane is still in Victoria.[22] Three days later, however, Jane sailed for England, on the *Renown*, to find on her return (as will be seen) a shocking development in her personal circumstances.[23]

Syme's negotiations with his nephews Joseph and William continued over the next two months or so, concluding at the end of July.[24] The difference between the positions taken by each side was not great and the demands made by the nephews were not unreasonable, while the uncle took pains to

---

[16] DS to A. Malcolm, 25 January 1877, LB2, pp. 14–17.
[17] 'Shipping Intelligence', *Argus*, 9 January 1877, p. 4.
[18] DS to Jane, 8 February 1877, LB2, p. 20.
[19] DS to Jane, 13 February 1877, LB2, pp. 21–22.
[20] Jane to DS, 17 February 1877, SFP Box 1180/1(d).
[21] Offer, 27 April 1877, LB2, p. 36.
[22] DS to Joseph Cowen Syme (hereafter JCS), 9 May 1877, LB2, p. 37.
[23] 'Shipping Intelligence'. *Argus*, 14 May 1877, p. 4.
[24] Extant are three letters (copies) from DS to JCS (LB2, pp. 44, 45–47 and 53–54); five from DS to W. Syme (LB2, pp. 52, 59, 60–62, 66 and 71); four from W. Syme to DS, SFP Box 1180/2(b); and two from JCS to DS, SFP Box 1180/3(a).

clarify and explain aspects and details of running the business that had a bearing on the value. On the whole, the tone of the letters is polite, Syme writing to William on 30 May, 'Joe & I are now in a fair way to settlement'.[25] Eventually David agreed to pay the sum of £8250 to Jane, as one quarter share, putting the total value of the business at £33,000, and it was arranged that Joseph would travel to England to procure Jane's and Palk's signatures on the contract of sale. William would pay Joseph's travel expenses, the sum to be refunded by the firm after the signatures were obtained; Joseph would have five or six months' absence on full pay. Joseph would in due course purchase another quarter, through buying his siblings' shares. All was not happy, however; here and there in the letters is evidence that Joseph bore grudges and was not convinced of his uncle's fair treatment, while Syme was provoked to protest 'what an egregious fool I have been in sacrificing so much on behalf of those who do not appreciate my conduct'.[26] There was a sore that later would fester.

The dissolution of the partnership with Jane was one matter. The formalising of a new one with Joseph another, albeit intricately related. The deed of the new partnership is dated 1 January 1877, for a seven-year term.[27] The articles of co-partnership define the respective areas of responsibility. David Syme is to have 'entire control of the Policy of the Age and Leader newspapers…the sole right of engaging and discharging the Editors SubEditors Contributors and Reporters employed in the Editorship and Literary Department', with Joseph not to interfere, provided that undue expenditure is not undertaken and there is appropriate communication. Joseph Cowen Syme is to have the management (unless manifestly not to the interest of both parties) 'of all Mechanical Departments including Machinery Printing Stereotyping and Composing Rooms Collection of Subscriptions Superintendence of Agencies Advertisements'. But all staff under him are only to be engaged and dismissed with the consent of both. Syme's salary is to be £1250 per annum; Joseph's £400 for the first four years, then £600. Significantly, David's eldest son, 18-year-old John Herbert Syme, is to be employed at an annual salary of not more than £250. Not then at issue, the role of son vis-à-vis nephew would in time become so.

Joseph left Melbourne by the *China* on 7 August, bound for Venice, taking the dissolution documents for signature and given several business

---

25   DS to W. Syme, 30 May 1877, LB2, p. 52.
26   DS to JCS, 1 June 1877, LB2, pp. 53–54.
27   Articles of co-partnership, SFP Box 1185/3(b)[i].

CHAPTER 8

matters to look into for Syme (dealt with below).[28] On 14 October Syme received, via a letter from William, the information from Joseph that Palk had left England three weeks before Jane's arrival and that his whereabouts were not known.[29] Syme was inclined to dispense with Palk's signature, provided the brothers gave him an indemnity in case he turned up again. In early December Syme received Joseph's letter of 15 October informing that Palk, presenting as a widower, in August bigamously married 33-year-old Anne Sophia Helmore in the Parish Church of St Pancras and soon after sailed with her for Port Elizabeth in the Cape Colony, South Africa.[30] Fathering two children with his new 'wife', Palk would live there until his death in 1890 (Armstrong 2011). Joseph having sent on the documents to the Cape for signature, Syme wrote to William on 5 December commenting revealingly that Joseph should have gone there with them: 'Nothing like doing business ones self'.[31] On 18 December he wrote to Joseph asking for full proof or disproof of Palk's marriages.[32] There the matter rested, to await the return of Joseph. Now Syme was all but free of this millstone that was the Palk connection, while Jane in Britain would be taking steps towards a new life.

During the first half of 1877, Syme followed up unfinished business from his 1876 trip to do with machines and paper, through a series of letters to Malcolm at McEwans, after which he handed the matters over to Joseph for attention in England, sending further instructions in his regular letters.[33] Printing machines were a priority. In May Syme had ordered a two-feeder 'Graphic' machine for the *Illustrated Australian News*, specifying one for printing fine woodcuts. It was to be the same size as the London weekly *Graphic* used, unless the rival *Australasian Sketcher* had a larger one![34] Joseph's letter of 23 November from London advised him that the Graphic machine would be ready in six to seven weeks and that he had arranged for various fittings and he supplied information about other equipment.[35] Invoiced on

---

[28] Shipping, *Age*, 8 August 1877, p. 2.
[29] DS to W. Syme, 17 October 1877, LB2, pp. 105–107.
[30] JCS to DS, 15 October 1877, SFP Box 1180/3(a); Family History Report, Ebenezer Syme and Jane Hilton Rowan, dated 23 October 2009, supplied by Pru Williams, descendant; B. Armstrong (2011).
[31] DS to W. Syme, 5 December 1877, LB2, p. 123.
[32] DS to JCS, 18 December 1877, LB2, p. 128.
[33] Six letters DS to JCS from [early August] (LB2, pp. 77–78) to 27 December 1877 (LB2, p. 131).
[34] DS to A. Malcolm, 12 May 1877, LB2, p. 40.
[35] JCS to DS, 23 November 1877, SFP Box 1180/3(a).

15 October 1878 (£633.14.5), the delivery may have been much later.[36] The second Victory machine, ordered by Syme when in Britain, arrived in the middle of 1877; it was invoiced on 17 June for £2025.11.8 and put to work at the end of March 1878.

Syme's many letters to Malcolm in London before Joseph's departure were mainly concerned with orders for paper from Spicer Brothers and from the Star Company, neither firm giving full satisfaction. With an inconsistent doggedness that must have been irritating and frustrating for the recipients, he issued and countermanded orders and made complaints and claims concerning poor quality, oversupply, etc. To Joseph he handed over the task of pursuing these matters in person, and his nephew clearly did a lot of investigating, and reporting. Syme's last set of instructions on record about paper supplies is in a letter of 27 December to Joseph, which he writes 'on the chance' it will reach him before leaving England. A cordial letter, in it he wishes 'My Dear Nephew' a 'very happy new year'.[37] Shortly, the burden of attending to the procurement and maintenance of machinery and supplies would be lifted from him and become Joseph's responsibility as junior partner.

Cable news service

A great achievement for Syme and his *Age* business in 1877 was the arrangement of a cable news service independent of the Australian Press Association, something he had wanted but failed to achieve in 1871 and 1872. A usage that was to become commonplace, Syme sometimes used the word 'cable' for messages from overseas in place of 'telegram' and 'telegraph', reserving these for telecommunications within Australia. In general, the climate and conditions were propitious for such a development. The intercolonial network was almost complete, New Zealand having been linked in 1876 and Western Australia to be connected in December 1877. The Australian Press Association arrangement with Reuters to end in October, Syme was in May worried that the dominant *Sydney Morning Herald–Argus* combination would set up its own direct service and so 'throw overboard' the *Age* and the other newspapers currently supplied.[38] Moreover, the need for up-to-date news from England and Europe was felt intensely in 1877. The long-festering so-called Eastern Question, centring on relations between

---

[36] Machinery Register, SFP Box 1186/1.
[37] DS to JCS, 27 December 1877, LB2, p. 131.
[38] DS to A. Malcolm, 15 May 1877, LB2, p. 42 (also LB2, pp. 41, 43 of same date).

CHAPTER 8

Russia and the Ottoman Empire, had developed into hostilities between the two parties, with the outbreak of the Russo-Turkish War on 24 April. The possibility existed that England, along with other European powers, might be drawn to support Turkey (in the event, Great Britain remained neutral) (Ensor 1936, 40–50).

In part, this need for cable news could be met by the State War Telegrams sent by the Secretary of State for the Colonies or by Agents-General to colonial governments and passed on to the press. In May Syme wrote to Chief Secretary John Macpherson requesting copies of telegrams from the Agent-General concerning the war between Russia and Turkey, and accordingly these were supplied.[39] The *Age* of 2 July, under the heading 'The War in the East', first carried cable news from 'Reuters–AAP' (that is, from the Australian Press Association). This was followed by a 'Government Telegram, By Submarine Cable, [from the Agent-General], Russian Movements on the Danube'. This particular example also illustrates the contrast in layout to the cramped dull presentation of cables and telegrams in 1872. Headings in large type, followed by a series of sub-headings, progressively smaller but still prominent, helped to lighten the appearance of the page as well as highlight the cable news.

The same month Syme sought advice from English contacts about securing a correspondent in London or India to supply the latest news.[40] He then wrote to Samuel Bennett of the Sydney *Evening News* and Thomas King of the *South Australian Advertiser* about forming an association to obtain news independently and to supplement it with some from Reuters.[41] In June he organised for J.H. Heaton of the Sydney *Evening News* to go to London and arrange a service.[42] He also sought information about Reuters service from the Sydney representative, Frederick Linden, which was duly supplied to him in a circular.[43]

By August Syme at last had a cable news correspondent in London, the *Age* of Friday 3 August featuring cable news 'From Our Own Correspondent', comprising the latest news of the war in the East, repeated in 'News of the Day': 'Today's cable news from our London correspondent announces a decisive defeat of the Russians at Nicopolis'. The advantage of one's own correspondent is demonstrated in that this same news was repeated in a

---

[39] DS to J. Macpherson, 10 May 1877, LB2, p. 39.
[40] DS to A. Malcolm 15 May 1877, LB2, p. 42 (also LB2, pp. 41, 43 of same date).
[41] DS to T. King, 21 May 1877, LB2, pp. 50–51.
[42] DS to J. McEwan and to A. Malcolm, 12 June 1877, LB2, pp. 56 and 57.
[43] DS to F. Linden, 1 August 1877, LB2, p.75.

Government Telegram made available for printing in the *Age* a day later! During August and September Syme was a driving force in taking the initiative with Bennett in Sydney and King in Adelaide to push for a shared service that, independent of Reuters, would offer both overseas cables and intercolonial telegrams. Syme claimed that there was never a better chance of defeating the *Argus–Sydney Morning Herald* combination. He proposed that Bennett take New South Wales and Queensland, he would have Victoria, Tasmania and New Zealand, and they would share South Australia.[44]

Syme gave Joseph some tasks and responsibilities relating to the cable news plans. En route to England he was to see King in Adelaide to discuss a shared arrangement, and at King Georges (now George) Sound (Albany), in anticipation of the Western Australian line being open, he was to engage a good correspondent. Giving the cable news matter a lot of thought and canvassing support in the weeks after Joseph's departure, he arrived at a more realistic position regarding Reuters. In a letter of 4 September he told Joseph that he expected to have to take Reuters service and supplement it (rather than use Reuters to supplement his own), and urged his nephew to make contact with a leading London morning newspaper such as the *Daily News*, as a source of news for cabling.[45] On 1 November Syme signed up with Reuters, and from 3 November Reuters cable news appeared in the *Age* directly, not via the Press Association. Very soon, however, he was complaining to the Reuters Sydney agent, Linden, about serious deficiencies in the service.[46] From London, on 23 November Joseph answered several of Syme's queries about rates and payments, and suggested that J.M. Hewick, assistant to the subeditor of the *Pall Mall Gazette*, would be a suitable cable agent.[47] Syme replied on 27 December, undecided whether to continue with Reuters, finding the news inferior. As for the cables despatched by his own correspondent, he required 'War news', rather than the 'matters affecting Catholics' as Heaton had instructed ('The Catholic question is of no interest here', he wrote).[48] He considered McLean (engaged by Heaton?) a good correspondent.

In the New Year of 1878 Syme was still trying to arrange a shared service to offer to country papers. On 4 February he wrote to Heaton, who was then back at the *Evening News* in Sydney, about arrangements, agreement, costs,

---

[44] DS to S. Bennett, 8 August 1877, LB2, p. 79.
[45] DS to JCS, 4 September 1877, LB2, pp. 89–91.
[46] DS to F. Linden, 8, 9 and 11 November 1877, LB2, pp.108–110, 114 and 115.
[47] JCS to DS, 23 November 1877, SFP Box 1180/3(a).
[48] DS to JCS, 27 December 1877, LB2, p. 131.

CHAPTER 8

payment, and concern over the slow progress; and again on 13 February, 'anxious to get this matter settled at once'.[49] On 2 March, with Joseph back again and able to answer various questions he wrote again, advising that he had arranged with two country newspapers, which would bring in £125 each, and had contacted the *Herald* about joining.[50] He hoped that he had 'answered all the points in your letter, & I hope to your satisfaction'. A service alternative to and in competition with the Australian Press Association was in the pipeline.

In the same letter Syme told Heaton 'What between conspiracies against the paper & libel actions together, I have had, as you surmise, a rather busy time of it of late'. The *Age* proprietor was no stranger to libel actions – the corollary of editorial plain speaking, they dogged him throughout his career. For the most part he dealt with them as an inevitable and almost routine part of his business. The latest was a writ for £10,000 damages brought by Alexander Fraser MLC on the basis of a claimed libellous leader in the *Age* of 22 February one week earlier and for which Fraser would eventually be awarded damages of £250.[51] More worrying and time-consuming was the earlier libel suit brought by Free Trade conservative politician Edward Langton relating to an editorial attack on 22 January 1877, two weeks after Syme's return (Sayers 1965, 115–121). Exacerbating the issue for Syme was the fact that his erstwhile editor, the vituperative George Paton Smith, was counsel for Langton. Battles were waged throughout the year, both in the courts and in columns of the *Age*. Twice verdicts were awarded against Syme. He wrote on 16 April 1877 to Malcolm: 'I have been in hot water since I came back, & had a verdict against the paper for libel.'[52] By June, a public subscription fund amounted to £750 (Sayers 1965, 120). Syme reported to Malcolm in July: 'You will see I had my revenge on Langton, the public subscribing the full amount of the damages awarded to him!'[53]

Politics

More satisfying for Syme in the political arena was the triumph of liberal–reformist Graham Berry, who held the same policies as Syme concerning land, tariff and constitutional reform. A onetime journalist and newspaper

---

[49] DS to J. Heaton, 4, 13 February 1878, LB2, pp.133, 135.
[50] DS to J. Heaton, 2 March 1878, LB2, p. 138.
[51] 'The Case of Fraser v. Syme', *Argus*, 22 June 1878, p. 5, 24 June, p. 6.
[52] DS to A. Malcolm, 16 April 1877, LB2, p. 34.
[53] DS to A. Malcolm, 10 July 1877, LB2, pp. 64–65.

proprietor, Berry had been an MLA since 1861, Premier and Chief Secretary briefly in 1875, and in 1877 was President of the National Reform and Protection League. Supported by a swathe of the Victorian newspaper press, led by the *Age*, he and his supporters won power at the 1877 elections. On 12 May Syme wrote jubilantly to Malcolm in London: 'The Age has just scored a tremendous Victory over the general Elections'.[54]

Later in the year Berry attempted to legislate for the permanent payment of members of parliament by attaching a measure for this to an Appropriations Bill. This caused the Legislative Council to block Supply, the deadlock amounting to a constitutional crisis. Berry retaliated on 9 January 1878, a date known in the history of Victorian politics as Black Wednesday, by sacking more than 200 public servants, judges, magistrates, public prosecutors, etc. (Morrison 1999; 2005, 222–237). The Melbourne *Daily Telegraph* announced in a dramatic and potentially inflammatory headline 'Commencement of the Revolution'. Compromise rather than revolution was the order of the day, however, and a modified Bill passed at the end of March. The close association between Syme and the *Age* on the one hand and Premier Berry and Governor George Bowen on the other during the aftermath of the sackings is evidenced by a letter from Bowen to Berry dated 3 February, containing detailed instructions for the Premier. Bowen had received despatches expressing support for the Government from the Colonial Office that he wished passed on to the *Age*. He wrote: 'You shd. give the enclosure (1) to the Age at once as materials for a leading article tomorrow. I do hope you will be reticent to other newspapers.'[55] Accordingly, the *Age* of 4 February announced (but in 'News of the Day', not an editorial) that the imperial authorities 'recognise the constitutional importance of [Bowen]…being guided by the advice of his responsible ministers'. Bowen's advice was repeated and enlarged upon in a separate article headed 'The Crisis. The Governor's Action Approved by the Home Government'.

An article in the *Age* on 19 January entitled 'The Manufacture of Public Opinion' describes the two rival press networks, led by the *Age* and the *Argus* respectively, showing that all the newspapers of Victoria, country and city, were locked into one or other daily, with their policies and opinions being echoed and crystallised through quotation and repetition, and played back in 'Opinions of the Country Press' columns.

---

[54] DS to A. Malcolm, 12 May 1877, LB2, p .40.
[55] G. Bowen to G. Berry, 3 February 1878, Sir Graham Berry Correspondence, MS 8894, Australian Manuscripts Collection, State Library of Victoria.

CHAPTER 8

Notwithstanding political crises, libel actions and partnership problems, publication of the four titles in the Syme stable continued smoothly, with Syme involved in a number of enlargements and improvements to layout and content made during 1877. The stallion of the Syme newspaper stable, the *Age*, was steadily penetrating the reading market. An advertisement in the *Age Annual 1876*, published early in 1877, claims a daily circulation of 28,000 for the *Age*; in February 1878, when the new era with Joseph was about to start, it had risen to 32,000, far higher than that of any other daily newspaper in Australia.[56] Foreshadowing enlargements to come, there were changes of format. In the issue of 27 December 1877, the monthly 'Summary for the English Mail' appeared as a two-page Supplement to the usual eight-column, four-page paper, a small increase that was paving the way for larger papers both on weekdays and Saturdays. Serial fiction continued as an established feature of Saturday issues, including works by the bestselling novelists Annie Edwardes and Wilkie Collins. We do not know if or to what extent Syme was involved now in selecting the fiction to be featured.

In August 1877 competition with the *Argus* management over sporting news developed into an unpleasant disagreement. Syme complained to general manager Hugh George on two counts. First, that the *nom de plume* Nomad had been used by the cricket commentator on the *Australasian* when it was already in use by the football contributor to the *Leader* (Syme's Nomad appears to be Ben Goldsmith, formerly writing as 'Fair Play' on football for the *Australasian*).[57] Further, Syme complained that Peter Pindar's football columns in the *Australasian* contained 'literary larceny' from the *Leader*'s Nomad. In a letter a week later to Hugh George, Syme expressed offence at the reply he had received from William Hammersley, sporting editor of the *Australasian*, whom he had believed until now to be a 'gentleman'. One might expect that oversight of such matters would be the responsibility of the *Leader* editor, but George Syme does not seem to have been involved. Nevertheless, Syme saw him as a valued asset on the staff. When in December 1877 George went to Fiji for a month's holiday, Syme was 'very busy', having 'his work to do in his absence', he wrote to nephew William.[58]

---

[56] 'Circulation of the Age', *Age*, 13 February 1878, p. 4.
[57] DS to H. George, 23 and 31 August 1877, LB2, pp. 86, 88.
[58] DS to W. Syme, 12 December 1877, LB2, p. 126.

The *Illustrated Australian News* continued to appear monthly, aimed now more at an Australian than English readership. In November 1877 Syme wrote to Malcolm of McEwans about engaging an artist for it, having found the person he brought back to Melbourne earlier in the year was not satisfactory. He wanted 'a man accustomed to the work of an illustrated paper', not a landscape painter as they were plentiful 'here'; he had to be an all-round man who was good at figures (human not numerical) and who could be recommended by the *Illustrated London News* or the *Graphic*; he did not want an amateur. He would pay £6 per week with time for private professional practice so long as this was not for another newspaper, and £50 towards the passage out.[59] This would lead to the engagement of English artist Julian Rossi Ashton, who would be attached to the *Illustrated Australian News* until 1881 (Dysart 1981, 15).

The *Age Annual* for 1877, published early in 1878 had double the number of pages as the previous edition, its preface claiming a resounding acceptance:

> The favour with which the Age Annual has been received in the first three years of its publication, with the certainty that the work has acquired a permanent place among the periodicals as a reliable record of the History and Progress of Victoria and the adjoining Colonies has induced the proprietors to enlarge the volume and greatly increase the number of subjects from which a compilation of useful and valuable information is made.

This issue includes municipal and educational statistics; religious and financial information, a list of Australasian Governors, details of Victorian municipalities listing office-bearers, lists of Victorian State Schools and their head teachers, and more.

The four publications – the daily, the weekly, the monthly and the annual – were securely established, and growing in size and circulation. Accordingly, the staff was enlarging. At this time Syme found that he needed to formalise the evolving organisational structure and assign clear responsibilities to his middle management people in the Literary Department, which was his responsibility. A spur to this autocrat's action was the impending addition of Joseph as junior partner, with responsibility for the Mechanical Department. While the *Age* had Arthur Windsor as editor, and the *Leader* had George Syme, there was a need for delegation and direction at subordinate levels.

---

[59] DS to A. Malcolm, 28 November 1877, LB2, p. 120.

CHAPTER 8

Staff management

When in March 1877 Syme appointed Reuben Quarrill to the key position of subeditor and A.J. Smith 'head of the Staff' (the position later to be termed chief of staff) he wrote a memo to each man enumerating and stressing certain tasks. Something new for the *Age* office staff, each memo was, in effect, a schedule of duties, albeit prefaced informally (to Smith, 'I wd like to suggest one or two things to you'; to Quarrill, 'I would ask you particularly to attend to the following') and not an exhaustive list of all tasks required.[60]. But he was not clear in his mind about the boundaries of the various positions. Wanting the 'sub-editorial columns up to the standard that I have fixed for attainment', in August Syme rejected a war news article Quarrill had written, telling him to '<u>devote the whole of your time</u> to subeditorial duties'.[61] Yet when Quarrill left in December and Syme offered the subeditorship to the reporter James Williams, he specified that in addition he was to continue to write drama reviews (the 'notice of any new piece that is put on the stage at any of the theatres'), because no one else was capable of doing this.[62] Similarly, in December when the incumbent commercial editor Downey was given a fortnight's notice date and Anthony Robinson, already on the staff, was offered the position at £7 per week, it was on the understanding that in addition he would be writing articles for the *Age* and *Leader* and be paid an additional £3 for these.[63]

A financial statement for 1876 that is difficult to interpret appears to show a modest net profit for the *Age* business of some £5000.[64] While there are no extant financial statements for 1877, presumably the finances were healthy, as this year Syme was contemplating considerable expenditure. The Elizabeth Street premises, occupied since March 1856, were now quite inadequate and he was looking for new ones. He made several offers that came to nothing – in June to lease and build on a block of land on the corner of Elizabeth and Bourke Streets; in August to purchase the Railway Hotel and other buildings on the corner of Elizabeth Street and Flinders Lane.[65]

---

[60] DS to A. Smith, 23 March 1877, LB2, p. 28; DS to R. Quarrill, 23 March 1877, LB2, pp. 29–30.
[61] DS to R. Quarrill, 16 August 1877, LB2, p. 81.
[62] DS to J. Williams, 10 December 1877, LB2, p. 125.
[63] DS to A. Robinson, 14 December 1877, LB2, p. 127.
[64] Balance sheet and profit and loss account, SFP Box 1191/1(a)[vii]
[65] DS to V. Williams, 8 June 1877, LB2, p. 55; DS to R. Ker, 20 June 1877, LB2, p. 58; DS to G. Petty, 31 August 1877, LB2, p. 88.

In October Syme tendered, with numerous provisos, for a property in Collins Street East, 'a magnificent site in the very centre of the best street in Melbne' he wrote to nephew William, whom he asked to join him in purchasing it.[66] Although withdrawing his offer in early November because the vendors had changed their terms, later in the month he considered leasing with a right to purchase, from the Modern Permanent Building Society, which was to buy it.[67] After correspondence with William on his mother's behalf he got permission from Jane via William to lease for up to £1000 a year, and in December proceeded to secure the tenancy, with the right to build.[68] Constructing and moving into a grand new purpose-built establishment was to be a highlight of the new partnership.

On 27 February 1878 Joseph returned to Melbourne on the *Siam*, and within a few weeks the formalities of his partnership with Syme were concluded.[69] That he had not obtained Palk's signature seems not to have been any longer an issue. Finances were sorted out: David to pay Jane for her quarter share and her children William, James and Minnie (with her husband Frank Johnson acting for her) their proportion of the other quarter. The renegade nephew George had forfeited his share to William. Joseph had to find extra funds, £5295.7.2, to bring his share up to the quarter. On 18 January 1878 the date of final settlement was set for 5 April, but must have occurred earlier, for the receipts of payments by David Syme and Joseph Cowen Syme are dated 8 March 1878, noting they are in terms with the agreement and on condition they are returned duly executed by Robert Palk and Jane Hilton Palk. There is no evidence they ever were. Nor is there evidence of wild celebrations, but reaching this stage must have been an immense relief for all parties. With a lump sum for Jane, to get her life in order, there was no need for David to contact her again, and no evidence that he did.

On 20 March 1878 the newspapers in the Syme stable were registered in the joint names of David and Joseph, with brother George and brother-in-law John Gourlay providing sureties (Darragh 1997, 94 [37.09], 100 [62.04], 117 [175.04]). The *Age* of 22 March 1878 carries the imprint: 'Printed and

---

[66] DS to F. Hunt, 10 October 1877, LB2, p.104; DS to W. Syme, 17 October 1877, LB2, pp. 105–107.

[67] DS to J. Graham, 8 November 1877, LB2, p. 113.

[68] DS to W. Syme, 23, 29 November, 5, 12 December 1877, LB2, pp. 119, 121, 122, 126.

[69] 'Shipping Intelligence', *Argus*, 28 February 1878, p. 4; Articles of co-partnership, SFP Box 1185/3(b); Draft of declaration, SFP Box 1185/3(c)[i].

CHAPTER 8

Published for the Proprietors, David Syme and Co., at the *Age* office, Elizabeth street, Melbourne.' A company in name only, as it would be during Syme's lifetime and for a period thereafter.

A new phase in the life of David Syme, newspaper proprietor, was about to begin. In relation to the phase now ending, country newspaper proprietor Mitchell Armstrong, who was employed in the *Age* in the early years, would later write: it was 'difficult to make even a feeble estimate of the indomitable tenacity, perseverance and energy which characterised… the first twenty years of his strenuous struggle for political and journalistic supremacy' (Armstrong 1908b).

PART III

NEGOTIATING WITH A NEPHEW

Chapter 9

'I AM THE MAN WHO HAS MADE THE FIRM A SUCCESS'

(April 1878 to July 1883)

Judging by the upbeat, almost chirpy tone of a letter to George Levey dated 30 April 1878, David Syme was enthusiastic, confident and cheerful at the start of his partnership with Joseph. It concludes: 'I must not forget to tell you I had an addition to my family the other day, & that Mrs Syme & the boy are "both doing well".'[1] Oswald Syme, born on 19 April at Woodside, Albert Park, the residence bought by Syme that year, was the last child for 40-year-old Annabella and her spouse.[2] There were now five sons and two daughters.

The business intent of the letter concerns the London correspondence, for which Levey then had responsibility. Syme characteristically kept strictly to the point, and often laboured it in letters; here, however, he is expansive and chatty. He gossips about public figures and politics, bespeaking close (perhaps privileged) knowledge, yet distancing himself from exercising control. 'Don't you wish you were an Irishman?' he asks Levey in unusually jocular fashion, naming Irish-born Victorians proposed for high places under the Berry premiership ('the programme is: Duffy, agent-general; Casey, Judge; Lalor, Speaker; O Hea, Chairman of Committees; O Loghlen, Attorney General with the mob racing on the benches'). He mentions having to be economical because of the 'combination against the paper to stop advertisements', but does not sound unduly worried.

At this start of a period of great prosperity and boom for Melbourne, planning for the new premises at 50 Collins Street East, on the south side between Swanston and Elizabeth Street, must have been exciting. In

---

1 DS to G. Levey, 30 April 1878, LB2, pp. 142–143.
2 Extract from register of births, O.J. Syme, SFP Box 1193/4(b)[i].

anticipation of the move, a registration of the business of David Syme & Co. dated 4 April 1878, and witnessed by the 'General Manager' of the *Age* office, (John Macdonald), gives both the Elizabeth and Collins Street addresses (Darragh 1997, 13 [410]). Collins Street was becoming a veritable Fleet-Street precinct, with the offices of the other two morning dailies, the *Argus* and *Daily Telegraph*, to the east at 76 and 86 respectively, and the evening daily, the *Herald*, just around corner in Swanston Street. It was also the 'fashionable business' area of the city, as described in the June 1878 issue of the *Illustrated Australian News*. Syme had planned this as a 'Special Edition' to be available at the Paris Exhibition held from May to November 1878. In preparing it he was assisted by the publisher William Clarson (who investigated printing machines for him in England in the early 1870s), Syme's diary entry for 24 April recording their agreement to share profits from sales and advertising.[3]

For his new building, Syme went to the top, hiring the architect firm of Reed and Barnes.[4] Joseph Reed is seen to have 'dominated the architectural profession in Melbourne' singly (Saunders 1976), and as a partner in Reed & Barnes, and 'during Melbourne's period of greatest growth…[to have been] responsible for some of the largest and most important building commissions in the city, and [thus] instrumental in making Melbourne one of the great Victorian cities' (Tibbits and Goad 2012, 586). When engaged by Syme, Reed had already made his mark on Collins Street, with the Melbourne Town Hall, churches, and the Bank of Australasia. During 1878, while drawing up plans for the *Age* office building, Reed and Barnes were also designing Wilson Hall at the University of Melbourne, and the following year would begin work on the Royal Exhibition Building in the Carlton Gardens, in anticipation of the Melbourne International Exhibition of 1880–81.

Syme had leased the property at 50 Collins Street East with a frontage of 30 feet, 6 inches (10.7 metres) for 25 years at £500 per annum.[5] The new five-floor building (fig. 9.1) designed by Reed would replace the long-outgrown one in Elizabeth Street, which Alfred Deakin, who began his connection with Syme and the *Age* in 1878 (see below), recalled as narrow and dirty (Deakin 1957, 7). The *Age* editorial department occupied a single dingy upstairs room, while George Syme edited the *Leader* in the middle of the machine room and, although separated by a low partition, was prey to heat, smells and noise.

---

[3] Entry for 24 April, DS diary 1878, SFP Box 1184/1.
[4] *Illustrated Australian News*, 21 February 1879, p. 26.
[5] 'The Age 1854–1954 Centenary', *Age*, 16 October 1954, Supplement, p. 39.

CHAPTER 9

Figure 9.1. The *Age* office, Collins Street, 1879. (Pictures Collection, State Library of Victoria, IAN21/02/79/20)

DAVID SYME

The *Illustrated Australian News* of 21 February 1879 carries an illustrated article, '*The Age* office', describing the exterior of the new building as 'classic Corinthian order' and detailing the layout of the interior. The basement, on a bluestone and brick foundation, housed the printing and machine rooms. On the ground floor were general offices with cedar fittings, the publishing department and the damping room. Staircases and lifts led to the three upper floors. The first comprised 14 rooms, for the proprietors, editor, subeditor, reporters and contributors; on it also were the lavatories; the second was given over to compositors, stereotypers, readers and assistants; the third and top was for artists and engravers. The Furniture Register, which gives the value of the furniture at the end of 1879 at almost £1000, conveys the division of duties and the components of the production line and shows the allocation of rooms.[6] There was one each for: David Syme (Room no. 1), the *Age* editor, the subeditor, the reporters; for the *Leader* editor (George Syme), the *Leader* agricultural editor (John Dow); for the cable news agency, the Sporting, the commercial editor; for the *Illustrated Australian News* editor; for the contributors, the readers, the compositors, the artists, the stereotypers. There was a room for Joseph Syme, and also the counting house, the publishing room, the damping room and the machine room. In addition, there were spaces for files and stores, and a hall and enquiry counter.

The cost of the new building and plant (but not land) was said to be some £20,000 (Sayers 1965, 133). Syme had written to Malcolm at McEwans in London during January 1879: 'we are now incurring a heavy expense in building new premises'.[7] One can imagine that he had a great deal of input to the planning, although I have found no extant records to establish this with certainty.

The new *Age* office was occupied and in business on Monday 3 February 1879, the *Age* of that day announcing, in a notice above the editorial, the removal to 'new and commodious premises'. An item in 'News of the Day' repeats this information, adding that the newspaper too appears in a 'new dress, the occasion having been taken to replace the old type', and the imprint on page 4 gives the address as 'Collins-street east'. The three Syme newspapers were registered at the new address on 24 February 1879 (Darragh 1997, 94 [37.10], 100 [62.05], 117 [175.05]).

Almost directly opposite the new *Age* building (where now is the Australia-on-Collins shopping precinct) was Gunsler's Café, a 'favourite

---

[6] Furniture Register, SFP Box 1186/4.
[7] DS to A. Malcolm, 13 January 1879, LB2, p. 159.

CHAPTER 9

rendezvous of clubmen, journalists, musicians and theatrical people' (Davison 2005, 214), advertised as 'one of the sights of Melbourne', with an 'elegant restaurant' and 'magnificent banqueting room'.[8] There, on 21 October 1879 more than 250 'influential and leading citizens', including Premier Berry and a large contingent of politicians, met to celebrate the 25th anniversary of the newspaper's founding.[9] Business manager John Macdonald presided, proposing continued prosperity and commenting that a quarter of a century was far beyond the average life of a newspaper.

The highlight was the presentation of two portraits in oils: one of David Syme to him; the other of Ebenezer Syme to son Joseph. Shipping reporter and long-time employee Charles Clark made the presentation to David, saying the portrait was intended as a lasting memorial for the family and descendants. It is now held at the *Age* premises.[10] The artist was German-born Louis Tannert who came to Melbourne in 1876, was admitted as a member of the Victorian Academy of Arts the following year and soon obtained painting commissions; several years later he moved to Adelaide as master painter at the Adelaide School of Design ('Louis Tannert' 2011). Responding at length, Syme recounted the history and aims of the *Age* and his early struggles to keep it afloat. He then summarised world history of the previous 25 years (wars in Europe, Germany united, Italy an independent nation, France a republic, slavery abolished, science to the fore) concluding, in relation to Victoria: 'We have within a quarter of a century effected a social and industrial revolution which it has taken many centuries to achieve elsewhere.' The proprietor could afford to be satisfied if not complacent. Partnership matters were settled for the present, as were the acute technical problems, which in any case were now Joseph's responsibility. And there were other favourable aspects.

The independent cable news service was expanding. In May 1878 Syme recommended to Samuel Bennett of the Sydney *Evening News* the allocation of more funds to the fledgling agency in England, which from 1 June was to supply the Launceston *Cornwall Chronicle*, the *Benalla Standard* and the Melbourne *Herald*, in addition to the Hobart *Mercury*.[11] In November he

---

[8] 'Cafe Gunsler' [advertisement], *Leader*, 15 November 1879, p. 16.
[9] 'Twenty-Fifth Anniversary of the Age', *Age*, 22 October 1879, p. 3.
[10] Tannert's portrait of Syme was exhibited at the Art Gallery of Ballarat, April to July 2014.
[11] DS to S. Bennett, 25 May 1878, LB2, p. 146; DS to A. Smith, 29 May 1878, LB1, pp. 147–148.

was able to tell Levey that arrangements for the cable service independent of Reuters had been completed.[12]

What to do about the Reuters service was clearly a problem, however, for a year later Syme was negotiating charges for the service with its Melbourne agent, Henry Collins, and appears to have been discussing with James Fairfax of the *Sydney Morning Herald* joining forces to obtain and supply a service[13] – something that did not come about then but would 17 years later (Putnis 2006). Joseph was in New Zealand in early 1880 with instructions from his uncle to attempt to recruit one or two leading papers in Dunedin and Wellington, to be supplied at a low rate to 'secure their independence' (from Australian Press Association and Reuters messages).[14] This did not prevent the New Zealand Press Association from procuring cable news both from the Association and Reuters, although it sometimes used the *Age* service, which the New Zealand manager praised as 'by far' the best.[15] With the intention of improving cable despatches at the London end, at the start of 1883 Syme sent 'home' as telegraphic correspondent the *Age* journalist Philip Mennell, formerly of the *Bairnsdale Advertiser* and on Syme's staff since 1882.[16]

Maintaining and improving the appearance of his newspapers was a paramount concern for Syme, requiring recruiting and management of suitable staff, especially a competent subeditor for the *Age*. Office correspondence reveals a problem with appointing and retaining the latter, something that would not be satisfactorily fixed until the mid-1880s. During the first five years of the new era, acting or very temporary subeditors included A.J. Smith, James Williams (who had earlier been offered the position but not taken it up), reporter Middleton, Mennell, and Gottfried Schuler, parliamentary reporter since 1879, whom Syme found unsuitable as a subeditor although years later would appoint as editor.[17] (Clearly, different though related aptitudes were and are required for the respective positions; some journalists were capable of both.) Most of the above names crop up in

---

[12] DS to G. Levey, 15 November 1878, LB2, p. 158.

[13] DS to H. Collins, 9 October 1879, LB2, p.172; DS to J. Fairfax, 3 November 1879, LB2, p. 175.

[14] DS to JCS, 5 February 1880, LB2, pp. 180–181.

[15] E. Gillon to DS, 30 July 1882, New Zealand Press Association Papers, Alexander Turnbull Library, National Library of New Zealand.

[16] DS to J. Harrison, 10 September 1883, LB2, p. 214; Trevena (1986).

[17] Evident from DS letters from 29 May 1878 to 3 November 1882, LB2, pp. 147, 155, 161, 172. 196.

CHAPTER 9

Syme's letters and memoranda instructing and complaining about matters of content and layout, but are not likely to comprise a complete list of subeditorial incumbents.

Syme has often been said to have no interest in literature and the fine arts. (Alfred Deakin wrote that he had 'no eye for art, ear for music, heart for poetry'.[18]) Nevertheless, he was always concerned to obtain reports and reviews of quality in the arts, particularly in the domains of theatre and literature, and frequently gave the matters his personal attention. Concern with quality of the theatrical notices is evident in a letter of 30 July 1878, and presumably improved when, a few months later, he installed James Williams as both subeditor for the *Age* and drama critic for the *Leader*.[19]

Pearson and Deakin join the *Age* team

The most significant and valuable human resources acquired for the Syme enterprise during this period were two part-time contributing journalists, paid by volume: Charles Pearson and Alfred Deakin. Both exceptionally talented, one was almost Syme's age and with a range of achievements, the other was a youth with potential. The duo boosted Arthur Windsor's editorial team immeasurably.

Charles Pearson in 1878 turned 48. Oxford educated with first class honours, he was the author of several works of history and had contributed to English, American and Australian periodicals and newspapers (Tregenza 1968). Like Syme's, his career had been anything but straightforward. Among his various occupations, he had been a professor of history at King's College London, a sheep farmer in South Australia, from 1872 until 1874 a lecturer in history in the Law Faculty of the University of Melbourne and then headmaster at the Presbyterian Ladies' College, during which period he was appointed to the University Council. During these years he had also given public lectures and contributed journalism on controversial reformist subjects that would have been dear to David Syme but which brought about an enforced resignation from the girls' school and the necessity to live by his pen until or in addition to obtaining other employment. In May 1877 he stood unsuccessfully for the Legislative Assembly seat of Boroondara, beaten to it by Syme's *bête noire*, his former editor George Paton Smith.

---

[18] Alfred Deakin, Autobiographical Notes, Series 3/290a, Alfred Deakin Papers, MS 1540, National Library of Australia.

[19] DS to A. Telo, 30 July 1878, LB2, p. 151; DS to J. Williams, 27 September 1878, LB2, p. 155.

Standing in June the following year for the seat of Castlemaine, Pearson was elected. The *Age* supported him in both campaigns.

It is not clear exactly when Syme and Pearson became personally acquainted or when the latter offered his services to the former. John Tregenza's biography (1968, 160) states that he began to write occasional articles for the *Age* and *Leader* in 1874, and that this journalism became his principal source of income from June 1878, the time at which he was elected to Parliament. References by Deakin indicate that he was a contributor in 1878.[20] He was away from Melbourne from December 1878 to mid-1879, accompanying Premier Graham Berry on his 'embassy' to England in a failed attempt to get the imperial government to legislate to increase the power of the Victorian Legislative Assembly in relation to the Legislative Council (Bartlett 1969).

Amongst Pearson's papers is a notebook that lists his 'literary contributions' (mainly leaders and sub-leaders) in the *Age* from August 1880 to early February 1884.[21] From August to December 1880 these number between three and eight a month for the *Age* and one in each issue of the *Leader*. The *Age* contributions increase in the following years, in 1882 usually ranging from 13 to 15 a month. At, say, two guineas an item (a rate Syme often offered to valued contributors) this journalism would have earned him more than the parliamentarian's salary of £300 a year.

Tregenza (1968, 195) sees Pearson having played a major role in the rising circulation of the *Age* at this time. Certainly, through his informed contributions on a wide range of subjects from the local to the universal, Pearson helped to transform Syme's newspapers from primarily vehicles of Victorian colonial political news and opinion to newspapers with an Australian, British imperial, and international reach. He was not simply an editorial mouthpiece for Syme's liberal–reformist policies for, while he was at one with him on matters of land legislation and constitutional reform, he completely avoided his proprietor's protective tariff theme, privately espousing the doctrine of free trade.[22] Moreover, he extended the *Age* reformist agenda to include many aspects of educational provision, a field in which he was a respected authority. Syme made the general observation in his memoirs that he was fortunate in having the services

---

[20] Autobiographical notes, Deakin Papers, Series 3/290a.
[21] Charles H. Pearson, Contributions to Age & Leader, C.H. Pearson Papers, MS 7107, Box 431/5, Australian Manuscripts Collection, State Library of Victoria.
[22] Pearson, Literary work, Pearson Papers, Box 438/3e.

CHAPTER 9

of 'the late Professor Pearson', seeing him, with Windsor, as standing out from the 'commonplace' literary staff.[23] This view is echoed by Deakin in his unpublished memoirs, writing of Pearson that his 'weight of learning & breadth of culture placed him high above most of the press contributors I have met & known' and that he outshone even the 'brilliant' Windsor.[24] Pearson's service to Syme went beyond his journalistic contributions, however, for by example and advice he fanned his employer's aspirations as an author (dealt with later in this chapter).

Melbourne-born Alfred Deakin was 21 when he and Syme met in 1878. It is likely that each already knew of the other through their being involved in activities of the Victorian Association of Spiritualists. Deakin wrote that a Mr Dempster, 'an ardent Spiritist', introduced them 'in the middle of the year', and that Syme was then 'interested in Spiritism tho always coldly non-committal'.[25] (In September Deakin would be elected President of the Association and Syme and his wife would be appointed committee members; he for only one year, she for longer (Gabay 1992, 14).[26]) Admitted to the Bar in September 1877, since February 1878 Deakin had been languishing in Chambers at Temple Court; while waiting for briefs he was reading and writing poetry, essays and literary criticism (La Nauze 1979, 20–23; Norris 1981). He had taken evening classes at the University of Melbourne to obtain the requisite certificate to practise as a barrister and during the day had earned a living from teaching and tutoring and participated in clubs and societies. At the University Debating Club he met Pearson, whose lectures and writings he greatly admired.

Deakin also recorded meeting Syme on 23 May, to offer contributions on art and literature and being engaged on a trial basis.[27]. On 8 June his first contribution, a review of an article on Australia in an English periodical, was published in the *Age*. The same day Deakin wrote to Pearson offering his 'most hearty & sincere' congratulations on his election as MLA and referred to the sympathy they both had for Free Trade principles.[28] Syme would soon convert Deakin to his protectionist cause, however. According to Deakin's autobiographical notes, he was groomed briefly by Windsor for

---

[23] DS notebooks.
[24] Autobiographical notes, Deakin Papers, Series 3/290a.
[25] Autobiographical notes, Deakin Papers, Series 3/290a.
[26] *Harbinger of Light*, October 1878.
[27] Autobiographical notes, Deakin Papers, Series 3/290a.
[28] Deakin to C. Pearson, 8 June 1878, Pearson Papers, Box 439/5a.

whom he produced his first full *Age* leader on 1 July; he was then 'handed on' to George Syme to be trained at painful length. David's brother, if a kindly, scholarly, admirable man was, as a mentor, indecisive and pedantic. Recognising this, David intervened and took the young man under his wing, giving him the 'lightest supervision'.

After what Deakin termed a 'stormy and painful apprenticeship of six months' (Deakin 1957, 5) he became a regular contributor to the *Age* and *Leader*, sometimes mimicking Windsor's or Pearson's writing style, he remarked mischievously.[29] He wrote that his articles did not need to be cut or altered, and he was, after Pearson, the highest-paid contributor. The record he kept of his earnings shows that the greater part came from contributions to the *Leader*.[30] For instance, in November 1880, he earned £6.15.0 for the *Age* and £25.8.0 for the *Leader*. For the weekly he wrote articles, the regular 'The Week' summary, and also from April 1881, 'Under the Verandah', when its regular contributor, Marcus Clarke, was ill. (Lamenting the loss of the capable writer with whom he had once shared lodgings, Clarke had replaced Telo, who died in 1879;[31] Clarke himself died in August 1881.) The majority of Deakin's four or five articles a month in the *Age* were sub-leaders; occasionally his was the leading article (editorial). He took over editing the *Leader* when George Syme was away, but does not say when this was or for how long. In 1879 he was writing the summary 'The Month' for the *Illustrated Australian News*. A further income supplement in October, November and December came from seven contributions to the *Otago Daily News* in Dunedin, New Zealand, invoiced by him at two guineas each – a foretaste of future moonlighting (unless this trans-Tasman transaction was sanctioned by Syme).

Deakin's connection with the *Age* office brought him friendship as well as remunerative employment. Windsor and Deakin became close, despite the difference in age of 23 years;[32] and with Syme, Deakin said, there developed an 'intimacy' during the years 1879 to 1883, before political responsibilities took him away from day to day contact. We have to rely on his version of the relationship, as Syme omits mention in drafts of his memoirs that I have seen, although the fact of their long association is evidenced in

---

29   Autobiographical notes, Deakin Papers, Series 3/290a.
30   Financial jottings, Deakin Papers, Series 7. 2.
31   M.C., 'Alfred Telo: A Reminiscence', *Leader*, 11 October 1879, p. 18.
32   Evident in A. Windsor to A. Deakin, undated [possibly 1900], Deakin Papers, Series 1/588.

CHAPTER 9

their correspondence on file stretching from 1890 to 1907 and Deakin's diaries from 1884. While testament to mutual affection, disagreements are also recorded, and one severe falling-out in the last years of Syme's life. Deakin's memoirs record not only privileged access to the Syme sanctum, the proprietor's first floor office in Collins Street, but also frequent visits to Syme's Albert Park residence, Woodside, where they had long conversations about books and ideas, and to Rosenheim at Mount Macedon. The first visit to the country retreat was from Thursday 2 to Saturday 4 January 1879.[33] Perhaps then he met the Syme offspring, including Herbert and Francis, both about to embark on study towards a degree in Law, the qualification that Deakin had completed in 1877.

In these early years of their acquaintance, Syme exerted considerable influence over his protégé, not least in converting him, through extended reasoning, from a free trader to a protectionist. The argument was put conclusively, Deakin recalled, while the two were walking over Princes Bridge, the major crossing point in Melbourne of the Yarra River, on a road that could have taken them to or from Syme's home at Albert Park.[34] The writing of protectionist articles came to be Deakin's province, and thus he was a complement to Pearson, who avoided the topic. Like Pearson he also became a politician. It was Syme's influence, initially, that drew or pushed him onto the Victorian political stage, suggesting him as a candidate for the electorate of West Bourke in early February 1879 after one of the two representatives died. The story of his entry to Parliament is told in some detail by biographer John La Nauze (1979, 39–48, 80). Deakin agreed to stand and, under pressure of time, his first campaign speech was drafted by Windsor. He was elected on 18 February but, because of a controversy about a shortage of voting papers, he used his maiden speech to resign on principle, thereby incurring hostility from some quarters. Standing again in August that year and in February 1880, each time he was defeated. Persuaded to stand yet again, he was re-elected and took up his seat in the Assembly in July 1880, the start of what would be an illustrious career in Victorian and Federal politics.

This was not the end of Deakin's journalistic work for Syme, however, for he continued as a regular contributor to the *Age* and *Leader* until his first Ministerial appointment in March 1883, in the Berry–Service coalition, and he maintained contact with Syme thereafter. During the early 1880s

---

[33] 'Crude index', Deakin Papers, Series 2/37.
[34] Autobiographical notes, Deakin Papers, Series 3/290a.

Deakin's career had three dimensions: the political; the journalistic; and, to a much lesser extent, the legal. From Syme's point of view, he now had – through both Deakin and Pearson – two more unofficial spokesmen in the government and sources of information from it, in addition to John Dow, agricultural editor of the *Leader*, who had been elected an MLA in 1877.

While Syme brought about a consistently high standard and greatly widened range to the journalism produced in the Melbourne *Age* office through engaging Pearson and Deakin as regular contributors, he also gave attention to the quality and scope of copy procured from overseas. This included the cabled news that came within 24 hours, mentioned earlier in this chapter, and the 'correspondence' sent by ship that took five to six weeks. From a letter of Syme's to Levey in April 1878, it appears that the regular 'letters' being sent by Levey and Harrison were still appreciated but sometimes covered the same ground ('they clash somewhat'), while in February 1882 he asked Harrison to send one less leading article and one less review per fortnight, surely a consequence of the improved local talent in the *Age* office.[35] By 1878 Syme was also receiving regular correspondence from Paris, supplied by R.L. Hobart, resident at 224 Rue de Rivoli.[36]

Largely thanks to Syme's initiatives, the world of the *Age* and its readers was expanding, beyond Britain and Europe. In particular, there were two projects launched by him in mid-1883 that will also be dealt with in the following chapter. One is part of Syme's abiding interest in agriculture, an interest that was both practical and theoretical. As will be seen, in his private life he was becoming a practising agriculturist and horticulturist. As a journalist, he wanted agricultural information researched, written about and disseminated in his newspapers, believing this vital to the development of Victoria. Doing so for the *Age* and *Leader*, he was in close competition with managers of the *Argus* and *Australasian* for journalistic coups in an international arena, a competition that intensified as the political policy differences were becoming less acute and prominent.

In 1874 Syme had sent John Dow on a fact-finding tour of rural South Australia. In 1883 he despatched the agricultural editor to the United States to report, as announced in the *Age* of 2 July, on 'Agriculture, Grazing and Horticulture', noting that the practice of publishing reports of actual farming operations was first introduced into Australia 20 years ago and

---

[35] DS to G. Levey, 30 April 1878, LB2, pp.142–3; DS to J. Harrison, 15 February 1882, LB2, p. 193.
[36] DS to R. Hobart, 16 April 1878, LB2, p. 140; DS diary, 1878, SFP Box 1184/1.

CHAPTER 9

that special reporters for the *Leader* had visited South Australia, New South Wales, Tasmania and New Zealand. Dow's instructions were set out in a memorandum, itemising 23 subjects to which 'special attention' was to be paid, and a 24th, which was to keep an account of all expenses.[37] Written in a spidery copperplate hand other than Syme's, it may have been a transcription of Syme's instructions, as it carries a partly legible note in Syme's hand reading 'The original par & letter [illegible word]'. On 17 May Dow sailed for San Francisco from Sydney, on the *Zealandia*.[38] His first weekly 'Agriculture in America' appeared in the *Leader* on 14 July, subtitled 'On the Pacific Slope – Notes by the Way'. While it is little more than an account of shipboard life, subsequent reports begin to address the topics of his mission, commencing in California.

Intriguingly, Dow's brother Thomas, agricultural writer for the rival *Australasian*, had already been sent by his employers to survey and report on agriculture in America, leaving Sydney one month earlier, on the *City of New York*.[39] His weekly reports in the *Australasian* also began appearing on 14 July, entitled 'Farming in America'. His first, from San Francisco, subtitled 'Across the Pacific', is less about the voyage and more an introductory comparison of agriculture in Australia and America. One wonders whether Syme, hearing of Thomas's assignment, made a swift decision to despatch John on a similar one. One wonders also whether the Dow brothers spent time together and shared notes. The *Leader* of 28 July reproduces from the *San Francisco Chronicle* of 5 June the report of an interview with John, noting that both journalist brothers were in San Francisco and that John Dow praises Americans, recommends the Californian route of travel and states his intention to visit Chicago and New York before returning to Australia in September.

The other project initiated by Syme in mid-1883 was a fact-finding expedition to the island of New Guinea north of Australia, which colonial powers, predominantly Britain and Germany, were developing interests in claiming. This became a political issue in Victoria and other Australian colonies, particularly following the Queensland Government's attempt to annex the territory by planting a flag at Port Moresby in April (Serle 1971, 180–182). Syme's expedition was to be carried out by Victorian-born

---

[37] Unsigned, to J.L. Dow, LB2, p. 199.
[38] 'Shipping', *Sydney Morning Herald*, 18 May 1883, p. 4 (as J. Lamont); 'The "Leader" Representative in California', *Leader*, 28 July 1883, p. 23.
[39] 'Shipping', *Sydney Morning Herald*, 20 April 1883, p. 4.

George Ernest Morrison, an adventure-seeking young man whose accounts of his local exploits had been published in the *Leader* since he was little more than a schoolboy. 'The Diary of a Tramp', for which he was paid seven guineas, appeared during May 1880, narrating his walk along the coast from Melbourne to Adelaide in the summer 1879–80. The following summer he paddled a canoe down the Murray River from the New South Wales–Victorian border-crossing at Wodonga to the sea in South Australia, then walked back home to Geelong. Deakin recommended to Morrison that he see *Leader* editor George Syme, and the young man's account subsequently appeared in the weekly in August and September 1881 as 'Down the Murray in a Canoe', by GEM.[40] George Syme, however, reportedly called it 'monotonous', finding that readers tired of it (Pearl 1967, 11–12; Thompson and Macklin 2004, 20–21).

The next venture, suggested and agreed to by David Syme, was to report on the Kanaka 'blackbirding', the sometimes fraudulent and forceful recruiting of Pacific Islanders as indentured labourers for the sugar and cotton plantations in Queensland. In early 1882, having given up medical studies at the University of Melbourne, Morrison signed on as crew of a blackbirder vessel, to get information first hand. His detailed series of articles entitled 'A Cruise on a Queensland Slaver, by a Medical Student' appeared in the *Leader* from 21 October to 9 December 1882, and an even stronger denunciation in the *Age* as a Letter to the Editor on 9 May 1883, 'The Queensland Slave Trade'. This gave rise to Pearson's editorial on 10 May, stressing that New Guinea and the islands should be put under the protection of the Crown, to stop the trade. Meanwhile, leaving the ship, Morrison had travelled to Port Moresby in New Guinea, on to Thursday Island, and then to Normanton on the Gulf of Carpentaria, from where he walked, without misadventure, back to Melbourne, roughly along the route taken in the reverse direction by the fateful Burke and Wills expedition some 22 years earlier. Syme paid him £4.10 for his story, published as a 6000-word article in the *Leader* of 19 May 1883 (Pearl 1967, 34).

With all Morrison's experience on the ground and in print, it is not surprising that in May 1883 Syme engaged him, as 'Special Commissioner to the *Age*', for an expedition to New Guinea. An added incentive was that the *Argus* proprietors were organising a similar one. Joseph Syme, taking responsibility for Morrison's organising of the expedition, wrote on

---

[40] A. Deakin to G. Morrison, 29 June 1881, microfilm of correspondence in George Ernest Morrison Papers, G28245, National Library of Australia.

CHAPTER 9

29 and again on 31 May urging him to hasten his departure so as to beat the *Argus*.[41] The expeditioner left Melbourne on 6 June, after which he was sent telegrams from the *Age* office to Cooktown, then the end of the telegraph line in north Queensland. On 19 June he was instructed to 'not study economy in men or equipment' and advised that the *Sydney Morning Herald* would be sharing the expenses; the next day the instructions were: 'avoid Argus expedition if possible use discretion in getting away & in forwarding articles here'.[42]

Morrison's mission was announced in the *Age* of 2 July under the heading 'Exploration of New Guinea', justifying the exploring because of the proximity to Australia, the interest to science and the fact that there had been no serious attempt hitherto to penetrate the interior (no allusion to the politics of annexation, although this topic made the news frequently in the *Age* and *Leader*). It said that 'Mr Morrison' was 'the stuff of which explorers are made'. The *Leader* of 21 July reported, in reference to 'the race to supply the public with news of and from New Guinea', that the explorer had reached Port Moresby on 7 July, the first of the 'specials' to get there, and his letters were awaited.[43] The *Australasian* of the same day reported that Captain William Armit, leader of the rival expedition, had reached the settlement on 10 July.[44] Indeed, the race was on! The next chapter will take these stories further.

Writing for the *Melbourne Review*

While running the newspaper business and prosecuting the intense competition with the *Argus* and *Australasian*, Syme had not neglected his part-time vocation as an author. In April 1879 he had written to Kegan Paul, disputing charges for his 1876 changes to the proofs of *Outlines of an Industrial Science*.[45] He also expressed concern that writers had used his ideas in the *Nineteenth Century* and the *Fortnightly Review* without acknowledgment, and he still wanted to get the book reviewed in the *Fortnightly*. The same day he repeated these complaints in a letter to noted English author Frederic Harrison, from whom he had received a congratulatory one when the book

---

[41] JCS to G. Morrison, 29, 31 May, Morrison correspondence.
[42] Telegrams David Syme & Co. to G.E. Morrison, 19, 20 June, Morrison correspondence.
[43] 'The Week', *Leader*, 21 July, 1883, p. 25.
[44] 'The Argus Expedition to New Guinea', *Australasian*, 21 July 1883, p. 84.
[45] DS to C. Kegan Paul, 16 April 1879, LB2, pp. 165–166.

came out.[46] He also gave vent to private frustrations, telling Harrison that he felt 'chagrined' at being neglected:

> I suppose I must consider myself an outsider out here in Australia, although I take a warm interest in all such subjects & carefully read everything that is written on them from mail to mail. But I am so far off here that I find I cannot join in the discussion, & that is the reason why no notice is taken of my contribution.

While making this accurate enough assessment of his failure to be taken into the English intellectual milieu, Syme was writing or would have already written an article for local publication and consumption. The *Melbourne Review*, which had begun in January 1876 as a quarterly modelled on English ones, published in its July 1879 issue a 16-page article by Syme on land values in Melbourne.[47] In a sense, Syme was joining a local debate. Land matters were frequently debated in print and there had been numerous articles dealing with questions of land tenure and legislation published in this quarterly, including one by Pearson (1877) and another by pastoralist Stuart Reid (1879). Syme's approach differed from that in his first published article in the *Westminster Review* nine years earlier. The latest article emphasises prices rather than tenure and deals with just one urban area. His approach is empirical rather than theoretical, illustrating the method he advocated in his article 'On the Method of Political Economy' and his book *Outlines of an Industrial Science*. Away with Berry for seven months prior to the article's publication, Pearson probably had no hand in its revision, but perhaps Syme had learned from his proficient style.

Through a thumbnail sketch providing the context of 44 years of British settlement, he gave his study historical as well as spatial parameters. He consulted a 'mass of material', the article states: journals of early colonists, historical records in the Lands Department, recent government documents, newspapers, and data supplied by the Town Clerk, auctioneers, estate agents, dealers and purchasers. His historical survey, which meticulously traces and demonstrates the 'extraordinary increase' in the value of land in private hands and consequent loss of revenue to the State, concludes with advocacy of a land tax to make up the deficit and 'put an end to land speculation'. Ironically, this was the eve of a decade of huge speculation, Melbourne's 1880s boom. It is also ironical that Syme himself was engaged in substantial

---

[46] DS to F. Harrison, 16 April 1879, LB2, pp. 167–168.
[47] 'On the Increment in the Value of Land in Melbourne'.

CHAPTER 9

real estate acquisition. No doubt the research he undertook informed his purchases. Whatever verbal debate the article occasioned is conjecture, but on record is a response from journalist and author Alexander Sutherland, whose letter in the *Argus* on 14 July describes it as having a 'noble tone', but containing a serious fallacy in the calculations. This claim was refuted in a letter in the same newspaper the following day, from Arthur Topp, one of the founders of the *Melbourne Review* and a member of its editorial committee.

Notwithstanding the discouragement he expressed to Frederic Harrison in April 1879, Syme was carrying the germ of a new writing project. It would eventuate with the publication of a book related to Harrison's own writing on the subject of parliamentary institutions, about which Syme had commented to him: 'In England it is all talk & no work, & so it is here'.[48] Syme's *Representative Government in England* would be published in 1881. It seems reasonable to conclude that he wrote it during 1880. There is a gap in his office correspondence, at least as copied into the letterbook, after 19 February until 19 November 1880. While there may have been letters not copied, it does seem that there were no major initiatives during this period, and with Joseph in charge of the technical side and a reliable, talented team in the editorial branch, the proprietor took some time to develop his ideas into the draft of a treatise about the function and working of British parliamentary government.

Syme had definite plans for travelling in 1880. He may even have been considering this as early as October and November 1878, when he wrote several letters to Premier Berry urging him to use his influence to appoint Levey as secretary to the Commissioners for the Melbourne International Exhibition in planning for 1880–81.[49] It is probably this intervention of Syme's that Berry resented. He was reported as having told a Cabinet meeting, about an 'attempt at dictation'.[50] While this 'urging for some time', as Syme described it, was a personal favour for Levey, the proprietor seems to have had in mind also that Levey in Melbourne would be available to help in the *Age* office.[51] In November 1880, by which time Syme had travel plans drawn up, he proposed to Joseph that Levey be engaged for a year at £10 a week to write four leaders and replace Windsor on Sundays.[52] Press

---

[48] DS to F. Harrison, 16 April 1879, LB2, pp. 167–168.
[49] DS to G. Berry, 8, 11 November 1878, LB2, pp.156, 157.
[50] DS to G. Berry, 20 November, 1879, LB2, p. 177.
[51] DS to G. Levey, 15 November 1878, LB2, p. 158.
[52] DS to JCS, 19 November 1880, LB2, p. 185.

reports show that Levey was very fully occupied with Exhibition duties and other appointments until he left for Europe at the end of November 1881, so he may not have fully taken on this commitment, but a reference in the *Argus* to his 'connexion with and influence over the Ministerial journal' (the *Age*) suggests that he did so at least in part.[53] Syme's letter to Joseph has an irritable undertone, as does one few days later.[54] Both are responses to the latter's queries and complaints about business and holiday entitlements. Syme reminded his nephew that he proposed going away to attend to some essential business and then to have a holiday on account of his health, and that Joseph would be entitled to the same leave and remuneration as he. He did not mention working on a book.

Syme and part of his family were to sail on Friday 24 December 1880. On the Saturday preceding, the proprietors David and Joseph Syme treated the staff, relatives and friends to a monster picnic at Mordialloc, on Port Phillip Bay some 25 kilometres south of Melbourne, a place fast becoming popular for such activities.[55] The gathering included Attorney-General William Vale, Minister of Railways J.B. Patterson, and numerous other politicians. A chartered steamer brought more than 400 passengers from Sandridge (now Port Melbourne), to the accompaniment of music. Others arrived independently. Activities during the afternoon included sporting races for men, women and children, with prizes awarded. There were cricket, football, croquet and rounders matches, an 'Aunt Sally' and other games, and there was dancing, with a band supplying music. Central to the proceedings was the presentation of a 'handsomely illuminated address', the work of prominent lithographic printer Charles Troedel, in recognition of the esteem in which Syme was held by his employees, and for his 'many acts of benevolence' and 'various other kindnesses' to them, and concluding in wishing him and his family 'God speed' on their journey to England. Syme responded expressing pleasure in receiving such a flattering testimonial from persons long in his employ, and hoped that the existing friendly relations would continue.

When Syme sailed on Christmas Eve for Pointe de Galle via Adelaide on the *Bokhara*, he expected to travel via Bombay, Egypt, Brindisi or Venice to London, as he informed the Secretary of the National Mutual with which company he had a life insurance policy.[56] His wife and two sons

---

53 'The Exhibition "Director" and the Ministry', *Argus*, 23 June 1881, p. 6.
54 DS to JCS, 25 November 1880, LB2, p. 189.
55 'The Age Picnic', *Age*, 20 December 1880, p. 3.
56 'Shipping', *Age*, 25 December 1880, p. 4; DS to Secretary, National Mutual, 24 November 1880, LB2, p. 188.

CHAPTER 9

accompanied him (the girls, Lucie 10 and Olive 5, are not mentioned in any shipping records, and must have stayed behind – in whose care is not known). Although unnamed, the sons must have been Francis, then at a loose end, and Arthur, having completed his secondary schooling, and not young Geoffrey and Oswald; nor Herbert, who had completed the second year of studies towards a Law degree at the University of Melbourne and would be enrolled in Third Year in 1881. Both he and his younger brother Francis had enrolled in 1879, also receiving coaching at home in Classics and Logic from young barrister Henry Bournes Higgins, then supplementing his income, later to be a prime mover in political and judicial circles.[57] Francis did not continue after Second Year, although he obtained better results – honours in Jurisprudence and English Language and Literature – than Herbert, who in October 1881 failed a Third Year subject.[58] Persisting, Herbert successfully sat a supplementary examination in February 1882, passed all exams in Fourth Year, got a third-class honour and had his LL.B degree conferred on 2 December 1882.

The Syme contingent arrived in late March 1881 and stayed until October. Whatever work Syme did in England for the newspaper business, the record is scant. He was to see to a paper contract for Joseph, he intended to seek the support of some London newspaper editors for the Reform Bill being presented to the Victorian Parliament (it would be passed in mid-June), and he learned that English and American newspapers were supplied with meteorological information by local weather bureaus, something he cited when wanting to obtain the same on his return to Melbourne.[59] We may assume that he made some use of the new London *Age* office, furnished and containing books for reference.[60] He may have met journalist Matthew Macfie, who would become a contributor to the *Age* and later be appointed *Leader* editor (Sutherland 1888, v. 2, 489). Possibly he and Thomas King of the *South Australian Advertiser* travelled together to the Continent in September, as mooted in a letter of 26 October to Syme & Co. from the Adelaide newspaper office.[61]

---

[57] Henry Bournes Higgins, Autobiography draft, c. 1927, Higgins Papers, MS 1057, Series 3, National Library of Australia.

[58] University of Melbourne Student records for Herbert John Syme and Francis George Syme, Melbourne University Archives.

[59] DS to R. Ellery, 18 January 1882, LB2, p. 192.

[60] London Office Furniture, Furniture Register, SFP Box 1186/4.

[61] Burden & King to DS & Co., 26 October 1881, J.L. Bonython and Company, Summary Record, Letter Books, BRG 10, Series 8, State Library of South Australia.

There is no indication that Syme had anything to do with his sister-in-law Jane – and no reason for him to do so. Filing for divorce from Robert Palk on 17 March 1880, on the grounds of his adultery with and bigamous marriage to Anne Helmore in 1877, she obtained a decree nisi on 10 May 1881 and a final decree 22 November 1881.[62] If the end of the unhappy Palk saga, this did not mark the end of upheavals for her. On 26 May 1882 she married Irish doctor William Galgey and travelled with him to the United States, where he died in 1884.[63] She then made New Zealand her home for the rest of her life, spending some of her years caring for children of her son James Syme (M. Syme 2013, 59), and dying herself in Auckland, in 1912.[64]

Reception of *Representative Government*

In a letter dated 9 April Syme told Pearson that he visited the publishing house of Kegan Paul with his manuscript.[65] Publication was agreed to, with autumn being considered the best time. He wrote from 'Bamboro Grange', a farmhouse where he had been for some weeks, in a 'very out of the way part of Yorkshire' perhaps at or near relatives of Annabella. He said his health was no better, but at least not worse. He had been spending the time rewriting his manuscript and was extremely grateful for Pearson's helpful annotations and revisions, which had enabled him to correct several serious errors. He would like to have talked with him more about the manuscript, and did not feel very confident.

The Publication Account Books of Kegan Paul, Trench & Co. (Kegan Paul took on the young Alfred Trench as a partner in 1881) show that 500 copies of *Representative Government in England: Its Faults and Failures* were printed and bound on 18 October 1881. The book did modestly well. The edition was quickly used up: in 1881 the number of copies for presentation, review and library legal deposit totalled 60; a further 266 were put on sale in Australia through George Robertson and 156 were sold in Britain. The book was re-issued in 1882, with 500 copies printed and 73 copies sold. In 1883 90 copies were destroyed in the fire at the publisher's warehouse; in Melbourne sales of 133 copies by George Robertson were recorded. Thereafter sales

---

[62] Divorce Court file 6785, wife's petition. Records of the Supreme Court of Judicature and related courts, J 77/239/6785, The National Archives.

[63] Family History Report, Ebenezer Syme and Jane Hilton Rowan, dated 23 October 2009, supplied by Pru Williams, descendant.

[64] Death certificate 1912/4074, www.dia.govt.nz/Births-deaths-and-marriages.

[65] DS to C. Pearson, 9 April 1881, Pearson Papers, MS 7498, Box 440/8b.

CHAPTER 9

dwindled to an annual handful, with 393 of the 1000 printed still on hand in July 1897. Kegan Paul advertised the book in December 1881, June 1882 and June 1885. We do not know what income Syme received from the publication (or if he paid a publishing fee, as he had for *Outlines of an Industrial Science*), as there is no contract or memorandum of agreement on file.

The subtitle of Syme's 220-page book indicates that it is a severe critique. Indeed, the introduction claims that modern British administrations are weak, due to the failure of party government, and advocates a return to 'pre-reform times' – that is, well before the Glorious Revolution of 1688. The next chapter traces the development of English parliamentary government from medieval times. Successive chapters analyse and attack, in turn: the composition and operation of present-day parliaments; government by 'party'; 'outside pressure' including the press; and Cabinet powers. A final chapter expands proposals hinted at in the introduction.

To a considerable extent these apparently backward-looking views were shared and had been publicised by Pearson in two articles on democratic government that had appeared in the *Fortnightly Review* during 1879 (Pearson 1879a–b). The topic would also be explored in his book *National Life and Character* (1893), published the year before his death. Greg Melleuish examines and points up similarities in the ideas propounded by the two men, calling Syme's 'very definite and interesting, if somewhat idiosyncratic' (Melleuish 2009, 214). He concludes that the ideas expressed by each amount to the view that 'the will of the majority found its true expression in the actions of a supervising state', a view of democracy that would 'have a big future in Australia' (227).

Syme's book was first advertised in the *Age* on 10 January 1882, as available from the bookshops of George Robertson and Samuel Mullen. A two-part summary, conjecturally written by Pearson, was published in the daily on 21 and 25 January. It presents Syme's book as a guide to remedying the chaotic state of government through providing systemic accountability to constituents, and welcomes it as an important contribution to constitutional discussion in 'this country' (Victoria), though written primarily for England. As to be expected, the *Argus* coverage, in its 'Current Literature' feature on 4 February, was dismissive, claiming that, while the system of government in England and the colonies was not perfect, it was doubtful there could be any better one, and pointing out that David Syme and his school of radical doctrinaires were in a great hurry that the world should be perfect.

During 1882 Syme's book and the ideas in it were discussed prominently in issues of the *Melbourne Review*. Reviewed by 'A.D.' (doubtless Deakin) in the 'Editor's Library Table' of the January number, it was praised for its 'finished literary workmanship', the style likened to that of John Stuart Mill (A.D. 1882). It was seen as 'pregnant with suggestions', the necessity for reform depicted 'in a masterly way'. The April issue has an article 'Personal Government' by New South Wales politician and writer William Forster (1882a), discussing Syme's ideas without naming him or his book; similarly, Forster's 'Democratic Government' in the October number discusses the declining standards of colonial governments without reference to Syme or his book (Forster 1882b). The same number has a lengthy review by Gilbert Elliot (1882), praising *Representative Government* for its 'laborious collection of facts and logical reasoning in using them' and regarding it as useful to students of the British Constitution but concluding that, while 'very much in agreement with Syme', he saw 'no earthly chance of obtaining a hearing' for his scheme.

But Syme was primarily addressing an English readership. One wonders how this censure from a colonial newspaperman would have been taken. It was hardly likely to have been well received from a person resident in the Antipodes and by no means in or close to the corridors of political power in the 'home' country or moving in learned and intellectual circles there. An advertisement for the book in the *Age* of 2 May 1882 includes favourable if guarded observations from reviews in seven English periodicals – the *Graphic* of 12 December 1881, ('well worth reading' and his chapter on early parliaments 'full of interesting facts'); the *Westminster Review* ('thoughtful and independent' but 'cannot agree with all conclusions'); the January issue of the *British Quarterly* ('interesting and instructive'); the *Academy* of 11 February (an 'interesting book', now that a new Reform Bill is 'the goal of the present Parliament'). However, a notice included in Syme's *On the Modification of Organisms*, published in 1890, quotes only the fairly faint praise in the *British Quarterly*, including the author's 'happy knack of writing on abstruse topics with force and felicity', and recognising 'that he has investigated as well as thought for himself'. The book found its way into several major libraries outside Australia: the British Library and the library of Oxford University (both would have received legal deposit copies), the library of the Sorbonne in Paris and the National Library of Canada.

There are some puzzling and unanswerable questions relating to Syme's *Representative Government*. In producing it for London publication, was the author yet again trying to be part of a discourse in England, in spite of having recognised the obstacles to this? That he does not appear to have followed up the reviewing of his book, as he had previously done, and there

CHAPTER 9

is nothing on file to indicate his views about his treatment by the publisher and the adequacy of publicity and reviewing (although there is always the possibility such material has been lost), suggest a certain disillusionment on his part after its appearance. And why the ferocity of his attacks on party government, which seem utterly at variance with his and the *Age*'s partisanship during the previous 20 or more years – albeit Victoria was entering a period of political depolarisation, with a Coalition government prevailing during the 1880s?

Not discussed by Melleuish, but very revealing of Syme's views about the role of the newspaper press, is his treatment of the press in Chapter IV of *Representative Government in England*, entitled 'Outside Pressure'. This is one of Syme's few writings on the subject. By no means idiosyncratic here, he is aligning himself with the mainstream view that had developed during the 1870s in Victoria, of the press as a beneficent educational influence, through the spread of ideas: 'The newspaper press has been especially useful as an educating agency, particularly of late years' (p. 122). This educational emphasis was part of a wider acceptance in the later 19th-century of the newspaper press as essential to the machinery and functioning of a parliamentary democracy, being a major means of informing the electorate. Stating that the press 'at once forms and expresses public opinion' (p. 123), Syme then proceeds to qualify this general and perhaps simplistic statement, pointing out the fact that, as manifested by divergent election results in Britain, the press does not always represent public opinion. He also stresses the great diversity of newspapers, and asserts that 'mere circulation' is no test of influence, some papers with a small circulation having a greater influence (p. 124). Considering his successful efforts to achieve a large circulation for the *Age*, and the accompanying pride expressed in the paper, this seems paradoxically disingenuous. A similar contradiction is apparent in the view expressed in the *Contemporary Review* in 1886 by W.T. Stead, editor of the London *Pall Mall Gazette* who is known to posterity for popularising 'new journalism', not to say sensationalism: 'Circulation is all very well, and the larger circulation any newspaper has the better for its proprietor; but influence depends not half so much upon quantity as upon the quality of its subscribers' (Stead 1886b, 671).

A striking element for the reader today of Syme's mini-disquisition is his imaginative evocation of the power of *en masse*, of simultaneous newspaper reading: '[The press] brings every day to every fireside information on every subject that can interest mankind, and on every event that transpires throughout the civilized world…every newspaper reader participates, becomes as it were, a member of that vast assembly which may be said to embrace the whole nation, so widely are newspapers now read' (pp. 122–123). Stead calls up a similar picture: 'The telegraph and the printing-press have converted Great Britain into a vast agora…in which the discussion of the affairs of State is carried on from day to day in the hearing of the whole people' (Stead 1886a, 654), and journalists have to 'write afresh from day to day the only Bible which millions read' (663). Both writers are conceiving the resultant effect of newspaper reading as arising from the aggregation of individual responses, much as expounded a century later by Benedict Anderson, in his *Imagined Communities*, seeing 'the newspaper as a mass ceremony' daily 'performed in silent privacy' yet 'replicated simultaneously by thousands (or millions) of others' (1991, 35). Syme would further enunciate his views about the newspaper press when drafting his memoirs some 26 years later. Therein more parallels with Stead are to be seen.

Joseph deputises

During Syme's absence, when his junior partner Joseph was in charge, there were several innovations. One was the installation of a telephone. In August 1880 the Melbourne Telephone Exchange came into operation, the first in Australia and very likely impelled by the imminence of the Melbourne International Exhibition to open in December. An engineering firm was the first subscriber, the Exhibition the second (Melbourne Telephone Exchange Co. 1882). There followed merchants, insurance companies, and banks. The first newspaper business to have a telephone, the *Age* office became subscriber no. 49 in 1881, with a 'set' there, and another at Reuters Melbourne agency.[66] The *Herald* Office followed soon after (no. 56); the *Daily Telegraph* was no. 113 and the *Argus* considerably later at no. 171. The *World*, a penny daily that would run from November 1881 to June 1885, was no. 191. Syme would always discourage use of the telephone by journalists, however. Thorold Waters, an *Age* reporter from 1899 to 1904, wrote that the single phone then in the editorial and literary department was not usually to be used, Syme's principle being that staff should 'go out after [the facts] and see and estimate [their] informants' (Waters 1951, 20).

Further communication devices were introduced to the office in 1881, surely instigated by Joseph in Syme's absence. Several speaking tubes were installed for inter-office communication: Joseph to manager Macdonald

---

[66] Furniture Register, SFP Box 1186/4.

CHAPTER 9

and to the Counter; Macdonald also to the Counter; and the printer to the reader.[67] In 1882 another two were fitted: Joseph to Syme, and Syme to the printer.

A *Leader* literary competition prize was awarded while Syme was away. First advertised on 13 November 1880, before his departure, was a *Leader* offer of a prize for an original tale set in Australia, something the weekly *Sydney Mail* had done in 1879. Scores of stories were submitted, among them, pseudonymously, Ada Cambridge's 'A Girl's Ideal'. Several of Cambridge's novels had been serialised in the *Australasian* and, a runner-up in the *Sydney Mail* competition, she was on the way to becoming a leading novelist of Australia's colonial period. This story was one of three commended but, seen as too short, not awarded the £100 prize.[68] In December 1881 and January 1882 it was serialised in the *Age* (not the *Leader*). This was the first of what would be several very successful serialisations of Cambridge's fiction in Syme's newspapers and the start of her being weaned away from the *Australasian*. 'A Girl's Ideal' also appeared in the *Australian Town and Country Journal*, weekly companion to the *Evening News* and rival to the *Sydney Mail*, while an offer to Burden & King for the *South Australian Advertiser* or *Observer* was provisionally declined because arrangements had already been made for 'stories'.[69] In these years serials (and the rights to them) were frequently offered to and shared amongst metropolitan newspapers of the several colonies. This is especially evident between David Syme & Co. and Burden & King (later Burden & Bonython).

Syme, his wife and three (not two) sons returned on 10 December 1881, on the *Carthage* from London, not via New York and San Francisco as he had contemplated before he left Melbourne 12 months before.[70] Herbert, who arrived in Adelaide from Melbourne on 7 December, joined the *Carthage* and his family there for the final leg of their return voyage.[71]

Scarcely back in Melbourne, Syme became the owner of Blythswood (fig. 9.2), a 14-acre property in the Melbourne suburb of Kew some six kilometres from the city centre, on the banks of the Yarra River.[72] It would be the David Syme family residence for the rest of his life. By 17 February

---

67 Buildings Register, SFP Box 1187/1.
68 'The "Leader" Prize Novel Competition', *Leader*, 8 October 1881, p. 16.
69 Burden & King to DS & Co., 18 October 1881, Bonython & Co. Letter Books.
70 'Shipping', *Age*, 12 December 1881, p. 2.
71 'Shipping News', *South Australian Advertiser*, 8 December 1881, p. 4.
72 For a detailed description, see 'Blythswood', in Condon (2005).

Figure 9.2. Blythswood, home of David Syme and family from 1882. (Courtesy of Fairfax Media, with permission from Dr Veronica Condon)

1882 he proposed making additions to the two-storey brick-rendered house and surrounds, providing a conservatory and various outbuildings.[73] The property was turned into virtually a small farm. With milking cows and an extensive kitchen garden, the family of seven children could be fed with a degree of self-sufficiency. When they moved in is uncertain. The 1882 *Sands & McDougall's* directory, which would have collected its information in late 1881 when Syme was still away, lists it as his residence. The first of Syme's letters on record to be explicitly written there is dated 19 October 1883.[74]

Age circulation breaks records

The partnership of the now prospering newspaper business of David Syme & Co. was due to expire on 1 January 1884. All three newspapers were growing in size, expanding in content and increasing in circulation. The circulation of the *Age* in July 1879 was 38,000 and rising, while that of the *Argus* was

---

[73] DS to National Fire Insurance Co., 17 February 1882, LB2, p. 193.
[74] DS to T. Watson, 19 October 1883, LB2, p. 217.

CHAPTER 9

11,400 and would remain about that figure to 1881.[75] A letter of 5 June from expatriate *Argus* proprietor Lauchlan Mackinnon to James Johnston, who in Melbourne represented his interests, expresses great concern about the *Age* success (with advertisements and circulation), seeing it as 'an opponent' that cannot be ignored.[76] Indeed, the *Age* in November 1881 published a 'certificate' from accountants Danby and Gilmour, that the circulation was now 45,306 daily, together with the claim that would be reiterated for the decade or so that it held true: 'Its issue is now the largest of any daily newspaper in the British Empire out of London, and is there exceeded by only five of the leading journals.'[77]

First published in Syme's absence, the claim may well have been supplied by him, based on information available from the newspaper directories with international reach that (targeted at potential advertisers) were beginning to appear (L. Brown 1985, 52; Morrison 2005, 250). However, it is unlikely that this grand assertion was then (or is now) completely verifiable. Certainly the circulations of leading Canadian dailies (the *Montreal Star* and *Toronto Globe*) were less than half that of the *Age* (L. Brown 1985, 49, 53, 59). But in the United Kingdom outside London (whose leading daily papers had circulations well over 200,000), dailies in Liverpool, Birmingham and Newcastle were at the least not far behind the *Age* – and by 1892 the *Newcastle Daily Chronicle*, at 120,000, would be well ahead. But it is highly likely that, although exact figures are not available, Glasgow daily newspapers would disprove the claim. In 1881 Glasgow had a population of 511,000 (Checkland 1989, 41) – almost twice that of Melbourne at 288,169 – and its *Herald* is noted in *Deacon's Newspaper Directory* of 1881 as having a 'great circulation'. Be that as it may, the *Age* claim, undoubtedly holding true in the 19th century for the British Empire *outside Britain*, has received unquestioning approbation and reiteration down the years.

By April 1883 the circulation had risen to 50,480.[78] The physical size of the *Age* was also on the increase. From 1881, issues frequently included supplements. By July 1883 most weekday issues were eight pages and the Saturday eight-page issues, with four-page supplements, were effectively enlarged to 12.

---

[75] 'Circulation of The Age', *Age*, 4 July 1879, p. 2; 'Circulation', 'Historical Records of "The Argus" and "The Australasian" ', compiled by C.P. Smith, [1924], MS 10727, Australian Manuscripts Collection, State Library of Victoria.

[76] L. Mackinnon to J. Johnston, 5 June 1881, James Stewart Johnston Correspondence, University of Melbourne Archives.

[77] *Age*, 25 November 1881, p. 2, col. 4.

[78] *Age*, 7 April 1883, p. 4, col. 6.

The *Leader* also was enlarged – to 48 pages on 30 September 1882. In 1884 it was acclaimed by an English newspaper for its 'journalistic enterprise' and to be 'peculiarly entertaining to Engishmen who have friends in Australia, or who are in any way concerned in the development of that promising and prosperous country'.[79] 'Under the Verandah', the weekly round-up of local, mainly political-personal news and gossip that began in 1867, continued to be much appreciated. Until early 1881 written by Marcus Clarke, journalist, novelist and *bon viveur*, who had contributed to Syme's papers from 1874, after falling out with the *Argus* management, as earlier mentioned, it was taken over by Deakin a few months before Clarke's untimely death.

The *Illustrated Australian News* benefited for a time from the services of English artist Julian Rossi Ashton, who had joined the *Age* office staff in 1878 (as noted in Chapter 8). Brought out from London with a first-class passage and the promise of an annual salary of £300 provided he remained for three years, he moved in 1881 to the rival *Australasian Sketcher*. Perhaps he had not found Syme's directives acceptable – mid-20th-century *Age* art critic Arnold Shore (1958, 18) alluded to a 'temporary "walk-out"' after one year. In February 1880, in a letter to Joseph (mainly about cable agency business in New Zealand) Syme seemed unconcerned about artistic sensitivities: 'I got Ashtons picture half finished & stopped him, & gave him a new idea which I liked better'.[80] Perhaps anticipating Ashton's departure, in the issue of 4 December 1880, 'Artists and Amateurs' were invited to 'forward sketches and subjects and water-colored paintings suitable for special coloured supplements'. Beginning with the issue for 2 January 1882, the masthead statement of the *Illustrated Australian News* that linked the publication date to the departure for England of the monthly mailboat was dropped. While this may mark the shift of primary readership to Victoria and Australia, it does not signal the abandoning of overseas consumers, for by January 1883 there were named agents for the periodical in London, Paris and New York. Rather, it may signal the diminishing dependence on that monthly mail service, with ships departing more frequently for Europe and (out of Sydney) the United States.

The business was beginning to provide sizeable returns for the partners. Clear profit for the year 1882 was £23,815.0.8, giving £17,861.5.6 to Syme and £5953.15.2 to Joseph.[81] To this must be added their annual salaries.

---

[79] *Ipswich Journal* (UK), 19 January, p. 11.
[80] DS to JCS, 5 February 1880, LB2, pp. 180–181.
[81] Financial statements 1881–1884, SFP Box 1191/2(a).

CHAPTER 9

Under the 1878 deed, Syme's was £1250 and Joseph's initially £400, but which would have increased by 1882; in 1884 they would be, respectively, £1650 and £1250 – a lessening of the disparity, reflecting the extent of Joseph's managerial responsibilities.[82]

Partnership issues

Notwithstanding the successes, there are hints of partnership pressures surfacing in 1882 and a tricky resolution the following year, which was not altogether satisfactory to either man. A letter from Joseph to Syme in September 1882 refers to previous discussions, not to say disputes, about the need for amending the list of respective duties as defined in the existing partnership document.[83] Whatever was at issue (not stated), Joseph said he would agree to for the 'sake of settlement', but wants what appear to be unintended omissions rectified: 'clerical' added to the list of departments under his management, and 'Country agencies' added to Town and Suburban ones.[84] More difficult and contentious was Joseph's *'sine qua non'* that his name be in the imprint of the newspapers. He insisted: 'If I am fit to be a member of the firm certainly it is fit also to make that fact known.' David's draft reply, filed with Joseph's letters to him, and which presumably was sent, states his implacable opposition, on several grounds, including 'usage & custom'.[85] He concludes, at some length, with telling, affronted dignity:

> I may, without egotism consider I am the man who has made the firm a success…Surely you cannot believe that your name wd lend any influence for the firm? Why attempt to depose me from my position as the head of a firm which I have attained by hard work and a long period of servitude?

One can imagine the junior partner being similarly affronted by this rejoinder.

Whatever negotiations ensued, the records are silent until June and July 1883, when the letterbooks record four letters from David to Joseph (Joseph's to David have apparently not survived).[86] The first, seemingly prompted by

---

[82] Articles of co-partnership 1877, SFP Box 1185/3(b)[i]; Articles of co-partnership, 1883, SFP Box 1185/4(a)[i].
[83] JCS to DS, 15 September 1882, SFP Box 1180/3(a).
[84] Articles of co-partnership, 1883, SFP Box 1185/4(a)[i].
[85] DS to JCS (draft), 22 September, SFP Box 1180/3(a).
[86] DS to JCS, 21, 22, 28 June, 2 July 1883, LB2, pp. 204–205, 206, 207–208, 209.

Joseph's desire to have a greater share in the business and by protracted wrangling about this and other matters, contains David's refusal to sell his nephew an additional interest ('I…find that I cannot comply with it for reasons which it will not be necessary to explain'). Perhaps as a concession, in the letter of 22 June he agrees to both names being in the imprint, and proposes either renewal for 7 years or for 14, conceding 'the matter of the sale of the paper, for the sum named by you'. David's next letter, dated 28 June, is a detailed, somewhat cantankerous response to Joseph's numerous late additions and alterations to the draft agreement. He particularly objects to Joseph's refusing his request that in the event of Herbert's death, another son be allowed to take his place in the office. Finally, on 2 July David wrote that he was sending the 'final' version of the draft agreement. He proposed renewal for 14 years from 1 January 1884 and a salary increase for Joseph from £1000 pa to £1250 and to £1500 five years later. There is no mention of the employment-of-a-son provision. With Herbert on the staff and only one son permitted employment there was no position for Francis (whether or not he wanted one), who had abandoned his legal studies.

The new deed of partnership is dated 4 July 1883.[87] It is for 14 years, from 1 January 1884. That is, it would expire on 1 January 1898, in David's 71st year. The new imprint first appeared on the *Age* on Friday 6 July 1883, reading: 'Printed and published for the Proprietors, David Syme and Joseph Cowen Syme, under the style of David Syme & Co, at the *Age* office, Collins-street east, Melbourne.' This was almost as Joseph had asked; only 'under the style of' was substituted for his 'trading as', a phrase ridiculed by David in his letter of 22 September 1882.

While Joseph has been considered an asset to the firm (Deakin wrote that he 'proved himself a 1st class business man')[88] and David must have benefited from his taking care of technical matters, leaving him freer to focus on the content and appearance of the newspapers, it seems that disputatious and acrimonious relations were inexorably developing. Although we cannot with any certainty fathom David Syme's motives and intentions relating to negotiations about partnership, we may have some idea of the complex of contradictory obligations and ambitions that virtually tied his hands. As brother and business partner of the late Ebenezer, he appears to have been as bound by family ties and a sense of equity as he had been when his brother died more than 20 years earlier; hence his acceptance of the bar

---

[87] Articles of co-partnership, 1883, SFP Box 1185/4(a).
[88] Autobiographical notes, Deakin Papers, Series 3/290a.

CHAPTER 9

on employment in the *Age* office for four of his five sons, surely a matter of deep concern. He had to accept Joseph's stake in the business, so long as the latter wanted it (as indeed he seemed to). Now a leading public figure in Victoria, producing influential newspapers for the masses, at which he had been outstandingly successful, continued to be the driving force of his life. But whether the partnership would help or hinder him over the years it had to run was by no means clear.

Chapter 10

'EXPEDITION IS EVERYTHING IN NEWSPAPER WORK'

(August 1883 to December 1887)

When the partners David and Joseph Syme were both working at the *Age* office and able to consult in person about managerial and operational matters, written communication between them was generally confined to issues relating to the partnership agreement. Thus, in August 1883 Joseph wrote to his uncle and senior partner that he wanted a year's holiday in 1884 with the same conditions as Syme had had for his absence from December 1880 to December 1881 – namely, full pay and £250 expenses.[1] Syme agreed in writing, pointing out this was in line with the terms of the existing agreement.[2] Joseph's absence for 1884 was actually very much a working holiday, however, with letters between the two mostly about the practicalities of running the business, including the procurement of staff and equipment. They are testimony to what was on the whole a productive working partnership. While there were points of difference, both were making efforts to cooperate for the sake of the business. Joseph appears to have managed it competently during Syme's absence of nine months in 1887, although no correspondence between the two survives for this period – only three letters from Syme to his son Herbert.[3]

Building expansion

Syme was energetically active during 1884 on several fronts. Early in the year he was looking for expanded or new premises for David Syme & Co., something he had discussed with Joseph before his departure. By letter

---

[1] JCS to DS, 16 August 1883, SFP Box 1180/3(a).
[2] DS to JCS, 17 August 1883, LB2, p. 212.
[3] DS to H. Syme, 11 April, 2, 23 June 1887, SFP Box 1180/5(f).

CHAPTER 10

he kept the junior partner informed and also was in contact with nephew William, who had power of attorney during Joseph's absence.[4] Joseph's responses to Syme's various proposals for leasing and purchasing additional property were cautious but not entirely negative.[5] Syme too had some reservations, eventually preferring simply that the firm buy the Collins Street property, which they had been leasing. In October the partners purchased it for £16,000. Syme told nephew William that he was short of money, understood Joseph was too, and had borrowed the sum at a favourable 5½ per cent interest from a client of his lawyer Samuel Gillott, and taken out a mortgage.[6] As profits from the newspaper business were quite handsome, and increasing (£20,126 in 1883, £22,945 in 1884), the cash-flow problems of the partners may well have arisen in part from their respective private real estate investing.[7]

Acquisition of freehold in the existing premises did not solve the need for additional space or provide for continued production in the case of fire (a severe hazard for newspaper and printing businesses). Housing was needed for the two new Hoe high-speed rotary printing machines, ordered by Joseph when in England in 1884. Following their arrival in January and March 1885 cranes were obtained to hoist and move these and the three Victory machines.[8] On 24 December tenders were called for the purchase and removal of the old building behind, which had a frontage to a lane (known informally as Monaghans Lane) accessed from Monaghans Place, parallel to Swanston Street.[9] Designed by William Salway, this 'Back Building', as it was named in the Buildings Register, was largely completed by November 1886, at a cost of £11,000. Syme had chosen his architect well. Salway, who had trained with Reed and Barnes, by the 1880s was recognised as a leader in the field. With a 'free Italianate classical style' his buildings ranged from imposing warehouses to institutional premises (the Athenaeum Club in 1889) and 'grand land boom residences' (Trethowan 2012).

---

[4] DS to JCS and W. Syme, 14 February to 27 October 1884: LB2, pp. 241, 251, 253–254, 271–273, 283–284, 289, 290–291, 306.
[5] JCS to DS, 24 May, 25 July, 15 August, SFP Box 1180/3(b).
[6] DS to W. Syme, 27 October 1884, LB2, p. 306.
[7] Financial statements 1881–1884 and 1885–1890, SFP Box 1191/2(a) and 1191/2(b).
[8] Machinery Register, 1871–1888, SFP Box 1186/1.
[9] Buildings Register, 1879–1937, SFP Box 1187/1; 'The *Age* New Premises, Monaghans Lane', *Illustrated Australian News*, 15 November 1886, pp. 186 (text), 188 (illustration).

Figure 10.1. The *Age* 'Back Building', 1886. (Pictures Collection, State Library of Victoria, IAN13/11/86/188)

The brick-and-iron Back Building (fig. 10.1), appeared much plainer than the main *Age* office fronting Collins Street, albeit in harmony with it. Flying bridges connected the different floors of the two. Able to be shut off and claimed to be fireproof, the new one was planned not only to provide extra storage, but more particularly to duplicate the essential components of production, thus to ensure uninterrupted operation in case of fire. While the basement was a machine room, the ground floor accommodated the machinists and had bathrooms and lavatories; a mezzanine floor housed literary staff (presumably in emergency). The first floor comprised a storeroom and offices; the second included the *Leader* composing room and stereotyping machines; the *Age* composing room occupied the top floor; and the roof (attic) provided (proof) readers' rooms and lavatories.

With Joseph taking responsibility for technical and practical matters, Syme was heavily involved in managing the editorial and literary side, working and scheming to broaden newspaper content and so keep pace with if not outrun the *Argus*. In these years of coalition government he was less directly involved in Victorian colonial politics than formerly, less challenged to drive forward political policies in the teeth of party opposition. From 1883 to 1886, Conservative James Service was Premier and the once radical Graham Berry, in whom 'the progressive…was in retreat', was Chief Secretary (Strangio 2006, 68). They were followed by the ministry of Conservative Premier Duncan Gillies with Liberal Deakin his deputy, in power until 1890. Deakin was no longer writing as regularly for the *Age*, but was in close touch with Syme and Windsor, calling at the newspaper office every week or so and also in contact outside it – in 1884, for instance, a visit to Macedon in February and a dinner at the Syme household in September, along with Pearson, Windsor and others.[10] We can only guess at the conversations, but may assume at least a communication channel for political developments and a two-way exchange of information and opinion.

While Syme had a huge capacity for hard work, he did not carry his responsibilities lightly. He was a constant worrier, particularly about obtaining suitable staff. He wrote about this to George Levey in 1883, when he did have some grounds of concern about editing of the *Age*.[11] Pearson was unsettled, contemplating joining his wife then in England (though he did not go). Syme was again anxious in 1884 when Windsor was ill and had several protracted absences.[12] For editorial and literary direction, Pearson was invaluable on all the major issues arising, whether local or international (Tregenza 1968, 159–197). He knew this, writing to a close friend in July 1884, when Windsor had been absent for two months: 'If either Robinson [commercial editor] or I broke down, I cannot conceive what would become of the *Age*' (Tregenza 1968, 195). It was fortunate that Windsor soon returned, because Pearson went to England for the first half of 1885. Syme refused to give him a retainer while away, but agreed to increase his

---

[10] Diary entries for 8 February, 7 September 1884, Alfred Deakin Papers, Series 2, MS 1540, National Library of Australia.
[11] DS to G. Levey, 23 October 1883, LB2, p. 222.
[12] DS to JCS, 19 May 1884, LB2, pp. 265–266.

rate of remuneration on return.[13] His continuing reliance on Pearson is indicated in August 1886, when he requested two leaders rather than one per week and wanted this increased to four or five, should Pearson's political commitments decrease;[14] this at a time when Windsor had been hinting at resigning — something that Syme discouraged, granting him instead a month's holiday.[15]

In April 1886 Syme made a formal arrangement with Charles Bright as another backstop for Windsor.[16] For several years, based in Sydney he had travelled intercolonially and overseas, delivering lectures on a range of subjects, including his speciality, spiritualism. In January 1886 he returned to Melbourne.[17] Not listed in the staff Wages Book until 1892, however, he must have been paid as a contributor, as was Pearson. In October 1886, at Robinson's suggestion Syme engaged Alexander Bell, also on a payment by contribution basis until he joined the staff from 8 January 1887 as an 'editor', his actual duties now unknown.[18] At £13 per week, he was paid less than Windsor (£20) and Robinson (£15) but more than *Leader* editor Macfie (£10) and agricultural editor Dow (£8).[19]

Syme's eldest son, Herbert, appears in the financial records as on the editorial and literary staff in 1884.[20] As the first partnership agreement with Joseph specifically allowed his employment in the business, the 1883 renewal implies his presence in the firm. Most likely Herbert started that year after his graduation in Law (there are no staff lists extant for the years 1881 to 1883 to check this). In 1884, when his annual salary was a lowly £109.4s (2 guineas a week), he may have been learning the ropes under the direction of his father and Windsor. He also had the opportunity to try his hand at journalism, being paid the quite considerable sum of £42 that year for contributions to the *Leader*. His salary was increased to £5 a week in 1886, and £7 in 1887 when he had more responsibility during his father's absence

---

[13] DS to C. Pearson, 1 January 1885, LB2, p. 317.
[14] DS to C. Pearson, 10 August 1886, LB2, p. 410.
[15] DS to A. Windsor, 23 July 1886, LB2, p. 407.
[16] DS to C. Bright, 15 April 1886, LB2, p. 397.
[17] 'Bijou Theatre' [advertisement], *Age*, 27 January 1886, p. 1.
[18] DS to A. Bell, 12, 15 October 1886, LB2, pp. 415, 416; David Syme & Co. Staff Wages Book 1886–1937, MS 10602, Australian Manuscripts Collection, State Library of Victoria (hereafter referred to as Wages Book), p. 27.
[19] Entries for Dow, Macfie, Robinson and Windsor in Wages Book, pp. 103, 339, 421, 525.
[20] Financial statement, 1884, SFP Box 1191/2(a).

CHAPTER 10

overseas.[21] In late 1887, after Syme was back and while Joseph was away, Herbert took charge of printing, machine maintenance and stock keeping, all of which he was interested in (perhaps more so than the editorial and literary side).[22]

As staff numbers increased, Syme's relationship with most of his journalists beyond hiring and firing became somewhat removed. More often than not, in correspondence with contributors he was conveying what he said were Windsor's decisions, requests, or recommendations. Given Syme's characteristic autocratic methods and minimal delegating, it cannot be determined to what extent he was simply using Windsor's name, and how much he had in fact delegated. In any case, it was he rather than Windsor writing to the contributing journalists. And it is to be inferred from letters he wrote from England in 1887 that he had accorded Herbert a degree of oversight and responsibility in his department, notwithstanding Windsor's seniority. Writing from London on 2 June, he advised his son: 'You will discover if you have not already, that the finding of suitable subjects [for editorials] entails a great deal of time, & that the sub-editing is a matter that wants a great deal of attention'.[23]

Syme's own attention is evident from the multitude of memos to his subeditors over the years. From November 1883 until he resigned in July 1885 subeditor Westlake received a series of written complaints, carping about contents and omissions, although paradoxically Syme expressed regret at his departure.[24] He was replaced by John Stephens, already on the reporting staff, who would receive the same treatment. Formal and fairly courteous for a few years, the tone of Syme's memos to him later became unremittingly querulous, amounting to complaints after the fact rather than instructions beforehand.[25] A memorable 'character' and undaunted by Syme's onslaughts, Stephens would hold the position until retirement in 1935. The flamboyant Randolph Bedford, suburban correspondent and contributor to the *Age* for several years from the late 1880s, called him the 'doyen of sub-editors' (1976, 332). To William Robinson (son of Arthur, the commercial editor) who joined the staff in 1897, he was the 'grand' Stephens

---

21 Entry for J.H. Syme in Wages Book, p. 441.
22 DS to JCS, 23 December 1887, LB3, pp. 26–28.
23 DS to H. Syme, 2 June 1887, SFP Box 1180/5(f).
24 For example, DS to Westlake, 9 November 1883, 1 July 1885, LB2, pp. 225, 351.
25 The first of some 125 from DS to J. Stephens, copied into the letterbooks, is LB2, p. 384, dated 9 November 1885.

(Robinson 1967, 22). A counter to Syme's acerbic, peremptory tone, from which one might infer a browbeaten subeditor, it is helpful to have George Cockerill's impressions. An *Age* reporter from 1898, he described Stephens as 'a fine figure of a man…nearly 6 ft high, square-shouldered, kindly blue eyes and the most generous of countenances', who had a keen sense of humour (Cockerill 1943?, 53). If Syme did not show his appreciation of Stephens in the workplace, he was indeed fortunate to have his services, and would mark this fact in his last will and testament.

Syme's abrasive manner to subordinates is seen also in his attitude to his head of the reporting staff, a position evolving into 'chief of staff', a term that would later become standard usage at the *Age* office. He seems to have slowly become aware of the need for such a position, from 1884 to 1886 dividing the oversight of the reporters between two men – C.G. Coulson, sporting writer for the *Leader*, and H. Humphries.[26] In May 1885 he gave a few instructions to Humphries, outlining duties that seem to overlap with those of the subeditor and containing a vague directive implying a need for change: 'I wish you to understand that you are to be guided in the management of your staff by no traditions of any kind, or by what may have been the style of doing things in this office.'[27] Both men resigned in 1886, Humphries, after demotion in April, leaving in May.[28] Possibly not appointed until 1888, reporter G. Allen was an unsatisfactory replacement.[29] The position was not settled until Syme made Gottfried Schuler chief of staff, most likely in 1890 after Allen left.[30]

Looking at the relations between Syme and his middle management staff, one has the impression of some muddle if not ineptitude – not about the desired outcomes, but about lines of responsibility, degrees of delegation and modes of management. Quick to assign blame, he interfered in matters that one would expect to be under the control of the editor – that is, Windsor. From today's perspective, as David Syme & Co. was evolving into a large organisation, there appears to have been a degree of disorder in the editorial and literary department, albeit more than offset by the considerable talents of the staff and by the policy input from the senior partner.

---

[26] DS to G. Coulson, 9 August 1884, LB2, p. 294.
[27] DS to H. Humphries, 29 May 1885, LB2, p. 344.
[28] DS to H. Humphries, 21 April 1886, LB2, p. 398.
[29] DS to JCS, 17 February 1888, LB4.16–19.
[30] Entry for Schuler in Wages Book, p. 441.

CHAPTER 10

In 1883 George Syme, who had edited the *Leader* for more than 20 years, turned 60 and contemplated retirement and a return to England.[31] Leaving the firm in 1884, he retained a keen interest in the *Age* and *Leader* and, settling again in Melbourne after a trip to England, continued to contribute to both papers. Beset by ill health throughout his life, on 2 April 1885 he wrote to David from London that he was never out of trouble, having fallen on a kerbstone, and developed a cold, rheumatic seizure and shivering fits.[32] By this time, Syme had engaged Matthew Macfie for two years to edit and subedit the *Leader* and be free to supplement his income with leading articles for it and the *Age*.[33]

Macfie had studied theology for many years in England and worked as an educationist in Canada. Returning to England he took up journalism for the London *Daily Telegraph* and then for the *Standard*, until a breakdown in health brought about his resignation and migration to Victoria (Sutherland 1888, v.2, 489). On Syme's invitation, perhaps after meeting him in London in 1881, he had become a contributor to the *Age*. In mid-1886 Windsor expressed some doubts about Macfie's continuing in this senior position on the *Leader*, thinking he should confine to himself to work for the *Age*.[34] There were problems in early 1887 when Syme was away, and Macfie was given a change of duties. Perhaps the trouble lay with editorial responsibility and staff supervision and not the actual journalism, for Syme wrote to Herbert in June that he wanted him to continue writing articles (for the *Age*?), and the 'Week' (for the *Leader*).[35] He resigned, however, in October 1887 after Syme's return, and moved to the less demanding task of editing the official catalogue for the 1888–89 Centennial International Exhibition.[36]

A congenial and more suitably resilient Henry Short replaced him in November and would edit the *Leader* for 36 years. Syme had actually approached him in 1879 about subediting it.[37] Having earlier worked for the *Argus*, Short had been news editor of the Melbourne *Daily Telegraph* for four years before he 'flitted across' to the *Leader*, leaving 'the aroma of many happy memories behind him', as Benjamin Hoare (1927, 133) recalled.

---

[31] DS to G. Levey, 23 October 1883, LB2, p. 222.
[32] G. Syme to DS, 2 April 1885, SFP Box 1180/4(a).
[33] DS to M. Macfie, 20, 21 January 1885, LB2, pp. 322, 323.
[34] DS to M. Macfie, 30 August 1886, LB2, p. 412.
[35] DS to H. Syme, 2 June 1887, SFP Box 1180/5(f).
[36] Entry for Macfie in Wages Book, p. 339.
[37] DS to H. Short, 5 March 1879, LB2, p. 161.

Hoare, in 1887 about to join the Melbourne *Daily Telegraph*, would move across to the *Age* office in 1892. Theodore Fink, then a solicitor and journalist, was recruited in July 1884 through his friend Deakin to write 'Under the Verandah' for the *Leader*, which he did for some years, as Atticus. Under the guidance of Windsor, he also wrote leaders for the *Age*, gaining valuable experience with a daily paper and an acquaintance with Syme that would prove useful later when he was chairman of directors of the *Herald* press group (Garden 1998, 32–33).

From the end of 1883 the *Age* was enlarged to 16 pages on Saturdays, and sometimes also on weekdays. The new Hoe printing machines facilitated the production of more and larger papers. The *Age* circulation was steadily rising – from 52,562 in October 1883 to some 72,000 in December 1887 – increased market penetration measured both in terms of Melbournian and Victorian demographics (for Melbourne a ratio of paper to persons of 1:6 becoming 1:5; for Victoria more dramatically, 1:17 to 1:14).[38] The *Age* circulation was still some four or more times bigger than that of the *Argus*, which was 11,400 in 1881 rising to 20,000 in 1889; no figures are available for the interim, in spite of its price reduction to twopence in July 1884.[39] Joseph's report from London of 15 August concludes with the hope that this reduction would not be 'hurting us'.[40] But Syme's letter of 11 July, which Joseph was yet to receive, would tell him that 'after a weeks trial of the Argus at 2d we find it has affected the Age less than 400 copies'.[41] Syme was never complacent, however, monitoring the volume of advertisements, as well as circulation. In mid-1884 he was temporarily worried that it was a 'dull time with advertisers'; in December 1887 he noted a 'large increase', requiring larger pages and even more of them.[42]

The *Leader* continued to contain 48 pages, with regular Easter, Melbourne Show (September), Cup Day (November) and Christmas supplements. While the cover price remained at sixpence, the intercolonial subscription rates were reduced in 1884. The Contents list was revamped, in new type, in June 1887. It was clearer to read, but carried less detail.

---

[38] 'The Age', *Age*, 25 October 1883, p. 4; DS to JCS, 23 December 1887, LB3, pp. 26–28.
[39] 'Circulation', Historical Records of "The Argus" and "The Australasian", 1846–1923, comp. C.P. Smith, [1924], MS 10727, Australian Manuscripts Collection, State Library of Victoria.
[40] JCS to DS, 15 August 1884, SFP Box 1180/3(b).
[41] DS to JCS, 11 July 1884, LB2, pp. 290–291.
[42] DS to JCS, 21 April 1884, LB2, p. 257; 23 December 1887, LB3, pp. 26–28.

CHAPTER 10

Syme wanted news and he wanted it fast. In December 1884 he instructed a correspondent sent to New Caledonia: 'pray bear in mind that <u>expedition</u> is everything in newspaper work – that the news must not only be got but must be dispatched by the quickest means of conveyance & at the shortest moment.'[43] The telegraph (cable) was relied on for prompt British and European news from London, for intercolonial news from the colonial capitals and large towns and, increasingly now also, for news from the Pacific region via the nearest colonial telegraph offices. Amplified news and considered opinion came later, by ship from overseas and through the post within Australia. Issues of importance ranged from weighty matters such as outbreaks of international hostilities affecting Britain and the activities of colonial powers in the Pacific region to the sportive recreational, particularly cricket matches and horse races. Syme believed he needed to take especial measures to obtain results of matches and races, although not personally interested in such pastimes. In October 1885 he wrote to the *Argus* general manager Lauchlan Charles Mackinnon (cousin of Lauchlan Mackinnon, the erstwhile expatriate *Argus* proprietor) about the 'undue prominence given to sporting matters' in the press, seeking agreement to reduce it (unsurprisingly, to no effect).[44] Moreover, and notwithstanding his own stables and use of horses, he strongly disapproved of the interest that his three older sons took in 'the Turf' (horseracing), and sought to discourage it. 'It is vulgar; but worst of all it is absorbing, distracting to the mind, & ruinous therefore to ones career in the world,' he wrote to Herbert from London on 2 June 1887, responding to his son's account of 'Easter holiday amusements'.[45]

Cable service staffing

Philip Mennell continued in charge of the London-based cable service, operated by the *Age* in conjunction with the *South Australian Advertiser*. In January 1884 Syme instructed him to resume the earlier expenditure of £250 a month, urging a need to surpass the *Argus*, which was making 'superhuman efforts to beat us'.[46] In March 1885 the Sydney *Daily Telegraph* joined the service as a full member.[47] Although he made some complaints,

---

[43] DS to A. Aucher, 29 December 1884, LB2, p. 315.
[44] DS to L.C. Mackinnon, 1 October 1885, LB2, p. 380.
[45] DS to H. Syme, 2 June 1887, SFP Box 1180/5(f).
[46] DS to P. Mennell, 2, 16 January 1884, LB2, pp. 229, 232.
[47] DS to P. Mennell, 23 June 1885, LB2, p. 350.

generally Syme was satisfied with Mennell's work for the cable service, in June 1885 giving rare praise: 'Altogether I am very pleased with the manner in which you perform your duties.' He was very sorry on hearing soon after that Mennell considered resigning, which he did in 1886.[48] Syme replaced him with G.J. Bones, formerly a reporter on his staff and now assistant subeditor in charge of telegrams.[49] Bones left for London with his family in December 1886.[50] The *South Australian Advertiser* people were soon to find his service 'indifferent', but tolerantly considered this probably due to Mennell's replacement not yet having 'got into harness'.[51] Matters did not improve, however. A series of letters written to Bones by Syme in late 1887 after his return from overseas constitutes a litany of complaints.[52]

The smooth operation of the cable service was complicated by the sometimes-inharmonious relations between the members of the newspaper triumvirate running it. Syme's manner of exercising control was resented by John Bonython of the *South Australian Advertiser* and by Watkin Wynne of the Sydney *Daily Telegraph*. In a letter of February to David Syme & Co., Burden & Bonython objected to paying expenses for the London office, which they saw as ' yours and Mennell's'.[53] Similarly, in August 1887 the Adelaide partners expressed surprise that Bones saw himself as the representative for the *Age* and only the telegraphic correspondent for the other two papers.[54] Bonython sent a copy of his letter to Wynne, saying that they should not allow the *Age* to have entire control of the London office.[55] Syme's authoritarianism was not the only problem. His meddling while in England in 1887 appears to have been another. With agreement from Joseph (then deputising at the *Age* office) and from Wynne, the firm of Burden and Bonython appointed J.B. Stephenson to assist Bones in London, where

---

48 DS to P. Mennell, 1 October 1885, LB2, p. 381.
49 Entry for Bones in Wages Book, p. 28; DS to Westlake, 30 January 1885, LB2, p. 328; DS to F.W. Ward, 31 August 1885, LB2, p. 376.
50 Outward Passengers to Interstate, UK, NZ and Foreign Ports, 1852–1923, Public Record Office Victoria.
51 Burden & Bonython to DS & Co., 3 March 1887, J.L. Bonython and Company, Summary Record, Letter Books, BRG 10, Series 8, State Library of South Australia.
52 DS to G. Bones from 27 October (LB3, pp. 14–15) to 9 December 1887 (LB3, p. 24).
53 Burden & Bonython to DS & Co., 24 February 1885, Bonython & Co. Letter Books.
54 Burden & Bonython to DS & Co., 17 August 1887, Bonython & Co. Letter Books.
55 Burden & Bonython to W. Wynne, 17 August 1887, Bonython & Co. Letter Books.

CHAPTER 10

he commenced duties on 13 March.[56] A letter from Bonython to Wynne in August conveys that Syme (then in London) 'interposed', objecting to Stephenson's presence; one to Bones in September implies that Syme instructed him not to cooperate, and it seems that newcomer Stephenson was indeed badly treated by him.[57]

In November (when Syme was back in Melbourne) Bonython wrote to Wynne saying that he was disgusted at the treatment of Stephenson and Syme's view of the matter.[58] The same day he wrote a conciliatory letter to Joseph ('My dear Mr Syme') about the Bones, Syme and Stephenson problem, obviously seeking to smooth it over.[59] But Joseph by this time was away on leave and his uncle back in charge. A letter of 11 November from Syme to Bones reveals his very different view of matters, referring to complaints by both Bones and Stephenson, and to a 'savage letter' written by Bonython.[60] So far as the archival record goes, this was the end of the matter, but was not the last of such troubles. Troubles that gave Syme a bad name with Bonython and Wynne and, furthermore, helped to drive a wedge between him and Joseph.

Notwithstanding the personnel issues, the cable service partners were cooperating to launch a new, expanded service to commence in 1888. Syme, back in harness in November, was struggling to come to grips with what Joseph had organised for the David Syme & Co. side of the proposed service, writing to Wynne on 10 November that he could not find the documentation: 'Mr J.C. Syme made a hurried departure from here & there were many things I shd have asked him about had there been more time, & this subject of the cable was one of them.'[61] With or without such documentation, Syme was in a position to write to Bones on 16 November with an unusually detailed and explicit set of instructions.[62] The total expenditure for 1888 was to be almost doubled, to £7500; the newspapers sharing the service would be the *Age*, Sydney *Daily Telegraph*, *South Australian Advertiser*, New Zealand Press Association, Tasmanian papers and the Brisbane daily *Telegraph*.

---

56   Burden & Bonython to JCS and W. Wynne, 27 July 1887, Bonython & Co. Letter Books.
57   Burden & Bonython to W. Wynne, 17 August, and to G. Bones, 17 September 1887, Bonython & Co. Letter Books.
58   Burden & Bonython to Wynne, 4 November 1887, Bonython & Co. Letter Books.
59   Burden & Bonython to JCS, 4 November 1887, Bonython & Co. Letter Books.
60   DS to G. Bones, 13 November 1887, LB3, p. 18.
61   DS to W. Wynne, 10 November 1887, LB3, p. 16.
62   DS to G. Bones, 16 November 1887, LB3, pp. 19–21.

The instructions to Bones included a code for commercial news, suggested abbreviations, how and when to send batches of cables. The arrangements were promising; an unresolved matter, however, was the competence of Bones.

In parallel with making these arrangements, Syme was involved in discussions with representatives of the newspapers of both cable services to dispense with Reuters. As Peter Putnis (2006) has explained, this was a step towards the demise of Reuters in Australia.

Procuring and sending intercolonial news was a further ongoing concern. Most of it came by telegram, although Syme did aim to have a regular correspondent by mail in Sydney. On 13 November 1884 he invited Sydney lawyer and journalist George Barton to write from 'the *Age* standpoint' rather than provide a 'diluted' *Sydney Morning Herald* one.[63] That the intercolonial telegraphic news (including New Zealand) was a sizeable budget item for the firm is demonstrated by the expenditure on it in 1884: £1840 (even more, £2415, was spent on European cables).[64] As with the overseas cable news, the *Age* cooperated with the *South Australian Advertiser* (for South Australian news) and the Sydney *Daily Telegraph* (for New South Wales and, forwarded, Queensland news). In November 1886 Syme arranged with Charles Davies of the Hobart *Mercury* to receive Tasmanian news, on a reciprocal basis.[65] No organised means of obtaining news regularly from Western Australia seems to have been available at this time.

The Syme Letterbooks contain a spate of letters from Syme about the intercolonial telegrams to Burden & Bonython and to Bonython personally, and to general manager Wynne and editor Frederick Ward of the Sydney *Daily Telegraph*, most comprising complaints. Syme was not alone in this. The Bonython Letter Books contain outgoing correspondence with like complaints from the *Advertiser* to the *Age* and the Sydney *Daily Telegraph* (for the latter there appear to be no corresponding records extant). Of frequent concern were such matters as the late supply of sporting results, inadequate information about railway accidents, the lack of vital commercial news. A noticeable difference between the two sets of letters is Syme's blunt language, sometimes to the extent of being gratuitously insulting. A sarcastic postscript to a letter of 17 August 1885 to Burden & Bonython, occasioned by hearing that the Melbourne *Daily Telegraph* had been

---

[63] DS to G. Barton, 13 November 1884, LB2, pp. 311–312.
[64] Financial statement, 1884, SFP Box 1191/2(a).
[65] DS to C. Davies, 23 November 1886, LB3, p. 8.

getting telegrams from the *Advertiser*, threatens: 'I presume you will have no objection to our supplying a duplicate of our telegrams to the Adelaide Register' (the opposition paper).[66] This elicited a prompt telegraphic reply, objecting to the tone and contents of Syme's letter. In responding, Syme conceded that he had been 'forcible' but said he could not detect anything 'in the slightest degree offensive'.[67] He seems to have had no idea of the offence that would be taken from his dictatorial and patronising words.

Expanded coverage

Central to the regular correspondence received by ship from London was the London Letter. Mennell, while running the cable service, was its author. Although Syme complained from time to time about the declining quality of the contributions, he was dismayed and at a loss in May 1885 after Mennell hinted that he might resign both cable service and correspondence.[68] As previously mentioned, he would leave in 1886, but be back in 1888. Possibly the journalist and author Arthur Patchett Martin filled in until the arrival of Bones (Syme's letters of May 1884 to Mennell and Joseph, mention 'Martin' as a possible replacement).[69] All the while, the consistently reliable James Harrison was sending much copy for the *Age* and the *Leader*. Syme wrote to him on 10 September 1883 to discontinue Pall Mall Echoes for the present, because of a clash with Mennell's topics.[70] In the same letter he asked him to include a wider range of topics, including biology, in his Scientific Gossip feature, as does 'Dr Taylor' in the *Australasian*, although having a too 'scrappy' treatment. 'Notes on Popular Science' in the *Australasian* was taken from the English *Hardwicke's Science-Gossip*, edited by John Ellor Taylor since 1872 (Brake and Demoor 2009, 268). Syme repeated this request in June 1885, also telling Harrison not to send any more leading articles, as Pearson and Macfie were on hand to write them (although Pearson had not then returned from his travels).[71] One month later he wanted no more book reviews from him, writing that he had plenty of staff to supply them.[72]

---

[66] DS to Burden & Bonython, 17 August 1885, LB2, p. 364–366.
[67] DS to Burden & Bonython, 25 August 1885, LB2, p. 370–371.
[68] DS to P. Mennell, 10 May, 1886, LB2, pp. 401–402.
[69] DS to P. Mennell and JCS, 19 May 1884, LB2, pp. 264 and 265–266.
[70] DS to J. Harrison, 10 September 1883, LB2, p. 214.
[71] DS to J. Harrison, 23 June 1885, LB2, p. 349.
[72] DS to J. Harrison, 23 July 1885, LB2, p. 359.

While it might be inferred from these directives that Harrison's scientific and general journalism was no longer required, in fact he continued to have an estimated four or more articles published regularly each week in the *Age* and the *Leader* (Morrison 1997). He was always there, as a steady, informed, urbane fallback. In late 1883 George Levey, who continued to contribute, but without a regular commitment, contacted Syme about a possible position in Melbourne. Syme's reply, while encouraging, was perhaps too indefinite and there is no evidence that Levey did in fact follow this up.[73] In late 1885 Levey sent Syme from London a prospectus of a new venture, the 'Anglo-Australian Literary Agency', perhaps an attempt to recoup his fortunes after he was declared bankrupt earlier in the year.[74] Syme wrote back that he should 'almost consider the *Age* booked' for the series of articles on 'The Colonial Exhibition', adding to this tentative order the vague offer that if he could 'put anything else in your way' he could be relied on to do it.

In 1884, in Joseph's absence, Syme took a new step for the firm, sending a reporter to England with the Australian cricket team that left in March for a series of matches in which there was keen interest. Since 1877 there had been regular matches between English and Australian teams, with Australia victorious in 1882, a win subsequently termed The Ashes (Harte 2008, 125). In the Australian summer of 1882–83 the defeated side, on tour in Australia, regained them. What would happen in 1884? Recommending H.W. Hedley as the best cricketing reporter in Australia, on 4 February Syme wrote to Alfred Bennett of the Sydney *Evening News* and to Barrow & King, then proprietors of the *South Australian Advertiser*, about sharing the cost.[75] Joseph, having received his uncle's letter of 26 February about his intentions, wrote from Chicago on 4 April that the proposal to send Hedley was a mistake – he was not 'steady enough' and, in any case, matches could be reported well enough by the men at home.[76] Syme, however, had no regrets, saying that he had consulted K.D. Bennett (now business manager), Windsor and commercial editor Robinson, and that already 'we have received a great deal of kudos' and he was sure Hedley would behave.[77] It seems that he did; a long-term employee, he

---

[73] DS to G. Levey, 23 October 1883, LB2, p. 222.
[74] DS to G. Levey, 18 November 1885, LB2, p. 384; 'Bankruptcy of Mr. George Collins Levey', *Argus*, 23 July 1885.
[75] DS to A. Bennett and to Barrow & King, 4 February 1884, LB2, pp. 236, 237.
[76] JCS to DS, 4 April 1884, SFP Box 1180/3(b).
[77] DS to JCS, 19 May, 16 June 1884, LB2, pp. 265–266, 271–273.

CHAPTER 10

was appointed sporting editor of the *Age* in 1886.[78] It appears that he had a gambling propensity, however, for William Robinson later wrote that Hedley usually lost money 'backing his own tips, but [was] a cheerful loser and also a joyful borrower' (Robinson 1967, 22).

The colonial team, Hedley with them, arrived in England at the end of April. From then until their departure on 25 September they played 32 matches including three Tests, two of which were drawn, the other won by the English team (Harte 2008, 133–134). Reuters Special Cricket Telegrams appeared in the colonial newspapers five or so days after the events. The information was doubtless sent in coded and abbreviated form, and decoded and enhanced in the newspaper offices, for the descriptions and results are lengthy and verbose. They appear in the *Age* side by side with accounts five to six weeks old by 'Mid On' (Hedley's pseudonym), a few days being saved by their being telegraphed from Albany and Adelaide, not without problems.[79] From today's perspective, and notwithstanding Syme's satisfaction, one is inclined to agree with Joseph that Hedley's excursion was not strictly necessary.

As Australia in the 1880s became more closely connected to and thus aware of the wider world, Syme was ever alert to broaden the range of correspondents. His letterbooks show him throughout 1886 taking available opportunities to supplement the now regular correspondence from London, Paris and New York. He was agreeable to Alfred Daniel's offer to write an occasional letter from Edinburgh, stressing that he should give English subjects from the Scottish standpoint.[80] He was pleased to get Stuart Cumberland's account of a journey on the New Canadian Railway,[81] but turned down a later offer from Cumberland, obviously on the move, to act as special correspondent from Berlin, saying that he had just recently made arrangements to receive European news 'in the case of war or other emergency' and that he would like to meet Cumberland when in London early 1887.[82] In addition to contracting with personal correspondents, Syme was open to procuring suitable syndicated material from the many agencies being formed to provide it. In December, choosing from a printed circular, he placed a year's subscription to a Ladies Letter, Agricultural Letter and

---

[78] DS to H. Humphries, 11 March 1886, LB2, p. 393; Entry for Hedley in Wages Book, p. 198.
[79] DS to J.L. Bonython, 21, 30 June 1884, LB2, pp. 276, 282.
[80] DS to A. Daniel, 10 March 1886, LB2, p. 392.
[81] DS to S. Cumberland, 1 June 1886, LB2, p. 405.
[82] DS to S. Cumberland, 27 December 1886, LB3, p. 12.

Literary Notes, all for the *Leader*.[83] It is not known whether he discussed this with the weekly's editor, Matthew Macfie.

When Syme first introduced serial fiction into the *Age* he was closely involved in the choice of novels, but within a very few years left this to others, possibly in Joseph's area. But he did not stay completely out of the action. In November 1887, following references in English newspapers, he asked Bones to identify fiction syndicates other than Tillotsons Fiction Bureau (with which David Syme & Co. had been dealing for years).[84] Usually the novels had been chosen from Tillotsons' circulars. Sometimes, when appropriate publication rights had been purchased, rights were on sold to other newspapers. One such example is Mary Braddon's bestselling *Ishmael*. The *Age* bought serial publication rights from Tillotsons and published it in weekly instalments for a year from 22 March 1884. At the same time, it sold copy and rights to the Brisbane Newspaper Company (publishers of the *Brisbane Courier*) for £30 and to the Sydney *Town and Country Journal* for £35.[85]

Occasionally novels by local colonial writers had been sought and obtained for the *Leader*. As seen in the previous chapter, one of these local creations, 'A Girl's Ideal' by A.C. (Ada Cross, who would later write as Ada Cambridge), had made it into the *Age* in 1881. The *Australasian* had been featuring fiction by this author since 1872, not long after her arrival in Victoria. But when David Watterston in 1885 replaced the affable Henry Gullett as its editor, she no longer had ready acceptance of her work. Offended by Watterston's attempts to edit it, she turned to the *Age* office (Morrison 2004, xxix–xxx). As a result *The Perversity of Human Nature*, her satirical novella about inadvertent bigamy, was published in the December 1887 *Illustrated Australian News*, an unusual, not to say risqué, Christmas tale. Moreover, early that year she had apparently been given an assurance by 'Mr Syme' that the *Age* was going to publish her next novel, which would be set in Sydney (Morrison 2004, xxvi–xxvii). Clearly not David, who was away in 1887, the Mr Syme was most likely Joseph – who would deal with Cambridge in 1889 – rather than Herbert, though this is not certain. In any case, obtaining her work when she was at the peak of her novelistic powers was a coup for David Syme & Co.

---

[83] DS to F. Connor, 23 December 1886, LB3, p. 12.
[84] DS to G. Bones, 13 November 1887, LB3, p. 18.
[85] Financial statement, 1884, SFP Box 1191/2(a).

CHAPTER 10

One of the two special overseas reporting projects for the *Leader*, set in train by Syme in early 1883, was also to be a great success – as indeed was the very similar, competing venture for the *Australasian*. As intimated in Chapter 9, the brothers Dow were in the United States for several months in later 1883 investigating and reporting on American agriculture, John for the *Leader* and Thomas for the opposition *Australasian*. Some material was suitable for sharing with intercolonial newspapers; some not, as seen when Burden & King decided against accepting John Dow's *Leader* articles offered for the *South Australian Advertiser*: 'all the kudos in the matter is yours' and everybody 'will know that the articles are from the pen of your reporter', was the response.[86] John Dow's 'Agriculture in America' began on 14 July and continued weekly until instalment no. 54 for 26 July 1884, long after his return to the *Age* office in October 1883. Thomas Dow's 'Farming in America' began in the *Australasian* also on 14 July, running to 3 May 1884, while his nine-part series, 'A Tour in America' ('Among the Millionaires', 'Among the Politicians', etc.) was published in November and December 1883. In June 1884 Syme wrote to Joseph that much notice had been taken of the *Leader* and that, while the public's attention had been divided between two papers, David Syme & Co. 'had the advantage of the Argus'.[87]

Whether or not Syme was wholly justified in this claim, it is clear that the earlier publication in book form of John Dow's articles was a coup. Printed in May 1884, *The Australian in America* was published by the 'Leader' Office on 1 June, while the author's series was still running in the newspaper. Paper-covered, comprising 170 pages, it was priced at one shilling. Including a subsequent reprinting, in all 2000 copies were produced, some of them sent to Mennell in London and to an agent in New York.[88] In 1884 the book brought in £203.8.0, through sales and advertisements (some in Sydney newspapers). Subtracting costs of production, this gave a clear profit of £11.9.6. Copies sold in smaller numbers over the next few years. But the justification for the effort was renown rather than money – newspaper producers valuing 'kudos' along with profits. Although Syme had doubted that the *Argus* would be able to publish Thomas Dow's articles, his *A Tour in America* did come out, albeit nearly three months later.[89] Published by the

---

[86] Barrow & King to DS & Co., 12, 25 July 1883, Bonython & Co. Letter Books.
[87] DS to JCS, 16 June 1884, LB2.271–273.
[88] Financial statement, 1884, SFP Box 1191/2(a).
[89] DS to JCS, 30 June 1884, LB2, pp. 283–284.

'Australasian' Office, comprising 207 pages, it was also paper-covered and priced at one shilling.

A sequel to the 1883 American tours, in 1885 the members of a Victorian Royal Commission on Irrigation, chaired by Deakin, visited the United States. John Dow was included in a dual capacity – politician, and correspondent for David Syme & Co. Reporter Edward Cunningham represented the *Argus* business (Serle 1971, 55). Deakin and Dow left Sydney on 1 January 1885, reaching San Francisco on 25 January, readers learned, from Dow's first article in his series, 'The Irrigation Commission in America', in the *Leader* of 21 March. The series ran until 18 July, one month after Dow was back in Melbourne. It was followed by another, entitled 'Among American Farmers', published from 25 July to 6 February 1886. One week after the series concluded, the *Leader* carried an article on 'Conservation of Water in Australia', by Oedipus, *nom de plume* used by London-based James Harrison for his science column. This, and the preceding two series to which it was a fitting conclusion, contributed substantially to the campaign that led to the passing of the major Irrigation Act in 1886, to help alleviate the problems of Victorian farmers. This *Leader* journalism also played a part in the inducement of the Chaffey Brothers from California to introduce an irrigation system to Mildura on the Murray River in northwest Victoria that would transform the arid land into a productive region for fruit growing and viticulture (Serle 1971, 54–57). Syme was abreast of, and considerably involved in, the legislative and practical developments, as the support given in his newspapers attests and entries in Deakin's diaries, noting meetings and discussions, reveal.[90]

Syme's other 1883 venture was concerned not with the agricultural and economic development of Victoria but with imperial, political considerations in the region. In mid-1883, as outlined in the previous chapter, he had despatched the George Morrison expedition to New Guinea. About the same time, the *Argus* expedition led by William Armit had set off. Both missions proved disastrous and had to be aborted after penetrating less than 40 miles inland, not even reaching the Owen Stanley Ranges (Ryan 1972, 385). Armit's set out from Port Moresby on 14 July and turned back a month later. On the return journey several of the party contracted fever and one, American Professor William Denton, died (Gibbney 1969). The *Australasian* of 20 October reported briefly the telegraphed facts of the return, fevers and death. The events were given a more positive spin in the issue of 8 December

---

[90] Diaries 1885, 1886, Deakin Papers, Series 2.

CHAPTER 10

1883, in an account under the headline 'The Expedition Reaches Its Furthest Point', dated Port Moresby 22 September. Ironically, by 1885 Armit, the failed expeditioner, was the *Age* correspondent from Cooktown, north Queensland.[91]

Morrison's party fared scarcely better. The men left Port Moresby on 11 July but, due to a couple of false starts, they were not on the way until the end of the month. Their experiences with hostile inhabitants were exacerbated by the lack of an interpreter (Gregory 1986; Pearl 1967, 46–49). After several thefts of food and equipment, Morrison retaliated by thrashing one of the thieves. This may have been a cause of his being speared on 3 October. He managed quickly to extract a spear near his eye but could not remove one in his groin. (He would have to wait until 1884 for its extraction by a surgeon in Edinburgh, where he finished medical studies and resumed his career of adventure, becoming famous as 'Chinese Morrison', correspondent of the London *Times*.) He and his party were back in Port Moresby about 13 October, from where he travelled to Melbourne and then to his parents and recuperation in Geelong. By this time he was suffering severely from fever (septicaemia?).

Meanwhile, Syme was becoming desperate to produce accounts for the reading public. The *Leader* of 4 August 1883 had a cabled report of the party having crossed the Lalokie River, and a week later published a letter from Morrison dated 9 July, describing Port Moresby. A silence ensued that Syme found 'inexplicable'. He cabled and wrote frantically, stressing to the agent in Cooktown the urgency of getting news and sending a letter care of missionaries at Port Moresby. To keep the readers engaged, 'Under the Verandah' in the *Leader* of 20 October opined that, although there had been no word from Morrison, one would rather bet on him than on the Melbourne Cup. Finally, the *Leader* of 10 November carried a brief cabled report of 8 November from Cooktown that the expeditioner had been 'speared by natives'. The 'Week' feature in the *Leader* of 17 November talks up Morrison's achievement as braver than that of the Armit group's unfortunate Denton. Further details were supplied in the issue for 24 November, a cable from Cooktown, dated 20 November, stating that Morrison was wounded when 100 miles (161 kilometres) from the coast (a distance that would be disputed) and praising the courage and endurance of John Lyons, a prospector of the party, who had cared for Morrison. A report one and a third columns in

---

[91] DS to W. Wynne, 30 November 1883, LB2, p. 386.

length, it must have been expanded, not to say embellished, in Melbourne (rather like the English cricket cables).

Finally, on 15 December the first of what would be nine articles, 'Exploration of New Guinea' by Morrison appeared, supplied by the sick young man. The series would run to 16 February 1884, but not without exceptional measures. Anxious, indeed desperate, to receive more than one article, not only for his own papers but also for the *Sydney Morning Herald* for which they had been contracted, on 14 December Syme had written to Morrison in Geelong asking to send copy for the second letter at once.[92] Morrison must have complied, for the next article appeared on schedule. But then there was a hiatus; Syme wrote on 26 December, suggesting he send a reporter to help, because all the articles were required. He also commented that Morrison would have seen the serious alterations that had to be made in the material published to date, saying it was unsatisfactory and contained contradictions. John Stephens, subeditor in the making, was despatched to assist. Apart from correspondence in March 1884 about paying Morrison's medical expenses, where Syme was somewhat churlish but materially forthcoming, that was the end of the *Age* office connection with the bright young adventurer.[93]

Undaunted – spurred on, rather – Syme was planning another expedition to New Guinea even before publication of Morrison's articles was completed. On 4 February 1884 he wrote to Bennett of the Sydney *Evening News* and to Barrow and King of the *South Australian Advertiser* to share the reports and the estimated cost of £800.[94] This time he had Joseph's support. In February his junior partner, proceeding on his travel overseas via Queensland, in Cooktown attempted but did not succeed in recruiting Lyons, hero of the failed Morrison venture.[95] On 14 March Syme wrote to Wilfred Powell, seasoned New Guinea explorer then in England and rumoured as having an interest in another expedition, offering to take him on as journalist.[96] In the event, the expedition, which left Melbourne on 28 March, was led by shipmaster ('Captain') John Strachan, accompanied by journalist David Barker Walker, naturalist Charles Stewart, gold miner W.H. Scott and sailor T.C. Kerry. Syme was soon to have misgivings, even to regret the

---

[92] DS to G. Morrison, 14, 26 December 1883, microfilm of correspondence in George Ernest Morrison Papers, G28245, National Library of Australia.
[93] DS to G. Morrison, 3 March 1884, LB2, p. 245.
[94] DS to A. Bennett and Barrow & King, 4 February 1884, LB2, pp. 236, 237.
[95] DS to Lyons, 14 February 1884, LB2, p. 242.
[96] DS to W. Powell, 14 March 1884, LB2, p. 247.

CHAPTER 10

Figure 10.2. Attack on the *Age* New Guinea expeditioners, as depicted by one of its members, 1884. (Pictures Collection, State Library of Victoria, IAN06/08/84/120–121)

undertaking, especially when he learned that the *Argus* was not sponsoring another New Guinea expedition.[97] By 4 April Joseph too had reservations.[98]

It was intended that the new expedition would sail from Thursday Island in Torres Strait and head north-west to the coast of New Guinea, then travel eastwards back to Port Moresby. Seven reports appeared in the *Leader* between 31 May and 16 August, telling a tale of disaster, even worse than that of the failed Morrison mission, the most dramatic part also described and depicted in the August number of the *Illustrated Australian News* (fig. 10.2). Travelling up the Mai Kasa [Kussa] River and threatened by inhabitants in canoes, the party set off fireworks and rockets to frighten their potential attackers. Fearing for their lives, the expeditioners abandoned their boat and Scott the miner set out on a makeshift raft for help. He paddled into the distance and was never seen again. Persevering through their privations, and getting some help from missionaries along the way, the survivors eventually got back to Thursday Island with intentions of returning to Melbourne then setting out afresh.

---

[97] DS to JCS, 21 April, 19 May, 16 June 1884, LB2, pp. 257, 265–266, 271–273.
[98] JCS to DS, 4 April 1884, SFP Box 1180/3(b).

A very different story again was later told in the Sydney *Daily Telegraph*, of some one hundred 'natives' deliberately killed by an explosion of a 'torpedo' launched at them. In May 1885, after an article based on this account was subsequently run in the Melbourne *Daily Telegraph*, the expedition journalist Walker launched a libel suit against the paper's proprietor, James McKinley.[99] Walker, who was represented by Fink (about to begin writing for the *Leader*), won his case, being awarded £100 damages. The naturalist Stewart subsequently also brought an action against McKinley, less successfully. In both cases appeals would ensue. But Syme was not a part of this litigation. Nor did he wish to be, on 11 August writing to Walker: 'what possible advantage cd I gain by your action. You know how keenly I suffer over the failure of the expedition, & yet you think that I cd possibly wish the matter revived in a court of law?'[100] In part he was constrained, one suspects, because of the role of the Sydney *Daily Telegraph*, partner in the cable service, and which had paid David Syme and Co. £45.10 in 1884 for New Guinea copy.[101] In the course of the trial it became known that Sydney *Daily Telegraph* news editor Lauchlan Brient (who will feature again, in the next chapter) apparently obtained the allegedly libellous information from sailor Kerry, and the version in the Melbourne *Daily Telegraph* was written by William Fitchett, respected minister of the church and educationist. Syme, one infers from his letter to Walker, was embarrassed not to say mortified by the turn of events. The truth of the matter is now unknowable. A colourful account in Strachan's *Explorations and Adventures in New Guinea* (1888) falls between the *Leader* and the *Daily Telegraph* versions. There are frequent mentions of shooting sessions and of the downing of shots of brandy. The latter would account for the item '1 case 3 star brandy' that Syme found exceedingly objectionable when disputing Strachan's accounts with Burns Philp & Company of Brisbane and Thursday Island, suppliers to the expedition.[102]

Syme would now engage on-the-spot correspondents, rather than sponsor expeditions to the region. In February 1885 he was happy to obtain New Guinea news from the Sydney *Daily Telegraph*, although in May he complained of an overlong report.[103] There was great concern in the

---

[99] 'The "Age" Expedition to New Guinea', *Argus*, 29 May 1885, p. 6, 30 May, p. 11.
[100] DS to D. Walker, 11 August 1885, LB2, pp. 362–363.
[101] Financial statement, 1884, SFP Box 1191/2(a).
[102] DS to W. Poole, 2 July 1884, LB2, p. 286–287.
[103] DS to W. Wynne, 23 February, 31 May 1885, LB2, pp. 336, 342–343.

CHAPTER 10

Australian colonies when in November 1884 Germany proclaimed north-east New Guinea and adjacent islands a German Protectorate. In the same month the British followed suit claiming south-west New Guinea and its adjacent islands (the western half of the island having earlier been claimed by the Dutch) (R. Brown 1986, 338). The *Leader* of 15 November reported the news in a cable from Cooktown of the hoisting of the British flag, something the Victorian government, and indeed the *Age*, had been urging, in the face of British indifference or reluctance to seek territories in the Pacific (Ward 1948, 315–323). In Victoria, general agitation followed news of these actions. The cover of the *Illustrated Australian News* for 21 January 1885 depicts a 'Monster Meeting' at the Town Hall and its 'Summary of Events' for the month comments that the annexation by Germany had 'created a profound sensation throughout the Australian colonies'. Imperialist Pearson explained some of the ramifications of the annexation issue when he was farewelled by parliamentary colleagues on 2 January 1885. He spoke to them about the threat to the Queensland sugar industry posed by the recent German annexation of north-east New Guinea, because it would reduce the amount of 'costless labor' available, and he stressed the need for the British Empire to be in Asia.[104]

Other areas of special interest in the Pacific-Oceanic region were New Caledonia, now a French possession, and the New Hebrides, its independence preserved under an Anglo-French agreement of 1870. In the Australian colonies there had been governmental and public concern for some time about French intentions. The *Leader* of 14 July 1883 reported a motion by the Premier, James Service, uniting the two houses of the Victorian parliament to urge England to annex the islands of the New Hebrides and establish a protectorate. New Caledonia attracted particular interest after the French Parliament passed the Recidivist Bill, providing for the transportation of increased numbers of convicts and raising fears of these ne'er-do-wells eventually finding their way to Australia. On 9 December 1884 French-speaking Arthur Aucher, left for Sydney and thence to New Caledonia as special correspondent for the *Age* and *Leader* (Gibbney and Smith 1987, v.1, 23). His first letter, 'New Caledonia. No. 1. Melbourne to Noumea' appeared on 24 January 1885 in both papers, under 'The Traveller' banner. The 11th and last was published on 18 April. Prompted by Wynne of the Sydney *Daily Telegraph*, Syme suggested that if, as was being rumoured, French vessels were sent to annex New Hebrides,

---

[104] 'Farewell to Mr. C.H. Pearson, M.L.A.', *Age*, 3 January 1885, p. 6.

Aucher should travel with them and report back.[105] There is no evidence, however, that he went further than New Caledonia. Syme's instructions to Aucher, already noted, reveal his news-gathering priorities at this time – take whatever measure necessary to send the news as fast as possible, for 'expedition is everything'.[106]

Syme continued to ensure that his readers would be informed about New Caledonia and the New Hebrides, the latter a potential trouble spot until the Anglo-French Condominium was established in 1906 (Ward 1948, 300–302). In 1886 the *Age* was publishing reports from correspondent Nixon in the New Hebrides, while the 18 September issue of the *Illustrated Australian News* featured (pictorial) 'Sketches in the New Hebrides', made especially for the newspaper.[107] Syme's concern about New Caledonia (and the rival newspaper taking a lead) surfaced whenever cabled information from London about 'recidivistes' for the French territory got into the *Argus*, but was not received by the *Age*.[108]

Syme was drawn into gathering news from yet farther afield in 1884 and 1885, because of happenings in the Sudan (then spelled Soudan) area of north-east Africa. British occupation of Egypt, including the Egyptian Sudan, was in jeopardy when the self-proclaimed Mahdi (Muslim leader) and his insurrectionary forces were uniting to assert control (Ensor 1936, 77–83). In January 1884 British General Charles Gordon was despatched to Khartoum. In March the Mahdi troops began a siege of the city. Syme, aware that the fortunes of the British in the Sudan were of general interest, upbraided Mennell in a letter of 19 May 1884 for failing to supply news of Gordon and Khartoum.[109] Gordon, who had secret instructions to evacuate the city, was perhaps planning to hold out. The Mahdi forces eventually launched a fierce attack, in which Gordon was killed on 26 January 1885.

The news created a stir in Britain and its colonies, eliciting an upsurge of patriotic fervour. On 2 April George Syme wrote to David from London about *Age* attacks on Prime Minister William Gladstone for his Egypt policy, objecting to the 'animus' of its criticism, for example in its

---

[105] DS to W. Wynne, 27 December 1884, LB2, p. 314.
[106] DS to A. Aucher, 29 December 1884, LB2, p. 315.
[107] DS to J. Stephens, 24 August 1886, LB2, p. 411.
[108] DS to Mennell, 23 June 1885, LB2, p. 350; DS to JCS, 23 December 1887, LB3, pp. 26–28.
[109] DS to Mennell, 19 May 1884, LB2, p. 264.

CHAPTER 10

7 February editorial.[110] It is hard to agree with gentle George. This leader, written before news of Gordon's death had reached Melbourne, does speak plainly, referring to a 'succession of diplomatic blunders by the Gladstone administration' and the 'cup' of his 'errors in foreign and colonial policy' now being 'full', but such criticism was widespread also in England. Otherwise, the contents of the leader, said to be based on a 'private letter received in Melbourne' from one of the officers of the British contingent sent to relieve Gordon, seem factual enough. News of Gordon's death would reach the *Age* by cable less than a week later. The New South Wales government's prompt offer to send a military contingent to the Sudan was accepted by the British government; offers from Victoria and other colonies were rejected by an imperial government wanting to defuse the crisis (Serle 1971, 199–201).

The New South Wales contingent of some 730 men was accompanied by a large number of press representatives, officially restricted to men from newspapers of that colony, although Joseph Melvin of the *Argus* managed to get on board in disguise (Anderson and Trembath 2011, 27–29). The best known of the New South Wales war correspondents-in-the-making was William Lambie of the *Sydney Morning Herald* who would join the *Age* staff in 1888 and in 1899 be sent to cover the South African war. The Sudan contingent sailed from Sydney in early March 1885, its embarkation depicted on the cover of the *Illustrated Australian News* for 18 March. The Sydney *Daily Telegraph*, through Wynne, invited David Syme & Co. to share in the cost of cables sent by its correspondent. Syme, in a climate of cooling public opinion in Victoria (the colony excluded from participation) now had reservations about the intensity of the New South Wales patriotic reaction. He wrote to Wynne on 20 February: 'We here look upon you all in Sydney as so many lunatics, & I am pretty sure you will look upon yourselves as such very soon, when you have time to cool down'.[111] He hoped that an inferior man would not be sent, he did not want to spend much on cables, for 'There will be really nothing to cable if your men are sent to guard the railway, as is proposed, except an occasional skirmish with the arabs'.

Four days later he wrote again, wanting more information before sharing one third of the cable costs and saying ungraciously: 'We are quite willing to co-operate with you, but we expect you shd not treat us like children.'[112]

---

[110] G. Syme to DS, 2 April 1885, SFP Box 1180/4(a).
[111] DS to W. Wynne, 20 February 1885, LB2, p. 335.
[112] DS to W. Wynne, 24 February 1885, LB2, p. 338.

Apparently he did accept Wynne's offer and share the costs, complaining on 7 July about a telegram from the 'special in the Soudan'.[113] The cables from Africa were channelled through Adelaide, on 27 March Bonython writing to the South Australian Superintendent of Telegraphs, Charles Todd, asking for Egypt cables to be forwarded to the *Age* and the Sydney *Daily Telegraph* as well as to the *South Australian Advertiser*.[114] In fact, the contingent, which arrived in May, would see very little action and stay a bare seven weeks.

It might be thought that Syme's time and energies were fully committed between 1883 and 1887, when he was making extraordinary efforts to transform the *Age* into a newspaper of international standing. Not so. In parallel with these exertions, he managed to carry out a packed program of real estate transactions and associated agricultural activities. Under Clause 12 of the partnership agreement, the partners were not to engage in any other profession or trade.[115] On 12 October 1883 he somewhat disingenuously asked Joseph in writing for his consent to invest in a rural property ('station') saying that he believed it might be necessary under the partnership agreement to obtain this, but did not have the document with him to check the wording.[116] Joseph replied in writing the same day, giving his consent and, tit for tat, informed David that he intended to be a partner in running a property in Queensland.[117] This was to be with Henry Davies, brother of Charles and George who owned the Hobart *Mercury*. Joseph also wrote that he wanted to help set up his errant brother George in business in that colony. But George may have been beyond help, and in January 1885 died in Brisbane aged only 34 (M. Syme 2013, 56).

David replied that he had no objection to Joseph's venture, provided it did not occupy much of his time and embarrass the newspaper business.[118] In spite of a veiled warning from the other Davies brothers to Joseph via his solicitor about Henry's prospects, the partnership was being finalised in December 1884, shortly before Joseph's departure on leave.[119] Before sailing to the United States and thence to Britain, he spent some time in Queensland, attending to newspaper business matters in Brisbane and in far north Cooktown, and presumably visited his newly acquired property.

---

[113] DS to W. Wynne, 7 July 1885, LB2, p. 356.
[114] J. Bonython to C. Todd, 27 March 1885, Bonython & Co. Letter Books.
[115] Articles of co-partnership, SFP Box 1185/4(a)[i].
[116] DS to JCS, 12 October 1883, LB2, p. 215.
[117] DS to JCS, 17 October 1883, LB2, p. 216.
[118] DS to JCS, 17 October 1883, LB2, p. 216.
[119] DS to Smith & Emmerton from Davies Bros, SFP Box 1180/5(e).

CHAPTER 10

Yarra Valley properties

Syme's letterbooks contain hints of various financial and real estate ventures contemplated but not taken up at this time. A major investment, however, was the purchase of land in the Yarra Valley 50 to 60 kms east of Melbourne, a farming and viticulture district then as now, from David Mitchell (father of the famed opera singer Nellie Melba) (M. Syme 2013, 61). This property he named Killara. In late 1884 he added to his Yarra Valley holdings with the purchase of Dalry, where he installed son Francis as manager in January 1885.[120] So doing, he was providing a home and a minimal income (a salary of £3 per week) for a young family. Francis, who had abandoned law studies and whom the partnership terms precluded from employment in David Syme & Co., had married Christina McDonald in July 1883, producing a first grandchild, Elsie, for David and Annabella some questionable six and a half months later. Another daughter, Lucy, would be born in March 1885 and a son, Vere, in 1887.[121] Syme and Francis had an uneasy relationship, letters showing the father to be strict and dictatorial, giving little opportunity for initiative, the son somewhat of a free spirit and apparently not good with money.[122]

Syme was to involve himself seriously in the agricultural and pastoral business. At Killara he installed a manager, exercising close supervision while trying to turn the property into a productive farm. In March 1884 he wrote to James McEwan in London asking him to order from his Chicago agent a new Automatic Hay Stacker and Gatherer, wanting it in time for the Melbourne agricultural show in September, doubtless wishing to be seen as an innovator. Duly arriving, the equipment was found to be incomplete and, lacking instructions, unusable for the Show.[123] In 1885 he bought a herd of prize Polled Angus cattle from a vendor in New Zealand. Letterbook entries between August 1885 and April 1886 record considerable attention to matters of shipping, freight, insurance, certificates, etc. for it.[124] A link between his hobby or private agribusiness and his newspaper enterprise, in May 1886 he offered to the National Agricultural Society of Victoria an

---

[120] DS to F. Syme, 9 January 1885, LB2, p. 320.
[121] Syme Family Date books, SFP Box 1193/6.
[122] DS to F. Syme, 7 July 1885, 28 April, 9 December 1886, LB2, pp. 355, 399, LB4, pp. 2–5.
[123] DS to J. McEwan & Co., 7 March, 25 August 1884, LB2, pp. 246, 296.
[124] DS to various addressees, 5 August 1885 to 28 April 1886, LB2, pp. 361, 367–368, 375, 400.

annual *Leader* prize of £20 for the best milch (milking) cow, in regard to both quality and quantity, at the Show.[125]

These were new beginnings and an end to the Mount Macedon phase. Rosenheim, now with a marvellously established, extensive garden, would cease to be the family residence and retreat that it had been in the 1870s. David Syme, in his late 50s, could well have used it, at least on weekends, for relaxing as a country squire, away from the stress of running the newspaper business. Instead, he was embarking on new challenges, where the 'Mount' had no place. Deakin visited the family at Rosenheim in the New Year 1884 as he had earlier done, but during the summer of 1884–85 the house was leased to the Government of Victoria for Governor Sir Henry Loch.[126] He must have remarked favourably on the experience of retreating to the Mount, for on 30 October 1885 the Victorian Government bought the property for the incumbent Governor's use, paying £5000, and an additional £300 for furniture.[127] A new two-storey Tudor-style house was built in 1886, adjacent to the original Syme house ('cottage'). How Annabella and the children felt about the displacement is not known.

Syme also owned a 959-acre property in the district, Valley Farm, acquired some years earlier. Adding to his income, on 26 October 1885 it was bought by P.W. Millane for £5350, allowing for the fencing not being completed. Syme, who had placed it on offer the previous January, had between October 1883 and June 1884 been conducting a protracted dispute with a neighbour about the fencing.[128]

At the end of 1886 Syme was about to travel overseas, ostensibly for his health – which indeed was not good. It had been a busy three and a half years since the quarrel with Joseph had been resolved by the inclusion of his name in the imprint on the David Syme & Co. newspapers. Accompanied by wife Annabella and 17-year-old daughter Lucie, he sailed from Melbourne, late in the afternoon of 4 January 1887, on the *Te Anau* for Hobart and Christchurch, New Zealand, travelling from there to San Francisco and eventually to England.[129] Earlier on the day of departure he attended a farewell luncheon at the Athenaeum Club, given by financier

---

[125] DS to Secretary, National Agricultural Society, 20 May 1886, LB2, p. 404.
[126] Diary entry for 8 February 1884, Deakin Papers, Series 2.
[127] Account sales for Rosenheim and Valley Farm, SFP Box 1188/1(b)[i].
[128] DS to T. Watson, 19 October 1883 to 30 June 1884, LB2, pp. 217, 267, 277–278, 288.
[129] 'Shipping', *Age*, 5 January 1887, p. 4.

CHAPTER 10

and MLC Simon Fraser.[130] Attended by 'some 60 fellow citizens... the company included prominent representatives of the commercial and financial interests as well as several members of the Government'. Joseph was not overlooked: he was toasted by Deakin, who noted the 'grave responsibility' he now had, and also the high esteem in which his father Ebenezer had been held. Before departing, Syme may have reunited, albeit briefly, with his brother George who, with wife and medico son George, arrived back in Melbourne the day before, on the *Sutlej*, from England.[131]

Syme expected to be in London about the end of February.[132] On 25 March he met Deakin, there as the principal representative of Victoria at the Colonial Conference, held from 4 April to 9 May. They dined together two days later and met again on 7 April (La Nauze 1979, 88–90). On 12 April, after visiting the South Kensington Museum, Syme and Annabella dined with him and Graham Berry, now Agent-General for Victoria.[133]

By this time Syme had settled paper contracts for the *Age* and *Leader* and had tried unsuccessfully to engage a machinist and stereotyper (Joseph would attend to this in 1888). He was now planning to take Annabella and Lucie to Paris, and perhaps beyond.[134] Back in London by June, they were able to witness celebrations for Queen Victoria's Golden Jubilee, Syme writing to Herbert: 'we have seen the Jubilee & yet survive' (a reference to the rumoured Jubilee Plot, or just wry humour?). 'We are thoroughly tired of London', he added, and would be leaving soon for 'the north'.[135]

It must have been during this northern journey that Syme made the visit to the *Newcastle Daily Chronicle* to which he would later refer, in correspondence with Joseph.[136] Known as the 'The *Times* of the North', the newspaper was owned by Joseph Cowen junior, son of the Joseph Cowen after whom his nephew was named (Brake and Demoor 2009, 148–149, 446). Cowen had invested heavily in new technology and his newspaper was claimed to be the largest-selling regional one of its kind, with sales over 40,000 (then still less than that of the *Age*, with its circulation of almost 72,000 at the end of 1887). It seems that Syme not only looked at printing machines in operation, but also exchanged ideas with the managerial staff.

---

[130] 'News of the Day', *Age*, 5 January 1887, pp. 4–5.
[131] 'Shipping Intelligence', *Argus*, 4 January 1887, p. 4.
[132] DS to S. Cumberland, 27 December 1886, LB3, p. 12.
[133] Diary entries for 25, 27 March, 7, 12 April 1887, Deakin Papers, Series 2.
[134] DS to H. Syme, 11 April 1887, SFP Box 1180/5(f).
[135] DS to H. Syme, 23 June 1887, SFP Box 1180/5(f).
[136] DS to JCS, 17 May 1888, LB4, p. 35–39.

And as already mentioned, in England he also attended to Bones and the cable service. Otherwise, there is no record of work done and contacts made in relation to his newspaper business.

While surviving letters to Herbert touch on the running of the editorial and literary department, mainly they are about family and private business matters.[137] Syme is concerned to hear that Francis had been very ill. He sends his 'best love' to Arthur, Geoff & Oswie & yourself'; he asks after 'Addie' – nephew George Adlington Syme.

But his overriding concern, not to say obsession, in the letters to Herbert is the running and productivity of his properties Dalry and Killara in the Yarra Valley. He worried that they had produced no profits, only losses, in the three years of his ownership. He requested information, sent instructions, commented on employees, livestock, crops and produce. He was dreadfully concerned about some cattle that had gone missing. And he reported on his purchases in Britain of fowls, ducks, pigeons and a stallion ('Gentleman George'), for all of which he was arranging shipment to Melbourne.

He intended to leave England at the end of July, in plenty of time to embark on the *Zealandia*, which sailed from San Francisco on 26 August and reached Sydney on 22 September.[138] Deakin, who tried but failed to meet him on arrival in Melbourne by the train from Sydney on 23 September, did make contact with him three days later.[139] How long Syme and Joseph had together in the Office to confer, debrief and hand over the reins before Joseph left for a year's leave is conjectural. He may have gone before his marriage to Laura Blair on 23 October 1887.[140] In a letter of 10 November Syme referred to his nephew's 'hurried departure', seeming to imply a less than satisfactory handover.[141] He was, however, most cordial towards his nephew in a letter written on 23 December, concluding: 'I wish you & Mrs. Joseph many happy returns of the season.[142]

But all was not well between the two partners. There are hints that, underneath the cordiality, trouble had been brewing for some years. Syme's curt note of 20 October 1883 to Joseph states: 'your letter of yesterday is to me quite incomprehensible'.[143] His letter three days later warns: 'This

---

[137] DS to H. Syme, 11 April, 2, 23 June 1887, SFP Box 1180/5(f).
[138] 'Shipping Intelligence', *Sydney Morning Herald*, 23 September 1887, p. 6.
[139] Diary entries 23, 26 September 1887, Deakin Papers, Series 2.
[140] 'Marriages', *Argus*, 3 November 1887, p. 1.
[141] DS to W. Wynne, 10 November 1887, LB3, p. 16.
[142] DS to JCS, 23 December 1887, LB3, pp. 26–28.
[143] DS to JCS, 20 October 1883, LB2, p. 218.

CHAPTER 10

correspondence had better at once cease unless it can be conducted in a tone different from what you have indulged in your note of yesterday'.[144] Unfortunately Joseph's letters are not on file, for us to know and assess his grounds for complaint. Nor do we know what he said at the end of 1886 to cause Syme to tell Herbert: 'I was very much put out the day I left with Joe & I cannot get over it'.[145] Clearly, Joseph harboured a grievance.

The division of responsibilities – crudely, David looking after content, Joseph after production – for the most part worked well. That their managerial styles were different – David's creative, *ad hoc* and somewhat chaotic; Joseph's systematic and somewhat cautious – did not in these years adversely affect the business and may, rather, have been a salutary complementation. But where responsibilities overlapped there was the potential for trouble. For instance, many extant memos show that Syme, when displeased with the layout of material appearing in his newspapers harangued the printer, who otherwise was under Joseph's direction. Another and more disturbing source of discord related to telegraphic and cable messages, arrangements for the procurement of which seems to have rested chiefly with Joseph. It would seem that the allocation of roles and duties had not been clarified, for Syme did not hesitate to make known his displeasure whenever he found messages to be sub-standard or not received at all.

Syme's complaints were not only to his staff but also to relevant personnel in outside organisations where, as seen with press colleagues sharing the cable service, his blunt and imperious manner militated against friendly cooperation. His impatient tendency to take precipitate action, without consultation and in the assumption that he was in supreme command, had led in the past to litigation over paper contracts and, in 1887, to an unfortunate disagreement with his press partners over the staffing of the cable service office in London. Fortunately, that the imperious manner belied both judgment that was usually sound and a sense of fairness came to be recognised, if not liked, by friends and colleagues who sometimes, however, found it easier to have dealings with Joseph. Deakin kept in touch with Joseph in Syme's absence, lunching with the junior partner on 30 June 1887 and seeing him again twice in September, shortly before Syme's return.[146]

---

[144] DS to JCS, 23 October 1883, LB2, p. 223.
[145] DS to H. Syme, 11 April 1887, SFP Box 1180/5(f).
[146] Diary entry, 30 June 1887, Deakin Papers, Series 2.

Thanks to both partners, the business was thriving, with profits ranging from £20,126 in 1883 to £28,819 in 1885.[147] The *Age* was always the big earner – in 1884 (for which a detailed financial statement is available) it brought in £102,170 of the total income of £132,536 for that year. The biggest, regular outgoings were always for wages and paper – in 1884 these were, respectively, £43,514 and £39,120. What would 1888 – Melbourne's boom year and the centenary of British settlement in Australia bring in? And would the uneasy elements of the partnership be resolved, or worsen?

---

[147] Financial statements 1880–1884 and 1885–1890, SFP Box 1191/2(a)(b).

Chapter 11

'EVERYTHING GOING ON WELL'

(1888)

Melbourne in the 1880s was experiencing an economic boom. Discussing the topic, the first issue of the *Age* for 1888 explained that '"boom" has been incorporated with our language to such an extent as to be commonly understood…[in relation to] land and property transactions', especially in the City of Melbourne.[1] Values in Collins Street had increased 'by leaps'. This was ascribed not so much to the inflow of 'vast amounts of English and foreign capital' as popularly believed, but to the increasing elasticity of revenue locally, to the absence of drought and to the prospect of a good harvest. Whatever the causes, in 1888 rising land values, unprecedented building activity and associated speculation reached a peak in Victoria's capital city, the good times celebrated in the grand International Centennial Exhibition that opened on 1 August (Davison 1978). It was a boom year also for Syme, and for the *Age* business, which was able to declare an astonishing profit of £98,421.[2] Deriving from a great spike in advertising volume as well as from a still increasing circulation, it was almost four times the amount for 1887; there was nothing remotely like it again in the proprietor's lifetime.

The circulation of the *Age* rose from 76,484 in June to 81,149 in November.[3] This latter figure represents one newspaper for every five persons in Melbourne or one in 13 for the whole of Victoria, more or less maintaining the market penetration of the previous year. Such calculations mask the increasing readership beyond Victoria, however. In April Syme visited Sydney, where he established an office for the *Age* in Pitt Street, opposite the premises of the *Sydney Morning Herald*. There he installed

---

[1] 'Great Rise in Property During 1887, Enormous Transactions', *Age*, 2 January 1888, p. 5.
[2] Financial statement, 1888, SFP Box 1191/2(b).
[3] 'Circulation of "The Age"', *Age*, 3 July 1888, p. 4, 6 November, p. 4.

DAVID SYME

Gabriel Montgomery, who for some time had been canvassing advertisements and subscriptions for the David Syme and Co. newspapers. Under a one-year agreement (which appears to have been extended) Montgomery would receive generous commission, but bear his own expenses, and pay the office rental[4] – certainly an incentive to produce results and an indication of sales opportunities in Sydney.

Advertisements related to land ventures and transactions increased almost overwhelmingly from August to October 1888. This, and the opening and first months of the Exhibition, caused the *Age* to be enlarged dramatically. At the beginning of the year the daily comprised 8 or 10 pages on weekdays and usually 16 or 18 on Saturdays. From June to October the weekday issues rose to 12 or 16 pages, and on Tuesdays from 14 August to 30 October a Melbourne Centennial Exhibition Supplement was included, while the Saturday issue increased to 20 or 24 pages. From November there was a cutting back, and by the end of the year the number of pages was more or less as it had been at the start. Other papers in the Syme stable were also enlarged. The 48-page *Leader* was sometimes issued with a supplement that ranged from four to 32 pages. The *Illustrated Australian News* too had supplements, largely devoted to the Exhibition and to the history of Victoria. The *Age Annual* for 1888 had 131 pages, with an additional 43 for advertisements; the next edition, published in February 1889, had 138 pages and 48 for advertisements. Syme's newspapers were not alone in enlarging. *The Argus* followed a similar path, with Saturday numbers of 28 pages in September and October, while the weekly *Australasian* also increased in size to 56 pages, with engravings in an eight-page supplement. While this alerted Syme, he did not think the first *Australasian* for 1888 a success.[5]

Syme wrote regularly to Joseph, away this year. On file are copies of 23 letters to him between 6 January and 26 October – at least one each month and sometimes four.[6] He reported in detail on business matters and sought his nephew's views on possible new moves. In March he sounded a rare positive note: 'The <u>Age</u> has been doing very well of late.'[7] By mid-year he was sounding uncharacteristically optimistic and buoyant, writing in late July, when the Exhibition was soon to open:

---

4   Entries for 17 January, 8 February DS diary 1888, SFP Box 1184/4; DS to JCS, 26 April 1888, LB4, pp. 30–31.
5   DS to JCS, 6 January 1888, LB3, p. 34.
6   DS to JCS from 6 January to 26 October in LB3, p. 34 to 128–130; from 17 February to 24 August in LB4, pp. 16–19 to 48–49.
7   DS to JCS, 2 March 1888, LB4, pp. 21–22.

CHAPTER 11

Figure 11.1. *Age* newsprint display at Melbourne Centennial International Exhibition, 1888. *Age*, 25 September 1888, Supplement, p. 2. (Newspaper Collection, State Library of Victoria)

The advts are increasing instead of falling off, last Saturday we had no less than 2 cols of reading matter in the second sheet, the advts coming in late in extraordinary force. So far every thing is going on well. The paper maintains its influence as well as it ever did.[8]

One month later he was equally enthusiastic:

Everything going on well. The Advts & circulation kept up. The Exhibition has been opened 4 weeks now…We have got a stand…As

---

8 DS to JCS, 20 July 1888, LB3, pp.109–112.

a set off against the Argus machine I have got an additional site & erected a sort of trophy, consisting of one days (Saturdays) paper – 50 reels on each in 5 tiers. It is an immense attraction & puts the <u>Argus</u> machine quite in the shade.[9]

The *Age* display in the Victorian court of the Exhibition was illustrated in the Exhibition Supplement for 25 September (fig. 11.1), accompanying a three-and-a-quarter column feature entitled 'A Popular Newspaper'. Against a background of British and Australian press history, it describes printing and production equipment and practices at the *Age* office, focusing on the 'full power of five machines…at work printing the popular newspaper'.

But, ever a realist, Syme did not allow himself to be carried away by success. In his letter of 28 September to Joseph he regretted that his nephew had not agreed to increase the charges for advertisements:

We shall never have such another opportunity. Auctioneers will pay almost any price to get their ads in the paper, so that it wd have been the easiest thing in the world to have got an increase…Later on it might be too late, for the spurt wont last.[10]

Sure enough, a week later he reported that advertisements had fallen off slightly (although still at abnormally high level; the crash would come later).[11]

For the whole year Syme was running the business, his own and Joseph's side, with a burst of energy that paid off. He rode the inflationary wave to his advantage and carefully, so that when the 'bust' came the newspaper business was not significantly touched and his private finances remained ample. But relations with his business partner, cordial at the outset, would take an unstoppable dive before the year was out.

Occupied as he was with the newspaper business, characteristically Syme also pursued other avenues of remuneration and satisfaction. While involved in the investing mania he was, however, cautious and conservative. When the engineering enterprise of David Munro was floated as a public company in early 1888 he politely declined to be a director and to take up shares 'so kindly reserved' for him.[12] This was a prudent move, for Munro was one of the 'new men' who, in their meteoric rise, had little business

---

[9] DS to JCS, 24 August 1888, LB4, pp. 48–49.
[10] DS to JCS, 28 September 1888, LB3, pp. 122–124.
[11] DS to JCS, 6 October 1888, LB3, pp. 128–130.
[12] DS to D. Munro, 26 January, 2 February 1888, LB4, p. 14, LB3, p. 52.

CHAPTER 11

training or judgment; in 1890 he was declared bankrupt, his firm one of the largest that went under (Serle 1971, 267; Davison 1978, 66; Cannon 1966, 105, 106, 228–229). Similarly, Syme refrained from joining the Kauri Timber Syndicate, a hugely ambitious venture launched in Melbourne to buy 430,000 acres of kauri timber land and a large number of sawmills in New Zealand, saying he was unable – and certainly he was unwilling – to find the £21,000 suddenly asked for.[13] This venture was a success, however; the Kauri Timber Company was registered in Melbourne in July 1888 and remained in Australian ownership for decades ('Kauri Timber Company' 2005). Syme conscientiously agreed to meet liabilities in a failed Queensland venture.[14] He did invest some of the firm's money at what he saw as a sound five per cent interest in two of the building societies that in the mid-eighties were 'rivalling the savings banks as savings institutions' (Serle 1971, 79).[15] So far as trading in debentures and shares was concerned, he was a cautious investor, and seems not to have been deeply interested. Through A.J. Malcolm in London, to whom he gave power of attorney, he had bought a small interest in McEwans, part of which he subsequently sold, in correspondence apologising for his 'blundering' and confessing to being in a 'complete state of confusion' about the money he originally paid.[16]

Syme was more astute and informed when it came to his country properties. In April he was pleased to be able to sell a property placed with his stock and station agent.[17] In May he put a £2000 deposit on another, but subsequently pursued return of the money which, he said, had been obtained by misrepresentation.[18] His largest property transaction this year was the acquisition of several thousand more acres in the Yarra Valley.[19] With his characteristic, persistence, through a series of letters over months, he pursued with the Healesville Shire Council his complaint about a roads contractor's damage to his Dalry fences.[20] He obviously did not delegate this

---

[13] 'The Kauri Timber Syndicate', *Argus*, 30 June 1888, p. 14; DS to D. Blair, 27 February 1888, LB4, p. 20; DS to J. Sharpe, 6 March 1888, LB4, p. 23.
[14] DS to Clarke & Co., 7, 16 August 1888, LB4, pp. 46, 47.
[15] DS to JCS, 28 September 1888, LB3, pp. 122–124.
[16] DS to A. Malcolm, 20 January 1888, LB4, p. 12; DS to J. McEwan & Co. Ltd, 18 May 1888, LB4, p. 40.
[17] DS to C. Hamilton, 16 April 1888, LB4, p. 28.
[18] DS to J. Howden, 30 May, 8 October, 21 November 1888, LB4, pp. 41, 54, 57.
[19] Victoria. Certificates of title 2076/104 and 2076/105, 25 August 1888. There may be others, not identified.
[20] DS to Healesville Shire Council, 7 May, 21 June, 4 August, 24 October 1888, LB4, pp. 33–34, 42, 45, 56.

to his son Francis, whom he had placed there as manager, and with whom relations continued to be uncomfortable. In December, when Francis did take an initiative in exchanging a horse at Dalry for one at Killara, his father wrote to reprimand him.[21]

More than a hobby, amounting to a passion, it seems, was his interest in procuring livestock for his rural properties. And not any creatures – breeding was paramount. Nor did he act in isolation. Appointed president of a new Polled Cattle Society in Victoria, he sought affiliation with an equivalent English body, identifying himself as an advocate of 'a pure descent from pedigreed stock' and lamenting the very few pedigreed and many 'half-bred' cattle in the colony.[22] In March he was reluctant to sell two heifers from his prized herd, advised to keep them because of the 'strain of blood'.[23] The same day he wrote to leading pastoralist William McCulloch, who was about to set off for Britain, telling him of success in getting a good farm manager (for Killara) – a Scot with New Zealand experience.[24] Following up a recent conversation, Syme asked McCulloch to buy for him a polled Angus bull in Scotland, wanting a 'thoroughly good animal'. By September 'young Eric' had arrived, been placed in quarantine and inspected by Syme, who proceeded to insure the animal, destined for Killara, with the Australian Mutual Livestock Association.[25] He had also asked McCulloch to purchase two pairs of Cayuga ducks, those he had bought himself when in England the previous year having died on the voyage back to Victoria, and a Scots Grey rooster for, although his fowls had survived that journey, he wanted a 'change of blood'.

A new development, in parallel with practical animal husbandry pursuits, Syme was immersing himself in questions of academic biology, and by the end of July had written an article that, focusing on the fertilisation of plants by insects, criticised aspects of Darwin's interpretation. He sent the piece to Dr Richard Garnett of the British Museum, whom he saw as a 'friend' of long standing, asking him to use his influence with journal editors to get it published promptly for he wished it to appear before George Henslow's forthcoming *The Origin of Floral Structures through Insects and other Agencies*; however, when Henslow's book came out with Kegan Paul very soon after,

---

[21] DS to F. Syme, 10 December 1888, LB4, p. 58.
[22] DS to A. Ramsay, 24 August 1888, LB4, p. 50.
[23] DS to D. Mitchell, 13 March 1888, LB4, p. 24.
[24] DS to W. McCulloch, 13 March 1888, LB4, p. 25.
[25] DS to W. McCulloch, 28 September 1888, LB4, pp. 54; DS to Secretary, Australia Mutual Livestock Association, 15 October 1888, LB4, p. 55.

CHAPTER 11

Syme saw to his relief that it had an approach different to that of his article.[26] He also noted that he would be asking Philip Mennell, back as a contributor (dealt with below), to read the proofs and check technical terms. Hearing of its rejection by the *Nineteenth Century*, Syme then wanted its submission to the *Contemporary*, the *Fortnightly*, the *Universal* or the *Westminster*, but on no account in the latter's 'Independent Section', where his somewhat heterodox 'On the 'Method of Political Economy' had appeared in 1871.[27] While it does not seem to have been published anywhere, this new article would become part of his book on evolution, published in 1890.

How did this radical departure from politics and government, economics and land tenure, and like fields of study and literary production come about? Perhaps Syme had thought about and partly written the article while away in 1887, when he had several weeks of shipboard existence. In the past he had used such time to work on manuscripts. But it could also have arisen in 1888, from thoughts about breeding related to his livestock and from the debates about evolution raging in the *Argus* early in the year, following a review in the 3 January issue of *The Life and Letters of Charles Darwin*, edited by son Francis Darwin, which had been published by John Murray in 1887. The review, which considered the book a 'model of a biography', provoked fierce controversy in letters to the *Argus* editor and in several leaders about the tenability of Darwin's theory of evolution, with more writers accepting than rejecting. David Blair, co-editor with Ebenezer Syme of the *Age* in the mid-1850s before David's involvement, was one of the outspoken proponents, writing that 'Evolution…as a scientific doctrine…has risen from being the challenged into the challenger'.[28] Moreover, there was a new scientific climate in learned circles and new blood at the University of Melbourne, with Baldwin Spencer installed as the foundation professor of biology. He and colleagues are seen to have 'ushered in the new biology based on sound evolutionary principles' (Mulvaney and Calaby 1985, 70, 147, 108). And in 1888 the Australasian Association for the Advancement of Science was founded.

If the above preoccupations were 'out of hours', Syme was no less energetic concerning the ongoing newspaper management, including attending to matters normally under Joseph's control. Taking charge of all details concerning machinery, equipment and supplies, with no suggestion of

---

[26] DS to R. Garnett, 27 July 1888, LB4, p. 44.
[27] DS to P. Mennell, 4 September, 20 December 1888, LB4, pp. 53, 59.
[28] 'The Progress of Evolution', *Argus*, 1 February 1888, p. 8.

delegation, he had much to master, and this was complicated by his having taken over without much briefing and by the inevitable delays in sea mail communication, which impaired decision-making.

Most of Syme's letters to Joseph in 1888 run to several pages, dealing in detail with matters of machinery, type and newsprint supplies, as well as numerous other aspects of the business. In February he wrote that the rising circulation of the *Age* called for another printing machine, and on 2 March informed his nephew that the printing workload was causing the *Age* to be late every day. He wanted him to order the best available equipment as soon as possible. During March and April he reiterated this and gave specific advice. In May he asked Joseph, by cable and letter, to inspect the Hoe machines at the *Newcastle Daily Chronicle*. But Joseph had already placed an order by the time he received this advice or instruction, and Syme acknowledged that he had to accept the *fait accompli*. Nevertheless, he quibbled, repeating his preference for the Hoes used by the Newcastle paper and, in another letter, reporting that he had favourable reports from other colonial newspapers about Foster machines. Joseph Foster & Sons of Preston, England, had developed their 'Prestonion' rotary printing machine soon after the appearance of the Victory (Wilson and Grey 1888, 208). The Hoe ordered by Joseph, was featured in the *Illustrated Australian News* of 13 October, the illustration showing the 'latest development' and a statement that the *Age* was now being printed by six machines (the three Victory ones bought in the 1870s and, now, three Hoes – not quite correct, for the third Hoe would not arrive until 1889).

Syme was no less concerned about the procurement of new type, which he wanted in time for the Exhibition, presumably to improve the appearance of the newspapers. And he preferred smaller type for more economical setting of the growing volume of advertisements. Twice in early January he asked Joseph to excuse the delay in drawing up the order that he was to have sent the previous month, and suggested that his nephew might in any case make contact with type foundries in anticipation of it. Finally, on 20 January he despatched a list of requirements. In February he wrote hoping that the order would he underway (presumably he meant by the time Joseph would be reading his letter, some four to six weeks later). Twice in March he stressed the urgency; in April he expressed relief that the type would be sent out in time, then in a letter two weeks later deplored some of the changes that Joseph had made. Two months later he was pleased to report that a consignment of the type had duly arrived and been put into use on Monday 16 July. In August, however, he complained that some of the type

CHAPTER 11

was wearing fast and Joseph would have to arrange for it to be taken back, and in October he made a similar complaint. Worry and carping, aggravated by the 10- to 16-week time lag between epistolary communication and response, characterise his treatment of what one imagines to be a relatively straightforward matter. As only a couple of Joseph's 1888 letters to Syme are extant, the junior partner's attitude to the issue can only be guessed at.[29]

Supply of suitable newsprint was yet another worry, expressed in four letters during January and February; paper obtained from Lloyds was unsuitable and would Joseph do something about this, and would Joseph follow a reported successful experiment in London into using the wood of Australian eucalypts for newsprint. On 9 March, having just heard by cable (via the *Argus*, not his own service) of the death of the German Emperor Wilhelm I, he was almost frantic about securing adequate supplies, with stocks running low. Presumably, with Queen Victoria's son-in-law Friedrich III to succeed his father Wilhelm, Syme expected public interest to set off a spurt in sales of the *Age*. He had cabled twice to send extra supplies and was going to do so again, but acknowledged that paper from a mill at Geelong was helping somewhat. While shipments from overseas must have arrived to allay his worries for a time (the same concern with paper supplies is not on record relating to the death just over three months later of the terminally ill Friedrich III), in September he was again agitating, having had to cable for an extra 5000 reams, noting that 'we are only in the beginning of summer yet, with the land boom in full swing & supplements increasing every week'.[30] Litigation involving a dispute with an Irish paper supplier and likely to involve hundreds of pounds he dealt with in four letters between March and June. He urged Joseph, on lawyer Gillott's advice, to settle ('<u>Now</u> is the time for compromise') and was relieved when he did.[31] And yet, following the satisfactory settlement each man later quibbled and took offence over the correct use of code words about the matter in their cables.

Syme wrote to Joseph on 6 January that K.D. Bennett had been seriously ill but was now better. As the highest paid staff member in the Counting House, Bennett would have been Joseph's right-hand man.[32] Syme's letters to Joseph throughout the year indicate that Bennett was a continual source of advice and information and the office ran smoothly. But in relation to

---

[29] JCS to DS, 27 June, 2 July, 4 July (extract only), 1888, SFP Box 1180/3(b).
[30] DS to JCS, 28 September 1888, LB3, pp. 122–124.
[31] DS to JCS, 2 March 1888, LB3, p. 67.
[32] Entry for Bennett in Wages Book, p. 27.

his own area of responsibility – the literary and editorial side – his letters in the early part of the year give a more negative impression. On 6 January he complained that Windsor was 'laid up again'. On 17 February he wrote at some length about his 'uphill work', with Windsor not even knowing when anything was wrong, commercial editor Robinson overwhelmed by the vastly increased activity in the share market, and Allen bad and the reporting staff under him even worse. These appear gratuitous comments, likely to make Joseph uneasy, and would have provided ammunition for later criticism. In fact, when Allen gave notice in March, Syme was taken by surprise, and on reflection persuaded him to stay on, which the chief of staff did, until 1890. One gains the impression of a moody and sometimes unwarrantedly pessimistic proprietor.

Syme was concerned also about staffing of the *Leader*, telling Joseph about this without referring to the editor, Henry Short. It would appear that John Dow, now Minister of Lands and Agriculture, although remaining on the staff, was no longer the agricultural editor, and in any case Syme considered that he knew little about agriculture and stock. He saw W. Elliott, the horticultural editor, who had been acting in the position, as only a makeshift, getting too old for the work and with a defective memory, and R. Dodds, who would in fact take up the position, as a very dull writer. Syme said he had been keeping a 'strict supervision' but this was getting too much for him.[33] He suggested that Joseph contact editors of agricultural papers to try to find a suitable person in London. This would lead to Charles Scott taking up the position of 'farm editor' in February 1889.[34] Syme had considered local recruitment of a Professor Brown, formerly at an agricultural college in Canada, but knew from Dow that he might be appointed to a new agricultural college in Victoria, and thus engaged him as an occasional contributor on agricultural topics. Indeed Brown joined the staff of the new Longerenong Agricultural College early in 1889.[35]

Subeditor Stephens continued to receive a stream of stern letters and memos, copied into the letterbook for reference in case of disputes, Syme informed him.[36] There are 17 on file for the period January to August, after which there is a hiatus for the rest of the year, perhaps an indication of Syme being in a better frame of mind, or preoccupied elsewhere.[37] A few were

---

[33] DS to JCS, 20 July 1888, LB3, pp. 109–112.
[34] Entry for Scott in Wages Book, p. 442.
[35] 'Another Agricultural College', *Kerang Times*, 15 February 1889, p. 3.
[36] DS to J. Stephens, 9 February 1888, LB3, p. 55.
[37] DS to J. Stephens from 28 January 1888 (LB3, p. 49) to 21 August 1888 (LB3, p. 118).

CHAPTER 11

directed also at the printer, J. Odgers, with whom Syme was increasingly dissatisfied, asking Joseph time and again to engage another, someone who could take a stand against the Age Chapel (the compositors' and printers' association). By September Joseph had engaged one, and a machinist, also requested. Less successfully, Syme asked Joseph to find a stereotyper, then obtained one locally and rescinded the request. He found, however, that the man he appointed 'neglects his work, gets drunk & is impertinent', and in October notified that he needed another stereotyper after all.[38] All the same, and in contrast to his despairing comments about the printing staff, in June he pointed out to Joseph that the printing was now very good (implying that it was superior now with Joseph away?).[39] It was better than that of the *Argus*, he claimed, and reprimanded his nephew for not giving credit for the improved appearance.

A dispute with the substantial body of compositors on his staff arose when the Melbourne Typographical Society resolved in April to raise the remuneration rate for typesetting.[40] This rate was to apply from July, as would a new set of new rules, which would act to increase costs for the newspaper business.[41] The *Argus* estimated these would amount to £4000 a year. The dispute with the Age Chapel persisted and Syme, dreading a strike, 'at the last moment' offered a compromise, entailing an increase of £1200 a year for the firm, a sum that might be reduced by one half if ruby type (at 5.5 point, small and therefore space-saving) was used for all the advertisements. This being accepted by the Chapel put 'the Argus people… in a towering rage', he told Joseph in July.[42]

As usual, this year Syme was the defendant in several libel actions. Two he mentioned to Joseph in March, being particularly worried about one brought by Joseph Winter, manager of the *Advocate*, a Catholic newspaper published weekly in Melbourne, covering matters of Irish interest as well as local general news. A letter published in the *Age* the previous November, signed 'Scrutator', accused Winter of misappropriating funds for the Irish National League.[43] The defence (Syme) argued successfully for more time to prepare

---

[38] DS to JCS, 26 October 1888, LB3, pp. 128–130.
[39] DS to JCS, 8 June 1888, LB3, p. 99–107.
[40] *Australasian Typographical Journal*, May 1888, p. 867; DS to JCS, 26 April 1888, LB4, pp. 30–31.
[41] *Australasian Typographical Journal*, June, p. 883, July p. 891; DS to JCS, 17 May 1888, LB4, pp. 35–39.
[42] DS to JCS, 20 July 1888, LB3, pp. 109–112.
[43] DS to JCS, 2, 9 March 1888, LB3, pp. 67, 69–70.

a case and, at the hearing in May, presented a litany of detailed questions that would require witnesses in England and Ireland and raised questions that shed doubt on the accounting practices at the *Advocate*.[44] It appears that the suit was subsequently dropped. Syme worked hard, and usually to good effect, to avoid verdicts against him on matters of major concern.

Syme's letterbooks attest to his continuing involvement in the procurement of news from afar. Intercolonially, he came to a satisfactory split arrangement with Davies Brothers of the Hobart *Mercury* for Tasmanian cables and with Charles Fox for occasional Tasmanian correspondence.[45] For some years Fox had been contributing to and editing the Davies Brothers' weekly *Tasmanian Mail* (Gibbney and Smith 1987, v.1, 240), but apparently was leaving that employment. Syme was less satisfied with the cable news from New South Wales and Queensland received via the Sydney *Daily Telegraph*. He found occasion to complain to Wynne about late messages and serious omissions, usually making comparisons with more satisfactory *Argus* coverage.[46]

Harrison continued to be a prolific contributor of correspondence from London. He could be relied upon, but had to be discouraged from overdoing it. On 27 April Syme wrote that he was sending too many 'International Notes'.[47] When he received Harrison's response more than three months later (illustrating the immense time lag for maintaining correspondence by sea mail), on 8 August he replied, clarifying his instruction. He assured Harrison that his International Notes were 'good', only there were too many of them.[48] He said that seven articles by him had appeared in two issues of the *Age* the previous week and pointed out that three of them were of little interest locally, and could have been compiled from blue books (official parliamentary reports). The seven articles presumably are: on 3 August, 'The Great Cities of the World' by 'Cosmopolitan', 'The Trade through the Suez Canal' (anonymous) and 'Emigration and Vital Production' by 'Mercator; and on 4 August, 'Modern Monopolies' by 'Mercator', 'Chips' by 'Oedipus' and, both anonymously, 'A Year's Progress in Bechuanaland', and 'The Food Supply of Great Britain'. In December he asked Harrison to slow the rate of supplying Scientific Gossip items, which were piling up at the *Leader*.[49]

---

[44] *Argus*, 6 April 1888, p. 7, col. 7, 'The Irish National League', *Argus*, 19 May 1888, p. 13.
[45] DS to Davies Bros, 22 May, 20 June, 1888, LB3, pp. 94, 106; DS to C. Fox, 20 June 1888, LB3, p. 105.
[46] DS to W. Wynne, 13 November, 14 December 1888, LB3, pp. 131–132, 137–138.
[47] DS to J. Harrison, 27 April 1888, LB4, p. 32.
[48] DS to J. Harrison, 8 August 1888, LB3, p. 116.
[49] DS to J. Harrison, 20 December 1888, LB3, p. 141.

CHAPTER 11

Tracing the authorship in 1888 of the London Letter regularly featured in the *Age* is difficult, and bound up with the fraught matter of the London cable correspondent, dealt with below. As seen in the previous chapter, Mennell resigned from both positions in 1886. His replacement, Bones, seems to have written the Letter as well as providing the cable messages, for in March Syme observed to Joseph that he would 'never make a good correspondent, either for cables or letters (the latter are getting worse & worse.)'.[50] In April 1888 Mennell was offered both positions back, at £500 a year, an attractive salary, and in May Syme expressed his gratification at again having his services.[51] In October, however, he wrote to Joseph that he had no idea about the correspondence arrangements now that Mennell was 'gone' and suggested that he try to recruit Levey again.[52] Mennell, however, was retained or brought back (relevant records are unclear), and in December Syme wrote him two letters with instructions about, and fairly severe criticism of, the correspondence that he had been sending.[53]

Also from London, a Miss Carpenter was sending contributions, including a regular Ladies Letter. In August, while accepting her contributions, Syme regulated the flow as he had done with Harrison, asking for no more than two short contributions or one long one per month.[54] He was happy to accept the regular London Town Talk, offered by James Payn, no stranger to David Syme and Co.[55] Editor of the *Cornhill Magazine*, journalist Payn also wrote novels, one of which had been serialised in the *Age* in 1875 and five in the *Leader* between 1868 and 1887 (Brake and Demoor 2009, 484; Johnson-Woods 2001, 124). As Payn had apparently been writing for the *Argus*, which now was running a feature called Social Gossip from Home, Syme suggested the title of his contribution be changed to Social London. It is not clear whether Payn took up this suggestion.

Besides the usual fortnightly (sometimes weekly) London Letter, there was one of similar frequency from Paris, a more or less monthly one from New York and similarly from New Zealand and, closer to home, usually a weekly one from Sydney. From time to time there was a series of articles by a traveller. In early 1888, for instance, 'Six Weeks in Japan', by Lex ran in

---

[50] DS to JCS, 23 March 1888, LB3, pp. 87–88.
[51] DS to JCS, 19 April 1888, LB4, p. 29; DS to P. Mennell, 18 May 1888, LB4, p. 41.
[52] DS to JCS, 26 October 1888, LB3, pp. 128–130.
[53] DS to P Mennell, 13, 21, December 1888, LB3, pp. 135–136, 140.
[54] DS to Miss Carpenter, 3 August, 9 October 1888, LB3, pp. 114, 124.
[55] DS to J. Payn, 28 May 1888, LB3, p. 95.

the *Age*. And true to his *nom de plume* 'The Vagabond', John Stanley James, aka Julian Thomas, who in 1887 had switched allegiance from the *Argus* to the *Age*, was in 1888 sending contributions from distant parts of the globe; in February a series of 'Californian Jottings' appeared in the *Age*, and in November a column from Paris.

Serial fiction for the *Age* and *Leader* continued to be sourced from England, with a bestselling novel by Walter Besant in the *Age* and similarly sought-after titles by Mary Braddon and David Christie Murray in the *Leader*. There was also a solid body of Australian fiction in the David Syme and Co. newspapers this year. What role Syme had in its procurement is not known, but clearly he did not reject the works. In the latter half of 1888 the *Leader* ran the notable *The Ladies' Gallery*, by Queensland-born Rosa Praed and English author Justin McCarthy, and *Bingley's Gap*, a never otherwise published early work by young Mary Gaunt, one of the first two women admitted to the University of Melbourne, who would become a prolific travel and fiction writer. Another Gaunt work not published in book form was 'A Man's Sacrifice', printed in full in the December *Illustrated Australian News* and described in the *Leader* of 2 December as a 'stirring and dramatic Christmas tale'.

The colonial fiction coup was the serialisation in the *Age* from 7 July 1888 to 5 January 1889 of Ada Cambridge's novel, *A Black Sheep* (later published as a book with the title *A Marked Man*). As noted in the previous chapter, this is the novel for which Cambridge in 1887 travelled to Sydney to obtain material, with the blessing of a Syme (probably Joseph, possibly Herbert). Soon making its author famous throughout the English-speaking world, this novel has been regarded ever since as her most outstanding (Wilde, Hooton and Andrews 1985, 137–138; Morrison 2004). Certainly it brought financial rewards. Writing later of the 'merry Boom time', with some pride she pointed to her participation in it: 'Those days! I too had my little boom on the Australian press…I received £197 for the serial rights of *A Marked Man*.' (Cambridge 2006, 124, 129). As the author 'A.C.', Cambridge already had a formidable reputation amongst Victorian newspaper readers; it can only have been enhanced by this latest work, its first instalment appearing in the lead-up to the opening of the Exhibition. Moreover, it may have contributed to the growing demand for the *Age* (although there is no way of finding evidence for this). Ironically, since its serialisation was synchronous with the Exhibition, *A Black Sheep* is set in Sydney, the true 'centennial' city, which had been unable to finance a celebratory exhibition. The Syme papers were not the only ones to feature significant Australian fiction in this centennial

CHAPTER 11

year, however; from January to May the *Australasian* serialised *The Pipers of Piper's Hill* by Tasma (Jessie Couvreur). Set in Melbourne, it was published to acclaim as a book in 1889 as *Uncle Piper of Piper's Hill*.

The revamped cable service that Joseph had negotiated and arranged with Wynne of the Sydney *Daily Telegraph* and *South Australian Advertiser* proprietors Burden & Bonython came into operation in 1888, and expanded during the year. The alliance of these three leading colonial capital dailies is underscored by the advertisements that appeared often in the *Age* during 1888: for the 'leading South Australian Paper, the *South Australian Advertiser*' with a circulation 'treble that of any of the Daily Morning Papers in South Australia'; and for the Sydney *Daily Telegraph*, with the 'Largest Circulation of any Morning Newspaper in New South Wales'. It is not clear whether the reciprocal arrangement that Burden and Bonython in Adelaide made with John Hackett of the daily *West Australian* in July for the supply of telegraphic news from their respective colonies extended to the other members of the cable service.[56] It is clear, however, that in November Wynne in Sydney signed up the *Australian Star*, a penny evening daily that, in the Sydney press ethos of free trade advocacy, stood for the protectionist cause dear to Syme, and numbered democrats and radicals amongst its directors.[57] Around the same time Syme was lining up the promoters of a new evening daily, the *Evening Standard*, being planned for Melbourne long in advance of its actual appearance – it would begin publication in April 1889.[58]

Following Joseph's departure in late 1887, Syme took some weeks to familiarise himself with arrangements for the revamped service. There was much to manage. One source of concern was the arrangement for telegraphing lists of passengers on ships arriving at Albany in Western Australia, to be shared with the *Argus*; another was stopping the news summaries that were being sent out with the mail ships and telegraphed from Albany and Adelaide. From January to July Syme sent a spate of letters about this to his cable service partners and to staff in London and Melbourne.[59]

---

[56] Burden & Bonython to J. Hackett, 14 January 1888, J.L. Bonython and Company, Summary Record, Letter Books, BRG 10, Series 8, State Library of South Australia.
[57] DS to W. Wynne, 22 November 1888, LB3, p. 134; Walker (1976, 88).
[58] DS to JCS, 24 August 1888, LB4, pp. 48–49; DS to W. Wynne, 22 November 1888, LB3, p. 134.
[59] DS to J. Stephens and to P. Mennell from 4 January (LB3, p. 29) to 6 July 1888 (LB3, p. 108).

Of more pressing concern, however, was the perceived inadequacy of the news cables from London. They were late, or omitted altogether, or seen as frivolous and irrelevant. All three intercolonial members of the service realised this and Syme was recipient of many complaints, for it was he who had selected Bones as cable correspondent.[60] Clearly he was not up to the task. Although telling Joseph that Bones was 'a fool' and thinking that Mennell should replace him, Syme persisted for weeks with detailed instructions for Joseph to pass on to him, as well as writing and cabling to Bones, suggesting ways of improving his work.[61] On 14 March, after complaints all round about the service failing to give news of the German Emperor's death, and demands from the directors of the Sydney *Daily Telegraph* for action, Syme wrote a placatory letter to Wynne, in which he seems to be deflecting attention by suggesting a protest to the Eastern Extension Telegraph Company about ordinary messages getting precedence over press ones.[62] The next day he despatched a fairly desperate letter to McEwan & Co. in London in an attempt to contact Joseph, then travelling on the Continent.[63] He seems to have been in a morass of indecision, leaving responsibility to Joseph, who was technically on leave.

Matters came to a head in April, when Bonython and Wynne came to Melbourne to consult with or confront Syme. According to Syme, at this 'conference' a decision was reached to remove Bones and replace him with Mennell, if Mennell was agreeable and, if he was not, to send Lauchlan Brient from Sydney to take over.[64] Brient (whose name Syme usually misspelled as Briant) was news editor on the Sydney *Daily Telegraph*, and the person apparently responsible for publishing in 1885 the sensational story (referred to in the previous chapter) about the disastrous New Guinea expedition led by the buccaneer-type Strachan. He had earlier been a leader writer for the *Sydney Morning Herald* and may at one time have worked on the *Age* (Waterhouse 1979). Accordingly, as noted above, Syme wrote and cabled Joseph to try and re-engage Mennell as cable and conventional correspondent and, to his pleasure and relief, Mennell was back on the job by mid-May. (Bones arrived back in Melbourne with family in May 1889, and

---

[60] For example, Burden & Bonython to DS & Co., 14 March 1888, Bonython & Co. Letter Books.
[61] DS to JCS, 20 January 1888, LB3, pp. 41–44.
[62] DS to W. Wynne, 14 March 1888, LB3, pp. 74–75.
[63] DS to J. McEwan & Co., 15 March 1888, LB3, pp.78–80.
[64] DS to JCS, 19 April 1888, LB4, p. 29.

CHAPTER 11

was not employed again on the *Age*.[65]) Meanwhile Wynne, before hearing of Mennell's appointment, and pressed by his directors, had despatched Brient, who sailed from Sydney with his wife on 14 May.[66] Once again a problem arose similar to the one caused the previous year when Bones was sent to London by Syme, and Stephenson was sent by Bonython to fill the same position. (In that case, although it came to be agreed that Stephenson would assist Bones, in January Burden and Bonython decided to terminate the former's engagement.[67]) While Wynne wanted Mennell dismissed, Syme continued to deal with him as their cable correspondent and told Joseph that when Brient arrived, to 'Treat him civilly but let him understand that he has no mission from the Association'.[68] In early June, before Brient would have arrived, Syme, Bonython and Wynne were all extremely dissatisfied with the cricket cables about the Australia–England matches being played in the run-up to the Tests that would begin in mid-July (Harte 2008, 154–155). Syme sent detailed instructions for correct and prompt match reporting.[69]

What happened in the London office when Brient did turn up in late June is not on record. In July Syme wrote to Mennell as if he were in charge.[70] But pressure was being put on Syme, who in August wrote to Henry Gorman, Chairman of the Daily Telegraph Newspaper Company, that he would advise him of his decision about Brient as soon as he heard from Joseph.[71] While records are incomplete for the next moves, one infers from Syme's letters that by 4 October Joseph had appointed Brient and Mennell had gone.[72] Syme, Bonython and Wynne were to meet in Melbourne on 29 October to settle the terms of Brient's appointment and perhaps to discuss an observed deterioration in the service under him. Once again, records are lacking, but it would seem that Brient was retained for the cable service and Mennell for the London correspondence sent by ship. Syme, who found Wynne 'abominably nasty since the Briant affair',

---

[65] Unassisted Inward Passenger Lists to Victoria 1852–1923, Public Record Office Victoria.
[66] DS to JCS, 17 May 1888, LB4, pp.35–39; 'Shipping', *Sydney Morning Herald*, 15 May 1888, p. 6.
[67] Burden & Bonython to DS & Co., 6 January 1888, Bonython & Co. Letter Books; DS to G. Bones, 11 January 1888, LB3, p. 38–40.
[68] DS to JCS, 17 May 1888, LB4, pp. 35–39.
[69] DS to JCS, 1, 8, 30 June 1888, LB3, pp. 97, 98, 99–105.
[70] DS to P. Mennell, 6 July 1888, LB3, p. 108.
[71] DS to H. Gorman, 13 August 1888, LB3, p. 117.
[72] DS to Burden & Bonython, 18 October 1888, LB3, pp. 125–127.

he told Joseph, does not seem to have realised that his precipitate action and lack of communication, worsened by the tyranny of distance, had largely contributed to the unpleasant situation.[73] The matter created much ill will and several employees – Stephenson, Bones, Mennell, and perhaps Brient also – arguably were rudely and unjustly treated.

If sundry employees and others in the press community had cause to be disaffected by Syme, this could seem as nothing compared to what might have been the effect on Syme of accusations made by Joseph during the course of the year, which would lead to the absolute breakdown of relations between the partners. Goodwill characterises Syme's letters to his nephew in January and February (always 'Dear Nephew'). The first ends: 'Wishing you a happy New Year. I am yours affectionately'.[74] Several that follow are signed 'affectionately' and that of 20 January adds: 'Aunt sends her love to Laura [Joseph's wife] & hopes you are enjoying yourselves'.[75] But one of 2 March, his sixth to Joseph so far in 1888, begins 'At last I have a letter from you'.[76] This seems to set a tone for the rest of the correspondence, with letters usually ending 'Yours sincerely' rather than 'affectionately', and no more family pleasantries. As seen earlier in this chapter, much routine newspaper management business was covered in the correspondence, punctuated now and then by seemingly gratuitous quibbles and niggles.

Syme introduced a significantly new topic, however, in his letter of 17 May, one that was consonant with Melbourne's boom ethos and activity. Reporting that he had received two offers from 'financial associations' to float the *Age* as a joint stock company, with one offering £250,000 to purchase the business, he told Joseph that he was 'disposed to let it go in certain conditions' believing he would 'never have a better chance'.[77] If Joseph was in favour he should cable immediately and return as soon as possible. Awaiting his response, Syme's six subsequent letters make no mention of the proposal.

Replying on 27 June, from Glasgow, Joseph judiciously refrained from committing himself until his return, set for 21 January 1889, but obviously he had given the matter serious consideration and was favourably inclined.[78] He said that in the meantime the balance sheet for 1888 should be ready

---

[73] DS to JCS, 26 October 1888, LB3, pp. 128–130.
[74] DS to JCS, 6 January 1888, LB3, p. 34.
[75] DS to JCS, 20 January 1888, LB3, pp. 41–44.
[76] DS to JCS, 2 March 1888, LB4, pp 21–22.
[77] DS to JCS, 17 May 1888, LB4, pp. 35–39.
[78] JCS to DS, 27 June 1888, SFP Box 1180/3(b).

CHAPTER 11

for him to look at on his return and the fact that 1888 was 'turning out a good year' should increase the selling price of the paper. Writing that the directors should be men of probity and a mixture of 'thorough liberals and good business men', he suggested Deakin, Windsor, William McLean, John Shillinglaw '& ourselves'. They seem sound choices of men to be relied upon; McLean was a committed protectionist with a very prosperous hardware business (Parsons 1974) and Shillinglaw a secretary to various government bodies and a respected author and historian (Jordens 1976). He added that James Mirams would not be suitable (as he was 'not strong enough' – presciently, for the politician and financier would go under with the failure of his Premier Building Association in 1889). Nor would he consider Pearson, as he was 'not popular'. Finally, he would prefer not to use a financial company to float the concern ('They are grasping').

Five days later Joseph wrote again on the subject, from Pitlochrie. This time he was more definite, saying that he was 'in favour' of a company.[79] His further remarks, however, were unpleasant: 'I am activated also by the feeling that we ought not to continue working together after our recent conversations respecting the manner in which my father's family was bought out.' The 'conversations' must have been in late 1887 after Syme's return to Melbourne and before Joseph's departure and, as many times before, to have been about Joseph's long-standing grievances. He went on to say that he didn't want to hurt Syme's feelings but his uncle was only 'widening the breach & losing a good opportunity of doing an honorable act of restitution'. Then came the thunderclap: 'No lawyer's sophisms will get over the fact that you are retaining what has come to you wrongly no matter how.' Joseph was convinced that his uncle had cheated Jane and family. The evidence shows that, on the contrary, Syme took responsibility for his brother's dependants and had been scrupulously fair and considerate in very difficult and trying circumstances. Joseph's accusation, not new but this time presented with a force that surely could not be deflected or ignored, reads as a deep insult to Syme's honour and sense of integrity. Joseph wrote two days later with financial calculations relating to the hypothetical company, seemingly unaware of any insult.

The first paragraph of Syme's letter of 24 August contains his dignified, polite response: 'That part of your letter having reference to a private matter I shall leave saying anything about till you return to Melbourne.'[80] He then

---

[79] JCS to DS, 2 July 1888, SFP Box 1180/3(b).
[80] DS to JCS, 24 August 1888, LB4, pp. 48–49.

noted Joseph's remarks about forming a company and said the balance sheet for 1888 would be ready by 31 January. The long letter went on to deal, as usual, under headings: <u>New stereotyper</u>, <u>New machine</u>, <u>The new Evening paper</u> and <u>Type.</u> The next two and final letters sent to Joseph while away are similarly businesslike, with no further mention of the public company proposal nor of the private difference of opinion.[81] The latter would be taken up upon Joseph's return in January 1889.

---

[81] While Peter Yule (2012, 68) has written that in 1897–98 William Baillieu and Theodore Fink made plans to take over the *Age* and that Syme was willing to sell, Syme's papers yield no mention of this.

Chapter 12

'NEITHER PLEASURE NOR PROFIT IN CONTINUING OUR PARTNERSHIP'

(January 1889 to March 1891)

Seen then and now as an icon of boom time Melbourne, the Centennial International Exhibition, which wound up at the end of January 1889, actually sustained a large financial loss (Serle 1971, 285). Perhaps this was an indicator of the hard times to come in the early 1890s. After the 'pricking of the land bubble' in late 1888, paper gains of speculators were wiped out, but otherwise there appeared to be a return to economic and social normality in 1889 (Serle 1971, 327). There were no credit restrictions, and land values were maintained, as was full employment. The 'first tremor of a financial earthquake' occurred in March 1890 with the collapse of James Mirams' Premier Building Society (Davison 1978, 185). More business failures, the Maritime Strike of August 1890 and further industrial disruption were part of the depression that deepened in 1891 and lasted for several years. While the bust was Australia-wide, Melbourne, which had the biggest boom, was its 'epicentre' (Dingle 2005).

The fortunes of David Syme and Co. from 1889 to early 1891 were a microcosm of Melbourne's. In July 1890 Syme wrote to Malcolm: 'Matters here are as well as can be expected after the enormous inflation of 1888, & we are gradually getting onto the right track again.'[1] While extant financial records are messy and conflicting, a table of Syme's three-quarters profit share that has been drawn on in earlier chapters to calculate total annual profits gives £26,397.4.8 in 1889 and £29,686.18.4 in 1890.[2] While each

---

[1] DS to A. Malcolm, 29 July 1890, LB4, p. 103.
[2] Profit and loss, 1885–1890, SFP Box 1191/2(b).

is a small fraction of the 1888 sum, both figures approximate the pre-land-boom year level.

The late 1880s, which Geoffrey Serle (1971, 340) saw as 'the last, dying days of Australia Felix', were also the dying days of a press partnership of more than a decade, which would finally be dissolved in March 1891. In early January 1889, when Syme was awaiting the return of Joseph, he spent five days at Killara with Deakin. The two men travelled together by train to Lilydale on 10 January then by horse-drawn carriage to the farm further east in the Yarra Valley. During their rural break they rode around the property, fired scrub, fished and, in Deakin's case at least, read. This spell was for Syme the calm before the storm.[3]

On 26 January 1889 Joseph arrived back in Melbourne from London on the P. & O. steamer *Rome*.[4] With him were wife Laura and baby Eveline, born at Thames Ditton three months earlier (to be in adulthood an esteemed artist). There is no record of the partners' first meeting nor, until mid-May, of any dealings between them. Until then there are only scant records of Syme in the office (a note to the printer in January and the subeditor in March) and none between the partners.[5]

Whether Joseph repeated his allegations that Syme dealt dishonestly with sister-in-law Jane or brought fresh accusations against his uncle, and how his uncle might have responded during these early months of 1889, have to be conjecture. Not only are any verbal exchanges unrecorded but also it is clear from references in extant documents that the files of office memos and letters are incomplete. (It is unsubstantiated Syme family lore that files were deliberately 'filleted' years after Syme's death.) The surviving items do show, however, that any residual 'gentleman's ties' of partnership were, by the middle of May, irrevocably broken and mutual respect gone. Protracted negotiations thereafter led to formal dissolution in March 1891, with Syme buying out Joseph's quarter share in David Syme and Co. for the huge sum of £140,000 – almost 17 times the £8250 that Joseph had paid in 1878, and putting the value of the business at £560,000. In 1878 it had comprised little more than machinery and relatively modest goodwill; now it was a highly capitalised enterprise, including the substantial real estate acquired and erected by David Syme and Co. during the partnership of uncle and nephew. Goodwill

---

[3] Diary entries for 10–14 January 1889, Alfred Deakin Papers, MS 1540, Series 2, National Library of Australia.

[4] 'Shipping Intelligence', *Argus*, 28 January 1889, p. 9.

[5] DS to printer, 23 January 1889, LB3, p. 141; DS to J. Stephens, 28 March 1889, LB3, p. 143.

CHAPTER 12

was the major component. There is an undated, unsigned memorandum about the sum proposed to pay Joseph. Carrying the comment, 'If purchase was made for £140,000 this would be giving for goodwill & c. £102,000 or valuing all goodwill at £408,000', it was probably written by John Packer who, appointed head of the Counting House in July 1889, was often called on thereafter for financial information.[6]

In spite of the bitter dispute, it was business as usual at David Syme & Co. While the premises remained the same, the address of the *Age* office was changed from 50 Collins Street East to 233 Collins Street when the street was renumbered in 1889.[7] Production schedules for the three newspapers were maintained and, notwithstanding the impending depression, the circulation of the *Age* increased – claimed to have reached 90,000 in 1890 ('Great Australasian Dailies' 1892, 98). While at least part of the disputatious correspondence about dissolving the partnership has been preserved, there are no records to show how tense if not poisonous the atmosphere in the *Age* office must have been during these protracted negotiations. There is, however, a wealth of documentation in the office letterbooks showing how newspaper publication continued on schedule despite the soured personal relationships.

As they had done in the past, the partners consulted in writing about their holiday entitlements. Joseph wrote in November 1889 that he would be taking three weeks' holiday the following January 1890; in December 1890 Syme notified Joseph his intended month-long vacation after the forthcoming Cable Conference.[8] But where previously the partners would have discussed and settled a host of issues in person, it appears that from May 1889, instead of verbal exchange, they put words on scraps of paper, usually unaddressed and sometimes undated. In a letter of 29 April 1890 to Malcolm in London Syme wrote that relations with Joseph were 'of a very unpleasant nature', he had 'not exchanged a word with him for the last six months', he could not 'conceive of circumstances' under which he could ever speak to him again, so 'abominable' had his conduct been towards him, and concluded that it was a 'bad day' when he took him into partnership.[9] This would place the silence from October 1889, but it was probably earlier, for

---

[6] Memo re DS & Co., SFP Box 1191/2(c)[ii].
[7] 'The Age 1854–1954 Centenary', *Age*, 16 October 1954, Supplement, p. 39.
[8] JCS to DS, 29 November 1889, SFP Box 1180/3(c); DS to JCS, 12 December 1890, LB4, p. 141.
[9] DS to A. Malcolm, 29 April 1890, LB4, p. 79.

the dated scrappy notes from Syme to Joseph that have been preserved range from May 1889 to March 1891, Joseph's to Syme from July 1889.[10] While containing chronic carping on both sides, these memoranda do testify to a grudging cooperation, in order to keep the show on the road every day. They also bespeak the deep and irreconcilable divisions between them about running the business.

Printing capability was increased with the arrival on 26 April 1889 of a third Hoe machine. The 'Double Stereotype Perfecting Press' ordered by Joseph on 23 May 1888, was invoiced at £6138.1.10, including 'extras'.[11] In September 1889 Joseph reported to Syme that neither the Hoe casting boxes nor the damping machine were satisfactory, but in January 1890 he considered that the machines were better than at any time in the past 25 years. He also pointed out that the Victory machines, now old, would need to be replaced, and the sooner they were got rid of, the better (in November 1890 the oldest of these was sold to the *Sportsman* for £400, including attachments).[12] As for paper, throughout the whole period of the generally deteriorating relationship Joseph was advising Syme about anticipated requirements and recommending particular suppliers and terms. In January 1890, when David Syme & Co. were being supplied by the local Barwon Mill at Geelong and overseas by Lloyds in London, Joseph prepared a table of quotes from numerous other British and American suppliers, advising that United States freight charges were high. While Joseph appears to have procurement of adequate stocks under control, Syme responded to his memos with his own recommendations, and sometimes complained about the quality of the paper in use.

The number of pages in an issue of the *Age* was usually eight on a weekday and 16 on Saturday, thus considerably less than at the height of the land boom. Three sheet sizes were used to print the *Age*, allowing seven, eight and nine columns per page, respectively. There is little discernible consistency or pattern in sizes used, as consultation of *Age* bound volumes for the period readily show. Several memos between the partners in 1890 about desirable numbers of columns and pages and whether to resort to supplements suggest a concern for regularity that was complicated by the desire to use paper

---

[10] DS to JCS, from 21 May 1889 (LB4, p. 65) to 9 March 1891 (LB3, p. 207); JCS; JCS to DS, 8 July 1889 to 28 April 1890, SFP Box 1180/3(c), 25 July 1890 to 11 March 1891 SFP Box 1180/3(d).

[11] Machinery [ledger], no. 2, 1889–1892, *Age* Archives, Melbourne.

[12] JCS to DS, 25 January 1890, SFP Box 1180/3(c); Machinery [ledger].

CHAPTER 12

economically in these hard times yet not allow the *Age* to be smaller than the *Argus*.[13]

The *Leader*, in accordance with its subtitle *A Weekly Journal of News, Politics, Literature, Science, Agriculture, and Sport*, contained a great range of contributions, including numerous travellers' tales. 'The Vagabond' sent articles from and about parts of Europe, Australia, New Zealand, Samoa and elsewhere, and an unidentified 'Travelling Correspondent' contributed from many countries of South America. And there were others. But sales were dropping and this was a source of some concern. The weekly remained the same size (48 pages) and format (five columns). Until February 1891 Syme and Joseph corresponded inconclusively about raising the wholesale or lowering the retail price of issues, but apparently took no action.[14]

The *Illustrated Australian News* was also in trouble. While advertised in the other Syme newspapers as the 'Oldest, Best, and Most Widely Circulated Illustrated Paper in the Colonies', with agents in London, New York and Ceylon, it was showing a heavy loss, Joseph reported on 25 January 1890, its circulation 'lower than ever'.[15] Some months earlier an innovation had been tried: the inclusion of music and musical news and reviews, reflected in the addition, from June 1889, of '*and Musical Times*' to the title of the monthly. This may well be related to the heightened popular interest in music, stimulated by the concerts and opera that were featured as part of the Centennial Exhibition. It was later observed, 'the orchestral and choral activities transcended all other musical festivals ever given in Victoria' (Carne 1954, 109). The June issue, with a new, plainer masthead includes, in addition to items about music, the actual music for 'Sérénade Andalouse', composed by Austrian born Alberto Zelman, conductor and composer who had settled in Melbourne and took part in Exhibition music programs (Radic 1976). This issue also features an engraved illustration from a photograph of singer Nellie Melba as Ophelia, the role in which she made her outstandingly successful début at the Paris Opéra the month before (but the photograph must have been made before then) (McLachlan 1998). From the August issue, a 'Musical Directory of Melbourne' became a regular feature. But the *Musical Times* innovation was deemed unsuccessful and stopped after a year, with May 1890 the final issue.

---

[13] JCS to DS, 28 April, 15 September, 29 September 1890, SFP Box 1180/3(c); DS to JCS, 1 October, 20 November 1890, LB4, pp. 128, 135.

[14] For example, DS to JCS, undated [February 1891], LB3, p. 189.

[15] JCS to DS, 25 January 1890, SFP Box 1180/3(c).

In play too was the question of illustrations. Believing that this matter had to be considered in relation to all three papers, in his letter of 25 January 1890 Joseph suggested, radically, that the *Age* have sketches and portraits to be re-used together with additional illustrations in the *Leader*, and that the illustrated monthly be simply a monthly reprint or 'budget' of the *Leader*.[16] Syme responded three days later, dismissing the *Age* proposal on the grounds of lack of time to prepare engravings,[17] seemingly unaware of the halftone process introduced by the *Illustrated Sydney News* and the *Sydney Mail* in 1888, its adoption by newspapers, including the *Illustrated Australian News* and the *Leader*, to spread in the 1890s (Dowling 1995). Indeed, the Christmas Supplement issued with the *Leader* of 27 December 1890 features a full-page illustration of 'The Australian Prima Donna, Madame Melba', apparently a half-tone reproduction. While admitting that he knew little of how the *Leader* compared with the *Australasian* (in earlier times he would have had his finger on that pulse), he stated that if the former were to have more illustrations, then a proper staff of artists would have to be recruited and machinery upgraded. Opposing the use of reprint material in the *Illustrated Australian News*, he thought anyway that its publication should be stopped, but wanted to see a financial statement first. The rival *Australasian Sketcher* had been pulled in December 1889, heralding the demise of Australian colonial illustrated newspapers, and Syme's view was in line with a general trend. One of the last, apparently unanswered, memos of Syme to Joseph asks: 'Please let me know what has been done about the sale of the A. News.'[18] Nothing was, then.

Cable correspondence issues

If the matter of falling revenues from the monthly and the weekly could be shelved, this was not so with the pressing and complicated matter of providing relevant and timely cable news in the *Age*, procuring it through the service run in conjunction with Sydney and Adelaide dailies for the benefit of subscribing newspapers throughout the Australian colonies and New Zealand. The position of cable correspondent in London was crucial. Filled in 1888 with the fraught appointment of Lachlan Brient, in August 1889, it was reported that he had been asked back to a position on the *Daily*

---

[16] JCS to DS, 25 January 1890, SFP Box 1180/3(c).
[17] DS to JCS, 28 January 1890, LB3, p. 160.
[18] DS to JCS, 5 March 1891, LB3, p. 205.

CHAPTER 12

Telegraph and was tired of living in England.[19] On 12 December he arrived back in Sydney on the *Mariposa*.[20] Mennell, who had replaced him as cable correspondent, resigned at the end of 1889 when planning an extended visit to Australia as a correspondent for the London *Daily Chronicle*; he also intended to finalise work on *The Dictionary of Australasian Biography* that Hutchinson would publish in 1892, and wanted to gather material for other publications.[21]

Two weeks before this resignation, representatives of the cable service partners – *Age*, *Advertiser* (*South Australian* was dropped from the title from 22 March 1889), Sydney *Daily Telegraph* and *Australian Star* – had met in Sydney to agree on terms and conditions.[22] Having represented the *Age*, Joseph on his return reported in writing to Syme on the discussions, including the decision to appoint a Mr Terry as assistant to cable correspondent Mennell at a salary of £300 a year. This sum did not include supply to the several interested capital city evening papers that, controversially, were to pay Terry directly.[23] This appointment is puzzling, seeming to indicate that the delegates were unaware of Mennell's impending departure, while references elsewhere suggest this not to be the case. When Syme on 9 January 1890 expressed his disapproval of and disappointment with some of the clauses, Joseph pointed out promptly the next day that signed agreement with the clauses had been reached at the Sydney conference, and that the *Age* was required to agree or 'stand out', adding added that if he had taken the latter course in Sydney, the Melbourne *Daily Telegraph* would have 'stepped in'.[24]

Terry replaced Mennell as London cable correspondent and continued in that position throughout 1890. During the year the question of how to supply the evening newspapers with cables and what to do when these papers pirated cables continued to concern members of the combination, and was the agenda for a Sydney meeting in December 1890, attended by Joseph.[25] The outcome is not clear, except that on 5 February 1891 Joseph asked Syme if he could do something about legislation to prevent Tasmanian and Sydney

---

[19] 'A Windfall to a Journalist', *Clarence & Richmond Advertiser*, 10 August 1889, p. 3.
[20] 'Shipping', *Sydney Morning Herald*, 13 December 1889, p. 6.
[21] 'Our Anglo-Colonial Letter', *Advertiser* (Adelaide), 11 February 1891, p. 5.
[22] JCS to DS, 10 December 1889, SFP Box 1180/3(c).
[23] JCS to DS, 16/18 December 1889, SFP Box 1180/3(c).
[24] DS to JCS, 9 January 1890, LB3, p. 157; JCS to DS, 10 January 1890, SFP Box 1180/3(c).
[25] DS to W. Wynne, 16 May 1890, LB3, p. 167; JCS to DS, 4 December 1890, SFP Box 1180/3(d).

evening papers getting *Age* and *Argus* cables for free.[26] No reply is on file. On 4 December, Joseph had told Syme that Terry was asking for a salary of £700 but he was offering £400. Syme, extremely dissatisfied with Terry's work, began to investigate getting rid of him and finding a replacement. Wishing to avoid a suit for wrongful dismissal, he took legal advice from his solicitor Samuel Gillott. Accordingly, as he wrote to Wynne in March 1891, he was prepared to pay Terry his contracted salary to 30 June, suggesting that he resume his former position, presumably as assistant.[27] Syme sounded out the stalwart George Levey, apparently available, and asked him to write a formal application, pointing out that he would have to agree to do the work himself, not delegate it, and recommended Levey in the strongest terms to Wynne.[28] When consulted, Joseph vehemently opposed the appointment of Levey saying he had in the past proved incompetent.[29] Syme also, on the suggestion of Bonython, wrote to a Mr Sowden of the *South Australian Register*, but no reply is on file.[30] Moreover, Syme was considering another Bonython recommendation, the *Advertiser* correspondent Rathbone, whose name had come up at the start of 1888 but whom Syme had then rejected.[31] The matter of Terry's dismissal and replacement appears to have been unresolved at the time of Joseph's departure.

Spheres of responsibility

As in the past, dealings were frequent between David Syme & Co. and newspaper businesses in other colonies, in particular with Burden & Bonython of the *Advertiser* in Adelaide and the *Daily Telegraph* firm in Sydney. Typically, these concerned the sharing of material offered for publication and running the cable service. It is not clear whether Burden and Bonython were addressing Joseph or his uncle when writing to 'My dear Syme' in November 1890. The letter is a request for mention in the *Age* of H.R. Wilkinson and E.B. Grundy who were coming to Melbourne to float

---

[26] JCS to DS, 5 February 1891, SFP Box 1180/3(d).
[27] DS to S. Gillott, 12 March 1891, LB3, p. 210; DS to W. Wynne, 12 March 1891, LB3, p. 211.
[28] DS to G. Levey, 9 December 1890, LB4, p. 136–137, 27 January, 24 February 1891, LB3, pp. 184, 199–200.
[29] JCS to DS, 11 March 1891, SFP Box 1180/3(d).
[30] DS to J. Bonython, 28 January 1891, LB3, p.186; DS to Sowden, 3 March 1891, p. 203.
[31] DS to JCS, 27 January 1888, LB3, pp. 46–48, DS to W. Wynne, 12 March 1891, LB3, p. 211.

CHAPTER 12

a Western Australian land company.[32] Whoever it was, Joseph was more proactive than Syme in promoting cooperation locally, with Melbourne newspapers. On 25 January 1890 he recommended a formal agreement with the *Herald* to share a backup printing plant, in the case of fire.[33] His concern followed the September 1889 'Great Fire' that swept through buildings on the opposite side of Collins Street, causing an estimated £200,000 of damage, including the destruction of the George and George building at no. 286, regarded as one of the finest buildings in Melbourne.[34] Indeed, north to Little Collins Street and west to Elizabeth Street, scarcely a building escaped. Witnessed from office windows, surely including those of the *Age* office, the blaze, in which three firemen died, was described as a scene 'of terrible grandeur'. On 28 January Syme responded to Joseph that some action was desirable, adding if the printing machines of the *Evening Standard* were not suitable then the *Herald* should be approached.[35] The archives reveal arrangements made with the *Herald* some years later, but not at this time.

Writing to Syme on 8 July 1889 about a replacement for K.D. Bennett, the head of the Counting House, who had died suddenly two days earlier, Joseph recommended that John Packer be installed as the new manager. He stated that as senior clerk, book-keeper and head of the Advertisement department, Packer had been Bennett's 'righthand man' and would be best suited 'to cope with discipline & duties of clerical staff', although having 'no presence & slightly nervous.[36] Syme agreed that Packer would suit, directing that his salary be increased from £6 to £7 a week (as Bennett had been paid £12 and Packer's salary would be increased little by little to only £10 in 1905, was Syme being miserly?).[37] While seen as 'timid' by assistant commercial editor William Robinson, Packer proved to be an excellent appointment indeed, being a source of sound financial advice to Syme soon thereafter and over the years (Robinson 1967, 21). Joseph's further suggestion, to engage a supervisor of general and technical work, Syme rejected out of hand, seeing 'no occasion for a second manager' as the head machinist and the printer should be capable of looking after their respective departments.

---

32   Burden & Bonython to 'Syme', 13 November 1890, J.L. Bonython and Company, Summary Record, Letter Books, BRG 10, Series 8, State Library of South Australia.
33   JCS to DS, 25 January 1890, SFP Box 1180/3(c).
34   'Great Fire in Collins-Street', *Age* 14 September 1889, pp. 9–10; 'Great Fire in Melbourne', *Leader* 21 September 1889, pp. 36–37.
35   DS to JCS, 28 January 1890, LB3, p. 160.
36   Entry for Bennett in Wages Book, p. 27; JCS to DS, 8 July 1889, SFP Box 1180/3(c).
37   DS to JCS, 2 August 1889, LB3, p. 146; Entry for Packer in Wages Book, p. 391.

When Joseph started a subscription fund for Bennett's widow and children Syme sternly rebuked him, stating that the firm, not its employees, would make any provision for the family.[38] There is no record that it did, although there is ample evidence that Syme could be generous to employees in adversity. It seems that he wished always to be in control of the finances, which Joseph obviously recognised when writing to Syme in November pressing for a doubling of the £1 per week sick fund for machinist M. Mahoney, who had slipped and broken his leg at work and had a wife and six children.[39] Arguing that it was necessary to 'encourage a feeling of contentment among the hands if we are to keep them quiet', his motive was of course not solely compassion.

Rarely did Joseph intrude in relation to reporters in the literary and editorial department, under Syme's control. Exceptionally, on 15 September 1890 the junior partner wrote that reporter George Aytoun should be removed unless he took more care; accordingly, on 26 September Syme dismissed him with two weeks' notice.[40]

To judge from the letterbooks, however, for the most part Syme acted alone in hiring, supervising and firing his reporters. In February 1890 he recruited as a leader writer Scottish Edmund Mitchell,[41] who had been a journalist in England and more recently assistant editor on the *Times of India* (Gibbney and Smith 1987, v.2, 108). In May, pleased with his services, he increased his salary by £2; in August, however, he reprimanded him for the latest outbreak of drunkenness and urged him to 'take the pledge' (abstain from alcohol).[42] Mitchell left David Syme & Co. in September, writing a letter expressing deep gratitude to Syme for giving him 'the start in this colony' when his wife was seriously ill and work an 'urgent necessity'.[43] Continuing to work as a journalist, he also wrote a novel, *The Temple of Death*, set in India, which the *Age* serialised in 1893 and Hutchinson of London published in book form the following year. In early 1890 not happy with G. Allen as head of the reporting staff, Syme considered offering the position to Thomas Courtney, who left the Sydney *Daily Telegraph* and was

---

[38] DS to JCS, 11 July 1889, LB4, p. 73.
[39] JCS to DS, 6 November 1889, SFP Box 1180/3(c).
[40] JCS to DS, 15 September 1890, SFP Box 1180/3(d); DS to G. Aytoun, 26 September 1890, LB3, unnumbered p. following p. 172.
[41] DS to E. Mitchell, 30 January 1890, LB3, p. 161.
[42] Entry for Mitchell in Wages Book, p. 303; DS to E. Mitchell, 15 August 1890, LB4, p. 125.
[43] E. Mitchell to DS, 3 September 1890, in possession of Dr Veronica Condon.

CHAPTER 12

now at the *Australian Star*.[44] The offer does not seem to have been taken up, and when Allen left in May 1890 Gottfried Schuler became chief of staff, the term now used (Hurst 1988).

Syme's critical memoranda to subeditor John Stephens, on a multitude of matters, continued. A couple of instances illustrate his close involvement in content and presentation. On 14 June 1889 he protested the inclusion in the *Age* of a 'case of incest, with all its minutely disgusting details' ('Do you think that any newspaper can do this sort of thing with impunity? Have you a wife & any young daughters?').[45] On 11 October 1890 he complained about a duplicate item in 'News of the Day' (adding: 'There are more duplicates in the Age than in all the other papers put together.')[46] While Joseph played no role in supervision of the subeditor, relations could be more complicated, and sometimes fraught, when matters of printing and production (his area) impinged on the subeditorial work. This is discussed in a separate section below.

Joseph seems to have played no part in Syme's engaging of non-salaried occasional contributors, when these did not involve additional expenses and long-term commitment. The letterbooks show Syme regularly in touch with literary figures local and overseas, sometimes passing on the judgments of their work by the *Age* and *Leader* editors Windsor and Short, sometimes stating his own. On 3 June 1889 he returned two contributions not accepted by the editor to Francis Adams,[47] an English author who wrote prolifically for colonial newspapers and magazines while in Australia from 1884 to 1890, and whose 'Mr Fletcher's Love Story' was published in three instalments in the *Leader* from 18 May to 1 June 1889 (Tasker 2001). In December 1889 he wrote to journalist Arthur Patchett Martin, an advocate of Australian literature, then living in London. Rejecting Patchett's 'Religion in England', Syme wrote: 'I wd never venture to have a series of articles on a subject of that nature. We have quite enough to do when we confine ourselves to social & political subjects, without stirring up the odium theologicum.'[48] In May 1890 he asked Charles Bright, writer of editorials and the *Leader*'s 'Under the Verandah', to reduce his

---

[44] DS to G. Allen, 30 January, 17 May 1890, LB3, pp. 162, 168; DS to T. Courtney, 30 April 1890, LB3, p. 166; 'A "Windfall" to a Journalist', *Clarence and Richmond Advertiser*, 10 August 1889, p. 3; Entry for Allen in Wages Book, p. 1.
[45] DS to J. Stephens, 14 June 1889, LB3, p. 145.
[46] DS to J. Stephens, 11 October 1890, LB3, p. 177.
[47] DS to F. Adams, 3 June 1889, LB3, p. 144.
[48] DS to A. Martin, 4 December 1889, LB3, p. 154.

contributions to four weekly, now that Edmund Mitchell had joined the staff (as already seen, not for long).[49] In September he wrote to Francis Augustus Hare, former Victorian Superintendent of Police, accepting his series 'Records of an Adventurous Life' on behalf of the *Leader* editor.[50] In December he turned down a review of 'Booth's book' from Catherine Spence, South Australian novelist and social reformer, as it had been out too long (presumably *In Darkest England and the Way Out*, by William Booth founder of the Salvation Army, published in 1890) but enclosed a cheque for 'Saturday's article' and stating that contributions would always be welcome.[51] By now there was a host of contributors, including Deakin and Henry Hyde Champion, mentioned below.

With Syme managing the 'literary' side, it is anomalous that responsibility for the serialisation of fiction seems to have been ill defined and sometimes muddled. It was probably Joseph (not Herbert) who in early 1889 helped Ada Cambridge send the text of her 1888 *Age* serial, *A Black Sheep*, to London, where it would be published to acclaim as *A Marked Man*. Cambridge later wrote that 'a younger Syme pasted all the newspaper story together like a scrapbook and shepherded its transfer to England'.[52] It was certainly Joseph who accepted another work for serialisation, *A Woman's Friendship*, from Cambridge. The novel is set mainly at the Centennial Exhibition and, through a personal 'boom and bust' narrative, deals ironically with 'the woman question' (feminism and female suffrage) and female sexuality. It was serialised in the Saturday *Age* from 31 August to 26 October 1889, but not before it was censored by Syme when reading it in proof. He told Joseph that he had excised a 'scene' that he found 'indecent', but refused to have any communication with the author about this. He chastised Joseph for accepting the work, which he considered 'the dullest & stupidest' the author had ever written.[53] This is not a view shared by posterity. While the content of the omitted section is not known, published as a book in 1988, the novel is now seen as one of Cambridge's most significant and accomplished works (Lever 2000, 28–32, 36). It was Syme and not Joseph, however, who concerned himself with a three-instalment serial by English

---

[49] DS to E. Mitchell and C. Bright, 22 and 23 May 1890, LB3, p. 169.
[50] DS to F. Hare, 9 September 1890, LB3, p. 170.
[51] DS to C. Spence, 2 December 1890, LB3, p. 183.
[52] A. Cross (Cambridge) to G. Robertson, 25 December 1924, Angus & Robertson Correspondence, ML314/20, Mitchell Library, State Library of New South Wales.
[53] JCS to DS, 10, 16 September 1889, SFP Box 1180/3(c); DS to JCS, 12, 16 September, LB3, pp. 149, 150.

CHAPTER 12

author David Christie Murray, with a 'scene laid in Australia'.[54] On 12 March 1891 he wrote to Wynne at the Sydney *Daily Telegraph* offering to share it for £50. This was 'Bob Martin's Little Girl', which ran in the *Leader* during 1892. Syme's involvement probably arose from dealings with Christie Murray in late 1889, when the author was travelling in Australia and contributing articles from far-flung parts.

The partners consulted each other about intercolonial and overseas correspondents and agents. In December 1889 Joseph asked Syme's opinion of their man at Broken Hill in western New South Wales,[55] where silver-lead mining was in full swing, and the Broken Hill Proprietary Company mining shares had risen exponentially (though the depression to come would change this for a time) (Cannon 1966, 49–50). He pointed out that the *Age* ought to have plans of the mines there, as did the *Argus*. Syme replied that he found the correspondent 'very indifferent' and thought a better man could be got.[56] Whether one was is not on record.

A perennial topic for decades was the appointment of a 'London Letter' writer. Mennell had held the position from 1888, but either he signalled his intention to resign when his contract expired at the end of 1890 or Syme desired not to renew it. Late in 1890 (the letter is not on file, only references to it) he wrote offering the position to Levey, who accepted.[57] In December Joseph objected, as he did to making Levey the cable correspondent.[58] He was also worried that Mennell owed some £108, for 'if he can't write for us, how will he get the money?' In February 1891 Syme wrote to express satisfaction with the correspondent's first letter, dated 16 January, and made many suggestions for the topics and type of coverage wanted in the future.[59] Joseph maintained his opposition, albeit chiefly on the grounds of the cable appointment, writing to Syme on 11 March: 'I have already expressed my opinion abt Levey. He is utterly unsuitable and will be a failure.'[60]

Highlighted against the background of repeated stalemate situations concerning measures other than those essential to continuing newspaper publication, the progressive decline in the relationship of the two partners may be traced through surviving relevant correspondence of the two men

---

54   DS to W. Wynne, 12 March 1891, LB3, p. 211.
55   JCS to DS, 10 December 1889, SFP Box 1180/3(c).
56   DS to JCS, undated [December 1889?], LB3, p. 156.
57   DS to G. Levey, 1, 9 December 1890, LB3, p. 181, LB4, pp. 136–137.
58   JCS to DS, 9 December 1890, SFP Box 1180/3(d).
59   DS to G. Levey, 24 February 1891, LB3, pp. 199–200.
60   JCS to DS, 11 March 1891, SFP Box 1180/3(d).

and their legal representatives (Gillott, Croker, Snowden and Co. acting for Syme personally as well as for David Syme & Co; Smith, Emmerton and Johnson for Joseph).[61] The first relevant extant documents date from May 1889 and show that Syme, feeling in 'a tight place', was seeking advice from Gillott about whether, under the deed of partnership, dissolution might be enforced.[62] At the same time, needing certain financial information for the years 1875 to 1877 before the partnership with Jane was wound up, Syme recruited Counting House employee John Macdonald, who had been business manager at that period, though now in a subordinate position, to help dig out the desired information from the accounts books.[63] Perhaps he wanted this to rebut past repeated accusations from Joseph that he had cheated Ebenezer's family out of their financial entitlements. He had trouble getting access to the books, held in Joseph's area.[64] In March 1890 he upbraided Gillott for not having assisted him gain access the previous July, writing that he was in an 'intolerable position', that it was 'quite impossible that things can go on as they are', and that he would never again go away and leave Joseph in charge.[65]

Syme was also holding a particular grievance against Joseph for allegedly being complicit in July and August 1889 with his father-in-law David Blair (not the erstwhile *Age* journalist but a timber merchant) in planting pseudonymous material published in the *Age*. Letters to the editor from 'Mechanic' and 'Protectionist' (the preserved originals clearly written by the same hand) promoted a rise in timber duties that would, to the detriment of his competitors, have greatly benefited Blair, who had already bought up an enormous supply of imported timber that would not be dutiable.[66]

Syme's continuing concern with the appearance of the *Age* – the layout and quality of the printing – is evident in his complaints to key members of Joseph's printing staff and to Joseph himself. From January 1889 to March 1891 and beyond, printer William Stewart, engaged by Joseph in 1888, was a

---

[61] Numerous letters and memos DS to JCS and to S. Gillott, 16 May 1889 (LB4, pp. 62–63) to 20 October 1890 (LB4, p. 131); two memos JCS to DS, 14 and 25 October 1890, SFP Box 1180/3(d) and two, 28 July and 4 August 1890, quoted in Sayers (1965), but not located; four lawyers' letters, 28 July to 10 September 1890, SFP Box 1180/4(b).

[62] DS to S. Gillott, 16 May 1889, LB4, pp. 62–63.

[63] DS to J. Macdonald, 16 May 1889, LB4, p. 64.

[64] DS to JCS, 21 May 1889, LB4, p. 65.

[65] DS to S. Gillott, 11 March 1890, LB4, p. 78.

[66] DS to JCS, 30 July 1890, LB4, pp. 107–112; letters and notes re timber duties, SFP Box 1180/7(b).

CHAPTER 12

focus of Syme's reprimands.[67] The tone of the memos to Joseph is aggressive and forceful, to say the least. The first fierce attack on file was in August 1889 after Syme had spent a week out of Melbourne, having uncharacteristically found it 'necessary to take some rest'.[68] There he scrutinised copies of the *Age* that were sent to him and, perhaps unwell, obviously brooded. On his return he complained to Joseph about the inadequate wrappers in which the papers had been sent and the 'wretched appearance' of the printed pages. He said that the printing, 'at least decent' under his own supervision, had gone from 'bad to worse' under the junior partner.[69] Syme was exaggerating. For years the print quality of the *Age* had been inferior to that of the rival *Argus* and the esteemed *Sydney Morning Herald*, whose pages generally had a crisper, cleaner appearance. Replying that the machinist W. Bleackley (or Bleakley), whom he had also recruited in England and whom both partners had found unsatisfactory, had now been dismissed (recorded as leaving in September 1889), Joseph also observed, justifiably, that Syme's remarks read like a personal attack on him.[70]

On 20 January 1890 Syme fired off another attack on 'continued bad printing', apparently enclosing readers' letters of complaint.[71] Joseph rebutted it five days later, saying that Herbert regularly examines the newspapers and his reports 'do not bear out your informants' statements'.[72] Doubtless this put both Herbert and his father in an invidious position. Syme could not stop interfering in an area that was not his direct responsibility, eliciting from Joseph on 28 April the severely provocative: 'It is to be regretted that in the management of a successful business like ours you shd cause so much additional friction by proposing to act out side the limits of your authority'.[73]

By July 1890 Joseph was prepared to sell his share and had nominated a price that Syme, in a letter to Gillott of 14 July and on the advice of an unnamed 'expert', rejected as exorbitant.[74] The next day he sent his nephew the most interfering extant memo, which took the dispute to a new and dangerous level. It concerned the makeup of advertisements in the *Age* of the

---

67   DS to printer, W. Stewart, 23 January 1889, 9 March 1891, LB3, pp. 141, 207.
68   DS to JCS, 2 August 1889, LB3, p. 146.
69   DS to JCS, 12 August 1889, LB3, p. 147.
70   Entry for Bleackley in Wages Book, p. 30; JCS to DS, undated [September 1889], SFP Box 1180/3(c).
71   DS to JCS, 20 January 1890, LB3, p. 159.
72   JCS to DS, 25 January 1890, SFP Box 1180/3(c).
73   JCS to DS, 28 April 1890, SFP Box 1180/3(c).
74   DS to S. Gillott, 14 July 1890, LB4, p. 92.

previous Saturday. Three closely written pages contain a litany of detailed specific complaints, together termed as 'gross' and 'grave' irregularities' and concluding 'I therefore see nothing for it but to undertake the duty of looking after the printers work myself'.[75] At this time Syme was thinking about changing solicitors for himself (not the firm), an intention prompted because Joseph's father-in-law Blair was also a client of Gillott.[76] In the event, however, he retained Gillott's services.

Three documents comprise Joseph's response. The first is a memo of 25 July referring to a 'crop of writs' (libel actions'): 'My firm wd save alike in reputation & in pocket if you wd devote more time and attention to ensuring greater accuracy in the cols of the Age' adding that Syme 'might not find it so necessary to expend [his] energies composing inaccurate letters of 7 or 8 pages over matters of minor importance'.[77] The second is a memo of 28 July, part quoted by Sayers (1965, 135) but not now to be found, in which Joseph observes: 'You appear to consider that you are licensed to criticise freely, and like some divinity to enjoy an immunity from criticism', and stresses that he expects 'to be consulted on all important questions of policy and expenditure'. The third item is a typed letter of the same date from Joseph's lawyers to Syme's, concerning the failure of negotiations for sale of Joseph's share and expressing concern with 'your client's mode of conducting the business, more especially the literary branch'.[78] It states that the partnership clause giving Syme entire control of policy was 'manifestly not to the interest of both partners' and that Syme had agreed to consult. Here Syme has pencilled in the margin 'NO'. It further claimed that Syme had 'systematically failed to conduct the business…in such a way as to avoid loss of repute and money'. The letter refers to Syme's 'intemperate memo' of 25 July, in which he implies that Joseph is 'meddlesome and aggressive' in regard to literary matters and calls on Syme to arrange times to confer with Joseph.

Syme complained to Malcolm on 29 July that his partnership relationship was 'anything but agreeable'.[79] The next day, he wrote a six-page memo to Joseph, stating, that he had trusted him, treated him well, had always given

---

[75] DS to JCS, 15 July 1890, LB4, pp. 96–98.
[76] DS to S. Gillott, 23 July 1890, LB4, p. 100; DS to JCS, 12 August 1890, LB4, p. 120.
[77] JCS to DS, 25 July 1890, SFP Box 1180/3(d).
[78] Smith, Emmerton & Johnson to Gillott Croker Snowden & Co., 28 July 1890, SFP Box 1180/4(b).
[79] DS to A. Malcolm, 29 July 1890, LB4, p. 103.

CHAPTER 12

'the fullest consideration to any suggestion' emanating from him, and was 'still ready to do so'.[80] He refuted criticisms of mismanaging the literary side. He reiterated that he was responsible for policy and asserted his altruism in regard to the policy of the *Age* on the Railway Bill (of which, more below). He launched an attack on what he saw would be Joseph's approach to management of the business: 'you wd reduce the number of staff below efficiency, cut down the salaries of those who remained to starvation point, print the Age in process paper…& let the advertising columns guide the general policy.' With a multitude of further harsh criticisms and refusing to concede Joseph's right to have any say on policy matters, he concluded: 'Under present circumstances you must see as well as I do that there can be neither pleasure nor profit in continuing our partnership' and requested that all future communications to be sent through his solicitor. It was no help to Syme that Gillott advised him on 1 August that Joseph had a contractual right to be consulted and that there was 'not the slightest "loophole" in the deed to take advantage of, to terminate the partnership'.[81]

Joseph's reply of 4 August, now lost, is also quoted by Sayers (1965, 135–136). It begins, 'There is no pleasure in continuing our partnership, but profit there certainly is.' The long, critical and defensive letter concludes with the wish to be more conciliatory and the hope that Syme would 'moderate' his tone. But, clearly, reconciliation was out of the question.

Matters came to a head on 10 September with Joseph's lawyers, through Syme's, issuing an ultimatum – since Syme had legally bound himself to consult, but refused to do so, then there must be a settlement or the matter would go public, to arbitration.[82] Eight days later, Joseph wrote, without reference to his solicitors he said, a relatively conciliatory letter to his uncle suggesting that Syme buy him out by 'splitting the difference' between the respective figures each had arrived at.[83] He said that he was proposing compromise 'with the best of motives' and that he did not favour litigation, but would not be deterred from it if necessary. Syme, in one of his subsequent noncommittal and evasive responses asked, on 6 October, for actual figures, which Joseph supplied in a memorandum of 14 October.[84]

---

[80] DS to JCS, 30 July 1890, LB4, pp. 107–112.
[81] S. Gillott to DS, 1 August 1890, SFP Box 1180/4(b).
[82] DS to JCS, 12 August 1890, LB4, p. 120; Smith etc. to Gillott etc, 10 September 1890 (copy), SFP Box 1180/4(b).
[83] JCS to DS, 18 September 1890, SFP Box 1180/3(d).
[84] DS to JCS, 22 September, 6 October 1890, LB4, pp. 126, 129–130; JCS to DS, 14 October 1890, SFP Box 1180/3(d).

With sundry small provisos, the junior partner suggested he sell his quarter share for £140,000, a figure more or less midway between Syme's 'last offer' of £122,000 and Emmerton's request for £160,000. With Syme still vacillating, on 25 October Joseph wrote that he was apparently not being taken seriously.[85] Sometime thereafter Syme clearly did agree for, although the archive is silent about this, in early March 1891 Syme was corresponding with Gillott about details of the settlement and arrangements for paying the £140,000.[86] In particular, Syme requested the omission from the draft agreement that he had been sent, of a 'ridiculous clause about [not] publishing anything against the vendor'. While the final agreement indeed has no such clause, Syme's newspapers never did publish anything against or in favor of Joseph, the vendor.

According to the contract of sale, which is dated 19 March 1891 and signed by both parties, the vendor Joseph Cowen Syme agreed to sell to David Syme his quarter share in the business for £140,000, with £40,000 to be paid him immediately and the balance, including interest, in 10 half-yearly instalments. Syme would duly make these payments, the last on 28 February 1896.[87] Under the contract, Joseph, was not to be engaged in newspaper business or be employed on a daily morning newspaper for 10 years or an evening or weekly paper for five in the City of Melbourne or a 150-mile radius of the General Post Office. Years later it was rumoured that this prohibition prevented him from purchasing the *Evening Standard* in October 1894, when the paper was 'tottering on its legs' before being taken over by the *Herald*.[88] Projected in 1888, this new Melbourne evening newspaper began publication in April 1889, published by journalist James Thomson, whose extensive experience included having worked for the Melbourne *Daily Telegraph* and the *Argus* (Birman 1990). Whatever the truth of this report Joseph, who was a man of some means in 1891, had other business pursuits for the rest of his life (he died in 1916), being on the board of directors of several large companies and having property interests in New South Wales.[89] There is no evidence of any contact between the erstwhile partners after March 1891. Syme's wife Annabella wrote to their

---

[85] DS to JCS, 20 October 1890, LB4, p. 131; JCS to DS, 25 October 1890, SFP Box 1180/3(d).
[86] DS to S. Gillott, 5, 12 March 1891, LB3, pp. 204, 210.
[87] Contract for sale of share, SFP Box 1185/4(b)[i].
[88] *Australasian Typographical Journal*, June 1907, p. 10.
[89] 'Personal', *Argus*, 13 November 1916, p. 8.

CHAPTER 12

son Arthur on 24 March that 'Joe' had been in the office for the last time three days earlier.[90]

What was the dispute *really* about? Not Joseph's inadequacy, for in managing the business side of David Syme and Co. he acquitted himself well. Annabella confided to Arthur that he would be missed for his desire and ability 'to practice economies', while Deakin thought highly of his business abilities.[91] Moreover, there is ample evidence of his informing, advising and reminding Syme about financial matters that needed attention. In mid-1889 the junior partner suggested he give a modest subscription to the Working Man's College.[92] In November 1889 he recommended an increase of travelling expenses for Scott (presumably farm editor Charles Scott).[93] In January 1890 he reminded Syme about several mortgage and banking matters needing attention.[94] Syme, on the other hand, was not well organised and systematic, often unable to lay hands on documents, and calling on solicitor Gillott to supply them.[95] Moreover, he was less in touch these days with press colleagues and developments than was Joseph. On 11 July 1889 Joseph passed on to Syme a suggestion from paymaster John Gourlay that the firm give a wedding present to *Leader* editor Henry Short – perhaps an indication that the brothers-in-law were not close as they had been in the past.[96]

Notwithstanding this regular, businesslike support, Syme complained to Malcolm on 29 April 1890 that his junior partner 'simply tries to make money'.[97] And yet, he blocked any attempts by his nephew to be present or take part in consultations about the policy of the paper. Records indicate two areas that were of particular concern to Joseph, one in relation to an industrial dispute; the other, about railway construction.

A major news item in the Melbourne press during August and September 1889 was the London Dock Strike (Morrison 2005, 290–299). Press reports expressed and elicited fellow feeling for British brothers and sisters in distress. But underlying this sympathy was the huge economic threat posed by the cessation of loading and unloading of cargo that brought shipping

---

[90] AS to Arthur Syme, 24 March 1891, in possession of Judith Adams.
[91] Autobiographical notes, Deakin Papers, Series 3/290a.
[92] JCS to DS, undated, [July or August 1889] SFP Box 1180/3(c).
[93] JCS to DS, 29 November 1889, SFP Box 1180/3(c).
[94] JCS to DS, 25 January 1890, SFP Box 1180/3(c).
[95] For example, DS to S. Gillott, 14 July 1890, LB4, p. 92.
[96] JCS to DS, 11 July 1889, SFP Box 1180/3(c).
[97] DS to A. Malcolm, 29 April 1890, LB4, p. 79.

to a halt. An *Age* editorial of 29 August is credited by Geoffrey Serle (1971, 335) as having led the movement in support of the dockers' cause (a claim for payment of sixpence per hour), which took the form of fund-raising meetings and subscriptions around the colony. However, whilst coming out strongest in support, the *Age* was actually the last Melbourne daily to comment on the strike editorially, the *Argus* five days earlier, on 24 August having warned of its possible dire economic consequences. There are no clues to indicate why the delay, or what part Syme played in taking this pro-worker line. The only correspondence between the two partners concerns the adequacy of paper supplies, given the shipping stoppage – these proved to be more than sufficient, however (Packer informed Syme in December 1890 that there were still excess stocks, because it had been expected that the land boom would last longer).[98].

The strike on the London docks was an early manifestation of a growing labour movement with international ramifications. No political party yet represented workers in any Australian colony, but developments in the trade union movement of the 1880s included intercolonial congresses and communications links. Exactly one year after the London disturbances, major industrial trouble erupted in Australia (Fitzpatrick 1944; Sutcliffe 1921). This was a terrible time for David and Joseph Syme to be fighting each other. In Melbourne the Mercantile Marine Officers' Association decided to affiliate with the Trades Hall Council and to press for improved pay and conditions from the ship owners. In Sydney the Shearers' Union and Wharf Labourers' Union united with other maritime trade bodies in New South Wales to boycott the handling of wool shorn by non-union labour. The Maritime Strike, as these troubles became known, lasted from 16 August to 17 October 1890. Shipping was paralysed and the strike spread to other industries.

British socialist, journalist and publisher Henry Hyde Champion, who arrived in Australia at a critical time for the Australian labour movement, gave speeches in Melbourne promoting international trade unionism. These were reported and praised in the *Age* (Dickenson 2006, 58–64). The first of his *Age* articles, appearing on 6 September, was accepting of non-union labour, which immediately put him at odds with the strike leaders and strikers, and led to him – and the *Age* – being seen in some quarters as betraying the labour cause. Joseph was worried at being left out of consultation about the

---

[98] JCS to DS, 28 August 1889, SFP Box 1180/3(c); J. Packer to DS, 3 December 1890, SFP Box 1180/4(b).

CHAPTER 12

line to be taken in the *Age* policy and, inferentially, he disagreed with the stance taken in its columns. His lawyers' letter of 10 September, mentioned above, stated that the absence of consultation with the junior partner during the present strike demonstrated the risks of not consulting.[99] Yet Joseph was not effectively sidelined in these commercially unstable times. It was he who reported to Syme on 29 September the reassuring news that Thomson of the *Evening Standard* had been in contact with John Hancock, Secretary of the Melbourne Typographical Society, and had been assured that compositors were not to be called out.[100]

By the time of the next critical assertion of worker power – the strikes by shearers in New South Wales and Queensland that began in January 1891 – Joseph was effectively out of the picture and Syme, unilaterally, was handling the procurement of information for his newspapers. He wrote in February to Wynne in Sydney that he badly needed Queensland strike information.[101] Three days later he complained to subeditor Stephens that while reports of the shearers' strike did have cross heading and subheadings (the subeditor's job to supply), there was no subheading for 'the most important item— the dispatch of the Military'.[102] In March he sent William Lambie to Queensland, to report for the *Age* on the shearers' strike.[103] Lambie, who had travelled to the Sudan for the *Sydney Morning Herald* in 1885, had joined the *Age* in 1888.[104]

Joseph's other major worry about policy was the continuing criticism in the *Age* and *Leader* of extravagance in railways construction and operation and of the Railways Commissioners for their crucial part in this. The direction having been set by Syme during the mid-1880s, not a week would pass thereafter without the subject being touched on, if not dealt with at length in the editorial and other columns of his newspapers. In July 1890 Joseph had objected to the *Age* policy of opposing a new Railway Bill and alleged or implied that Syme sought to benefit personally from such opposition – a claim that Syme dismissed, pointing out to his partner that, in opposing the Bill, he was rejecting personal gain from a line proposed through his Yarra Valley property.[105] Joseph raised the railways policy matter again on

---

[99] Smith etc. to S. Gillott etc, 10 September 1890 (copy), SFP Box 1180/4(b).
[100] JCS to DS, 29 September 1890, SFP Box 1180/3(d).
[101] DS to W. Wynne, 18 February 1891, LB3, p. 195.
[102] DS to J. Stephens, 21 February 1891, LB3, p. 198.
[103] Letter of introduction for W. Lambie, 17 March 1891, LB3, p. 213.
[104] Entry for Lambie in Wages Book, p. 281.
[105] DS to JCS, 30 July 1890, LB4, pp. 107–112.

Figure 12.1. Joseph Syme. (Courtesy of Dr Veronica Condon)

7 November, objecting to 'the tone of personal animosity in pursuing Speight and his colleagues' (the Railway Commissioners).[106] He noted that £1500 had already been spent in 1890 on libels 'of a wantonly stupid character' and that Syme seemed determined to invite an action that would be 'as unjournalistic and expensive as the Times & Parnell cases' (a recent, long-running and complex libel action in London). He advised that if the firm were to be put to expense over this matter, he would hold Syme responsible, and pointed out that Commissioner Richard Speight was stating openly that he was waiting for an opportunity to put Syme in court. Joseph was prophetic, Syme undeterred.

The sum total of these grievances and differences is of little moment in comparison with the root cause of the inability of the parties to reconcile. This has to be the intractable family situation, the legacy of Ebenezer. From

---

[106] JCS to DS, 7 November 1890, SFP Box 1180/3(d).

CHAPTER 12

Joseph's point of view, he was entitled to carry on his father's half share in the enterprise once jointly owned by his father and uncle. Over the years he believed that his uncle had cheated his mother, his siblings and himself out of their due. As David saw it, he had laboured ever since 1860 to 'do the right thing' financially and in other practical ways by his brother's dependants, in the face, as it transpired, of duplicity by his widow and hateful allegations by his nephew. Moreover, these actions of Syme's fraternal loyalty to Ebenezer worked directly against any obligations and plans for his own sons, who could well feel *their* entitlements were being utterly disregarded – an impossible situation, which had to be terminated.

Disputing Darwin

It may seem strange that Syme, during this dreadful last phase of the nephew and uncle association, had the time to complete the writing of a third book and arrange for its publication, distribution and promotion. This activity could have provided refuge and solace, however, from the angst associated with the disintegrating partnership. The subject of Syme's monograph is far removed from the quotidian demands of running a newspaper business, for *On the Modification of Organisms* is an elaboration of the essay that was rejected by the *Nineteenth Century* in 1888, in which he disputed aspects of Darwinism through an examination of the fertilisation of plants by insects. When he began the book is not known. In December 1890 he claimed that study of the subject and writing the book were 'the labour of years'.[107] It is very likely that he was bringing it to completion in 1889. It may be relevant to his scholarly pursuit that this year, 1889, he became a Trustee of the Melbourne Public Library, Art Gallery and Museum and that, through McEwans in London, he purchased volumes of the *Encyclopaedia Britannica*.[108] This would be the ninth edition, published from 1875 to 1889 and seen as a landmark one for scholarship and literary style. The *Academy* of 24 August 1889 contains a note that David Syme of Melbourne, known in England and Germany as a political and economic author of originality, was now engaged on a scientific work. In February and March 1890 Syme was arranging with the Melbourne publisher and bookseller George Robertson to publish his work; at the end of June, he returned the corrected proofs.[109]

---

[107] DS to Kegan Paul, Trench Trübner & Co., 23 December 1890, LB4, p. 146.
[108] DS to J. McEwan & Co., 4 July 1889, LB4, p. 70.
[109] DS to G. Robertson & Co., 5 March, 30 June 1890, LB4, pp. 77, 86.

Possibly editor Windsor and perhaps also George Syme had some part in checking the proofs. According to Deakin, Syme always handed them to friends for advice, with Windsor 'bristling up his phrases' and breaking up long sentences, Pearson advising on and revising style, and Deakin reading and making comments.[110] Deakin and Pearson may have been too caught up in political commitments to oblige this time, although Syme told Levey that Deakin read some chapters that were serialised in the *Age* on Saturdays from 2 August to 6 September, before the book itself was published.[111] He also informed his London correspondent that these chapters had also been read by his brother George, by anti-Darwinist University of Melbourne professor Frederick McCoy, and others, and all of them considered that Syme had 'pretty well disposed of Darwinism'.

If Syme's view of the importance of his book as a contribution to scientific and philosophical thought appears inflated, his approach to its publication seems arrogantly unorthodox. In July 1890, the very time his dispute with Joseph was reaching crisis point, he was making arrangements that would seem to reflect a disturbed mind and faulty judgment. Deciding to have his book published in England as well as Australia, in June he instructed George Robertson to add the name of the London publisher Kegan Paul to the title page and make the binding of copies identical with that of his earlier Kegan Paul book, *Representative Government in England* (1881).[112] On 4 July (an afterthought?) he asked the Melbourne publisher what 'steps were needed to secure the copyright in England of a book published in Australia'.[113] On 14 July he wrote to Kegan Paul, presenting this *fait accompli* and advising that he would be sending the first batch to be announced, advertised and sold, at five shillings a copy.[114] He explained that he had 'put forth a theory of the origin of species which is neither Darwins nor Lamarcks', that his views were 'quite original' and 'likely to provoke hostility on the part of the high priests of the Darwinian cult', and that, if in consequence there was 'a run on the book', the publisher should cable for additional copies or arrange to publish a second edition. He enclosed an unbound copy.

Copies were despatched from Melbourne in August, as was Syme's list of persons and organisations to receive complimentary ones. In several letters

---

[110] Autobiographical notes, Deakin Papers, Series 3/290a.
[111] DS to G. Levey, 9 December 1890, LB4, pp. 136–137.
[112] DS to Robertson & Co., 30 June 1890, LB4, p. 86.
[113] DS to Robertson & Co., 4 July 1890, LB4, p. 89.
[114] DS to Kegan Paul & Co., 14 July 1890, LB4, p. 94.

CHAPTER 12

to George Robertson and to Kegan Paul during July and August Syme gave instructions about the numbers of copies to print, bind, and despatch that were conflicting and contradictory to an extent that could indicate that he was not thinking clearly.[115] Kegan Paul's Publication Books record receipt on 3 October of the first lot of bound copies and quires (sets of printed sheets), and the binding of copies in November and December.[116] The books also show, by 31 December 1890, some expenditure on advertisements, and the distribution of review and presentation copies. On file also is an undated publishing agreement, setting out a publishing fee of five guineas and 10 per cent commission. While taking on this title, the London publisher was, apparently, not happy about having George Robertson's name on the title page imprint as well as his own, and would be further displeased later to find that many copies lacked their name altogether, requiring the printing by them of a replacement title page.[117]

At the same time as Kegan Paul in London were attending to the publishing and publicising of Syme's book, its author in Melbourne became greatly and, it would appear, unreasonably aggrieved and agitated. In December he wrote to Levey that Kegan Paul had failed to carry out his instructions, amounting to suppression of his book, perhaps due to 'contempt of anything Colonial' and extremely annoying. His book was not only 'worthy of notice in its relation to Darwinism' but provided a 'substitute' for it. He asked Levey to investigate the matter.[118] He also wrote twice to Kegan Paul in December, complaining that the only notice he had seen of his book was in *Nineteenth Century*, their own publication, asking that the situation be remedied and enclosing again his list for sending review and presentation copies.[119] His concern was ill founded, however, for as early as August 1890 numerous English periodicals and newspapers were carrying advance notice of this 'new work on evolution', and from November it was being listed as among newly published works.[120] By the

---

[115] DS to Robertson & Co., 25 July, 1 August, 8 August 1890, LB4, pp. 101, 114, 117; DS to Kegan Paul & Co., 11 August 1890, LB4, pp. 118, 119.
[116] Publication Books, *Archives of Kegan Paul*.
[117] DS to G. Levey, 9 December 1890, LB4, pp. 136–137; DS to Kegan Paul & Co, 5 May 1891, LB4, p. 153.
[118] DS to G. Levey, 9 December 1890, LB4, pp. 136–137.
[119] DS to Kegan Paul, 16, 23 December 1890, LB4, pp. 142–143, 146.
[120] Advance notices in, for example, *Athenaeum* and *Academy* (23 August 1890), *Leeds Mercury* (26 and 30 August), and in 'New Books' listing, *Birmingham Daily Post* (28 November).

end of January 1891 Syme had settled down, writing to Levey: 'I note that you have at last received a copy of my book so I hope to see the publication of it announced soon.'[121]

What is to be made of Syme's attempt to depose Charles Darwin from the evolutionist throne? Syme described himself as an evolutionist, but he thought that he had arrived at a more convincing argument about evolutionary processes than had Darwin. In brief, his clearly, concisely and logically presented short (164-page) book criticises Darwin for being imprecise in theorising about natural selection and survival of the fittest. Relating to the latter concept, Syme's book argues that struggle is, on the whole, pernicious, tending to produce disease. In relation to selection, it sees that the process of adaptation is critical; crudely, that cooperation is more significant than competition. Evidence of its author's extensive reading, a great many scientific writings are cited, including works by eminent English scientists Thomas Huxley, Herbert Spencer and Alfred Wallace, in support of his postulates.

The catalogues of holding libraries, both in Australia and Europe, vary in presenting *On the Modification of Organisms* as published in 1890 or 1891. The exact date of issue in each place is not evident, imprints on the title page lacking a date. As noted above, the book was in the public domain in England in November 1890, and indeed was reviewed in the *Glasgow Herald* of 28 November, disparagingly, as 'an abortive attempt to upset a deduction of science as great indeed as is the law of gravitation itself'. The Adelaide *Advertiser* of 1 January 1891 carries a long review, stating that the book was 'just published in Melbourne and London'. While presenting Syme's arguments in some detail, it does not criticise or evaluate them. The *Westminster Review* of February 1891 has a fairly dismissive assessment, observing that the book appears a quarter of a century too late, contains little that has not been advanced before, and does not weaken Darwin's fundamental doctrines.

Besides individuals, Syme's distribution list had included leading scholarly and literary periodicals and two newspapers – the London *Times* and the *Scotsman*.[122] Reviews in newspapers were generally favourable. As reproduced by Syme in a letter of 5 May 1891 to Kegan Paul, the *Times* had seen it to be 'a vigorous criticism, not so much of Darwinism in general as of some portions of Darwin's writings and reasonings' and considered

---

[121] DS to G. Levey, 27 January 1891, LB3, p. 184.
[122] DS to Kegan Paul, 16 December 1890, LB4, pp. 142–143.

CHAPTER 12

that 'Mr Syme is strong in dialectic and powerfully sustains his thesis'; and the London *Daily Chronicle* stated that 'No earnest student…can afford to neglect the strictures of this acute critic.'[123]

In this letter Syme stated he was 'particularly desirous to have the criticisms of the Scientific Press'. The individuals on his list included eminent scientists such as Thomas Huxley, John Tyndall and Alfred Wallace, along with intellectuals and leading public figures such as Sir Charles Dilke and William Gladstone. He did not have long to wait for a scientist's review that would seem to deliver the *coup de grâce*. Wallace, arguably Darwin's peer in theorising evolution, assessed Syme's book in the 9 April issue of *Nature*, which would have reached Melbourne around the end of May. His forceful, adverse criticism concludes:

> Mr Syme has a considerable reputation in other departments of literature as a powerful writer and acute critic; but he has entirely mistaken his vocation in this feeble and almost puerile attempt to overthrow the vast edifice of fact and theory raised by the genius and the life-long labours of Darwin (Wallace 1891a, 529–530).

Unbowed, on 2 June Syme sent a rejoinder to *Nature* in which he asserted his justification for criticising Darwin and categorically refuted Wallace's observation that he has misquoted.[124] This was published in the 12 November issue, along with the last word, from Wallace, who pinpointed several examples of Syme's incorrect quotation and misrepresentation (Wallace 1891b).

Surprisingly – and perhaps Kegan Paul had after all been less than comprehensive in its advertising – Syme's book was not listed in the *Review of Reviews* 'New Books' section until September 1891, where it is described as 'An attempt to disprove Darwin's theory of Natural Selection, with all its attendant consequences and corollaries' ('Science, Medicine' 1891). Yet in the *Dublin Review* of July 1892 it was seen as a valuable contribution to the rapidly growing stock of anti-Darwinian literature, its ruthless criticism showing that Darwin's terms were inexact. In sum, while *On the Modification of Organisms* did not become a bestseller (sales recorded by Kegan Paul are scarcely more than 100 copies) or bring about a paradigm shift in evolutionary thinking, it did receive some serious attention and occasional modest praise. Reading it today, one sees that an author,

---

[123] DS to Kegan Paul & Co., 5 May 1891, LB4, pp. 153–154.
[124] DS to Editor, *Nature*, 2 June 1891, LB4, p. 156; 'Topical Selection and Mimicry'.

thinking outside the mould of the period, actually ventured into territory that some biologists of more recent times have been exploring and which are summarised and reviewed in *What Darwin Got Wrong*, published in 2010 (Fodor and Palmarini 2010).

This intellectual endeavour of Syme's seems out of kilter with his life in the day-to-day world of journalism, newspapers, business and politics, which occupied so much of his time and attention. It is also relevant that Syme had no scientific education or training; in fact, apart from the months at Morison's unorthodox theological academy when a youth, and attendance at some public lectures in Heidelberg, Germany, when he was scarcely more, Syme was never in a milieu of rigorous intellectual enquiry. Rather, he was an amateur, an autodidact and, as such, lacked schooling in the extended processes of argument and counter-argument, verification, legitimisation required for new knowledge to be accredited and accepted.

Of more significance than his assaults on aspects of Darwin's arguments, however, is Syme's further consideration of the implications for the spiritual nature of human existence. Seeking to identify the 'designing agent' that sets the 'modifying' mechanism in motion, in his book he posited that each of the cells of which the organism is constituted is a psychical unit and source of all change. The community of psychical units, he claimed, make up the 'Soul', which pervades and maintains every part of the organism, and may modify it when necessary. The Ego, as part of the Soul but not conscious of its operations, has its seat in the brain. This part of Syme's theorising amounts, fundamentally, to claiming a scientific basis for a belief in a sort of afterlife for human beings – a subject he would pursue in his fourth and last book, *The Soul*, published in 1903. This aspect of Syme's 1890 book, however, was not dwelt on by reviewers, who focused on the author's critique of Darwin's theories, and passed over his tentative, quasi-religious theory about the basis of human life. These concluding chapters of the book comprise what seems a manifestation of an underlying, persistent existential preoccupation – one that plagued him during the days at Morison's Academy, intrigued him during the height of the spiritualism fervour in Melbourne during the 1870s, and would surface again in the last years of his life.

As for private life and personal relationships during this period, the annual New Year excursion with Deakin may have provided some relaxing diversion if not solace. In 1890 this took place from Saturday 22 to Monday 24 February, and as in 1889, at Killara horse riding, burning off, and

CHAPTER 12

reading.[125] Deakin's diary entries record regular contact with Syme and visits to the *Age* office throughout the period covered in this chapter. There was no Syme and Deakin summer excursion in 1891 because Deakin was touring overseas with Herbert Syme, dealt with below.

Family

Of Syme's home life and family relationships during these difficult years, surviving records yield scattered clues. His sister Margaret Gourlay died aged 74 on 5 December 1889. Buried the next day in the Boroondara Cemetery, her passing was lamented at a meeting early January of the Committee of the Victoria Seaman's Mission, of which she and her daughter Mary Jane Lormer and a Mrs Syme (Annabella?) were members.[126] There are glimpses of the men of the family. Brother-in-law Frank Johnson (brother of Annabella and husband of Ebenezer's daughter Minnie) was asked by Syme in March 1890 to return shares that had been put in Frank's name, apparently to improve his employment prospects in the issuing company. Now, Syme wished to sell, seeing a poor future for them.[127]

Syme was involved with the careers of his sons. At the start of 1889, 10-year-old Oswald and 15-year-old Geoffrey were at school. Arthur, 24, was studying medicine at the University of Melbourne. Francis, 28, who had been managing Dalry had a falling out with his father and left the farm that year (M. Syme 2013, 62); Herbert, 29, was employed in the Counting House at the *Age* office, under his cousin Joseph's oversight. Supported by his father, in 1891 Geoffrey began studies towards a Bachelor of Arts degree at the University of Melbourne.[128] Also supported by his father, Arthur in 1890 travelled to Britain to complete his medical studies at the University of Edinburgh and gain some hospital experience in London, sailing on 17 January on the *Orient* mail steamer.[129] Syme arranged for Malcolm at McEwans to pay Arthur an allowance, stipulating that it should be sufficient to cover fees and some pocket money, and requiring a statement of expenses.[130]

---

[125] Diary entries for 22–24 February 1890, Deakin Papers, Series 2.
[126] 'Deaths', *Argus*, 6 December 1889, p. 1; 'Victorian Seamen's [sic] Mission', *Argus*, 4 January 1890, p. 8.
[127] DS to F. Johnson, 11 March, 1 May 1890, LB4, pp. 77, 80.
[128] University of Melbourne Student record for Geoffey Syme, Melbourne University Archives.
[129] 'Shipping Intelligence', *Argus*, 18 January 1890, p. 8.
[130] DS to A. Malcolm, 24 January, 29 April 1890, LB4, pp. 75, 79.

Presumably satisfied with the reported expenditure statements, after several months Syme was prepared to send payments directly to Arthur, who apparently preferred to continue receiving them through Malcolm (perhaps indicating a desire to avoid being subject to paternal control?).[131]

Francis and wife Christina had another child in 1889, making four grandchildren for Syme and Annabella. In 1889 and until July 1890 Francis was a partner in the firm of Merry and Syme, which advertised in country newspapers as Farmers' Commission Agents with premises at 533 Flinders Lane West.[132] Sundry newspaper items refer to the firm and to J.W. Merry singly as judges and exhibitors in various country district agricultural shows.[133] In addition the partners appear to have experimented, possibly through contractors, with flax growing in Gippsland and in western Victoria near the town of Colac, on the property 'Corunnun', where they were renting 20 acres.[134] In guaranteeing an overdraft at the National Bank, David Syme provided support to the Merry and Syme business, but cancelled this liability in July 1890 because Francis was 'selling out' of it.[135]

Syme's eldest son, Herbert, an employee of David Syme and Co. at a relatively lowly level, in Joseph's area of supervision and without a clear role and avenues for advancement, must have been uncomfortable during the crescendo of hostility between his father and his cousin. On 25 January 1890 Joseph referred to Herbert's regular task of checking printing quality.[136] But he was sometimes occupied outside the newspaper office. In June 1889 he was at Killara, perhaps sent there by Syme to be acting manager after the dismissal of unsatisfactory James Souter in May.[137] Admitted as a barrister in the Supreme Court on 1 September 1890, Herbert may have been contemplating switching to a career in the law, but there is no indication that he ever engaged in legal practice.[138]

In late November, in the company of Alfred Deakin, Herbert was on a ship bound for Ceylon and India, a venture that may have been suggested,

---

[131] DS to A. Malcolm, 29 July 1890, LB4, p. 103.
[132] For example, in issues of the *Camperdown Chronicle* for January 1890.
[133] For example, *Alexandra and Yea Standard*, 7 February 1890, p. 2; *Gippsland Times* (Sale), 24 March 1890, p. 3.
[134] 'In the Colac District', *Maitland Mercury*, 31 December 1889, p. 7.
[135] DS to National Bank, 9 July 1890, LB4, p. 90.
[136] JCS to DS, 25 January 1890, SFP Box 1180/3(c).
[137] DS to Souter, Rappanzini, J. McIntyre, PMG Melbourne, 30 May, 1, 17 June, 1889, LB4, pp. 66–67, 68, 69.
[138] *Argus*, 2 September 1890, p. 5, col. 4.

CHAPTER 12

organised, and perhaps paid for by his father, to have him out of the way during the collapse of the partnership. There is no hard evidence for this, although it was clearly Syme who suggested and financed Deakin's trip. On 31 October, the day that the Gillies–Deakin Coalition government was defeated, Syme wrote to Deakin regretting the inevitable fact and commenting that the *Age* had not supported Gillies as Minister of Railways.[139] The main intent of his letter, however, was to propose that Deakin take a trip to Egypt for several months and report for the *Age* on irrigation there. By 14 November the destination had been changed to India, but not the journalistic purpose.[140] Opposing the proposal, Joseph considered the expense unwarranted and unsuitable; Deakin was no expert and, moreover, the subject had already been reported on and he 'would only make a globe trotters rehash'.[141] Syme went ahead anyway, giving Deakin a set of instructions, overruling Joseph's objections and giving Wynne of the *Daily Telegraph* first Sydney offer for use of the articles for a third of the cost, while noting that the *Sydney Morning Herald* had expressed interest.[142] The Adelaide *Advertiser* was also interested, but was not prepared to pay Syme's price and the offer lapsed.[143]

Deakin and Herbert sailed from Adelaide on 26 November 1890, Herbert for Colombo, Ceylon, Deakin for Calcutta.[144] Deakin was soon sending back articles, the first appearing in February in the *Age* and the *Leader*. He collected a large amount of information and impressions, enough for his articles to run well into 1892. He and Herbert returned to Australia together from Bombay on the *Arcadia* arriving in Adelaide on 16 February.[145] Deakin disembarked in Adelaide and took the train to Melbourne, arriving the next day and meeting Syme.[146] Herbert, who had greatly enjoyed his travels (as he would recall some years later), arrived in Melbourne a day later, by ship.[147] This was one month before the partnership dissolution came into effect, but after the formalities had been set in train.

---

[139] DS to A. Deakin, 31 October 1890, Deakin Papers, Series 10.
[140] DS to JCS, 14 November 1890, LB4, p. 132.
[141] JCS to DS, 17 November 1890, SFP Box 1180/3(d).
[142] DS to A. Deakin, 18 November, W. Wynne, 27 November, LB3, pp. 178, 179; DS to JCS, 19 November 1890, LB4, p. 134.
[143] DS to W. Wynne, 2 December 1890, LB3, p. 182.
[144] 'Shipping', *Advertiser* (Adelaide), 27 November 1890, p. 7 (gives Syme for Calcutta, but names Colombo in an item elsewhere in the issue).
[145] 'Shipping Intelligence', *South Australian Register*, 17 February 1891, p. 4.
[146] 'Crude index', Deakin Papers, Series 2/37.
[147] H. Syme, Diary 1895, MS 6751, National Library of Australia; 'Shipping Intelligence', *Argus*, 19 February 1891, p. 4.

Sole proprietor

Following the signing on Thursday 19 March of the contract of sale of Joseph's quarter share in David Syme and Co., the now sole owner attended to the legalities required by the ownership changes. A new imprint statement, 'Printed and published for the proprietor, David Syme, at the *Age* office, Collins-street east' appeared in the *Age* of Saturday 21 March and in the next issue of the *Illustrated Australian News*, 1 April. Slightly slower to fall into line (someone failing to pass on an instruction?), the *Leader* began to carry the new imprint two weeks later, on 4 April. On Monday 23 March the three newspapers were re-registered in the name of 'Syme, David of "Blythswood", Carson Street, Kew' as proprietor (Darragh 1997, 94 [37.11, 37.12], 100 [62.06, 62.07], 117 [175.06, 175.07]). This time the obligatory sureties were provided by Samuel Gillott, 'Solicitor', and John Herbert Syme, 'Journalist'.

At last Syme was free to give Herbert a senior position in David Syme & Co. He appointed his eldest son to take over Joseph's duties, formalising this in a letter on the same day as the registration. He wrote that Herbert's weekly salary would be increased from £7 to £10, and raised again as soon as his son had 'qualified…for the work'.[148] Reading today as patronising if not overbearing, the long letter to the 31-year-old reveals, nevertheless, Syme's awareness of his son's 'very anomalous position in the office', with desultory and part-time duties, and the father's desire to provide a career opportunity for him. There were four conditions: hours of work from 9.30 am to 5.30 pm with half an hour for lunch; giving up many of his present associates and dressing properly; giving up attendance at horse races ('except on rare occasions, perhaps') and public billiards playing; and for the first three months submitting *all* matters of business to Syme, even the unimportant. The first and last seem unexceptionable; the middle two perhaps uncalled for. Belying the condescending tone, however, the letter is signed 'Your affectionate father, David Syme'. The 64-year-old father was also anxious to obtain what sounds like desperately needed assistance ('at an age when most people retire from business I have thrown upon my shoulders new duties & responsibilities which I wish you to share with me'). Little did Syme then know of the further challenges he was to face.

Another letter of 23 March is a reply to contributor Champion about the rate of payment for his contributions.[149] By this time Champion was on the

---

[148] DS to H. Syme, 23 March 1891, LB4, pp. 150–151.
[149] DS to H. Champion, 23 March 1891, LB3, p. 214.

CHAPTER 12

high seas bound for London, having sailed on 4 March from Adelaide on the *Valetta* (by the end of May he was reported as back in England in 'excellent health and spirits from his visit to the antipodes').[150] Syme told the journalist that he had been 'awfully busy', had purchased his partner's share of the business and was now sole proprietor. He further hinted at possible next moves, adding the intriguing information that he would have to postpone his plans for a London paper for some time – in fact, whenever this notion was conceived (this seems the only mention on record), it must have been abandoned altogether. He also said that he would try to 'get a run home' in six or eight months' time. But a carefree getaway was not to be.

---

[150] 'Shipping Intelligence', *South Australian Register*, 5 March 1891, p. 4; 'Miscellaneous', *Argus*, 30 May 1891, p. 6.

PART IV

A FREE HAND

VI

Chapter 13

'I AM NOT PREPARED TO MAKE ANY COMPROMISE WHATEVER'

(April 1891 to July 1896)

Single owner of the *Age* business from April 1891, Syme at 64 was at last free to run it as he chose, without objection. According to biographer Sayers (1965, 185) and numerous historians, he was immersed in politics, using the *Age* to 'put men into office, and remove them from office'. It is said that he made and unmade three short-term, fairly ineffectual Victorian premiers: James Munro (in office 5 November 1890 to 16 February 1892); William Shiels (16 February 1892 to 23 January 1893 whom, according to Macintyre, Syme 'installed as Premier'); and James Patterson (23 January 1893 to 27 September 1894) (Macintyre 1991, 218). Outlining and documenting what he calls the 'David Syme and the three stooges' thesis, historian John Lack (2006) has discredited this entrenched view, claiming it exaggerates the newspaper's undoubtedly considerable influence. Not only may that be so, but the view also rests on the reductive proposition that Syme and the *Age* were one and the same. Accordingly, any influence the *Age* might have exerted through its editorial advocacy has been ascribed directly to dictation from its proprietor.

While Syme did set the general policy course and for the most part kept an eye on the day-to-day routines of newspaper production, his talented and experienced leader-writing team, with Arthur Windsor at the helm, could and often did carry on without him. Attending to policy was now a relatively small part of the proprietor's activities, for he had many other matters to pre-occupy him, in and away from Melbourne, sometimes at crucial political moments. He was constantly involved with his agricultural pursuits, real estate acquisitions and mining enterprises, and he undertook overseas trips in 1892 and 1895. In addition, and overwhelmingly, for some four years he was dogged by a series of libel actions arising from the criticisms expressed in the *Age* and *Leader* of extravagant railways development and inept, wasteful operation. Defending these drew on an inordinate amount of his time and energies.

Without Joseph around to object, strongly worded editorial criticism of railway plans and management continued to appear in the *Age* and *Leader*. This put great pressure on the government and the Minister for Railways on the one hand and on the Railway Commissioners led by Richard Speight, on the other. On 17 March 1892 the new Shiels Government, responding to journalistic and parliamentary pressures and after lengthy discussion in Cabinet, resolved to suspend the Commissioners for 'alleged inefficiency and mismanagement' and appoint temporary commissioners in their place, decisions that were duly ratified by the Governor-in-Council that day.[1] A few days earlier Speight had made known his intention to bring a libel action against Syme as proprietor of the newspaper that had allegedly inveighed against him – something that Joseph, back in November 1890, had warned his senior partner might come about.[2] With his characteristic stoicism and persistence (along with increased irritability and acerbity of which colleagues and staff took the brunt), Syme and his business rode out the turbulence and survived, but it was a heavy and difficult time. There were five related trials, two of them very long, and more actions attempted and contemplated, until July 1896 when Syme was finally free of the railway litigation.

Killara and Dalry

In the lead-up to the trials, and during them, the Yarra Valley was more than ever a place of retreat. Syme regularly spent weekends at Killara. By 1894, he was usually there from Friday afternoon until Monday morning, sometimes accompanied by Annabella.[3] When Arthur took up a medical practice at Lilydale his father often stopped there en route to and from Melbourne.

Syme's activities at Killara and his other Yarra Valley properties were manifold. For instance, in April 1891 he was arranging for the auction of 30 horses, advertised as 'Annual Draft of the Killara Horses'.[4] For several

---

[1] 'The Management of the Railways', *Argus*, 18 March 1892, p. 5.
[2] 'Summary for Europe', *Argus*, 21 March 1892, p. 11; JCS to DS, 7 November 1890, SFP Box 1180/3(d).
[3] DS to McFarlane, 7 June 1 1894, LB5, p. 115; AS to Arthur Syme, 22 May 1894, in the possession of Judith Adams.
[4] 'Sales by Auction', *Argus* 25 April 1891, p. 3; DS to J. Clarke & Co., 18 April 1891, LB4, p. 152.

CHAPTER 13

days in January 1892, as was customary each summer, Deakin came to stay. This time the two men roamed the district, calling at his Dalry property.[5] On Friday 25 March the Upper Yarra District Racing Club held its annual races at Killara. Whether or not Syme was present, he must have given permission for the event to be held there, and very likely his horseracing enthusiast son Herbert attended.[6] In August, when Syme was overseas, the Killara herd of Polled Angus cattle was auctioned, giving rise to a comment in the *Australasian* that his 'retirement' from the Polled Angus competition was 'a conspicuous defect' at the Melbourne Show, although his Romney Marsh sheep had carried off all the prizes.[7]

Items in Syme's letterbooks give some indication of his dealings in livestock over these years. In particular, various mentions of selling a bull, a stallion, and rams suggest his continued interest in breeding.[8] Sales of pork for freezing and export indicate his great interest in promoting by example Victoria's primary production, as do the references to milk production and the cheese-making that he organised at Dalry, and his plans to grow maize at Killara.[9] Herbert took responsibility for these matters when Syme was out of the colony.[10]

Although he spent much time at Killara and Dalry, Syme by now owned or had a stake in numerous other properties, not all of which are readily identifiable, and was alert both to further acquisitions and to opportunities for disposing profitably. His interests, covering real estate in city and country Victoria, extended beyond the colony also. In May 1891 he was considering an offer of forested blocks in South Australia.[11] He may have inspected these in July 1891, when he spent time in the colony looking at dairy farming and stock. It is significant that an Adelaide *Advertiser* news item about this visit identifies Syme not only as the *Age* proprietor but more prominently as a well-known writer whose evolution book was recently published and who

---

[5] Diary entries for 7–10 January 1892, Alfred Deakin Papers, MS 1540, Series 2, National Library of Australia.

[6] 'Upper Yarra Races', *Argus*, 28 March 1892, p. 10.

[7] *Australasian*, 27 August 1892, Supplement, p. 4 ('Polled Angus'), 5 ('Romney Marsh').

[8] For example, DS to S. Hoot, 18 November 1895, LB5, p. 156; H. Syme to J.M. Peck & Sons, 25 August 1892, LB3, p. 296.

[9] DS to R. Davidson & Co., 27 August 1894, LB5, p. 126; DS to [no addressee, undated, February? 1895], LB5, p. 141.

[10] H. Syme to J.M. Peck & Sons, LB3, p. 296.

[11] DS to W. Marshall, 28 May 1891, LB4, p. 155.

also devoted himself to farming and cattle-breeding – information probably supplied by Syme himself.[12] In late 1892 or early 1893 he visited his 900-acre 'Barr Park', property at Cohuna in northern Victoria close to the Murray River, which in February 1889 he had been arranging to buy.[13] His manager there was Jesse Timmins, mining partner from the early 1850s, whom Syme helped financially over the years (the last on record a postal order for £10 in February 1903) and who was then supervising the raising of the livestock (bullocks and sheep) that were sold periodically at Melbourne Markets.[14] But Timmins found the climate too hot, and appears to have left in 1895 or earlier, replaced by Syme's son Francis, no longer at Dalry. Evidence of his activities, Francis is named as the Barr Park livestock vendor in a 26 February 1896 *Argus* Markets report and in April 1896 became actively involved in the Cohuna Irrigation Trust.[15]

Timmins, who did not take up a suggestion from Syme that he move to Killara, by February 1895 was working for another concern in which Syme had a stake.[16] This was the Spa Proprietary Company on a gold-mining claim in southern New South Wales, on the Shoalhaven River near Nerriga.[17] In May 1893 Syme had expressed interest in taking up a share in this venture. By October he was clearly involved, concerned about managerial disorder, and intending to visit the claim during a temporary recess of the Speight trial.[18] Entries in Deakin's diary would indicate that the two men went there in January 1894, taking the Sydney express train to Goulburn, proceeding on to Bungonia, and camping out.[19] Troubles continuing at this mine in February and March 1895, Syme was worried about non-payment of the workers, including Timmins, while dissociating himself from reported complaints about his onetime partner.[20]

---

[12] *Advertiser* (Adelaide), 24 July 1891, p. 4, col. 7.

[13] DS to Robertson, Caper & Co., 21 February 1889, LB4, p. 61; DS to J. Timmins, 11 January 1893, LB4, p. 162.

[14] DS to J. Timmins, 20 February 1903, LB5, p. 463; 'An Old Omeo Identity', *Bairnsdale Advertiser*, 18 February 1909, p. 2; sales of DS's stock reported periodically in 'Markets' *Argus*, 1891–1893.

[15] 'Our Country Service', *Bendigo Advertiser*, 7 April 1896, p. 2.

[16] DS to Timmins, 11 January 1893, LB4, p. 162.

[17] 'The Shoalhaven Valley', *Bathurst Free Press*, 30 June 1893, p. 3.

[18] DS to [no recipient] 4 May 1893, LB5, p. 47; DS to R. Stamp, 23 October 1893, LB5, p. 89.

[19] Diary entries for 11–18 January 1894, Deakin Papers, Series 2.

[20] DS to [addressee indecipherable] 20 February 1895, LB5, p. 140; DS to J. Armstrong, 4 March 1895, LB5, p. 142.

CHAPTER 13

Syme became a shareholder in other new mining ventures. One such followed investigations by the government from late 1892 (hoping to reduce dependence on imports), which opened up a rich black-coal seam in South Gippsland. The township that developed was subsequently named Outtrim, after the then Minister for Mines, Alfred Outtrim. Syme bought shares in the Outtrim coal-mining company in June 1893.[21] Another was one of the many mining projects of politician John Wallace MLC, the Wallace-Bethanga gold and copper mining and smelting enterprise, reviving the Yackandandah goldfield in north-east Victoria and visited by Premier Patterson and a delegation in July 1894.[22] By May 1895 Syme had 2000 shares in Wallace-Bethanga.[23]

During these years of economic depression, when many of his contemporaries suffered financial loss (brother George for one, and Deakin another) (M. Syme 2013, 73–74; La Nauze 1979, 138–139) and some were declared bankrupt, Syme had money to put into causes he believed in strongly, in particular, the development of resources in Victoria and other Australian colonies. At the same time he was building up his own assets. He was, however, ready to sell stocks and call in loans whenever he needed substantial ready cash, whether for other purchases, or for the buy-out instalments due to Joseph, or for legal expenses associated with the libel actions.[24] And while he gave serious thought to deciding what enterprises to support, he was somewhat cavalier about the actual state of his portfolio and finances, born out by sundry requests to Gillott and others for relevant paperwork, and information therein.[25]

Six weeks after Speight had instructed his solicitors to issue a writ for libel, Syme embarked on the overseas trip that he had long intended. Having mentioned it in a letter to Henry Champion in March 1891, in October he wrote him again that he expected to be 'coming home' in about four months.[26] On 30 April 1892 he left on the French mail steamer *Australien*, for Marseilles and London.[27] While there is no record of a farewell function

---

[21] DS to R. Stamp, 30 June 1893, LB5, p. 68.
[22] 'A Pioneer in Mining', *Argus*, 30 July 1894, p. 4.
[23] DS to L. Robinson, undated [May 1895], LB5, p. 146.
[24] For example, DS to R. Stamp, 23 October 1893, LB5, p. 89; DS to J. Macdonald, 31 January 1894, LB5, p. 99.
[25] For example, DS to S. Gillott, 17 February 1892, LB4, p. 161; fragment of letter, undated [October? 1893] LB5, p. 82.
[26] DS to H. Champion, 23 March, 19 October 1891, LB3, pp. 214, 268.
[27] 'Shipping Intelligence', *Argus*, 2 May 1892, p. 4.

for him, the *Age* of 2 May reported that 'several public men' were present to see off the 'many prominent citizens' who were on board. Doubtless Syme would have been considered one of them. Travelling with him was wife Annabella and a young woman, possibly Lucie, Olive, or a niece (shipping records are unclear). He would be away until early November.

In his father's absence, Herbert managed all aspects of the business, signing correspondence either in his name or as attorney for his father, some of it typed. He sacked reporter W.B. Melville after only three months' employment, part of reducing the staff and therefore costs.[28] He had to field a letter from Burden and Bonython in Adelaide about sharing a Rudyard Kipling Christmas story and several from them about a libel action brought by James Williams against the *Advertiser*, apparently for publishing information supplied by the *Age* (no replies are on file).[29]

Railway litigation

Most significantly, in the absence of his father, the defendant, he oversaw developments in the Speight libel case. On 2 June he met with Deakin and lawyer Arthur Snowden of Gillott, Crocker and Snowden to discuss it (Samuel Gillott, the usual contact, then being overseas) and on 6 June a retainer was arranged for Deakin, for legal services.[30] While still an active and prominent member of parliament, Deakin did not hold ministerial office at this time and was conducting a legal practice along with parliamentary responsibilities. Whether Syme requested his services, either before his departure or via cables, or whether this was Herbert's doing, is not known. Deakin had been in contact with Syme and the *Age* office regularly since his return from India in 1891. He also had occasional social contact with Herbert and, his diary shows, in July 1891 with Annabella Syme, in relation to 'Indian Curios'.[31]

On 9 June Syme's legal team, led by barrister John Madden, regarded as 'the doyen of the bar for many years', and to be appointed Chief Justice and knighted in 1893 (Campbell 1986), applied for time to gather evidence in

---

[28] Entry for Melville in Wages Book, p. 303; DS to W. Melville, 25 June 1892, LB3, p. 294.

[29] Burden & Bonython to DS & Co., 31 May, 15 June, 9 August. 13 August 1892, J.L. Bonython and Company, Summary Record, Letter Books, BRG 10, Series 8, State Library of South Australia.

[30] Diary entries for 2, 6 June 1892, Deakin Papers, Series 2.

[31] Diary entry for 7 July 1891, Deakin Papers, Series 2.

CHAPTER 13

England in defence of Speight's action for £25,000 damages.[32] Successive hearings in the months following led to the establishment of a Committee to examine witnesses in England, and for the ensuing evidence to be forwarded to Melbourne.[33] This meant that the case proper would not be heard until the following year, well after Syme's return. Whether Syme foresaw and planned this, either before his departure or in correspondence after it, also cannot be established.

Syme could hardly have anticipated the bandwagon action instituted in July by Arthur Groom, former MLC for West Gippsland, seeking damages of £10,000 for alleged libelling in several editorials published in April issues of the *Age*, claiming that Groom attempted to influence railway construction. Heard before Mr Justice Holroyd and a jury of 12, the *Groom v. Syme* case ran from 26 September to 28 October 1892. Appearing for the defence were James Purves, known as a brilliant barrister, highly skilled in cross-examination (Aveling 1974), and Madden. The jury brought in a verdict for Syme, on the basis of the statements being true, and fair comment. The *Age* leader of 29 October commented that politicians were free to interfere, but must be open to scrutiny.

Far away during these initial legal manoeuvres, Syme was otherwise engaged. In July, soon after his arrival in England, and after extensive travelling and sightseeing on the Continent, particularly in Switzerland, he undertook a whirlwind trip to Norway.[34] With him was Gillott. There is no hint of what led him to go there, and it may have been at the solicitor's suggestion. Relations were slight between Victoria and Norway, no longer the source of timber for the colony that it had been. Syme's London newspaper contact Frank Lloyd bought two paper mills in Norway, but that would be almost a decade later, in 1902 (D. Griffiths 1992, 377). The two men, presumably leaving their wives in England, spent about a week in the Scandinavian country. In a letter of 29 July Syme told Deakin that they visited Christiana (now Oslo), saw something of the countryside and travelled on a 'fastboat', before embarking from Bergen on a ship bound for Hull.[35] This 'hurried visit' was solely for his health, Syme wrote, adding that he felt 'all the better' for what was 'really a nice trip' and he wished he could have stayed longer.

---

32 'News of the Day', *Age*, 10 June 1892, p. 5, *Argus*, 10 June 1892, p. 4, col.1.
33 'Speight v. Syme', *Argus*, 3 August 1892, p. 10, 25 November, p. 5, 'Special Telegrams', 31 December, p. 7.
34 AS to Arthur Syme, 5 June 1892, from Zurich, in possession of Judith Adams.
35 DS to A. Deakin, 29 July 1892, Deakin Papers, Series 6.

This letter, replying to one from Deakin dated 6 June, the day that Herbert had engaged him to act in the impending Speight lawsuit, reveals that Syme was following developments as reported in the *Age*, although he was not being briefed in detail from the Office. From copies of weeks-old papers, he had learned that Deakin, wearing his parliamentarian's hat, had expressed support for a move to establish a joint committee of both Houses to examine the charges against the Railway Commissioners. This would have been Deakin's speech in the Assembly on 2 June, the day he had met with Herbert and solicitor Snowden. Syme had also read the *Age* editorial of the next day, which was critical of Deakin for this support and for being involved in railway development during the Gillies Premiership.[36] Implying Deakin was not a detached observer, in strongly worded albeit courteous words, Syme expressed his strong opposition to a committee and justified the *Age* editorial in the light of what he read as Deakin's 'not friendly' remarks in his Assembly speech, adding that Gillott agreed with him (Syme). Obviously concerned not to fall out with his friend, erstwhile journalist and putative legal counsel, he added the mollifying 'I hope the remarks in the paper on you will not prevent you from seeing George and Herbert'.

In the concluding paragraph Syme turned to a quite different subject. Apparently undeterred by Alfred Wallace's denunciation in *Nature* the previous year, he still sought to spread his evolutionist gospel, through his *On the Modification of Organisms*. He told Deakin he had consulted Philip Mennell about an abridged edition, for he would be 'pleased to keep it on as much as in my power'. At this time there was an unresolved dispute with Kegan Paul over the publisher's request for payment of £27 to cover costs of reprinting the title page, because the copies sent by George Robertson lacked the name of the English publisher.[37] There is no indication that he visited Kegan Paul to sort out the matter when in London (and it was still unresolved in December 1892).[38] In any case, by then, at Syme's written instruction in January, some 200 surplus copies had been handed over to agent George Street, to whom he had given yet another list of recipients of complimentary copies.[39] Copies remaining after this distribution had been transferred to the London bookseller and publisher Simpkin & Marshall,

---

[36] Editorial, *Age*, 3 June 1892, p. 4.
[37] DS to Kegan Paul, Trench, Trübner & Co., 12 August 1891, 30 January 1892, LB3, pp. 254, 284–285; DS to G. Robertson & Co., 12, 26 August 1891, LB3, pp. 255, 256.
[38] DS to Kegan Paul & Co., 5 December 1892, LB5, p. 13.
[39] DS to G. Street, 30 January 1892, LB3, p. 286.

CHAPTER 13

who in October 1892 was advertising them for sale at 3s 6d.[40] The original publisher, George Robertson, suggested this move to Syme, who may have arranged it personally. What sales were made is not known, although Syme wrote in 1894 enquiring about this.[41] Nor was there ever another edition, either full or abridged.

There is little on record about the newspaper business matters that Syme would have attended to when in London. Letterbook items provide a couple of clues: that he met with at least one paper supplier, A.L. Poulter; and that he saw Philip Mennell and discussed the publication of Deakin's book on irrigation in India, a collection of his *Age* articles.[42] He would have visited his London *Age* office and his agents, particularly George Street and McEwan & Co. He would have seen James Harrison, who was old (76) and ill, lending him funds to enable a return to Victoria.[43] And he very likely also saw his long-standing correspondent George Levey.

On 4 November 1892 Syme returned to Melbourne, on the *Thermopylae*.[44] A few days later he wrote to Levey in London: 'Got here on Friday after a rough passage. Hope to get over it soon.'[45] At a time of economic adversity yet to worsen, he was back in the saddle and marshalling his energies for the legal battle to come. Following the collapse of building societies, many banks failed, including the Federal Bank on 28 January 1893. More disastrously, on 6 April the Commercial Bank of Australia stopped payment. Thus 'Melbourne's days as the financial capital of Australia were numbered' and 'Victoria was no longer the powerhouse of the Australian economy' (Merrett 2005). The reduction of the *Argus* price to a penny on 1 April posed an additional worry – a threat to the circulation of the *Age* and, thus, to revenue for the business. Two days later, however, Syme sounded fairly sanguine, writing on 3 April to Watkin Wynne in Sydney that the 'Argus so far, has not affected us in the least'.[46] But he was not complacent, adding that, with the 'intense competition' between the two papers, the Sydney correspondent should be instructed to send 'sensational accounts of sensational events'. The *Argus* circulation did rise, from a daily average

---

40   For example, in *Athenaeum*, 22 October 1892.
41   DS to Simpkin & Co. 6 August 1894, LB5, p. 123.
42   DS to A. Poulter, 12 November 1892, LB5, p. 9; DS to P. Mennell, 16 January 1893, LB5, p. 25.
43   DS to J. Harrison, 17 November 1892, LB5, p. 12.
44   'Shipping Intelligence', *Argus*, 5 November 1892, p. 6.
45   DS to G. Levey, 11 November 1892, LB5, p. 8.
46   DS to W. Wynne, 3 April 1893, LB5, p. 41.

for the year 1892 of 20,000 to 31,000 in 1893 and 40,000 in 1894;[47] and it probably did have a retarding effect on the *Age* circulation, which at 101,346 in 1892[48] was more than five times than that of the *Argus* but for some months from July 1893 was prominently stated in the *Age* to be 'now four times larger than any other Melbourne morning paper'. It may be indicative of a decline that actual circulation figures were not published after 1892 and gross revenue from sales of the *Age* for the years 1893 to 1905 was drastically below those for previous years (£162,916 in 1892, £132,391 in 1893, £126,657 in 1895).[49]

With the Speight action looming, Syme worked to raise his public profile and reputation overseas and locally. He asked Levey, in his first letter to him after returning from England, to get the outcome of *Groom v. Syme* reported in the leading columns of leading dailies, in particular, the *Times* or the *Daily Chronicle*. He saw it as 'a subject that will bear trenchant treatment, & wd also be of vast importance to us in Speights case'.[50] In February 1893 he wrote to Levey that he would be paid six guineas for his three articles about the case that had appeared in the *Daily Chronicle*.[51] In May, when the trial was about to commence, he offered a '*Leader* prize' of £10.10s for the Melbourne Agricultural Show (for what entries is not apparent).[52] In September, when the trial was in full swing, he nominated himself as a Life Governor of the Working Men's College (established by philanthropist Francis Ormond in 1887, today RMIT University).[53]

He sought information that might be relevant to the trial. In November 1892 he asked Levey to find out if Speight's wife was related to Sir James Allport, onetime manager of the English Midland Railway, where Speight had been employed before he arrived in Melbourne in 1884 to head the new Board of Railway Commissioners. He stated that such information would be 'of very great importance'.[54] If he was seeking to uncover preferential treatment for Speight through his wife's connections, the investigations made

---

[47] 'Circulation', 'Historical Records of "The Argus" and "The Australasian"', compiled by C.P. Smith, [1924], MS 10727, Australian Manuscripts Collection, State Library of Victoria.
[48] 'Circulation of The Age', *Age*, 1 February 1892, p. 4.
[49] Profit and loss accounts, 1891–1900, SFP Box 1191/3.
[50] DS to G. Levey, 11 November 1892, LB5, p. 8.
[51] DS to G. Levey, 21 February 1893, LB5, p. 32.
[52] DS to F. Patterson, 17 May 1893, LB5, p. 52.
[53] DS to Secretary, Working Men's College, 14 September 1893, LB5, p. 79.
[54] DS to G. Levey, 13 November 1892, LB5, p. 10.

CHAPTER 13

by Levey came to nought.[55] Also in November, Syme requested London agent Street to send him a recently published article on American Railways in a recent issue of the *Investors Guide*.[56]

Syme's behaviour in the six months after his return and before the trial suggests that he was deeply concerned and apprehensive, these feelings exacerbated by the worsening economic conditions and the worry about the effect of the *Argus* price reduction. This manifested in several unprovoked outbursts in letters and memos to regular and respected colleagues (one can only guess at unrecorded verbal ones). In December 1892 he wrote a most querulous letter to James Thomson about shared cable messages, when typically his letters to the publisher of the *Evening Standard* on this subject were polite, if firm.[57] In January 1893 a letter to his correspondent, confidant and unofficial agent, Levey, began with an insultingly aggressive dressing down. No business of Syme's, it concerned Levey's apparently inept involvement as a go-between to negotiate a loan in London for the Melbourne and Metropolitan Board of Works Chairman, Edmund Fitzgibbon, which had been reported sarcastically in the *Age* and *Argus* of the same day, 11 January.[58] There followed criticism of the quality of both Levey's regular correspondence and his 'specials' articles, ending with the statement that his contributions would not be paid for without his (Syme's) authorisation. Levey must have protested at this unwarranted attack, for a later letter from Syme opened with 'Am awfully sorry to have vexed you over that correspondence business. I must have written you that letter in a moment of irritation'.[59] He nevertheless repeated his complaints, albeit in a milder tone. Also in January, Syme sent an annoyed letter to Mennell, unreasonably criticising him for allowing the *Daily Telegraph* and the *Advertiser* to be acknowledged alongside the *Age* in the preface to Deakin's *Irrigated India*, whose publication he was helping organise.[60]

Strain showed also in dealings with the editorial department. Earlier memos on file from Syme to editor Windsor are courteous, while the numerous references to him in Syme's letters to others are consistently respectful. In contrast, a memo in January berates him for editorials not being up to standard, one in particular being 'feeble & inconsequential'; one

---

[55] DS to G. Levey, 12 February 1893, LB5, p. 28.
[56] DS to G. Street & Co., 15 November 1892, LB5, p. 11.
[57] DS to J. Thomson, 31 December 1892, LB5, p. 16.
[58] DS to G. Levey, 11 January 1893, LB5, p. 22.
[59] DS to G. Levey, 29 March 1893, LB5, pp. 38–39.
[60] DS to P. Mennell, 16 January 1893, LB5, p. 25.

in February critical at length of his 'haphazard' handling of policy and the 'disorganised state' of his staff.[61] In June Syme wrote that he was renewing his contract for two years, at a salary of £800 per annum, substantially less than the £1040 he had been earning since 1886.[62] As no reduction is recorded either in the Wages Book or in Syme's own notes on the salaries of his staff, it may be assumed that Syme had second thoughts.[63] Subeditor Stephens, habitually taken to task in streams of memos – Syme's *ex post facto* method of quality control – was much more severely treated in January 1893, when Syme cancelled his holiday pay, and in May when Syme gave him two weeks' notice of dismissal.[64] This edict too must have been rescinded, for Stephens remained on the staff, while continuing to receive a regular litany of complaints about his work. The burden would have been lightened, however, for from November 1892 he had an assistant, J. Nicholson.[65]

In fact, Syme had a strong *Age* editorial and literary team, and knew it. Besides the body of reporters headed by Gottfried Schuler, the staff classified as 'editorial' included Windsor, Charles Bright, Alexander Bell (who would leave at the end of 1893), Benjamin Hoare (of whom at first Syme despaired but would come to rely on heavily and who in turn became a great admirer of his chief) and Anthony Robinson, long-time commercial editor.[66] In addition, there were contributing leader writers, not on staff but paid by volume. These included Charles Pearson, who was in London from late 1892 and sent contributions from there, the last published on 9 May 1894, shortly before his death on 29 May.[67] There was a great array of correspondents and contributors from near and far, whose work Syme monitored, telling some it was no longer wanted. In July 1891 he provisionally accepted travelling Walter Bell's offer to send descriptive letters from Mexico, but not from New Zealand and California (about which 'we fear nothing fresh can be said').[68] In October 1891 he advised Champion to discontinue his articles

---

[61] DS to A. Windsor, undated [January 1893] LB5, p. 20, 3 February 1893, LB5, pp. 26–27.
[62] DS to A. Windsor, 3 June 1893, LB5, p. 57.
[63] Entry for Windsor in Wages Book, p. 525.
[64] DS to J. Stephens, [?] January, 25 May 1893, LB5, pp. 24, 55.
[65] Entry for Nicholson in Wages Book, p. 355.
[66] DS to B. Hoare, 24 February 1892, LB3, p. 288; Hoare (1927, 149–150).
[67] DS to C. Pearson, 28 March 1893, LB5, p. 37; 'Memorials of C.H. Pearson', Charles H. Pearson Papers, Box 438/3e, Australian Manuscripts Collection, State Library of Victoria.
[68] DS to W. Bell, 8 July 1891, LB3, p. 243.

CHAPTER 13

from England because 'their contents are invariably anticipated' (presumably by cables).[69] He was alert to recruiting new contributors. In August 1894 he welcomed the offer of letters from a D.V. Piccoli, on his retirement to Italy, stressing that in the 'present depressed conditions as a colony any information as to a market for our produce' would be acceptable.[70] He was tolerant of personal failings, provided that his correspondent supplied copy that was of good quality, timely and relevant. Thus, while he was accepting articles from Edmund Mitchell, former *Age* reporter with a drinking problem, he was wary, as seen in the postscript to an April 1893 letter to Wynne: 'Was Ed Mitchell sober when he wrote his last paper from San Francisco? You know his failing I suppose. Is he to be trusted with our Chicago cables?'[71]

Contrasting with his eruptions of irritability in the stressful period from late 1892 to mid-1893, Syme's treatment of James Harrison was generously compassionate. Sailing from Southampton on 7 August by the German mail steamer *Hohenzollern*, Harrison, with his wife and his four youngest children, had arrived in Melbourne on 21 September.[72] He went with his family to live in a cottage on windswept tidal flats at Point Henry on Port Phillip Bay several kilometres south of Geelong, from where he wrote to Syme on 12 November 1892 with proposals for repaying the loan. These Syme, himself just back in Melbourne from his overseas trip, found acceptable.[73] Possibly they entailed repayment through written contributions, for he went on to discuss future ones from Harrison, stating that, in addition to his regular science column, a second feature could be acceptable, and suggesting that he call in to discuss this with Windsor. Whether or not he did so, living inconveniently far away, the 'Scientific Gossip' contributions continued to appear in the *Leader*, although clearly becoming less substantial.

In July 1893 Harrison was in Melbourne, attending a Committee meeting of the benevolent Caxton Commemoration Fund that he had helped set up back in 1871 and of which Syme was a Trustee.[74] A couple of weeks later 'The Vagabond' sought him out at Point Henry and interviewed him in

---

[69] DS to H. Champion, 19 October, 1891, LB3, p. 268.
[70] DS to D.V. Piccoli, 28 August 1894, LB5, p. 126.
[71] DS to W. Wynne, 3 April 1893, LB5, p. 41.
[72] Unassisted Inward Passenger Lists to Victoria 1852–1923, Public Record Office Victoria; 'Shipping Intelligence', *Argus*, 22 September 1892, p. 4.
[73] DS to J. Harrison, 17 November 1892, LB5, p. 12.
[74] 'The Caxton Fund', *Argus*, 25 July 1893, p. 6; David Syme, Caxton Commemoration Fund, Declaration of Trust 1894, MS 10602, Australian Manuscripts Collection, State Library of Victoria.

Geelong the following day, describing him, in the *Age* of 12 August, as 'hale and hearty'.[75] But his days were numbered, for he soon became seriously ill, and died on 3 September, the last of his science contributions appearing some two weeks later (Morrison 1997). A news item from Geelong in the *Age* of 4 September notes that he was at one time editor and, later, in England a 'valued contributor' to the *Age* and the *Leader*.[76] The editorial in the *Age* of 5 September is an obituary that recognises his considerable contribution to journalism from his establishing of the *Geelong Advertiser* in 1840 and his early advocacy of protective tariffs to his rising on the day of his death decades later 'with the intention of writing an article for the columns of this journal'. It pays tribute to the journalist's 'moral heroism and fine sturdy independence' but not to the manifold service he did for Syme through his robust, informed journalism and his knowledge about newspaper publication when *Age* editor from 1867 to 1873.

On 1 June 1893 *Speight v. Syme* finally came to trial in the First Civil Court before Mr (later Sir) Justice Henry Hodges, known to be able to 'sit for long hours without showing fatigue' (J. Young 1983), which is just as well, as the case would run for 90 days of hearings over a seven-month period, including a six-week adjournment.[77] Damages of £25,000 were sought for alleged libels amounting to accusations of incapacity and mismanagement in 11 *Age* editorials published between 20 March 1891 and 14 March 1892.[78] (There was arguably libellous material published at times during the previous few years, but citing it could have brought up the curly question of Joseph's liability.) Syme's solicitors were Gillott, Snowden & Crocker. Their employee George Moir was clerk to the solicitors. Purves was senior counsel and Deakin, whose diary records his day-to-day involvement, was junior counsel. Corresponding regularly with Pearson since he went to London, on 13 June writing from Parliament House during a day's respite from the Speight case Deakin expressed pessimism to him (probably with a candour he did not show to his client, Syme).[79] He considered that the case might ruin Syme unless he was 'helped to maintain it for the 3 or 4 months for which it may last', also that it threatened to be 'the biggest ever tried in Australia & perhaps the costliest too'. From a different angle, he

---

[75] 'About Geelong', No. 1, *Age*, 12 August 1892, p. 15.
[76] 'A Pioneer Journalist', *Age*, 5 September 1893, p. 4.
[77] '"The Age" and the Railway', *Age*, 2 June 1893, pp. 5–6; 'Important Libel Action', *Argus*, 2 June 1893, pp. 5–6
[78] Summarised in Sayers (1965, 167–169).
[79] Deakin to Pearson, 13 June 1893, Pearson Papers, MS 7323, Box 439/5(a).

CHAPTER 13

expressed the 'fear that [it] will wreck the reputations of our Railways with English investors [for] the disclosures of reckless extravagance…are simply appalling'. For 'every reason' he wished it could be settled.

Syme immersed himself in the case, with every indication of seeing it through. He sought the support of key politicians, a few days into the trial writing to former Premier Shiels, asking him to be a witness.[80] Shiels had opposed much railway development and in March 1892 been responsible for suspending Speight and his fellow Commissioners. In July Syme communicated with Premier Patterson seeking common ground against an *Argus* attack of three days earlier.[81] During a fortnight's recess granted late June he made his services and those of chief of staff Schuler and experienced and reliable reporter E.G.L. Sweet, who had done stints as parliamentary reporter, available to assist the legal team in gathering information, much of it detailed and technical; and he found other avenues to obtain financial data.[82]

Traceable through reports in the *Age* and *Argus*, the hearings ground on day after day, being mercifully adjourned between 27 September and 1 November. On 19 December, the 85th day, the judge announced that he wished for a verdict so the jury would not be locked up on Christmas Day. But due to his 'indisposition', the case was adjourned on 21 December for a week. Finally, on 2 January 1894 a verdict was brought in, albeit an inconclusive one: £100 damages for plaintiff Speight on the eighth count, relating to charges of extravagance in the Stores Branch. On the other 10 counts the jury were unable to agree. The judge duly thanked the jurors and discharged them.

Syme moved swiftly to convey appreciation of assistance in gathering evidence. On 3 January he sent a cheque for £100 to George Moir, managing clerk at his solicitors, for 'exceptional valuable' services rendered, the 'zeal, the industry & the extraordinary ability you manifested' calling forth his gratitude and admiration.[83] The next day he sent one for £25 to chief of staff Schuler, as a 'slight acknowledgement' of 'very valuable service' and another for £20 to reporter Sweet, as a 'slight recognition' of his 'valuable service'.[84]

---

[80] DS to W. Shiels, 5 June 1893, LB5, p. 58.
[81] DS to J. Patterson, 4 July 1893, LB5, p. 70.
[82] DS to S. Gillott, 25 June 1893, LB5, p. 65; DS to Gillott & Snowden, 27, 29 July, LB5, pp. 72, 74.
[83] DS to G. Moir, 3 January 1894, LB5, p. 94.
[84] DS to G.F. Schuler and E. Sweet, 4 January 1894, LB5, pp. 95, 96.

The *Argus* of 3 January noted that the plaintiff, Speight, was disappointed, and on the following day reported that he was instructing his solicitors to continue the action on the outstanding 10 counts, with a new jury. Somewhat prematurely, the *Age* of 3 January, under the heading 'Feelings in the Country', claimed the verdict as 'practically a triumph for the defendant'. It noted also that the costs of the trial for the defence amounted to nearly £21,000, for the plaintiff £8000. The rival *Age* and *Argus* newspapers moved fast to encourage and report on public subscriptions towards these costs. On 4 January the *Age* announced a 'Proposed National Subscription', to which Syme's friend William McCulloch MLC had already contributed £100 and John Bonython of the Adelaide *Advertiser* £25. Two days later the formation of a Committee was announced, of which McCulloch became treasurer and professional organiser Robert Walpole secretary. Subscribers were listed and fund totals supplied in successive issues of the *Age*. On 13 January receipt of £100 from the Father of the *Age* Chapel was noted; in donating towards Syme's expenses, the body of printers, compositors and proofreaders wished to express their 'sympathy and goodwill'. By 16 January the total received was £609.17.6.

On 29 March the 'Defence Fund' Executive Committee met Syme at the *Age* office to hand over the moneys subscribed, and a handsome testimonial on behalf of subscribers in 113 places in Victoria, 34 country newspapers, and well-wishers associated with the *Australasian Typographical Journal*.[85] Syme's long acceptance speech, as reported in the *Age* of 31 March, is a magnificent encomium to press freedom. Expressing thanks for the 'handsome' sum, especially in a time of depression, he launched into an assertion of his motives, stating that the 'welfare of the whole community… should be the paramount object of an honest newspaper'.[86] He then reiterated criticisms of extravagance as expressed in the *Age*, pointing out that the public acts of public men should be open to scrutiny and that there was no personal antipathy involved. He led into his conclusion with the rousing 'What is the use of a Press which is unobservant of affairs, and dumb when it ought to speak out; and what think you, must be the fate of the country when such is the case?' As outlined below, publication of this stirring speech would soon have severe consequences, but not for Syme.

The actual sum is not named on the testimonial or in the report of the presentation. As a revenue item in the financial statement for 1894, it is

---

[85] Testimonial, in *Age* Archives, Melbourne.
[86] '"The Age" National Defence Fund', *Age*, 31 March 1894, p. 9.

CHAPTER 13

£1021.17.5 – a small fraction of Syme's legal costs to date, but strong evidence of the rallying of widespread community support.[87] In parallel, there was support for Speight through the *Argus*, with the flowing in of letters of sympathy reported in its issue of 5 January and daily thereafter. By 9 January a Speight Testimonial Fund Committee was formed and funds progressively subscribed were reported in the *Argus*. By 27 February the subscriptions exceeded the final total for the Syme fund. The last and largest amount published is £1237.9.0 on 20 April, the day before the second Speight action began. There are no more reports in the *Argus*, and it is not now known whether further moneys were subscribed, nor if and when the total amount was presented. Obviously the litigation had a polarising effect. From time to time during the period of subscription, the *Argus* also published disparaging remarks about the *Age* Fund (something the *Age* did not reciprocate).

While the subscriptions were being collected, a second bandwagon action was launched (not that the last had been heard of Groom, who brought the first in September 1892). In February 1894 former locomotive engineer Allison Dalrymple Smith issued a writ for damages of £15,000 for alleged libels in the *Age* between 3 March 1892 and 14 June 1893.[88] This case would not be heard until June 1895, after a second Speight action had been tried.

On 2 April 1894 Speight applied for a new trial, wanting a review of the verdict on the eighth count because it was not unanimous, and pronouncements on the 10 undecided ones. The first matter was settled on 4 April, the verdict of £100 damages to stand. Trial on the others began on 17 April before judge Hartley Williams, knighted that year, well-known and respected for common sense (Miller 1976). With the same legal team, it went for five months, examining a mass of detailed administrative, financial and technical evidence, as in the first trial. While it was running, two related matters were raised in the law courts. On 6 April Speight applied for a writ against the *Age* publisher for contempt of court in relation to publication on 31 March of Syme's subscription acceptance speech. This matter was to be dropped while the second *Speight v. Syme* trial was proceeding. On 4 May Groom made application for a new trial in the case of *Groom v. Syme* on the grounds that the jury had been misdirected. A small but significant victory for Syme, this was dismissed, with costs.

Sayers (1965, 173–174), quoting Deakin's introduction to Pratt's biography of Syme, wrote that midway through the second Speight trial

---

[87] Profit and loss accounts, 1891–1900, SFP Box 1191/3.
[88] *Argus*, 24 February 1894, p. 9, col. 2.

an offer of compromise was made that Syme considered and rejected. This is not identifiable from Deakin's diary entries nor is it mentioned in Syme's letterbook correspondence, although there is reference to a later offer (discussed below). In any case, all indications are that he was staying the course that Speight had set. On 13 August he wrote to Levey that the second Speight case was still proceeding. This time his tone was most conciliatory ('It is a long time now since I had any word from you. Hope you have not forgotten me altogether').[89] Some six weeks later the hearings ended and on Monday 24 September the jury was locked up to consider its verdict, which it returned on 26 September. This time there was unanimity, the jury finding for defendant Syme on nine of the 10 counts and for plaintiff Speight on one, with token damages of one farthing. On 27 September the *Age* editorialised on the 'victory' in what was 'virtually a State trial'. That day Deakin had a 'drive to Francis Syme', presumably with David Syme to Dalry, and three days later had 'the Symes and Purves to tea'.[90] For several days following, the *Age* carried, prominently, congratulatory opinions from the country press.

The show was not over, however, for there was the matter of awarding costs, which was heard from 12 to 16 October, with the result that Syme had to bear all but those relating to Speight's one farthing. The next day he wrote to Francis, telling him that 'poor Grandpa' (Annabella's father John Johnson) had just died and that shortly he would be 'going away for a fortnight's holiday (so called)'; the day after he wrote to his bank manager that he would be leaving the colony for two weeks, authorising his wife to operate one of his accounts in his absence.[91] Where exactly he went is not known – somewhere in New South Wales according to another letterbook item.[92]

A contempt of court case against the *Age* publisher was heard over three days, 22 to 25 October. The defendant this time was not Syme. For on 28 April 1891, just one month after he had registered the *Age*, the *Leader* and the *Illustrated Australian News* in his name as proprietor and publisher, he had them re-registered, naming as publisher the firm's accountant, John Packer (Darragh 1997, 94 [37.13–14], 100 [62.08–09], 117 [175.08–09]). Otherwise, the entries for the three newspapers were unchanged (Syme

---

[89] DS to G. Levey, 13 August 1894, LB5, p. 123.
[90] Diary entries for 27, 30 September 1894, Deakin Papers, Series 2.
[91] DS to F. Syme, 17 October 1894, LB5, p. 129; DS to Manager, Bank of Victoria, 18 October 1894, LB5, p. 132.
[92] DS to Willing, 17 October 1894, LB5, p. 130.

CHAPTER 13

as proprietor, with Samuel Gillott and Herbert Syme providing sureties). While there is no reason on record for the change, it conveys that Syme was loosening his tight control over some aspects of business. It also meant that Packer, as publisher, could – and indeed would – be in the firing line of legal action against the newspaper business. It was alleged that publication in the *Age* of 31 March 1894 of the Syme's speech accepting the subscriptions was likely to have influenced the jury.[93] Fund secretary Walpole testified in court that the donations were intended to reimburse the defendant for legal costs and that a similar collection had been made for the plaintiff, Speight. Packer swore that he had no intent to bias (indeed, he would have had nothing whatsoever to do with publishing the material in question). He was found guilty, nevertheless, fined £150, and to be held in custody until the fine was paid. Half an hour later the sum, in sovereigns, was brought from the *Age* office and the hapless Packer was released.[94]

This was not the end of the railway-related litigation. The Allison Smith action was pending and would come to trial in June 1895, and moreover, Speight was to persist with his claims. But Syme may well have felt that the tide of public opinion had turned in his favour. There are no recorded irritable outbursts like those in late 1892 and early 1893. As dealt with later in this chapter, in the months before the *Smith v. Syme* trial, he was caught up in family happenings, devoted considerable time to his agricultural and financial concerns, and attended to two developments in relation to the newspaper business: the advent of linotype and the amalgamation of the two competing Australian cable services.

The *Smith v. Syme* action for £15,000 damages related to a series of allegedly false and malicious libels published in the *Age* between 3 March 1892 and 10 June 1893. It was claimed that these caused the erstwhile locomotive engineer to be deprived of his professional status and livelihood. It began on 4 July 1895, with a jury of six empanelled. As in earlier trials, Syme was represented by Purves, Deakin and the legal firm of Gillott and Bates. Syme took the witness stand on 9 July, testifying no personal animosity against Smith, whom he knew personally and professionally and pointing out that he was out of the colony for nine of the 15 months during which the alleged libels were published, though acknowledging that he took an active part in framing the policy of his paper and read all copies when away.[95]

---

[93] 'Speight v. Syme', *Age*, 23 October 1894, p. 5.
[94] 'Alleged Contempt of Court', *Age*, 26 October 1894, p. 5.
[95] 'Another Railway Action', *Age*, 10 July 1895, p. 5.

Cross-examined, he refused to name journalists who wrote the offending leaders. He stood by all the statements in the allegedly libellous articles. Three days later, in a letter about the cable service, he told Wynne 'My case still dogs on'.[96] On 19 July he wrote to Gillott that he was unhappy about the judge's 'adverse directions to the jury'.[97] Nevertheless, the *Age* of 22 July, reporting the outcome, claimed that the third 'great trial' had ended disastrously for the plaintiff, who was awarded one farthing on each of four out of 25 counts. That is, on 21 of 25 the jury found for the defendant. Shortly thereafter, the *Age*, in parallel with the Australasian Institute of Journalists, would take up the matter of libel law reform, dealt with later in this chapter.

Japan

On 24 July Syme left the colony. It may have been a spur of the moment move, for the only record of his intentions is a letter to Deakin on the morning of his departure, where he writes that he is about to leave for Sydney and thence to Japan, being fed up with 'perpetually defending myself in the law courts' and requesting that he 'keep an eye on my interests while I am away, like a good fellow, & on those of my family should I not return.'[98] Deakin, whose diary entry for 24 July is 'Goodbye to Syme', may have been one of the number of friends who, the *Age* of the following day reported, assembled at Spencer Street station to farewell the proprietor as he boarded the express train for Sydney.[99] The news that he was travelling to Japan for the benefit of his health and would be away about three months was relayed over the next few days in numerous country papers.[100] On 27 July he sailed on the *Tsinan* from Sydney for Hong Kong and Japan.[101]

That the besieged proprietor was run down and needing a break from the strains of the protracted litigation is understandable, but why Japan? In the late 19th century, this Asian country was opening up to the outside world, one indication being the study of English becoming part of the Japanese common school curriculum in 1884 (Dickson 1900, 363–372). Conversely, material about Japan was appearing in Australian newspapers

---

[96] DS to W. Wynne, 12 July 1895, LB5, p. 153.
[97] DS to S. Gillott, 19 July 1895, LB5, p. 155.
[98] DS to A. Deakin, 'Wednesday Morning'[1895], Deakin Papers, Series 1/3668.
[99] 'News of the Day', *Age*, 25 July, p. 4.
[100] For example, *Euroa Advertiser*, 26 July 1895, p. 3.
[101] 'Shippping, Passengers per *Tsinan*,' *Sydney Morning Herald*, 26 July 1895, p. 4; 'Shipping', *Sydney Morning Herald*, 29 July 1895, p. 4.

CHAPTER 13

and periodicals, not least the *Age*, which in 1892 featured 'Travels in Japan' by Lafcadio Hearn, the American-born journalist who had settled there and become a Japanese citizen. It was becoming what today is termed a 'tourist destination', with 'Tourist tickets' to India, China and Japan advertised in Melbourne newspapers in 1895.[102] While this publicity may have had some bearing on Syme's choice, his interest may also have been aroused by the perceived need in the mid-1890s to develop export markets in and obtain a supply of labour from the Asian region (Broinowski 2000).

The *Age* of 26 April had run a feature 'The Export of Fruit Trade with Japan'. There was also particular interest in opening up the wool trade with Australian colonies, and the implications for this of the recently concluded trade treaty between Great Britain and Japan were matters of public interest. The *Argus* of 22 November 1894 had pointed out that the treaty was of vital importance to Australian colonies regarding the future of commerce in the Pacific Ocean, and a future Commonwealth of Australia would be a Pacific power together with Japan and Chile, and California representing the United States. Indeed, while Syme was away, the South Australian premier was stressing to the other Australasian colonial premiers the need for a conference to discuss Australian relations with Japan.[103] Ultimately, however, the premiers saw that trade benefits would be outweighed by problems associated with Japanese immigrants, and the restrictive controls associated with the hardening 'White Australia' policy precluded further consideration of trade relations with Japan.

Bonython, in a letter of 4 October to Herbert from Adelaide, asked after Syme, and whether he was enjoying his trip, hoping 'sincerely…that he was recovering from the effects of the worrying time he has had'.[104] Syme, who, arrived back in Sydney on Saturday 2 November, by the *Changsha*, has left no mention of his state of health.[105] He was back in the office by the Thursday following, when Deakin called on him.[106] His first letter in the office letterbooks, dated 18 November, does not refer to newspaper matters, however, but is an offer to sell a thoroughbred stallion and 20 to 25 mares.[107] The next letter, dated the day following, is to Levey in London, responding

---

[102] For example, in *Argus*, 1 May 1895, p. 1.
[103] 'Australian Relations with Japan', *Argus*, 1 October 1895, p. 5, 22 October, p. 6.
[104] J. Bonython to H. Syme, 4 October 1895, Bonython Letter Books.
[105] 'Shipping', *Evening News* (Sydney), 4 November 1895, p. 4.
[106] Diary entry for 9 November 1895, Deakin Papers, Series 2.
[107] DS to S. Hoot, 18 November 1895, LB5, p. 156.

to several from him and saying about Japan simply that he had returned from there 'about ten days ago'.[108] The only other clue to his experiences is an anecdote in Pratt's biography, said to have come from Syme himself, and at odds with his typically controlled behaviour (Pratt 1908, 266–268). Returning by mail steamer to Hong Kong from Japan, he tossed overboard the English captain's deck chair when commanded to vacate it, a story he apparently told Pratt with some delight. One imagines that he was letting off steam, misbehaving, after the protracted strain of lawsuits. This was the normally unamused Scotsman, who reportedly told his agricultural editor, when slashing his article that contained a bit of humour, 'Y'will na' jok' here, Mr Dow' (Bedford 1976, 266).

Syme was back in Melbourne to hear the Full Court decision against Speight for his appeal against the judgment of September 1894. The appeal had commenced on 23 September 1895 and the rejection was handed down on 18 November. The *Age* editorial of 19 November observed that one consoling reflection from the protracted battle was its importance for the 'very financial life of the colony', saving it from 'a few more years of reckless spending'. The defence team must have considered the battle over, for on Saturday 7 December Purves hosted a grand celebratory dinner for Syme, attended by leading politicians who were also his friends, and by editor Windsor and leading members of the *Age* office staff.[109] Paying tribute to Syme, the host observed that, although he himself was politically a conservative, he could see 'the community, stricken with a summer madness, was awakened to appreciation of the danger into which it was drifting by a quiet, upright, self-sacrificing man'. Syme expressed his gratitude to his legal team and to officials of the Railway Department. Gillott toasted the health of Parliament. Sundry anecdotes were told, and the party broke up near midnight.

But the battle continued, on two fronts. Though financially ruined, Speight was undaunted. On 18 December he was given leave to appeal to the Privy Council of the United Kingdom, the Court ordering that security of £3000 be provided and granting him three months to obtain the funds.[110] On 31 December Syme wrote to Levey about this, saying that the Speight case seemed 'interminable' and again asked him to look into any connection

---

[108] DS to G. Levey, 19 November 1895, LB5, p. 157.
[109] 'The Age and the Railways', *Age*, 9 December 1895, pp. 5–6.
[110] 'Speight v. Syme', *Age*, 19 December 1895, p. 5.

CHAPTER 13

with Sir James Allport of the Midland Railway.[111] Nor had Allison Smith given up. In the New Year Syme got wind of some talk of a settlement being reached with him, writing about it on 22 January 1896 to reporter Sweet, and referring to the possible involvement of John Hancock, MLA and President of the Trades Hall Council, who had earlier been opposed to the stance of the *Age* on labour issues. Syme stated unequivocally: 'I am not prepared to make any compromise whatever on this matter. I trust you will not fail to make this clear without any unnecessary delay.'[112]

The *Smith v. Syme* application for a new trial ran from 6 to 28 February, when it was dismissed and costs awarded against the appellant.[113] On 5 March Speight applied for a further extension of time to obtain funds for the requisite security for his Privy Council appeal, and was granted four months, provided he paid the defendant's costs of this application.[114] Between 17 and 19 June many newspapers throughout Australia (but not the *Age*) reported that Speight's solicitors, Malleson, England and Stewart, had made known that their client had abandoned proceedings. This really was the end of the railway litigation. Syme's role in the saga finished on 27 July 1896, when he sent a cheque to politician and financier Ephraim Zox, towards a relief fund for Speight, writing in an accompanying letter that he knew this action might be misconstrued but was 'ready to run that risk so long as I know that you will not misunderstand me'.[115]

Syme was sufficiently wealthy and his business sound enough for him to weather the multiple financial onslaughts of the early 1890s: the effects of the general economic depression; the *Argus* price reduction; the imposition of income tax in Victoria from 1895; the large repayments to Joseph twice-yearly to February 1896; and, not least, the huge legal expenses. The account books are not easy to follow, containing sums in the detailed annual financial statements that differ from those in a summary table of expenses 1891 to 1899.[116] Moreover, for the years 1892 to 1895 the summary table provides a 'declared' profit and a sum representing 'property written down'. The declared profits, which roughly correspond with the entries in the respective annual statements, were drastically down from £47,447 in 1891 to £20,394

---

[111] DS to G. Levey, 31 December 1895, LB5, p. 163.
[112] DS to E. Sweet, 22 January 1896, LB5, p. 169.
[113] '"The Age" and the Railways', *Age*, 29 February 1896, p. 7.
[114] 'Speight v. Syme', *Age*, 6 March 1896, p. 5.
[115] DS to E. Zox, 27 July 1896, LB5, p. 190.
[116] Profit and loss accounts, 1891–1900, SFP Box 1191/3.

in 1892 and hit bottom at £16,322 in 1893 and £17,794 in 1894. Recovery began in 1895 with £35,849 and profits would rise steadily in subsequent years.

While these figures appear to be in line with general economic trends, and gross revenue for the *Age* was down, a major contributing factor was, of course, the legal expenses. Sayers (1965, 178) refers to the costs of the Speight trials as an 'estimated' £50,000, adding that the 'true figure is not known and was never revealed'. Indeed it is impossible to pin it down: adding up the 'law expenses' entries in the financial statements for the years 1892 to 1895 gives a total of £44,923 (an annual average of £11,231); adding items in the summary table for the same period gives a much lower £29,588 (an annual average of £7397). Either average is vastly in excess of the £913 recorded consistently for 1891, before the railway actions were brought and the records of legal costs become messy. Whatever the accuracy or otherwise of the account books, it is conceivable that Syme met some of the legal expenses from his own pocket. As for income tax, introduced by Premier Turner and passed by parliament in late 1894, it was a scarcely significant £696 in 1895. As for the contracted payments to Joseph for buying out his share, only some are recorded, with the note that they were made from Syme's 'private funds'. In sum, despite heavy expenses, the business continued to make a profit, albeit reduced, this entailing economies rather than expansion and outlays. The Speight matter was not ever about money so much as reputation.

Age Annual and *Illustrated Australian News* terminated

Some economies were effected by doing away with two of the firm's four publications. In both cases this was long overdue. The *Age Annual* was discontinued after the 20th issue in 1894, having shown a loss for some years: £23.18.6 in 1890; £71.19.6 by 1894, when, 436 of the 1000 copies printed were unsold.[117] Stopping further publication was not before time, for now there were numerous directories and yearbooks covering much of the ground, not least the *Victorian Municipal Directory*, while what had been a key feature of the *Age Annual*, a summary of new legislation, lacked the interest it had earlier attracted. By 1890 a basic set of laws had been enacted, and were published in consolidated form in that year.

More significantly, the *Illustrated Australian News*, which had been a leading exponent in Australia of the 19th-century illustrated newspaper,

---

[117] Profit and loss accounts, 1885–1890, SFP Box 1191/2(b), 1891–1900, SFP Box 1191/3.

CHAPTER 13

ceased after the issue of 1 July 1896. Its future had been considered inconclusively by David and Joseph in 1890, but it was six years before action was taken. It had turned a modest profit for the years 1891 to 1894, but in 1895 sustained a loss of £46.6.5, while in 1896 to July the deficit was a severe £183.11.5. Clearly demand was falling, with 7800 copies printed in January 1891 but only 4000 in December 1895.

Its demise would be offset by increased demand for the *Leader*, with which it was incorporated. Its circulation, 10,879 in 1891, had fallen to 10,011 in 1893. This was a worry, especially when that of the rival *Australasian* was 18,500.[118] If accurate, the claim made by the *Age* of 23 June 1896 that the *Leader* was the largest circulating weekly in Victoria (unsubstantiated by figures) means that there had been a great circulation leap forward to overtake the *Australasian*. A key factor in this must have been the reduction in price from sixpence to threepence on 6 October 1894. In 1893 the *Leader* had been reduced in size from 48 to 44 pages, albeit sometimes carrying a supplement. In 1894 and after, the number of pages in an issue ranged down from 44 to 40, 36 and even 32. But issues usually had supplements, sometimes very long, and illustrated – on 5 October 1895, a 32-page one on New Zealand. From the next issue, 13 October, the subtitle was modified to include 'mining' (*Weekly Journal of News, Politics, Agriculture, Sport, Mining, Science & Literature*), reflecting the revival of interest in some Victorian gold-mining sites and developments on the Western Australian goldfields. On 30 May 1896 the Leader had a 'Western Australia' 48-page supplement, the outcome of a visit by the Vagabond and artist-photographer Edmund Luke, who had joined the staff in 1893.[119] Stylish changes – decorated rubrics for sections – appeared in the issue of 4 July, three days after the last *Illustrated Australian News*.

Syme's letterbook copies for the years 1891 to 1895 have no mention of either discontinued title, so his part in their demise has to be guessed at. Perhaps he set little store by them, in contrast to his quite frequent references to the *Leader*. In July 1891 he wrote to its editor Henry Short that in future he had to be consulted about subjects to be illustrated and see drawings to be engraved.[120] A photographer, A. Jordan, joined the staff in December 1894, perhaps indicating a major shift from engravings to the swift and convenient half-tone reproduction of photographs.[121]

---

[118] 'Circulation', 'Historical Records of "The Argus" and "The Australasian"'.
[119] Entry for Luke in Wages Book, p. 282.
[120] DS to H. Short, 10 July 1891, LB3, p. 245.
[121] Entry for Jordan in Wages Book, p. 245.

If matters of illustration involved both the weekly and the monthly, Syme's directives about literary content often applied to both the weekly and the daily and reflect his perpetual worry about the *Age* and the *Leader* being outdone by the *Argus* and *Australasian*. This is especially evident in a letter to London cable correspondent James Morgan in December 1893 about new sources of 'tales' for serialisation and feeling 'overshadowed' by the *Argus*, which had begun to feature serial fiction, and not just on Saturdays but twice weekly (in 1893 it serialised novels by noted authors Gilbert Parker, Rider Haggard and Rudyard Kipling).[122] His concern appears an unwarranted overreaction; his newspapers had recently run new Australian fiction (short stories by Mary Gaunt and a novel, *The Silent Sea*, by South Australian Catherine Martin), had obtained Mark Twain's *The American Claimant* by arrangement with the *Auckland Star*, had habitually (as correspondence shows) shared rights to novels and other material with the Adelaide *Advertiser* and appear to have had no shortage of titles by bestselling English novelists, procured from Tillotsons.[123] It is typical, however, of the persistence that so often paid off.

In mid-1894, in the interests of economy in hard times, Syme instructed James Williams, formerly a reporter on staff, now a contributor, to reduce his Drama feature in the *Leader* to one column.[124] Four weeks later he acted similarly for music coverage, citing as justification that the *Argus* and the *Australasian* 'have both made extensive reductions in this department' and advising contributor A.M. Nesbitt that 'the Age & Leader have to keep pace with the times'.[125] However, recognising Nesbitt's ability and standing (an Oxford-educated mathematician and musician) he took him onto the staff in July as 'Musical Editor', apparently finding sufficient work for him until May 1896, when 'reluctantly compelled' to give him notice because there was so little of importance in the musical 'line' to report.[126] Once again, the employer must have had second thoughts, for Nesbitt was on the payroll until 1911[127] and his 'Musical Notes' in the *Age* were later deemed 'excellent…recognising a public requirement' (Carne 1954, 130).

---

[122] DS to J. Morgan, 21 December 1893, LB5, p. 92.

[123] Profit and loss, 1892, SFP Box 1191/3 (re *Auckland Star*); for example, Burden & Bonython to DS & Co., 31 May 1892, 5 February 1895, Bonython Letter Books.

[124] DS to J. Williams, 31 May 1894, LB5, p. 114.

[125] DS to A. Nesbitt, 28 June 1894, LB5, p. 120.

[126] DS to A. Nesbitt, 28 May 1896, LB5, p. 183; 'An Accomplished Musician', *Australian Town and Country Journal*, 6 October 1888, p. 705.

[127] Entry for Nesbitt in Wages Book, p. 355.

CHAPTER 13

One of two major developments involving the Australian press in the 1890s was the introduction of linotype machines. David Syme & Co. was slower than many Australian newspaper businesses to obtain the labour-saving innovation that rendered obsolete the letter-by-letter hand composition carried out by armies of compositors and was thus a cost-effective investment for large circulating dailies. Ottmar Mergenthaler, the naturalised American who had invented a machine to set and cast lines of type, in 1886 established a company in New York to manufacture and market it ('Mergenthaler Linotype Company' 2011; Hagan 1966, 101–102). The invention was taken up by several dailies in Australia early in the 1890s. The Sydney *Daily Telegraph* had machines operating in April 1894, and in the next 12 months, so did the Sydney *Evening News*, the Brisbane *Courier* and the *Launceston Examiner* (Hagan 1966, 104). In Melbourne the *Herald* 'installed a battery of eleven' in early 1895. The *Argus* followed suit a year later, with 10 machines used for the first time on 12 May 1896.[128]

Then abreast of innovations overseas, in 1872 Syme introduced web-fed rotary machines for the printing of major newspapers in Australia. Some two decades later he was anything but a frontrunner, for linotypes would not be operating at the *Age* office until 1897. He seems to have known very little of developments, asking Levey in a letter of 13 May 1895 for information about patents rights of 'a type setting machine…Higgins is the patenter… said to be in Manchester'.[129] Syme had probably heard something of the Linotype Company formed in 1889 by Joseph Lawrence in Manchester after he and Mergenthaler representative Hutchins (not Higgins!) had taken three experimental machines there ('Mergenthaler Linotype Company' 2011). But he found Levey's letter of reply 'about the type setting machine at Manchester…quite unintelligible' and asked him to make further enquiries.[130] Whatever Syme's subsequent sources of useful information (not evident), he did move soon, for a memorandum of agreement dated 1 April 1896 shows that David Syme & and Co. placed an order through the Sydney agent Henry Franks for 20 Mergenthaler Linotype Machines, and in July two more were ordered.[131]

---

[128] 'Machinery', 'Historical Records of "The Argus" and "The Australasian"'.
[129] DS to G. Levey, 13 May 1895, LB5, p. 147.
[130] DS to G. Levey, 19 November 1895, LB5, p. 157.
[131] Unlabelled ledger containing records relating to linotype introduction, *Age* Archives, Melbourne.

That Syme had clearly lost his pre-eminence in press circles as a technological innovator is evident in letters from Bonython in July 1895, seeking information about Hoe printing machines, to Wynne of the Sydney *Daily Telegraph* ('I regard you as the greatest machine expert within the circle of my acquaintance') and to Joseph Syme ('There is no one in Melbourne who knows more about printing machines than you').[132] That he also wrote, 'I trust that you and Mrs Syme and the children, including the Baby, are well' and reminded him to send the 'promised photographs' perhaps suggests a closer camaraderie with the former junior partner than with the now sole proprietor. That Syme did not give priority to the linotype matter may be understood in the light of the many competing demands for his attention, the libel suits not least, but it also raises the question of Herbert's authority. He was assigned management and oversight of the technical side of the business, but how aware was he of the advent of the linotype and did he raise the subject with his father who, in 1895, seemed to have only a vague idea of the technical details? As will be seen in the next chapter, in 1897 Syme would have to focus on and come to grips with the human realities of the large-scale redundancies that were a corollary of the revolution in typesetting and casting.

United Cable Service

The other development concerned the amalgamation in 1895 of the two Australian services providing overseas cable news. The *Age–Advertiser–Daily Telegraph* service was extremely well served from July 1891 for about a year by Frederick Ward as London cable correspondent. New Zealand born Ward, a former clergyman, had substantial experience with Fairfax as a journalist and editor of the *Sydney Mail* and *Echo,* and then with the Sydney *Daily Telegraph*, which he left in 1890 for London after a falling out over editorial independence (Moignard 1990). Having in April 1891 asked Wynne about his capacity as subeditor or editor, Syme recruited him as London cable correspondent.[133] Although making a somewhat patronising observation to Wynne – 'Ward is doing fairly well, for a beginner' – Syme gave uncharacteristic praise to Ward himself: 'your cable messages on the whole give great satisfaction.'[134] Ward was assisted in the London office by

---

[132] J. Bonython to W. Wynne and JCS, 17 July 1895, Bonython Letter Books.
[133] DS to W. Wynne, 21 April 1891, LB3, p. 221; DS to F. Ward, 20 July 1891, LB3, p. 251.
[134] DS to W. Wynne, 14 July 1891, LB3, p. 249; DS to F. Ward, 30 November 1891, LB3, p. 272.

CHAPTER 13

(John) Desmond Byrne, who had been a reporter on the *Age* from November 1890 and left for London in September 1891.[135] But Ward gave up the job after a year, the strain of night work and the cold winter affecting his health (Moignard 1990); perhaps, also, because it was a more junior position than he merited. He was replaced by James Morgan, who had been on the *Age* reporting staff from June 1891 and left for London in April 1892 to take up the position.[136]

Morgan was still in the employ of the *Age–Advertiser–Daily Telegraph* cable service when in September 1895 it amalgamated with that of the *Argus–Sydney Morning Herald* (Walker 1976, 205–206). This had been in the wind for more than two years, Syme in April 1893 writing to Sydney *Australian Star* manager Sanders about the 'proposal to amalgamate the two services'.[137] In 1895 serious negotiations were taking place, with meetings in Sydney and Melbourne, and the prospect obviously welcomed by Bonython ('a united cable service will be a great relief', he wrote in March) and by Wynne (Bonython in May writing to him that 'your dream of many years ago will be realised').[138] Syme devoted his energies in June and July to discussing with Bonython and Wynne and arguing with Lauchlan Mackinnon, manager of the *Argus*, about the salary and status of Morgan in the united service, and objecting to its being located at the *Argus* London office.[139] His manner may have been unpleasant, for on 16 July Bonython wrote to Wynne that he was astonished at Syme's attitude and hoped that nothing would prevent the arrangement coming into force in September.[140] All was well, however, for on 18 July Syme sent a formally worded typed letter to Mackinnon accepting the conditions, albeit with some reluctance.[141]

Syme left for Japan nine days later. In his absence Bonython wrote on 4 October to Herbert, who obviously had been trying to smooth things over: 'Having read your letter I am quite ready to say that as far as I am concerned, there shall be an end to strained relations', adding that the fault was not 'with

---

[135] Entry for Byrne in Wages Book, p. 30.
[136] Entry for Morgan in Wages Book, p. 303.
[137] DS to M. Sanders, 21 April 1893, LB5, p. 44.
[138] J. Bonython to DS & Co., 22 March 1895, J. Bonython to DS & Co. and Wynne, 15 May 1891, Bonython Letter Books.
[139] DS to L.C. Mackinnon, 13 June 1895, LB5, p. 148; DS to J. Bonython, 10 July 1895, LB5, p. 150; DS to W. Wynne, 12 July 1895, LB5, p. 153.
[140] J. Bonython to W. Wynne, 16 July 1895, Bonython Letter Books.
[141] DS to L.C. Mackinnon, 18 July 1895, LB5, p. 154.

me'.¹⁴² He went on to praise the 'magnificent' supplement in the day's *Leader*. (Unlike Syme, Bonython was a great flatterer, having written to Mackinnon 10 days before that his *Australasian* was 'splendid' and that its contemporaries – which would include the *Leader* – were 'not in the running'!)¹⁴³ The United Cable Association service went into operation with no significant problems, although Syme, after his return from Japan, would find faults from time to time – in December asserting that 'Morgan's telegrams are more intelligible than the others', and in June 1896 that Levey was having trouble getting information from the cable office for his letters from London.¹⁴⁴

Adverse discussion of Speight matters in the *Argus* was an irritant to Syme, who complained to Mackinnon in December 1895 that 'Twice within the week some very ugly words have been used in the Argus with reference to the case', and in June 1896 that 'I am still held up in your trading column as a "persecutor" of Speight & improper motives are imputed to me. I think this very unfair, as there is not a particle of evidence'.¹⁴⁵ The main import of both letters was, however, the joint cable service, Syme now forced into cooperating with the former competition, a mode that suited him less than fierce competitiveness. Such cooperation would be called for on several fronts, as the press network became increasingly organised and complex.

Australasian Institute of Journalists

In January 1892 a professional organisation for journalists was established in Melbourne. An initiative from within the informal Victorian Reporters' Association and aired in the press the previous November, the Australian Institute of Journalists was established in January 1892.¹⁴⁶ By June, 'Australian' had become 'Australasian', thus allowing for New Zealand participation. Though essentially a Victorian body, for there were parallel moves in some other colonies, it did envisage intercolonial links and the establishment of a Federal Council. With growing enthusiasm in Melbourne and the country, it flourished for a time, with 133 members in June and 167 in November

---

142   J. Bonython to H. Syme, 4 October 1895, Bonython Letter Books.
143   J. Bonython to L. C. Mackinnon, 23 September 1895, Bonython Letter Books.
144   DS to L.C. Mackinnon, 2 December 1895, LB5, p. 158; DS to G. Levey, 2 June 1896, LB5, p. 185.
145   DS to L.C. Mackinnon, 16 December 1895, 25 June 1896, LB5, pp. 162, 187.
146   'Victorian Reporters' Association', *Argus*, 9 November 1891, p. 3, 11 January 1892, p. 5, col. 2. The summary history of the Institute is drawn from minutes of the Australian Institute of Journalists, in Australian Journalists Association Victorian Branch Records, University of Melbourne Archives, and Lloyd (1985, 13–39).

CHAPTER 13

1892. Apparent from extant records of the Institute, it was inspired by and largely modelled on the English Institute of Journalists; its aims included monitoring legislation affecting journalists, organising examinations and certification for journalists, and assisting those in financial distress, this last involving reactivation of the benevolent Caxton Fund. In April 1893, there were 95 non-financial members, a situation that only got worse, with the *Daily Telegraph* ceasing publication in May 1892 and the *Evening Standard* in October 1894. In August 1896, the 'bulk' of members were not paying and the question of dissolution arose. The last document on file is pencilled, incomplete minutes of the Annual General Meeting held on 10 October 1896, recording an attendance of only 11 and indicating the end of the Institute. Hard economic times indeed were a major cause of its demise. But arguably, it might have folded sooner, were it not sustained by *Age* and *Leader* employees who used it as a lobbying medium during the railway litigation.

Throughout the Institute's brief life, members of Syme's staff were to the fore. *Age* editor Arthur Windsor was President, albeit an inactive one, except for donating £50 to the Provident Fund; as Vice-Presidents and alternately chairing meetings were *Leader* editor Short and Samuel ('Stormy') Winter of the *Herald*. Syme was a Trustee of the Institute, *Age* reporter William Briggs an auditor, Syme's legal team of Purves and Deakin the Institute's legal advisers. An undated newspaper clipping names 25 *Age* and *Leader* journalists as members, with David and Herbert Syme heading the list. This is a much larger number than from any other newspaper business, which is not surprising, in that Syme's enterprise was the biggest; but, more significantly, several of them were particularly prominent as Council and/or committee members. Schuler and Morgan were active for a few months before resigning from Council – the former perhaps because of heavier duties at the *Age*, the latter to be cable correspondent in London and also to represent the Institute in Great Britain (soon after his arrival he would attend the British Institute's annual meeting in Edinburgh). Members especially active throughout the Institute's existence included John Dow, Benjamin Hoare, John Stephens, William Lambie and Henry Short.

Minutes of General and Council Meetings of the Institute show that amending the libel law was a recurring concern, raised first in July 1892 when the Speight action was pending and Syme was overseas. At issue was the perceived need to extend protection to journalists reporting public meetings as well as parliamentary deliberations, and thus be in line with English legislation of 1881. This was not new: Dr John Quick, MLA, had sought such an amendment in the late 1880s. Within the Institute, *Leader* editor and Institute Vice-President Short seems to have been chiefly responsible for its carriage. In the Legislative Assembly it was Isaac Isaacs, who introduced the Libel Law Amendment Bill in September 1892, July 1893 and June 1894, each time without passage through to law, debates showing vocal opposition as well as strong support.[147] A petition from the Institute, headed by Windsor as President, was introduced into parliament by Dow in November 1892, but failed to make the desired impact.[148] Deputations and letters to Premier and Attorney-General Shiels were of no avail.[149] Nor were approaches to Premier Patterson, whose Attorney-General Bryan O'Loghlen was violently opposed.[150]

On 7 October 1893, Winter reported to the Institute Council that Isaacs, now Attorney-General in the Turner government, was doubtful the Bill would be passed and had advised Herbert Syme (in charge of the *Age* while his father was touring Japan) and *Argus* manager Mackinnon to push the amendment, believing it would be best secured by individual newspapers. The draft (a new one?) of a Bill to amend the libel law, agreed to by Isaacs and, representing the three Melbourne dailies, Mackinnon, Winter and Syme, was endorsed by the Institute at its Annual General Meeting on 29 August 1896, when the organisation was about to fall apart. The Institute's 1896 and final annual report states that, due to 'the political exigencies of the times', no further parliamentary action was taken, despite Isaacs having urged the Cabinet to make it a 'government measure'. In fact, with Syme's court cases behind him, the urgency of action had passed – if indeed it ever went to the heart of the matter. Under existing Victorian libel legislation of 1856, there could be no action against a person for faithful reporting. It was the 'fair comment' interpretation rather than the letter of the law that had been pivotal in the protracted suits against Syme, which he finally bested.

Contrarily, when the depression was deepening and two Melbourne dailies failed, the status of the press Australia-wide was rising. This was manifested in and doubtless encouraged by a series, 'The Great Australian Dailies', published in the new *Review of Reviews, Australian Edition* from August

---

[147] Libel Law Amendment Bill, VPP, Legislative Assembly, 1892–3, pp. 142, 179, 448; *Victorian Parliamentary Debates* (hereafter VPD), Vol. 70, 28 September 1892, pp. 1894–1906, Vol. 72, 11 July 1893, p. 253, Vol. 74, 1894, 6 June 1894, p. 139, 21 June, pp. 389–418.

[148] VPP, Legislative Assembly, 1892–3, p. 227; VPD, Vol. 71, 22 December 1892, pp. 3721–3741.

[149] Minutes of AGM, 26 October 1892, Australian Institute of Journalists.

[150] Minutes of Council meeting, 24 June 1893, Australian Institute of Journalists.

CHAPTER 13

1892 until July 1893. (The word 'Australian' was used in the title of the first two in the series – August and September 1892 – and in the title of the first six issues of the periodical – July to December 1892 – after which the change to 'Australasian' reflected the similarities and multiple connections between the seven colonies, including New Zealand, and the possibility, then, that it might become part of the envisaged federation.) In July 1892 the periodical began publication in Melbourne, priced at ninepence. Imperial advocate William Henry Fitchett (1841–1928), a journalist and former clergyman, who had been consulting editor for the Melbourne *Daily Telegraph* when it ceased two months before, found employment as editor of the new monthly (Zainu'ddin 1981). As its title conveys, it comprised a reprint of W.T. Stead's English *Review of Reviews* plus coverage of Australian current affairs.

The *Age* may have been by far the largest circulating and politically most powerful paper, but it was dealt with fourth in the series on daily papers, appearing in November after the *Sydney Morning Herald* (August), the *Argus* (September) and the Sydney *Daily Telegraph* (October). Later issues featured daily newspapers of Brisbane, Hobart, Dunedin, Auckland and Wellington. The *Age* article was written in house – as, presumably, were all the others – for Herbert on 24 November returned a payment cheque to Fitchett, because the work had been 'done by a member of the staff in office hours'.[151] Whoever the author (Windsor?), the article provides an accurate summary history (except that 1858 not 1868 is given as the date of reduction to a penny – a misprint?) and account of processes behind the current mass production. It concludes that the '*Age* has fought with magnificent energy and endurance for Liberal reforms'. It carries photographs of Ebenezer, David and George Syme, editor Windsor and commercial editor Robinson. Having had no part in its preparation, Syme returned from Japan in time to see the finished product. What he thought of it is not on record.

The Australian press was getting some notice in English periodicals. Francis Adams, having returned to England in 1890 after six years in Australia wrote several articles on Australia for the *Fortnightly Review*. 'Some Australian Men of Mark', published in February 1892, dealt at length with politicians then turned to men of the press. Adams singled out J.F. Archibald of the *Bulletin,* and the expatriates Frederick Ward (formerly with Sydney *Daily Telegraph*, now Syme's cable correspondent) and W. Kinnaird Rose (formerly of the Brisbane *Courier*) as leading journalists. He then called the *Age*, the *Bulletin* and the Sydney *Daily Telegraph* the 'most characteristic

---

[151] H. Syme to W. Fitchett, 21 November 1892, LB3, p. 298.

and powerful expressions of place and people', and the *Argus* and *Sydney Morning Herald* of a higher literary standard, but politically insignificant 'mouthpieces of the antique Anglo-Australia'. He was misinformed about Syme, however, in saying that he started out as a compositor (confusing with Syme's namesake in the printing department). And if his description of the 'Australian Greeley' being a 'medium-sized, thick-set, middle-aged colonial man of business' is meant to refer to the *Age* proprietor, he can never have met the lean, six-foot man with a mission, probably confusing him with Joseph Syme. Evidence that the role of the *Age* was recognised in England, the *Age* of 6 January 1894 printed a cable from London about reactions there to the outcome of the second Speight trial, quoting the politically liberal penny daily *Westminster Gazette* terming the *Age* 'the one real force in Victorian journalism'.[152]

Having survived the heavy legal onslaughts, the *Age* at the end of 1895, clearly was an established not to say esteemed institution. That its proprietor, likewise, was a socially accepted establishment figure, not an upstart pariah, is witnessed in his and his family's appearance in the social gossip pages of periodicals. The December issue of the *Australian Journal* reports the attendance of Mrs Syme and her daughter (Lucie?) at the Melbourne Cup in early November, describing their costumes and headgear. The *Australasian* of 14 December notes the attendance of David Syme and wife at a dinner party on 9 December given by Governor Lord Brassey and Lady Brassey.

Family developments

By this time there had been generational changes in the Syme family. As already noted, Syme's father-in-law John Johnson died in October 1894. He left a very small estate, but had been a significant source of financial support in the early years of his son-in-law's marriage (M. Syme 2013, 89). The same year Syme lost his brother-in-law, John Gourlay, who had retired 'through sickness' on 23 June, and died shortly after.[153] The *Age* of 29 June praised his 'devotion to duty, business capacity and consideration for those with whom he came into official contact' and noted his connection 'by marriage with the proprietor'.[154] A third bereavement, Syme's brother George, never robust, died on 31 December, aged 78, the cause of death given as enteritis, vascular

---

[152] '"The Age: and the Railways', *Age*, 6 January 1894, p. 7.
[153] Entry for Gourlay in Wages Book, p. 177.
[154] 'News of the Day', *Age*, 29 June 1894, p. 5, col. 1.

CHAPTER 13

degeneration and a thrombosis.[155] The *Age* obituary identifies him as 'the eldest of three brothers who have figured prominently in the journalistic world of Melbourne' who was 'of a rather too retiring and reserved a nature' yet 'as interesting and instructive a companion as Carlyle himself, with a good deal of the rugged Carlylean manner in his speech'.[156] Perhaps it was written by Windsor, who had known him for more than 20 years.

There were developments with the younger generation. Within three months of each other, two of Syme's sons married. First was the eldest, Herbert, on 29 November 1894 in St John's Church, Camberwell.[157] His bride Ethel was daughter of the late Thomas King, a founder of the *South Australian Advertiser*, subsequently a member of the South Australian Parliament, and well known to Syme. Possibly it was through this newspaper connection that Herbert met her. Lucie was the chief bridesmaid, and a reception was held at the residence of Ethel's married sister. The bonus of £500 that Herbert received in 1894 may have helped with the expenses of the honeymoon.[158] The couple were to undertake a short country tour then embark on a three-month trip to India, duly sailing on the *Oceana* for Colombo in early December. Herbert's unpublished account, 'To India and Back', which is unfinished and undated, refers to his visit four years previously with Deakin, and his wish to go again.[159] It reveals that he and Edith travelled in Ceylon, India and Burma. Recording various experiences, Herbert also noted thoughts they gave rise to – jottings that indicate he was no shallow tourist: that 270 million Indians were ruled by a handful of whites; that Anglo-Indians look down on tourists; that at the ruins of the Residency at Lucknow, there were headstones to the English killed at the deadly siege of 1857, but no there was memorial to the more than 2000 rebels who were killed by the British in a couple of hours. The couple returned to Melbourne on 12 March 1895. Two weeks later Deakin had the newlyweds to dinner.[160]

Herbert was still away with Ethel when his brother Arthur was married, on 13 February, to Amy Horne, daughter of George Horne, manager of the

---

[155] George Alexander Syme, Death certificate, Registry of Births, Deaths and Marriages, Melbourne.
[156] 'Death of Mr. G.A. Syme', *Age*, 1 January 1895, p. 5.
[157] 'Our Melbourne Ladies Letter', *Mercury* (Hobart), 8 December 1894, Supplement, p. 1.
[158] Profit and loss account, 1894, SFP Box 1191/3.
[159] H. Syme, Diary, 1895, MS 6751, National Library of Australia.
[160] Diary entry for 29 March 1895, Deakin Papers, Series 2.

National Bank of Tasmania.[161] A reference in a November 1892 letter of Annabella's to Arthur about Amy Horne being in town, seeing Lucie and coming to tea, suggests the bride and her family had been well known to the Symes for some years.[162] Herbert had been best man the previous August at the marriage of Amy's brother Richard in Melbourne.[163] The ceremony was at St Johns in Launceston, a quiet affair with only a few friends because of family sadness on both sides: the Symes were in mourning for Arthur's Uncle George and Amy's father was gravely ill. Geoffrey was best man and, once again, Lucie was bridesmaid. It is not now known whether Syme and Annabella travelled to Tasmania for the occasion. Arthur went back with his bride to his residence and medical practice at Lilydale.

Foreshadowing yet another aspect of generational change, and no longer prohibited as it was during the David–Joseph partnership, Syme's two youngest sons came to work at the *Age* office. Whether decreed by Syme or on his own initiative, Geoffrey abandoned his university studies and in August 1893, aged 20, joined the staff as a reporter, with the meagre salary of 30 shillings per week.[164] Oswald, who in 1894 was engaged in matriculation studies that his father was anxious for him to pass as soon as possible, started in the Counting House on 20 June 1896, aged 18, at the minute sum of 10 shillings per week.[165] Syme now had three sons employed in his business, available to relieve the load of running it and, in due course, take over.

---

[161] 'Weddings, Syme-Horne', *Australasian*, 23 February 1895, p. 375; 'Launceston', *Mercury* (Hobart), 15 February 1895, p. 3.

[162] AS to Arthur Syme, 14 November 1892, in the possession of Judith Adams.

[163] 'Woman's World', *Brisbane Courier*, 24 August 1894, p. 6.

[164] Entry for Geoffrey Syme (hereafter GS) in Wages Book, p. 443.

[165] Entry for Oswald Syme in Wages Book, p. 443; DS to Begg, 17 October 1894, LB5, p. 131.

Chapter 14

'I AM SENDING FORTH ON THEIR TRAVELS MY TWO YOUNGEST SONS'

(August 1896 to December 1901)

Approaching 70, Syme was in a position to enjoy prosperity and personal fulfilment after almost a decade of conflict and stress from the protracted fight with Joseph and the drawn-out railways litigation. While the years leading up to Federation and into the new century would be eventful for Victoria and Australia, this was a period of unwonted tranquillity for him. As in the past, there were recurrent health problems, but they seem to have been relatively brief, without anxiety or fuss and with recuperative measures taken. A man of property and repute, he had many commitments and a panoply of engagements; also, and not least, a growing patriarchal role. As the branches of the paternal tree grew and blossomed, the father moved to shape and organise the lives of his offspring as part of the dynasty he was founding and, while still actively overseeing and innovating, to think realistically about succession for his newspaper business.

Two more children found life partners. Lucie, at 27, was the fourth child to marry – to William Macalister on 9 February 1898, at Holy Trinity Church, Kew, with brother Geoffrey the best man.[1] Deakin's brief diary entry suggests that he, as a long-time family friend, attended.[2] After the marriage, Syme, who came to rely quite heavily on his son-in-law 'Willie' for help with farm matters, made him manager of his Tarrawarra estate in the Yarra Valley, providing a residence for the newlyweds. While in England in 1901, Geoffrey became engaged to 18-year-old Violet Garnett. The couple would marry there in January 1902 before embarking for Australia.

---

[1] 'Weddings', *Australasian*, 12 February 1898, p. 381.
[2] Diary entry for 9 February 1898, Alfred Deakin Papers, MS 1540, Series 2. National Library of Australia.

Figure 14.1. Annabella Syme. (Courtesy of Dr Veronica Condon)

Many grandchildren arrived between 1896 and 1901.³ Two more (Cecil and Winifred) for Francis and Christina, who were again living at Dalry. Urged by Syme, who considered it had been a burden, they had sold their Cohuna property.⁴ There were three for Arthur and Amy (Kathleen, Hilda

---

3   Family tree, showing descendants of David Syme, copy held by great-grandson Michael Dennis.

4   *Bendigo Advertiser*, 4 February 1899, p. 5, col. 1; DS to F. Syme, undated, in the possession of Judith Adams.

CHAPTER 14

and Edith), two for Herbert and Ethel (Annabel and Brenda) and a son, Rupert, for Lucie and William. Surviving letters suggest a substantial grandmotherly role for Annabella at Blythswood. If less directly involved with his growing brood of grandchildren, Syme was comfortable in his patriarchy and proud of his descendants. When Annabella (fig. 14.1) wanted a beach house for them all to enjoy, he bought land at the bayside settlement of Mordialloc, some 24 kilometres south-east of Melbourne, and in 1901 arranged for the building of a holiday residence, Seaforth (Condon 2005).[5]

In September 1897 a New South Wales country newspaper reported that Syme was 'wearied of late' and no longer 'the invincible fighter', preferring the 'calm and seclusion' of his fine country estate.[6] The observation is not accurate. Certainly Syme continued to visit Killara and maintain an active interest in crops (grain, fruit, vegetables), dairy products, and livestock and win prizes for the latter at the Melbourne Agricultural Show – including for his stallion 'Gentleman George' and Romney Marsh Sheep in 1897, and a Dexter Kerry Bull in 1898.[7] He also monitored his investments, with particular interest in mining enterprises. But as ever these were only a part of his many-sided life.

Now Syme was very much a public figure. Newspaper reports and magazine social jottings have him, sometimes with his wife, attending significant public functions, especially several related to Federation. The foremost man of the Melbourne press, he was now a leading citizen. In June of 1897, the year of the Queen's 60th Jubilee, it was reported in newspapers all over Australia, but with little amplification, that the *Age* proprietor had been offered but declined a knighthood.[8] Previously, Queen's honours had been given to Australians prominent in politics, the public service, the judiciary and the financial sector; this offer was the first to an Australian press personage. That he turned it down was no imperial snub, however, for on the day of the Jubilee public holiday, 22 June, the *Age* expatiated on 'A Glorious Reign', describing the marvellously decorated David Syme & Co. building – outlined with electric lights and carrying a huge portrait of the Queen surrounded by English roses, Scottish thistles and Irish shamrocks

---

5   GS to DS, 12 December 1901, held by Veronica Condon.
6   'Personal and Political', *Queanbeyan Age*, 8 September 1897, p. 2.
7   'The Show', *Age*, 2 September 1897, p. 9, 'The Agricultural Show', *Bendigo Advertiser*, 31 August 1898, p. 3.
8   Most capital city dailies and many country papers carried the item on 14 June 1897, for example, 'Victoria', *Sydney Morning Herald*, p. 5, 'Epitome of News', *Mercury* (Hobart), p. 2.

and flags, including the Australian ensign, also flown in Sandhurst (Bendigo) for the celebrations and favoured, especially in New South Wales as a future Australian flag (in fact quite similar to the flag eventually adopted).[9]

Syme's decision places him in distinguished company, for in the later 19th century several notable Victorians declined imperial honours. In the early 1870s George Higinbotham, then MLA and journalist, had aroused controversy with his publicly expressed strong aversion, claiming the honour was a 'base, contemptible distinction' (quoted in Macintyre 1991, 58). In 1887 Deakin rejected a knighthood, and in 1900 evinced a similar lack of interest (La Nauze 1979, 91, 202). Syme recalled in a memoir entry that he, J.G. Francis and Deakin had each turned down offers. Outlining the conditions under which honours were given – automatically to persons in high positions and able to be 'bought' through philanthropy – Geoffrey Serle (1971, 219–220) considers it 'well recognized…that a knightage was a political handicap', referring to views in several *Age* and *Leader* editorials during the 1880s. Sparked by news that politician James Service was to be thus honoured, the editorial in the *Age* of 21 May 1884 referred disparagingly to the 'colonial aristocracy', claiming that knighthoods were out of place in modern society and naming several notable Englishmen who had turned them down. Yet that several of Syme's associates had been or would be knighted was no bar to friendly contact – with politician and sometime premier George Turner, knighted in January 1897, and with his lawyer Gillott, who would be Mayor of Melbourne and MLA in 1900 and become 'Sir' in 1901.[10] Pastoralist and politician friend Simon Fraser would make the grade, only much later, in 1918 aged 85.[11] Australian newspaper persons were first knighted in May 1898 – Syme's close associate John Langdon Bonython of the Adelaide *Advertiser* and James Reading Fairfax of the *Sydney Morning Herald*.[12] Syme's withholding was consonant with his personality – ambitious to prove his worth, but not through membership of a privileged class; rather, as a uniquely perceptive and powerful individual.

A setback occurred six months after the knighthood offer was apparently dealt with smoothly. On 15 December 1898 MLA Frank Madden, in the course of a debate on a Land Bill returned from the Legislative Council with amendments, alleged that Syme had had shady dealings in relation to

---

[9] 'The Celebration in Bendigo', *Bendigo Advertiser*, 23 June 1897, p. 2; 'The Proposed Federal Flag', *Sydney Morning Herald*, 24 May 1898, p. 9.
[10] 'News of the Day', *Age*, 2 January 1897, p. 6; 'City Council', *Argus*, 30 May 1901, p. 8.
[11] 'New Year Honours', *Sydney Morning Herald*, 1 January 1918, p. 5.
[12] 'New Knighthoods', *Advertiser* (Adelaide), 23 May 1898, p. 4.

CHAPTER 14

the Mount Macedon property he acquired in 1868 and sold in 1885.[13] As parliamentary proceedings were published verbatim in the daily newspapers, this was a very public slander. Madden, an extreme conservative, is on record as 'tactless and pugnacious', a man of 'hysterical outbursts' (Ingham 1986). Under parliamentary privilege, his unprovoked and, as it transpired, unjustifiable attack, refuted in a long letter signed 'David Syme', published in the *Age* of 19 December, could not be challenged through a libel action.[14]

The besmirching of Syme's name was the subject of a public inquiry five months later, possibly the shortest Victorian Royal Commission on record.[15] It sat for only two days, 29 May and 9 June 1899, taking evidence mainly from Syme, who strongly contested all charges, from a stock and station agent who had acted for him, and from Land Department employees and sundry others involved in the transactions 30 or so years back. Madden declined to appear; indeed he never did elaborate on, or substantiate, his charges. Commissioner Sir Hartley Williams concluded, in effect, that there was no case to answer, all actions by Syme having been validated by the Land Act of 1869. The *Age* leader of 12 June described the result as a 'triumphant vindication' of governments, officials and David Syme. A coda to this outcome, in the Assembly on 2 August Madden's motion protesting against the Commission as interference with parliamentary privilege was lost.[16]

Syme had powerful support. If Premier Turner was instrumental in setting up the Royal Commission, it appears that Deakin was the prime mover. Five days after Madden's attack in the Assembly, he met with Syme and Turner to discuss it,[17] and of his regular, frequent meetings with Syme, those of 26 May and 1 and 2 August 1899 were specifically about the Madden affair. The whole matter was finally and fully disposed of a good week before a major event in the life of the Syme newspapers enterprise – the official opening of the renovated premises (see below). Compared with the Speight railway litigation, the Madden affair was a minor upset.

Relatively minor too were the sundry libel cases that cropped up from time to time, as they did for the producers of the other Melbourne dailies – an occupational hazard, dealt with easily, and normally not costing

---

[13] 'Parliament', *Age*, 16 December 1898, p. 7; Sayers (1965, 246–249).
[14] 'A Baseless Charge', *Age* 19 December 1898, p. 5.
[15] Royal Commission into Certain Allegations against the Lands Department 1899, *Land Selection at Mount Macedon: Commission, Report and Evidence*, VPP 1899–1900, no. 33.
[16] VPD, v. 91, 2 August 1899, p. 426.
[17] Diary entry for 20 December 1898, Alfred Deakin Papers, MS 1540, Series 2, National Library of Australia.

hugely. The David Syme & Co. accounts for the years 1896 to 1901 show 'Law expenses and alleged libels' to be a fraction of the outgoings in the earlier 1890s – low £00s rather than £000s [18] Actions in the latter part of 1901, for instance, had minimal or no impact on Syme. In September the jury acquitted him in a £1000 damages action by failed financier James Mirams for articles in relation to his Federal candidature the previous March, the judge directing that the newspaper had been exercising its rights to express opinions.[19] A £750 damages action brought in November by Thomas Ashworth, president of the Victorian division of the Free Trade and Liberal Association, for misquotation in the *Age* was apparently settled by the end of the year, with negotiations by letter between the two parties, Syme appearing to concede liability.[20]

Syme was becoming a philanthropist of note. He set up and donated to numerous subscription lists for worthy causes in the *Age* and continued the annual *Leader* dairy prizes. In February 1897, when the Government had turned down a request for £2000 for the Victorian Rifle Association to attend the annual Bisley championships in England, he wrote to Premier Turner offering to provide the amount in full.[21] The offer was accepted, and Syme's generosity was widely reported in the Australian press. At Bisley, the Victorian team won several prizes, the most notable being the Kolopore Cup in July, and the accolades continued throughout the year, with a welcome home banquet for the team in December at which Governor Brassey, to cheers, acknowledged Syme's gift.[22] He continued his interest in the rifle shooting, in 1901 offering, through Colonel Templeton of the Victorian Rifle Association, £100 yearly for five years for the 'best shot…open to all comers within the Commonwealth'.[23] In July 1901 he was made a Governor of the Melbourne Church of England Grammar School, for having donated £100.[24] Whatever his motive in these and other instances of liberality, it was not purchase of a knighthood.

The newspaper business in these years was prospering as Syme's papers went from strength to strength, annual profits rising from £44,889 in 1896

---

[18] Profit and loss accounts, 1891–1900, SFP Box 1191/3, and 1901–1910, SFP Box 1192/1.
[19] 'Alleged Libel', *Argus*, 21 September 1901, p. 13.
[20] DS to J. Ashworth, 18 December 1901, LB5, p. 425.
[21] DS to G. Turner, 22 February 1897, LB5, p. 216.
[22] 'Bisley Rifle Matches', *Age*, 16 July 1897, p. 5; 'The Bisley Rifle Team', *Age*, 18 December 1897, p. 9.
[23] DS to Colonel Templeton, 4 September 1901, LB5, p. 420.
[24] Governor's Certificate, dated 9 July 1901, SFP Box 1193/3(a)[iv].

CHAPTER 14

to £60,282 in 1901.[25] Along with detailed political coverage in the lead-up to Federation and the subsequent federal elections, the contents diversified, with more literature, music and art, and a growing emphasis on Australian works and performances. On the production side there were innovations to keep pace with technological change, while the premises were renovated and expanded to signal a new era. Moreover, Syme's management style changed for the better. It was less autocratic, at a distance rather than hands-on, and with more delegating.

Editorial and literary staff

Relations with his editorial and literary staff relations were harmonious and productive. In his memoirs *Herald* journalist Bertie Cook, who disliked Syme's 'dictatorial attitude on public affairs', conceded nevertheless that although the *Argus* paid higher salaries, it had a 'stricter discipline' and its journalists 'did not seem to be as happy' as the *Age* men, who all seemed to be 'very proud of the paper'.[26] There was an excellent combination of mature, experienced men and enthusiastic, talented young ones. The former, who knew what Syme wanted and how to deliver it, included *Age* editor Arthur Windsor and its commercial editor Anthony Robinson, who were personal friends outside the office, subeditor John Stephens and chief of staff Gottfried Schuler, and for the *Leader*, editor Henry Short and agricultural editor John Dow. When at the end of 1900, after nearly 30 years with the *Age*, the urbane and witty Windsor retired, he was replaced by the competent 46-year-old Schuler, less colourful a personality but with years of experience as a leader writer and well-schooled in Syme's policies.

Five years younger than Syme, in 1900, 67-year-old Windsor was not well. Self-effacing, he offered to refund his salary for his times away from work: 'When did you ever hear of me deducting a mans salary from absence through ill health?' Syme responded on 30 January, suggesting several alternatives to lighten his load.[27] At the end of 1900 Windsor made a clean break from the *Age* office, sailing on the *Damascus* for London via Capetown on 20 February 1901, farewelled at Port Melbourne by a gathering of friends.[28] Four days earlier Syme, who had granted him a generous £3000

---

25 Profit and loss accounts, 1891–1900, SFP Box 1191/3, and 1901–1910, SFP Box 1192/1.
26 B.S. Baxter Cook, Memoirs of a Pioneer Pressman, MS 1453, National Library of Australia.
27 DS to A. Windsor, 30 January 1900, LB5, pp. 357–358.
28 'About People', *Age*, 21 February 1901, p. 5.

'bonus', held a farewell dinner at the Grand Hotel (today's Windsor Hotel, long associated with Australian politics).[29] The gathering included former and present *Age* and *Leader* journalists, notably Deakin, with whom Windsor had a close professional relationship and particular affinity.[30] Syme and colleagues maintained friendly contact with Windsor thereafter, and while there were some offers of further work, his days as a journalist and editor seem to have been over.

Another change, and in accord with the times, in 1897 a female journalist was appointed to the regular staff to write a 'ladies' column and comment on general and local women's affairs. From time to time Syme had accepted contributions from various women journalists, mostly in England, but found the new arrangement much better.[31] She was Henrietta McGowan, daughter of the late Samuel, the Canadian who had introduced telegraphy to Victoria. With the pseudonym 'Viola', her 'Feminine Fads and Fancies' (the title previously used for a contribution from actress and journalist Emily Soldene of London), appeared weekly from Saturday 10 July, the heading before long changed to a perhaps less patronising 'Feminine Facts and Fancies'. 'Viola' also contributed sundry other articles on topics concerning the 'woman question', in particular, the campaign for female suffrage, which the *Age* supported, but which would not become law in Victoria until March 1908 (Clarke 1988, 220). In May 1902 Mary Grant Bruce, a contributor of short stories for some years, was appointed editor (as 'Cinderella') of a feature for children in the *Leader*.[32]

Numerically, a striking change was the influx of a new generation of young men as reporters or leader writers. All were born in the 1870s, and most in Australia. Among this large cohort of men in their 20s was Frank Fox, whom Syme made chief of staff in 1901 when Schuler vacated the position to become *Age* editor.[33] Colleague Thorold Waters (1951, 45) remembered him as 'tall, erect, dignified', a 'crafty political reporter high in the graces' of Syme. There was (John) Desmond Byrne, who returned from London and resumed work at the *Age* office in August 1896. The renowned publisher

---

[29] Entry for Windsor in Wages Book, p. 525.
[30] A. Windsor to A. Deakin, undated, Series 1/588; diary entry for 16 February 1901, Series 2, Deakin Papers.
[31] DS to E. Soldene, 11 March, 25 June, 13 July 1897, LB5, pp. 219, 228, 230; DS to F. Hoey, 17 April, 1899, LB5, p. 294.
[32] Entry for Bruce in Wages Book, p. 34.
[33] Entry for Fox in Wages Book, p. 157 (the *Age* Fox is not the Frank Fox of the Sydney *Bulletin*, with whom he has been confused).

CHAPTER 14

Bentley had brought out his *Australian Writers*, reviewed very favourably in the *Age* of 2 January 1897. While Syme was not entirely satisfied with him ('I cannot keep up my efforts to galvanise you into action any longer', he wrote on 8 September 1896) Byrne did stay with the *Age* until 1899, then returned to London, where he was a useful contact, just as George Levey had earlier been.[34] There was reporter Leonard Biggs who, long after Syme's death, would succeed Schuler as editor. Talented and very promising reporter Robert Burt died from tuberculosis in 1899 aged 27. Syme was compassionate about his illness, attended to funeral arrangements, and may have arranged for the obituary in the *Leader* on 1 July.[35] There were two sons of staff members: reporter David Dow, son of the *Leader* agricultural editor, and William Robinson, son of the commercial editor and assistant to him.[36] Towards the end of a career in the financial world Robinson junior published a memoir that conveys pride in being part of the *Age* and *Leader*, provides insights into the office workings and thumbnail sketches of the key figures. He recalled that in 1897 Syme was a 'tall, gaunt, grey haired, and grey bearded man' who 'looked forbidding, but was just a human being suffering from a definite inferiority complex. Alleged to be cruelly unfair and ungenerous, he was in fact quite the opposite' (Robinson 1967, 22). Also, and importantly, he stressed that he had the merit of being receptive to new ideas (23).

Several other young reporters of this time later wrote about their experiences in the *Age* office, similarly conveying feelings of respect for their awe-inspiring boss while suggesting that, beneath the stern exterior, there was a vulnerable person. George Cockerill, who joined in 1898, remembered Syme's appearance as 'tall, spare, big-boned…jaw strong, his mouth hard, his nose Roman and his eyes suggested those of an eagle', who always backed his reporters when their work was questioned by outsiders, but who was shy and without social qualities (Cockerill 1943, 57, 61, 64). Monty Grover, a reporter from 1895 to 1897, who transferred to the *Argus* when offered a higher salary, remembered a very capable staff and found Syme a 'hard man', but 'just', who 'knew the work of every man as well as that man knew it himself' and never sacked without reason (Grover 1993, 76). One such

---

[34] DS to D. Byrne, 8 September 1896, LB5, p. 201; Entry for Byrne in Wages Book, p. 30.

[35] Entry for Burt in Wages Book, p. 30; DS to Mrs Burt, 26 February 1898, 28 June 1899, LB 5, pp. 262–263, 317; DS to Curator, Estates of Deceased Persons, 22 November 1899, LB5, p. 348.

[36] Entries for Dow and Robinson in Wages Book, pp. 104, 422.

example is Syme's treatment of headstrong if not wayward Joseph Melvin, the onetime *Argus* reporter who had tricked his way to the Sudan in 1885. On the *Age* staff since 1893, he had a weakness for drink and in 1897 was warned by Syme of dismissal if he again imbibed at work. Tolerated for two years, in April 1899 Melvin was asked by Syme regretfully but firmly, to resign after 'having exhausted the patience of everyone in the office'.[37]

Another *Age* employee and memoirist was Benjamin Hoare. Older than the young men mentioned (born in 1842), he had joined Syme's team some years earlier and, after a rocky relationship with his employer, was becoming a protégé, somewhat as Deakin had been two decades earlier. Hoare later described Syme's expounding to him the deficiencies of parliamentary democracy and giving him a copy of his 1881 book *Representative Government* to read (Hoare 1927, 152–155). Hoare's judicious responses apparently pleased his employer, as surely did his advocacy of protection. Hoare was a member and in the late 1890s secretary of the Protectionists' Association of Victoria, which published his pamphlets extolling the benefits to the colony from 25 years of protective tariffs.[38] His sizeable monograph *Preferential Trade*, published in 1904, makes clear how thoroughly he had absorbed Syme's economic theories, favouring the 'profounder reasonings of the German school of economists' and referring frequently to the arguments in Syme's 1876 monograph *Outlines of an Industrial Science* (Hoare 1904, iv, 11, 15, 16, 37, 41, 44, 234). It is likely that Hoare wrote many or all of the articles on protection, including its adaptation into 'new protection', enunciated for instance in the *Age* leader of 20 November 1900, to encompass not only tariffs but welfare measures such as a minimum wage and an old-age pension.

Linotype introduced

Son Herbert, in charge of the business and technical side, was responsible for the operation of the linotype machines ordered in early 1896. It is likely that he had a key part in their installation, which was systematic and relatively smooth, unlike his father's somewhat fraught and frantic, albeit effective, moves when introducing rotary presses in the 1870s. Expected

---

[37] DS to J. Melvin, LB5, 9 March, 1897, 19 April 1899, pp. 218, 297; Entry for Melvin in Wages Book, p. 303.

[38] Hoare's essays published as pamphlets by Protectionists Association of Victoria are *Twenty-Five Years of Protection* (1896), *Slaying a Slander* (1897), and *Farmers and Federation* (1899).

CHAPTER 14

in December 1896, the machines must have arrived in January 1897.[39] The whole operation took some 16 months. Most straightforward, if time-consuming, was their setting up, testing, making modifications, and ordering extra fittings. More complex and demanding were three questions involving the workforce: who of the compositors to deem redundant? who to retrain as linotype operators? what rates and conditions to apply to the linotype workforce? For the introduction of the linotype in the 1890s caused as massive a change in newspaper production as did computer typesetting in the late 20th century.

Three reports, all typed, helped the decision-makers. 'Report and Suggestions, Introduction of Linotypes', dated 19 January 1897, was written by H. Clarke, the *Age* printer. Stressing the need for copy to be legible and carefully subedited, it singles out Grover, P. Dinley and Schuler as the worst offenders. It then names five persons from the printing staff who could be 'learners' for daytime work, suggesting that a Mr Woods at the stationers Sands & McDougall be engaged to teach them, while for night work, there could be a ballot since nearly all the compositors were anxious to learn although 10 or more were unsuitable.

The second report, undated, is by *Leader* printer J. Dummelow. He records having interviewed the head reader on the *Argus* about the system used for the *Australasian* and the printer of the *Weekly Times* and refers frequently to their views, including a preference for the use of apprentices. He too stresses the importance of copy in a 'complete state' and gives his opinion of some of the *Leader* printing staff. (He also outlines the duties of 'Mr Syme', who must be the proprietor's namesake, on the staff from the earliest days, who resigned in November 1900 shortly before his death.)[40]

The third, 'Report Suggesting Improvements in the Successful Working of the Linoytpe Machines', dated 27 April 1897, is by 'Linotype Expert' J.T. McAlpine, an outsider. It seems to have been written when the new machines were operating on a trial basis. While McAlpine thinks work at the *Age* compares favourably with that at the Sydney *Daily Telegraph*, he does have a lot of constructive suggestions, in the interests of saving time and maintaining standards. There should be one staff of regular operators; 'takes' should be larger; machines should be kept running during suppertime, possibly by supernumerary compositors. Most importantly, a

---

[39] Unlabelled ledger, containing records relating to linotype introduction, including the reports discussed, *Age* Archives, Melbourne.
[40] Entry for the other David Syme in Wages Book, p. 444.

'great alteration' was needed in the Literary Department – copy must be legibly written, carefully subedited and submitted early; at present it takes too long to read.

The first page of a typed three-page 'List of Regular Operators, Grass Operators, Frameholders and Grass Compositors' is date-stamped 17 May 1898, by which time the fates of these men had been decided. Some of the detailed annotations and markings on the list are explained ("* old men'; '‡ not likely to be eligible'); some are now impenetrable. Standing out from the several marks in black and red ink are big blue-pencil ones that appear to be in Syme's hand. This document suggests there was careful, reasoned and consultative decision-making, while the Wages Book shows more clearly what happened to the army of compositors between 21 April 1897 and 14 January 1898. More than 50 who were laid off received bonuses ranging from £5 to £25, most commonly £20 or in the case of older men, a pension of 10 shillings or £1 a week. Many others were transferred to other sections and duties. Some left without any extra payment recorded. While there are no corroborative records, these may be the 'remainder' described by biographer Pratt (1908, 265–266) for whom Syme 'found other employment; he set up several in independent businesses, and many others he helped to settle on the land'. Syme's treatment of the redundant men bespeaks not only a sympathetic generosity but also an awareness that the need for old-age pensions from the state was a matter being raised in some quarters, and which the Victorian Government under Premier George Turner, in a climate of post-Depression meliorism, had begun to investigate and which would be legislated for in 1900 (Rickard 2006).

Comments on the unemployment resulting from the introduction of linotypes appeared in the *Australasian Typographical Journal* long before the machines were in use at David Syme & Co. The January 1896 issue laments that the New Year brings 'wholesale dismissals'; the February one notes a great 'labour displacement' with many men out of work. The August one records an exodus of printers to Western Australia. By contrast, the April 1897 issue, in mentioning dismissals at the *Age*, notes the liberality with which this has been done and reports the Father of the *Age* Chapel having stated that the proprietor had been generous to the 'dismissed elderly'. Subsequent issues record further batches of *Age* redundancies to February 1898, the last in February 1898, when the body of compositors had been reduced by 50 per cent. With the matter of pensions in the wind, and given further airing by Syme's actions, the August 1899 *Australasian Typographical Journal* carried an editorial on the subject.

CHAPTER 14

While records relating to Syme's linotype staff are unclear and incomplete, there is some indication of negotiations about their duties and conditions. In 1896 a subcommittee of the Melbourne Typographical Society was framing new rules, the *Australasian Typographical Journal* reporting in November 1896 that a document had been sent to the three dailies for consideration. It reported a year later that linotype staff in the *Age* office were unsettled about their terms and conditions, while two letters from Syme to the 'Age Chapel Father' (spokesperson for the *Age* printing staff) at this time imply a dispute, which led to a conference with the Master Printers, in which Herbert Syme was involved and which had a 'good outcome'.[41] It would appear that Syme and his son worked together well to secure the resolution. Another beneficiary was Bonython at the Adelaide *Advertiser*, who in April 1898, January 1899 and August 1900 sought advice and information from Syme concerning linotype installation and operation, and in November 1900 sent a letter of thanks for same.[42]

Western Australia visited

With the linotype now under Herbert's competent control, Syme in mid-June 1898 travelled to Western Australia with son Geoffrey and illustrator Edmund Luke, who had been there with the Vagabond two years earlier and produced the illustrations for the 52-page 'Western Australia' supplement to the *Leader* of 30 May 1896. The continuing population migration to Western Australia from the early 1890s was frequently noted and deplored in Syme's papers – the overall loss to Victoria in the *Age* of 13 October 1896, the exodus of farmers on 24 March 1897 and the 'Westralian Boom' on 30 March. Syme went to see for himself the developments arising from the lucrative gold discoveries. On 15 June the three men left Melbourne on the *Australien*, arriving in Albany five days later.[43] Interviewed there, Syme said he had come to the colony for a holiday during which he wished to find out about the resources – timber, agricultural, and above all mineral – of which he had heard so much.

---

[41] DS to Father, Age Chapel, 4 October 1897, 21 April 1898, LB5, pp. 247, 268; *Australasian Typographical Journal*, February 1898.

[42] J. Bonython to DS & Co., 28 April 1898, 19 January 1899, 11 August and 17 November 1900. J.L. Bonython and Company, Summary Record, Letter Books, BRG 10, Series 8, State Library of South Australia.

[43] 'Shipping Intelligence', *Age*, 16 June 1898, p. 4; 'Mr. David Syme', *West Australian* (Perth), 21 June 1898, p. 5.

During the next 24 days he visited timber forests and mills at Denmark (which he found impressive but not equal to the South Gippsland timber) and mines in and around Kalgoorlie, Boulder and the town of Northam.[44] He was in Perth for several days, entertained by leading politicians and public servants and taken down the Swan River in the government launch to inspect harbour works and make an unscheduled visit to the Fremantle prison. He visited the newly incorporated Canning Jarrah Timber Company in the Darling Ranges on Perth's eastern outskirts.[45] By 14 July he and Geoffrey were in Albany for their departure the next day on the *Polynesien* for Adelaide.[46] Arriving in the South Australian capital on 18 July, they lunched with Ebenezer Ward, MLC in the South Australian parliament. A former journalist and proprietor of several South Australian newspapers, he had a brief stint with the *Age* in 1863 (Hirst 1976; Kirkpatrick 2013, 63, 77, 78). Symes senior and junior were welcomed by the Premier, the Speaker of the Assembly and other politicians.[47] They then took the afternoon express train to Melbourne.

While newspaper reports enable the tracking of Syme throughout his holiday, occasional references to Geoffrey indicate that he was with his father for much if not all of the time. Artist Luke was with Syme during the first segment, but seems not to have gone to Perth but instead continued inspecting mining operations, in the Kalgoorlie area and north on the Murchison fields. He left for Melbourne a few days after Syme and Geoffrey. His was not a holiday. Rather, he was taking photos and sketching for a planned *Leader* supplement on the mines of Western Australia, to be published simultaneously in London as a supplement to the *Financial Times*. According to an Adelaide *Advertiser* report, it was he who suggested the Western Australia excursion to Syme, surely with the production of a supplement in mind.[48] (No longer could the Vagabond be called upon, having died in September 1896, four months after co-authoring the 'Western Australia' Supplement in May of that year.[49]) In fact two sizeable, profusely illustrated 'Western Australia' supplements were issued

---

[44] 'Local and General', *Kalgoorlie Western Argus*, 30 June 1898, p. 19; 'Kanowna', *West Australian*, 24 June 1898, p. 5, 'Northam', 29 June 1898, p. 5; 'Coolgardie', *Inquirer* (Perth), 1 July 1898, p. 3.

[45] *Inquirer* (Perth), 15 July 1898, p. 6, col. 3.

[46] *Albany Advertiser*, 16 July 1898, p. 3, col. 2.

[47] 'The Mail Steamers', *Advertiser* (Adelaide), 19 July 1898, p. 4.

[48] 'Perth', *Advertiser* (Adelaide), 18 July 1898, p. 5.

[49] 'Death of the Vagabond', *Age*, 5 September 1896, p. 7.

CHAPTER 14

with the *Leader* in 1898, both gratis, the first on 24 September, chiefly about goldfields of the colony, and the second on 29 October, with a more general coverage – agriculture and industries. In addition, the *Age* ran a related series, 'Goldfields of West Australia' in September and October. Exactly what part Syme or Geoffrey played in planning the content and writing the detail that accompanies Luke's illustrations is not known, but it seems reasonable to assume that their input was considerable.

During Syme's time in the West, newspapers reported the 'Importation of Pure-Bred Stock', the 'Valuable Shipment' including two prize Dexter-Kerry bulls that Alexander Crawford, former Victorian agriculturalist and now working for the Western Australian Bureau of Agriculture (Lomas 1981) had purchased from Syme on a trip back to Victoria.[50] It is possible that this contact, too, may have whetted his appetite to see the West, an experience that he kept telling reporters at places visited impressed him. In any case, the visit appears to have been a beneficially stimulating experience for Syme and an opportunity to develop a close working relationship with Geoffrey.

New look premises

Back from the West, Syme had soon to set in motion the enlargement and remodelling of the newspaper premises. From July 1897 if not earlier he had been considering expansion, with an eye on the building adjacent at 235 Collins Street, formerly occupied by the Victorian Permanent Building Society.[51] In February 1898 he purchased it for £27,500, *Melbourne Punch* observing that this sum 'to a certain extent fixes the value of properties today in the celebrated bank and financial block of the city'.[52] That the business was outgrowing the 233 Collins Street building designed by Joseph Reed almost 20 years earlier probably became very obvious when the linotypes were acquired. Besides, the premises were becoming run down. William Robinson (1967, 21) recalled that when he started in 1897 there were a battery of earth closets on the first floor facing the stairs and 'rats galore'.

As architect, Syme engaged Robert Gordon Hyndman, giving him 'a free hand' provided the work of newspaper production could be carried on 'without interruption'.[53] Grandson of artist and diarist Georgiana McCrae,

---

50 'Stud Cattle for the West', *Advertiser* (Adelaide), 5 July 1898, p. 4.
51 DS to Vale & Son, 22 July 1897, LB5, p. 233.
52 'Financial', *Melbourne Punch*, 17 March 1898, p. 229.
53 'The Evolution of a Newspaper…The New Building', *Leader*, 12 August 1899, Supplement, p. 4.

Hyndman was involved in the Arts and Crafts movement of Melbourne. Having worked in the 1880s at the firm of Syme's earlier architect Reed, he was now a principal in Hyndman and Bates, which at the time was also doing work for Gillott – possibly he and Syme compared notes (Edquist 2012, 44; Willis 2012, 350).[54] On 27 July, less than two weeks after Syme's return from Western Australia, a contract was signed for major renovations – a makeover of two buildings into one, to be undertaken by the builders Murray and Crow.

The renovations took a year and cost £15,000. The exterior result was a single Italianate façade (fig. 14.2), described in Syme's newspapers as a 'broad, imposing front', contributing to the 'picturesque attractiveness' of Collins Street.[55] A 'grand' central arch connected the old and new sections, which inside were completely remodelled with ample fire precautions – the printing machines, including a 'huge' new sextuple Hoe, in the basement; public office and manager Herbert's room on the ground floor; the literary and editorial branch and proprietor Syme's office on the first; art work, photography and stereotyping on the second; and on the third the composing branch and linotype room.

The crowning glory was outside. A graceful statue adorned the centre of the top of the building, a figure over 12 feet high. Made of sheets of beaten copper, reinforced internally by a steel rod embedded in the stone of the wall, it appeared about to fly up and away. A representation of Mercury, the Roman messenger god, it elicited responses that were not only aesthetic. Many observed at the time,[56] as reporter Waters (1951, 63) later explained, that it was Syme's 'one and only public jest', alluding to the rivalry between the *Age* and its Melbourne daily rival – Mercury mythologically known for having put to death the god Argus of 100 eyes. That Mercury was also the god of thieves and liars, the *Australasian* pointed out, other papers echoed and Waters later noted. At the time, Syme was quick to protest in writing to co-proprietor of the rival weekly, William Spowers.[57]

Inspiration for the statue atop the *Age* building was a bronze Mercury created by the Italian sculptor Giambologna in the 16th century. The National Gallery of Victoria held a plaster replica, from which sculptor Charles Richardson must have worked.[58] A founding member of the

---

[54] DS to J. Mathieson, 21 August 1899, LB5, p. 330.
[55] 'The New Building', *Age*, 11 August, 1899, p. 8, *Leader*, 12 August, Supplement, p. 4.
[56] For example, 'Without Sentiment', *Sunbury News*, 13 May 1899, p. 3.
[57] DS to W. Spowers, 24 April 1899, p. 298.
[58] Information from Museum Victoria, 21 February 2012.

CHAPTER 14

Figure 14.2. The *Age* office, Collins Street, 1899. (Courtesy of Fairfax Media)

Victorian Artists' Society and leading painter and sculptor in Melbourne – having taken part in the groundbreaking 9 x 5 Impression Exhibition of 1888 – Richardson carried out many significant commissions in Melbourne and Victoria, including the creation of a bust of Gillott as Lord Mayor (Rose 1988; Fysh 1933; Betley 1973). His Mercury is a close copy of the Renaissance original, with the addition of a circle of Cupid figures at the base. The figures of Literature, Science and Art modelled in relief on the face of the building below the statue and above the central arch, were also his work.

The new-look *Age* building, illustrated in the *Leader* of Saturday 12 August 1899, had a grand formal opening at 3 pm on the Thursday before.

Attended by 350 invited 'leading citizens', politicians and senior public servants, including Syme's close friend Gillott and nephew Dr George Adlington Syme. All were given a tour of the building and Mayor Malcolm McEachern opened proceedings.[59] Thanking him, Syme then praised his 'able' staff, especially editor Windsor, who said in response that in his years as editor there had seen no better staff than at present and that he liked his job, especially appreciating Syme's policy of non-intervention. Herbert then proposed a toast to the architects and builders, noting their difficult task of working while the business had to be carried on and that there had been harmonious relations and no accidents. Finally, architect Hyndman thanked the staff for their help and patience. These splendid premises, virtually unaltered, would grace Collins Street and serve David Syme and Co. for the next 60 years.

Around the time of the building's completion, Syme and Hyndman had been investigating the erection of a hoarding, presumably to advertise the *Age* and *Leader*, on a building at Princes Bridge, the railway station terminus for suburban lines.[60] But permission was refused by railways engineer G.R. Simms, as Syme wrote to John Mathieson, Railways Commissioner, with whom he had a more amicable relationship than with predecessor Richard Speight. The *Age* editorial on 8 January 1898 had urged that Mathieson be given a free hand from political interference, for he was an 'astute and capable railway expert'. Along with Gillott, he was one of Syme's regular 'lunchtime cronies', reporter Waters (1951, 67) noted. No recluse in his office, Syme customarily walked to Scott's Hotel, two blocks to the west from the *Age* building, on the other side of Collins Street, to lunch with various 'men of the city' (Sayers 1965, 217–218).

War in South Africa

Scarcely had Syme and his staff settled into the remodelled premises, when the proprietor had to take note of a matter beyond the bounds of Melbourne, the borders of Victoria, and indeed the shores of Australia – the war that was brewing in South Africa between British settlers of the Cape Colony and Natal and Boer (Dutch-Afrikaner) farmers in the republics of the Orange Free State and the Transvaal. Cabled via London, the telecommunications nerve centre for the far-flung parts of the British Empire, up-to-date news

---

[59] '"The Age" and "Leader"', *Leader*, 12 August 1899, pp. 22–23.
[60] DS to J. Mathieson, 21 August 1899, LB5, p. 330.

CHAPTER 14

of distant wars was provided regularly and prominently in the *Age*, as in all major Australian dailies. In 1897 the conflict in Europe between Turkey and Greece was boldly headlined; in 1898 it was the hostilities between the United States and Spain over possession of Cuba and the Philippines. In 1899 it was the simmering enmity in South Africa that cables in June termed 'The Boer Crisis' and by October 'The Boer War',[61] and in which an estimated 16,000 men from Australia would fight, 606 of them dying from wounds or the diseases that were rampant (Australian War Memorial 2012).

Responding to a British request in July for troop assistance, but ready in any case to participate, the Victorian and Tasmanian governments sent their first contingents on the *Medic*, which sailed from Melbourne for Cape Town on 28 October.[62] The troops arrived on 1 December, in time to take part in what would be a successful counter-offensive after earlier severe British losses (assisted subsequently by further contingents from all colonies). Battles raged until September 1900; by October major Boer cities and towns were in British hands. These tide-turning successes were followed by protracted Boer guerrilla attacks and British 'mopping up', including pre-emptive moves against Boer civilians that lasted into 1902. But only in May 1910 did the British colonies and the former Boer republics officially become the Union of South Africa, a self-governing (by whites) dominion of the British Empire.

Press coverage of this conflict was at first seen as absolutely vital in the Australian colonies. With no direct cable link across the Indian Ocean, the war news was cabled via London, with relative immediacy, but briefly, and not tailored for particular readerships. Fuller news by ship for eastern colonies was a month old on arrival, although telegraphing from Albany or Adelaide could save a few days. There were three forms of such news: items in Cape Town newspapers; letters from a correspondent already in situ; and letters from a correspondent especially despatched by an Australian newspaper.

Australian daily newspaper proprietors used all sources, especially the last, a large contingent of journalists travelling to South Africa in mid-1899 (Anderson and Trembath 2011, 32–38). Most had returned by October 1900, but not Syme's star reporter, whose calamitous story is below. Syme, acting not only for the *Age* but also for the Sydney *Daily Telegraph* and the Adelaide *Advertiser*, was proactive about news procurement by all possible

---

[61] For example, cables in *Age* 16 June, 14 October 1899.
[62] 'The Victorian Contingent', *Age*, 30 October 1899, pp. 56.

means. Supplied with cables as a matter of course from the now united service he, nevertheless, wrote to the *Argus* proprietors in October when war broke out, requesting that the cable service be increased to the fullest extent under the agreement 'so that war news may be ample and worthy of the united service'.[63] Months earlier, when the crisis was brewing, he had arranged for George Ralling (or Railling), subeditor of the daily *Cape Argus*, 'the leading Cape paper' he told Wynne, to send news and a letter by every steamer from Cape Town.[64]

In August he canvassed, with Wynne for his Sydney paper and Bonython for his Adelaide one, their sharing the cost of sending a war correspondent. He strongly advocated *Age* reporter William Lambie, of whom he thought highly, being 'well up in military matters', having reported from the Sudan for the *Sydney Morning Herald*. He may also have had the right temperament, for reporter Waters (1951, 45) later termed him a 'rifle butts enthusiast'. Initially sceptical of the likelihood of war, Bonython eventually came round, although peeved and apprehensive that Lambie would write for Victorians and Frank Wilkinson, being sent by the *Daily Telegraph*, for a New South Wales readership, and thus South Australian readers would be left out.[65] On 28 October Lambie sailed from Melbourne for Cape Town, on the *Medic*. Wilkinson left Sydney around the same time, with the first New South Wales contingent (sent in two drafts – 30 October on the *Kent* and 3 November on the *Aberdeen*).[66]

Fate gave Lambie a short time to report. His first article, 'With the Australian Troops', current to 30 November and describing shipboard life en route to the war, appeared in the *Age* on 2 January 1900. During the next six weeks there were more of his contributions, all written about a month earlier. Then a cable from London in the *Age* of 12 February reported the alarming news that he was missing as a result of a 'severe skirmish' on Friday 9 February near Colesberg, when 50 Australian and Tasmanian Mounted Infantry on reconnaissance 'drew the fire…of a large force of Boers'.[67] A cable

---

[63] DS to *Argus* proprietors, 10 October 1899, LB5, p. 342.
[64] DS to W. Wynne, 17 August, 10 October 1899, LB5, pp. 327, 340–341.
[65] DS to W. Wynne and J. Bonython in letters ranging from 17 August 1899 (LB5, pp. 327) to 10 October 1899 (pp. 340–341); J. Bonython to DS & Co. and to W. Wynne from 31 August to 10 November 1899, Bonython Letter Books.
[66] 'The New South Wales Contingent', *Argus*, 30 October 1899, p. 5; 'Departure of the Kent', *Sydney Morning Herald*, 31 October 1899, p. 5; 'Shipping', *Sydney Morning Herald*', 4 November 1899, p. 8.
[67] 'Australians in Action', *Age*, 12 February 1900, p. 5.

CHAPTER 14

the next day informed that the journalist had been 'killed in Friday's fight',[68] and one the day after that he had been shot in the head. Disconcertingly, this 14 February issue of the *Age* also carried Lambie's 12 January instalment of 'With the Australian Troops', and several more appeared over the following month. The last, dated 8 February, the day before he died, appeared on 14 March.

A full account of Lambie's death had to wait for a letter by sea mail from Major William Reay, war correspondent for the Melbourne *Herald*. The *Age* of 14 March published Reay's 'How Mr. Lambie Met His Death…specially written for The *Age*' – Reay's *Australians in War*, published later in 1900, would provide a fuller account. Reay wrote that Lambie and A.G. Hales, correspondent for the London *Daily Mail*, on horseback, in the company of Tasmanian soldiers and wearing clothes resembling battle dress, were accosted by a party of Boer soldiers. Ignoring a command to halt, the reporters were shot as they galloped off, Lambie fatally; Hales was taken prisoner, released after a few weeks. Tasmanian Lieutenant Francis Heritage, who took a truce flag to enemy lines, seeking further information, was given Lambie's watch and told that he had been 'decently buried'. Permission was subsequently given for the grave to be visited and Reay, accompanied by J.A. Cameron from the West Australian press and carrying an improvised white flag, crossed into enemy lines. Blindfolded, they were taken to the burial site. Reay met Boer General Jacobus de la Rey, who courteously explained that the war correspondents had been mistaken for military men and asked for his regrets to be conveyed to Lambie's wife.

Three months later Reay, with the chaplain of the Victorian forces, found his way back to Lambie's grave and marked it with a marble slab. (In 1905 the body was reburied in the military cemetery at Colesberg, Cape Province (Watson 2012).) Lambie was the first Australian war correspondent to lose his life in the field of battle (Anderson and Trembath 2011, 376). According to the *Age* of 13 February, he was also the 'first Victorian to fall in the cause of the Empire in South Africa'.[69] The next few days, however, would see the start of heavy casualties.[70]

There were widespread public expressions of sympathy in Australia – in newspapers and in colonial houses of parliament. There were also immediate practical concerns. Lambie had no life insurance, although the

---

68 '"The Age" War Correspondent', *Age*, 13 February 1900, p. 5.
69 '"The Age" War Correspondent', *Age*, 13 February 1900, p. 5.
70 For example, 'Victorian Losses', *Age*, 19 February 1900, p. 6.

three newspaper representatives had agreed that he would have cover and Syme had instructed him to obtain it in Cape Town.[71] Whether or not Lambie had attempted to get it there is not known. He had been refused in Melbourne, possibly because of being wounded in the Sudan. A Lambie Memorial Fund was promptly set up at the *Age* office, with Geoffrey Syme its treasurer. Numerous *Age* employees contributed as did staff from other newspapers, notably the rival *Argus* and the Sydney *Daily Telegraph*.[72] Considering that the *Age* was then collecting for several other funds – the Bushmen's Corps Fund, the Empire Patriotic Fund, the Indian Famine – the contributions for the Lambie one were generous, although probably totalling less than £50, and thus, relatively small relief for Lambie's dependants. Syme wanted each of the three newspaper businesses to put in £333 for his widow and thus make up the £1000 that would have been an insurance payout. In fact Syme contributed more – £375. But, though he tried to persuade Bonython and Wynne to do likewise, urging the 'moral aspect', rather than legal liability (he pointed out to proprietor Bonython that he was a free agent, not a 'board of directors'), he only succeeded in getting from them a total of another £375, making £750 in all for Mrs Lambie.[73] 'Proprietors of "The Age"' (ie. Syme) had also contributed an initial £105 to the War Relief Fund initiated by the Lord Mayor of London, for which the *Age* from late December 1899 had been accepting subscriptions.[74] A further indication of his concern for war casualties was his attendance in late May 1900 at a Parliament House reception for invalided soldiers.[75]

Fairness and compassion apart, Syme moved immediately to replace Lambie, cabling Ralling in Cape Town to appoint a successor for one month and writing to Bonython and Wynne suggesting his chief of staff Fox, whom he had consulted and was willing.[76] Nothing further is on record about this, Fox remaining in Melbourne. The war news subsequently supplied for the syndicate came from Wilkinson and sundry other sources mostly arranged by Wynne and Bonython, financial records showing the *Age* share of these

---

[71] DS to Mrs Lambie, 22 March 1900, LB5, p. 374; Entry for Lambie in Wages Book, p. 281
[72] Reports in *Age*, 20 February to 24 March 1900.
[73] DS to Bonython, 11 April 1900, LB5, p. 376.
[74] 'Patriotic Fund', *Age*, 22 December 1899, p. 5.
[75] *Melbourne Punch*, 31 May 1900, p. 527, col. 3.
[76] DS to Bonython, 15 February 1900, LB5, p. 363; DS to W. Wynne, 15, 17 February 1900, LB5, pp. 364, 365.

CHAPTER 14

expenses to be a sizeable £7311, plus some £143 for war cables.[77] Following the end of open warfare in October 1900, interest in the bitter endgame waned, with desultory reporting of the Boers' rearguard activities and scant mention of the British depredations that have come to light in later history-writing (Australian War Memorial 2012).

Rebellion in China

In mid-1900, while the battles in South Africa were raging, a conflict broke out elsewhere, so that for a time there were two lots of war news running concurrently. Press coverage of the new one, an uprising in China known as the Boxer Rebellion, displaced that of the older. For several years there had been attacks on foreign missionaries and diplomats in various parts of northern China by Chinese nationalists, many of peasant origins (designated 'Boxers') who were opposed to a foreign presence in China and to Christian proselytising. Matters came to a head in June 1900, with a siege of foreign legations in Peking (Beijing), where hundreds of foreign diplomats, businessmen, missionaries and their families, and several thousand Chinese Christians, were holed up ('Boxer Rebellion' 2012; Anderson and Trembath 2011, 30–32). Following an ineffectual armistice with Chinese authorities in July, relief for the legations came in August from an eight-nation alliance – of Austria-Hungary, Britain, France, Germany, Italy, Japan, Russia and the United States. A force said to be 38,000 strong (British, Russian and Japanese the largest component) gathered at Tsientsin (Tianjin), marched on Peking and liberated the besieged.[78] While violence and reprisals on both sides continued in China for many months, the crisis was past well before the arrival of the Victorian and New South Wales Naval Contingents that sailed from Sydney on 8 August, with them the *Sydney Morning Herald*'s journalist J.R. Wallace (*Century of Journalism* 1931, 351).

Before, during and after the Rebellion the *Age* and other papers were receiving cable news via London, its major source being George Morrison. A youthful contributor to Syme's papers in the early 1880s, and coming to grief on the New Guinea expedition, he had been the London *Times* correspondent in Peking since 1897. There were also reports sent by George Wynne, son of the Sydney *Daily Telegraph* manager Watkin, 'embedded' in the city (Souter 1981, 103–104). Clearly Syme was concerned to improve

---

[77] Profit and loss accounts, 1891–1900, SFP Box 1191/3.
[78] 'The Allied Forces' and 'The War in China', *Argus*, 13 August 1900, p. 5.

the quality of news from China. In January 1898 he had written to Wynne senior that he wanted to be supplied with the China news that the *Daily Telegraph* was receiving by mail (from George Wynne?), complaining about 'the poor figure we cut as compared with the Argus in this respect'.[79] In July 1900, during the siege crisis, Syme wrote again to Wynne asking that Hong Kong papers be sent regularly to the Darwin correspondent for the speedy telegraphing of news, which would be more up to date than in the Shanghai papers from which the *Argus* had quoted.[80] In August, days after the relief of the legations, he sent to then London correspondent William Garnett (of whom more below) detailed criticisms of the news he was supplying, including his treatment of Chinese issues – 'Chinese plot. Seems to mix up mahomedans & boxers – cannot make out your meaning'.[81] But the *Age* proprietor made no moves to dispatch a special correspondent to the battlefront, instead relying on arrangements made by his Adelaide and Sydney counterparts. Perhaps he had learned a lesson from the Lambie disaster; perhaps he perceived public disenchantment with war.

Syme's letterbooks show that he was very concerned with regular correspondence arrangements, however, being aware of significant events and developments overseas and wanting proper coverage. When he was in Japan in 1895, reports from New Zealand correspondent Grey had been discontinued; in September 1896 he re-engaged Grey, pointing out that there were now in that colony 'so many experiments of a social character'.[82] He employed Thomas Dow, brother of *Leader* agricultural editor John, as Sydney correspondent in 1899 but, as seven letters of complaint between June and December show, found him unsuitable in this position and discontinued the arrangement.[83]

As ever, London correspondence was of paramount importance. Evident in several letters carrying explicit instructions, he wanted a huge range of issues covered, from sport to society, military to political to economic, agricultural to 'Literary and Scientific'.[84] He was alarmed in March 1900 when mainstay Levey took 'French leave' (Syme's words), going to Paris as secretary to the colonial committee of the British Commission of the Paris

---

[79] DS to W. Wynne, 10 January 1898, LB5, p. 259.
[80] DS to W. Wynne, 30 July 1900, LB5, p. 396.
[81] DS to W. Garnett, 16 August 1900, LB5, 398–399.
[82] DS to Grey, 10 September 1896, LB5, p. 202.
[83] DS to T. Dow between 21 June (LB5, p. 312) and 28 November 1899 (LB5, p. 352).
[84] For example, DS to G. Levey, 25 April 1900, LB5, pp. 383–384; DS to W. Garnett, 11 July, 16 August 1900, LB5, pp. 392–393, 398–399.

CHAPTER 14

Exhibition (Exhibition Universelle) of 1900. He considered the replacement arranged by Levey – James Morgan, employed in the cable service – quite unsatisfactory, and regretted that Byrne had not been engaged, for he 'knows exactly the sort of letter we require'.[85]

For the rest of the year Syme was the key cause of a confusing situation, where he juggled Levey and a potential alternative for the London correspondence, William Garnett, former employee on the *Age* and relative of Annabella.[86] Learning that Levey had been seriously ill, he sounded out Garnett in a letter of 25 April, wrote on 11 July to confirm his engagement, on 16 August to discontinue as his contributions were not up to standard, wrote and cabled on 24 October to re-instate him and, ending the saga, wrote on 2 January 1901, 'happy to compliment him' on a 'manifest improvement'.[87]

By this time, Levey was permanently out of the picture, but not before epistolary unpleasantness. Letters of 18 and 25 April 1900 show Syme attempting to ascertain Levey's availability and, somewhat perfunctorily, sorry about his sickness while upbraiding him for the poor quality of the recent London letters he had resumed sending, intimating he might be replaced.[88] On 4 July he wrote and cabled reinstatement, but on 17 July contradicted, advising that he had 'written to a gentleman in London' (Garnett, of course) to take over.[89] On 18 September he severely rebuked Levey for sending 'countermanded' letters, complaining of having to pay two correspondents, and describing Levey's letters as 'arid'.[90] Finally, on 3 October Syme terminated his services.[91] This seems extremely discourteous at least, and undeservedly abrupt after a decades-long relationship, although there may be more cordial and appreciative communication, not preserved. An accounts record for 1901 shows Levey was paid 18 guineas (£18.18.0) for unspecified literary work in London, the last such entry on record.[92] A paragraph in the 'London' column of the Adelaide *Advertiser* of 15 October 1900 notes that Levey had severed his connection with the *Age* after 'friendly

---

[85] DS to W. Wynne, 15 March 1900, LB5, p. 371; DS to W. Turner, 18 April 1900, LB5, p. 378.
[86] Entry for Garnett in Wages Book, p. 177.
[87] DS to W. Garnett, 25 April, 11 July, 16 August, 24 October 1900, 2 January 1901, LB5, pp. 382, 392–393, 398–399, 407, 408.
[88] DS to G. Levey, 18, 25 April 1900, LB5, pp. 379–380, 383–384.
[89] DS to G. Levey, 11 July 1900, LB5, p. 391.
[90] DS to G. Levey, 18 September 1900, LB5, pp. 403–404.
[91] DS to G. Levey, 3 October 1900, LB5, p. 405.
[92] Profit and loss accounts, 1901–1910, SFP Box 1192/1.

relations of thirty-two years', that he was now 'heavily occupied with the Paris Exhibition', and that Syme regretted the 'parting with his old friend and colleague'.[93] The item describes Levey's successor, Garnett, as 'a quiet man, spending most of his time amongst his books', conversant with military matters but most interested in art criticism. As with earlier complicated double-dealing over appointments at a remove, this episode demonstrates Syme's pushing for a solution, impatient of delay and insensitive to personal niceties.

Besides the regular correspondence Syme, as usual, was arranging for fact-finding missions, reports of which were usually to be shared with his Adelaide and Sydney newspaper fellows. In April 1898 he was arranging to receive reports from John Dow, who was undertaking a tour of the United States. Bonython agreed to take them; Wynne this time was not interested.[94] The series 'America Revisited' appeared as 52 articles in the *Leader* from 30 July 1898 to 22 July 1899, some after Dow's return to Australia earlier in the year.

Antarctic exploration during these years called for press coverage. The Belgian Antarctic Expedition of 1897–98, was the first to spend a winter in the southern polar region, when the *Belgica*, was trapped in pack ice (T. Griffiths 2007, 162–172). Syme and the *Argus* proprietors were asked to submit their offers for the publishing rights, but appear not to have acted.[95] In any case, there was slight press coverage of this venture, although the *Sydney Morning Herald* ran a two-part series by its leader, Dr Adrien De Gerlache, on 24 and 26 March 1898, the second written in Punta Arenas, Chile, before the expedition went further south, out of contact, and came to grief.

By contrast, a British expedition was covered widely and often in the Australian press.[96] Sponsored by the Royal Geographical Society and substantially funded by publisher Sir George Newnes, it was led by English–Norwegian Carsten Borchgrevink, who had spent several years in Australia from 1888. In mid-August Borchgrevink and his co-expeditioners sailed from England in the *Southern Cross*. They were feted in Hobart and Launceston before arriving in Melbourne, where an interview 'A Chat with

---

[93] 'Personal Notes from London', *Advertiser* (Adelaide), 15 October 1900, p. 5.
[94] DS to J. Bonython, 21, 30 April 1898, LB5, pp. 268, 269; J. Bonython to DS ('My dear Syme'), 28 January 1899, Bonython Letter Books.
[95] DS to [no addressee] 30 July 1897, LB5, p. 235.
[96] For example, for 1898 'The Expedition to the South Pole', *Sydney Morning Herald*, 9 June 1898, p. 6.

CHAPTER 14

Mr Borchgrevink' was published in the *Age* on 8 December and appeared also, by prior agreement, in the Adelaide *Advertiser*.[97] From Australia, the *Southern Cross* visited New Zealand then made for Cape Adare, Victoria Land on the Antarctic mainland. Left there with a prefabricated hut and supplies for almost a year, the party was picked up again by their ship in early 1900 and taken to New Zealand, Australia and, by the end of May, England. From June, newspapers in several colonies published 'copyrighted' accounts written by Borchgrevink, possibly with Newnes's assistance. Publishing-savvy, he may have been active in signing up the numerous papers, including the Launceston *Examiner*, which, with rights for 'Northern Tasmania', ran a series 'The Great Ice-Land', while 'Amid Antarctic Ice' was coming out in the Adelaide *Advertiser* and 'A Winter in the Antarctic' in the *Age*. Syme, Bonython and Wynne appear to have negotiated a one-third share each, as was their custom, but not to have had any part in agreements reached by other papers.[98]

Spencer and Gillen expedition

Perhaps Syme was tiring of collaboration, for in funding the 1901 Spencer–Gillen anthropological expedition to the Northern Territory he acted alone, thus gaining sole rights to the reports sent back and published as a series, 'Aborigines of Australia', comprising 26 articles in the *Leader* from 25 May 1901 to 12 April 1902. A few also had simultaneous publication in the Saturday *Age*, under the series heading 'Across Australia' (later to be reused as the title of a Spencer and Gillen book). The expeditioners, Professor Baldwin Spencer of the University of Melbourne and Francis Gillen, until 1899 postmaster at Alice Springs, had met on the 1894 expedition led by W.A. Horn, and collaborated as authors of *The Native Tribes of Central Australia* (Mulvaney and Calaby 1985, 162–180). Published in 1899, this work received international praise and favourable notice in Australian newspapers into 1900, when Spencer was contemplating another expedition, to continue his studies of Aboriginal 'tribes'. For this there was much support from England, the *Argus* of 31 August reporting that a petition, signed by classical scholar and anthropologist James Frazer and many English scientists who held the Spencer–Gillen research in high regard, had been forwarded via their Agents-General in London to the Victorian and South Australian Governments asking that the men be

---

[97] J. Bonython to DS & Co., 25 October 1898, Bonython Letter Books.
[98] J. Bonython to DS & Co., 16 December 1898, Bonython Letter Books; DS to W. Wynne, 12 April 1899, LB5, p. 294.

granted 12 months' leave to undertake field work amongst Aborigines. As widely reported in the press in early September, both men were given leave, the Victorian Government promising £500 to pay a locum for Spencer, but declining to fund the expedition itself.

Journalist and author Alexander Sutherland, in a letter to the editor in the *Argus* of 25 September, deplored the meanness of the Victorian Government in contrast to the English, which had spent £100,000 on Antarctic exploration, and pointed out that it was a chance for an anthropologist to study Aboriginal tribes before they were 'contaminated' by civilisation. But by this time funding had been secured. A deputation from the University Council had sought help from Syme, who made an offer in writing on 28 September to pay the whole of the expedition expenses,[99] which he took to be the £1000 sought from the Government (Adams 1966, 58). This generosity was reported and acclaimed in newspapers around Australia, from 29 September onwards.

Spencer and Gillen left Adelaide by train in mid-March 1901 for inland Oodnadatta, from where their expedition would depart. Their route and progress can be roughly traced through press reports, as for the most part they were in telegraphic contact at their stopping points. They had a base camp at Alice Springs in April and May, at Barrow Creek further north in July, at Tennant Creek in September. Thereafter, newspaper reports are scant until the expeditioners fetched up at Borroloola on the Gulf of Carpentaria in late November. Frustratingly, they were unable to obtain transport south for nearly three months, but could get mail out and thus report, albeit anticlimactically, on their *in*activity. Gillen's diary entries ('camp jottings') for the months away indicate that Spencer worked almost relentlessly, not only on his anthropological surveying, including taking photographs and, innovatively, making audio (phonographic) and video (cinematographic) recordings, but also writing articles and preparing illustrations for despatch to the *Age* office (Gillen 1968). The expedition itself was getting press coverage from telegraphed reports and private contacts as well as Spencer's articles in the *Leader* and *Age*. Several newspapers reproduced some articles, with attribution to the *Age* or *Leader* but with no indication of permission given.

With his £1000 subsidy Syme in effect was paying more than £38 for each article, a generous amount compared with the going rate of £2.2s. for a contributed leader, even taking into account the greater length of the Spencer–Gillen articles. But more than a matter of securing copy for his newspapers

---

[99] John Mulvaney's photocopy of letter from Syme to E.E. Morris 28 September 1900 (original held privately).

CHAPTER 14

– for yesterday's news is soon forgotten – Syme's outlay was substantially a philanthropic contribution to scholarship and gave him some kudos in the world of books and scientific research. Data gathered during 1901 fed into the scholarly *The Northern Tribes of Central Australia*, published by Macmillan in 1904. The named authors, Spencer and Gillen, dedicate the book to 'David Syme, Whose Generosity Rendered our Work Possible', while their preface expresses 'warmest thanks', in the hope that results would justify the help received. Spencer later drew upon the *Leader* articles for two works for a general readership – *Across Australia* (1912) and *Wanderings in Wild Australia* (1928) – although without acknowledgment of their first publication. As early as June 1901 Gillen had considered that Spencer's articles, which embodied their findings in a 'highly popular form…should make an interesting and highly saleable volume'. Having been treated generously as a joint author, he nevertheless developed a hatred for Syme and his newspapers, vented in several letters to Spencer over the next few years. On 21 July 1902 he wrote: 'I loathe that old beast Syme simply because he insisted upon dragging his pound of flesh off your bare bones' (Gillen 1968, 130; 1997, 378). Spencer's biographer John Mulvaney considers that Gillen's uncharacteristic crticism possibly related to sympathy for the hot and weary hours that Spencer spent writing and developing photographs to meet article deadlines. Also, Syme's donation failed to cover expedition costs that Spencer met personally.[100]

Perhaps influenced by the publication of Spencer's contributions, John Gregory, Professor of Geology and Mineralogy at the University of Melbourne, late in 1901 offered to supply several of his reports as the outcome of his forthcoming trip with geology students to examine fossil remains at Lake Eyre in South Australia. Syme responded guardedly on 5 December that he would need to see the contributions before deciding, while Gregory's party left Adelaide by train for the north on 13 December.[101] The matter would be taken up again in 1902.

Federation

With his wide span of interests and continual claims on his time, Syme nevertheless was involved in celebratory–social functions leading up to Federation on 1 January 1901 and linked with the opening of Federal Parliament in May. He and Annabella and other leading newspaper men and

---

[100] Personal communication, 13 October 2013.
[101] DS to J. Gregory, 5 December 1901, LB5, p. 425; 'Personal', *Advertiser* (Adelaide), 14 December 1901, p. 8.

their wives were part of the 'Federal Theatre Party' at the Princess Theatre in January 1898.[102] He attended a dinner at Parliament House, hosted by Sir William Zeal, President of the Legislative Council, a gathering 'of a purely private nature', for the Lieutenant Governor in July 1900.[103] Present also were other newspaper people, including country press proprietor Mitchell Armstrong, who knew Syme from his earliest years at the *Age* in the 1850s. Syme and Annabella were at a reception at Government House on 8 May 1901, the eve of the opening of Federal Parliament, reported in the *Age* the next day as 'A Brilliant Gathering' attended by 'over 2000 Guests'. These included a sizeable Syme contingent: besides David and Annabella, also his sons Arthur and Herbert and their wives, and his nephew Dr George Syme. Geoffrey and Oswald were then overseas; Francis apparently did not make the grade, nor did Lucie and spouse William. Nephew Joseph Cowen Syme was absent, but had earlier attended a similar function, perhaps an exercise of tact on the part of the organisers.

Syme's presence at the opening of the first Commonwealth Parliament by the Duke of York (later King George V) on 9 May is depicted in the painting of the occasion by the official artist, Tom Roberts ('Key to Tom Roberts' 1903 [no. 51]). The ceremony took place in the imposing Melbourne Exhibition Building, designed by Reed for the International Exhibition of 1880 and extended for the 1888 Centennial one but which, as observed in the *Age* of 30 November 1900, had come to be seen as a 'white elephant' until the decision to use it for this purpose (which helped its preservation; in 2004 it was placed on the World Heritage Register) ('Royal Exhibition Building' 2010). In Roberts' painting Syme is shown standing to the left of the Royal dais with 10 other prominent men of the Melbourne, Sydney and Brisbane press (excluding Bonython, recently elected Member of the House of Representatives and thus grouped with other novitiate Federal politicians). This cannot, however, be taken as conclusive proof of where Syme stood, and perhaps not even of his attendance. Waters, there to report the occasion for the *Age*, later wrote that he stood left of the dais, and did not notice Syme (Waters 1951, 57). Moreover, Roberts told Waters (the two had become friends) that in his work of art he had replaced a group of working journalists by citizens of 'high transient renown or solid monetary pull' who had attended, but less conspicuously. Whether or not Syme was actually

---

[102] 'The Federal Theatre Party', *Melbourne Punch*, 27 January 1898, p. 82.
[103] *Melbourne Punch*, 19 July 1900, p. 73, col. 2; 'Personal', *Argus*, 18 July 1900, p. 7.

CHAPTER 14

present, the painting is witness to the contemporary regard for the press and its leading personages.

Syme's involvement in the politics of Federal union is evident from Deakin's diary entries and his retrospective accounts of events (Deakin 1944), read together with relevant *Age* editorials. One instance is the success of the 'how to vote' recommendation for Victorian delegates to the Adelaide Federal Convention of March 1897, first published in the *Age* editorial on 25 February that year. From 29 nominations, 10 delegates were to be elected, their task to help frame and amend a constitution for popular acceptance. The 10 names listed in the *Age* include Premier Turner and six MLAs aligned with him: Deakin; Henry Higgins (tutor to Herbert and Francis Syme during their first year at university); Isaac Isaacs (Attorney-General, who had promoted the proposed libel legislation for the Australasian Institute of Journalists in the early 1890s); Alexander Peacock (Chief Secretary); Graham Berry (champion of liberal reform in the 1870s, now frail and soon to lose his seat); and William Trenwith (of labour leanings, advocating welfare measures that the *Age* supported, but who would run foul of Syme and his paper in 1902). There was lawyer Dr John Quick, on the *Age* staff in the 1870s and already heavily involved in planning for Federation. Although termed the 'Liberal Ten', the list also included two conservative MLCs, Simon Fraser and William Zeal, both friends of Syme (Deakin 1944, 65).

Victorians voted on 4 March. The *Age* 10 were elected, trumpeted in the paper the next day as a 'Great Liberal Victory', with the comment a day later that 'the people at large are to be congratulated'. More than resulting simply from overweening power of Syme and the *Age*, the 'victory' arose from the fact that the *Age*, with a circulation probably well over 100,000, cleverly provided specific, unambiguous guidance to a vast number of people as to how they might vote, if interested (voting not then compulsory). The *Argus*, by contrast, was less clear and consistent. On 25 February it too published guidance – a 'classified list' giving names of *all* nominations, with its 10 recommendations, those for a 'free, uncoerced Australian Parliament', in capital letters. Only one candidate, Fraser, was also an *Age* selection. The following day, and repeated until polling day, the *Argus* carried two different lists: that of the anti-socialist, patriotic Australasian National League, which it advocated; and of the Trades Hall, which it strongly opposed. The favoured list, printed in bold type, included the *Age*'s Turner, Fraser and Zeal; the Trades-Hall one had eight of its 10 in common with the *Age*. The *Argus* also had several letters to the editor (planted?) with varying general and specific suggestions. In addition to its somewhat confusing approach, its circulation of 43,500 was surely less than half that of its rival.[104] Little wonder that the generally respectable and competent 'Liberal Ten' were victorious.

Deakin, himself a nominee for Adelaide, implied that it was Syme (not Windsor or one of the leader writers) who drew up the list, its members all being associates and friends (Deakin 1944, 65). There is no indication that he advised or influenced Syme in so doing, but the two, in regular contact, surely discussed it when meeting, as Deakin's diary records, on 17 February 1897. Deakin did exert influence a year later, however, in relation to the Constitution Bill, drafted at meetings in Adelaide, Sydney and Melbourne. While generally favouring Federation, Syme and Windsor had reservations about the Bill, particularly in relation to tariff protection for Victorian manufacturers. The Victorian referendum to accept or reject it looming in early 1898, the *Age* had been generally negative in its leaders.[105] Meeting with Syme and Hoare (presumably standing in for a sick Windsor) on 14 March, Deakin was asked to put the *Age* view to the Australian Natives Association, whose members he was to address at Bendigo the next day (Deakin 1944, 93).

Contrary to Syme's instructions, when Deakin spoke to the membership at a banquet following the annual meeting he resoundingly endorsed the 'yes' view for which the Natives Association had already opted. During the weeks following, the *Age* continued to express reservations and, relatively impartially, put the case for both sides. As historian John Hirst (2000, 79) has written, it 'would be hard for the Victorian ministry to carry federation with the *Age* opposed'. Only too aware of this, Deakin, over the course of several meetings in late May, persuaded Syme to modify his views and was able to record in his diary for 31 May: 'Age declares for bill.'[106] Hirst (2000, 184) has stated that Deakin did, at Syme's invitation, draft the editorial; Deakin's biographer La Nauze (1979, 176) has doubted that this was so, although Deakin's diary entries show that at this time and for several months afterwards he was responsible for some of the *Age* 'articles' (leaders and sub-leaders).[107] As for authorship of the 3 June polling day leader recommending the 'Yes' vote, Hoare (1927, 166) implied it was Windsor, while reporter Cockerill (1943, 102) has written that it

---

[104] 'Circulation', 'Historical Records of "The Argus" and "The Australasian"', compiled by C.P. Smith, [1924], MS 10727, Australian Manuscripts Collection, State Library of Victoria.

[105] For example, editorials in *Age*, 12 and 14 March 1898.

[106] Diary entry for 31 May 1898, Deakin Papers, Series 2.

[107] Several diary entries between 27 May and 11 August 1898, Deakin Papers, Series 2.

CHAPTER 14

was (uncharacteristically) Syme. In any case, the desired outcome eventuated: For 100,520, Against 22,029 (*Australian Encyclopaedia* 1927, v.1, 450).

By September 1899, five of the six colonies had declared for the Bill and Western Australia would do so on 31 July 1900, by which time it had passed in the imperial parliament. The delegation of representatives of five colonies in London to monitor its passage and ensure it was not altered was led by Edmund Barton, representing New South Wales; Deakin spoke for Victoria. The Act received Royal Assent on 9 July. On 13 July Queen Victoria approved the appointment of Australia's first Governor General, the Earl of Hopetoun, who had been Governor of Victoria 1889 to 1895 (Cuneen 1983). Unwell from a bout of typhoid en route, Hopetoun arrived in Sydney on 15 December. His immediate task was to name a Prime Minister who would then form a Ministry, this to be accomplished by 1 January 1901. Elections for members of the House of Representatives and the Senate were to take place early in the New Year.

Syme, again urged by Deakin, played a key part in the choice of Prime Minister. Syme had favoured Sir William Lyne, Premier of New South Wales and a protectionist who, like Syme, had been lukewarm about Federation (Sayers 1965, 222). Hopetoun, on 19 December, invited Lyne to fill the position. This invitation has since been termed the 'Hopetoun blunder' made by a man 'ill and poorly advised', for Lyne was not able to attract a suitable Ministry – Barton would not serve under him and Turner would not serve without Barton! (Hirst 1998). Accordingly, Lyne returned his commission and on 25 December, Christmas Day, the Governor-General sent for Barton to assume the Prime Ministership.[108]

Once again, Deakin had involved Syme. On 22 December, when it was known that Hopetoun had summoned Lyne, Deakin, as his diary shows, 'persuaded DS to wire Barton essential'. Similarly, for 24 December Deakin recorded 'Met DS his office. Persuaded him telegraph ultimatum'. Subsequently (and presumably telegrams from Syme played a part) Lyne removed himself from the scene (La Nauze 1979, 209–210). Deakin was contacted by Turner – 'Turner telegraphs Barton wants me at once', he recorded in his diary for 24 December – and accordingly on 26 December travelled to Sydney, remaining there for the inauguration pageant on 1 January 1901 ('Birth of a New Nation', the *Age* of 2 January headlined its coverage). The summoning of Lyne, his difficulties and resignation, and the subsequent choice of Barton are progressively reported in issues of the

---

[108] Editorial, *Age*, 26 December 1900, p. 4.

Age, together with cautious – certainly not rabble-rousing – comment. The editorial of 21 December noted that numerous 'leading politicians' supported Barton over Lyne for the position. On 26 December came the explanation that Lyne was unable to form a sufficiently strong government, the Victorian and South Australian Premiers unwilling to serve under him. As with the Constitution Bill, Deakin used his relationship with Syme to have views that he came to see vital expressed in the influential *Age*. Under Deakin's influence, no longer was Syme the prime mover in political plotting.

Syme's concern that the new Australian government adopt a tariff policy to his liking was manifested in the 9 January *Age* editorial, 'A Federal Tariff', and items on the topic in issues of the following days. Later in the month, however, the illness of Queen Victoria, her death on 22 January and memorial services, etc. captured the headlines, while pages and columns were marked with heavy black borders. A Fund for a National Monument was soon launched by the Mayor of Melbourne, with the *Age* on 29 January announcing its 'Shilling Fund' towards this, and Syme's donation of 2000 shillings (£100) to set an example. By the end of May contributions had risen to almost 34,000 shillings (£1700). Some £7000 would be raised from various sources, including the fund set up by the *Argus*, and lengthy, conflicting deliberations about a site ensued. Eventually, after the Queen Victoria Memorial Gardens were established beside St Kilda Road near Princes Bridge, a white marble and granite monument was erected there, unveiled in 1907 ('Queen Victoria Memorial' 2012).

By mid-March the leading topic in newspapers was the coming Federal elections, the *Age* proffering voting advice for polling day 29 March – advocacy of pro-protection candidates for seats in the House of Representatives and Senate. On Saturday 30 March the paper announced 'Great Liberal Triumph. Overwhelming Protectionist Vote', repeating these perhaps overstated observations on Monday 1 April. Following the excitement Syme apparently needed a rest, accepting an invitation from Simon Fraser (who had topped results for the Senate) to stay at his property, Nyang, in the Riverina district of southern New South Wales. In April he was there for 10 days, then went to Killara for several more, before returning to Melbourne and the office.[109] Perhaps it was also the strain of political involvement that had caused him to take to his bed for two days at the end of 1900 – 'a very

---

[109] DS to GS and O. Syme, undated [inferentially April 1901], quoted in Sayers (1965, 253–254).

CHAPTER 14

unusual circumstance', he had written to London correspondent William Garnett on 2 January.[110]

Geoffrey and Oswald to learn the ropes

Syme wrote on 13 March to Frank Lloyd, son of the late Edward and now proprietor of the *Daily Chronicle*, that he was sending his two youngest sons 'forth on their travels…[to] see something of the old world before settling down to work in the new'.[111] He explained that he had hoped to accompany them but could not, because the forthcoming elections would keep him in Melbourne, and he would be 'greatly obliged' if Lloyd would give them 'facilities for examining the making of a first class London newspaper' including going out with reporters on their rounds. This organising and support for the two sons contrasts strongly with Syme's own early independence and self-sufficiency: at Oswald's age (almost 23) he would soon take himself from Scotland to California; at Geoffrey's (28) he had been remuneratively prospecting on the Victorian goldfields for some three years.

On 26 March Geoffrey and Oswald sailed in the *Britannia* for London.[112] A scattering of letters between sons and parents written during their absence survives, some held privately, some in the Syme Family Papers held at the State Library of Victoria, a few quoted by Sayers but not located. Together these letters, affectionate and newsy, convey warm and close relations between family members. Several refer to photographs taken by Herbert that were sent to the brothers and shown around to relatives in Britain. Obviously, there were many more written and received. For instance, that very early in their voyage, Geoffrey and Oswald each wrote from Fremantle to their parents is clear from their father's reply.[113]

Apart from their commitment at the *Daily Chronicle* office, the sons made many family visits – to Garnetts in Yorkshire and Lancashire, to a Johnson cousin in Aberdeen – and travelled in Europe. Geoffrey went to the Continent in late October, spending a month mostly in Italy. Oswald, who had earlier in the year been to Holland, Germany and perhaps other countries, was back in Britain by mid-September and wanting to go home.

---

[110] DS to W. Garnett, 2 January 1901, LB5, p. 408.
[111] DS to F. Lloyd, 13 March 1901, LB5, p. 413.
[112] 'Shipping Intelligence', *Argus*, 27 March 1901, p. 6.
[113] DS to GS and O. Syme, undated [inferentially April 1901, quoted in Sayers (1965, 253–254).

Although Geoffrey wrote reassuringly on 20 September to his father that Oswald had made lots of visits and good use of his time, it would appear that Syme's youngest son was not making the most of the career opportunity arranged for him.[114] Indeed, Syme was worried that he might acquire 'idle habits' and, in a letter of 10 September, asked Geoffrey to arrange return home 'in good company'.[115] Oswald arrived in Melbourne in December, over three months before his brother.[116]

Geoffrey was dutiful and diligent. Syme wrote to him on 7 July with supplementary advice: 'You should get to know as many literary people as you can: attend lectures, hear all the prominent preachers [meaning speakers, not clergymen] and acquaint yourself with the intellectual life of London.'[117] Indicating a more practical focus, on 12 September Geoffrey wrote to his mother that he had been busy in London, visiting 'several of the large offices, Hoe's printing works & so on' and the paper mill at Sittingbourne, Kent, established by Edward Lloyd in the 1870s, from which he had 'copious notes to transcribe'.[118] He took up the *Daily Chronicle* arrangement for two to three weeks in December, reporting to his father on 12 December that he had seen *Daily Chronicle* editor W.J. Fisher, had a first interview with the chief of staff and would be spending more time with him and then with subeditors and editorial branches.[119] By 20 December he had gained a 'thorough insight' into the editorial department, he wrote to his mother, with heads of branches 'affording me every information'.[120] He thought there was no point in actually joining the staff unless he could be there for a month or two, which was 'out of the question' – as will be seen, he had other plans for the New Year.

If Geoffrey's period of work experience was relatively short, he was very active on several fronts, some on his father's behalf. On 28 September he wrote asking Syme what to do with two bundles of unbound copies of his book.[121] This was probably the 100 copies of *Representative Government* that Syme had asked publishers Kegan Paul to be forwarded to agent Edward

---

[114] GS to DS, 20 September 1901, held by Dr Veronica Condon
[115] DS to GS, 10 September 1901, quoted in Sayers (1965, 254–255).
[116] Unassisted Inward Passenger Lists to Victoria 1852–1923, Public Record Office Victoria.
[117] DS to GS, 7 July 1901, quoted in Sayers (1965, 255).
[118] GS to AS, 12 September 1901, held by Dr Veronica Condon.
[119] GS to DS, 12 December 1901, held by Dr Veronica Condon.
[120] GS to AS, 20 December 1901, held by Dr Veronica Condon.
[121] GS to DS, 28 September 1901, held by Dr Veronica Condon.

CHAPTER 14

Lloyd, instructing them to pulp the remainder of unsold copies.[122] Syme, in his letter of 7 July, asked Geoffrey to think about new London office premises, preferably for the *Age* only.[123] But when, soon after, Bonython secured a building for the *Age* and its syndicate partners, Syme, in his 24 September letter, then asked his son to arrange signage, with the *Age* in a prominent position.[124] This seems not to have been feasible, for on 12 December Geoffrey wrote that the building was unsuitable for advertising.[125] On 24 October he wrote to his parents that he had tried to contact Windsor and met Byrne.[126] He may have played some part in having the *Age* in July advertise prominently 'The Library of Famous Literature', edited by Richard Garnett, who had retired from British Museum in 1899. Containing more than 1000 'masterpieces', it was claimed to be 'a huge treasury of the finest and most interesting pieces of literature' from the dawn of civilisation to the authors of today'.[127] Distributed in Victoria and Tasmania by Gordon and Gotch, volumes could be examined and orders placed at the *Age* office. And just possibly Geoffrey had some part in the 'Australian Affairs Viewed from London' column that in July began to appear in the *Age*, although the feature continued after his return to Melbourne. He did write a letter to the *Daily Chronicle* about the newspaper's unfair representation of Australia, not yet published he wrote his mother on 20 December.[128]

In their letters, father and son exchanged news and views on current political issues. Syme kept him informed about tariff matters and sent interesting snippets, such as that Edward Findley had been defeated in the August State elections – a freedom of the press matter of interest to them both.[129] Politician Findley was also a printer and publisher who, earlier in the year, had been expelled from the Assembly for his association with the weekly *Tocsin*, in which an article critical of the new King, Edward VII, had been reprinted from the Dublin *Irish People*, causing that newspaper to be suppressed (Marshall 1981).[130] Geoffrey commented frequently on

---

[122] DS to Kegan Paul, Trench & Co., 20 March 1900, LB5, p. 372.
[123] DS to GS, 7 July 1901, quoted in Sayers (1965, 255).
[124] DS to GS. 24 September 1901, quoted in Sayers (1965, 254–255).
[125] GS to DS, 12 December 1901, held by Dr Veronica Condon.
[126] GS to DS, 24 October 1901, held by Dr Veronica Condon.
[127] For example, in full-page advertisement, *Age*, 31 July, 1 August 1901, p. 5.
[128] GS to AS, 20 December 1901, held by Dr Veronica Condon.
[129] DS to GS, undated, [inferentially August], quoted in Sayers (1965, 254) where it is erroneously dated 17 March.
[130] 'Foul Libel on the King', *Argus*, 26 June 1901, p. 5.

the news from Melbourne, read in weekly packages of the *Age*. Altogether, Syme was pleased with his son, writing on 10 September that he was 'looking forward to the time when you will relieve me from some of my duties and make a name for your self as a journalist'.[131] In the same letter he advised him that he planned to put him in charge of the reporting staff, with Fox heading the Parliamentary reporters (a demotion for the latter, surely). Syme's professional and personal closeness to this son he articulated in his letter of 7 July: 'I miss you very much in many things, both in the office and elsewhere'.[132] Father and son sharing interests also in agricultural matters, Geoffrey found time, evident from several letters, to attend agricultural shows, inspect milking machines and stock, and enquire about breeds and availability of goats and pass on relevant information to Syme.

For Geoffrey the most momentous outcome of his time in England was his engagement to young Violet Garnett to whom, through his mother, he was distantly related. Annabella's mother, Martha Johnson, was born a Garnett, and Violet and Geoffrey had as common ancestor William Garnett (1760–1832), a paper manufacturer and father of Jeremiah Garnett, co-founder of the *Manchester Guardian* (Condon 2005). Born 3 May 1883, Violet was the eldest daughter of Tom Garnett, who lived at Radclyffe, Clitheroe, Lancashire, where Geoffrey probably met her when doing the rounds of the extended family (which, more distantly, included the brothers William, *Age* reporter and correspondent, and Richard, formerly of the British Museum). Apparently Violet and Geoffrey were instantly attracted and by July had decided to become engaged to marry.

It seems that Geoffrey wrote to and cabled his parents in early July of his engagement, conditional on their consent, with Syme replying favourably by letter on 10 September, 'having full faith in your judgement in making your choice' and also cabling his approval.[133] He suggested they prolong the engagement to get to know each other. But two weeks later he was urging haste rather than delay: 'If it is to be, why not sooner than January?'[134] His offer of Conisbro, his Kew property adjacent to Blythswood, as a residence for the couple, Geoffrey gratefully accepted. Financially dependent on his father, he had at least twice to ask him for more funds, sending thanks in November and again in December for £500

---

[131] DS to GS, 10 September 1901, quoted in Sayers (1965, 254–255).
[132] DS to GS, 7 July 1901, quoted in Sayers (1965, 255).
[133] DS to GS, 10 September 1901, quoted in Sayers (1965, 254–255).
[134] DS to GS, 24 September 1901, quoted in Sayers (1965, 255–256).

CHAPTER 14

received.¹³⁵ In spite of Syme's urging, he and Violet did not alter their intention to marry in January 1902 and leave for Melbourne in February. In the meantime, Geoffrey was made welcome at his prospective in-laws' Radclyffe, where he spent Christmas.

In 1901, besides aiming to shape the future of the new nation, Syme, nearing his mid-70s, clearly was giving thought not only to the immediate future of his family and his business concerns, but to their future after his demise. In his letter of 10 September he told Geoffrey that the business income, about £50,000 a year, would on his death be equally divided between the five brothers, while his sisters and their mother would be provided with annuities from outside sources.¹³⁶ It is not known whether at this stage he had legalised this in a will. It seems he was then in good health and spirits, Annabella writing to Oswald on 17 September that 'Papa' was 'much as usual', receiving compliments on how well he looks, and to Geoffrey on 5 November describing a busy round of social engagements involving her and Syme.¹³⁷ He apparently had a bout of ill health in late November, but by 2 December was 'better', his mother wrote to Oswald.¹³⁸

Together with his multifarious public and personal pursuits, Syme had been reflecting on and writing about the big questions of the meaning of life, the nature of existence. In late 1901 he was readying a draft of his latest and last book, *The Soul*, to submit to a publisher. Its subject matter was a natural extension of ideas sketched in his earlier *On the Modification of Organisms*. If he had come across the favourable, albeit brief, reference to the book in an article on 'Darwinian Botany' by author and journalist Alexander Japp in the *London Quarterly Review* of October 1901 he would have been gratified to find his ideas still in circulation. In September 1897 he had sent a copy of *Modification* to plant pathologist Daniel McAlpine, Scottish-born, who had come to Melbourne in 1844; in it he stated that he had learned of his interest though a 'mutual friend' and remarked that, unlike Darwin, he and McAlpine saw Nature as a 'living force'.¹³⁹

By the end of August 1901 Syme had a draft of the new book, conveniently set in linotype, which he asked Deakin to 'cut and mangle'

135	GS to DS, 21 November and 12 December 1901, held by Dr Veronica Condon.
136	DS to GS, 10 September 1901, quoted in Sayers (1965, 254–255).
137	AS to O. Syme, 17 September 1901, SFP Box 1180/6(a); AS to GS, 5 November 1901, quoted in Sayers (1965, 224).
138	AS to O. Syme, 2 December 1901, SFP Box 1180/6(a).
139	DS to D. McAlpine, 20 September 1897, LB5, p. 244.

as he saw fit.[140] He explained that since his brother George was no longer around to consult, he would trust in Deakin's judgment. Two weeks later he set about having a chapter from the draft published as an article in the English periodical *Nineteenth Century and After*.[141] He explained to the owner-editor James Knowles that it was about 'the psychical basis of life' and set in linotype, and that he required no remuneration but wished to reserve right of republication. He identified himself as the author of three books ('one on Political Economy, a second on Parliamentary Government, & a third on Biology') and as 'the proprietor of the Age, a journal which has the largest circulation in this part of the world'. He said that his agent (possibly Byrne, who in 1902 would deal on Syme's behalf with his publisher) would call after Knowles had time to peruse the article. Knowles's response is not known, but in any case the article was not published. *The Soul*, however, would appear, in 1903.

Syme at the end of 1901 had several more years of active life, but he would be less concerned with his newspaper business and would expend a last burst of energy in different directions.

---

[140] DS to A. Deakin, 31 August 1901, Deakin Papers, Series 1.
[141] DS to J. Knowles, 17 September 1901, LB5, p. 422.

Chapter 15

'I WILL SEE THE THING THROUGH'

(January 1902 to February 1908)

In the last chapter of his life Syme withdrew from day-to-day control of his newspapers, although officially in charge of the business and liable to intervene at any time. Integral to this retreat was his disillusion with and relative marginalisation from politics at all three levels – municipal, state and federal. A critical point was reached in 1904, the *Age* golden jubilee year, in a *contretemps* with Deakin that served to clarify for both men the limits to the influence each could exert on the affairs of the other and to crystallise for Syme the role of the press in the political process and society in general. Far from retiring into the relative inertia of the elderly, however, during this final phase of some seven years he continued to be active on many fronts. He shepherded his final book, *The Soul*, through to publication and distribution. Absorbed as ever in his numerous financial, real estate and agricultural interests, he also initiated and carried through two innovative, challenging and costly property projects. Aware, however, that he was nearing the end of his life's span, in 1907 he commissioned his biography and provided recollections for it, and made binding, detailed arrangements for the future of his family, his firm, his extensive property holdings and, not least, his mortal remains.

Syme's progressive withdrawal from regular active engagement with the production of his newspapers is reflected in the falling-off of correspondence preserved in his letterbooks. For 1902, there are 20 letters from him relating to the business, seven in 1903 and only two in 1907. While not necessarily the whole story (there may have been letters not copied and there may have been more letterbooks, now lost, while of personal contacts and telephone conversations there are no records), seen in conjunction with the evidence of other growing preoccupations, it is strongly indicative. Business did not suffer, however, with profits soaring from £56,021 in 1902 to £69,493 in 1906

Figure 15.1. David Syme in later life. (Courtesy of Dr Veronica Condon)

and, though falling back in 1907, a still rewarding £68,112.[1] Advertising was a huge revenue source – the great volume of classifieds and the increasing prevalence of large block advertisements, sometimes running to a whole page.

On 9 December 1905 the Saturday *Age* was again 24 pages, as it had been in October 1888 at the height of the boom, and from late 1906 this size became standard for Saturday issues. The *Leader*, its jubilee noted on 6 January 1906, when it claimed to have fulfilled promises to be 'popular, impartial, and independent', was enlarged to 56 pages four months later and advertised in the *Age* of 22 May as the best illustrated paper in the Commonwealth for the price – thus implying superiority to the *Weekly Times*, also threepence per copy and 56 pages, but not necessarily to the *Australasian*, priced at sixpence.

---

[1] Profit and loss accounts, 1901–1910, SFP Box 1192/1.

CHAPTER 15

The *Age* stated the *Leader* to be the 'best and most widely read weekly journal in Australia', but circulation figures are not available to corroborate. The *Age* does not appear to have published its own circulation figures after the 1892 figure of 101,346, until September 1906, when it announced a daily average 106,343 from June to August.[2] In November 1906 the circulation was given as 109,616; in September 1907 as 113,476, a figure supplied repeatedly up to and for a short time after Syme's death in 1908.[3] Circulation of the perennial rival *Argus* was also rising steadily but, at 66,040 in 1907, still lagged far behind that of the *Age*.[4] In July 1907 printer and publisher Thomas Shaw Fitchett, son of journalist William Fitchett, when interviewed at Fremantle on returning to Australia, claimed the *Age* the most quoted Australian daily in England.[5]

Most of Syme's letterbook correspondence from 1902 to 1907 concerns relatively trivial matters. Some items are written directly to reporters rather than, as one might expect, to their chief of staff, Frank Fox – for example, complaints that the mining and bowling reports were too long.[6] The majority are nagging memos to subeditor Stephens, the last in February 1907.[7] There is no indication that Syme was in contact with Professor Gregory, whose Lake Eyre expedition of summer 1901/02 resulted in six articles entitled 'The Central Australian Steppes', published from 11 January to 8 March 1902 in the *Leader* and later as part of his *The Dead Heart of Australia*, published in London by John Murray in 1906. Nor is there any record of his involvement with the delayed return of Spencer and Gillen from their anthropological expedition in Central Australia, reported in issues of the *Age* in the early months of 1902 while their articles were still appearing in the *Leader*, the last on 12 April. The *Age* of 6 August 1904 carried a review of their scholarly *The Northern Tribes of Central Australia*, and Spencer's two-part 'The Steppe Lands of Central Australia' appeared in the daily on 7 and 21 October 1905.

In 1902 and 1903 but tapering off in 1904, Syme dealt with offers from some potential correspondents and contributors – guardedly willing to

---

2 'Circulation of "The Age"', *Age*, 5 September 1906. p. 8.
3 '"The Age" Circulation. A Record Week', *Age*, 26 November 1906, p. 5; 'Circulation of "The Age"', *Age*, 26 October 1907, p. 12.
4 'Circulation', 'Historical Records of "The Argus" and "The Australasian"', compiled by C.P. Smith, [1924], MS 10727, Australian Manuscripts Collection, State Library of Victoria.
5 '"The Age" Most Widely Quoted Paper in England', *Age*, 24 July 1907, p. 7.
6 DS to L. Klissa, 20 August 1902, LB5, p. 445; DS to J. Stephens, W. Wright, 24 November 1902, LB5, p. 456.
7 DS to J. Stephens from 13 March 1902 (LB5, p. 426) to 20 February 1907 (LB6, p. 31).

accept certain contributions from Sir John Bonython, who was travelling to Britain, declining reports from New Guinea and from the New Hebrides as both already covered (these letters written by son Oswald on his behalf), and enthusiastic about receiving contributions from a Hermann Woolf in Germany on agricultural subjects relevant to Australia.[8] Judging by items in his letterbook, he was particularly concerned on two fronts. One was the Sydney correspondence, at least until 1904, which inferentially he saw as more important than reports from other State capitals. Dissatisfied with Sydney-based W. Ely, he terminated his services August 1904.[9]

The other was news from the United States. Where formerly he regularly monitored 'Our London Letter' and various other generally less frequent features from the imperial centre, now it was the adequacy of news from the United States that seems to have become of particular importance – in addition to American news in cables still transmitted via London. (Hopefully awaited, the Pacific Cable from Vancouver in Canada to Southport in Queensland that opened on 9 December 1902 was deemed a failure – a long predicted deficit of £21,564 was reported in the *Age* of 21 September 1906 – and was not used at this time for direct despatch of news bulletins from North America.) Syme had not found it possible to retain a satisfactory correspondent in the States, and relied on bulletins compiled from latest American newspapers to hand. In June 1902 he ordered subscriptions to three additional newspapers – *Washington Post*, *Kansas City Journal* and *Boston Globe*.[10] While this may have been in part as source material for the new weekly *Every Saturday* (described below), these papers would also have served as a basis for the compilation of the somewhat irregular column of American news. Several times from mid-1902 he complained about its non-appearance, and its quality when it did appear. In August 1903 he secured a satisfactory San Francisco correspondent – Walter Smith, who had been a reporter for the *Age* from March 1901 to June 1903.[11] Syme continued to monitor this news; his last memo on file to Stephens, dated 20 February 1907 asks: 'Have you had time yet to send me your opinion about the American files?'[12]

---

[8] DS to J. Bonython, 24 March 1902, LB5, p. 428; DS to C. Sievewright, 19 May 1902, LB5, p. 436; DS to A. Foot, 5 June 1902, LB5, p. 439; DS to H. Woolf, 2 March 1903, LB5, p. 468.
[9] DS to W. Ely, 7 May 1903, 5 September 1904, LB5, pp. 473, 495.
[10] DS to J. Packer, 2 June 1902, LB5, p. 438.
[11] DS to J. Stephens, 22 August 1902, 28 April, 8 August 1903, LB5, pp. 448, 472, 480; DS to W. Smith, 19 August 1903, LB5, p. 479; Entry for W. Smith in Wages Book, p. 445.
[12] DS to J. Stephens, 20 February 1907, LB6, p. 31.

CHAPTER 15

With an Australian book publishing industry in its infancy, the Australian newspaper press was still a major outlet for literature, particularly fiction, long and short, which the *Age* and *Leader* continued to publish. Many of the authors were Australian, some of them later to achieve classic status. The *Age* in September 1902 had two Henry Lawson stories: 'His Brother's Keeper' and 'Barney, Take Me Home Again'.[13] Rosa Praed's 'The Lost Earl of Ellan' was serialised in the *Age* from 9 December 1905 to 26 May 1906. There were stories by Mary Grant Bruce – 'A Christmas Misadventure' in the 1905 Christmas number of the *Leader*, 'A Gippsland Sketch' in the *Age* of March 9 1906, and many more. In January 1908 Ethel Turner's 'That Girl' began in the *Leader*. It is not evident who had responsibility for procuring these novels and short stories. Syme does not appear to have appointed a deputy to manage the editorial and literary department during his absences, and on whom the work of commissioning and monitoring contributions devolved when he was otherwise occupied is not clear, although from mid-1905 son Geoffrey did progressively assume some responsibility.

The sons sent away to learn about the newspaper business came home in 1902. Returning first, Oswald was back on the payroll from 3 February, recorded as employed in the Counting House at a salary of £3 per week.[14] His duties were not confined to that area, for Syme's letterbook contains copies of several business letters written and signed by him on his father's behalf, dated between April 1902 and March 1903; moreover, from 1903 Oswald's salary was charged to 'Miscellaneous', rising in May 1905 to £4 per week, when for a year at least he had been full-time at Killara, possibly as manager, a situation he may have preferred – and his father may have deemed him more suited to rural pursuits. He told Geoffrey that, while pleased with Oswald, he had 'everything to learn' and he (Syme) did not want a 'repetition of Dalry' – alluding to mismanagement by son Francis.[15] (Ironically, almost half a century later Oswald would return to and play a significant role in securing the viability of David Syme and Co.)

During January 1902 Geoffrey kept his parents informed from England about his family and travel matters and his final dealings with the *Daily Chronicle*.[16] He wrote that the paper had published his letter about the

---

[13] *Age*, 6, 13, 20 September 1902.
[14] Entry for O. Syme in Wages Book, p. 443.
[15] DS to GS, 10 May 1904, held by Dr Veronica Condon.
[16] GS to DS, 2, 16 January 1902, held by Dr Veronica Condon.

Figure 15.2. Geoffrey Syme, 1908. (Courtesy of Dr Veronica Condon)

treatment of Australia in the English press, but with 'a great deal' excised. He reported having finally caught up with Windsor, who was planning a return to Melbourne, and having seen editor Fisher about taking on Windsor as a contributor. On 15 January he married young Violet Garnett at St Helens Church, Waddington, near Clitheroe. Reported briefly in the *Argus* of 22 February, the wedding is described in detail by Geoffrey's daughter Dr Veronica Condon (2005). On 24 February the newlyweds sailed on the *Australia* (also *Australien*) from Marseilles, disembarking in Melbourne on 1 April.[17]

---

[17] Unassisted Inward Passenger Lists to Victoria 1852–1923, Public Record Office Victoria; 'Shipping Intelligence', *Argus*, 2 April 1902.

CHAPTER 15

Every Saturday launched

Geoffrey was on the Syme payroll from 7 April, being paid £8 per week, more than double his younger brother.[18] Employed in the editorial and literary department, he did not after all displace Frank Fox as chief of staff as his father had earlier intended, but was made editor of a new magazine-cum-newspaper, *Every Saturday*. Scheduled to appear weekly from Saturday 21 June, it was flagged in the *Age* a week earlier by a notice above the editorial banner: 'Look Out For Every Saturday' and advertised in the paper the following Tuesday as a new, non-political weekly, not competing with any local journal and to contain all sorts of news in a 'concise and attractive form'. A small-format newsprint publication of 32 pages, priced at one penny, it contained a miscellany of light reading matter drawn mainly from American, French and English newspapers – 'a careful selection of news gathered from the press of the world…to supply instructive and entertaining matter', readers of the first issue were told. It could be seen as a greatly amplified, illustrated and popularised version of the 'Notes from Various Sources' column that had been appearing in the Saturday *Age*.

The idea for the new publication may have been sparked by the Sydney *World's News*, published from 21 December 1901 by the Daily Telegraph Newspaper Company and appraised in the *Liverpool Herald* as a 'journalistic enterprise' that was 'completely successful', 'the emphatic hit in the journalism of the Commonwealth'.[19] The Sydney *Bulletin* considered *Every Saturday* an inferior imitation, a 'snippet weekly…set up to give Geoffrey a congenial job and not giving the Australian writer a chance'.[20] However, the new Melbourne publication was widely advertised in newspapers throughout Australia and generally praised in a wide range of them, urban and rural, a few also pointing out its similarity to the English *Tit-Bits* (subtitled: *from all the Interesting Books, Periodicals and Newspapers of the World*), published from 1881 by George Newnes.[21] Indeed both *World's News* and *Every Saturday* were phenomena of the times, part of the popular mass journalism associated particularly with the English press baron Lord Northcliffe (Alfred Harmsworth) and, in these instances, being the production of periodicals that have been seen as 'not dedicated to news at all, but to digestible snippets of popular information'; published in parallel with mass-circulating dailies, they were a good source of income (A. Smith 1979, 156).

---

[18] Entry for G. Syme in Wages Book, p. 443.
[19] *Liverpool Herald*, 8 March 1902, p. 6, col. 3.
[20] 'The Inky Way', *Bulletin*, 12 July 1902, p. 28.
[21] For example, *Mercury* (Hobart), 24 June 1902, p. 5, col. 2.

Figure 15.3. Cover of *Every Saturday*, 12 October 1907
(Newspaper Collection, State Library of Victoria)

Despite losses for the first 18 months, incurred through a large expenditure on publicity in a great range of Australian newspapers and on posters displayed in railway stations, *Every Saturday* did prove to be a modest money-earner. In 1904 there was a net profit of £598, in 1905 it was £1112, in 1906 £1399, and in 1907 £1355.[22] Circulation peaked at 30,900 in 1908, declining thereafter, as did profits, and in 1912 *Every Saturday*,

---

[22] Profit and loss accounts, 1901–1910, SFP Box 1192/1.

CHAPTER 15

where Geoffrey had cut his editorial teeth, was sold to the Daily Telegraph Newspaper Company and incorporated into the rival *World's News*.

The editorial in the first number of *Every Saturday* states that original tales and other contributions would be welcome and, initially, the weekly contained several items on Australian subjects; however, the proportion of local content soon dwindled. The quantity of illustrations, mostly photographs, increased. This aspect would have suited Geoffrey's interest in photography, which manifested as early as 1887 when Syme sought information on behalf of the 14-year-old about the new Eastman camera.[23] But above all considerations, including profits, being editor of *Every Saturday* was invaluable experience for Geoffrey that would be applied in later years, after his father's death. Very likely Syme had this in mind when embarking on the new publishing venture and putting his son in charge. Geoffrey held the position until February 1904, when he left for England.[24] By this time he had established the weekly on a sound and potentially profitable footing. Reporter J.J. Darbyshire was appointed to replace him; reporter G.R. Brickhill took over in 1907.[25]

The Soul

Newspaper work apart, from 1902 to 1904 Syme was often preoccupied with getting his fourth and last book, *The Soul*, to publication and adequate distribution. Deakin was again called on for help, spending several days in February and March 1902 reading through the linotyped draft and making corrections.[26] On 15 April Syme dispatched the corrected linotyped document to Macmillan & Co. with a lengthy letter in which he expressed the hope it would meet with approval and set out detailed procedural instructions and advice, named London correspondent Desmond Byrne as his agent and stated that he might be in England 'in a month or two' (which did not eventuate).[27]

Macmillan did approve, after receiving a favourable reader's report, dated 23 May, from Henry Jones (later Sir), professor of moral philosophy at Glasgow University. Jones deemed it 'a small book on a very great subject',

---

23   H. Lustone to DS, 14 June 1887, SFP Box 1180/4(a).
24   Entry for G. Syme in Wages Book, p. 443.
25   Entry for Darbyshire in Wages Book, p. 105.
26   Diary entries for 14, 20, 21 February 1902, Alfred Deakin Papers, MS 1540, Series 2, National Library of Australia.
27   DS to Macmillan & Co., 15 April 1902, LB5, pp. 432–433.

with unusual if not 'fantastical' views that were, however, soundly argued and clearly expressed.[28] In sum, he found it 'quite a pleasant & intelligent little work to read', but 'not <u>weighty</u> enough to…raise much serious discussion in scientific & psychological circles'. On 5 June the publisher wrote informing Syme that the book would be printed and sent a memo of agreement, which the author signed and despatched on 16 July.[29] The work was overlooked for a time, however, for on 26 August the publisher instructed the printer to 'put this small book in type as quickly as possible', because this should have been done some time ago.[30]

Whenever Syme received proofs of *The Soul* (and apparently there was some delay), he put one corrected set in the mail for England on 26 November, telling Macmillan that he had rethought 'the whole subject' and made many corrections and additions.[31] One week later he despatched a duplicate set to the publisher, including an appendix, and instructions for advertising ('only literary & scientific journals, & newspapers of a large circulation') and a list of persons (in addition to Macmillan's own distribution of copies for review) to be sent complimentary copies.[32] Among the 13 named were several Garnett family members, Sir Charles Dilke, and Frank Lloyd at the *Daily Chronicle*. The same day he wrote to Deakin that he had modified his views on the theory of life and instinct and asked him to promote the book to literary friends in England and America; he said that Windsor, who had been through the book twice 'with enthusiasm', had pronounced it the best he'd read on the subject for 20 years.[33] In an undated letter to Syme, Windsor stated that he wanted to read the manuscript again, praising the 'perfection of scientific exposition, cogent, lucid, and incisive', but also expressing a caveat – 'All our reasoning <u>can be but provisional</u> after all'.[34]

In his letter of 2 December to Deakin, Syme commented that he had experienced 'a good deal of worry lately', was 'very much out of sorts' and would be leaving for New Zealand on the *Moeraki* the next day. Possible this was unease associated with the *Fox v. Trenwith* slander case, mentioned below, rather than concern about his book. It may also account for the

---

[28] 'David Syme's "The Soul"', in Readers' Reports, Part I, *Macmillan Archives* (1982)
[29] DS to Macmillan & Co., 16 July 1902, LB5, p. 441.
[30] 'Symes The Soul', Out Letterbooks, Other Printers 1902–1903, *Macmillan Archives* (1982).
[31] DS to Macmillan & Co., 26 November 1902, LB5, p. 457.
[32] DS to Macmillan & Co., 2 December 1902, LB5, pp. 459–460.
[33] DS to A. Deakin, 2 December [1902], Deakin Papers, Series 1.
[34] A. Windsor to DS, undated, held by Dr Veronica Condon.

CHAPTER 15

carping and irritable tone of three fairly inconsequential memos to Stephens sent during the preceding weeks.

To judge from the numerous items in New Zealand newspapers from 9 December 1902 to 10 January 1903, this trip, the last of several made there by the couple over the years, was enjoyably restorative. The Symes were reported disembarking at the southernmost port of Bluff on 8 December. The next day Syme attended the agricultural show at nearby Invercargill. On 13 December the couple arrived in Dunedin, staying at the Grand Hotel for several days. While in the South Island, they visited the alpine village of Queenstown, and reportedly liked the cool temperature after leaving a Melbourne that was baking in 100 degree Fahrenheit (37.8 C) heat. They took the express train to Christchurch on 26 December, and left there four days later for the boat trip to Wellington in the North Island. While there, they visited Wanganui to the north. Their last mention located is in the *Free Lance* of 10 January 1903. Describing Syme as a 'tall, dour-looking, softly-spoken, active Scottish Victorian' who does not look his age, it is accompanied by a sketch of a jaunty, youthful-looking Syme holding a copy of 'The Age'. When exactly and how they returned to Melbourne is not established, but Syme was there, attending to his business, by 26 January 1903.[35] If they were the Mr and Mrs Syme reported as attending Melba's 'reception at Myoora' House, Toorak, they had resumed social activities by 6 February.[36]

The Soul: A Study and an Argument had London publication in April 1903, listed in the *Review of Reviews* for that month, under 'Education, Science and Philosophy', as containing 234 pages and priced at 4/6. Copies had apparently reached Australia by June.[37] The book, which illustrates Syme's persistent underlying sense of the spiritual and his search for ultimate truths about the meaning of life, expounds a densely argued scientific basis for the existence of the soul, and for its afterlife independent of bodily structures. His preface is disingenuously self-effacing, positing 'no expectation that [the book] will prove much of an attraction to the general reader'; then stating that it is directed to those like himself who are 'profoundly dissatisfied with current opinion' on its subject matter and suggests that his heterodoxy may be 'a sin past praying for'. Throughout, Syme is conscious of being unorthodox,

---

[35] DS to A. O'Callogan, 26 January 1903, LB5, p. 461.
[36] 'Melbourne Lady's Letter', *Australian Town and Country Journal*, 11 February 1903, p. 43.
[37] DS to Macmillan & Co., 2 June 1903, LB5, p. 474.

referring in the introduction to 'breaking new ground', writing that 'modern civilised man' is ignorant as to ultimate destiny, and considering the history of religious thought 'pathetic'. *The Soul* sits well within the context of established theorising about the relation between mind and matter, drawing on evolutionary science, including his own *On the Modification of Organisms*. As summarised in the contents outline, he has presented arguments 'from instinct, from the persistency of memory and from the organising power of mind.'

Widely advertised by Macmillan, *The Soul* was extensively and favourably reviewed in British newspapers and journals, to judge from the clippings sent to Syme by the publisher and used for advertising the book in Australia.[38] An advertisement first appearing in the *Age* of 20 June 1903 quotes from eight British and four Australian newspapers. The *Times* reviewer found the book 'lucidly written and suggestive', the *Sheffield Telegraph* that it 'should receive respectful consideration', the *Glasgow Herald* that it was 'marked by acuteness'. Over the months following, into January 1904, comments from many more newspaper and periodical reviews were added to the *Age* advertisement, notably from the *Athenaeum* (praising an 'honest thinker' and 'independent thought') and the *Critical Review* (written, with sufficient knowledge, from a scientific, not theological view).[39] Endorsement came also from Christian religious quarters: to the reviewer for the London *Christian World* the work was 'original and very important'; the London *Church Times* reviewer perceived a 'call to destroy much loose theorising that passes as materialism'. From May to July 1903 short items about the book appeared in a wide range of Australian newspapers, while most of the leading papers carried long and favourable reviews. One in the Adelaide *Register* of 23 May praised Syme's 'excellent grasp of scientific facts and lucidity of expression'; one in the *Sydney Morning Herald* of 27 June stated that few would argue with Syme's conclusions.

Overall, Syme's last book got serious – but passing – mention. It was never going to overturn Darwinian or religious orthodoxies and become an authoritative work. Moreover, arguing the case for life after death was less revolutionary than expounding the atheistic opposite, and Syme's hope for a second edition (printing) was not met.[40] There are no records extant of the print run, or of sales, in Britain or Australia. Syme's several letters

---

[38] DS to D. Byrne, 1 July 1903, LB5, p. 476.
[39] For example, *Age*, 7 November 1903, 23 January 1904.
[40] DS to Macmillan & Co., 2 June 1903, LB5, p. 474.

CHAPTER 15

from December 1902 to November 1903 include orders for a total of 115 copies to be sent out – a modest number (of course this does not include any separate booksellers' orders).[41] More than once in correspondence Syme referred to a 'great demand' for his book in Australia, in connection with his concern that it was not being adequately publicised in England.[42] He wanted Macmillan to run new advertisements to include favourable press notices, such as had been done in the *Age*, and pursued the matter repeatedly until September 1904.[43]

Syme went to great lengths to maximise the distribution of his book, but never sought or received monetary reward from its publication and sales (instead, he had accounts to pay). The whole project seems to have been carried out with a missionary zeal, in the aim of expressing and spreading the truths he believed he had arrived at. In the last letter on file to Macmillan, dated 14 September 1904, he wrote that he 'never expected to make money by the book' and all he wanted was to 'have it read'.[44] He also stated that he had received letters from England and elsewhere that indicated it was well thought of. To one, from a J.H. Thompson, he replied at length, pleased to engage with the series of detailed points that the writer had raised and obviously open to further correspondence (though none is on record). In concluding that 'there is very little demand for books of a serious character now-a-days', he does not give the impression of being dissatisfied; rather, a sense is conveyed of mission accomplished.[45]

Other matters were coming to the fore in 1904, a climactic and transitional year for Syme. Geoffrey was away from February for 12 months. That Syme missed him is understated in a letter of 29 November: 'I won't be sorry when you return.'[46] Geoffrey and Violet went to England for the birth of their second child, Violet, later known as Hilaire, a name said to derive from Hilaria, as grandfather Syme called the happy, laughing child (their first, Marjorie, had been born in 1902).[47] Sailing on 9 February for London, on the mailboat *Moldavia*, Geoffrey would have had a chance to

---

[41] Six letters DS to Macmillan & Co., between 2 December 1902 (LB5, pp. 459–460) and 4 November 1903 (LB5, p. 484).

[42] DS to D. Byrne, 1 July 1903, LB5, p. 476; DS to Macmillan & Co., 4 November 1903, LB5, p. 484.

[43] DS to Macmillan & Co., 14 September 1904, LB5, p.497.

[44] DS to Macmillan & Co., 14 September 1904, LB5, p. 497.

[45] DS to J. Thompson, 14 July 1904, LB5, pp. 489–491.

[46] DS to GS, 29 November 1904, quoted in Sayers (1965, 256).

[47] Information from Dr Veronica Condon.

extend his press connections, for several leading newspaper men were on board – among them *Argus* editor Frederick Haddon, sometime *Age* cable correspondent Frederick Ward, reinstated as editor of the *Daily Telegraph*, and newly retired partner in the *Sydney Morning Herald* business, Charles Burton Fairfax.[48] Indicative of the closeness between father and son, Syme took the ship to Adelaide. There farewelling the young family, he went on to Port Victor and inspected a herd of Holstein cattle, then spent a few days with Bonython at his property *Carminow* in the Adelaide Hills (Prest 2011, 129). (The *Advertiser* proprietor must have set aside any offence given by Syme in the past.)

Disillusion with politics

In the middle of 1904 Syme's relationship with Deakin foundered. The falling out is best understood in the context of Syme's attitudes to and involvement with post-Federation politics, characterised by the pessimism into which leader writer Benjamin Hoare (1927, 155) saw him habitually drift. Assuming Syme was still directing editorial policy, this gloom was behind the *Age* leader of 1 January 1902, which saw the first year of the Commonwealth 'a disappointment to most' and a 'disillusion to many'.

If that is how Syme felt, then a pamphlet by Irish-born Edmund Fitzgibbon published in late January would have deepened his negativity. Chairman of the Melbourne and Metropolitan Board of Works, Fitzgibbon had been for many years Town Clerk of the City of Melbourne (as noted in Chapter 13, under scrutiny in 1893, when George Levey tried to negotiate a loan in London on his behalf). Titled *Letter to David Syme, Esq.*, it addresses the newspaper proprietor in his 'paternal dialect' (broad Scots), mocks his past behaviour, implying underhand dealings, and claims that he and related municipal affairs have received appalling treatment in Syme's newspapers over the past 46 years, most recently through a 'skit in a weekly rehash of your newspaper that is little read'. This referred to a portrait in words and picture (photograph) in the *Leader* of 18 January 1902, part of a series entitled 'Representative Men'. While acknowledging Fitzgibbon's public status and achievements, the tone is sarcastic and taunting, harping on the contrast between the glamour of high office and the lowliness of sewers and, in relation to Fitzgibbon's previous municipal position, terming him 'Town Despot'. Moreover it generalises about 'the egotism of nonentities in the

---

[48] 'Shipping Intelligence', *Argus*, 10 February 1904, p. 6; 'Personal', *Advertiser* (Adelaide), 12 February 1904, p. 4.

CHAPTER 15

force of municipalities'. Fitzgibbon, in his perhaps understandable public rejoinder, claimed that Syme had borne him a grudge since April 1856 (before David joined the *Age*) for assaulting Ebenezer Syme over comments made in the *Age* (for which Fitzgibbon was convicted and fined).[49] His parody, which is devastatingly clever, more than a match for the 'skit' in the *Leader*, may well have wounded its target. While there is no record of Syme's response, an obituary for Fitzgibbon in 1905 stated that he was 'perhaps the only public man in Victoria who successfully defied the majestic might' of Syme.[50]

Further pessimism was conveyed in March 1902 through 'Papers for the Times', a series of eight articles in the *Age*, in April reprinted in the *Leader* and issued as a 32-page pamphlet priced at one penny. This time the target was state, not municipal, governance. Aspects of Victorian state administration were fiercely attacked and sweeping, cost-cutting reforms advocated. The criticisms were part of, and stimulated some, popular reformist agitation in the coming months. They were detailed in the *Age*, with an inflated claim on 29 April, that the movement for reform was 'sweeping Australia'. To the extent that Syme was involved, he was focusing more on State than Federal politics in this period. This led to trouble – to the so-called Syme–Trenwith controversy. Snobbery and extravagance were imputed in the *Age* of 22 March to Labourite MLA for Richmond, William (Billy) Trenwith, when he was Minister for Railways in the Victorian government. They elicited rebuttals by Trenwith, an attack on John Dow, MLA and *Leader* agricultural editor, and allegations of shady land dealings by Syme. An unholy exchange of attack and counter-attack, ensued, conducted through the *Argus* (including accusations against Dow) and the *Age* (including a letter of rebuttal in the *Age* of April 23, in Syme's name), and relayed by papers throughout Victoria. Finally, on 24 September Trenwith published a selection from the press coverage as a 32-page pamphlet (Trenwith 1902). It did not, however, contain his abusive, derogatory remarks about the *Age* chief of staff Fox, made in a speech to an estimated 10,000 Richmond electors on 29 June, in which he belittled him as a 'bilious, dyspeptic-looking…mangy dog' and made derogatory mention also of *Age* employees, Henry Champion and John Dow.[51]

---

49 'Assault on an Editor', *Argus*, 3 May 1856, p. 5.
50 'Peeps at People', *Sunday Times* (Perth), 17 December 1905, p. 12.
51 'Action for Slander', *Age*, 20 November 1902, p. 8.

In April, when the furore erupted, Syme told Dow (in a letter about another matter) that his response to Trenwith (published as a letter to the editor in the *Age* of 24 April) was not satisfactory.[52] Otherwise there is no record of his views and actions about Trenwith's attacks on his staff, and it was Fox who issued a Supreme Court slander writ against him. The case for £1000 damages was heard in November, Trenwith stating in court that he spoke the offending words because of the *Age* attacks on him and should have acted against Syme himself (who surely was alarmed about the course the matter was taking). A verdict was brought in for Fox who, however, received only a token one shilling in damages.[53] Trenwith planned to appeal but by April 1903 had abandoned the case. At that time Syme replied, with stiff courtesy, to complaints from Mackinnon at the *Argus* about articles in the *Age*, and made a counter-claim of biased reporting of the Trenwith matter in the *Argus*. He pointed out that the arrangement between the *Age* and *Argus* was that both should 'abstain from offensive remarks on each other', a 'compact' that he was willing to abide by.[54]

Syme's personal connection with Federal politics was largely through Alfred Deakin, now a leading Federal politician. Attorney-General in the Barton government, he was also Acting Prime Minister from May to November 1902, when Barton went to England for a Colonial Conference and the Coronation of Edward VII. From 24 September 1903 until 27 April 1904 he was Prime Minister. During these early Federation years he was heavily involved in attempts to form stable, majority government out of three groupings of roughly equal numbers – Protectionists, Labourites and Free Traders. Following the brief reigns of Labourite John Watson and Free Trader George Reid, on 5 July 1905 Deakin again became Prime Minister, retaining the position until 13 November 1908, his Liberal Protectionists having the informal support of Watson's Labour group. The difficulties for the parliamentary government of these embryonic political parties gave rise to the *Age* series 'The Evils of Party Government', revised and reissued as a supplement to the *Age* of 6 August 1904. Syme may have suggested content for the articles, for many of the arguments and proposals in them resonate with those in his 1881 *Representative Government in England*.

---

52   DS to J. Dow, 25 April 1904, LB5, p. 434.
53   'Slander Action', *Argus*, 26 November 1902, p. 7.
54   DS to L.C. Mackinnon, 9 April 1903, LB5, pp. 470–471.

CHAPTER 15

Deakin wrote of being in a 'continuous relationship' with Syme from 1902 until his death.[55] His diaries record regular contact through meetings, usually at the *Age* office, and, for the first few years, through occasional lunches that sometimes included leading politicians and *Age* journalists. More than friends' keeping in touch, there was on Syme's side the desire to urge policies and actions upon government. This was consonant with the view, expounded in the *Age* leader on 7 November 1903, of the press vying 'with the statesmen in shaping the legislation of the nation', except that this was personal and not journalistic intervention. On Deakin's side was the desire to get his policies expounded and promoted in Syme's influential daily, and to avoid adverse publicity. Through letters to Deakin, Syme gave advice sometimes verging on instructions, for instance in relation to the resignation in July 1903 of South Australian Charles Kingston, Minister for Trade and Customs, over clauses in the Conciliation and Arbitration Bill.[56]

Falling out with Deakin

Relations were not always harmonious, however, and resentments erupted after Deakin gave an address in his Ballarat constituency on 1 August 1904 to launch the National Political League (which did not spread much beyond Ballarat) (La Nauze 1979, 374–376). It was reported verbatim in the *Age* of 2 August and editorially damned on 3 August as 'a series of windy speeches – not the leadership which a virile Protectionist party demands', with Deakin having 'lost himself in the clouds of politico-philosophical questions'. The same day Deakin protested in writing to Syme that his speech had been treated with derision.[57] Syme's prompt and apparently lengthy reply, not copied into his letterbook, is not preserved in the Deakin papers, for when in a stern rejoinder Deakin stated that the correspondence might have to be published, Syme requested return of his letters, uncopied, and Deakin appears to have complied.[58] Deakin's next two letters express bitterness and hurt, with that of 9 August drawing a parallel between the hypothetical situation of Deakin having cordially endorsed Syme's views in *The Soul*, then writing a scathing review; he concluded that he had suffered without word of regret or explanation.[59] Syme's very brief reply (on file) conveyed that he did

---

[55] Autobiographical notes, Deakin Papers, Series 3/290a.
[56] DS to A. Deakin, 24 July, 27 August 1903, Deakin Papers, Series 14.
[57] A. Deakin to DS (draft), 3 August 1904, Deakin Papers, Series 16.
[58] A. Deakin to DS (draft), 4 August 1904, Deakin Papers, Series 16.
[59] A. Deakin to DS (drafts), 5, 9 August 1904, Deakin Papers, Series 16.

not understand this letter and was not disposed to offer an apology. Rather, he expected one;[60] but he did not get it.

On 26 August Deakin met *Age* reporter Leonard Biggs to talk about Syme.[61] A reporter of note, Biggs had been on the staff since 1899, was also Melbourne correspondent for the London *Daily Chronicle*, and would take over as *Age* editor after Schuler's death in 1926.[62] The ice may have been broken at (William?) McCulloch's lunch on 5 October for Syme and Deakin (noted in Deakin's diary) and in 1905 regular contact resumed, but with fewer social engagements; the diary entries indicate that visits to the *Age* office were often to see Schuler, Fox or Biggs. Sometimes he visited Blythswood – in April 1905, when Syme was ill, and later, when he was dying.

Syme's letters to Deakin from 1905 to 1907 contain his views, not to say advice, on what he saw as pressing political matters, particularly in relation to tariffs and imperial preference. When the *Age* of 15 March 1906 praised Watson's speech in Launceston, Syme had already written to Deakin that Watson, in not alluding to protection, had 'thrown him over' and his friends were 'in despair'.[63] Relations between the two then verging on the unpleasant, Deakin wrote that he would go to the election without the *Age*, and Syme replied that he was 'sick of the whole affair'.[64] Each backing off from an impasse like that of August 1904, their ensuing letters were cordial, with Syme frequently soliciting visits. In October 1907, when Deakin complained to Syme about a discouraging leader in the *Age*, he added that he did not 'seek to influence *Age* policy', but wanted to put himself right with Syme and avoid misunderstandings, for he was determined to discharge his responsibility as Prime Minister.[65]

Clearly intimacy had been lost after the August 1904 breakdown, and each had reservations about the other. Syme wrote to Geoffrey in November 1904 that 'Poor Deakin is quite in the background now' and to Deakin himself in November 1905, 'as a friend', warning that he was on the way to 'break[ing] up the Liberal Party' and should give attention to 'Protection and Fiscal Preference'.[66] Deakin, on the other hand, recollected years later

---

[60] DS to A. Deakin, 9 August 1904, Deakin Papers, Series 16/114.
[61] Diary entry for 26 August 1904, Deakin Papers, Series 2.
[62] Entry for Biggs in Wages Book, p. 33.
[63] DS to A. Deakin, 14 March 1906, Deakin Papers, Series 15.
[64] DS to A. Deakin, and Deakin's draft reply, 26 March 1906, Deakin Papers, Series 15.
[65] A. Deakin to DS (draft), 7 October 1907, Deakin Papers, Series 15.
[66] DS to GS, 29 November 1904, quoted in Sayers (1965, 256–257); DS to A. Deakin, 16 November 1905, Deakin Papers, Series 15.

CHAPTER 15

that, although they remained on good terms till the end, they drifted apart in political views, with Syme relying on his fixed ideas of 20 years earlier and having an 'uncertain memory'.[67] To an extent Deakin seems to have been humouring Syme in the last years, not only out of respect but also to keep the *Age* on side. As for Syme's influence, in fact the *Age* editorial team that he had set up was now able to run the show with or without his specific instructions – in fact had to, for he was frequently otherwise engaged and sometimes ill. The disagreement of August 1904 did serve to show each man that private friendship was one thing and public relations as representatives of press and parliament another.

For Syme, this had two sides. First, there was to be no external dictation whatsoever of what was to be written in his papers – nor any justification for reprimanding the expression of editorial opinion. Secondly, he felt himself free, however, to proffer advice and guidance to parliament via Deakin out of his own convictions, seemingly as a private thinking person, not a press proprietor – which he continued to do until the last illness took over. As for Deakin, he recognised that the *Age*, and the press generally, must remain free from interference in editorial lines or language. In future he was more guarded in his reactions to adverse coverage, while maintaining contact with Syme and receiving though not necessarily acting on his advice. While the lines between the public and the private continued to be somewhat blurred and overlapping in action, after the upset of August 1904 each man arrived at his own workable concept of press freedom and parliamentary duty.

One curious if not ironic aspect of Deakin vis-à-vis the *Age* is the placement above the editorial columns of a quotation from the English *National Review*: 'The Melbourne Age is one of the ablest papers written in the English language'. First appearing on 7 December and running well into 1905, the header was taken from an article in the October 1904 number of this conservative monthly. The suspicion arises that Deakin, perhaps to mollify Syme, may have drawn attention to this favourable mention in the journal to which he had begun to contribute as Australian correspondent, under the pseudonym 'C.R.' (standing for 'Commonwealth Representative'), his first article appearing in the December issue (La Nauze 1979, 199–201, 347–351). Posing as an anonymous Sydney correspondent, the Federal politician and sometime Prime Minister was already sending a weekly column to the also conservative daily *Morning Post*, to which he contributed until 1914. The arrangement, which had been finalised through friend Philip Mennell

---

[67] Autobiographical notes, Deakin Papers, Series 3/290a.

in 1900 and carried remuneration of £50 a year, was apparently unknown to the public at large, including Syme and the *Age* personnel. Claimed as a way of bringing Australian affairs and outlook insightfully to English readers (something Geoffrey Syme had argued for in his *Daily Chronicle* piece), the contributions also served to present Deakin and his policies in a favourable light to Australian readers, when endorsed by establishment journals in the 'home' country. Thus the *National Review* of September 1904 quoted the *Morning Post* 'Sydney correspondent' (Deakin of course, anonymously) on Watson's 'hopeless parliamentary position' (out-of-date information by then). And the *Age* sub-leader of 28 November 1907, on fiscal controversies in British journals, stated that the *Morning Post* 'takes a trenchant part in the protectionist crusade in England'. Readers of the *Age* did not know that journalistic support for the protectionist crusade actually came from the Australian Prime Minister!

In October 1904 the *Age* had been in publication for 50 years. To mark the jubilee year, Syme provided £3000 to the University of Melbourne to endow a 'David Syme Research Prize' that, he wrote to Geoffrey with a note of pride, 'got a little kudos'.[68] Worth £100 and to include a gold medal, it was to be awarded annually for Australian research in the fields of biology, chemistry, geology, or natural philosophy. The first award was made in March 1906 to anaesthetist Dr Edward Embley for research with chloroform.[69] Confusingly (and perhaps intentionally so), an article in the *Age* a few weeks later, by 'Medicus', gave some background to Embley's research, describing the earlier work of noted surgeon and anaesthetist Sir James Syme, thus allowing the reader to surmise a familial connection (although there was none).[70]

Otherwise, the daily did little to celebrate its half-century. On the actual day, 17 October 1904, the *Age*, in 'News of the Day', included a brief mention of the opening on 17 October 1854 of the Melbourne Exhibition by Governor Hotham, but had nothing about the paper's first appearance. The omission was rectified in the *Age* editorial of Tuesday 18 October 1904, with the comment that the *Age* came into being at the right time and the somewhat erroneous observation that it *began* with whole-hearted espousal of the diggers' cause (although this came *after* the Eureka uprising). The *Age* of the following Saturday made more of a fuss, with a 'Jubilee of the

---

[68] DS to GS, 29 November 1904, quoted in Sayers (1965, 256).
[69] 'Scientific Research', *Age*, 20 March 1906, p. 5.
[70] 'Scientific Research', *Age*, 7 April 1906, p. 4.

CHAPTER 15

Age' item, which noted that congratulatory letters and telegrams had been received, and made the unverifiable claim that the paper reached its high-water mark in 1903 with a circulation of 135,000 (far higher than published audited figures for 1906 and 1907, quoted above). It is hard to believe that Syme contributed in any way to this sloppy journalism.

Nor, apparently, were there any jubilee celebrations, unlike those in October 1879 for the 25th anniversary. There was a public function later in the year, on 22 December – the official opening of an electric plant, manufactured by Westinghouse, which supplanted existing steam-driven machines. It was claimed to be a first in Australian newspaper offices. The 'party of gentlemen' invited to view and take part, included Chief Secretary (now Sir) Samuel Gillott, several State parliamentarians, newly elected Lord Mayor Charles Pleasance and several aldermen.[71] Syme thanked Gillott as acting Chair of the Electric Supply Committee for having suggested the innovation. Herbert also gave thanks, and proposed a toast to the health of Lord Mayor Pleasance.

Little is knowable about Geoffrey's activities while away in England in 1904. A letter dated 10 May from Syme to him, held by Dr Veronica Condon, expresses concern that his son has been very ill. The 1904 correspondence between Geoffrey and parents, available to Sayers in the early 1960s, has not been located. Extracts quoted by Sayers from two of Syme's letters indicate that Geoffrey had an employment plan vetoed by his father, who urged him instead to get some reporting experience on the *Daily Chronicle*, and kept up with Australian affairs through reading the Melbourne papers.[72] Anticipating the return of Geoffrey and family travelling to Melbourne on the *Marmora*, Syme sailed to Adelaide on the *Mongolia* to meet them, arriving on 23 February 1905. (A fellow passenger was Lauchlan Mackinnon of the *Argus*, bound for Marseilles – a brief opportunity for cordial conversation between the two pressmen?) The reunited Symes travelled together back to Melbourne in the *Marmora*, which berthed on 28 February.[73] Sometime after this he may have become unwell, his friend William McCulloch, in a letter of 21 April, pleased to learn that he was much better.[74]

After 10 months' leave without pay, Geoffrey was back on the payroll from the start of 1905. His weekly salary was increased to £10, the same

---

[71] 'Electrical Installation at "The Age" Office', *Age*, 23 December 1904, p. 5.
[72] DS to GS, 7 June and 29 November 1904, quoted in Sayers (1965, 256–257).
[73] 'Personal', *Advertiser* (Adelaide), 24 February 1905, p. 4, 28 February, p. 4.
[74] W. McCulloch to DS, 21 April 1905, held by Dr Veronica Condon.

as subeditor Stephens was receiving.[75] From January 1906 it was raised to £796 a year (more than £15 weekly), exceeded only by the salaries of editor Schuler (£1004), his older brother Herbert as business and technical manager (£1400) and Syme himself (£2500).[76] Geoffrey settled back with his wife and two young daughters into Conisbro, the home that his father had provided adjacent to Blythswood, and soon set to work in compiling a topic index to editorials and selected articles in the *Age*, ranging in date from 3 March 1905 to 5 September 1906. The handwritten index is recorded in a small black notebook with tabs A to Z, presumably a way of learning about *Age* policies and practices.[77] The index is preceded by a few rough notes relating to the *Age*, *Leader* and *Every Saturday*. Followed these are floor plans of Melbourne Mansions, discussed below.

Delegating to Geoffrey

On 1 April 1905 Geoffrey was formally appointed secretary to his father. Entries in the first of Geoffrey's three extant letterbooks, dating from 30 August 1905, reveal that from this date, if not earlier, he handled much of his father's business correspondence.[78] Up to 14 January 1908, the last entry before Syme's death, there are carbon copies of some 315 handwritten letters. Only 20 of these concern newspaper business matters. Many of them are replies to letters received, and their import if not their exact wording appears to have been dictated by Syme, except when they simply state that Mr Syme is out of town. Several decline offers to contribute, one notifies a reporter of a salary rise, another that there are no vacancies on the reporting staff. A letter of 20 February 1906 to London correspondent Byrne complains of the inadequacy of books being sent out for review and asks him to rectify – to see publishers, and get important works, not light novels. It also asks him for a confidential report on the new appointment to the *Age* London Office. This was W.E. Robinson (not to be confused with assistant commercial editor William S. Robinson). The *Age* of 21 September 1905 had announced, in its 'News of the Day', new arrangements at 160 Fleet Street with Robinson in charge, stating that Australians could give this address when visiting London. An order of 17 March 1906 to the United States Department of Agriculture for publications may have been as much for Syme's personal

---

[75] Entries for G. Syme and Stephens in Wages Book, pp. 441, 443.
[76] Profit and loss account 1906, SFP Box 1192/1.
[77] GS, Notebook 1905–1906, SFP Box 1184/7.
[78] GS, Letterbook, 30 August 1905–18 September 1914, SFP Box 1183/1.

CHAPTER 15

edification as grist for his newspaper mill. By 1907, however, Geoffrey could act independently of his father, and give directions to staff of the Editorial and Literary department. In any case, Geoffrey was not entirely under his control, and would have a more open, gentler manner in personal dealings. In a postscript to his letter of 12 February 1906 stating that Syme could not give a reference for the correspondent's son, Geoffrey had added: 'I can give you information personally'.

Several of Geoffrey's letters deal with Syme's philanthropic activities, for during these final years the proprietor continued to make donations – among them, to field naturalists and rifle clubs – and to offer prizes in the *Leader* (for example, an 'Orchard Prize' for the best kept orchard in the Doncaster district of outer Melbourne).[79] He continued to set an example through heading *Age* subscription lists for disaster relief, in 1906 giving £21, together with £50 from Governor General Lord Northcote, to launch the *Age* Gippsland Fires Relief Fund.[80] A more personal benefaction was the £100 he provided in 1905 for a William Best, who had been wounded in a gun accident. At one time employed on a Syme property, he was the financial support for his widowed mother and siblings, despite having previously lost an arm. A newspaper in Best's locality observed: 'Although a strict man of business Mr. Syme has the reputation of being just and generous whenever a case of destitution is brought under his notice.'[81]

The contents to February 1908 of Geoffrey's letterbook are testimony to the great spread of Syme's involvements and his need for secretarial assistance therewith. Geoffrey's first letter on file, dated 30 August 1905, concerns a possible purchase of land at Mooroolbark some 30 kilometres east of Melbourne (now a suburb, then rural). Indeed many of the letters written for his father, and indeed most of Syme's in these final years, relate to property and agricultural interests. They are evidence of keen property purchasing, mostly in rural areas, of acquisition of new mechanical equipment and good quality seeds and livestock, and of produce and stock marketing. They also show that some properties were profitably tenanted and that some were occasionally sold off. A proportion of Geoffrey's correspondence is to Oswald ('Oswie'). Chiefly concerning the management of Killara, the letters show Geoffrey a go-between, transmitting instructions from 'the Pater', as

---

[79] DS to Secretary, Doncaster Fruitgrowers Association (signed by Oswald Syme for DS & Co.), 27 May 1902, LB5, p. 437; GS Letterbook.
[80] 'The Gippsland Fires', *Age*, 27 January 1906, p. 11.
[81] *West Gippsland Gazette*, 26 December 1905, p. 2, col. 7.

he referred in them to his father. Exhibiting gentle tact and humour, they are friendly letters from a caring, affectionate, older brother. One dated 24 September 1905 intimated that he could give Oswald two 'certainties' for the 'Cup'. Dear to the hearts of brothers Herbert and Arthur, betting on horse races was not to be countenanced by their father.

Melbourne Mansions

Of Syme's property dealing and developments, two of the many that engaged him in the last years of his life, stand out – one urban, one rural. The former was the construction and management of 'Melbourne Mansions' at 91 to 101 Collins Street (fig. 15.4), a six-storey building comprising professional suites on the ground floor and residential apartments above, with electric lighting, heating and refrigeration, and a communal dining room in addition to kitchens in individual apartments. It and the Albany building in Macquarie Street, Sydney are seen as the first purpose-built apartment blocks for the well-off in Australia (Pickett and Butler-Bowden 2012, 252). Syme had the project in mind by October 1903 when writing to leading architect Charles D'Ebro who had produced a sketch for him.[82] In the event, following his purchase of a suitable site in June 1904 with the condition that the building on it be demolished, Syme commissioned the firm of Inskip and Butler.[83] Walter Butler was the dominant partner and, like Robert Hyndman who revamped the *Age* building in 1898 (and died in 1901), was involved with the Arts and Crafts Movement (Dernelley 2012, 128). Also, he was highly regarded by the many wealthy pastoralist and businessman clients, for whom he had produced grand residences (Tibbits 1979).

Documentation relating to this project, dating from 8 November 1904, is in a dedicated section of the Syme Family Papers.[84] The builders, Murray and Crow from the 1898 *Age* office makeover, were contracted on 28 October 1904, to complete the apartments by 28 January 1906.[85] Foundations were laid by the end of November 1904 and Melbourne Mansions was a landmark by late 1905 (a dentist regularly advertising in the *Gippsland Times* his Collins Street premises 'next Melbourne Mansions').[86] Although the completion

---

[82] DS to C. D'Ebro, 9 October 1903, LB5, p. 483.
[83] DS to Inskip & Butler, 7 September 1904, LB5, p. 496; DS to J. Barrett, 7 November 1904, SFP Box 1190/4.
[84] 'Melbourne Mansions', 1904–1911, SFP Boxes 1190/4–5.
[85] Contract dated 28 October 1904, SFP Box 1190/5.
[86] DS to GS, 29 November 1904, quoted in Sayers (1965, 256–257).

CHAPTER 15

deadline was not met, with furnishings and lift installation unfinished, a ground-floor suite was leased from 1 February 1906 and the *Age* from 24 February ran a prominent block advertisement for: 'Melbourne Mansions Collins-Street. Magnificent Professional and Residential Chambers.'[87] From 7 July 1906 the *Age* advertisement provided more details: suites of two to six rooms from £90 per annum and some single rooms for £35. A new advertisement from 25 April 1907, proclaiming Melbourne Mansions the 'Finest Site in Melbourne', was for suites of five to 11 rooms, with electric lights, lifts, etc. By 12 February 1908 only one two-room suite, two six-room suites and two single rooms were advertised as vacant.

Geoffrey had been acquainted with this project from almost the outset, his father alluding to it in his letter of 10 May 1904, saying that he was 'over head and ears now grappling in Collins St', not sure that he would go ahead, and having received 25 designs, none suitable without 'great alterations'.[88] However, on 7 December Syme sent him material from the architects concerning the building which, he said, was to have doctors' rooms on the ground floor and 27 residential suites above, but which he had no time to read. He wanted advice from Geoffrey on many aspects, especially management and tenancy arrangements, about which he wrote again some weeks later.[89] Geoffrey, back at the *Age* office, was heavily involved with this as with all of Syme's business projects. While Syme closely followed all details, from tenancy and management arrangements and staff recruitment to heating, fire alarms, electric lighting and refrigeration, furnishings and leasing, he frequently delegated responsibility for them to Geoffrey, especially during his various absences from Melbourne. References in Geoffrey's letters indicate that staff at the *Age* office were sometimes called upon, as when commercial editor Robinson was to receive applications for manager at the Mansions in October 1905. Annabella too helped, probably with painting and furnishing arrangements.[90]

Syme was demanding and meticulous, calling for many alterations to the plans after the tender and contract had been signed, and incurring added expense, as architect Butler explained in a letter to Geoffrey in January 1907.[91] In April 1906 Geoffrey wrote to Butler that Syme 'utterly'

---

[87] GS to G. Henderson, 1 February 1906, SFP Box 1183/1.
[88] DS to GS, 10 May 1904, held by Dr Veronica Condon.
[89] DS to GS, 7 December 1904, 24 January 1905, SFP Box 1190/5.
[90] W. Butler to DS, 30 October 1906, SFP Box 1190/4.
[91] W. Butler to GS, 29 January 1907, SFP Box 1190/4.

Figure 15.4. Melbourne Mansions, Collins Street, 1950s. (Courtesy of Fairfax Media)

condemned the electric wiring; in October Syme directly complained of defective workmanship.[92] This was a difficult time, for earlier in the year Inskip and Butler had acrimoniously dissolved their partnership (a 'blessing in disguise', Butler later wrote) and by 6 June were 'not speaking'.[93] This complicated the completion of the building, dealing with contractors and making payments, as Syme's correspondence with each architect shows. Butler, however, emerged as the main person with whom Syme dealt, and not for the last time, as will be seen.

Syme's total outlay for the land and the equipped building to 14 February 1908 was £52,285.[94] Rental income began modestly in 1906, with a net profit of £167, rising the year following to £1757 and to over £2500 in 1908 and bringing income to David Syme and Co. for the next 50 years. More than an income source, Melbourne Mansions should also be seen as one of Syme's triumphant achievements, with stunning form as well as clever function.

---

[92] GS to W. Butler, 21 April 1906 and DS to Butler 30 October 1906, SFP Box 1183/1.

[93] G. Inskip to DS, 6 June 1906 and Butler & Bradshaw to DS, 19 April 1907, SFP Box 1190/4.

[94] Two-page document noting progressive costs re Melbourne Mansions, SFP Box 1190/5.

CHAPTER 15

Historian of Collins Street Judith Buckridge wrote that it 'had style – a touch of discreet Mayfair' (Buckrich 2005, 239). Architectural historian Harriet Edquist (2003, 15) has placed it in a wider international context, effusively describing 'an urban palazzo with sinuous, scalloped parapet, lavish ornamental carving of Australian plants festooned across its façade and wrought iron interwoven gum leaves' and sees it in the tradition of the Viennese modern art Secession movement as well as the 'contemporary *modernista* movement of Barcelona.' Now vanished and forgotten, it would grace the 'Paris' end of Collins Street for half a century, until sold in 1958, demolished, and replaced by the 26-storey CRA 'skyscraper', itself to be pulled down in 1988 to make way for the grandiose 57-storey '101 Collins'.

Mellool

Syme's major rural enterprise was Mellool Station in the Riverina district of New South Wales. Located several kilometres east of the Victorian river town of Swan Hill, it had Murray River frontage. Syme embarked on this project while Melbourne Mansions was under construction, buying the property on 29 June 1905 through Melbourne Stock and Station Agents Macleod and Kettle.[95] For £42,201.13.11 he acquired some 25,172 acres, 21,000 sheep and 323 cattle and horses.[96] That the vendor had installed irrigation channels on this huge grazing property was of particular interest to Syme at a time when irrigation schemes were being trialled elsewhere in the Riverina. The *Age* of 26 April 1906 reported the opening of one such scheme. The *Leader* of 8 June 1907 described 'Irrigation, Fruit Growing around Lake Boga', in the vicinity of Mellool.

Two weeks after the purchase Syme set up the Mellool Irrigation Company, with his five sons holding shares, and proceeded to extend and upgrade the irrigation system, installing a large pumping plant.[97] A pamphlet produced for the sale of Mellool many years later states 'with characteristic breadth of outlook he launched a scheme of improvements regardless of expense', his project being to make Mellool 'a model irrigation settlement'.[98] The *Argus* of 4 October had a report from Kerang of two 12-horsepower traction engines being landed at Mellool, from Mildura, and Syme's intention to go in largely for fodder-growing (lucerne, paspalum grass and maize to be

---

[95] Sale document, SFP Box 1190/6(a).
[96] 'Sale of a Riverina Station', *Argus*, 14 July 1905, p. 8.
[97] Contract, 12 July 1905, SFP Box 1190/6(a).
[98] *Mellool, 'The Land of Plenty'*, SFP Box 1190/6(e); Sayers (1965, 210).

grown under irrigation) and rearing fat lambs for the export trade.[99] With a hands-on interest, he was at Mellool with Annabella in October 1905. Her letters from there, quoted by Sayers, describe Syme's planned dam building and irrigation engineering.[100] There must have been several later visits, for Geoffrey's letterbooks have frequent mention of Syme being 'out of town', and some or all of these excursions were surely to his Riverina property.[101] Most of the 39 entries in Syme's last letterbook, begun 4 October 1905, relate to Mellool matters – hiring a manager, engineering requirements for dams, sale of fat lambs and purchase of lucerne seed. Son-in-law Willie Macalister was called on for assistance – in November 1906 acting for him in installing a new manager; in May 1907 selling lambs.[102] At the *Age* office Geoffrey provided secretarial assistance (for instance, engaging a book-keeper, enquiring about a pumping plant), but was less involved than with Melbourne Mansions.[103]

In November 1907 the Adelaide *Advertiser* reported on a river trip taken by the South Australian Premier and some of his ministers: 'on the New South Wales bank was the broad and fertile expanse of Mellool Station, belonging to Mr. David Syme, whose sheep were to be seen in great numbers'.[104] The purpose of this journey and of a similar excursion by Victorian legislators in October was not simply to note significant land-holdings. As Victorian Premier Thomas Bent was reported saying to the people of Echuca on the Murray, it was 'neither a picnic nor an invasion'.[105] Both river trips were in relation to pending Federal and State legislation to allocate and regulate water usage for the three States bordering the Murray, that would eventually become law and be ratified in 1914–15.[106]

A border dispute

In 1905 and 1906, Syme, through the *Age* and personal contacts, had promoted a view that would have placed much of the Murray River *within*

---

[99] 'Kerang', *Argus*, 4 October 1905, p. 8.
[100] AS to GS, 15, 25 October 1905, quoted and mentioned in Sayers (1965, 210).
[101] For example, GS letters, 17 October 1905, 15 October 1906, 9 April 1907, SFP Box 1183/1.
[102] DS to McCutcheon, 9 November 1906, and to W. Macalister, 27 May 1907, LB6, pp. 27, 38.
[103] Evident from GS letterbook, SFP Box 1183/1.
[104] 'The Murray', *Advertiser* (Adelaide), 7 November 1907, p. 7.
[105] 'The Murray', *Advertiser* (Adelaide), 7 November 1907, p. 7.
[106] 'New South Wales and Murray Agreement', *Advertiser* (Adelaide), 31 October 1907, p. 8.

CHAPTER 15

Victoria and take in the Riverina area of New South Wales (and Mellool). Two months before he purchased this property in 1905, the *Age*, seemingly out of the blue, noted an 'interesting paper' had been read to the Royal Geographical Society in October 1902.[107] The author, retired magistrate John Ogier had been collecting relevant documents and arguing his case for years, and indeed would continue to do so until his death in 1913. Syme and the *Age* took up his claim that the Victoria–New South Wales border, initially intended to start in the east at Cape Howe and to run in a straight line to the Murray River, ought to have been drawn not to its upper reaches known as the Indi Creek but to the Numerella River further north, which runs into the Murrumbidgee, which in turn joins the Murray far to the west, near Boundary Bend. Ogier claimed Victoria stood to gain an additional 35,000 square miles.

In October 1905 Syme wrote to Henry Higgins, Federal member for North Melbourne and recently Attorney-General in the short-lived Watson government, and to current Attorney-General Isaac Isaacs, whose electorate of Indi took in the border area at issue. He sought the opinion of each on this matter 'of immense importance to the State' although it was 'the fashion to sneer at Ogier's views'.[108] Syme was calling on persons of legal standing, who would both in 1906 join the High Court Bench. While it is not known if either replied, the matter was aired in the *Age* through the six-part series 'Who Owns the Riverina', published from 4 May to 18 June 1906. Some public interest was stirred in Victoria, eliciting a protest, reported in the *Argus* of 1 June, from the Borough Council of the New South Wales border town Albury.[109] The *Argus*, which ran commentary on the issue, on 11 June editorialised that, while this was a serious question, it might end in Victoria being made to look foolish. Undismayed, Ogier, now 85, on 27 August repeated his case at a meeting of the Geographical Society.[110]

By this time the Victorian Government had sought and been provided with a legal verdict. On Saturday 6 October Melbourne newspapers advised that the government endorsed the advice of counsel – that the territory in question belonged to New South Wales, and no further action would be taken. The *Age* that day noted that its articles had led to the government's seeking the legal opinion. On the Monday following the paper carried a long

---

[107] 'New South Wales Land Grab', *Age*, 22 April 1905, p. 4.
[108] DS to H. Higgins and I. Isaacs, 4 and 6 October 1905, LB6, pp. 1, 2.
[109] 'The Riverina', *Argus*, 1 June 1906, p. 5
[110] 'Riverina Question', *Argus*, 28 August 1906, p. 7.

refutation, claiming the matter was *not* settled. Refusing to take no for an answer, Syme wrote to Byrne in London asking him to 'hunt up documents bearing on the subject', which would 'no doubt be found in some government departments', saying he would get help from Victoria's Agent-General and was getting a letter from the Premier (Bent) to be sent to him.[111] This is the last word extant of what in hindsight was clearly a hopeless cause and a gross error of judgment by Syme. For once his independent, not to say idiosyncratic views, carried no sway with the powers that be.

Syme was still seen as leader of the press in Victoria and Australia but, compared with his position in the 1890s, was less prominent amongst the public men of Melbourne. No longer was he regularly named as an important guest in reports of official social functions, although he may well have attended. For the stage was larger now, with a third level of government in Melbourne, the temporary seat of the Federal Parliament. Public office outside the newspaper business did not claim much of his attention and time. When in April 1902 he was reproached for neglect of the affairs of the Melbourne Public Library, of which he was a Trustee, he responded defiantly, attacking recent acquisitions and asking 'how many of the members know anything about literature either ancient or modern'.[112] His aggressive letter was probably to his old adversary, the politician Edward Langton, who had countered *Age* allegations of corruption in 1867, brought successful libel actions against him in 1877, and was now President of the Trust.

More than ever, Syme was closely involved with members of his large and growing family. Five of his seven children were married (Oswald would wed in 1908 after his father's death; Olive, mildly impaired, remained single) and six more grandchildren were born during his final years – Marjorie and Hilaire for Geoffrey and Violet; Ursula for Arthur and Amy; Hugh, Maisie and David for Herbert and Ethel – a total of 21 at their grandfather's death (M. Syme 2013, 238–244). A hint of his relations with this brood is provided by Arthur's elder daughter, Elaine, born in 1897. In her late 60s she recalled as a child being invited to Killara by her grandfather, being often at Blythswood and walking round the garden with him, and being at Seaforth for holidays where Syme came on weekends.[113] Elaine stated that Syme, while 'shy and reserved', loved to have children about, provided they were not afraid of him.

---

[111] DS to Byrne, 17 October 1906, LB6, p. 26.
[112] DS to [no addressee] 1 April 1904, LB5, p. 429.
[113] E. Dennis to C. Sayers, 11 May 1964, SFP Box 1196/1(a).

CHAPTER 15

Syme provided livelihood and residences for most of his offspring and their families: for Geoffrey work at the *Age* office and a home, Conisbro, adjacent to Blythswood; for Francis, Oswald and Lucie, at his Yarra Valley properties Dalry, Killara and Tarrawarra; and for Olive at Blythswood. Herbert was provided with a very senior position in his father's newspaper business and his residence, Rockingham, was also in close proximity to Blythswood. Arthur, with his medical practice in Lilydale and less beholden to his father was, however, in regular contact, with Syme calling in at Arthur's for breakfast en route to Killara, daughter Elaine remembered. Besides his descendants, there were contacts with his nieces and nephews – his late brother's medico son George and his sister Margaret Gourlay's son John Ebenezer and daughter Mary Jane Lormer – and with a bevy of Johnsons on his wife's side. Above all, there was Annabella, his life partner and support. 'Grandma' was 'very clever', Elaine believed, and a 'wonderful companion' for Syme.

Last months

When Syme commissioned *Age* reporter Ambrose Pratt to write his biography is not recorded. Pratt, who had joined the staff in January 1906, very swiftly had his salary raised from £8 to a relatively high £10 per week, although less than that of valued reporter Hoare, at £12.12.[114] Syme may have preferred Pratt, because of his growing reputation as an author, albeit of fiction. Probably this was towards the middle of 1907, following publicity for *The Counterstroke*, his sixth novel published in book form, claimed one of the best from an author 'rapidly taking a high place as a writer of fiction'.[115] Another novel, *The Invasion of Australia: A Forecast*, predicting a German invasion of Australia in 1914, had been serialised in the *Age* from 10 November to 1 December 1906. Work on the biography must have been in train for some months, with Syme writing and dictating Pratt's chief source material, when Deakin agreed to write a preface – his diary entry for 7 October 1907 is 'Wrote Syme finally re Preface' and for 10 October, 'Final reply to DS'.[116]

In October Syme was sliding inexorably into his final illness. An undated letter to Deakin, filed with others dated 8 and 9 October 1907 containing his final exhortations on matters of tariff and imperial preference, expresses the hope that Deakin's health is better (he had been under stress and unwell since returning in August from the Imperial Conference in London) and states

---

[114] Entries for Hoare and Pratt in Wages Book, pp. 200, 394.
[115] 'New Books', *Age*, 2 February 1907, p. 6.
[116] Diary entries for 7, 10 October 1907, Deakin Papers, Series 2.

that his own is 'very bad'.[117] Though he may not have known it, Syme was suffering from cancer of the oesophagus, then an incurable disease and still often terminal today. The first successful surgery was carried out in 1913; later treatments include radiation and chemotherapy ('History of Esophageal Surgery' 2010; 'Stomach and Oesophageal Cancer' 2014). Early symptoms are difficulty in swallowing (dysphagia) and associated loss of weight, also heartburn and acid reflux. A recognised associated factor is tobacco smoking, in which Syme may have continued to indulge (a letter of November 1897 concerns an order for 1000 cigars, to be delivered to his home).[118]

Syme was under the care of his surgeon nephew George, who told his uncle that neither he nor the eminent specialists whom he had consulted (physician Sir Henry Maudsley, radiologist Frederick Clendinnen and physician David Grant) could offer a cure. George was to regret their having been 'frankly honest', writing to Annabella on 26 October that it seemed some of the family thought he was not sufficiently interested in Syme's condition.[119] He protested on the contrary to have taken the deepest interest and professed his 'lifelong affection and deep obligations'. By this time Syme, having rejected the experts' opinion, was undertaking a 'cure' in the country town Shepparton, offered by the local doctor William Gaze. On 16 October, a fortnight after his 80th birthday (there is no record of how he spent it), he travelled to the country town and took a room at the Court House Hotel. He wrote to Annabella of being amused by the local paper's report of 'the millionaire journalist' having arrived and 'taken a suite of apartments'.[120]

Writing frequently to his wife, he reported days good and bad, but didn't want her to visit until he was better. He mentioned vomiting (a later symptom of the cancer), attention to diet, and 'electric' treatment on his throat. He wrote to Herbert that he would 'see the thing through, however' and to Annabella that he would give the process a 'thorough trial'. So doing, he engaged in other activities too, visiting farms in the district and on 22 October attending the local show. He sent instructions to Herbert and Geoffrey, mainly about shares and sheep and crops, with just one about newspapers – that *Leader* illustrations compared unfavourably with those in the *Australasian*. But clearly he was failing, writing on 12 November that he

---

[117] DS to A. Deakin, 'Monday' [October 1907?], Deakin Papers, Series 15.
[118] DS to Levy, 13 November 1897, LB5, p. 251.
[119] G.A. Syme to AS, 26 October 1907, in the possession of Dr Veronica Condon.
[120] The source for Syme's stay in Shepparton are photocopies of some 30 letters from him to family members, mostly to his wife, in the possession of Dr Veronica Condon. Dated ones range from 17 October to 12 November 1907.

CHAPTER 15

would be coming home, had lost weight, and a nurse was needed to treat him as an invalid for at least a month. It is not clear if he knew that his illness was terminal.

Wherever he was nursed – in Shepparton or elsewhere – he had been bedridden for some time when he returned to Blythswood on 10 December – in 'middling health', Herbert wrote to Deakin, who tried unsuccessfully to see him on 17 December.[121] Deakin made what appears to have been his last visit on 22 December, for a 'chat', recording that Syme was 'weak'.[122] On 2 January 1908 Geoffrey wrote to the secretary of the Irrigation League, declining on Syme's behalf the offer of Vice-Presidency, saying that his father was at present confined to his bed through illness and could not reply.[123]

Whether Syme still had input to the *Age* editorials is not known. Mildly positive in tone, the New Year leader conveys none of Syme's characteristic pessimism. It states that the governments, state and federal, can begin 1908 with a 'fair sense of satisfaction', with the 'great strong commonsense of the Australian Democracy' steering a course between the 'extremes of visionary socialism' and the 'reactionary timidity' of socialism.

While the archives yield no clues to Syme's condition during the next few weeks, the sub-leader in the *Age* of 18 January 1908 encapsulates his ideas about the status and function of the press, expounded to Pratt for use in the biography. The modern newspaper promises to have an extraordinary influence on the drama of daily life in the 20th century, it stressed. It canvassed the history of the fourth estate, asserting that the power of journalism is growing – debating great questions of reform before parliament puts them into law, moulding public opinion and giving shape to legislation. Seeing the press as a moral force, the editorial claims that the 'highest form of journalism of the future' will be 'the best transcript of human life as it is, and the highest index to what it may become'. This is a more eloquent expansion of Syme's unpublished notes on 'The Press' – that it 'not only records public opinion but helps to form it', that it 'takes initiative in all legislation, Parlt never moves unless urged by the press'.[124] Speculatively, if this leader was not conceived *by* Syme, it may well have

---

[121] H. Syme to A. Deakin, 11 December 1907, Deakin Papers, Series 15; GS to R. McKnight, 11 December 1907, SFP Box 1183/1.
[122] Diary entry for 22 December 1907, Deakin Papers, Series 2.
[123] GS to Secretary, Irrigation League, 2 January 1908, SFP Box 1183/1.
[124] Syme's notes on 'The Press' in 'Work-Book of Some David Syme Manuscripts', pp. 327–373, compiled by and in the possession of Dr Veronica Condon.

been written *for* him (by Pratt?), as a tribute to what he had aimed to do in the *Age* while he was still *compos mentis* and able to appreciate it.

He must have been still lucid, for there are entries dated 18 and 19 January (apparently additions and revisions) in one of his notebooks of memoirs. Moreover, his last will (discussed in the concluding chapter) is dated 19 January and signed. At this time, Melbourne was experiencing a raging heatwave. The *Age* of Monday 20 January noted that the temperature reached 112.6 degrees Fahrenheit (almost 45 C) in the shade on the previous Friday (17 January), and that Melbourne, since becoming a city, had never gone through a worse five days, drastically affecting the sick, the fragile and the very poor, with numerous deaths from heat exhaustion. On the Friday night Annabella wrote to daughter-in-law Amy of a 'frightful' day and 'fearful' night, with no great prospect of a change, but noted that Syme had endured 'not so badly' after all.[125]

Mercifully, the cool change came on the Tuesday. However, by Monday 27 January it became known through the press that Syme was one of the sufferers of the heatwave, the Hobart *Mercury* reporting that he had become seriously ill. More precisely, the *Gippsland Times* stated that he was dangerously ill. On 10 February Annabella wrote again to Amy that she expected this to be her husband's 'last night', that 'all must be thankful for his sake' and that 'we have chosen the Boroondara Cemetery as our last home'.[126] Not a word of his condition appeared in the *Age* until 13 February, when the 'About People' column spelled out the true state of affairs: 'With deepest regret we have to announce that the serious illness of Mr. D. Syme, now extending over several weeks, has reached such a critical condition that no hope of his recovery is entertained.' Perhaps he had lapsed into a coma for, as reported in the *Age* of 15 February, he 'succumbed quietly' the next morning, Friday 14 February, at 7.30 a.m.[127] Kew physician Dr. Cowen supplied three causes on the death certificate: 'Carcinoma of oesophagus, Dysphagia, Exhaustion'.[128] To 'see the thing through', starving to death, must have drawn unconscionably on his remarkable powers of endurance.

On Saturday 15 February the *Age* had heavy black borders to the columns of the front page and to the editorial spread of pages 12 and 13. The editorial

---

[125] AS to Amy Syme, 'Friday night' [17 January 1908], in the possession of Judith Adams.
[126] AS to Amy Syme, 10 February 1908, in the possession of Judith Adams.
[127] 'Death of Mr. David Syme', *Age*, 15 February 1908, p. 13.
[128] David Syme, Death Certificate, Registry of Births, Deaths and Marriages, Melbourne.

CHAPTER 15

mourned the loss of the services of a man who had been a household word for over half a century, a great journalist and a great nation builder. It observed that he had found seats in parliament for four or five staff and thus brought the *Age* into closer relationship with government; it likened Syme to Thomas Delane, famed editor of the London *Times* from 1841 to 1877. Noting that his death came at an auspicious time when important matters were on the statute book – protection, women's suffrage, old-age pensions, payment of members – it quoted Shakespeare's Othello: 'I have done the State some service and they know it'. The facing page carried a long article headed 'Death of Mr. David Syme. A Great Journalist'. It conveyed that Syme had suffered from heart and digestive disorders for three months past, had been in a critical condition, and had succumbed quietly. Under subheadings, his achievements in various fields besides journalism were enumerated. The article contains a few factual errors relating to the early years of Syme's connection with the *Age* business – no one from that time around to correct them. The brief death notice appeared on Monday 17 February, the day of the funeral.

The weather was fine that day, with a pleasant temperature that reached 75.3 degrees Fahrenheit (about 24 C) in the afternoon and light cool southerly winds.[129] Flags were at half-mast on the Melbourne Town Hall and other public buildings. Some 250 employees from the *Age* office went to Blythswood to see their chief for the last time. A service was conducted there by two Scottish-born Presbyterian ministers: Patrick Murdoch of Trinity Church, Camberwell, a theologian of the liberal Free Church tradition, and Dr Alexander Marshall of Scots Church, Collins Street. As was customary, the widow and other women and children of the family stayed behind, while the menfolk escorted the cortège to the Presbyterian section of the Boroondara Cemetery. (Syme's sister Margaret and husband John Gourlay were buried in its Baptist section.) It was reported that hundreds of people lined the route.

The employees walked at the head of the long procession. Then came the hearse, followed by a floral carriage, and after, five mourning coaches, with Syme's immediate male family in the first three: Herbert and Francis, and the officiating clergy in the first; Arthur, Geoffrey and Oswald in the second; Vere and Norman, the young adult sons of Francis, with son-in-law William Macalister and long-time friend Samuel Gillott in the third. Nephew Dr George Syme, out of favour or disaffected, was apparently not

---

[129] 'Funeral of Mr. David Syme', *Age*, 18 February 1908, p. 5.

with these family mourners, though reported as attending the service. The eight pallbearers were *Age* editor Schuler, retired commercial editor Anthony Robinson, *Leader* editor Short, *Every Saturday* editor G.R. Brickhill, publisher Packer, printer Clarke, head of the Machine Department Fred Kruger and president of the News Agents' Association Flintoff. At the grave in the Presbyterian section, Reverend Murdoch read the service and Reverend Marshall offered a prayer. Luminaries present included the Lieutenant Governor of Victoria Sir John Madden, Prime Minister Deakin, Premier Bent, the Melbourne Lord Mayor, scores of federal, state and municipal politicians and leading public servants, and many representatives of the press, including Sydney and London newspapers. Mitchell Armstrong of the *Kyneton Guardian*, one of the cooperative that bought the *Age* in 1855, was probably the only person there who had known Syme when he first came to the *Age*.

The *Age* this day carried the first of a series of appreciations, under the heading, 'The Late Mr. David Syme. Tributes by Public Men'. Deakin's, with pride of place, states that during the 30 years he had known Syme acquaintance had deepened into intimacy. He remarked that Syme, in his own home, was 'exceptionally amiable, courteous, and of warm affections'. He pointed out his many sides: newspaper proprietor, editor-in-chief, and supervising business manager, participant in all public movements, farmer, breeder, irrigator and speculator, manufacturer, head of a large family. Accompanying Deakin's tribute were contributions from the Minister for Customs, the Chair of the Commonwealth Council of Rifle Associations, and the New South Wales Institute of Journalists, which called him a man of 'strong convictions and unfailing courage', an 'original thinker of the philosophic class'. More tributes and reports of motions of sympathy at public meetings (professional associations, trade unions, municipal councils, etc.) appeared in the *Age* every day until the first week of March. Newspapers throughout Australia and New Zealand – in total, scores if not hundreds – published obituaries, frequently sourced from those in the *Age*, or the *Argus* of 15 February (which stressed Syme's ill-health and noted that he 'pushed protection too far'), or the evening *Herald* of the day he died, 14 February, headed 'A Great Man Passes'.[130] A valuable exception was the obituary in the *Kyneton Guardian* of 15 February, written by Armstrong, providing personal

---

[130] GS, Scrapbook containing obituaries of David Syme, SFP Box 1194/1; Obituaries of David Syme, collected from Australian Newspapers, MS MSB 526, Australian Manuscripts Collection, State Library of Victoria.

CHAPTER 15

knowledge and views. On 18 February it reported the funeral and published Armstrong's 'The Early History of "The Age" By One of the Co-Partners', providing precise details and unique observations.

In London the *Daily Chronicle*, with which Syme had been closely associated, observed on 15 February that the announcement of his death would be received 'with great regret by his many friends in England'. The *Morning Post*, the newspaper for which Deakin covertly wrote, on 17 February carried an obituary by Bernhard Wise, former New South Wales politician and now barrister in London and promoter of Australian culture (Ryan 1990), claiming that 'Australia has lost in David Syme one of her great men'. The *Manchester Guardian* of 15 February wrote of him as 'perhaps the most notable journalist that our colonies have produced…a political thinker of originality…founder of colonial liberalism'. Giving a nationalistic twist, the *British-Australasian*, which Syme's erstwhile cable correspondent Philip Mennell had owned and edited from 1892 until his death in 1905, on 20 February described him as 'the most redoubtable journalist that the Commonwealth has known…[a person of] tremendous intellectual power, tremendous energy and tremendous determination'.

In Melbourne memorialising of the late proprietor in the *Age*, *Leader* and *Every Saturday* tapered off within weeks, while publication of the papers continued without a blip. *Sic transit gloria mundi.*

Chapter 16

AFTERWORDS

David Syme was a quintessentially typical and an exceptionally singular man of Victoria's golden age. A goldrush immigrant, imbued with the ethos of progress and development, he helped 'make' Victoria and, in turn, with an estate worth over £900,000 at his death, made himself into one of the wealthiest men in Australia. A controlling and caring family man, he exemplifies par excellence the paterfamilias of Queen Victoria's era. Like fellow intellectuals he pursued and pondered on the faith and doubt issues of the age. Australia's acknowledged leading man of the newspaper press, he was of the cast and calibre to be classed with the press barons seen to have dominated British and American journalism for a century from the 1830s (Brendon 1982, 1). It is easier to consider these four facets than to encapsulate an essence, to describe the 'inner' man, for how can the mind of another be known, especially by a biographer more than a century later? And yet, through these disparate aspects, common threads of personal belief and motivation may at least be conjectured.

Arriving at a valuation of Syme's estate for probate took several calculations, over time. The day after his death widowed Annabella and the five sons met informally at Blythswood with solicitor Sir Samuel Gillott, who provided them with an 'epitome' of his will.[1] On 18 February, the day after the funeral, they met to hear him read it, and have formally confirmed that they were to be the executors and trustees of his estate.[2] At this meeting, arrangements were made to open new bank accounts for 'office' and 'private' use. At the next meeting, three days later, documents were completed for re-registering the *Age*, *Leader*, and *Every Saturday* in the names of the trustees (accomplished on 22 February) (Darragh 1997, 94 [37.15], 100 [62.10], 282 [1018.03]), and preliminary arrangements were made for probate valuation.

---

[1] Geoffrey Syme, Notes of Meetings of Executors/Trustees, Ledger in possession of Dr Veronica Condon.

[2] Trustees and Executors, Notebook of Oswald Syme (Secretary), SFP Box 1193/1.

CHAPTER 16

Valuing the newspaper business was relatively straightforward – freehold, plant and materials, goodwill, all of which comprised about half of the total assets. The private real estate – town and beach residences of the family, working farms, numerous city and country properties rented out – comprised the greater part of the other half. Valuing it, taking into account various liabilities and outstanding debts, was far more difficult. And there was the extensive portfolio of shares and debentures. On 15 April the estate was sworn for probate at £779,535, the figure adjusted upwards to £882,801 by an affidavit of 26 May, a 'Final Balance £979,480' arrived at on 16 October, and duty of £92,846.15.8 certified on 5 November 1908 as paid (10 per cent of the value, excluding a £50,000 bequest to establish a David Syme Charitable Trust, and other non-dutiable gifts).[3] Over the next nine years there were sundry very minor adjustments to the total.

Then approaching one million pounds, Syme's estate in today's Australian dollars would class him a multi-millionaire; indeed, almost a billionaire by some conversion rates. His assets far exceeded those of his contemporaries. The *Age* of 28 March 1903 reported two 'large' deceased estates that, at £268,335 and £90,400, were a fraction of Syme's. Published sworn for probate amounts for personages dying between 1890 and 1920 rarely exceed £50,000, and most are much less.[4] Amongst the estates of Victoria's public men of the time are: Sir Archibald Michie's, £19,700 in 1899; Sir William Zeal's, £74,804 in 1912; and that of Syme's close associate, solicitor Samuel Gillott, who died in 1913, £291,864 – about one third of Syme's. As for Australian men of the press, Samuel Winter of the Melbourne *Herald* died in 1903 leaving £31,000 and Sir Robert Kyffin Thomas of the Adelaide *Register* in 1910, leaving £38,202. Watkin Wynne, manager of the Sydney *Daily Telegraph*, left £265,113. Sir Lauchlan Charles Mackinnon of the rival *Argus* died in 1925 leaving only £50,000. A notable exception to this pattern is Syme's Adelaide newspaper counterpart, Sir John Langdon Bonython, who died decades later, in 1939, leaving some £4 million, and whose career has some parallels with Syme's.

Evidently, Syme was never penniless. Arriving in Melbourne from California in September 1852, he had funds sufficient for a cabin passage from Sydney and overnight accommodation before setting out for the goldfields where, though he did not make his fortune and indeed was taken down more

---

3   David Syme, newspaper proprietor, Probate and Administration Files, VPRS-28-PO and P2, Public Record Office Victoria.

4   Figures obtained through searching 'sworn for probate' in the *Australian Dictionary of Biography* (adb.anu.edu.au).

than once, he remained solvent. His ensuing roads contracting enterprise was promisingly profitable. Taking over the struggling *Age* newspaper business in 1860, he discharged the mortgage within 18 months, while for all of the 48 years of his control the enterprise showed a net annual profit. Fluctuating in the 1860s from a dangerously low £53 to a more comfortable high of £3016, it had risen to between £20,000 and £30,000 in the 1880s except for the remarkable figure of £98,421 in 1888, the year of boom. Although falling back during the depths of the depression and the financially draining railways litigation of the early 1890s, from 1895 the profits increased by leaps, reaching over £60,000 for 1901 and approaching £70,000 for each of the two years before Syme's death.

By the end of the 1860s Syme was financially comfortable enough to begin investing in real estate and financial enterprises, choosing to buy and sell only when the market was advantageous to him – seen for instance in his acquisition in 1869 of land at Mount Macedon, building a house (Rosenheim) on it, and selling the property profitably to the Victorian Government in 1885. He kept informed about land values, as his 1879 *Melbourne Review* article shows, and over time amassed a large collection of titles to properties in the heart of Melbourne, throughout Victoria and some beyond its borders. He built up a sizeable portfolio of shares and debentures, investing carefully in a range of mining enterprises (including coal, copper, gold) and developmental projects.[5] In financial transactions he always drove a hard bargain and, after his goldfields reverses in the early 1850s, seems never to have been taken down. While augmenting his assets, he received income from rents and dividends that increased over the years. A summary of income for 1904 that totals £11,348 (£6655 bank interest; £3163 dividends; £1529 rents) may not take into account considerable outgoings; in addition, he was then receiving an annual salary of £1650 (raised to £2500 in 1906) and, moreover, had the newspaper business profits at his disposal – in 1904 amounting to £66,424.[6]

Syme was one of the immigrant Scotsmen seen to have brought to Victoria 'elements of industry, fortitude, tenacity, courage, thrift and shrewdness' (Serle 1971, 337). A Lowlander, he left a swiftly industrialising, urbanising society, centred in Glasgow where he had his first employment (Checkland 1989, 38–42). His financial acumen and acquisitiveness have

---

[5] Probate Jurisdiction, Statement of Assets and Liabilities [April 1908], SFP Box 1193/2(b).

[6] Profit and Loss Accounts, 1910–1910, SFP Box 1192/1.

been interpreted in the context of the Protestant 'work ethic', specifically applied to Calvinism (Presbyterian Scots), with his belief in and acting on a duty to make money driven by secularised Calvinist values (Reed 1991). The interpretation is persuasive, particularly considering the example of the Calvinist commitments and conflicts of his father, and of his older brothers in their early adulthood.

Syme's capitalist drive may also be viewed in the context of the imperial project. That is, identified with the building and development of the colony of Victoria by a cohort of ambitious Britons, most particularly, a generation of young goldrush immigrants. Serle wrote that the lure of gold 'remade Victoria, and peopled it…with men of more diverse talents, skills and backgrounds, and perhaps more vigour, than Australia had yet seen', and singled out George Higinbotham, Graham Berry, David Syme and Charles Gavan Duffy as thus having taken their places in Australian history (Serle 1977, 381). All liberals of reformist–radical inclinations who helped shape the Victorian political system and legislative framework, three did so substantially as parliamentary representatives, while Syme exerted influence from his base as a newspaper proprietor, and for a longer period, when the post-goldrush generation was coming to the fore. He also stands out for his extensive involvement in promoting industry and agriculture, not only through his newspapers, but also through his own experimenting with irrigation, his breeding and marketing of livestock and his development of agricultural products. In a completely different setting, through architecture and construction, he contributed to the landscaping of urban Melbourne. Arriving in Victoria just after its creation, and when the colony was promising to be enriched by gold finds, he seized and optimised opportunities to take part in development and 'progress'.

Syme's testamentary disbursement of his wealth indicates the central importance of family for him, his widow and offspring well provided for in various ways, and some close relatives receiving legacies or annuities. In the weeks before his death he had made gifts to Oswald (on 28 December 1907, the household goods at Killara in consideration of his 'natural love and affection') and to Geoffrey (on 16 January 1908 an outright sum of £10,000 as 'absolute gift', bespeaking gratitude for his assistance during his decline).[7] In his will, dated 19 January 1908, he left his estate in trust to his widow and five sons until the death of all, when, excluding the newspaper business,

---

[7] Will of David Syme, 19 January 1908, Wills, VPRS-7591-P2, Public Record Office Victoria (typed copy, SFP Box 1193/2(a)).

it would be sold and distributed to the children of the sons. Additionally, widow Annabella was granted an immediate £500, an annuity of £3000, the household effects and lifetime residence at Blythswood and Seaforth. Daughter Lucie was granted the income from and lifetime residence at Tarrawarra and could receive any rents and incomes from the property. The sum of £10,000 was to be invested, to provide an income for the care of Olive, with Annabella to be her guardian. Son Francis was to pay his debts, for which he had given promissory notes, and accrued interest (this latter subsequently waived by the Trustees). There were legacies of £1000 each to his nephew Dr George Adlington Syme, niece Mary Jane Lormer and niece Jane Mary Johnson (daughter of Ebenezer and widow of Annabella's brother), and an annuity of £100 for an unmarried niece of Annabella's.

Earlier, Syme had helped all sons with their vocations, taking Herbert and Geoffrey into the business, and also Oswald, then finding another occupation for him when that apparently did not suit. He supported Arthur's medical studies in Britain. From the mid-1880s, and in the face of personality clashes, he had continued to help Francis, who was more successful in growing a family than generating an adequate income and managing finances. Annabella wrote perceptively to Arthur in 1894 about the relationship of father and son:

> [I]t would be utterly hopeless to try for him & Papa to get on intimate connection. The only chance of peace is not to be within easy reach. Both are mistaken in their notions of each other, but Francis is so irritable & touchy that it is like a match to gunpowder to talk to him & when he is in the right it is just as bad as when he is wrong. I often wonder how I can get on at all with such clashing dispositions.[8]

Nevertheless, Syme persisted with advice and support, his last extant letter to his son addressed 'My dear Francis' and concluding 'Your affectionate father'.[9] This and other traces indicate deep reciprocal caring.

Syme was exceedingly fortunate with his family. While basically nuclear (children living with parents), as was the norm in 19th-century Australia though not then in Britain (G. Young 1960, 153; Kingston 1988, 142), there was a significant extended component. In Melbourne there were three of the four grandparents to Syme and Annabella's children, and numerous aunts, uncles and cousins on both sides; and there was much socialising

---

[8] AS to Arthur Syme, 22 May 1894, in the possession of Judith Adams.
[9] DS to F. Syme, 'Tuesday', in the possession of Judith Adams.

CHAPTER 16

amongst them. When adult, with children of their own, Herbert, Geoffrey, and their respective families lived in close proximity to Blythswood, Francis, Lucie and Oswald were established at Syme's Yarra Valley properties, Dalry, Tarrawarra and Killara, and Arthur at Lilydale was regularly visited by his father en route to Killara. Family cohesion was thus maintained.

Like many other colonists in Australia, and his two brothers before emigration, Scottish Syme married 'out', to an English girl (McDonald and Quiggan 1985). Fortunately, he was not subject to spousal desertion or death. Surviving letters of Syme to his wife, expressing his love and emotional dependence and sharing with her a range of business problems and proposals attest the suitability of the match. No letters from Annabella to him have been located, but hers to Arthur and his wife Amy and to Geoffrey and Oswald reveal that, notwithstanding her separate sphere of domestic responsibilities, she was intelligently interested in and conversant with her husband's business matters, and also concerned for his fluctuating health. She was involved with numerous charities, the secretary of the Austin Hospital for Incurables committee describing her as a 'splendid business woman, thorough and practical in everything' and with patients, of 'winning gentleness and sympathy'.[10] Apparent from a letter to Arthur of 28 July 1891, she was very affected by the drawn-out break-up of the partnership with Joseph, but managed to conceal the symptoms of her emotional upset, while two letters she wrote to Arthur's wife Amy during the testing time of Syme's final illness display great strength of character.[11] In the first 20 years of their marriage she gave birth to nine children. Given the infant mortality rates of the era, that two died in infancy was not unusual, although occasioning sadness and suffering at the time. One of the surviving offspring had a mild intellectual disability; the other six were mentally and physically normal. Syme presided over them in Victorian patriarchal mode, somewhat heavy-handed, remote and sovereign. Knowing best, he carried out a 'duty' to inculcate values and habits, and expected the obedience he did not get from Francis at one extreme but did at the other, from gentle, malleable Geoffrey. Through his last will and testament, the control was to extend beyond the grave.

That, at a deeper level, family had for Syme a quasi-religious significance, is suggested by the directive in his will that a sum not exceeding £700 be expended on 'the construction of a family vault in or over my grave in the

---

[10] 'Death of Mrs. David Syme', *Leader*, 4 September 1915, p. 49.
[11] AS to Amy Syme, 28 July 1891, 10 February 1908 and 'Friday night 10.15 p.m.' [17 January 1908], in the possession of Judith Adams.

form of a Doric temple or any such other structure as my trustees may consider suitable or appropriate'. He may have discussed this with Walter Butler in early 1907, two letters from the architect at this time referring to but not specifying a new project.[12] Supporting this is that plans for the vault were considered at the first meeting of the trustees on 21 February 1908 and found unsuitable.[13] At the meeting of 13 March Butler presented a drawing that was said to be 'an improvement on the Temple of Phylae'. It was approved, with the details to be left to Annabella. Estimated to cost about £1500, the additional £800 would be paid by the Trustees. A history of the Boroondara Cemetery states the tomb to have been constructed in 1912/1913 (Turnbull 2008, 6). A long undated letter from Butler to Annabella must have been written thereafter, describing the structure and its architectural and symbolic significance.[14] Inferentially, she had not after all been involved with the 'details'. Nor had Syme, it would seem, been privy to Butler's departure from the specified Doric tomb to what would be an outstanding example of Egyptian revival architecture and, according to architectural historian Harriet Edquist (2003, 26), 'a key work of the Australian Arts & Crafts movement'.

The granite tomb with bronze decorations (fig. 16.1), one of two striking temple-like edifices dominating the cemetery (the other is the Greek-influenced granite Springthorpe memorial, erected 1899–1907, which perhaps sparked Syme's idea), is based on an ancient Egyptian temple, Trajan's Kiosk. In Syme's time known to travellers as 'Pharaoh's Bed', it was 'the most beautiful part', Butler told Syme's widow, of the Temple of Isis, located on the island of Philae in the Nile River (later badly affected by flooding from the Aswan dams, and re-erected on the higher island of Agilkia) (Morkot 2005, 88, 312–316). Butler stated that the Egyptian building was 'comparatively light & graceful in its lines & nearer anything else in Egypt it approaches to the grace & charm of Grecian architecture'. He saw it as suitable because Syme's views in *The Soul* had affinity with the Egyptian tradition of care of the souls of the dead. Butler also asserted, unverifiably, that Syme 'probably' had this in mind. He described the decorative motifs used, most significantly the 'hooded python' embodied in the design of the gates and on the stone cornice around the top, telling her it was the emblem of leadership and power.

---

[12] W. Butler to GS, 29 January 1907, Butler and Bradshaw to DS, 19 April 1907, SFP Box 1190/4(d).

[13] Trustees and Executors, Notebook of Oswald Syme (Secretary), SFP Box 1193/1.

[14] W. Butler to AS, undated, SFP Box 1180/5(d).

CHAPTER 16

Figure 16.1. Syme tomb in Boroondara Cemetery, the 'last home' for David and Annabella. (Photographed by the author in June 2007)

Photographs (such as that in Mehling (1990, 376)) attest the astounding likeness of Syme's tomb to the Egyptian 'kiosk'. Annabella, who died on 30 August 1915, is the only other Syme listed as buried in what her husband envisaged as the 'family vault'. Affixed to the interior are several memorial plaques: one each for the infant daughters Caroline, who died in 1864, and Gabrielle, in 1871, perhaps arranged for by Annabella; one for the intransigent son Francis, who died in 1931 (was the plaque his wish?); and three for descendants more recently deceased – in 1991, 1996 and 2010. Although not the final resting place of Syme's own children, the impressively graceful memorial to him and Annabella is obviously valued by some later Symes.

The temple as family vault can be seen as consonant with Syme's search for truths about the human condition and the basis of life, and the solitary spiritual questing throughout his life. Immersion at 17 in theological studies at James Morison's Kilmarnock Academy left him directionless two years later, with neither answers to questions about the meaning of life nor the skills for making a living. For some 10 years thereafter, by trial and error, he made his way in the world, fetching up in Australia and, virtually by accident, was propelled into the arena of newspapers and journalism, which became his lifelong profession. In mid-life and mid-career, when business was booming, in parallel he was analysing the underlying causes and effects of current happenings. Through his writings on political economy and on governance published from 1870 to 1881, he sought, in tracing historical developments, to uncover and expound principles or laws, as the basis for the policies he advocated in his papers. During this time also, he was involved with the spiritualism movement, seeking to corroborate the claims made for contact with the dead, an activity probably eventually unfruitful, and quietly dropped.

Syme's books published late in his life, in 1890 and 1903, show a renewed if not continuing search for meaning beyond the here and now. One focusing on evolution, the other making a case for the immortality of the soul, both advance arguments with impeccable logic, but they lack elements of faith and belief beyond the scientifically demonstrable. In an age when religious certainties were being questioned and challenged, in colonial intellectual circles no less than in Britain (Helmstadter and Lightman 1990; Serle 1971, 127–152), Syme sought, through science, answers usually provided by religion. One wonders if this was satisfactory enough for him, and whether the notion of the family tomb was an unconscious attempt to fill a void. Possibly Syme, who was averse to organised religion and avoided religious content in his newspapers, was compensating for an unresolved dimension of his lived experience, thus exemplifying historian Beverly Kingston's view of colonial belief: 'What was really missing from religion in the colonies was grandeur or style built on the inheritance of the ages in older societies, or that intensity of belief, evident in societies less secure materially, and less committed to the use of reason to solve human problems' (Kingston 1988, 88). Valorising reason and science as the answers not only to human affairs and the ways of the world, but as avenues to eternal truths, Syme, in his driven restlessness, could be seen to embody the irreconcilable mix of contrasting traditions that shaped the society in which he spent his first 23 years – Calvinism in all its tortured forms, and the rationalist Scottish manifestation of the 18th-century Enlightenment (Checkland 1989, 133–137).

Syme is known as a newspaper proprietor of legendary political influence, which was strongest in the later 19th century and tailed off after Federation. As discussed in Chapter 1, this is the basis of most biographies, long and short. Formulating editorial policies for his *Age* and, to a lesser extent, participating personally in political movements and intervening with politicians, he was centrally involved in promoting vital issues of the time. He both sensed and

CHAPTER 16

experienced the needs of the newly enfranchised immigrant goldminers-turned-settlers – needs that could be translated into legislative programs in a colony where responsible government was established only four years before he took control of a newspaper to advocate them. He arrived on the Melbourne newspaper stage at an exceptionally favourable time, conducive to the mushrooming of newspapers, with the first 30 years of his incumbency – spanning goldrush to boom – a period of great prosperity, without the problems of transported felons or armed conflicts between settlers and Aborigines of earlier times and other colonies.

The *Age* was the newspaper that Victorians had to have, and Syme was fortunate to have been on the spot. This is not to diminish his stature or achievements. He was the right man for the upstart daily. Not only did he have his finger on the colonial political pulse, but he also kept abreast of press developments in the wider world, and was quick to innovate to advantage – utilising new technology to expand production, lowering the paper's price to widen its affordability, recruiting talented journalists, and broadening content beyond the political and parochial. In the 1860s and 1870s he progressively gained ascendancy for the *Age* over the other, longer established morning dailies, the *Argus* and *Herald*, through ferociously hard work in the *Age* office and several trips to Britain, where he visited leading provincial newspaper businesses and established useful links with their personnel, especially with the large-circulating *Newcastle Daily Chronicle*.

Competing with the *Argus*, particularly concerning news procurement, he constantly monitored the perennial tension between getting it first and getting it right. In these crucial years, two *Argus* proprietors Edward Wilson and Lauchlan Mackinnon had retired to rural England, from where they sent their directives, via their Melbourne representative, James Johnston, to the *Argus* on-the-spot management. Their correspondence, particularly concerning their opposition to emulating the *Age*, reveals their ignorant complacency.[15] This management by tyrannous distance only ended effectively when Mackinnon's cousin Lauchlan Charles Mackinnon became manager in 1881, by which time the *Age* had established its massive market share. The *Argus* only began to erode it after reducing its price to one penny in 1893. The other morning daily, the *Herald*, seen as a threat by Syme in the earlier 1860s, was bedevilled by the financial straits of its series of proprietors, and effectively neutralised when Syme bought it in 1868 and turned it into an evening paper.

---

[15] James Stewart Johnston, Correspondence, University of Melbourne Archives.

DAVID SYME

In the boom years of the 1880s and beyond Syme spread some of his workload. While he retained ultimate control, his nephew Joseph, and later his son Herbert, looked after the day-to-day management of the business and technical side. The collaborative relations that had been developing with Bonython of the *Advertiser* in Adelaide and Wynne at the *Daily Telegraph* in Sydney were well established. These included arrangements for obtaining and sharing news from other Australian colonies (Queensland, Western Australia), for sharing the costs of and reports from expeditioners and war correspondents, and of rights to syndicated features. Moreover, the combined cable news service based in London and operated by the three papers became a viable and often preferred alternative to the *Argus–Sydney Morning Herald* service, until the rivals found common interest against Reuters and amalgamated in 1895. For the editorial and literary department, Syme recruited an outstanding team of journalists, and began the in-service training of his son Geoffrey for eventual succession. With the *Age* having established a seemingly unassailable circulation in Melbourne, and exceeding that of most newspapers throughout the British Empire, Syme looked more to London press contacts than to British provincial ones. From 1887, if not earlier, his main Fleet Street contact was with Edward Lloyd, who bought the *Daily Chronicle* in 1876, transforming a small local paper into one of international standing. Later dealings were with son Frank Lloyd, whose *Daily Chronicle* was a source of news for the *Age* combination cable service for many years and in 1901 a London base for Geoffrey Syme to gain valuable experience.[16]

Other Australian newspapermen centrally important in establishing the metropolitan daily press include Edward Wilson, actively involved with the Melbourne *Argus* from 1848 until 1857 before he retired to England, and John Fairfax, owner of the *Sydney Morning Herald* from 1841 to 1877. Playing such a part for the *Age*, Syme's tenure was longer, extending into the changed environment of an expanding, internationalised press network that saw Bonython of the Adelaide *Advertiser* and John Winthrop Hackett of the *West Australian* come onto the press stage. Like Syme, each had a key role in conducting their metropolitan dailies, first in partnership, Bonython moving to full ownership in 1893, Hackett in 1912. Like Syme, both became extremely wealthy. Unlike Syme, who was often severely critical of parliamentary functioning, each also became a politician, Hackett in the Western Australian colonial, later state, Legislative Council from 1890 until

---

[16] DS to G. Bones, 11 January 1888, LB3, pp. 38–40.

CHAPTER 16

his death, Bonython a Member of the Federal House of Representatives from 1901 to 1905 (Pitcher 1979; Hunt 1983). The big difference between these two and Syme, however, is their sphere of operations. The man in Melbourne was operating in a vastly more populous metropolis and colony, South Australia having less than a third its population, while that of Western Australia, even after the goldrushes of the 1890s, was a tiny fraction. Much remains to be studied, however, about the cadre of leading journalists and the circumstances that gave rise to and shaped their Australian capital daily newspapers, providing uniquely vital news coverage until the advent of radio and television killed off all but a handful of hardy survivors.

Syme's role in the newspaper world is comparable to that of the so-called press barons beyond Australia, said to have 'transformed newspapers from servile little propaganda sheets into real organs of information and opinion' (Brendon 1982, 1) during the 'golden age' of independent newspaper owners and illustrious editors (Douglas 1999). Referring to the huge influence exercised by the *Age* upon some 100,000 readers, Deakin likened Syme, by implication, to Thomas Delane, editor of the London *Times* from 1841 to 1877 and to Horace Greeley of the New York *Tribune* from 1841 until 1872: 'the *Times* in its palmiest days was not more omnipotent in London nor the *Tribune* of Horace Greeley in New York' (Deakin 1944, 92) – a somewhat inflated comparison, for while Melbourne in 1870 had a population just over 200,000, that of New York approached 1,000,000 and London's was three times that number.

For the scale of operations, a more meaningful comparison is with powerful proprietors of the major English provincial newspaper concerns, to which colonial newspaper managers, Syme included, looked for models. One is Joseph Cowen (son of the radical politician, after whom Joseph Cowen Syme was named), owner from 1859 until his death in 1900 of the *Newcastle Daily Chronicle*, introducing technological and stylistic improvements and transforming it into the '*Times* of the North' (Brake and Demoor 2009, 148–149). Another is C.P. Scott, editor of the *Manchester Guardian* from 1871 to 1929, seen to have 'brought the paper into its glory' (Brake and Demoor 2009, 395), much as Syme did for the *Age*. There are marked and specific parallels with W.T. Stead, a journalist usually associated with the 'New Journalism' of the London *Pall Mall Gazette*, which he edited from 1883 to 1889 (Brake and Demoor 2009, 598; Robinson 2012, 14 and 256). Like Stead, Syme was self-educated, with a belief in his own infallibility. Like Stead, he adapted his newspaper to changing times and readerships. Broadening the range of topics covered, including controversial issues, both fostered investigative journalism. Most significantly, the two journalists were in tune concerning relations between the press and parliament, seeing the former as an initiator of change and reform, with a greater role than the latter, rather than the generally accepted reciprocal relationship.

A corollary of Syme's autocratic management style, his employees sometimes feared but always respected and admired him. His often abrupt manner, seen in written communications, could sometimes be extremely insulting to them, as also to his counterparts in charge of other newspapers – a contrast with the ingratiating tone of Bonython in correspondence. But that he valued staff who had held senior positions loyally for many years and wished, paternalistically, to reward them, is suggested by legacies in his will: £500 each to *Age* editor Schuler, leader writer Hoare and accountant Packer; £250 to agricultural writer Dow, *Leader* editor Henry Short and subeditor Stephens (the recipient of invective over decades). Biographer Pratt was not included, but perhaps was separately remunerated. Some junior employees were also singled out: cashier, printer and messenger each received £100; coachman and gardener each £50.

The core of Syme's 16-page closely handwritten will concerns disposal of the 'residuary and real estate', in particular, the newspaper business, which was to 'remain in the possession of my sons and of the survivors…until the death of the last survivor', with the imprints on the *Age* and *Leader* to be unchanged (no mention of *Every Saturday*, which inferentially could be dispensed with, and in 1912 was) and Herbert and Geoffrey to be retained for its 'conduct and management', the 'capacities and salaries' to be decided by the trustees. While appearing to give power to the trustees to sell and acquire property and to advance capital out of the trust monies for employing newspaper business staff, these provisions were hedged around with extensive, detailed, specific conditions and requirements for investments and other uses of income that would discourage actions – if indeed the trustees could come to the majority decisions deemed necessary.

After Syme's death the David Syme Trust provided for in his will administered the Syme newspapers enterprise, with Herbert as business manager until 1939 and Geoffrey managing editor to 1942 (Serle 1990; Condon 2005). From the 1920s several Syme grandchildren were on the staff, notably Kathleen Syme (daughter of Arthur) and Hugh Randall Syme (son of Herbert). After the death of all his brothers, in 1943 the sole surviving trustee, Oswald, took over management at the *Age* office, launching a successful action in the Supreme Court in 1948 to vary provisions of the will and thus enable the newspaper business to be floated

CHAPTER 16

on the Melbourne Stock Exchange, with a share issue to raise desperately needed capital (David Syme & Co. 1949–1986). Several Syme descendants were on the Board of Directors of the formally incorporated David Syme and Co. Ltd, and Oswald's grandson Ranald Macdonald was managing director from 1964 to 1983 (Tidey 1998), but the independent existence of the firm was increasingly in doubt after a partnership was negotiated with the Sydney based John Fairfax & Sons in 1966. The percentage of Fairfax holdings steadily increasing, a takeover was accomplished in 1983 and the Melbourne-based newspaper came under Sydney ownership. It was not an outcome that Syme could have foreseen or welcomed, but one which the inflexible arrangements decreed in his will, requiring continuance of the business as a family concern for decades come what may, surely helped to bring about.

Comparing him with the English newspaper proprietor Alfred Harmsworth, better known as Lord Northcliffe, shows that by the turn of the century Syme was no longer in the vanguard of developments, his half-century involvement with the press coming to an end when major changes were in the wind. In 19th-century Britain the newspaper industry was built on the basis of family businesses; towards the end of the century and beyond, there would be a shift from small-scale newspapers run by editor-proprietors to large companies owning newspaper chains (Lee 1976, 79; Wiener 1988, 57). The beginnings of the transition are seen markedly in the career and achievements of Harmsworth, more of a 20th-century media magnate than a 19th-century press baron. With a first publishing venture in 1888, in 1894 he 'burst upon Fleet Street' (Koss 1981, 356), built up a chain of newspapers and magazines, and in 1905 acquired the 'signature paper of Fleet Street', the *Times* (Brake and Demoor 2009, 270). He is viewed as 'a consummate journalist who changed the whole course of British journalism by making it both lively and prosperous' (*Concise Dictionary* 1992, v. 2, 1326).

By contrast with the huge Harmsworth empire, Syme's stable of newspapers was modest, comprising one daily and, at varying times, one to three weekly 'companion' newspapers and a monthly illustrated paper. In 1860 he inherited two weeklies (*Weekly Age* and *Leader*), experimentally started two more (the weekly *Farmers' Journal* and monthly *Australian News for Home Readers*), amalgamated the weeklies by stages into the *Leader*, developed the monthly into the outstandingly successful *Illustrated Australian News*, and in the 20th century started the popular lightweight *Every Saturday*. (Taking the same steps with their companion weeklies and monthlies, the *Argus* proprietors were generally slower to do so, as indeed they were with any change to the status quo.) While Syme's illustrated monthly was at first intended primarily for readers in Britain ('home') and for a time was issued in some intercolonial editions, the daily and weekly papers were for distribution primarily in Melbourne and Victoria. Otherwise, there were no trans-border ventures, no chains, and seemingly Syme had no such ambitions, except (as noted in Chapter 12) for toying briefly with the notion of starting a paper in London when he became sole proprietor in 1891. Moreover, though he had a good sense of the world around him and took his enterprise along the road from small partisan papers to mass-circulating enterprises, he seems to have had no vision of or plans for a world that was radically changing.

David Syme and Co. was a family concern and a company in name only until long after Syme's death. The family that broke up in Scotland when Syme senior died came together in Melbourne around the *Age* business. In the early years, the gifted journalist Ebenezer was joined by the reliable brother-in-law John Gourlay, and then by brother David bringing funds and entrepreneurship, followed by George, bringing intellectual weight. After Ebenezer's death, his widow Jane became a partner for almost two decades, followed by her son Joseph as junior partner. More significantly, three of David's sons came into the business, two of whom would carry it on, establishing the basis of a press dynasty (albeit one that barely lasted into the next generation). This was very much the Australian colonial model, maintained well into the 20th century, particularly in the non-metropolitan press. For instance, Mitchell Armstrong, who worked at the *Age* office in the 1850s, went on to found the *Kyneton Guardian* and an Armstrong dynasty producing the country newspaper until 1965 (Kirkpatrick 2011). Only in the heady year of 1888 (as noted in Chapter 11) did Syme appear briefly to entertain the idea of incorporation as a public company, after this was suggested to him. He sounded out his junior partner, who responded favourably, with many suggestions about directors and steps to be taken. It may have been a passing impulse, for it seems that he took the matter no further.

Is it possible to gain an understanding of the man who was so outstandingly fortunate and successful, and yet seems to have been shortsighted relating to the future of the *Age* and *Leader*? Seeing him as a product of his Scottish origins, the standards of the Victorian era and the heady opportunities offering in colonial Victoria may be historically enlightening, but does not take us closer to the individual person. *Age* leader writer Hoare (1927, 155) puzzled about a man who was 'essentially masterful, mastering even

CHAPTER 16

the fitful circumstances of life' yet was drifting into 'an habitual pessimism', perhaps glimpsing a side of Syme that even Deakin, who knew him for much longer, seems not to have recognised. Biographer Sayers (1965, 219), who did not know Syme personally, wrote that he was 'a lonely man, nervously individualist'. Without qualification, this can mislead. He worked constantly, with many heavy, parallel commitments to discharge and a restless drive for achievement, leaving little time for relaxation or socialising. But that he was not cut off from personal contact is evident in his various club and committee memberships, his sometimes expansive letters to Levey and Malcolm in London over many years, and references in correspondence to associates and people he called friends (such as William McCulloch, Simon Fraser). Moreover, he had a mentoring role with some of his editorial staff (particularly Hoare), and enduring friendships with Deakin and Gillott (testifying to his regard, the trustees were instructed to spend £20 on a 'ring or other article of jewellery' to give his lawyer and friend). And there was family.

Ranald Macdonald (1982, 37–39) has written, persuasively, that his great-grandfather was driven by an 'intense, almost obsessive, belief in the individual and the individual's duty to society [and was] convinced…that a man must make his own decisions and remain true to them'. He stressed that Syme 'exercised his power in the public interest', had 'great qualities of leadership which are needed in any age…and a profound sense of public duty'.

Accepting the view that Syme's actions were driven by a moral imperative, some aspects of his behaviour call for further interpretation. These may be summarised as self-reliance, sometimes combined with mistrust to a fault, and fixed, often idiosyncratic points of view, not to be challenged by employees, business associates or even family. The first may be seen as a Scottish trait of independence, exaggerated by the collapse of his home at 16, albeit having the example of and some support from his older brothers, with whom he had strong bonds. The mistrust could have been engendered or exacerbated by the deception of his sister-in-law Jane and hostility of nephew Joseph, in the face of his deep sense and generous recognition of family ties. The rigid views could derive in part from his being largely self-taught, lacking the formal university education of his brothers. And there is something more. Study of the records relating to Syme's life – his letterbooks and the numerous descriptions by members of his editorial and literary staff – has shown a push to control that permeated the man's personal dealings and plans, becoming evident in the later 1870s.

For this controlling behaviour, and notwithstanding all his demonstrated virtues, talents and achievements, Syme might, in today's general parlance, be labelled a control freak. Or, in the light of current personality theory, be seen to exhibit some of the features associated with paranoid personality disorder, in particular, being 'generally difficult to get along with and often [having] problems with close relationships', and further described:

> Because individuals with paranoid personality disorder lack trust in others, they have an excessive need to be self-sufficient and a strong sense of autonomy. They also need to have a high degree of control over those around them. They are often rigid, critical of others, and unable to collaborate, although they have great difficulty accepting criticism themselves. They may blame others for their own shortcomings. Because of their quickness to counterattack in response to the threats they perceive around them, they may be litigious and frequently become involved in legal disputes (*Diagnostic and Statistical Manual* 2013, 650–651).

As the theory goes, and arguably applicable to Syme, persons with 'paranoid' behaviour can function quite competently, but need to do so on their own terms (Millar and Davis 2000, 397). The paranoid character structure has been explained as resulting from the warping of 'native talent', that is

> [of a] cognitive substrate in which there is a well-developed capacity to scan, search, and locate fine detail in the environment. The paranoid character would seem to possess natural talents for perceptivity in noting incongruity, legalistic mastery of detail, elaborate theory-building that accounts for detail and incongruity, and strategic planning based upon complex theoretical understanding (Josephs 1992, 221).

These positive qualities Syme displayed in abundance. If indeed his controlling behaviour resulted from 'warping' of his capacities, this might in part be ascribed to the influence of his authoritarian father and to the misdealings he experienced on the goldfields. But there is an evidentially based and compelling case for its being also and more forcefully part of trauma resulting from the shocking, stressful dealings with his sister-in-law Jane and his nephew Joseph Syme.

However, what is considered normal behaviour, or tolerably eccentric, or unacceptable, varies over time, a phenomenon reflected in the revising of criteria for mental disorder classification in successive editions of medical texts.[17] No one has suggested that Syme suffered from a mental disorder (although, as noted in Chapter 14, assistant commercial editor William Robinson (1967, 22) thought he had a 'definite inferiority complex'). The crucially important point is that Syme's exercising of omnipotent control – whether seen now as pathological or not – fitted well with structures and behaviours of his time. A case might be made for seeing it as a distinguishing trait of a media magnate of the 20th century and beyond, and Syme, therefore, as a proto-tycoon. Be that as it may, his controlling predisposition was in absolute accord with patriarchy in the family and autocracy and paternalism in the workplace in a way that would scarcely be possible today. These aspects of control, plus the intelligent prudence of his financial transactions, doubtless facilitated the achievements for which he is famous.

The *Lone Hand* of June 1907, the second issue of the popular new Australian literary monthly, has a feature on Syme. An engaging caricature (fig. 16.2, overleaf) prefaces the article, in which he is labelled 'the last of the old order of newspaper-makers in Australia'. The writer sees him to be 'iron-willed but with imperfect sympathies'; indeed 'a law unto himself, and with will and strength to enforce that law on others' ('David Syme' 1907, 117). As to strength, biographer Pratt termed him 'that rugged old Titan'.[18] The mythological Titans, giants of enormous (titanic) might, were overthrown by Zeus and supplanted by the gods of Olympus. Just so, Syme and his Australian 19th-century peers gave way to the media Fairfaxes, Murdochs and Packers of the 20th, who in turn have or will become yesterday's men. But in Queen Victoria's time, in colonial Victoria, David Syme was, in every sense of the phrase, man of the age.

---

[17] Discussed in Haslam (2013).
[18] A. Pratt to R. Jebb, 8 July 1908, Ambrose Pratt Papers, MS 6325, Australian Manuscripts Collection, State Library of Victoria.

DAVID SYME

A caricature of David Syme by Phil May

Figure 16.2. David Syme depicted for readers of the *Lone Hand*, June 1907. (Courtesy of Fairfax Media)

APPENDIX A

Newspapers and Periodicals Published by the *Age* Business Under David Syme

Already in publication 1860

Age. Daily. First issue Tuesday 17 October 1854. Still being published (2014).

Melbourne Weekly Age. Weekly. First issue 3 February 1855. From 31 January 1862 title is *Weekly Age*. 30 September 1864 incorporates *Farmers' Journal and Gardeners' Chronicle* (see below). Last issue published 24 July 1868; from 1 August 1868 incorporated into *Leader*.

Melbourne Leader. Weekly. First issue 4 January 1856. From 4 January 1862, title changes to *Leader*. 1 August 1868 incorporates *Weekly Age*. Last issue published 26 June 1957.

Begins publication 1860

Victorian Farmers' Journal and Gardeners' Chronicle. Weekly. First issue 7 July 1860. From 11 January 1862, title is *Farmers' Journal and Gardeners' Chronicle*. Last issue published 23 September 1864. From 30 September 1864 incorporated into *Weekly Age*.

Begins publication 1861

Australian News for Home Readers. Monthly. First issue possibly March 1861 when it is first advertised. (First issue seen is 21 April 1862, pages 1–2 only.) 27 July 1867 title changes to *Illustrated Australian News for Home Readers*. 1 January 1869 incorporates *Illustrated Melbourne Post* (see below). 26 January 1876 title shortened to *Illustrated Australian News*. 22 January 1879 drops statement that it was published expressly for mailboat. 1 June 1889 to May 1890 title is *Illustrated Australian News and Musical Times* then reverts to *Illustrated Australian News*. Last issue published 1 July 1896 states 'For the future it will be amalgamated with the *Leader*'.

DAVID SYME

Acquired 1868

Herald. Daily. First issue published 3 January 1840 as *Port Phillip Herald*, several other title changes thereafter. David Syme is behind the purchase as part of buying *Herald* business in late 1868. From 4 January 1869, it is an evening paper. Duration of Syme–*Age* business ownership uncertain: at least to September 1870, but certainly no longer than August 1872. Last issue published 5 October 1990.

Illustrated Melbourne Post. Monthly. First issue for 'January Mail' 1862. Purchased late 1868 as part of *Herald* business. Last issue published 7 December 1868. From January 1869 incorporated in *Illustrated Australian News for Home Readers*.

Begins publication 1875

Age Annual. First issue published 1875 with title *Age Annual for the Year 1874*. From 1879 the year of the title is the year of publication, and includes advertisements. The 20th and last issue published 1894.

Begins publication 1902

Every Saturday. Weekly. First issue 21 June 1902. Still published at Syme's death, February 1908. Last issue 10 February 1912.

APPENDIX B

David Syme's Personal Publications

'The Land Question in England.' *Westminster Review*, 38, October 1870: 233–262. Reprinted as a 32-page pamphlet entitled *Landlordism: In its Moral, Social, and Economic Relations*. London: Trübner, 1871. A 15-page abbreviated version, with original title, was issued as Tract No. 2. of the Land Reform League, Victoria. (Melbourne: Printed by Mason, Firth and M'Cutcheon, 1871).

'On the Method of Political Economy.' *Westminster Review*, 40, July 1871: 206–218 (in the 'Independent Section').

'Restrictions on Trade: From a Colonial Point of View.' *Fortnightly Review*, 13, April 1873: 447–464. Reprinted as a 16-page pamphlet in the United States, in Boston, according to La Nauze (1949, 124).

Outlines of an Industrial Science. London: Henry S. King & Co., 1876. xii, 195 pp. Second edition [i.e. printing] 1877. American edition, Philadelphia: H.C. Baird & Co., 1876. Republished 1996 by David Syme College of National Economics, Public Administration and Business, Flemington, Vic.

'On the Increment in the Value of Land in Melbourne'. *Melbourne Review* 4 (15), July 1879: 221–236.

Representative Government in England: Its Faults and Failures. London: Kegan Paul, Trench & Co., 1881. xxv, 220 pp. Second edition [i.e. printing] 1882.

On the Modification of Organisms. Melbourne: George Robertson, [1890?] vii, 164, 89 pp. Also published in London by Kegan Paul, Trench, Trübner & Co., 1890.

'Topical Selection and Mimicry.' *Nature*, 45: 30–31, 1981.

The Soul: A Study and an Argument. London: Macmillan, 1903. xxxi, 234 pp.

SOURCES

Archives and manuscripts

Age archives, Melbourne
David Syme Testimonial, 1894.
Machinery [ledgers] 1889–1914.
Records relating to linotype introduction, 1896–97.

Alexander Turnbull Library, National Library of New Zealand
New Zealand Press Association. Papers.

Monash University Library, Clayton
Archives of Kegan Paul, Trench, Trübner, and Henry S. King, 1853–1912 1974, Bishop's Stortford: Chadwyck-Healey (microfilm).
Macmillan Archives, 3rd series 1982, Cambridge: Chadwyck-Healey (microfilm).
Dowling, Peter 1997, 'Chronicles of Progress: the Illustrated Newspapers of Colonial Australia, 1853–1896', PhD, Monash University.

National Library of Australia
Cook, B. S. Baxter. Memoirs of a Pioneer Pressman. MS 1453.
Deakin, Alfred. Papers. MS 1540.
Higgins, Henry Bournes. Autobiography draft, circa 1927, in Higgins Papers. MS 1057, Series 3.
Morrison, George Ernest. Microfilm of correspondence in Morrison Papers, G 28245.
Syme, Herbert. Diary 1895, MS 6751.

Public Records Office Victoria
Central Roads Board. Register of Tenders 1853–1860.
Probate and Administration Files; Wills.
Shipping Records.

State Library of New South Wales
Angus & Robertson. Correspondence. ML314/20.
Parkes, Henry. Correspondence. A907.

State Library of South Australia
J.L. Bonython and Company, Summary Record. Letter Books, BRG 10, Series 8.

State Library of Victoria
Berry, Sir Graham, Correspondence. MS 8894.

Caxton Fund, Records, 1871–1912. MS 6272.
Historical Records of "The Argus" and "The Australasian", 1846–1923, compiled by C.P. Smith. MS 10727.
Pearson, Charles Henry. Papers. MS 7093–MS 7522.
Pratt, Ambrose. Papers. MS 6325.
Rundle, James. Political and Social Tensions in Victoria, 1875–1880, Melbourne, 2010. Unpublished manuscript.
Syme, David. Obituaries; Wages Book 1886–1937; Caxton Commemoration Fund. MS 10602.
Syme, Ebenezer. Papers. MS Box 132.
Syme, George. Letters to the Reverend George Alexander Syme. MS 4576/7–9.
Syme Family. Papers. MS 9751 (referred to throughout as SFP).

University of Melbourne archives
Australian Institute of Journalists. Records in Australian Journalists Association Victorian Branch Records.
Johnston, James Stewart, Correspondence 1836–1911.
Student Records.

Held privately
David Syme notebooks, correspondence (originals and some photocopies) held by Dr Veronica Condon (granddaughter of David Syme) (Referred to as DS notebooks).
David Syme to E.E. Morris, 28 September 1900 (John Mulvaney's photocopy of original held privately).
Letters from Annabella Syme, and one from David Syme, held by Judith Adams (great-granddaughter of David Syme).
Family tree, showing descendants of David Syme, copy held by Michael Dennis (great-grandson of David Syme).
Family History Report, Ebenezer Syme and Jane Hilton Rowan, dated 23 October 2009, copy supplied by Pru Williams (descendant of Ebenezer Syme).
Transcripts of Letters to the Reverend George Alexander Syme (originals in State Library of Victoria) made and held by Marten Syme (descendant of George Syme).

Newspapers and periodicals
The *Age*, the *Leader*, the *Illustrated Australian News* and the other newspapers owned by David Syme (listed in Appendix A) have been heavily used, as has the rival Melbourne *Argus*. Runs of the spiritualist periodical *Harbinger of Light* and of the *Australasian Typographical Journal* and the *Melbourne Review* have been read.
Relevant material in a wide range of other Australian metropolitan and country newspapers has been located via searches of the online Trove Digitised Newspapers database. Relevant material in New Zealand newspapers was

accessed via the Papers Past: New Zealand Newspapers and Periodicals database.

Items in English newspapers and periodicals and some Australian titles were found through searches of the online databases Nineteenth Century British Library Newspapers and Nineteenth Century UK Periodicals.

Parliamentary papers and debates

1856 VPP. Legislative Council 1855–56, no. C 26, Quartz Claim of Messrs Syme and Co.

1892–1893 Libel Law Amendment Bill, dealt with in VPP and VPD 1892 & 1893.

1899 Royal Commission into Certain Allegations against the Lands Department 1899, *Land Selection at Mount Macedon*, VPP 1899–1900, no. 33. Discussed in VPD 1899.

Published books and articles

Note: David Syme's personal publications are listed in Appendix B (p. 407).

ABS (Australian Bureau of Statistics) 1986, *Historical Statistics of Victoria*, Melbourne: ABS, Victorian Office.

A.D. [Alfred Deakin?] 1882, 'Editor's Library Table', *Melbourne Review*, 7 (25) January: 106–110.

Adams, Nancy 1966, *Family Fresco*, Melbourne: Cheshire.

Adamson, Graeme 1984, *Century of Change: the First Hundred Years of the Stock Exchange of Melbourne*, South Yarra, Vic: Currey O'Neil.

Anderson, Benedict 1991, *Imagined Communities: Reflections on the Origin and Spread of Nationalism*, rev. ed., London: Verso.

Anderson, Fay and Richard Trembath 2011, *Witnesses to War: the History of Australian Conflict Reporting*, Carlton, Vic: Melbourne University Press.

Anderson, Patricia J. and Jonathan Rose (eds) 1991, *British Literary Publishing Houses, 1820–1880*, Detroit: Gale Research.

Armstrong, Barbara 2011, 'Palk', *History of Homoeopathy in Australia*, www.historyofhomeopathy.com.au/people/item/127-palk.html, accessed 20 February 2013.

Armstrong, Mitchell 1908a, 'Death of David Syme', *Kyneton Guardian*, 15 February.

Armstrong, Mitchell 1908b, 'The Early History of "The Age"', *Kyneton Guardian*, 18 February.

The Australian Enyclopaedia 1927, edited by Arthur Wilberforce Jose, Herbert James Carter with T.G. Tucker, Sydney, Angus & Robertson.

Australian War Memorial, 'Australia and the Boer War, 1899–1902', www.awm.gov.au/atwar/boer/, accessed 24 April 2012.

Aveling, Marian 1974, 'Purves, James Liddell (1843–1910)', *Australian Dictionary of Biography*, adb.anu.edu.au/biography/purves-james-liddell-4419/text7215, accessed 13 March 2013.

Baker, Mark 2012, 'Honouring the Newsbreakers of a Nation', *Age*, 8 December: 17.
Bartlett, Geoffrey 1969, 'Berry, Sir Graham (1822–1904)', *Australian Dictionary of Biography*, adb.anu.edu.au/biography/berry-sir-graham-2984/text4355, accessed 10 February 2013.
'Bathgate', *Wikipedia*, en.wikipedia.org/wiki/Bathgate, accessed 17 November 2009.
Bedford, Randolph 1976 (1944), *Naught to Thirty-Three*, Carlton, Vic: Melbourne University Press.
Betley, John 1973, 'Touch of Our Art in Old English Pub', *Age*, 4 August: 14.
Birman, Wendy 1990, 'Thomson, James (1852–1934)', *Australian Dictionary of Biography*, adb.anu.edu.au/biography/thomson-james-8796, accessed 16 July 2011.
Blainey, Geoffrey 1983, *The Tyranny of Distance: How Distance Shaped Australia's History*, rev. ed., Sydney: Pan Macmillan.
Bonwick, James 1890, *Early Struggles of the Australian Press*, London: Gordon & Gotch.
'Boxer Rebellion', *Wikipedia*, en.wikipedia.org/wiki/Boxer_Rebellion, accessed 24 April 2012.
Brake, Laurel 2008, 'The Leader (1850–1859)', *Nineteenth-Century Serials Edition*, www.ncse.ac.uk/headnotes/ldr.html, accessed 20 March 2014.
Brake, Laurel and Marysa Demoor (eds) 2009, *Dictionary of Nineteenth-Century Journalism in Great Britain and Ireland*, Gent and London: Academia Press and British Library.
Brendon, Piers 1982, *The Life and Death of the Press Barons*, London: Secker & Warburg.
Broinowski, Alison 2000, 'The Japanese in the Big Picture', in *Makers of Miracles: the Cast of the Federation Story*, edited by David Headon and John Williams, 199–211, Carlton, Vic: Melbourne University Press.
Brown, Lucy 1985, *Victorian News and Newspapers*, Oxford: Clarendon Press.
Brown, Robin 1986, *Milestones in Australian History: 1788 to the Present*, Sydney: Collins.
Brown-May, Andrew and Shurlee Swain (eds) 2005, *The Encyclopedia of Melbourne*, Melbourne: Cambridge University Press.
Buchanan, Rachel, *Stop Press: The Last Days of Newspapers*, Melbourne, Scribe, 2013.
Buckrich, Judith Raphael 2005, *Collins: The Story of Australia's Premier Street*, Melbourne: Australian Scholarly Publishing.
Cambridge, Ada 2006 (1903), *Thirty Years in Australia*, Sydney: Sydney University Press.
Campbell, Ruth 1986, 'Madden, Sir John (1844–1918)', *Australian Dictionary of Biography*, adb.anu.edu.au/biography/madden-sir-john-7453, accessed 13 March 2013.
Cannon, Michael 1966, *The Land Boomers*, Carlton, Vic: Melbourne University Press.
Carne, W.A. 1954, *A Century of Harmony: the Official Centenary History of the Royal Melbourne Philharmonic Society*, Melbourne: The Society.
Carrington, Thomas 1911, *The Yorick Club: Its Origin and Development*, Melbourne: Atlas Press.

SOURCES

A Century of Journalism: the Sydney Morning Herald and its Record of Australian Life, 1831–1931 1931, Sydney: John Fairfax & Sons.

Checkland, Olive and Sidney 1989, *Industry and Ethos: Scotland 1832–1914*, 2nd ed., Edinburgh: Edinburgh University Press.

Clarke, Patricia 1988, *Pen Portraits: Women Writers and Journalists in Nineteenth Century Australia*, Sydney: Allen & Unwin.

Cockerill, George 1943?, *Scribblers and Statesmen*, Melbourne: J.R. Stevens.

The Concise Dictionary of National Biography 1992, 3 vols, Oxford: Oxford University Press.

Condon, Veronica 2005, *Geoffrey Syme*, www.sirgeoffreysyme.com.au, accessed 27 March 2014.

Crail, Martin (comp.), 'Chartists in Australia and a Eureka Moment for Democracy', www.chartists.nt/Chartists-in-Australia, accessed 23 July 2010.

Cuneen, Chris 1983, 'Hopetoun, Seventh Earl of (1860–1908)', *Australian Dictionary of Biography*, adb.anu.edu.au/biography/hopetoun-seventh-earl-of-6730, accessed 18 May 2012.

The Cyclopedia of Victoria 1903–1905, edited by James Smith, Melbourne: Cyclopedia Co.

Darragh, Thomas A. 1997, *Printer and Newspaper Registration in Victoria, 1838–1924*, Wellington, NZ: Elibank Press.

'David Syme' 1907, *Lone Hand*, June: 116–120.

David Syme & Co. 1949–1986, *Annual reports*, Melbourne.

Davison, Graeme 1978, *The Rise and Fall of Marvellous Melbourne*, Carlton, Vic: Melbourne University Press.

Davison, Graeme 2005, 'Doing the Block', in Brown-May and Swain 2005, 214–215.

Davison, Graeme, John Hirst and Stuart Macintyre (eds) 1998, *The Oxford Companion to Australian History*, Melbourne: Oxford University Press.

Deacon's Newspaper Handbook and Advertisers' Guide 1881, 5th ed., London, Samuel Deacon and Company.

Deakin, Alfred 1944, *The Federal Story: the Inner History of the Federal Cause*, Melbourne: Robertson & Mullens.

Deakin, Alfred 1957, *Crisis in Victorian Politics, 1879–1881: a Personal Retrospect*, edited by J.A. La Nauze and R.M. Crawford, Carlton, Vic: Melbourne University Press.

Dernelley, Katrina 2012, 'Butler, Walter', in Goad and Willis 2012, 128.

de Serville, Paul 2013, *Athenaeum Club, Melbourne: a New History of the Early Years, 1868–1918*, Melbourne: Athenaeum Club, 2013.

Diagnostic and Statistical Manual of Mental Disorders 2013, 5th edition (DSM-5), Washington, DC: American Psychiatric Publishing.

Dickenson, Jacqueline 2006, *Renegade and Rats: Betrayal and the Remaking of Radical Organisations in Britain and Australia*, Carlton, Vic: Melbourne University Press.

Dickson, Walter 1900, *Japan*, New York: Peter Fenelon Collier.

Dingle, Tony 2005, 'Depressions', in Brown-May and Swain 2005, 204–206.

Donaldson, Gordon 1990, *The Faith of the Scots*, London: B.T. Batsford.
Douglas, George H. 1999, *The Golden Age of the Newspaper*, Westport, Conn: Greenwood Press.
Dow, Hume 1972, 'Dow, John Lamont (1837–1923)', *Australian Dictionary of Biography*, adb.anu.edu.au/biography/dow-john-lamont-3433/text5227, accessed 7 February 2013.
Dowling, Peter 1995, 'Destined not to Survive: the Illustrated Newspapers of Colonial Australia', *Studies in Newspaper and Periodical History*, 3: 85–98.
Dysart, Dinah 1981, *Julian Ashton: Essay on the Artist*, Canberra, Australian National Gallery.
Eastwood, Jill 1976, 'Wood, John Dennistoun (1829–1914)', *Australian Dictionary of Biography*, adb.anu.edu.au/biography/wood-john-dennistoun-4883/text8169, , accessed 5 February 2013.
Edquist, Harriet 2003, '"He Who Sleeps in Philae": Walter Butler's Tomb for David Syme at Kew', *Fabrications*, 13 (1): 15–31.
Edquist, Harriet 2012, 'Arts and Crafts', in Goad and Willis 2012, 44–46.
Elder, David, undated, *Ebenezer Syme and the 'Westminster Review'*, (no place of publication or publisher; copy held in the *Age* Library).
Eliot, George 1954, *The George Eliot Letters*, edited by Gordon S. Haight, 9 volumes, London: Oxford University Press.
Elliot, Gilbert 1882, 'Syme on Representative Government', *Melbourne Review*, 7 (28): 443–453.
Elliott, Brian 1958, *Marcus Clarke*, Oxford: Clarendon Press.
Ensor, R.C.L. 1936, *England 1870–1914*, Oxford: Clarendon Press.
Escott, Harry 1960, *History of Scottish Congregationalism*, Glasgow: Congregational Union of Scotland.
Finlay, E.M. 1976, 'Supple, Gerald Henry (1823–1898)', *Australian Dictionary of Biography*, adb.anu.edu.au/biography/supple-gerald-henry-4670/text7723, accessed 5 February 2013.
Fitzpatrick, Brian 1944, *A Short History of the Australian Labor Movement*, Melbourne: Rawson's Bookshop.
Fodor, Jerry and Massimo Piattelli Palmarini 2010, *What Darwin Got Wrong*, London: Profile.
Forster, William 1882a, 'Personal Government', *Melbourne Review*, 7 (26) April: 169–183.
Forster, William 1882b, 'Democratic Government', *Melbourne Review*, 7 (28) October: 359–372.
Fysh, Ernest (comp.) 1933, *Memoir of C.D., Sculptor and Painter*, Melbourne: Industrial Printing and Publishing.
Gabay, Al 1992, *The Mystic Life of Alfred Deakin*, Cambridge: Cambridge University Press.
Gabay, Al 2001, *Messages from Beyond: Spiritualism and Spiritualists in Melbourne's Golden Age 1870–1890*, Carlton, Vic: Melbourne University Press.
Garden, Don 1984, *Victoria: a History*, Melbourne: Nelson.
Garden, Don 1998, *Theodore Fink: a Talent for Ubiquity*, Carlton South, Vic: Melbourne University Press.

SOURCES

Gibbney, H.J. 1969, 'Armit, William Edington (de Margrat) (1848–1901)', *Australian Dictionary of Biography*, adb.anu.edu.au/biography/armit-william-edington-de-margrat-2897/text4157, accessed 13 February 2013.

Gibbney, H.J. and Ann G. Smith 1987, *A Biographical Register 1788–1939*, 2 volumes, Canberra, Australian Dictionary of Biography.

Gillen, F.J. 1968, *Gillen's Diary: Camp Jottings…Expedition Across Australia, 1901–1902*, Adelaide: Libraries Board of South Australia.

Gillen, F.J. 1997, *'My Dear Spencer': the Letters of F.J. Gillen to Baldwin Spencer*, edited by John Mulvaney, Howard Morphy and Alison Petch, Melbourne: Hyland House.

Goad, Philip and Julie Willis (eds) 2012, *The Encyclopedia of Australian Architecture*, Melbourne: Cambridge University Press.

'The Great Australasian Dailies, No. IV, the Melbourne "Age"' 1892, *Review of Reviews, Australian Edition*, 1 (5).

Gregory, J.S. 1986, 'Morrison, George Ernest (1862–1920)', *Australian Dictionary of Biography*, adb.anu.edu.au/biography/morrison-george-ernest-chinese-7663/text13405, accessed 13 February 2013.

Griffiths, Dennis (ed.) 1992, *The Encyclopedia of the British Press, 1422–1992*, New York: St Martin's Press.

Griffiths, Tom 2007, *Slicing the Silence: Voyaging to Antarctica*, Sydney: UNSW Press.

Gronn, Claus 1981, *Gold! Gold! Diary of Claus Gronn, a Dane on the Diggings*, edited by Cora McDougall; translated from Old Danish by Gullevi Ubbersen, Melbourne: Hill of Content.

Grover, Monty 1993, *Hold Page One*, edited by Michael Cannon, Main Ridge, Vic: Loch Haven Books.

Hagan, J. 1966, *Printers and Politics: a History of the Australian Printing Unions 1850–1950*, Canberra: Australian National University Press.

Haight, Gordon S. 1969, *George Eliot & John Chapman, with Chapman's Diaries*, 2nd edition, Hamden, Conn: Archon Books.

Hancock, W.K. 1930, *Australia*, London: Ernest Benn.

Harte, Chris, with Bernard Whimpress 2008, *The Penguin History of Australian Cricket*, rev. ed., Camberwell, Vic: Viking.

Haslam, Nick 2013, 'DSM-5 and the Mental Illness Makeover', *Monthly*, May: 32–39.

Helmstadter, Richard J. and Bernard Lightman (eds) 1990, *Victorian Faith in Crisis: Essays on Continuity and Change in Nineteenth-Century Religious Belief*, London: Macmillan.

Hills, Ben 2010, *Breaking News: the Golden Age of Graham Perkin*, Melbourne: Scribe.

Hirst, J.B. 1976, 'Ward, Ebenezer (1837–1917)', *Australian Dictionary of Biography*, adb.anu.edu.au/biography/ward-ebenezer-4799/text7995, accessed 16 March 2013.

Hirst, John 1998, 'The Hopetoun Blunder', in Davison, Hirst, and Macintyre 1998, 324.

Hirst, John 2000, *The Sentimental Nation: the Making of the Australian Commonwealth*, South Melbourne, Vic: Oxford University Press.

'History of Heidleberg University' 2013, www.uni-heidelberg.de/university/history/history.html, accessed 25 April 2014.

'History of Esophageal Surgery' 2010, www.lwwoncology.com/Textbook/Content.aspx?aid=8058216, accessed 26 April 2014.

Hoare, Benjamin 1904, *Preferential Trade: Study of its Esoteric Meanings*, Melbourne: George Robertson.

Hoare, Benjamin 1927, *Looking Back Gaily*, Melbourne: E.W. Cole.

Howsam, Leslie 1998, *Kegan Paul: A Victorian Imprint*, London: Kegan Paul International.

Hunt, Lyall 1983, 'Hackett, Sir John Winthrop (1848–1916)', *Australian Dictionary of Biography*, adb.anu.edu.au/biography/hackett-sir-john-winthrop-6514, accessed 22 May 2013.

Hurst, John 1988, 'Schuler, Gottlieb Frederick Heinrich (1858–1926)', *Australian Dictionary of Biography*, adb.anu.edu.au/biography/schuler-gottlieb-frederick-heinrich-8360/text14589, accessed 11 September 2013.

Hutchison, I.G.C. 1986, *A Political History of Scotland: Parties, Elections and Issues*, Edinburgh: John Donald.

Ingham, S.M. 1986, 'Madden, Sir Frank (1847–1921)', *Australian Dictionary of Biography*, adb.anu.edu.au/biography/madden-sir-frank-7452/text12979, accessed 13 March 2013.

Jericho, Greg 2012, *The Rise of the Fifth Estate: Social Media and Blogging in Australian Politics*, Melbourne: Scribe.

Johnson-Woods, Toni 2001, *Index to Serials in Australian Periodicals and Newspapers: Nineteenth Century*, Canberra: Mulini Press.

Jordens, Ann-Mari 1976, 'Shillinglaw, John Joseph (1831–1905)', *Australian Dictionary of Biography*, adb.anu.edu.au/biography/shillinglaw-john-joseph-4575/text7511, accessed 16 February 2013.

Josephs, Lawrence 1992, *Character Structure and the Organization of the Self*, New York: Columbia University Press.

'The Kauri Timber Company Ltd (1888–)' 2005, *Guide to Australian Business Records*, www.gabr.net.au/biogs/ABE0100b.htm, accessed 19 February 2013.

'Key to Tom Roberts' Historical Painting' 1903, *In the Artists' Footsteps*, www.artistsfootsteps.com/html/Roberts_picturenames.htm, accessed 18 February 2013.

King, J.E. (ed.) 2007, *A Biographical Dictionary of Australian and New Zealand Economists*, Cheltenham UK: Edward Elgar.

Kingston, Beverly 1988, *The Oxford History of Australia, Volume 3, 1860–1900: 'Glad, Confident Morning'*, Melbourne: Oxford University Press Australia.

Kirkpatrick, Rod 2011, 'Mitchell King Armstrong, Editor and Exemplar', *Australian Journalism Review*, 33 (2): 27–34.

Kirkpatrick, Rod 2013, *A Short History of the Australian Country Press*, Mount Pleasant, Qld: Australian Newspaper History Group.

Koss, Stephen 1981, *The Rise and Fall of the Political Press in Britain, Volume 1, the Nineteenth Century*, London: Hamish Hamilton.

SOURCES

Lack, John 2006, 'David Syme and the Three Stooges? The Bust Premiers: James Munro, William Shiels and JB Patterson', in Strangio and Costar 2006, 94–108.

La Nauze, J.A. 1949, *Political Economy in Australia: Historical Studies*, Carlton, Vic: Melbourne University Press.

La Nauze, J.A. 1979 (1965), *Alfred Deakin: a Biography*, Sydney: Angus & Robertson.

Lee, Alan J. 1976, *The Origins of the Popular Press in England, 1855–1914*, London: Croom Helm.

Lever, Susan 2000, *Real Relations: the Feminist Politics of Form in Australian Fiction*, Sydney: Halstead Press with the Association for the Study of Australian Literature.

Livingston, K.T. 1996, *The Wired Nation Continent: the Communication Revolution and Federating Australia*, Melbourne: Oxford University Press.

Lloyd, Clem 1985, *Profession Journalist: a History of the Australian Journalists' Association*, Sydney: Hale & Iremonger.

Lomas, L. 1981, 'Crawford, Alexander (1857–1935)', *Australian Dictionary of Biography*, adb.anu.edu.au/biography/crawford-alexander-5810/text9861, accessed 16 March 2013/

'Louis Tannert' 2011, *Design & Art Australia Online*, www.daao.org.au/bio/louis-tannert/, accessed 4 January 2013.

Macdonald, Ranald 1982, *David Syme*, Cheltenham, Vic: Vantage House.

Macdonald, Ranald 2012, 'David Syme (1827/1908)', www.melbournepressclub.com/sites/melbournepressclub.com/files/images/ranald_speech_to_mpc_hall_of_fame_2012.pdf, accessed 17 March 2014.

Macintyre, Stuart 1991, *A Colonial Liberalism: the Lost World of Three Victorian Visionaries*, Melbourne: Oxford University Press Australia.

Macleod, Donald 2001, 'Scottish Calvinism: a Dark Repressive Force?', *Scottish Bulletin of Evangelical Theology*, 19 (2): 226–256.

Marshall, Tony 1981, 'Findley, Edward (1864–1947)', *Australian Dictionary of Biography*, adb.anu.edu.au/biography/findley-edward-6170, accessed 20 May 2012

McCaffrey, John F. 1998, *Scotland in the Nineteenth Century*, Basingstoke: Macmillan.

McDonald, Peter and Patricia Quiggan 1985, 'Life Course Transitions in Victoria in the 1880s', in *Families in Colonial Australia*, edited by Patricia Grimshaw, Chris McConville and Ellen McEwen, 64–82, Sydney: Allen & Unwin.

McKay, Claude, 1961, *This Is the Life*, Sydney: Angus and Robertson.

McLachlan, Noel 1998, 'Melba, Nellie', in Davison, Hirst and Macintyre 1998, 422–423.

'Media House' supplement 2010, *Age*, 21 June.

Mehling, Marianne (ed.) 1990, *Egypt: a Phaidon Cultural Guide*, Oxford: Phaidon.

Melbourne Press Club 2012, *Victorian Media Hall of Fame*, www.melbournepressclub.com/halloffame, accessed 12 December 2012.

Melbourne Telephone Exchange Co. 1882?, [List of subscribers], Melbourne: McCarron, Bird. (Held at National Library of Australia.)

Melleuish, Gregory 2009, 'David Syme, Charles H. Pearson and the Democratic Ideal in Australia', *Australian Journal of Political Science*, 44 (2): 213–228.
Mellor, Suzanne G. 1974, 'Levey, George Collins (1835–1919)', *Australian Dictionary of Biography*, adb.anu.edu.au/biography/levey-george-collins-4014/text6363, accessed 21 March 2014.
Men of the Time in Australia 1882, Victorian Series, 2nd ed., Melbourne: McCarron Bird.
'Mergenthaler Linotype Company', *Wikipedia*, en.wikipedia.org/wiki/Mergenthaler_Linotype_Company, accessed 3 December 2011.
Merrett, D.T. 2005, 'Banking and Finance', in Brown-May and Swain, 58–60.
Millar, Theodore, and Roger Davis 2000, *Personality Disorders in Modern Life*, New York: John Wiley.
Miller, Robert 1976, 'Williams, Sir Hartley (1843–1929)', *Australian Dictionary of Biography*, adb.anu.edu.au/biography/williams-sir-hartley-4856/text8111, accessed 14 March 2013.
Mitchell, Charles 1851, *Newspaper Press Directory, 1848–50*, London: C. Mitchell and Co.
Moignard, Kathy 1990, 'Ward, Frederick William (1847–1934)', *Australian Dictionary of Biography*, adb.anu.edu.au/biography/ward-frederick-william-8982/text15807, accessed 14 March 2013.
Morkot, Robert 2005, *Egypt: Land of the Pharaohs*, Hong Kong: Odyssey Books and Guides.
Morrison, Elizabeth 1995, 'Serial Fiction in Australian Colonial Newspapers', in *Literature in the Marketplace: Nineteenth-Century British Publishing and Reading Practices*, edited by John O. Jordan and Robert L. Patten, 306–324, Cambridge: Cambridge University Press.
Morrison, Elizabeth 1997, 'Grub Street Inventor: James Harrison's Journalism, Old and New, in Geelong, Melbourne and London', in *Disreputable Profession: Journalists and Journalism in Colonial Australia*, edited by Denis Cryle, 55–77, Rockhampton, Qld: Central Queensland University Press.
Morrison, Elizabeth 1999, 'Black Wednesday 1878 and "The Manufacture of Public Opinion" in Pre-Federation Victoria', in *Journalism: Print, Politics and Popular Culture'*, edited by Ann Curthoys and Julianne Schultz, 36–55, St Lucia, Qld: University of Queensland Press.
Morrison, Elizabeth 2004, Editor's introduction, in Ada Cambridge, *A Black Sheep: Some Episodes in His Life*, Canberra: Australian Scholarly Editions Centre.
Morrison, Elizabeth 2005, *Engines of Influence: Newspapers of Country Victoria, 1840–1890*, Carlton, Vic: Melbourne University Press.
Mulvaney, D.J. and J.H. Calaby 1985, *'So Much that Is New': Baldwin Spencer, 1860–1929, a Biography*, Carlton, Vic: Melbourne University Press.
Norris, R. 1981, 'Deakin, Alfred (1856–1919)', *Australian Dictionary of Biography*, adb.anu.edu.au/biography/deakin-alfred-5927/text10099, accessed 14 May 2013.
'North Berwick', *Wikipedia*, en.wikipedia.org/wiki/North_Berwick, accessed 17 November 2009.

SOURCES

O'Donnell, Penny, David McKnight and Jonathan Este 2012, *Journalism at the Speed of Bytes: Australian Newspapers in the 21st Century*, Redfern, NSW: Media, Entertainment and Arts Alliance, www.thefutureofjournalism.org.au/2012_journalism_speed_of_bytes.pdf, accessed 17 March 2014.

Parsons, George 1974, 'McLean, William (1845–1905)', *Australian Dictionary of Biography*, adb.anu.edu.au/biography/mclean-william-4124/text6597, accessed 16 February 2013.

Pearl, Cyril 1967, *Morrison of Peking*, Sydney, Angus & Robertson, 1967.

Pearson, Charles Henry 1877, 'On Property in Land', *Melbourne Review*, 2 (6) April: 129–148.

Pearson, Charles Henry 1879a, 'Democracy in Victoria', *Fortnightly Review*, 25 May: 688–717.

Pearson, Charles Henry 1879b, 'The Functions of Modern Parliaments', *Fortnightly Review*, 26 July: 68–81.

Pearson, Charles Henry 1893, *National Life and Character: A Forecast*, London: Macmillan.

Pickett, Charles and Caroline Butler-Bowden 2012, 'Flats and Apartments', in Goad and Willis 2012, 252–254.

Pitcher, W.B. 1979, 'Bonython, Sir John Langdon (1848–1939)', *Australian Dictionary of Biography*, adb.anu.edu.au/biography/bonython-sir-john-langdon-5286, accessed 23 May 2013.

Pratt, Ambrose 1908, *David Syme: the Father of Protection in Australia*, London: Ward Lock.

Prest, E.J. 2011, *Sir John Langdon Bonython: Newspaper Proprietor, Politician and Philanthropist*, North Melbourne, Vic: Australian Scholarly Publishing.

Putnis, Peter 2004, 'Reuters in Australia: the Supply and Exchange of News, 1859–1877', *Media History*, 10 (2): 67–88.

Putnis, Peter 2006, 'How the International News Agency Business Model Failed – Reuters in Australia, 1877–1895', *Media History*, 12 (1): 1–17.

'Queen Victoria Memorial, Melbourne', *Public Art Around the World*, www.publicartaroundtheworld.com/Queen_Victoria_memorial_Melbourne.html, accessed 24 May 2012.

Radic, Thérèse 1976, 'Zelman, Alberto (1832–1907)', *Australian Dictionary of Biography*, adb.anu.edu.au/biography/zelman-alberto-4910, accessed 15 July 2011.

Reed, Rosslyn 1991, 'Calvinism, the Weber Thesis, and Entrepreneurial Behaviour: the Case of David Syme', *Journal of Religious History*, 6 (3): 292–303.

Reid, Stuart 1879, 'Victorian Land Acts and Large Estates', *Melbourne Review*, 4 (15) July: 257–271.

'Richard March Hoe', *Wikipedia*, en.wikipedia.org/wiki/Richard_March_Hoe, accessed 6 February 2013.

Rickard, John 2006, 'The Quiet Little Man in a Brown Suit: George Turner and the Politics of Consensus', in Strangio and Costar 2006, 109–118.

Robinson, W.S. 1967, *If I Remember Rightly: the Memoirs of W.S. Robinson*, edited by Geoffrey Blainey, Melbourne: F.W. Cheshire.

Robinson, W. Sydney 2012, *Muckraker: the Scandalous Life and Times of W.T. Stead, Britain's First Investigative Journalist*, London: Robson Press.
Roe, Jill 1969, 'Blair, David (1820–1899)', *Australian Dictionary of Biography*, adb. anu.edu.au/biography/blair-david-3011/text4407, accessed 3 February 2013.
Rose, Margaret 1988. 'Richardson, Charles Douglas (1853–1932)', *Australian Dictionary of Biography*, adb.anu.edu.au/biography/richardson-charles-douglas-8201/text14347, 16 March 2013.
'Royal Exhibition Building and Carlton Gardens' 2010, World Heritage List, whc. unesco.org/en/list/1131, accessed 8 May 2012.
Ryan, J. A. 1990, 'Wise, Bernhard Ringrose (1858–1916)', *Australian Dictionary of Biography*, adb.anu.edu.au/biography/wise-bernhard-ringrose-9161, accessed 26 April 2014.
Ryan, Peter (ed.) 1972, *Encyclopedia of Papua and New Guinea*, Carlton, Vic: Melbourne University Press.
Sands & McDougall's Melbourne and Suburban Directory, 1863–1901, Melbourne: Sands & McDougall.
Sands, Kenny & Co.'s Commercial and General Melbourne Directory 1860, Melbourne: Sands, Kenny & Co.
Saunders, David 1976, 'Reed, Joseph (1823–1890)', *Australian Dictionary of Biography*, adb.anu.edu.au/biography/reed-joseph-4459, accessed 4 January 2013.
Sayers, C.E. 1965, *David Syme: a Life*, Melbourne: F.W. Cheshire.
Sayers, C.E. 1976, 'Windsor, Arthur Lloyd (1833–1913)', *Australian Dictionary of Biography*, adb.anu.edu.au/biography/windsor-arthur-lloyd-4872/text8149, accessed 7 February 2013.
'Science, Medicine and Education' 1891, *Review of Reviews*, 4 (21): 309.
Serle, Geoffrey 1971, *The Rush to be Rich: a History of the Colony of Victoria, 1883–1889*, Carlton, Vic: Melbourne University Press.
Serle, Geoffrey 1977 (1963), *The Golden Age: a History of the Colony of Victoria, 1851–1861*, Carlton, Vic: Melbourne University Press.
Serle, Geoffrey 1990, 'Syme, Sir Geoffrey (1872–1952)', *Australian Dictionary of Biography*, adb.anu.edu.au/biography/syme-sir-geoffrey-8732/text15289, 23 May 2013.
Shore, Arnold 1958, 'Julian Ashton', *Age*, 14 June.
Smith, Anthony 1979, *The Newspaper: an International History*, London: Thames & Hudson.
Smith, F.B. 1969, 'Bright, Charles (1832–1903)', *Australian Dictionary of Biography*, adb.anu.edu.au/biography/bright-charles-3055, accessed 7 February 2013.
Souter, Gavin 1981, *Company of Heralds: a Century and a Half of Australian Publishing by John Fairfax Limited and Its Predecessors*, Carlton, Vic: Melbourne University Press.
Spurgeon, Dickie A. 1984, 'The Fortnightly Review', in *British Literary Magazines: the Victorian and Edwardian Age, 1837–1913*, edited by Alvin Sullivan, 131–135, Westport, Conn: Greenwood Press.
Stead, W.T. 1886a, 'Government by Journalism', *Contemporary Review*, 49: 653–674.
Stead, W.T. 1886b, 'The Future of Journalism', *Contemporary Review*, 50: 653–679.

SOURCES

Stearns, Peter N. 1974, *The Revolutions of 1848*, London: Weidenfeld and Nicolson.

'Stomach & Oesophageal Cancer' 2014, www.cancervic.org.au/about-cancer/cancer_types/stomach_and_oesophageal_cancer, accessed 26 April 2014.

Strachan, John 1888, *Explorations and Adventures in New Guinea*, London: S. Low, Marston, Searle & Rivington.

Strangio, Paul 2006, 'Broken Heads and Flaming Houses: Graham Berry, the Wild Colonial', in *The Victorian Premiers 1856–2002*, in Strangio and Costar 2006, 51–73.

Strangio, Paul and Brian Costar (eds) 2006, *The Victorian Premiers 1856–2006*, Leichhardt, NSW: Federation Press.

Stuart, Lurline 1979, *Nineteenth Century Australian Periodicals: an Annotated Bibliography*, Sydney: Hale & Iremonger.

Stuart, Lurline 1989, *James Smith: the Making of a Colonial Culture*, Sydney: Allen & Unwin.

Sutcliffe, J.T. 1921, *A History of Trade Unionism in Australia*, Melbourne: Macmillan.

Sutherland, Alexander 1888, *Victoria and Its Metropolis: Past and Present*, 2 volumes, Melbourne: McCarron Bird.

Syme, Ebenezer 1977 (1854), 'Letter…to John Pascoe Fawkner Concerning the Diggers' Advocate', *La Trobe Library Journal*, 19 (April): 63.

Syme, Marten 2013, *It's an Itch I've Got to Scratch: a History of the Descendants of George & Jean Sime*, Port Fairy, Vic: The author.

'Systems of Land Tenure' 1871, *Edinburgh Review*, 134 (October): 449–483.

Tasker, Meg 2001, *'Struggle and Storm': the Life and Death of Francis Adams*, Carlton South, Vic: Melbourne University Press.

Thompson, Peter and Robert Macklin 2004, *The Man Who Died Twice: the Life and Adventures of Morrison of Peking*, Crows Nest, NSW: Allen & Unwin.

Thomson, Kathleen and Geoffrey Serle 1972, *A Biographical Register of the Victorian Parliament, 1851–1900*, Canberra: Australian National University.

Tibbits, George 1979, 'Butler, Walter Richmond (1864–1949)', *Australian Dictionary of Biography*, adb.anu.edu.au/biography/butler-walter-richmond-5451/text9257, accessed 24 March 2013.

Tibbits, George and Philip Goad 2012, 'Reed & Barnes', in Goad and Willis 2006, 586–588.

Tidey, John 1998, *The Last Syme: Ranald Macdonald's Impact on* The Age, *1964–1983*, Brisbane: Dept of Journalism, University of Queensland.

'The Tradition Established, 1841–1884' 1939, *The History of the Times, v. 2*. London: The Times.

Tregenza, John 1968, *Professor of Democracy: the Life of Charles Henry Pearson, 1830–1894, Oxford Don and Australian Radical*, Carlton, Vic: Melbourne University Press.

Trenwith, W.A. (comp.) 1902, *Extracts from the Syme–Trenwith Controversy*, Richmond, Vic: W.A. Trenwith.

Trethowan, Bruce 2012, 'Salway, William', in Goad and Willis 2012, 613–614.

Trevena, Bill 1986, 'Mennell, Philip Dearman (1851–1905)', *Australian Dictionary of Biography*, adb.anu.edu.au/biography/mennell-philip-dearman-7557/text13187, accessed 10 February 2013.

Turnbull, Glen (ed.) 2008, *Triangle of Tranquillity: 150 Years of the Boroondara (Kew) Cemetery 1859–2009*, Kew, Vic: Friends of Boroondara (Kew) Cemetery.

Veitch, Don 2001, *David Syme: the Quiet Revolutionary*, Flemington, Vic: David Syme Foundation.

'Vincenz Priessnitz', *Wikipedia*, en.wikipedia.org/wiki/Vincent_Priessnitz, accessed 3 March 2013.

Walker, R.B. 1976, *The Newspaper Press in New South Wales, 1803–1920*, Sydney: Sydney University Press.

Wallace, Alfred R. 1891a, 'Another Darwinian Critic', *Nature*, 43: 529–530.

Wallace, Alfred R. 1891b, 'Mr Syme Now Says…', *Nature* 45: 31.

Wallins, Roger P. 1983, 'Westminster Review, The', in *British Literary Magazines: the Romantic Age, 1789–1836*, edited by Alvin Sullivan, 424–433, Westport, Conn: Greenwood Press.

Ward, John M. 1948, *British Policy in the South Pacific (1786–1893)*, Sydney: Australasian Publishing Co.

Waterhouse, Jill 1979, 'Brient, Lachlan John (1856–1940)', *Australian Dictionary of Biography*, adb.anu.edu.au/biography/brient-lachlan-john-5356/text9057, accessed 16 February 2013.

Waters, Thorold 1951, *Much Besides Music*, Melbourne: Georgian House.

Watson, R.A. 2012, 'Australian Journalism's First War Victim', *Australian*, 23 April, Media section: 25.

Waugh, John 2006, '"The Inevitable McCulloch" and His Rivals, 1863–1877', in Strangio and Costar 2006, 30–50.

Wiener, Joel (ed.) 1988, *Papers for the Millions: the New Journalism in Britain, 1850s to 1914*, New York: Greenwood Press.

Wilde, William H., Joy Hooton and Barry Andrews 1985, *The Oxford Companion to Australian Literature*, Melbourne: Oxford University Press.

Willis, Julie 2012, 'Hyndman & Bates', in Goad and Willis 2012, 350.

Wilson, Fred J.F. and Douglas Grey 1888, *A Practical Modern Treatise upon Modern Printing Machinery and Letterpress Printing*, London: Cassell.

Work, T.L. 1898, 'The Early Printers of Melbourne', *Australasian Typographical Journal*, May.

Wylie, William Howie 1853, *Old and New Nottingham*, London: Longman, Brown Green, and Longmans.

Young, G.M. 1960 (1953), *Victorian England: Portrait of an Age*, 2nd ed., London: Oxford University Press.

Young, J.McL. 1983, 'Hodges, Sir Henry Edward (1844–1919)', *Australian Dictionary of Biography*, adb.anu.edu.au/biography/hodges-sir-henry-edward-1092/text11549, accessed 14 March 2013.

Yule, Peter 2012, *William Lawrence Baillieu (1859–1936): Founder of Australia's Greatest Business Empire*, Melbourne: Hardie Grant.

Zainu'ddin, A.G. Thomson 1981, 'Fitchett, William Henry (1841–1928)', *Australian Dictionary of Biography*, adb.anu.edu.au/biography/fitchett-william-henry-6179/text10621, accessed 6 December 2011.

INDEX

Bold type indicates an illustration.

Aborigines, 97; Spencer and Gillen study, 335–337
Adams, Francis, 247, 305–306
Advertiser (Adelaide), 10, 141, 193, 195, 196, 243; *see also* sharing of copy
Advocate (Melbourne), 227
Age, 11, 305–306, 395; beginnings, 32–40; circulation, 10, 40, 50, 83–84, 110, 145, 160, 178–179, 192, 217, 224, 239, 282, 351, 396; editors, 37, 38, 48, 69, 70, 82, 115–116,
 see also Windsor, Arthur Lloyd; jubilee 1904, 368–369; masthead and royal coat of arms, 34, 39, **60**; ownership *see Age* newspaper business ownership; price, 34, 39, 41, 46, 49, 83–84; serial fiction in, 107–108, 145, 200, 230–231, 248; subeditors, 158–159, 189–190, 247; *see also* sharing of copy
Age, policies, 395; under Cooke brothers, 33, 35–36; under co-operative, 36, 38; under Ebenezer Syme, 48, 49, 69; under DS, 71, 114, 119, 130, 144, 160, 166, 342, 363, 364; on strikes, 256–257; on railways, 257–258; on Federation, 339–342
Age Annual, 113, 146, 218, 296
Age Chapel (compositors and printers association), 227, 288, 320
Age newspaper business esprit de corps, 40, 77; presentation of staff photo, 116–**117**; farewell to Harrison, 114; 'monster' picnic, 170; 25th anniversary and presentation of DS and Ebenezer Syme portraits, 156–157; Speight Defence Fund presentation, 288; farewell to Windsor, 315–316
Age newspaper business finances, 388; 1850s, 36, 45–46; 1860s, 72, 91; 1870s, 127–128, 147; 1880s, 180–181, 185, 216, 220, 237; 1890s, 237–239, 254, 295–296, 314–315; 1900s, 349–350, 387; joint stock proposal 1888, 234–236, 400
Age newspaper business ownership: Cooke brothers, 33–36; co-operative, 36–40; Ebenezer Syme, 40–42; Ebenezer Syme and DS, 42–45, 49–50; DS and Jane, 56–57, 79–80, 92, 123–125, 127, 130, 131, 135, 137–139, 148; DS and JCS (as David Syme and Co.), 125–126, 130, 131, 138, 148, 153, 181–183, 184, 238–240, 249–255; DS sole proprietor, 268–269, 273; David Syme Trust, 398; David Syme and Co. Ltd, 3, 9, 398–39
Age newspaper business premises: 21 Elizabeth Street, 33; 67 Elizabeth Street, 37, 46, 54, **55**, 116; 50 Collins Street East, 147–148, 153–157, **155**; 'Back Building', 184–187, **186**; renumbered 233 Collins Street, 239, 311–312; expansion and makeover, 315, 323–326, **325**; London office, 345, 370; Sydney office, 217; London paper mention, 269, 400; Media House, 5, **6**
Akhurst, William, 90, 108–109
Allen, G., 190, 226, 246
Anderson, Benedict, 176
Anglo-Australian Literary Agency, 198
Anglo-Australian Telegraph Agency, 106–107
Antarctic exploration, 334–335
Archibald, Jules François, 305
architects *see* Butler, Walter; Hyndman, Robert Gordon; Reed, Joseph; Salway, William
Argus, 10, 31, 102, 176, 306, 315, 384; Ebenezer Syme employed on, 36–37; comparisons with *Age*, 289, 315, 395; circulation, 40, 71, 110, 178–179, 192, 281; London office, 301; policies, 33, 36, 119, 144, 339–340; price, 192, 281, 395
Armit, Captain William, 167, 202, 205
Armstrong, Mitchell King, 37, 149, 338, 384–385, 400
Arts and Crafts movement, 324, 372, 392
Ashton, Julian Rossi, 146, 180
Ashworth, Thomas, 314
Athenaeum Club, 118, 212
Aucher, Arthur, 207–208
Auckland Star, 102, 298
Australasian, 65, 100, 112, 319; in competition with *Leader*, 84, 85, 108, 111, 145, 197, 302, 350; serial fiction in, 177, 200
Australasian Institute of Journalists, 292, 302–304
Australasian Sketcher, 69, 112, 139, 180, 242
Australasian Typographical Journal, 288, 320–321
Australian Journal, 103
Australian News for Home Readers see Illustrated Australian News
Australian Press Association *see* cable news services

Australian Star (Sydney), 231, 243, 301
Australian Town and Country Journal (Sydney), 101, 106, 177, 200
Aytoun, George, 246

Baker, Mark, 3
Ballarat Times, 36, 37
Barrow and King, 198, 204
Barton, Sir Edmund Toby, 341–342, 364
Barton, George Burnett, 196
Bedford, Randolph, 189
Bell, Alexander, 188, 284
Bell, Walter, 284
Benalla Standard, 157
Bendigo Advertiser, 26, 116
Bennett, Alfred, 198, 204
Bennett, K.D., 198, 225, 245, 246
Bennett, Samuel, 106, 141, 142, 157
Bent, Sir Thomas, 376, 378, 384
Berry, Sir Graham, 169–170, 187, 213, 339, 389; liberal-reformist government of, 119, 130, 143–144, 153; 'embassy' to England, 160, 168
Berry–Service Coalition, 163
Best, William 371
Biggs, Leonard, 317, 366
Bisley rifle championships, 314
'Black Wednesday', 9 January 1878, 144
'blackbirding', denunciation of, 166
Blair, David (journalist), 38, 40. 45, 48, 223
Blair, David (timber merchant), 250, 252
Bleackley, W., 251
Blythswood, 6, 177–**178**, 378, 379
Boer War, 326–331
Bones, G.J., 194–196, 197, 200, 214, 229, 232–234
Bonython, Sir John Langdon, 10, 321, 338, 387, 396–397; ambivalent relations with DS, 288, 321, 330, 352, 362; cable service problems, 194–197, 232–233, 244; contact with Herbert Syme, 293, 301–302; knighthood, 312; seeks advice from JCS and Wynne, 300; *see also* cable news services; sharing of copy
Boroondara Cemetery, 265, 383, 392, 393
'boom' and 'bust', Melbourne, 216, 217, 230, 237–238, 248, 281, 396
Borchgrevink, Carsten, 334–335
Bowen, Sir George Ferguson, 144
Boxer Rebellion, 331–332
Braddon, Mary, 107, 108, 200, 230
Brassey, Lord Thomas, and Lady Brassey, 306, 314
Brickhill, G.R., 357, 384
Brient, Lauchlan, 206, 232–234, 242–243
Briggs, William, 303
Bright, Charles, 115, 122, 188, 247–248, 284
Bright, Thomas Lockyer, 33, 36, 38, 48, 115

Brisbane Newspaper Co., 200
British-Australasian (London), 385
Brooke, Henry, 73
Brotchie, Richard, 88
Bruce, Mary Grant, 316, 353
Buckridge, Judith, 375
building societies, 128, 148, 221, 235, 281, 323
Bulletin (Sydney), 305–306, 355
Burt, Robert, 315
Butler, Walter, 7, 372, 373–374, 392; Inskip and Butler, 5, 372, 374
Byrne, Desmond (John Desmond), 301, 316–317, 333, 345, 348, 370, 378

cable connection to London, 103, 104–105
cable news correspondents, London, 194–195, 229, 232–234, 242–244, 298, 300–301, 333
cable news services, DS plans and beginnings, 101, 105–107, 130, 140–143, 157–158; *Age–South Australian Advertiser–Daily Telegraph* (Sydney) service, 193–196, 231, 396; Australian Press Association (*Argus–Sydney Morning Herald*) service, 105–106 140, 158, 396; Reuters, 101, 105, 106, 107, 140, 199, 396; Melbourne agency, 158, 176; Sydney agent, 141, 142; United Cable Service, 291, 300–302, 396
California: DS gold prospecting in, 23–24; J. Dow study tour, 164–165; The Vagabond's 'Jottings' from, 230; DS rejecting news from, 284
Calvinism, 13–14, 18, 388–389
Cambridge, Ada, 177, 200, 230, 248
Cameron, J.A., 329
Canada, account of railway journey, 199
Cape Argus (Cape Town), 328
Carey, Henry, 134
Carpenter, Miss, 229
Casey, James Joseph, 153
Caxton festival 1871, 118
Caxton Fund, 118, 285, 303
Champion, Henry Hyde, 248, 256, 268–269, 277, 284–285, 363
Chapman, John, 28, 30, 96, 120
Chevalier, Nicholas, 69
China *see* Boxer Rebellion
Clark, Charles, 157
Clarke, H., 319, 384
Clarke, Marcus, 162, 180
Clarson, William, 103, 111, 154
Cockerill, George, 190, 317, 340–341
Collins, Henry, 158
Commonwealth Parliament opening 1901, 338–339
Conisbro, 346, 370, 379
Constitution Bill 1898, 340–341

INDEX

constitutional reform, 48, 143, 160
Cook, B.S. (Bertie) Baxter, 315
Cooke brothers (Henry & Francis), 33, 34, 36
Cornwall Chronicle (Launceston), 157
Coulson, C.G., 190
Couvreur, Jessie *see* Tasma
Cowan & Co., 101, 102, 135
Cowen, Joseph, 213, 397
cricket news, **60**, 145, 193, 198–199, 233
Cross, Ada *see* Cambridge, Ada
Cumberland, Stuart, 199
Cunningham, Sir Edward Sheldon, 202

D'Ebro, Charles, 372
Daily Chronicle (London), 282, 366, 385; GS placement, 343, 344, 353–354, 368; DS obituary, 396
Daily Mail (Glasgow) *see North British Daily Mail*
Daily Mail (London), 329
Daily News (London), 142
Daily Review (Edinburgh), 100, 135
Daily Telegraph (Melbourne), 89, 102, 110, 176, 191–192, 196–197, 303; begins fiction serialisation, 108; publishes libellous account of New Guinea expedition, 206,
Daily Telegraph (Sydney), 193, 195, 196, 206, 232, 305–306; *see also* cable news services; sharing of copy; Wynne, Watkin
Dalry, 211, 214, 221, 265, 275, 310, 353, 379
Daniel, Alfred, 199
Darbyshire, J.J., 357
Darwinism *see* evolution, theories of
David Syme and Co. *see Age* newspaper business ownership
David Syme Charitable Trust, 4
David Syme Research prize, 4, 368
David Syme Trust *see Age* newspaper business ownership
Davies, Charles, 196, 210, 228
Davies, George, 210, 228
Davies, Henry, 210
Deakin, Alfred, 166, 192, 215, 235, 255, 277, 281, 283, 312, 316, 379; writes for DS's newspapers, 81, 154, 159, 161–164, 180, 187, 316; writes for London *Morning Post* and *National Review*, 367–368; reads MSS of and promotes DS books, 173–174, 260, 347–348, 357; provides legal services for Speight litigation, 278, 286–287, 291, 303, 364; politician, 163–164, 187, 213, 364, 368; engages with DS on political issues, 313, 339, 340–342, 364–367, 379; friendship with DS and family, 212, 213, 214, 238, 264–265, 266–267, 275, 276, 278, 290, 292, 293, 307, 309, 381, 401; view of DS, 8, 384

Delane, Thomas, 397
Dennis, Elaine, 378, 379
Denton, William, 202, 203
Dilke, Sir Charles Wentworth, 358
Dinly, P., 319
Dodds, R., 226
Dow, David, 317
Dow, John Lamont, 110–111, 188, 226, 294, 303, 315, 398; reports from United States, 164–165, 201–202, 334; advocates libel law amendment, 304; Trenwith attack, 363
Dow, Thomas, 165, 201–201, 332
Duffy, Sir Charles Gavan, 71, 153, 389
Dummelow, J., 319
Duncan and Wilson, 101, 102, 103, 104
Duncan, James, 101

Edinburgh, news from, 199
Edquist, Harriet 375, 392
Education Act 1872, 118
elections, federal, 342, 366
Eliot, George, 29, 108
Elliot, Gilbert, 174
Elliott, W., 226
Ely, W., 352
Embley, Edward, 368
Eureka Stockade, 28, 35, 36, 47
Evans, Marian *see* Eliot, George
Evening News (Sydney), 101, 106, 141, 142–143, 157
Evening Standard, 231, 245, 254, 303
Every Saturday, 352, 355–357, **356**, 399
evolution, theories of, 222, 223, 259–264, 280, 360
expeditions and tours, United States, 164–165, 201–202, 334; New Guinea, 165–167, 202–206; Antarctica, 334–335; Central Australia (Spencer and Gillen), 335–337

Fairfax, Charles Burton, 362
Fairfax, Sir James Reading, 158, 312
Fairfax, John, 396
Farmers' Journal and Gardeners' Chronicle, 61–65, **64**, 399
Fawkner, John Pascoe, 36
Federal Convention, Adelaide 1897, 339–340
federal elections, 342, 366
Federation, 309, 315; DS and celebrations, 311; DS and politics of, 337–342
fiction in newspapers, 85, 107–108, 145, 177, 200, 230–231, 278, 298; Australian authors, 230–231, 248, 298, 353
Financial Times (London), 322
Findley, Edward, 345
Fink, Theodore, 192, 206
fire danger and prevention, 99, 185, 245, 324

– 425 –

Fisher, W.J., 344, 354
Fitchett, Thomas Shaw, 351
Fitchett, William Henry, 206, 305
Fitzgibbon, Edmund, 283, 362–363
Flintoff (president, News Agents' Association), 384
Forster, Charles, 122
Forster, William, 174
Fortnightly Review, 96, 120, 121, 122, 167, 223, 305–306
Fox, Charles, 228
Fox, Frank, 346; chief of staff, 316, 330, 351, 355, 366; *Fox vs. Trenwith*, 358, 363–364
Francis, James Goodall, 312
Fraser, Alexander, 143
Fraser, Sir Simon, 212–213, 312, 339, 342, 401
free trade *see* protection vs. free trade

Garnett, Jeremiah, 346
Garnett, Dr Richard, 109, 222, 345, 346
Garnett, Tom, 346
Garnett, Violet *see* Syme, Violet
Garnett, William (1760–1832), 346
Garnett, William (*Age* reporter), 332, 333–334, 343, 346
Gaunt, Mary, 230, 298
Gaze, William, 380
Geelong Advertiser, 35, 50, 82, 91, 286
George Robertson (bookseller and publisher), 54, 172, 173; publishing DS, 259, 260–261, 280, 281
George, Hugh, 106, 107, 122, 145
Germany, agricultural news from, 352
Gillen, Francis, 335–337
Gillies–Deakin Coalition, 187, 267
Gillott, Sir Samuel, 185, 278, 324, 325, 383, 386, 387, 401; advice to DS, 225, 244, 277; acting for DS in JCS partnership dissolution, 250, 251, 252, 253; provides sureties, 268, 291; acting for DS in railway litigation, 291, 292, 294; at opening of renovated *Age* premises, 326; at installation of electrical plant, 369; knighthood, 312; Gillott, Crocker, Snowden, 250, 278, 286; Gillott, Bates, 291
Goldsmith, Ben, 145
Goodier, Susan *see* Syme, Susan
Gorman, Henry, 233
Gourlay, John, 19, 24, 47, 49, 255, 306, 383; employed in *Age* Office Counting House, 47, 95; provides sureties, 72, 88, 148
Gourlay, Margaret, 13, 16, 19, 24, 47, 265, 383
Gourlay, Mary Jane *see* Lormer, Mary Jane
government advertisements, withdrawal of, 71
Graphic (London), 108, 113, 135
Graphic printing machine, 135, 139–140

Gray, Moses William, 46
Greeley, Horace, 30, 122, 306, 397
Gregory, John, 337, 351
Grey (New Zealand correspondent), 332
Groom, Arthur, 279, 282; *see also* railway litigation
Grover, Monty, 317, 319
Gullett, Henry, 122, 200

Hackett, John Winthrop, 231, 396–397
Haddon, Frederick, 118, 362
Haggard, Rider, 298
Hales, A.G., 329
Hammersley, William, 145
Hancock, John, 257, 295
Hancock, Keith, 8
Hare, Francis Augustus, 248
Harmsworth, Alfred Charles William (Lord Northcliffe), 355, 399
Harrison, Frederic, 167–168
Harrison, James, **117**; in Geelong, 37, 91; at *Age* Office, 81–83, 85, 100, 114–115; London correspondent, 109, 164, 197–198, 228, 281; last days, 285–286
Hearn, Lafcadio, 293
Heaton, J.H., 141, 142–143
Hedley, H.W., 198–199
Herald (Glasgow), 179, 360
Herald (Melbourne), 71, 90, 102, 110, 176, 192, 245, 384; price reduced to 1d, 59; DS takes over, 86–89, 395; uses *Age* cable service, 157; takes over *Evening Standard*, 254
Heritage, Lieutenant Francis, 329
Higgins, Henry Bournes, 171, 339, 377
Higinbotham, George, 73, 118, 119, 312, 389
Hills, Ben, 9
Hirst, John, 340
Hoare, Benjamin, 191–192, 303, 340, 379, 398; protection advocate, 318; view of DS, 362, 400–401
Hobart, R.L., 164
Hodges, Sir Henry Edward, 286, 287
Hoe printing machines, 83, 100, 224, 300, 344; in *Age* Office, 104, 185, 192, 240, 324
Holyoake, George Jacob, 30, 39, 70
Holyoake, Henry, 30, 32
Hope, Jane *see* Syme, Jane
Hopetoun, Lord (Governor General), 341
horse-racing: DS seeks reports, 111–112, 193; disapproves sons' interest in, 193, 268, 372
Horne, Amy *see* Syme, Amy
Hoskyns, Chandos Wren, 97
Humphries, H., 190
Hyndman, Robert Gordon, 5, 323–324, 326, 372; Hyndman and Bates, 324

INDEX

Illustrated Australian News, 86, **87**, 89, 146, 180, 296–297, 399; as *Australian News for Home Readers*, 4, 61, 66–69, **67**, 72, 80–81; intercolonial editions, 80, 89, 112; engraved blocks for, 112–113; printing machine for, 139–140; *Musical Times* innovation, 241; special issues and supplements, 154, 218
Illustrated Melbourne Post, 68, 87, 89
illustrations in newspapers, **60**, 61, 66, 242; reprographic techniques, 112–113, 242, 297, 357
India: DS seeks cable correspondent in, 141; Deakin tours with Herbert Syme, 266–267; Deakin's *Age* articles and book, 281, 283; Herbert tours with wife Ethel, 307
industrial disruption, 237, 255–257, 319, 320–321
Inskip and Butler, 5, 372, 374
Ireland, Richard Davies, 72
Irish News (Dublin), 102
irrigation: DS promotion of, 202, 375, 389; J. Dow reports on United States use, 202; Deakin writes on Indian use, 281, 283
Isaacs, Sir Isaac Alfred, 304, 339, 377
Italy, market for Victorian produce, 285

Jacobus, General de la Rey, 329
James, John Stanley *see* The Vagabond
Japan, 229–230; DS visit, 292–294
John Fairfax and Sons, 399
Johnson, Francis (Frank), 127, 137, 148, 265
Johnson, John William, 45, 128, 290, 306
Johnson, Martha (née Garnett), 45, 346
Johnson, Minnie (Jane Mary), 123, 126–127, 137, 148, 390
Johnston, James, 395
Jones, Sir Henry 357–358
Jordan, A., 297
Jordan, Dr Robert, 92

Kegan Paul (publisher), 133, 167, 172–173, 261–263, 280
Kelley, William Darrah, 121–122
Kerry, T.C., 204
Killara, 6, 211, 214, 274–275, 311, 342, 378; DS visits with Deakin, 238, 264–265, 274–275; Herbert managing, 266; Oswald managing, 353, 371–372, 379
King, Ethel *see* Syme, Ethel
King, H.S. (publisher), 133
King, Thomas, 133, 141, 142, 171, 307; Barrow and King, 198, 204
Kingston, Charles Cameron, 365
Kipling, Rudyard, 298
knighthoods, 311–312
Knowles, Sir James Thomas, 348

Kruger, Fred, 384
Kyneton Guardian, 384–385

La Nauze, John, 5, 8, 134, 340
labour movement, 255–257, 364
Lack, John, 273
ladies column, 109–110, 199, 229, 316
Lake Eyre expedition, 337, 351
Lalor, Peter, 153
Lambie, William, 209, 257, 303, 328–330
Lambie Memorial Fund, 330
Lamonby, William Farquharson, 112
land legislation and acquisition, 48, 69, 71, 91, 95, 143, 160; DS on tenure, 96–98, 120–121; DS on values in Melbourne, 168–169, 388;
see also Mount Macedon land
Land Reform League, 122
Langton, Edward, 82, 143, 378
Lawson, Henry, 353
Leader (London), 30, 39
Leader (Melbourne), 4, 30, 46, **60**, 80, 103, 241, 319, 362, 380, 399; editors, 39, 77, 110, 154, 171, 191; begins as family magazine, 39, 47, 61; becomes primarily rural paper, 4, 84–85, 111, 201; agriculture prizes; 211–212, 282, 314, 371; science, 85, 109, 228, 285; literary competition, 85, 177; 'Under the Verandah' political comment', 85, **86**, 111, 162, 180, 192, 203, 247–248; supplements, 218, 297, 322–323; jubilee 1906, 350–351
Leeds Mercury, 102
Leslie, Thomas Edward Cliffe, 133
Levey, George (senior), 87
Levey, George Collins, 71, 81, 89–90, 198, 283, 401; associated with *Herald*, 87, 88, 89–90; on *Age* editorial staff, 115, **117**, 169–170; unofficial London agent for DS, 108–109, 260, 261, 262, 282, 290, 294–295, 299; receives newsy letters from DS, 111, 153, 293–294; contributes London Letter, 164, 229, 249, 302, 332–334; sounded out for cable correspondence, 157–158, 244
Levey, Oliver, 87, 88
Levey, William, 87
libel actions: against DS, 73–74, 91–92, 143, 227–228, 252, 313–314; *see also* railway (Speight) litigation; *Walker vs. McKinley*, 206; *Williams vs. Advertiser*, 278; *Fox vs. Trenwith*, 358, 363–364
libel law amendment moves, 292, 303–304;
The Library of Famous Literature, 345
Linden, Frederick, 141, 142
linotype introduced, 291, 299–300, 318–321; used for Syme's *Soul* draft, 347, 357

– 427 –

Lloyd, Edward, 343, 344–345, 396
Lloyd, Frank, 279, 343, 358, 396
Loch, Sir Henry Brougham, 212
London correspondence: 1870s, 90, 108–109, 164; 1880s, 193, 197–198, 199, 228–229; 1890s, 249, 302; 1900s, 332–334, 352
London Dock Strike 1889, 255–256
Lone Hand, 403
Lormer, Mary Jane, 265, 390
Luke, Edmund, 297, 321, 322
Lyne, Sir William John, 341
Lyons, John, 203, 204

Macalister, Lucie, 93, 136, 306, 307, 308; overseas with parents, 212, 213; marriage, 309; at Tarrawarra, 379, 390
Macalister, William (Willie), 309, 376, 383
McAlpine, Daniel, 347
McAlpine, J.T., 319
McCarthy, Justin, 230
McCoy, Frederick, 260
McCulloch, James (businessman), 111–112
McCulloch, Sir James (politician), 73
McCulloch, William, 135, 222, 288, 366, 401
Macdonald, Ranald (Chesborough Ranald), 3, 9, 399, 401
McDonald, Christina *see* Syme, Christina
Macdonald, John, 88, 95, 113, 136, 154, 176–177, 250
McEachern, Malcolm, 326
McEwan, James, 40, 45; London branch, 59, 102, 103, 134, 211
Macfie, Matthew, 171, 188, 191, 197
McGowan, Henrietta, 316
Macintyre, Stuart, 5, 8, 129, 273
Mackay, Angus, 116
Mackay, Robert, 116
McKinley, James, 206
Mackinnon, Lauchlan (1817–1888), 64, 85, 90, 112, 395
Mackinnon, Sir Lauchlan Charles (1848–1925), 193, 302, 304, 387, 395; dealings with DS, 301, 364
McLean, William, 235
Macmillan and Co. (publisher), 131, 132, 357, 360–361
Madden, Sir Frank, 312–313
Madden, Sir John, 278, 384
Malcolm, Alexander John, 123; acts as agent for DS, 102, 136, 139, 140, 146, 221, 265–266; DS writes to, as confidant and friend, 134, 143, 144, 156, 237, 401; DS complains to about JCS, 239, 252, 255
Manchester Examiner and Times, 84, 102
Manchester Guardian, 84, 102, 346, 384, 397
Maritime Strike 1890, 237

Marshall, Revd Alexander 383, 384
Martin, Arthur Patchett, 197, 247
Martin, Catherine, 298
Martin, W.S., 111–112
Mathieson, John, 326
Media Hall of Fame, Victorian, 3, 9
Media House, Collins Street, 5, **6**
Melba, Nellie, 211, 241, 242, 359
Melbourne Centennial International Exhibition, 217, **219**–220, 237, 241, 248; *see also* Royal Exhibition Building
Melbourne Church of England Grammar School, 314
Melbourne Leader see Leader (Melbourne)
Melbourne Mansions, Collins Street, 5, 372–375, **374**
Melbourne Press Club, 3
Melbourne Public Library, Art Gallery and Museum, 259, 378
Melbourne Review, 168–169
Melbourne Typographical Society, 227, 257, 321
Melbourne Weekly Age see Weekly Age
Melleuish, Gregory, 5, 173
Mellool Station, NSW, 375–376
Melville, W.B., 278
Melvin, Joseph, 209, 318
Mennell, Philip Dearman, 158, 385; cable correspondent and writer of London Letter, 193–194, 197, 208, 229, 232–234, 243, 249; consulted by DS about publications, 223, 280, 281, 283; arranges for Deakin to write for *Morning Post*, 367–368
Mercury (Hobart), 157, 195, 196
Mercury (statue on *Age* building), 324–**325**
Mexico, news from, 284
Michie, Sir Archibald, 387
Mirams, James, 235, 237, 314
Mitchell, David, 211
Mitchell, Edmund, 246, 248, 285
Moir, George, 286, 287
Modern Permanent Building Society, 148
Montgomery, Gabriel, 218
Montreal Star, 179
Morgan, James, 298, 301, 302, 333
Morison, James, 15, 20; theological academy, 17, 18
Morison, Robert, 17–18, 19, 20–21
Morley, John, 96, 120, 121
Morning Post (London), 367–368, 385
Morrison, George Ernest, 166–167, 202–204, 331
Mount Alexander Mail, 116
Mount Macedon land, 6, 94–95, 97, 388; Rosenheim (house), 6, 126, 128, 163, 212, 388; Royal Commission, 94–95, 312–313
Murdoch, Revd Patrick, 383, 384

INDEX

Munro, David, 220–221
Munro, James, 273
Murray, David Christie, 230, 248–249
Murray and Crow (builders), 324, 372
Murray River water usage, 376
My Note Book, 48

National Political League, Ballarat, 365
National Reform League, 119, 128
National Reform and Protection League, 144
National Review (London), 367–368
Nature (London), 263
Nesbitt, A.M., 298
New Caledonia, news from, 193, 207–208
New Guinea: annexation issue, 207; expeditions, 165–167, 202–206, **205**, 232; news from, 206, 352
New Hebrides, news from, 207–208, 352
New York correspondence, 199, 229
New Zealand, 61, 297, 302; news from, 196, 229, 241, 284, 332; DS travels 358–359
New Zealand Press Association, 158, 195
Newcastle Daily Chronicle, 179, 213, 224, 395, 397
Newnes, Sir George, 334, 335, 355
news, intercolonial, procurement of, 193, 196–197; New South Wales, 196, 228, 229, 332, 352; Queensland, 196, 228; South Australia, 196; Tasmania,196, 228; Western Australia, 196, 231; *see also* New Zealand, news from
news, overseas, procurement of, 193, 199, 241, 351–352; *see also* London correspondence; New York correspondence; Paris correspondence *and* names of countries and cities; cable news services
newspapers, American, subscriptions to, 352
newspapers, English and Scottish: *Age* to be advertised in, 107; models for DS, 76–77, 84, 102, 343–344, 397–398; DS dealings with personnel of, 100, 102, 213, 396
newspapers, 1850s Melbourne, 31–33, 37; *see also Age*, *Argus*, *Leader*, *Weekly Age*
newspapers, 1850s Victorian goldfields, 26–27
newsprint and suppliers of, 101, 103, 171, 213, **219**, 240, 256, 279, 281, 344; concern over adequacy of stocks, 225, 256; lawsuits, 135, 136, 225
Nicholson, J., 284
Nineteenth Century, 167, 223, 259, 261; *Nineteenth Century and After*, 348
North British Daily Mail (Glasgow), 100, 102, 104
Northcliffe, Lord *see* Harmsworth, Alfred Charles William
Norway, DS tour of, 279

O'Loghlen, Bryan, 153, 304
O'Hea, William Joseph, 70, 115, 153
O'Shanassy, John, 48, 71, 72
Ogier, John 377
Odgers, J., 227
Outtrim, Alfred, 277
Oxenpoint, George, 110

Packer, John, 239, 245, 256, 290–291, 384, 398
Palk (Hope) children: Alice 58, 76; Robert, 59, 75; Reginald, 80; Margaret, 93, 131; Lilian, 123, 127
Palk, Jane *see* Syme, Jane
Palk, Robert: relationship with Jane Syme, 58–59, 80, 123, 125, 131, 172; with Anne Helmore, 139, 148
Pall Mall Gazette, 397
paper supplies *see* newsprint
Paris correspondence, 109, 164, 199, 229
Parker, Gilbert, 298
Parkes, Henry, 116
Patterson, Sir James Brown, 170, 273, 277, 287, 304
Payn, James, 108, 229
Peacock, Sir Alexander James, 339
Pearson, Charles Henry, 81, 159–161, 168, 187, 197, 235, 286; contributes to *Age*, 159–161, 187–188, 284; advises DS on writing style, 172, 260; on democratic government, 173; on New Guinea annexation, 166, 207
pensions, old-age, 320
Perry, Charles, 33–34
Piccoli, D.V., 285
Pindar, Peter, 145
Pleasance, Charles, 369
Plummer, John, 106, 108–109, 110, 128
Poole, William, 56, 87–88, 92
Powell, Wilfred, 204
Praed, Rosa, 230, 353
Pratt, Ambrose, 8, 379, 398, 403
Premier Building Association, 235
Premier Building Society, 128
press, public view of, 91, 99, 304–306, 338–339
Prime Minister, choice of Barton as, 341–342
printing technology, 10, 213, 315; steam machines, 38, 46, 61, 83; rotary machines, 83, 224; Victory rotary, 100–104, 135, 185, 240; Hoe rotary, 185, 192, 224, 240, 324; Graphic machine, 135, 139–140; linotype machines, 299–300, 318–321; electric power, 369
protection vs. free trade, 49, 91; Harrison's early advocacy in *Geelong Advertiser*, 82, 286; DS 'Restrictions on Trade' article, 121–122; Pearson a free trader, 160; DS 'converts' Deakin, 161,163; Victorian politics, 48–49, 69, 73, 119, 143, 318; federal politics, 342, 345, 366, 379

– 429 –

Protectionists' Association of Victoria, 318
Purves, James Liddell, 279, 290, 291, 294, 303
Putnis, Peter, 196

Quarrill, Reuben, 106–107, 147
Quick, Sir John, 303, 339

railway (Speight) litigation, 273–274, 277, 278–279; *Groom vs. Syme*, 279, 282, 289; *Smith vs. Syme*, 289, 291–292, 295; *Speight vs. Syme*, 73, 277, 278–279, 282–283, 286–292, 294–295, 306; Contempt of Court, 289, 290–291
railways and Railway Commissioners, 257–258, 273–274, 287, 326
Ralling (or Railling), George, 328, 330
Reay, Major William, 329
Reed, Joseph, 5, 154, 323, 324, 338; Reed and Barnes, 154,185
registration of newspapers, 33, 41, 72; J. Packer as publisher, 290
Reid, Sir George Houstoun, 364
religion, Scotland, 13–14, 15, 18
responsible government *see* self government for Victoria
Reuters *see* cable news services
Review of Reviews, Australian Edition, 304–305
Richardson, Charles, 324–325
Riverina ownership *see* Victoria–New South Wales border claim
Roberts, Tom, 338
Robertson, George *see* George Robertson (bookseller and publisher)
Robinson, Anthony Bennett, commercial editor from 1877, 147, 187, 188, 198, 226; 1890s, 284, 305, 315; 1900s, 373, 384
Robinson, W.E. (*Age* London office representative), 370
Robinson, William, 189, 199, 245, 317, 323
Rockingham, 379
Rose, W. Kinnaird, 305
Rosenheim, 6, 126, 128, 163, 212, 388
Royal Commission into Certain Allegations against the Lands Department, *Land Selection at Mount Macedon*, 94–95, 312–313
Royal Commission on Irrigation, Victoria, 202
Royal Exhibition Building, 338
Royal Melbourne Show, 282, 311

Salway, William, 185
Sayers, C.E., 8, 401
Schuler, Gottfried, 158, 287, 319, 366, 384, 398; chief of staff, 190, 247, 284, 315; *Age* editor, 317, 366, 370
science journalism, 83, 85, 197, 228, 285, 286
Scott, Charles, 226, 255 (*Leader* journalist)

Scott, Charles Prestwich (of *Manchester Guardian*), 397
Scott, W.H., 204, 205
Seaforth, 6, 311, 378
Seebohm, Frederic, 97
Seekamp, Henry, 36, 37
self-government for Victoria, 43, 47–48
serial fiction *see* fiction in newspapers; *Age*, serial fiction in
Serle, Geoffrey, 8–9, 238, 312, 389
Service, James, 187, 207, 312
sharing of copy (*Age* and *Leader* with newspapers intercolonially), 244; Antarctic expedition, 334; Boer War, 327–328; Boxer Rebellion, 331–332; England–Australia cricket, 198; fiction, 177, 200, 249, 278, 298; irrigation in India, 269; New Guinea expedition, 204, 206; Sudan, 209; agriculture in United States, 201, 334
shearers' strikes 1891, 257
Shiels, William, 273, 274, 287
Shillinglaw, John, 235
Short, Henry, 255, 303, 304, 384, 398; *Leader* editor, 191, 226, 247, 297, 315
Sime, George Alexander (father of DS), 12–16, 122
Sime, Jean *see* Syme, Jean
Simpkin and Marshall, 280–281
Smith, Emmerton and Johnson (law firm), 250
Smith, A.J., 147, 158
Smith, Allison Dalrymple, 289; *see also* railway litigation
Smith, George Paton, 70, 73, 77, 115, 143, 159
Smith, Henry J., 70, 77
Smith, James, 39, 46
Smith, Walter, 352
Soldene, Emily, 316
Souter, James, 266
South African War *see* Boer War
South America, travel reports of, 241
South Australia, agricultural tour of, 111
South Australian Advertiser see Advertiser (Adelaide)
South Australian Register, 197
Speight, Richard, 274, 282–283, 294–295, 302; *see also* railway (Speight) litigation
Spence, Catherine, 248
Spencer, Sir Baldwin (Walter Baldwin), 223; expedition with Francis Gillen, 335–337, 351
spiritualist movement, 118, 122, 161
sporting news, **60**, 111–112, 145, 193, 198–199, 233
Spowers, Allan, 64
Spowers, William, 324
Star (Glasgow), 100
Stead, W.T., 175–176, 305, 397–398

INDEX

Stephens, John, 189–190, 204, 303, 352, 369–370, 398; complaints from DS, 226, 247, 284, 351
Stephenson, J.B., 194–195, 233, 234
Stewart, Charles, 204
Stewart, William, 250
Strachan, Captain John, 204, 206
Street, George, 102, 106, 108, 121, 122, 280
Sudan campaign, 208–210, 328, 330
Supple, Gerald, 70
Sutherland, Alexander, 8, 169, 336
Sweet, E.G.L., 287, 295
Sydney Morning Herald, 105, 113, 158, 204, 267, 306
Syme, Amy, 307–308, 310–311, 338, 378, 382
Syme, Annabella (Annie), 45, **310**, 373, 379, 391, 392, 393; birth of children, 45, 74, 93, 124, 126, 153; looking after nephews, 93; grandmother, 310–311, 378; at the Mount, 94, 126, 130; VAPS member, 161; with DS on travels, 77, 212, 213, 278, 359; at Killara, 274; at Mellool, 376; social engagements, 306, 337–338; illness and death of DS, 380, 382
Syme, Dr Arthur Edward, 74, 136, 171, 307–308, 310–311, 338, 378, 383, 390; DS supports medical studies, 265–266; practice at Lilydale, 274
Syme, Caroline Alice, 74, 124, 393
Syme, Christina, 211, 310
Syme, David, 10, appearance, 7, **53–54**, **117**, 157, 305, 306, 317–319, **350**, **404**; behaviour and personality, 7, 149, 153, 218–219, 274, 283–284, 294, 317, 358–359, 262, 401–403; early years, 12–18, 20–22; education, 16, 20–22, 264, 401; friendships, 326, 401, *see also* Deakin, Alfred; Fraser, Simon; Gillott, Samuel; Levey, George Collins; Malcolm, Alexander John; gold prospecting, 23–24, 25–28; health, 20–21, 75, 77, 79, 81, 117–118, 170, 172, 212, 251, 279, 292, 309, 342–343, 347; memberships, 118, 119, 259, 282, 303, 314, 378; philanthropy, 4, 255, 295, 314, 330, 336, 342, 368, 371; political connections, 119, 143–144, 153, 169–170, 273, 287, 313, 349, 362–364, *see also* Deakin, Alfred *and* libel actions; public works contractor, 44–45; travels, 77–81 *passim*, 100–101, 130, 136, 170–171, 177, 212–213, 277–278, 279, 281, 292–294, 358–359; final illness and death, funeral and obituaries, 379–385
Syme, David, as capitalist, 273, 387–389; investments, 128, 220–221, 277, 311, 380; mining ventures, 276-277, 311; urban development, 5, 154–156, 323–326, 372–375; real estate transactions, 97, 168–169, 221–222, 275, 371, 388; personal wealth, 10, 295, 386–387

Syme, David, as family man, 9, 12, 74, 94, 124, 136, 214, 265, 309, 361, 378–379, 390–391, 400; relations with parents, 13–15, 24; relations with siblings, 15–18 *passim*, 23, 31, 56, 136, 306–307; relationship with wife Annabella, 45, 94, 135–136, 379, 391; family residences, 6, 54, 74, 93, 126–128, 163, 177–178, 311; provisions in will, 389–390; *see also entries for* Arthur, Francis, Geoffrey and Oswald Syme
Syme, David, as man of the land, 273, 371, 380, 389; country properties, 210, 275–276, *see also* Dalry, Killara, Mellool Station, Rosenheim; irrigation experiments, 375–376; livestock and breeding, 222, 274–275, 293, 311, 323; *Leader* Show prizes, 211–212, 282, 314
Syme, David, as newspaperman, 3, 7–9, 96, 149, 311–312, 338–339, 378, 396–398, 399–400, 403; early experience, 22–23, 41; decision to manage *Age* business, 50, 55–56; assumes autocratic role, 113–114, 181, 252, 273, 367; rationalises and expands newspaper stable, 61–69, 86–89, 113, 296–297, 335; carries out program towards *Age* ascendancy, 81, 83–91 *passim*; introduces rotary printing machines, 10, 100, 114; solicits literary, arts and music features, 107–108, 109, 110, 112–113, 147, 159, 200, 241, 298; seeks 'sensational' but not 'indecent' accounts, 247, 248, 281; sponsors expeditions and tours, 111, 164–165, 165–167, 201, 203–206, 335–337; recruits range of correspondents and contributors, 90, 108–110, 111–112, 116, 159–164, 199–200, 207, 228–230, 247–248, 285, 328, 333–334, 336–337; management style, 146–147, 158–159, 180, 187, 190, 194–195, 215, 232–234, 245, 246, 255, 268, 315, 318, 320–321, 349; relations with editorial and literary staff, 83, 115–116, 226, 283–284, 315–318, 398; provisions for future of business, 398–399; *see also entries beginning Age* newspaper business
Syme, David, as thinker, 96, 98, 119, 167–168, 386; distancing from organised religion, 14, 15–16, 17, 20, 22, 247; sounding out spiritualism, 122, 118, 161; theorising evolution, 222–223; arguing immortality, 264, 347, 359; wanting a temple for a tomb, 7, 20, 391–394
Syme, David, publications: 1870, 'The Land Question in England', 96, 98, 120–121; 1871, 'On the Method of Political Economy', 120, 133, 134, 169, 223; 1873, 'Restrictions on Trade. From a Colonial Point of View', 121–122; 1876, *Outlines of an Industrial Science*, 131, 132–134, 167, 169, 318;

1879, 'On the Increment in the Value of Land in Melbourne', 168–169, 388; 1881, *Representative Government in England*, 169, 172–176, 260, 318, 344–345, 364; 1890, *On the Modification of Organisms*, 259–264, 275, 280, 347, 360, 394; 1891, 'Topical Selection and Mimicry', 263; 1903, *The Soul*, 264, 347–348, 357–361, 391, 394

Syme, Ebenezer, 13, 15, 24, 25, **29**, 49–50, 157, 213, 305, 363; religious vocation, 14, 16–19; with London bookseller–publisher, 28–30; to Australia, 30–32; joins *Age*, 36–39; buys *Age* business, 40, 41; takes DS into partnership, 42–43; into politics as MLA, 43, 49; illness and death, 49

Syme, Elaine *see* Dennis, Elaine

Syme, Ethel, 307, 311, 338, 378

Syme, Francis (George Francis), 74, 211, 214, 266, 276, 290, 310, 383, 390, 393; law studies, 163, 171, 182; manager at Dalry, 211, 379; relations with DS, 136, 221–222, 265, 353, 390

Syme Gabrielle, 124, 393

Syme, Sir Geoffrey, 126, 265, 308, 353–**354**, 361–362, 378, 379, 383, 390; joins *Age* staff as reporter, 308, 330, 369–70; WA tour with DS, 321–323; newspaper experience in England, 343–346, 369, 396; engagement and marriage in England, 309, 346–347, 354; editor, *Every Saturday*, 355; secretary to DS, 370–372, 373, 376, 381; *Age* managing editor, 398

Syme, Sir George Adlington ('Addie', Dr), 75–76, 213, 214, 326, 338, 380, 383–384, 390

Syme, George Alexander (brother of DS), 13, 24, 47, **75**–77, 148, 208, 213, 277, 305, 306–307; ill health, 20, 136, 176, 191; religious vocation, 14, 16, 17, 19–20; joins *Age* business, 77; deputises for DS, 78, 80–81, 130, 136; edits *Leader*, 77, 145, 146, 154, 162, 166; proofreads DS writings, 260, 348

Syme, George Alexander (father of DS) *see* Sime, George Alexander

Syme, George Alexander (nephew of DS), 19, 93, 95–96, 123, 124–125, 126, 148, 210

Syme, Herbert (John Herbert), 45, 177, 268, 291, 303, 307, 311, 338, 343, 378, 381, 383; studies law, 163, 171, 188, 266; joins *Age* Office staff, 182, 251, 265; tours India, 266–277, 307; business and technical manager, 268, 300, 318, 321, 326, 369, 370, 396, 398; deputises for DS, 278, 293, 301, 304, 305; letters from DS, 184, 213, 214, 380

Syme, Hilaire (Violet),361

Syme, Hugh Randall, 398

Syme, James (brother of DS), 13, 14, 16, 18

Syme, James (Jimmie, nephew of DS), 123, 124, 125, 126–127, 148, 172

Syme (also Hope, Palk, Galgey), Jane, 19, 30, 50, **57**, 76, 126; business partnership with DS, 56–57, 79–80, 92; proffers managerial advice to DS, 57, 59, 65, 68, 71–72, 73, 74, 76–77, 88–89, 91–92, 99, 123–124, 125; urges DS to help sons, 75, 92–93, 95, 124, 127, 131–132; dissolution of partnership, 130, 131–132, 137–138, 148; relationship with Palk, 57–59, 80, 93, 123, 131, 139, 172; conceals relationship from DS and AS, 75, 92, 123, 124, 132; effect on DS, 258–259, 401, 402

Syme, Jean (mother of DS), 12, 16, 24, 47, 93

Syme, Joseph Cowen, 30, 93, 131–132, 214, 238, **258**, 338; mother urges DS assist, 79, 92–93, 95; works in *Age* Counting House, 95, **117**; negotiations for share in business, 123, 124, 126, 131–132, 137–138; partnership, quarter share, with DS, 138, 148, 210, 213; areas of responsibility, 138, 140, 142, 166–167, 187, 200, 215, 231, 243–246, 248, 249, 396; deputises for DS, 176–177; disagreements with DS, 181–183, 184, 195, 198, 214–215, 234, 325–236, 239–240, 255–259, 401, 402; dissolution of partnership, 238, 249–255; praise for abilities, 95, 182, 255, 300

Syme, Lucie *see* Macalister, Lucie

Syme, Margaret *see* Gourlay, Margaret

Syme, Minnie (Mary Jane) *see* Johnson, Minnie

Syme, Olive, 126, 136, 378, 379, 390

Syme, Oswald, 153, 265, 378, 383, 389, 390; works in *Age* Counting House, 308, 353; travels to England, 343–344; manager at Killara, 353, 371–372, 379; as surviving Trustee, takes over *Age* business management, 398–399

Syme, Susan, 59, 75, 213

Syme, Violet, 309, 346–347, 354, 361, 378

Syme, Dr William Holland, 19, 93, 123; assumes head-of-family responsibilities, 95, 126–127; with power of attorney, negotiates for mother, 124–125, 137–138, 148; power of attorney for JCS, 185

syndication *see* sharing of copy

Tannert, Louis, 157
Tarrawarra, 309, 379, 390
tariffs *see* protection vs. free trade
Tasma, 231
Taylor, John Ellor, 197
Telegraph (Brisbane), 195
telephone in newspaper offices, 176
Telo, Alfred, 111, 162

INDEX

Terry (cable correspondent), 243–244
Thomas, Julian *see* The Vagabond
Thomas, Sir Robert Kyffin, 387
Thompson, J.H., 361
Thomson, James, 254, 257, 283
Tillotsons Fiction Bureau, 108, 200, 298
Times (London), 100, 282, 360, 399
Timmins (also Tymons), Jesse, 26, 27, 28, 276
Topp, Arthur, 169
Toronto Globe, 179
Town and Country Journal (Melbourne), 116
Town and Country Journal (Sydney) *see* Australian Town and Country Journal (Sydney)
Trenwith, William Arthur (Billy), 339, 358, 363–364
Troedel, Charles, 170
Trollope, Anthony, 108
Turner, Ethel, 353
Turner, Sir George, 296, 304, 312, 313, 314, 320, 339, 341
type, printers', 224–225, 227

'Under the Verandah' (*Leader* column), 85, **86**, 111, 162, 180, 192, 203, 247–248
United Cable Service *see* cable news services
United States, news from, 199, 229, 284, 352; reports of tours, 164–165, 201–202, 334

The Vagabond, 230, 241, 285–286, 297, 321, 322
Vale, William Mountford Kinsey, 170
Victoria–New South Wales border claim, 376–378
Victoria, Queen: Golden Jubilee, 213; death, 342
Victorian Association of Progressive Spiritualists, 118, 122, 161
Victorian Farmers' Journal and Gardeners' Chronicle see Farmers' Journal and Gardeners' Chronicle
Victorian Permanent Building Society, 323
Victorian Press Association, 118
Victorian Protection League, 119
Victorian Rifle Association, 314
Victory rotary printing machines, 100–104, **101**, 117, 135, 240

Walker, David Barker, 204, 206
Wallace, Alfred Russel, 262, 263, 280
Wallace, J.R. (journalist), 331
Wallace, John (MLC), 277
Walpole, Robert, 288, 291
war news, 326–327; *see also* Boer War, Boxer Rebellion, Sudan campaign
Ward, Ebenezer, 322

Ward, Frederick William, 196, 300–301, 305, 362
Waters, Thorold, 316, 338
Watson, John Christian (Chris), 364, 366, 368
Watterston, David, 200
Weekly Age, 37, 39, 46, **60**, 61, 65, 85, 399; circulation, 85
Weekly Times (Melbourne), 4, 89, 103, 319, 350
West Australian, 231
Western Australia: news from, 196, 231; tours of, *Leader* special issues on, 297, 321–323
Westlake (subeditor), 189
Westminster Gazette, 306
Westminster Review, 28–30, 96, 119–120, 223
Williams, Sir Hartley, 289, 313
Williams, James, 147, 158, 159, 278, 298
Wilkinson, Frank, 328, 330
Wilson, Edward, 33, 39, 64, 106, 395, 396
Windsor, Arthur Lloyd, 81, 115–116; *Age* editor later 1870s, 136, 146, 161, 162, 163, 169; editor 1880 to 1887, 187–192 passim, 198; editor 1888 to 1900, 226, 235, 247, 260, 273, 283–284, 294, 303, 304, 305, 326, 340; retirement, 315–316, 345, 354, 358
Winter, Joseph, 227–228
Winter, Samuel Vincent, 303, 387
women journalists, 109, 229, 316, 353
Wood, John Dennistoun, 73–74
Woolf, Hermann, 352
Working Men's College, 282
World (Melbourne), 176
World's News (Sydney), 355
Wynne, George, 331–332
Wynne, Watkin, 300, 301, 330, 387; cable service problems, 194–195, 196, 209, 232–233; *see also* sharing of copy

Yarra Valley properties *see* Dalry; Killara; Tarrawarra
Yates, Edmund, 108
Yeoman and Australian Acclimatiser (Melbourne), 64
Yorick Club, 118

Zeal, Sir William Austin, 338, 339, 387
Zimmern, Miss, 109
Zox, Ephraim Laman, 295